Intelligent Multimedia
Information Retrieval

PN 9134737 8

Intelligent Multimedia Information Retrieval

Edited by

Mark T. Maybury

AAAI Press / The MIT Press

Menlo Park, California / Cambridge, Massachusetts / London, England

Copublished and distributed by The MIT Press, Massachusetts Institute of Technology, Cambridge, Massachusetts and London, England.

Chapter one originally appeared in *IEEE Computer,* September 1995, 23–31. It is reprinted here with permission from IEEE.

Chapter seven originally appeared in *Proceedings of ACM Multimedia '95.* It is reprinted here with permission.

Chapter seventeen is reprinted here with permission of User Modeling, Inc.

Library of Congress Cataloging-in-Publication Data
Intelligent multimedia information retrieval / edited by Mark T. Maybury
      p.   cm.
  Includes bibliographical references and index.
    ISBN 0-262-63179-2 (pb : alk. paper)
    1. Multimedia systems. 2. User interfaces (Computer systems)
3. Artificial intelligence.   I. Maybury, Mark T.
QA76.575.I577   1997
025.04—dc21   97-591
                                               CIP

Printed on acid-free paper in the United States of America.

Contents

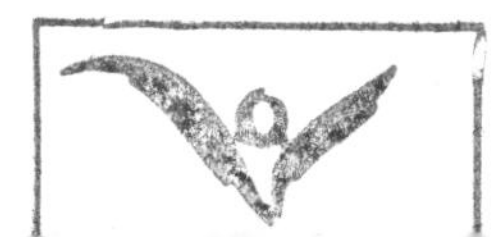

Section 6: Intelligent Hypermedia

Section 7: Empirical Evaluations

Some of the illustrations in this book can be viewed in color on
the AAAI Press web page (http://www.aaai.org/Press/Books/
Maybury-2/

Contributors

Robert Adams
Department of Computer Science, 773 Anderson Hall, University of Kentucky, Lexington, KY 40506-0046, adams@dcs.uky.edu

Philippe Aigrain
European Commission, DGIII/F6 N105 4/63 rue de la Loi, 200, B-1049 Brussels, Belgium, philippe. aigrain@dg3.cec.be

Thom Blum
Muscle Fish, LLC, 2550 Ninth Street, Suite 207 B, Berkeley, CA 94710, thom@musclefish.com, http://www.musclefish.com

Mei C. Chuah
Carnegie Mellon University, School of Computer Science, Pittsburgh, PA 15213-3890, mei+@cs.cmu.edu, http://www. cs.cmu.edu/~mei

Shih-Fu Chang
Center for Image Technology for New Media, Columbia University, 530 West 120th St, New York, NY 10027, sfchang@itnm. columbia.edu

W. Bruce Croft
Computer Science Department, University of Massachusetts, Amherst, MA 01003-4610, croft @cs.umass.edu

Ann Doubleday
School of Informatics, City University, Northampton Square, London EC1V OHB, A.Doubleday@city.ac.uk

Florence Dubois
Institut EURECOM, 2229 Route Des Cretes, B.P. 193, 06904 Sophia-Antipolis Cedex France, duboisf@eurecom.fr

Josef Fink
GMD FIT — German National Research Center for Information Technology, Schloss Birlinghoven, 53754 St. Augustin, Germany, Josef.Fink@gmd.de

Myron Flickner
IBM Research, 650 Harry Road, San Jose, CA 95120-6099, flick @almaden.ibm.com

Jonathan Foote
Department of Engineering, University of Cambridge, Trumpington Street, Cambridge CB2 1PZ, United Kingdom, jtf@eng.cam. ac.uk

Brian Frew
Code CS/Rp, Department of Computer Science, Naval Postgraduate School, Monterey, CA 93943

Morgan Green
School of Computer Science, Carnegie Mellon Universoty, Pittsburgh, PA 15213, USA, green+@andrew.cmu.edu

James Griffioen
Department of Computer Science, 773 Anderson Hall, University of Kentucky, Lexington, KY 40506-0046, griff@dcs.uky.edu

Jon Atle Gulla
GMD-IPSI, Dolivostrasse 15, D-64293 Darmstadt, Germany, gulla@darmstadt.gmd.de

Matt Hare
Land & Environmental Management Systems Group, Macaulay Land Use Research Institute, Craigiebuckler, Aberdeen, Scotland AB15 8QH, m.hare@mluri. sari.ac.uk

Alexander G. Hauptmann
Carnegie Mellon University, School of Computer Science, Pittsburgh, PA 15213-3890, alex@cs.cmu.edu

Stacie L. Hibino
Electrical Engineering & Computer Science Department, Software Systems Research Lab, The University of Michigan, Ann Arbor, MI 48109-2122, hibino@ eecs.umich.edu

Helmut Horacek
Universitaet des Saarlandes, FB Informatik, AG Siekmann, PO Box 15 11 50, D-66041 Saarbruecken, Germany, horacek@ cs.uni-sb.de

David House
Artificial Intelligence Center, The MITRE Corporation, 1820 Dolley Madison Blvd, McLean, VA 22102, dhouse@mitre.org

Takafumi Inoue
NTT Human Interface Labs, 1-1 Hikarinooka, Yokosuka-Shi, Kanagawa 239, Japan, inoue@ aether.hil.ntt.co.jp

Philippe Joly
Institut de Recherche en Informatique de Toulouse, Université Paul Sabatier, 118 rou de Narbonne, F-31062 Toulouse Cedex, France, joly@irit.fr

Gareth Jones
Department of Engineering, University of Cambridge, Trumpington Street, Cambridge CB2 1PZ, United Kingdom, gjtj@eng.cam.ac.uk

Stephan Kerpedjiev
Carnegie Mellon University, School of Computer Science/RI, 5000 Forbes Ave, Pittsburgh, PA 15213, kerpedji@cs.cmu.edu

Alfred Kobsa
GMD FIT—German National Research Center for Information Technology, Schloss Birlinghoven, 53754 St. Augustin, Germany, Alfred.Kobsa@gmd.de

Chien Young Low
Institute of Systems Science, National University of Singapore, Kent Redge, 0511 Singapore, cylow@iss.nus.sg

Inderjeet Mani
Artificial Intelligence Center, The MITRE Corporation, 1820 Dolley Madison Blvd, McLean, VA 22102, imani@mitre.org

R. Manmatha
Computer Science Department, University of Massachusetts, Amherst, MA 01003, manmatha@cs.umass.edu

Mark Maybury
Artificial Intelligence Center, The MITRE Corporation, Bedford, MA 01730, maybury@linus.mitre.org

Bernard Mérialdo
Institut EURECOM, 2229 Route Des Cretes, B.P. 193, 06904 Sophia-Antipolis Cedex France, merialdo@eurecom.fr

Adrian Müller
GMD-IPSI, Dolivostrasse 15, D-64293 Darmstadt, Germany, amueller@darmstadt.gmd.de

Wayne Niblack
K54/B2, IBM Research, 650 Harry Road, San Jose, CA 95120, niblack@almaden.ibm.com

Andreas Nill
GMD FIT — German National Research Center for Information Technology, Schloss Birlinghoven 53754 St. Augustin, Germany, Andreas.Nill@gmd.de

Alex "Sandy" Pentland
Perceptual Computing Section, MIT Media Laboratory, 20 Ames Street, Cambridge, MA 02139, sandy@media.mit.edu

Dragutin Petkovic
K54/802, IBM Research Center, 650 Harry Road, San Jose, CA 95120, petkovic@almaden.ibm.com

Steven F. Roth
Carnegie Mellon University, School of Computer Science/RI, Pittsburgh, PA 15213-3890, steven.roth@cs.cmu.edu, http://www.cs.cmu.edu/~roth

Neil Rowe
Code CS/Rp, Department of Computer Science, Naval Postgraduate School, Monterey, CA 93943, rowe@cs.nps.navy.mil

Elke A. Rundensteiner
Software Systems Research Lab, Electrical Engineering & Computer Science, The University of Michigan, Ann Arbor, MI 48109-2122, rundenst@eecs.umich.edu

Michele Ryan
Centre for HCI Design, School of Informatics, City University, Northampton Square, London, EC1V OHB, M.Ryan@city.ac.uk

John R. Smith
Center for Image Technology for New Media and Department of Electrical Engineering, Columbia University, 530 West 120th St, New York, NY 10027, jrsmith@itnm.columbia.edu, http://www.ctr.columbia.edu/, ~jrsmith

Stephen W. Smoliar
FX Palo Alto Laboratory, 3400 Hillview Avenue, Building 4, Palo Alto, CA 94304, smoliar@pal.xerox.com

Karen Spärck Jones
Computer Laboratory, University of Cambridge, New Museums Site, Pembroke St, Cambridge CB2 3QG, United Kingdom, ksj@cl.cam.ac.uk

Adelheit Stein
GMD-IPSI, Dolivostrasse 15, D-64293 Darmstadt, Germany, stein@darmstadt.gmd.de

Oliviero Stock
Istituto per la Ricerca, Scientifica e Tecnologica, I-38050 Povo, Trento, Italy, stock@irst.it

Carlo Strapparava
Istituto per la Ricerca, Scientifica e Tecnologica, I-38050 Povo, Trento, Italy, strappa@irst.itc.it,

Alistair Sutcliffe
Centre for HCI Design, School of Informatics, City University, Northampton Square, London EC1V 0HB, United Kingdom, {a.g.sutcliffe, sf328}@city.ac.uk

Atsushi Takeshita
NTT Hokkaido Business Communications Headquarters, Kita 1 Jou Nishi 6 Chome, Chuo-ku, Sapporo-Shi, Hokkaido 060-19, Japan, takesita@hokkaido.ntt.co.jp

Kazuo Tanaka
NTT Human Interface Labs, 1-1 Hikarinooka, Yokosuka-Shi, Kanagawa 239, Japan, tanaka@aether.hil.ntt.co.jp

Ulrich Thiel
GMD-IPSI, Dolivostrasse 15, D-64293 Darmstadt, Germany, thiel@darmstadt.gmd.de

Julita Vassileva
Institute for Technical Computer Science, Federal Armed Forces University Munich, 85577 Neubiberg, Germany, jiv@informatik.unibw-muenchen.de

Michael J. Witbrock
Carnegie Mellon University, School of Computer Science, Pittsburgh, PA 15213-3890, witbrock@cs.cmu.edu

Rajendra Yavatkar
Department of Computer Science, 773 Anderson Hall, University of Kentucky, Lexington, KY 40506-0046, raj@dcs.uky.edu

Steve Young
Department of Engineering, University of Cambridge, Trumpington Street, Cambridge CB2 1PZ, United Kingdom, sjy@eng.cam.ac.uk

Massimo Zancanaro
Istituto per la Ricerca, Scientifica e Tecnologica (IRST), I-38050 Povo, Trento Italy, zancana@irst.itc.it

HongJiang Zhang
Broadband Information Systems, Hewlett Packard Labs, MS 1U-17, 1501 Page Mill Road, Palo Alto, CA 94304, hjzhang@hpl-hjz.hpl.hp.com

Foreword

Karen Spärck Jones

Intelligent multimedia information retrieval is an exciting idea. With this timely book, displaying the state of the art, the reader can judge how far the idea is a reality. In particular, while technology has supplied the opportunity for retrieval through making multimedia resources available to users at their terminals, it has also, simply through bringing such vast masses of miscellaneous stuff on stream, created the problem of making retrieval effective. The interface tools that are currently part of every computer user's standard kit, and that grep can be taken to represent, do not provide effective information access—i.e. discriminating, thorough, and convenient access—even for text, and there is no reason to suppose that technicolor grep would suffice for multimedia either. Indeed the variety of information media and modes would make it a comparatively even less adequate tool.

To some extent, in our present encounter with new technology, we are seeing a rerun of earlier episodes in automatic information supply, management, and search. Thus when computing was first applied to library catalogues, one of its incidental but very valuable benefits was its ability to provide multiple copies of the file, sorted in different ways. There was a similar revolution when windows became the norm, because they allowed users parallel operations, effectively supporting and facilitating, and thus enhancing, the user's own activities in seeking or creating information.

From this point of view, powerful general-purpose computing (and communication) facilities have finessed the apparent need to address real issues about how to characterize and reach information, i.e. the content of items in the file. Thus if you can make several differently-ordered copies of a single book catalogue, the question "What is the natural hierarchy of information types, or of information classes?" disappears. Again, if you can look at a lot of different things at once on your screen—and pictures as well as text, directories as well as end-points—the question "Is a picture worth a thousand words?" doesn't need answering. You can have both.

The multimedia revolution thus promises to carry this process forward another stage. Forget about just one photograph and a page of text on your screen. You can have different videos as well if that will smooth the process of preparing a crispy marketing report for your boss, make the way insect pests take over a cornfield only too clear, or even just trigger a new burst of dress design creativity.

But the problem of retrieving the right information content for your needs—whether these are more or less well-defined—does not disappear, and it is intensified by both the increasing volume of material available and by the nature of the materials themselves. Old-fashioned picture archives had plenty of indexing challenges: who would think of indexing a street scene in, say, Glasgow in 1900, in such a way that, a century later, a historian interested in changes in the quality of clothing worn by the mass of the European population would get a highly relevant photograph showing everyone's clothes were patched? This historian already has to know, or suspect, that looking at photographs labeled "street scene, Town T, Date D" can provide such information and that they can leverage searching by using aids like town directories.

One of the holy grails of hypertext, and now hypermedia, is automatic content-based indexing, including indexing adapted to the individual user's behavior. One group of chapters in this volume illustrates how far adaptive hypertext can currently be provided. Another group illustrates how far we have progressed with direct automatic indexing and searching of images and graphics using general rather than application-specific techniques. One of the new problems multimedia has brought with it is retrieval from speech files (audio or video) without any concurrent written text stream. Speech recognition technology is far from being able to transcribe natural conversation in noisy conditions and thus provide the basis for indexing. Spoken language is also sequential and impermanent, so listening to it in order to assess the value of retrieved items is much more effort for the user than skimming text. The same issue arises with video, stimulating work on selecting key clips and frames. One group of chapters addresses retrieval from speech files, but in so doing also serves to emphasize the critical difference between the speech and image cases as far as content-based indexing (especially with general-purpose techniques) is concerned. This is that speech is merely one modality for an especially good and familiar way of conveying content, namely through natural language, so providing for content-based retrieval is far easier than for the image or graphics case.

Indeed, work on retrieving spoken documents already illustrates how automatic indexing and search strategies that meet the needs of convenient access to vast, heterogeneous files when applied in the text case can be used, with the necessary adaptation, to the speech case. In particular, these methods exploit the fact that there is redundancy in information transmission, in order to compensate for local glitches. Thus in the simplest case, using many different words to search overcomes both mismatches and missing matches in connecting users with what they want. The same approach, buttressed by the use of statistics about key occurrences, which become valuable when files are large, can clearly apply at the most general level to different media. However it is a major intellectual question whether the kind of simple, yet sophisticated, technique that has been shown to work for text retrieval can be successfully applied in these other cases, giving a uniform style of operation for multimedia retrieval.

This can at best, moreover, be only an underpinning strategy. At the interface surface, for the user, media are different and hence require distinct interpretation. The historical development mentioned earlier illustrated the persistent tension, though on shifting ground, between the work the system can do and the work it can rely on the user doing. In particular, as hypertext demonstrates, the user makes a crucial contribution in recognizing and marking content; but while this becomes more onerous as files became ever larger and more varied, in every way, system and interface technology has in turn kept pace and succeeded in lessening the load: processor speed, buttons, colour screens, and so forth.

The implicit issue behind this book is thus whether the quantitative and qualitative impact of high-volume multimedia will simply provoke a further step in a familiar direction or require a new path in quite another one. Can we cope if we get a few more gadgets, like a child made happy by another bright toy? The implicit message in the chapters in the book is no: the child has to grow up. However when we consider how we may reach to desired goal of intelligent multimedia retrieval, it seems that this will be so hard to reach, if indeed it can be reached, that the only way forward is to respond, as some chapters in this book suggest, by strategies that apply the notion of redundancy in a new form. That is, by combination strategies. Thus just as in the text case, where indexing redundancy compensates for the weakness of individual keys (and regardless of the reasons, good or bad, for this weakness), so in the multimedia case the user has to be supported with a range of access strategies to different media which can be effectively used in combination, though they may be limited for any one medium or mode alone.

This approach of course presumes that in general the user's need for information can in principle be met from several media sources, either alternatively or collectively, even if on some occasions there are particular media gaps. Thus if I want information about good kitchen layouts, I can learn from plans, photographs and text descriptions; similarly if I am interested in the pathology of some disease. There is of course nothing especially novel about this general approach. The important point is to recognize that it may not just be the only practicable approach right now, but the only correct one. It is robust, and flexible. Specifically, it is compatible with many different distributions of human effort across file indexing or search formulation, and with many forms of partnership between system and human. Thus there is nothing wrong with having human tagging, or captions, supplied for file items if tags and captions cannot be automatically assigned, and the human tagging can be a low cost enterprise because any defects can be overcome by exploiting other access routes to the end-item. At the same time, we should try to develop as many specific indexes as we can automatically, especially of the cheap and cheerful sort.

Such a strategy will of course still rely heavily on the user's contribution, so users will still have to be supplied, along with many different information sources and many alternative means of access to these (just as for text, one may search title text and/or classification codes), as well as many different ways of linking source files or individual items, with all the gadgets on their terminals they may find it nice to use: not just colour screens and handy mice, but microphones or whatever else. One important aspect of the resources available is that they will cover not only the end-resources (e.g., news files) but the intermediate directory ones as well, which can be searched just as if they were end ones. There is nothing novel about this idea: it just has to be carried through in a whole-hearted way.

Finally, in the context of truly vast resources, even if intelligent, i.e. discriminating automatic retrieval may be unattainable, we should not worry too much. Because there is so much there, the user will find something; and if this is not enough, we should rely on the user's own rich information resources and initiative, provoked by what they get, to drive further, effective searching. However as the last group of chapters in the volume reminds us, this does not imply that the need for system evaluation diminishes or disappears. Rather, evaluation becomes more complex. Even with a single-medium system there are many environment variables to consider and many system parameters. In the multimedia case evaluation will be called for to establish the best ways of offering and exploiting several media at once; and evaluation will be harder because there are many more context and implementation possibilities, and interactions between these, to examine.

But overall, therefore, the right model for supporting multimedia retrieval is "in combination there is strength": a picture and a thousand words together will really do a lot for you, and when both are in the file you have two ways of reaching the information they can give you.

Preface

Intelligent multimedia information retrieval is a multidisciplinary area that
lies at the intersection of artificial intelligence, information retrieval, human
computer interaction, and multimedia computing. It involves systems that
enable users to create, process (e.g., index, profile), summarize, present (e.g.,
visualize, customize), interact with (e.g., query, browse, navigate), and organize information within and across heterogeneous media such as text, speech,
non-speech audio, graphics, imagery, animations, and video. Intelligent multimedia information retrieval includes those systems which go beyond traditional hypermedia or hypertext environments and analyze media, generate
media, or support intelligent interaction with or via multiple media using
knowledge of the user, discourse, domain, world, or the media itself.

This collection originated from the International Joint Conference on
Artificial Intelligence (IJCAI) Workshop on Intelligent Multimedia Information Retrieval held in Montreal, Canada in August of 1995. The purpose of
the IJCAI workshop was threefold: (1) to bring together researchers and
practitioners to report on current advances in intelligent multimedia information retrieval systems and their underlying theories, (2) to foster scientific interchange among these individuals, and (3) to evaluate current efforts and
make recommendations for future investigations. The extended and additional chapters in this resulting peer reviewed collection address a broad range of
issues spanning disciplines of image and video processing, speech and non-
speech audio processing, computational linguistics, computer graphics and
visualization, human computer interaction, user and discourse modeling, intelligent agents, knowledge representation, cognitive science, adaptive hypermedia, software design, and information retrieval.

Following a foreword by Karen Sparck Jones, known for her many achieve-
ments in information retrieval and language processing, the book begins with
an introduction that outlines the purpose and scope of the book, its theoretical
foundations, an overview of the collection, and key remaining problems. The
book is organized into seven sections: (1) Content-based Retrieval of Imagery,

(2) Content-based Retrieval of Graphics and Audio, (3) Content-based Retrieval of Video, (4) Speech and Language Processing for Video Retrieval, (5) Architectures and Tools, (6) Intelligent Hypermedia, and (7) Empirical Evaluations. The chapters in the first section report techniques for automated indexing of images. Those in the second section describe techniques for indexing and retrieving graphics and non-speech audio. The chapters in the third section focus on methods for automated video indexing to support search and browsing. The fourth section reports techniques for video indexing based on spoken language or closed caption language processing. Section five reports on the application of agent technology, architectural frameworks and visualization techniques to improve the processing and analysis of video. Section six describes the use of user and discourse models to customize interaction with hypermedia. Finally, because insufficient attention has been paid to the way users actually interact with multimedia, section seven reports on empirical investigations into the retrieval of multimedia information.

The range and depth of the chapters in this collection reflects the interdisciplinary nature of intelligent multimedia information retrieval. The authors and I hope this collection will foster necessary scientific interchange to enable the development of fundamental advances in multimedia information access. These techniques will become increasingly important to broaden the range of potential users, and to improve interaction quality for all users, so that they can more effectively and efficiently exploit the increasing volume, range, and complexity of information and knowledge we face in our global village.

I would like to thank the American Association for Artificial Intelligence (especially Ken Ford and Mike Hamilton) and The MIT Press (especially Bob Prior) as well as The MITRE Corporation for their support and cooperation. I thank the authors and reviewers for their individual and, more importantly, collaborative efforts to provide an integrated collection. I thank Karen Sparck Jones not only for her contributions herein, but also for having made an indellible mark on my personal development as a graduate student at Cambridge. Special recognition is deserved for my expert assistant, Paula M. MacDonald, who spent endless hours, day and night, weekday and weekend, typing, drawing, faxing, converting, express mailing, e-mailing, and proofing the many versions of this collection. I thank my parents Ed and Stella for their unqualified love and support. Most important, I am indebted to my extraordinary wife Michelle for her continual support, encouragement and advice in this and all endeavors. Finally, for helping me edit the book late nights and weekends, and keeping me focused on what is truely important, I dedicate this collection to our boys, Zachary and Maximilian.

Mark Maybury
Bedford, Massachusetts
April, 1997

Introduction

Mark T. Maybury, The MITRE Corporation

Abstract

Our lives are increasingly surrounded by data, information and knowledge captured in multiple media: text, graphics, imagery, audio, and video. These media are frequently combined or structured to form complex artifacts (e.g., hypermedia documents, interactive CD-ROMs) which exploit multiple perceptual modalities (e.g., auditory, visual, haptic/gestural). This book focuses on tools and techniques that support efficient and effective indexing, browsing, retrieval, interaction with and visualization of multimedia. Multimedia digital libraries which incorporate text, graphics, audio, and video are central to many applications areas including information access, training, and decision support. This chapter introduces the need for intelligent multimedia information retrieval, outlines its theoretical foundations, outlines the current state of the art, describes the structure of this collection, and outlines some remaining fundamental problems.

1. Purpose and Scope

Increasing use and expansion of the information highway has created requirements for new and improved access to global and corporate information repositories. These repositories increasingly go beyond free text and structured databases to include graphics, imagery, audio (speech, music, sound), and video artifacts. The advent of large, multimedia digital libraries has focused attention on the problem of enabling more efficient and effective multimedia information access.

Traditionally, largely independent research communities have focused on the automated processing of single media including text processing (Grosz, Sparck Jones and Webber 1986; MUC-6, 1995), spoken language processing (Waibel and Lee 1990), and image and video processing (Niblack and Jain 1993-95; Chen, Pau and Wang 1993; IFIP 1989, 1992; Furht, Smoliar and Zhang 1996). The challenge of massive, multimedia digital libraries has turned attention toward the problem of integrated access to structured data and textual sources as well as media with spatial and temporal properties (e.g., sound, maps, images, video), the focus of this book. This collection differs from previous works focused on the more general issues of human computer interaction (Baecker et al. 1995), multimedia or intelligent interfaces (Blatner and Dannenberg 1992, Sullivan and Tyler 1991), intelligent multimedia interfaces (Maybury 1993) or multimedia systems issues such as standards, compression/storage, communications and networking (Furht 1996). In contrast, this edited collection targets fundamental issues in processing and providing content-based, tailored access to multimedia artifacts (e.g., documents, video mail, and broadcasts), typically using intelligent or knowledge based techniques to do so. The reported investigations aim to create a broad spectrum of new capabilities for a range of media including multimedia information browsing, search, extraction, visualization, and summarization. Results of these endeavors promise new applications such as customized television, interactive radio, and content-based multimedia authoring tools.

As such, solutions to some of the fundamental problems in this area need to draw upon and integrate results from many disciplines. These include information retrieval, cognitive science, software design, human computer interaction, computer graphics, database management, and artificial intelligence and its subareas (e.g., vision, speech and language processing, knowledge representation and reasoning, machine learning/knowledge discovery, planning and agent-modeling). Only through a collaborative effort will we make the necessary advancements to more toward a more principled understanding of multimedia information processing.

2. Theoretical Foundations

The analysis of information includes several key processes: detecting relevant sources, translating/converting them, extracting information from them, and exploiting this information (see figure 1). Detecting information could include identifying a relevant document as the result of a keyword search of several text databases, spotting keywords in a spoken language stream, or recognizing a face in a set of images. Having detected a relevant source, it may require translation from a source to a target natural language (e.g., English to Spanish text), conversion from one media to another (e.g., speech-to-text spoken language transcription), or mapping from a statistical representation to a symbolic one. Having the information in a common form, content (i.e., objects and their properties) can then be extracted. Examples of information exploitation include browsing a document collection, visualizing retrieved documents to detect patterns, looking up specific extracted facts,

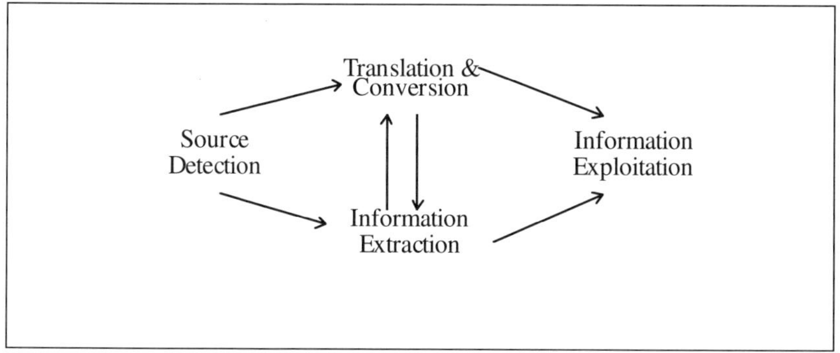

Figure 1. Information analysis.

summarizing extracted information, or further processing it to identify correlations and trends.

Most research and commercial development in document detection has focused on text retrieval. In the traditional information retrieval model (Salton 1988, van Rijjsbergen 1979), an index (I) is constructed from a set of documents (Di) to which queries (Qi) are applied by users to satisfy some information need. Document indices can be constructed by a variety of methods including statistical means (e.g., creating histograms of letter or word frequencies in documents) and linguistic analysis (e.g., parsing and interpreting natural language found in the documents). As a consequence, indices found in commercial and research systems range from a simple inverted index (i.e., words or word-stems and pointers to their occurrence in Di), to vectors of linguistic features found in documents (e.g., inferred document subjects) to structured databases of entities extracted from the source text from natural language processing (i.e., the who, what, when, where, why described in the documents). Queries can range from simple keywords to free form, natural language text. Query processing is often performed using the same techniques used for document indexing, although specialized processing is sometimes performed (e.g., term expansion using thesauri). Retrieval is the process of matching queries to documents. Evaluation of system effectiveness in satisfying user information needs (as characterized by Qi) is typically measured with large annotated corpora using *recall,* a measure of the ability of the system to retrieve all relevant documents in Di and *precision,* a measure of the system's ability to return only relevant documents. In other terms, system precision is one minus the number of false positives; system recall is one minus the number of false negatives. Current areas of research include the use of language processing to deepen the level of document processing, scaling to massive document collections, dealing with heterogeneous collections, and foreign language document retrieval/information extraction.

Extensions of the above model are required to deal with documents in forms other than text and to deal with access across heterogeneous document collections. Following Maybury (1993), I define *medium* as material centered—entailing both the physical media objects (e.g., ink on paper, soundwaves, video tape) as well as the logical means by which information is conveyed (e.g., natural language, sign language). The interpretation of media relies upon human centered processes, namely sensory *modalities* such as visual, auditory, and tactile perception as well as of course higher level cognition. Complementary production modalities in humans include: writing, speaking and gesture (to include hand, head, eye, and body motion). Consequently, a particular media (e.g., language) can be conveyed in multiple modalities (e.g., spoken or written language). *Multimedia information retrieval,* then, is the use of computer programs to access digital libraries of multiple media (e.g., text, audio, imagery, video). *Intelligent* multimedia information retrieval goes beyond traditional hypertext or hypermedia environments to provide content based indexing of multiple media and management of the interaction with these materials by representing and reasoning about models of the media, user, discourse and task.

As figure 2 illustrates, principal multimedia information processes include:

- *Analysis* of the multimedia artifacts (e.g., text, graphics, video) to index them or extract information from them (e.g., the objects, relations, and events contained in or communicated via the media).

- *Retrieval* of indexed information from single and multiple media document collections using single and cross-media query languages to support viewing of, interaction with, or generation of multimedia documents.

- *Generation* (planning or realization) of new, possibly multimedia artifacts from existing repositories.

- *Interaction* with existing collections, drawing upon the above processes but also dealing with tailoring access to the user, task, and/or situation.

Standard techniques for mapping between Q, D, and I are text-centric and need to be extended to address different media. For example, the document index, I, will need to be extended to include non-text media characteristics, such as the intonation and pitch contours of spoken language, the color, size, and shape characteristics in graphics and still imagery, and the camera-effects, lighting and motion captured in video. Creation of a multimedia index needs to address the fact that different media have different information carrying properties (e.g., static vs. dynamic, ease of representing quantitative vs. qualitative or temporal versus (geo)spatial information). This raises the need to mediate among media specific representations. For example, because of an inability to perform object and event recognition in all media, some indices will remain statistical (e.g., color histograms from images) whereas others

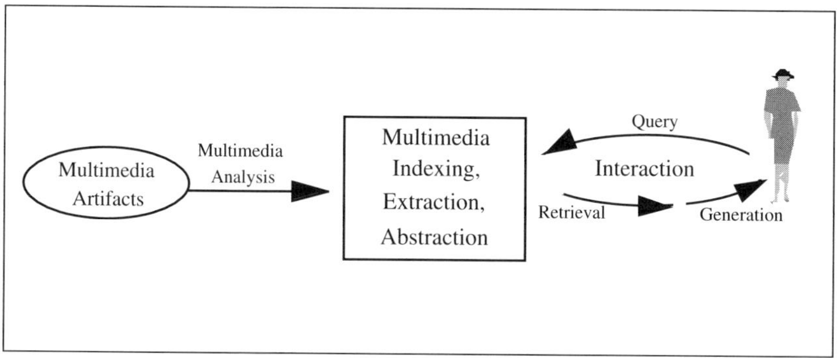

Figure 2. Multimedia processes.

will be symbolic (e.g., extracted names, organizations, and locations mentioned in text documents). Providing an integration of representations—a *media interlingua*—or at least access across heterogeneous media representations, remains an important challenge.

Figure 3 illustrates how media can be described and/or represented at multiple levels of abstraction, each increasingly higher level of which could be used for indexing for retrieval (up arrows) or presentation generation (down arrows). That is, as you proceed from the bottom to the top of the figure, which can be viewed as a set of transformations among representations, you reach successively deeper levels of representation, moving from surface forms to underlying intentions (if they exist). Each media has basic elements (which have associated attributes or features), a syntactic means of grouping, ordering and structuring these (e.g., a natural language grammar, a grammar of spatial or temporal constraints), and an associated semantic and/or conceptual meaning. At the highest level, an artifact in a media can serve an intentional purpose, e.g., a sentence can inform or request, a graphic can persuade, an image can shock or delight. While there remains debate regarding the basic unit of speech (e.g., phone, syllable), in text the word and its morphological variants and associated orthographic attributes (e.g., font, size, color) generally serve as basic elements. Words can be structured into (syntactic) phrases, utterances or sentences, and interpreted using compositional semantics. Analogously, in line graphics, visual elements such as pixel, lines, and regions have associated features (e.g., size, location, color) and can be organized into visual objects which in turn may encode some conceptual meaning (e.g., a person, location, or event), which in turn might perform some communicative action (e.g., inform, surprise).

Important relations can exist across media at all levels. For example, text labels on a map can be encoded using color coordinated with a graphic or

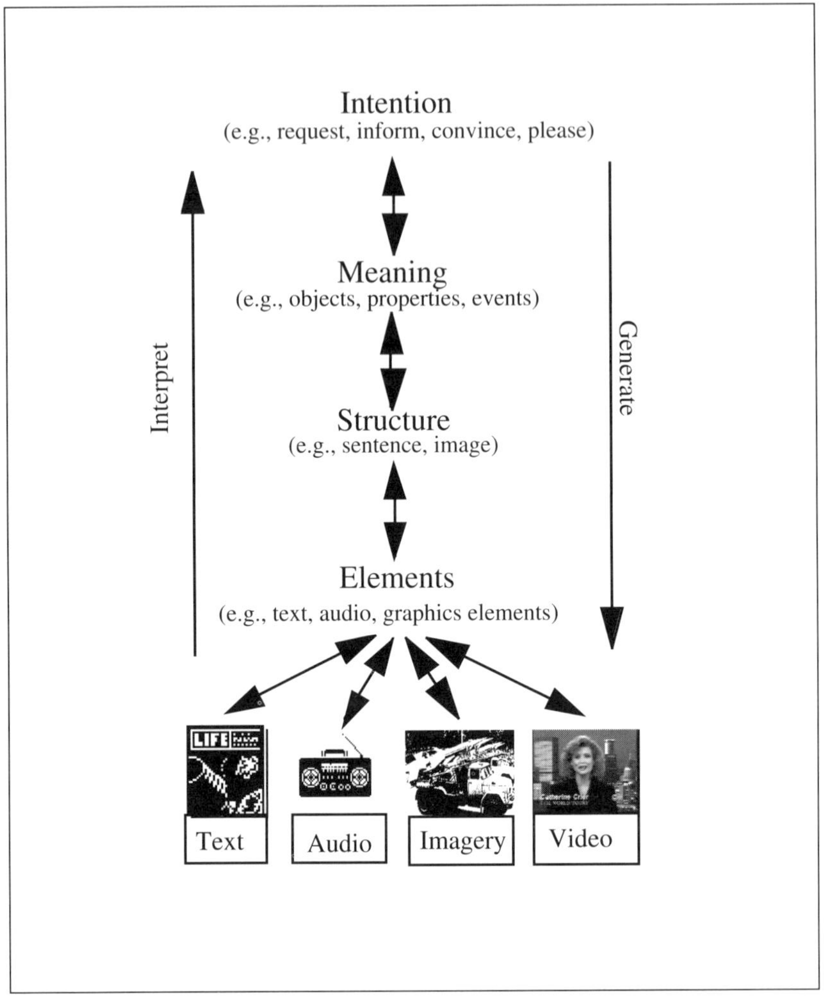

Figure 3. Levels of representations for media.

image. A sound or image could be used to convey linguistic content (e.g., a handwritten image; a text scrolled in a video). Cross media references might call out images by using text or graphics with an audio overlay. The state of the art is characterized by varying degrees of ability to both explicitly represent and automatically process media at these various levels of abstraction. For example, whereas there exist a broad range of text processing methods for lexical, morphological, syntactic, semantic, and, to a more limited extent, discourse and pragmatic analysis, we do not have agreed upon methods of describing the basic elements of imagery and audio. For example, as Blum et al. (this volume) address automated indexing of sounds, features such as pitch, loudness, and duration are readily describable and computable, however, timbre (related to the amplitude envelope, harmonicity, and spectral envelope), characterizing for example the tonality of an instrument, is primarily a perceptual concept, and thus derived from acoustic properties. Blum et al. are thus led to develop both acoustic and perceptual indices of audio. Similarly, whereas image properties such as color and shape are directly computable, as noted in this volume by Flickner et al. and Zhang et al., more sophisticated notions such as texture do not have agreed upon definitions, rather they are associated with multiple properties, including the directionality, granularity or coarseness, and contrast of an image. Thus, it is to be expected that terminological refinements will occur as we begin to increase our understanding of respective media and their relations. Experience with higher levels of representation (e.g., discourse, pragmatics) in non-textual media (e.g., video, animation) will expand our previous text-centric notions to take on new dimensions. For example, traditional models of focus of attention and discourse (Grosz and Sidner 1986) will need to be extended to address spatial and temporal focus of attention (Maybury 1991) as well as multimedia co-reference; models of communicative actions will need to incorporate visual and auditory actions; and user models will need to capture skills with and preferences for various media types and properties.

Document and query analysis techniques similarly need to be extended to enable, for example, users to posit queries not only by keyword and topical interest but also by color, shape, and texture for imagery; by gender, intonation, or rate of speaking in a spoken language stream; by characterizing the pitch, tone, and timbre for retrieval of sounds. Similarity based retrieval (i.e., "its like this image, sound bite, or video clip"), relevancy ranking of results, and results visualization will become important aspects of multimedia information access as the scope and complexity of the media space increases. When positing cross media queries (e.g., "find me all documents containing moving pictures of or spoken references to the President that have a duration of more than 2 minutes"), the multimedia index must support retrieval of non-text media via temporal, spatial, and visual properties.

3. State of the Art: An Overview of the Collection

This collection is organized around the following seven sections which, collectively, offer mechanisms to index, browse, search, visualize, and interact with imagery, graphics, audio, and video. The first five sections focus primarily on indexing multimedia, the sixth focuses on interacting with previously indexed or structured material, and the last focuses on empirical assessments of user performance in multimedia information spaces.

3.1 Content-based Access to Imagery

The chapters in the first section of the book focus on methods for automated indexing of imagery to support search and browsing. The first chapter by Flickner et al. describes the Query By Image Content (QBIC) system (now in IBM's DB2 Image Extenders), which indexes imagery and video on the basis of visual properties such as color, shape, and texture as well as motion analysis. In the second chapter, Smith and Chang describe indexing of imagery based on visual features, including color and spatial layout, reporting precision and recall experiments on 3,100 images that demonstrate the value of query by example. Manmatha and Croft next describe the use of image equivalence classes of scripted words together with affine transformations to support more effective retrieval of hand written historical manuscripts. In the last chapter, Rowe and Frew comparatively evaluate two techniques for image classification (case based and neural network) in a large, real world database of natural photographs. They show how associations between a "visual focus" computed from the image and a "linguistic focus" computed from the image captions can together improve classification performance.

3.2 Content-based Audio and Graphics Retrieval

The second section of the book addresses content based access to graphics and audio. In the first chapter, Roth et al. describe indexing of data-graphics to support indexing and retrieval based on graphical objects and relationships as well as structural similarity (e.g., find all graphs containing a descending line and an ascending one). Blum et al. then describe a user-extensible sound classification and retrieval system that computes both acoustic and perceptual properties to enable content based audio clip access.

3.3 Content-based Access to Video

In the first chapter in section three, Zhang et al. describe their video parsing algorithms for broadcast news which take advantage of models of anchor and reporter shots to go beyond transition detection (e.g., cuts, fades) to classify shot segments. The second chapter by Phillipe Aigraine presents a rule-based approach that infers the macrostructure of such videos as documentaries using a number of low level cues (e.g., color shifts, shot rhythm, music onset). In all of these efforts, results of image processing serve as important guides to select keyframes for browsing or summary presentations. Pentland's chapter concludes this third section by aiming at deeper semantic representations of video content of humans (e.g., tracking heads, hands, feet; classifying facial expressions).

3.4 Speech and Language Processing for Video Access

The fourth section of the book addresses content based access to video via indices of associated streams of spoken and written language (e.g. closed caption text). The first chapter by Jones et al. report techniques for video mail retrieval using spoken language indexing. Hauptman and Witbrock also investigate large vocabulary, continuous speaker independent broadcast news transcription, however for broadcast news retrieval and skimming. The last two chapters of this section turn to language processing of text transcripts. Mani et al. segment broadcast news using discourse cue based processing to enable story-based browsing of broadcast news. Takeshita et al. similarly report on discourse and lexical language processing to support "semantic based skim structures."

3.5 Architectures and Tools

Developing reusable architectures and tools is an important development in any field and is the focus of the fifth section. Whereas primary emphasis has been placed on algorithmic development, given the complexity of media analysis, researchers have begun to address the issues of developing frameworks and facilities to support both integration and analysis of multimedia data and processing. In the first chapter, Mérialdo and Dubois describe their Multimedia Flow Browser and related Agent Editor that enables users to both visualize agent interactions and combine existing agents into new agents. In the second chapter, Adams et al. present MOODS, a framework for developing content-based retrieval applications that allow users to go beyond searching for features such as colors and textures by combining a database, processing engine, and knowledge base. Their framework is illustrated in its application to music note recognition and ancient manuscript analysis. In addition to tools and frameworks to control and coordinate processing, multimedia systems also require multimedia query and analysis tools that go beyond the visual query reported in earlier sections. In the final chapter of this section, Hibino and Rundensteiner report their development of a visual temporal query mechanism and a visualization tool that supports temporal analysis of data from computer supported cooperative work environments.

3.6 Intelligent Hypermedia Access

Chapters in the sixth section of the book shift from indexing material to improving user access through human computer interfaces that support more effective multimedia interaction. The vision of conversational multimodal access necessarily entails user models and discourse models, and their application to either adapting hypertext or more directly managing interaction.

In the first chapter, Kobsa et al. describe work on adaptive hypertext and hypermedia systems that are tailored to a users' knowledge, interests and abilities, relying upon the services of a networked user modeling shell. In the second chapter, Vassileva presents a user and role adaptive, task-based hypermedia interface and shows how this improves the performance of both novice and expert users. The final two chapters both deal with multimedia dialogue in the context of art information access. In the first, Stock et al. describe the integration of a mediated information access paradigm (based on natural language dialog) and a navigational one (exploiting hypermedia), incorporating the use of attentional state and associated communicative acts to improve the effectiveness of multimodal information access. Finally, Stein et al. present a conversational approach to interactive retrieval which allows for an active role of the system, employing abductive reasoning to interpret ambiguous queries and to maintain coherent dialogue.

3.7 Empirical Studies

The final section of the book addresses empirical studies of multimedia information retrieval systems which aim at a deeper understanding of the strengths and weaknesses of various media and the way users interact with these. In the first chapter in this section, Horacek reports results of experiments with users of multimedia on-line documentation from which he derives design guidelines for object and action descriptions and information organization (e.g., "make cross media references explicit"). In the final chapter, Sutcliffe et al. report empirical studies of multimedia information retrieval which show that users may be misled into searching inappropriate media by the way a question is expressed, how explicit cross references between media can help in the extraction of information, and that well known information retrieval problems such as null result sets are exacerbated by multimedia. Like Horacek, the authors present design guidelines to overcome these challenges.

3.8 Content Index

Because many of the chapters in this collection address issues which cut across the above section distinctions, in order to facilitate access for the reader, table 1 cross references chapters by:

- Media data types investigated (e.g., text (captions or transcriptions), speech, sounds or music, graphics, imagery, video) and if the investigations examine cross stream or multiple media analysis.
- The media application they address, e.g., indexing broadcast video news, video teleconferences, or video mail; supporting hypermedia information access.

CHAPTER	1	2	3	4	5	6	7	8	9	10	11	12	13	14	15	16	17	18	19	20	21	22
Text			√	√						√	√	√	√		√							
Speech										√	√	√		√								
Sound						√		√														
Graphics					√																	
Imagery	√	√	√	√					√						√							
Video	√						√	√	√	√	√	√	√	√		√						
Multistream								√			√	√	√	√								
News Access							√				√	√		√								
Teleconference															√							
Video Mail										√												
Documentation																	√			√		
Hypermedia																	√	√	√	√	√	√
Indexing	√	√	√	√	√	√	√	√	√	√	√	√	√	√	√							
Search	√	√	√	√	√	√	√	√	√	√	√	√	√	√	√	√	√	√	√	√	√	√
Browse	√	√		√	√		√	√				√	√	√								
Visualization															√							
Statistical	√	√	√	√		√	√		√	√	√											
Rule based								√														
Case based			√																			
Model based	√		√		√				√	√	√						√	√	√	√		
Agent based													√									
User Models																	√	√	√			
Discourse											√	√					√	√				

Table 1. Content Index of Chapters.

- Principal functional area addressed (e.g., multimedia indexing, browsing, searching).
- Reported techniques, such as statistical-, rule-, case-, model-, or agent-based processing; the application of user or discourse models to tailor interaction.

For example, if a reader is interested only in techniques for multimedia processing exploiting tex, figure 1 points to Chapters 10-13, which exploit closed caption , but also leads the reader to Chapter 4, which deals with integrated processing of text captioned images, as well as Chapters 3 and 15, which deal with image processing of text manuscripts. All chapters address, from an algorithmic or analytic perspective, multimedia information access (e.g., to support browsing, search, or extraction).

4. Key Remaining Problems

Whereas this collection presents techniques for graphics, audio, imagery, and video information detection, extraction, and/or interaction, many problems must be solved in order to enable multimedia indexing, search, and navigation for large scale, heterogeneous collections. The most significant remaining systems level challenges include:

- *Scalability and Performance:* Dealing with orders of magnitude larger volumes of multimedia information, that support (storage and time) efficient indexing and real-time retrieval.

- *Portability:* Creating algorithms which rely minimally on domain-specific knowledge and can rapidly be applied to new multimedia corpora. Unfortunately, there remains a dearth of multimedia (e.g., audio, imagery, video) annotated data sets for experimentation. These data sets are fundamental to be used as training and test sets for machine learned indexing algorithms. And because of their creation expense, we require tools to support efficient corpora creation and annotation (either automated, semi-automated, or manual).

- *Robustness:* Dealing with increasing levels of irrelevance, dirty data and unstructured data.

- *Extensibility:* As new processing algorithms emerge (e.g., for indexing, search, extraction, summarization), system architectures should be sufficiently flexible to support seemless integration with existing approaches (e.g., augmenting a video indexing system with a speaker identification or face identification algorithm).

- *Usability:* Increasingly sophisticated processing will drive a need for mechanisms that can mitigate complexity to ensure natural and learnable interfaces that ameliorate and do not exacerbate task accomplishment.

I next consider challenges in the active research areas of media representation, reasoning (including algorithms), interaction, and evaluation.

4.1 Representation

One fundamental issue is the definition of primitives for the representation of data, information, and knowledge within and across different media, such as video, speech and audio. Media dependent and independent indices must be created to enable seemless cross media integration in order to support multimedia browsing, search, extraction and summarization. Figure 3 above alludes to some common ground. However, the designer of such representations needs to be aware of several distinct, often conflicting, objectives. There will be tradeoffs between completeness and timeliness of processing, expressiveness and compactness of representations, and computability and communicability of indices (i.e., if necessary, is the representation intuitive to the end-user).

Unfortunately, in many cases the indices automatically generated by current methods (e.g., shape, color, texture for imagery) are not rich enough to support more advanced processing, such as media understanding and generation. For example, to support content based audio access, Blum et al. (this volume) found the need to represent both measurable acoustic/perceptual properties (e.g., brightness, pitch, loudness) as well as subjective, user supplied attributes (e.g., "a shimmering" or "buzzing" sound). In many cases we must integrate heterogeneous representations. For example, how do we reconcile statistical image processing which involves representations at the depth of perceptual properties (e.g., color, shape, size, motion vectors) with the semantic or object properties that language processing systems yield from principally symbolic processing (e.g., named entities such as people, places, and things, their relationships, and associated events)? Additional remaining research questions include, What are the elements of media and mode (e.g., languages for visual, auditory, tactile primitives), and what are their associated syntax, semantics, and pragmatics?, What are appropriate formal languages in which to capture these? Does a media interlingua exist?, How can efficient but effective indices be organized (e.g., as a hybrid of statistical and semantic elements, as a casebase)?, Will these representations be scalable, for example, to millions of cases?

4.2 Reasoning and Architectures

Assuming we understand how to represent media, what algorithms or methods will prove valuable for browsing, search, extraction, and summarization? Techniques for media segmentation, classification, and parsing include purely statistical ones as well as symbolic ones, using rules, cases, and models. While research has primarily focused on single channel analysis (e.g., the image, audio, or closed-caption streams of a video), researchers are now beginning to investigate cross-channel analysis. Also, as Fickner et al.'s chapter points out, there exist indexing techniques for exact matching or range searching of tabular data which assure sublinear search for indexing (e.g., binary trees). However, what is required are fast and storage efficient techniques that support queries that include similarity matching together with spatial constraints. Finally, in part because of an inbalance between media analysis and generation techniques, there is a general lack of reversable methods, that is, algorithms that support both media analysis and generation. To be a good reader you must be a good writer and vice versa.

In addition to challenges with processing individual media, multiple media reveal special challenges such as the need for multistream alignment of heterogeneous data. However, these can also be viewed as opportunities, in which exploitation of cross channel cues can yield enhanced algorithmic performance as shown in several chapters in this volume (e.g., Aigraine et al.'s multiple cue macrostructure detector, Rowe et al.'s use of captions to improve image classification, Mani et al.'s demonstration of the value of speaker ID to improve text-based topic segmentation). Griffioen et al.'s framework approach and Mérialdo and Dubois' agent based approaches are mechanisms that can enable this kind of integrated processing.

Strongly related to these processes is the issue of what are the basic building blocks and processes within multimedia information retrieval systems (e.g., for indexing, searching, merging media elements). From an architectural standpoint, we need to understand a number of issues, including: What are the key components?, What functionality do they need to support?, What processes are most appropriate for each of these functions (e.g., statistically-based, knowledge-based)?, What are the appropriate integrating architectures (e.g., distributed vs. centralized, use of agent technology)?, What is the proper flow of control?, and How should they interact (e.g., serially, interleaved, co-constraining)?, What is the appropriate degree of automation vs. manual annotation/intervention?, How general will these architectures be across multiple applications and domains?

4.3 Interaction with Multimedia Information

Interaction tailored to the user, task, and situation will be necessary to support interaction with large scale and complex digital libraries. Heterogeneous media sources/services may require different methods of access, including distinct query languages and profiles (e.g., keywords for text data, structured query for relational data, visual query), however these should be as intuitive and uniform as possible, supporting cross media query. The notion of integration is important but this can mean different things: at one end of the spectrum it can mean a single, integrated representation system working across different media (a challenging and perhaps impossible objective, as discussed in Section 4.1 above); at the other end it can mean an integrated modus vivendi for the user at her terminal to enable shifting easily from one medium to another.

Important multimedia information interaction research questions include: What is the role of the user model in a multimedia interactive context? What is the role of discourse structure and multimedia structure? What is the role of managing models of attention, including global and local context? Is there a role for tasks if the domain or information is not defined or ill-defined? Is information negotiation a useful concept in an exploration environment? What common communicative devices found in human communication appear in multimedia (e.g., discourse context, anaphora, co-reference, elision)?

What will be the requirements and supporting tools and techniques for automated presentation design? What are effective multimedia displays and/or visualization/browsing of time-based media and in differing information seeking tasks? How can automated agents support and mediate conversational interaction to move toward a digital information retrieval assistant?

4.4 Evaluation

Finally, we need to better understand from an empirical standpoint how well our multimedia information retrieval systems will function. This entails designing metrics and conducting evaluations, often contrasting human and machine performance or integrated human-machine performance. While traditional metrics of precision and recall will remain important in information seeking contexts, we need to develop evaluation approaches which include humans in the loop.

Unfortunately, there remains a limited amount of reported experimentation in this area. Whereas scientific endeavors in areas such as vision, speech recognition, and text processing have made progress by creating large scale training and test corpora (e.g., the TIPSTER text retrieval and message understanding collections), collection and annotation of multimedia corpora is expensive and remains a bottleneck. Unfortunately, without such corpora, many issues of scalability, portability, extensibility and robustness cannot be properly investigated. As a consequence of the lack of large scale multimedia corpora, much of the current experimentation results in important but merely indicative conclusions, as discussed by several authors in this collection, including Jones et al. and Mani et al.

In addition to multimedia data, we need carefully defined multimedia tasks and experiments. Researchers have suggested the need for explicit task definitions (i.e., well-defined user and context centered goals), explicit separation of media, and the application of the scientific method in which one adds or subtracts dependencies (e.g., media, tasks, user classes) and runs controlled experiments where the goal is to lead to usability and performance criteria by comparison with some baseline (e.g., versus use of a conventional library). It is also necessary to have not only well defined but also large scale evaluations (e.g. hundreds of queries and relevancy judgments, gigabytes of data) with the ultimate objective of discerning principles of multimedia interaction which can be both prescriptive and predictive.

4.5 General Issues

As with any new technology, there are a range of economic and social challenges beyond the above technical ones that will arise in the context of multimedia information retrieval. On one hand, the technology promises information retrieval that can be more natural and personalized while at the same time more exact and richer in content and form. On the other, the power of information manipulation raises legal and economic issues (e.g., how to track and price derived works such as an extraction or summary or media translation), social issues (e.g., how to ensure all citizens have equal access to multimedia data and advanced tools), and privacy issues (e.g., how to manage models of a user and their information retrieval interactions), although these are not necessarily unique to this research area. Traditional concepts such as intellectual property and copyright will require new operational definitions as slight modifications of content or form using media editing tools might dramatically alter the message of a presentation and, by some, be considered novel artifacts.

5. Conclusion

Many open research issues remain in this nascent, interdisciplinary area. Lessons learned from more long standing research communities (e.g., information retrieval, image processing, speech processing, language processing) regarding user-centered design, corpora development, and evaluation strategies can be leveraged to make more rapid progress in research and applications. Only by addressing the above key questions will underlying progress be made to support future applications such as video archive search, video and audio teleconferencing archiving, and content-based multimedia access. A key challenge will be the development and transition of techniques to the many domains with needs for multimedia archive access including medical records, retail marketing, stock photo and video management (e.g., for advertising), museum and library collections, scientific applications (e.g., environmental analysis, weather prediction), law enforcement (e.g., face, voice, handwriting recognition), and content based clip art (e.g., images, sounds, graphics).

If successful, intelligent multimedia information retrieval will improve information access in three principal ways. First, it promises more effective access to content: getting the right stuff and tailoring it to the context of the user, their task, and their environment. The goal of achieving context sensitivity will be limited only by the richness of models that can be created. Second, by providing only the most relevant information, together with high performance browsing and search tools, this not only enables more comprehensive and higher quality search, it saves time, thus saving money. Finally, enabling the user to ask for and receive information in a natural manner (e.g., by speaking, drawing, or pointing to similar artifacts) promises a less stressful and more pleasant interaction.

In short, this area has the potential to improve the quality and effectiveness of interaction for everyone who communicates with a machine in the future. To achieve these benefits, however, we must overcome the remaining fundamental problems outlined above. The contributions in this book aspire to provide initial solutions.

Acknowledgments

I would like to thank all the workshop participants and authors for their ideas, many of which have been adopted above, especially Ed Hovy for an earlier concept for figure 2, Wolfgang Wahlster, Philippe Aigraine, and Stephen Smoliar.

References

Baecker, R. M.; Grudin, J.; Buxton, W.; and Greenberg, S., eds. 1995. second edition. *Readings in Human-Computer Interaction: Toward the Year 2000.* San Mateo, CA: Morgan Kaufmann.

Blattner, M. and Dannenberg, R., eds. 1992. *Multimedia Interface Design,* Reading, Mass.: ACM Press.

Chen, C. H.; Pau, L. F.; and Wang, P. S. P., eds. 1993. *Handbook of Pattern Recognition and Computer Vision.* Singapore: World Scientific.

Furht, B.; Smoliar, S.; and Zhang, H. J., eds. 1996. *Video and Image Processing in Multimedia Systems.* Boston: Kluwer.

Furht, B. ed. 1996. *Multimedia Systems and Techniques.* Boston: Kluwer.

Grosz, B. J., Sparck Jones, K., and Webber, B., eds. 1986. *Readings in Natural Language Processing.* Los Altos, CA: Morgan Kaufmann.

Grosz, B. J. and C. Sidner. July-September, 1986. Attention, Intentions, and the Structure of Discourse. *Computational Linguistics* 12(3): 175-204.

IFIP, 1989 and 1992. *Visual Database Systems I and II,* North-Holland: Elsevier Science Publishers.

Maybury, M. T. 1991. Topical, Temporal and Spatial Constraints on Linguistic Realization. In Pattabhiraman, T. and Cercone, N., eds. *Computational Intelligence:* Special Issue on Natural Language Generation. 7(4): 266-275.

Maybury, M. T. 1993. *Intelligent Multimedia Interfaces.* Menlo Park, CA/Cambridge, MA: AAAI/MIT Press.

MUC-6, Proceedings of the Sixth Message Understanding Conference. Advanced Research Projects Agency Information Technology Office, Columbia, MD, 6-8 November, 1995.

Niblack, W. and Jain, R., eds. 1993, 1994, 1995. Proceedings of IS&T/SPIE. Conference on Storage and Retrieval for Image and Video Databases I, II, and III, Vols. 1908, 2185, and 2420. Bellingham, WA: SPIE.

van Rijjsbergen, C. J. 1979. *Information Retrieval.* London: Butterworths.

Salton, G. *Automatic Text Processing. Reading,* MA: Addison-Wesley, 1988.

Sullivan, J. and Tyler, S., eds. 1991. *Intelligent User Interfaces.* Reading, MA: Addison-Wesley, ACM Press.

Waibel, A. and Lee, K., eds. 1990. *Readings in Speech Recognition,* San Mateo, CA: Morgan Kaufmann.

Intelligent Multimedia
Information Retrieval

Content-based Imagery Retrieval

Increasing amounts of imagery have made explicit the need for more effective and efficient imagery indexing and search of not only the metadata associated with the imagery (e.g., captions, annotations) but also retrieval directly on the content of the imagery. Initial algorithm development has focused on the automatic indexing of visual features of imagery (e.g., color, texture, shape) which can be used as a means for retrieving similar images without the burden of manual indexing, although the ultimate objective is semantic based access to imagery. Whereas the first two chapters of this initial section of the collection focus on retrieval of images of more conventional content, the third chapter focuses on retrieving images of handwritten language and the last chapter focuses on exploiting captions associated with images to improve retrieval. Collectively, these systems enable new forms of interaction with imagery.

In the first chapter, Flickner et al. (IBM Almaden Research Center, San Jose, CA) describe their Query By Image Content (QBIC) system, which supports access to imagery collections on the basis of visual properties such as color, shape, texture, and sketches. In their approach, query facilities for specifying color parameters, drawing desired shapes, or selecting textures replace the traditional keyword query found in text retrieval or structured query found in databases (e.g., "find images with a red round object and a green square, coarsely textured object"). Because robust, domain independent object identification remains difficult and manual image annotation is tedious, the authors developed automated and semiautomated object outlining tools (e.g., foreground/background models to extract objects) to facilitate database population. Results from this research have been transitioned into commercial products (e.g., IBM's Ultimedia Manager and DB2). For video, the authors describe their shot detection, representative frame (r-frame, sometimes called keyframe) creation for each shot, and derivation of a layered representation of moving objects. This enables queries such as "find me all shots panning left to right" which yield a list of relevancy ranked r-frames (which acts as a thumbnail), selection of which retrieves the associated video shot. Content based access to video is a subject we return to in sections three and four of the collection.

In the second chapter of the section, John Smith and Shih-Fu Chang (Columbia University) describe VisualSEEk, a content based imagery retrieval system for World Wide Web imagery access. In addition to searching traditional keyword annotations associated with images, query mechanisms include the ability to query by color and spatial layout of color regions. Using a 3,100 image database, in searching for sunset images, the authors demonstrate how color region retrieval (measured using precision and recall) can be improved by providing an example sunset image to support similarity-based color region searching.

The third chapter by R. Manmatha and Bruce Croft (Center for Intelligent Information Retrieval, University of Massachusetts) focuses our attention on retrieval of hand written historical manuscripts. Key challenges include the variability of single writer script and the small sample sizes available for historical documents (e.g., only one page per writer in this case). They first segment documents into words (measuring vertical and horizontal distances between characters, smoothing and thresholding, and computing a minimum bounding rectangle). They attempt to overcome OCR performance limitations by matching images of words rather than recognizing characters. Next, an image-based equivalence classes of scripted words is created by:

1. Providing a word image to use as a template
2. Filtering all words in the document based on area and aspect (width/height) ratios
3. Matching the template against the filtered list using Euclidean Distance Mapping (which is fast and accounts for translation shifts). They also experiment with affine matching, a linear transformation between two point sets, each point set representing the image of a word (this is slow, but models scaling, shear, and rotation)

This process yields equivalence classes of word images, the most frequently occurring of which are assumed to be stop words (e.g., articles, conjunctions, prepositions) which are pruned. These are then labeled by the user. The authors describe the application of their algorithms to both a neat and a difficult to read document, reporting a 79.7% average precision for the neat document and a 57.9% average precision for the difficult document using the Euclidean distance match. In contrast, the affine matcher, which models distortions, not only improves performance (e.g., 86.3% average precision on the easy to read document), but also has more effective discrimination between valid and invalid words. These techniques are useful not only for indexing content, but also in supporting human recognition efforts of hard-to-read or illegible documents. Thus, this work is related to Griffioen, Yavatkar, and Adams' chapter which appears later in the collection, however, their focus is on image processing frameworks, exemplified in character (in contrast to word) recognition from ancient manuscripts.

In the final chapter of this first section, Neil Rowe and Brian Frew (Naval Postgraduate School, Monterey, CA) illustrate the benefit of captions in classifying images. The authors comparatively evaluate two techniques for image classification (case based and neural network) in a large, real world database of natural photographs, in which traditional image understanding techniques such as shape templates fail because of the nature of the subject. In particular, Rowe and Frew compute a *visual focus* as follows:

1. Compute the visual focus of the image using visual properties of the regions (e.g., size, center of mass, surrounding color/texture discontinuity)
2. Classify regions into 25 predefined object classes
3. Compute the linguistic focus of the captions (e.g., using Wordnet to obtain word senses and superconcepts)
4. Consider a region the visual focus if visually classified regions are matched to the linguistic focus

Evaluation yielded 38% visual focus classification success (random guessing results in 10% success), however this in turn yielded a 48% shape classification success rate on randomly selected test images.

Taken as a group, these chapters contribute important approaches and solutions to the challenges of representing, processing, and retrieving imagery data. They also suggest interesting potential tools that could support imagery browsing and retrieval. Both indexing image content itself as well as enhancing this processing by exploiting correlated sources of information (e.g., image captions) are important approaches to processing this data. Indeed, just as captions can enhance image indexing, so too processing related channels of information in video (e.g., closed captions) can enhance video indexing, as illustrated by the articles in the fourth section of this collection. But first we turn to indexing non-speech audio and graphics.

Query by Image and Video Content: The QBIC™ System

Myron Flickner, Harpreet Sawhney, Wayne Niblack, Jonathan Ashley, Qian Huang, Byron Dom, Monika Gorkani, Jim Hafner, Denis Lee, Dragutin Petkovic, David Steele, and Peter Yanker
IBM Almaden Research Center

Abstract

QBIC lets users find pictorial information in large image and video databases based on color, shape, texture, and sketches. This article describes the QBIC system and demonstrates its query capabilities. QBIC technology is part of several IBM products.

1. Introduction

Picture yourself as a fashion designer needing images of fabrics with a particular mixture of colors, a museum cataloger looking for artifacts of a particular shape and textured pattern, or a movie producer needing a video clip of a red car-like object moving from right to left with the camera zooming. How do you find these images? Even though today's technology enables us to acquire, manipulate, transmit, and store vast on-line image and video collections, the search methodologies used to find pictorial information are still limited. Typically, available methods depend on file IDs, keywords, or text associated with the images. And, although powerful, they don't allow queries based directly on the visual properties of the images, are dependent on the particular vocabulary used, and don't provide queries for images similar to a given image.

Research on ways to extend and improve query methods for image databases is widespread, and results have been presented in workshops, conferences (Visual Database Systems 1989, 1992; Niblack and Jain 1993-95) and surveys.

Semantic Versus Nonsemantic Information

At first glance, content-based querying appears deceptively simple because we humans seem to be so good at it. If a program can be written to extract semantically relevant text phrases from images, the problem may be solved by using currently available text-search technology. Unfortunately, in an unconstrained environment, the task of writing this program is beyond the reach of current technology in image understanding. At an artificial intelligence conference several years ago, a challenge was issued to the audience to write a program that would identify all the dogs pictured in a children's book, a task most 3-year-olds can easily accomplish. Nobody in the audience accepted the challenge, and this remains an open problem.

Perceptual organization—the process of grouping image features into meaningful objects and attaching semantic descriptions to scenes through model matching–is an unsolved problem in image understanding. Humans are much better than computers at extracting semantic descriptions from pictures. Computers, however, are better than humans at measuring properties and retaining these in long-term memory.

One of the guiding principles used by QBIC is to let computers do what they do best—quantifiable measurement–and let humans do what they do best–attaching semantic meaning. QBIC can find "fish-shaped objects," since shape is a measurable property that can be extracted. However, since fish occur in many shapes, the only fish that will be found will have a shape close to the drawn shape. This is not the same as the much harder semantic query of finding all the pictures of fish in a pictorial database.

We have developed the QBIC (Query by Image Content) system to explore content-based retrieval methods. QBIC allows queries on large image and video databases based on example images, user-constructed sketches and drawings, selected color and texture patterns, camera and object motion, and other graphical information. An interactive demonstration of QBIC is available on the world wide web at http://wwwqbic.almaden.ibm.com.

Two key properties of QBIC are (1) its use of image and video content—computable properties of color, texture, shape, and motion of images, videos, and their objects, and (2) its visual query language in which queries are posed by drawing, selecting, and other graphical means. Related systems, such as MIT's Photobook (Pentland et al. 1994) and the Trademark and Art Museum applications from ETL (Kato et al. 1991) also address these common issues.

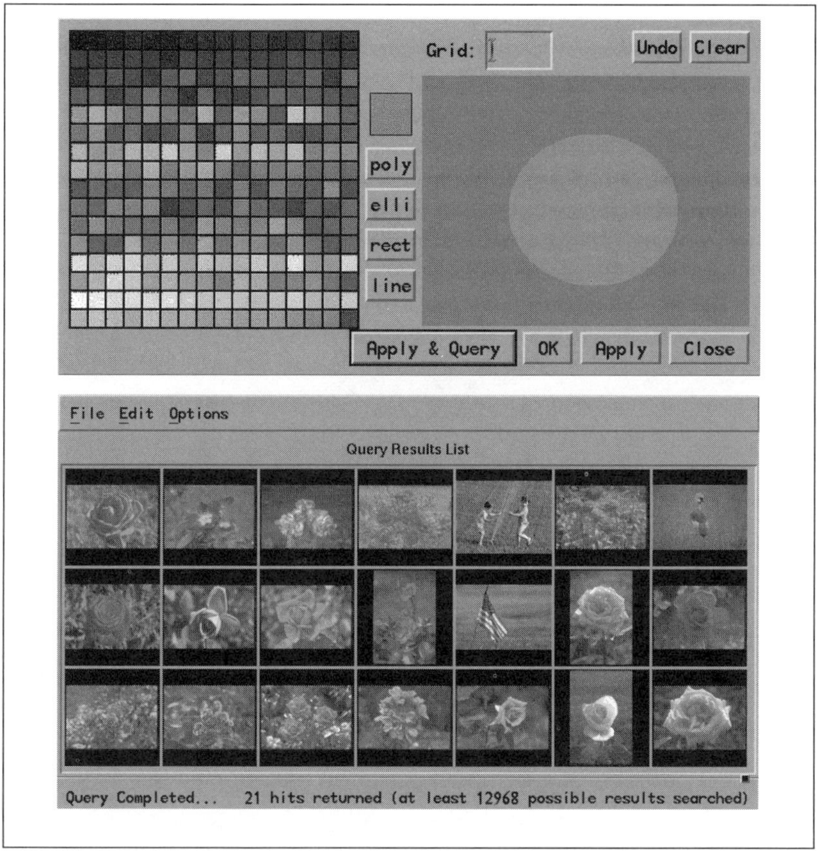

Figure 1. QBIC query by drawn color.
(Drawn query specification on top; best 21 results sorted by similarity to the query
on bottom. The results were selected from a 12,968-picture database.)

2. QBIC System Overview

Figure 1 illustrates a typical QBIC query.[1] The top shows the query specification, where the user painted a large magenta circular area on a green background using standard drawing tools. Query results are shown on the bottom: an ordered list of "hits" similar to the query. The order of the results is top to bottom, then left to right, to support horizontal scrolling. In general, all queries follow this model in that the query is specified by using graphical means–drawing, selecting from a color wheel, selecting a sample image, and so on–and results are displayed as an ordered set of images.

To achieve this functionality, QBIC has two main components: database

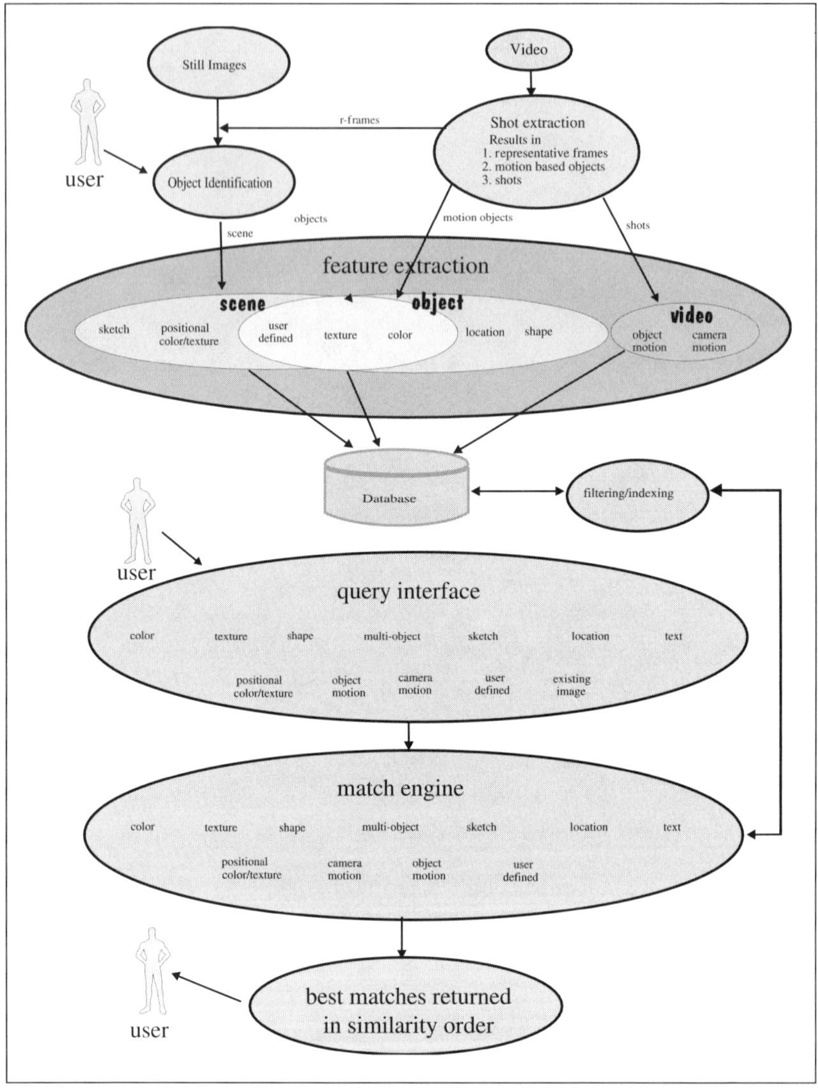

Figure 2. QBIC database population (top) and query (bottom) architecture.

population (the process of creating an image database) and database query. During the population, images and videos are processed to extract features describing their content—colors, textures, shapes, and camera and object motion—and the features are stored in a database. During the query, the user composes a query graphically. Features are generated from the graphical

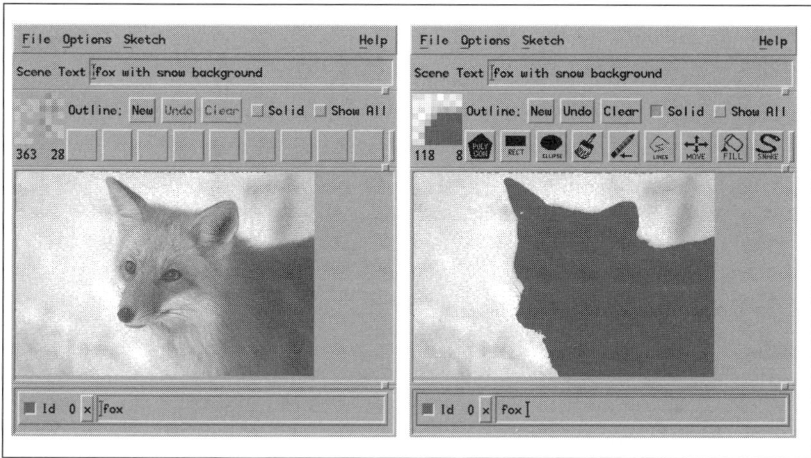

Figure 3. QBIC still image population interface. Entry for scene text at top. Tools in row are polygon outliner, rectangle outliner, ellipse outliner, paintbrush, eraser, line drawing, object translation, flood fill, and snake outliner.

query and then input to a matching engine that finds images or videos from the database with similar features. Figure 2 shows the system architecture.

2.1 Data Model

For both population and query, the QBIC data model has still images or scenes (full images) that contain objects (subsets of an image), and video shots that consist of sets of contiguous frames and contain motion objects.

For still images, the QBIC data model distinguishes between "scenes" (or images) and "objects." A scene is an image or single representative frame of video. An object is a part of a scene—for example, the fox in figure 3—or a moving entity in a video. For still image database population, features are extracted from images and objects and stored in a database as shown in the top left part of figure 2.

Videos are broken into clips called shots. Representative frames, or *r-frames,* are generated for each extracted shot. R-frames are treated as still images, and features are extracted and stored in the database. Further processing of shots generates motion objects—for example, a car moving across the screen.

Queries are allowed on objects ("Find images with a red, round object"), scenes ("Find images that have approximately 30-percent red and 15-percent blue colors"), shots ("Find all shots panning from left to right"), or any combination ("Find images that have 30 percent red and contain a blue textured object").

In QBIC, similarity queries are done against the database of pre-extracted features using distance functions between the features. These functions are intended to mimic human perception to approximate a perceptual ordering of the database. Figure 2 shows the match engine, the collection of all distance functions. The match engine interacts with a filtering/indexing module (see Section 5 of this chapter) to support fast searching methodologies such as indexing. Users interact with the query interface to generate a query specification, resulting in the features that define the query.

3. Database Population

In still image database population, the images are reduced to a standard-sized icon called a thumbnail and annotated with any available text information. Object identification is an optional but key part of this step. It lets users manually, semiautomatically, or fully automatically identify interesting regions—which we call objects—in the images. Internally, each object is represented as a binary mask. There may be an arbitrary number of objects per image. Objects can overlap and can consist of multiple disconnected components like the set of dots on a polka-dot dress. Text, like "baby on beach," can be associated with an outlined object or with the scene as a whole.

3.1 Object-outlining Tools

Ideally, object identification would be automatic, but this is generally difficult. The alternative—manual identification—is tedious and can inhibit query-by-content applications. As a result, we have devoted considerable effort to developing tools to aid in this step. In recent work, we have successfully used fully automatic unsupervised segmentation methods along with a foreground/background model to identify objects in a restricted class of images. The images, typical of museums and retail catalogs, have a small number of foreground objects on a generally separable background. Figure 4 shows example results. Even in this domain, robust algorithms are required because of the textured and variegated backgrounds.

We also provide semiautomatic tools for identifying objects. One is an enhanced flood-fill technique. Flood-fill methods, found in most photo-editing programs, start from a single object pixel and repeatedly add adjacent pixels whose values are within some given threshold of the original pixel. Selecting the threshold, which must change from image to image and object to object, is tedious. We automatically calculate a dynamic threshold by having the user click on background as well as object points. For reasonably uniform objects that are distinct from the background, this operation allows fast object identification without manually adjusting a threshold. The example in figure 3 shows an object, a fox, identified by using only a few clicks.

Figure 4. Top row is the original image. Bottom row contains the automatically extracted objects using a foreground/background model. Heuristics encode the knowledge that objects tend to be in the center of the picture.

We designed another outlining tool to help users track object edges. This tool takes a user-drawn curve and automatically aligns it with nearby image edges. Based on the "snakes" concept developed in recent computer vision research, the tool finds the curve that maximizes the image gradient magnitude along the curve.

The spline snake formulation we use allows for smooth solutions to the resulting nonlinear minimization problem. The computation is done at interactive speeds so that, as the user draws a curve, it is "rubber-banded" to lie along object boundaries.

3.2 Video Data

For video data, database population has three major components: shot detection, representative frame creation for each shot, and derivation of a layered representation of coherently moving structures/objects.

Shots are short sequences of contiguous frames that we use for annotation and querying. For instance, a video clip may consist of a shot smoothly panning over the skyline of San Francisco, switching to a panning shot of the Bay meeting the ocean, and then to one that zooms to the Golden Gate Bridge. In general, a set of contiguous frames may be grouped into a shot because they depict the same scene, signify a single camera operation, contain a distinct event or an action like a significant presence and persistence of an object, or are chosen as a single indexable entity by the user.

Our effort is to detect many shots automatically in a preprocessing step and provide an easy-to-use interface for the rest.

3.2.1. Shot Detection. Gross scene changes or scene cuts are the first indicators of shot boundaries. Methods for detecting scene cuts proposed in the lit-

*Figure 5. Scene cuts automatically extracted
from a 1,148-frame sales demo from Energy Productions*

erature essentially fall into two classes: (1) those based on global representations like color/intensity histograms without any spatial information, and (2) those based on measuring differences between spatially registered features like intensity differences. The former are relatively insensitive to motion but can miss cuts when scenes look quite different but have similar distributions. The latter are sensitive to moving objects and camera. We have developed a method that combines the strengths of the two classes of detection. We use a robust normalized correlation measure that allows for small motions and combines this with a histogram distance measure (Nagasaka and Tanaska 1992). Results on a few videos containing from 2,000 to 5,000 frames show no misses and only a few false cuts. Algorithms for signaling edit effects like fades and dissolves are under development. The results of cut detection on a video containing commercial advertisement clips are shown in figure 5.

Shots may also be detected by finding changes in camera operation. Common camera transformations like zoom, pan, and illumination changes can be modeled as unknown affine 2x2 matrix transformations of the 2D image coordinate system and of the image intensities themselves. We have developed an algorithm (Sawhney et al. 1995) that computes the dominant global view transformation while it remains insensitive to local changes resulting from independently moving objects and local brightness changes. The affine transformations that result from this computation can be used for camera operation detection, shot boundary detection based on the camera operation, and creating a synthetic r-frame wherever appropriate.

Shot boundaries can also be defined on the basis of events: appearance/disappearance of an object, distinct change in the motion of an object, or similar events. For instance, segmenting an object of interest based on its appearance and/or motion, and tracking it throughout its significant presence may be used for defining shots.

3.2.2. Representative Frame Generation. Once the shot boundaries have been detected, each shot is represented using an r-frame. R-frames are used for several purposes. First, during database population, r-frames are treated as still images in which objects can be identified by using the previously described methods. Secondly, during query, they are the basic units initially returned in a video query. For example, in a query for shots that are dominantly red, a set of r-frames will be displayed. To see the actual video shot, the user clicks on the displayed r-frame icon.

The choice of an r-frame could be as simple as a particular frame in the shot: the first, the last, or the middle. However, in situations such as a long panning shot, no single frame may be representative of the entire shot. We use a synthesized r-frame (Tonomura et al. 1993, Teodosi et al. 1993) created by seamlessly mosaicking all the frames in a given shot using the computed motion transformation of the dominant background. This frame is an authentic depiction of all background captured in the whole shot. Any foreground object can be superimposed on the background to create a single, static visual representation of the shot. The r-frame mosaicking is done by using warping transforms that result from automatic dominant motion computation. Given a video sequence with dominant motion and moving object(s), the 2D motion estimation algorithm is applied between consecutive pairs of frames. Then, a reference frame is chosen, and all the frames are warped into the coordinate system of the reference frame to create the mosaicked r-frame.

Figure 6 illustrates mosaic-based r-frame creation on a video sequence of an IBM commercial. Three frames of this sequence plus the final mosaic are shown. Two dominant-component-only mosaics of the Charlie sequence are shown in figure 6. In one case, the moving object has been removed from the mosaic by using temporal median filtering on the frames in the shot. In the

Figure 6. Top: Three frames from the Charlie sequence and the resulting dynamic mosaics of the entire sequence with and without the moving Charlie figure. Below that is a mosaic from a video sequence of Yosemite National Park. Bottom: Original images and segmented motion layers for the flower garden sequence in which only the camera is moving. The flower bed, tree, and background have been separated into three layers shown in different shades of gray.

other case, the moving object remains from the first frame in the sequence. We are also developing methods to visually represent the object motion in the r-frame.

3.2.3. Layered Representation. To facilitate automatic segmentation of independently moving objects and significant structures, we take further advantage of the time-varying nature of video data to derive what is called a layered representation (Wang and Adelson 1993) of video. The different layers are used to identify significant objects in the scene for feature computations and querying. Our algorithm divides a shot into a number of layers, each with its own 2D affine motion parameters and region of support in each frame (Ayer and Sawhney 1995).

The algorithm is first illustrated on a shot where the scene is static but the camera motion induces parallax motion onto the image plane due to the different depths in the scene. Therefore, surfaces and objects that may correspond to semantically useful entities can be segmented based on the coherence of their motion. Figure 6 (bottom row) shows the results for the layers from the flower garden sequence.

4. Sample Queries

For each full-scene image, identified image object, r-frame, and identified video object resulting from the above processing, a set of features is computed to allow content-based queries. The features are computed and stored during database population. We present a brief description of the features and the associated queries. Mathematical details on the features and matching methods can be found in Ashley et al. (1995) and Niblack et al.(1993).

Average color queries let users find images or objects that are similar to a selected color, say from a color wheel, or to the color of an object. The feature used in the query is a 3D vector of Munsell color coordinates. Histogram color queries return items with matching color distributions—say, a fabric pattern with approximately 40 percent red and 20 percent blue. For this case, the underlying feature is a 256-element histogram computed over a quantized version of the color space.

Figure 7 shows a histogram query on still images and a color query on video r-frames. Note that in the query specification for the histogram query of figure 7, the user has selected percentages of two colors (blue and white) by adjusting sliders. Using such a query, an advertising agent could, for example, search for a picture of a beach scene, one predominantly blue (for sky and water) and white (for sand and clouds); or find images with similar color spreads for a uniform ad campaign. The average color query demonstrates a query against a video shot database where the user is searching for red r-frames. Again, the query specification is on the left and the best hits are on the right.

Figure 8 shows an example texture query. In this case, the query is specified by selecting from a sampler—a set of prestored example images. The underlying texture features are mathematical representations of coarseness, contrast, and directionality features. Coarseness measures the scale of a texture (pebbles versus boulders), contrast describes its vividness, and directionality describes whether it has a favored direction (like grass) or not (like a smooth object).

An object shape query is shown in figure 8. In this case, the query

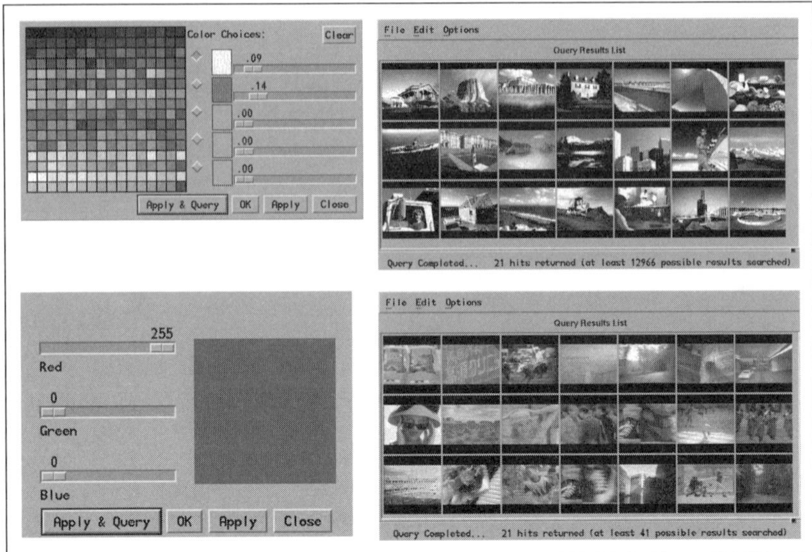

*Figure 7. Top: Query by histogram color. Histogram color query specification on left;
best 21 results from a 12,966-picture database on right.
Bottom: A query for a red video r-frame. The color picker is on the left;
the resulting r-frame thumbnails of the best matches are shown on the right.
Each thumbnail is an active button that allows the user to play the shot.*

*Figure 8. Top: Query by texture. Texture sampler on left (query specification is right
middle texture); best 21 results from a 12,966-picture database on right. Bottom:
Query by shape. User input shape on left and query results on right.*

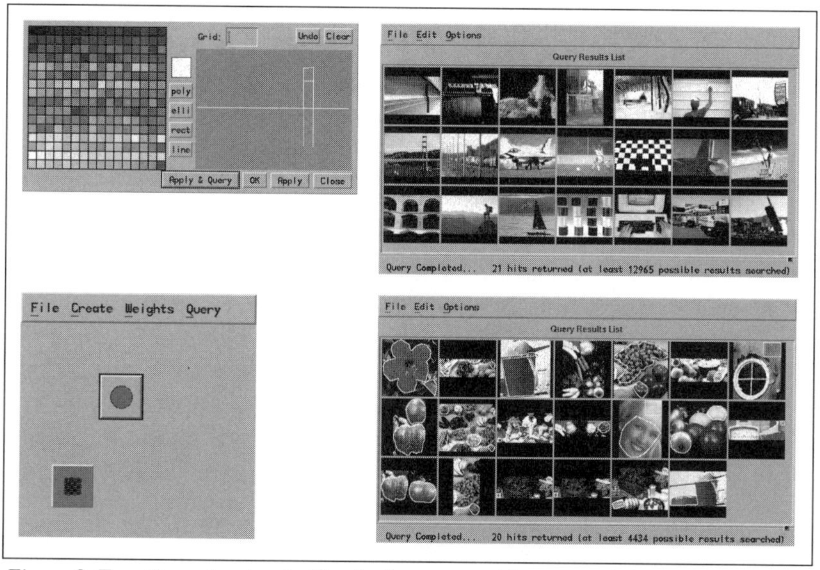

Figure 9. Top: Query by sketch. Sketched query specification on left; best 21 hits from a 12,965-image database on right. Bottom: A Multi- object query. The query specification on the left describes a query for images with a red round object and a green textured object. Best 20 matches shown on right.*

specification is the drawn shape on the left. Area, circularity, eccentricity, major-axis direction, features derived from the object moments, and a set of tangent angles around the object perimeter are the features used to characterize and match shapes.

Figure 9 illustrates query by sketch. In this case, the query specification is a freehand drawing of the dominant lines and edges in the image. The sketch feature is an automatically extracted reduced-resolution "edge map." Matching is done by using a template-matching technique.

A multiobject query asking for images that contain both a red round object and a green textured object is shown in the bottom of figure 9. The features are standard color and texture. The matching is done by combining the color and texture distances to implement logical "AND" semantics.

5. Fast Searching and Indexing

Indexing tabular data for exact matching or range searches in traditional databases is a well-understood problem, and structures like B-trees provide efficient access mechanisms. In this scenario, indexing assures sublinear search while maintaining completeness; that is, all records satisfying the query are returned without the need for examining each record in the database. However, in the context of similarity matching for visual content, traditional indexing methods may not be appropriate. For queries in which similarity is defined as a distance metric in high-dimensional feature spaces (for example, color histogram queries), indexing involves clustering and indexable representations of the clusters. In the case of queries that combine similarity matching with spatial constraints on objects, the problem is more involved. Data structures for fast access of high-dimensional features for spatial relationships must be invented.

In a query, features from the database are compared to corresponding features from the query specification to determine which images are a good match. For a small database, sequential scanning of the features followed by straightforward similarity computations is adequate. But as the database grows, this combination can be too slow. To speed up the queries, we have investigated a variety of techniques. Two of the most promising follow.

5.1 Filtering

A computationally fast filter is applied to all data, and only items that pass through the filter are operated on by the second stage, which computes the true similarity metric. For example, in QBIC we have shown that color histogram matching, which is based on a 256-dimensional color histogram and requires a 256 matrix-vector multiply, can be made efficient by filtering. The filtering step employs a much faster computation in a 3D space with no loss in accuracy. Thus, for a query on a database of 10,000 elements, the fast filter is applied to produce the best 1,000 color histogram matches. These filtered histograms are subsequently passed to the slower complete matching operation to obtain, say, the best 200 matches to display to a user, with the guarantee that the global best 200 in the database have been found.

5.2 Indexing

For low-dimensional features such as average color and texture (each 3D), multidimensional indexing methods such as R*-trees can be used. For high-dimensional features—for example, our 20-dimensional moment-based shape feature vector—the dimensionality is reduced using the K-L, or principal component, transform. This produces a low-dimensional space, as low as two or three dimensions, which could be indexed by using R*-trees.

6. Conclusions

We have described a prototype system that uses image and video content as the basis for retrievals. Technology from this prototype has already moved into a commercial stand-alone product, IBM's Ultimedia Manager, and is part of IBM's Digital Library and DB2 series of products. Other companies are beginning to offer products with similar capabilities. Key challenges remain in making this technology pervasive and useful.

Annotation and database population tools: Automatic methods (such as our Positional Color query) that don't rely on object identification, methods that identify objects automatically as in the museum image example, fast and easy-to-use semiautomatic outlining tools, and motion-based segmentation algorithms will enable additional application areas.

Feature extraction and matching methods: New mathematical representations of video, image, and object attributes that capture "interesting" features for retrieval are needed. Features that describe new image properties such as alternate texture measures or that are based on fractals or wavelet representations, for example, may offer advantages of representation, indexability, and ease of similarity matching.

Integration with text and parametric annotation: Query by visual content complements and extends existing query methods. Systems must be able to integrate queries combining date, subject matter, price, and availability with content properties such as color, texture, and shape.

Extensibility and flexibility: System architectures must support the addition of new features and new matching/similarity measures. Real applications often require new features, say a face-matching module, to add to their existing content-based retrieval capabilities.

User interface: The user interface must be designed to let users easily select content-based properties, allow these properties to be combined with each other and with text or parametric data, and let users reformulate queries and generally navigate the database.

Indexing and performance: As image and video collections grow, system performance must not slow down proportionately. Indexing, clustering, and filtering methods must be designed into the matching methods to maintain performance.

With these technologies, the QBIC paradigm of visual content querying, combined with traditional keyword and text querying, will lead to powerful search engines for multimedia archives. Applications will occur in areas such as decision support for retail marketing, on-line stock photo and video management, cataloging for library and museum collections, and multimedia-enabled applications in art, fashion, advertising, medicine, and science.

Note

1 The database used in this and subsequent figures consists of about 7,450 images from the Mediasource Series of images and audio from Romtech Corp., 4,100 images from the PhotoDisc sampler CD, 950 images from the Corel Professional Photo CD collection, and 450 images from an IBM collection.

References

Tonomura, Y; Akutsu, A.; Otsuji, K.; and Sadakata, T. 1993. VideoMAP and VideoSpaceIcon: Tools for Anatomizing Video Content. In Proceedings of ACM IN-TERCHI, 131-136. Amsterdam: ACM.

Ayer, S. and Sawhney, H. S. 1995. Layered Representation of Motion Video Using Robust Maximum-Likelihood Estimation of Mixture Models and MDL Encoding. In Proceedings of the Fifth International Conference on Computer Vision, 777-784. Los Alamitos, Calif.: IEEE CS Press, Order No. PRO7042, http://www.almaden.ibm.com/pub/cs/reports/vision/layered_motion.ps.Z.

Ashley, J.; Barber, R.; Flickner, M.; Hafner, J.; Lee, D.; Niblack, W.; Petkovic, D. 1995. Automatic and Semiautomatic Methods for Image Annotation and Retrieval in QBIC. In Proceedings of Storage and Retrieval for Image and Video Databases III, Vol. 2420: 24-35, Bellingham, WA: SPIE.

IFIP, 1989 and 1992. *Visual Database Systems I and II,* North-Holland: Elsevier Science Publishers.

Kato, T.; Kurita, T.; and Shimogaki, H. 1991. Intelligent Visual Interaction with Image Database Systems—Toward the Multimedia Personal Interface. *Information Processing* (Japan), 14(2): 134-143.

Nagasaka, A. and Tanaka, Y. 1992. Automatic Video Indexing and Full-Video Search for Object Appearances. *Visual Database Systems, II, IFIP Trans. A-7,* 113-127. North-Holland: Elsevier Science Publishers.

Niblack, W.; Barber, R.; Equitz, W.; Flickner, M.; Glasman, E.; Petkovic, D.; Yanker, P.; Faloutsos, C.; Taubin, G. 1993. The QBIC Project: Querying Images by Content Using Color, Texture, and Shape. In Proceedings of Storage and Retrieval for Image and Video Databases, Vol. 1908: 173-187. Bellingham, WA: SPIE.

Niblack, W. and Jain, R. eds. 1993, 1994, and 1995. In Proceedings of Storage and Retrieval for Image and Video Databases I, II, and III, Vols. 1908, 2185, and 2420. Bellingham, WA: SPIE.

Pentland, A.; Picard, R.W. and Sclaroff, S. 1994. Photobook: Tools for Content-Based Manipulation of Image Databases. In Proceedings of Storage and Retrieval for Image and Video Databases II, Vol. 2185: 34-47, Bellingham, WA: SPIE.

Sawhney, H. S., Ayer, S. and Gorkani, M. 1995. Model-Based 2D & 3D Dominant Motion Estimation for Mosaicking and Video Representation. In Proceedings of the Fifth International Conference on Computer Vision, 583-590. Los Alamitos, CA: IEEE CS Press, Order No. PRO7042. http://www.almaden.ibm.com/pub/cs/reports/vision/dominant_motion.ps.Z.

Teodosio, L. A. and Bender, W. 1993. Salient Video Stills: Content and Context Preserved. In Proceedings of the First ACM International Conference on Multimedia, 39-46. New York: ACM.

Wang, J. Y. A. and Adelson, E. H. 1993. Layered Representation for Motion Analysis. In Proceedings of the Computer Vision and Pattern Recognition Conference, 361-366. Los Alamitos, CA: IEEE CS Press.

Chapter 2

Querying by Color Regions Using the VisualSEEk Content-Based Visual Query System

John R. Smith and Shih-Fu Chang
Center for Image Technology for New Media
and Department of Electrical Engineering, Columbia University

Abstract

VisualSEEk is a highly functional image database manipulation system that provides advanced user tools for searching, browsing and retrieving images. VisualSEEk is distinct from other content-based image query systems in that the user may query for images using both the visual properties of regions and their spatial layout. Furthermore, the image analysis for region extraction is fully automated. VisualSEEk uses a novel system for region extraction and representation based upon color sets. Through a process of color set back-projection, the system automatically extracts salient color regions from images. This chapter describes the implementation of the color query system and examines its role for content-based visual query in image and video databases. The next phases of the VisualSEEk implementation will provide additional tools for querying by texture, shape, embedded text and motion features.

1. Introduction

This chapter describes the design, implementation and operation of the VisualSEEk content-based visual query system. VisualSEEk is a new content-based image query system that enables querying by both the visual properties of image regions and their spatial layout. VisualSEEk is easy to use and provides power and flexibility in the expression of visual queries. As the primary means for querying, the system utilizes visual features that are extracted from the images and videos using automated scene analysis. The integration

Figure 1. Image decomposition into localized color regions (a.) Original target image, (b.) Decomposed target image. (c.) Sample query image.

of feature-based similarity and spatial querying relies on the representation of color regions by color sets. Color sets provide for a convenient system of region extraction through back-projection (Smith and Chang 1996b). In addition, the color set distance function can be decomposed into terms that are easily indexed. This allows for the efficient computation of color set distance and the indexing of color regions. As a result, the system decomposes unconstrained images into near-symbolic images that lend to efficient spatial query, as depicted in figure 1.

In this chapter we briefly describe the processes for extraction, representation and spatial query of the color regions. We also describe other components of VisualSEEk such as the Give Me More color search tools and text-based search and annotation tools. These components also have critical roles in the query system. For example, clustering the images and videos using visual features greatly accelerates the annotation process. Finally, we demonstrate the query tools and show some example queries. Color is just one visual modality we are investigating. We will soon integrate into the query system other visual features such as texture, shape, motion and embedded text.

1.1 Image and Video Storage and Retrieval Systems

An image and video storage and retrieval (IVSR) system manages, stores and provides tools for search and retrieval of images and videos. Applications of IVSR include on-line stock photography, video-on demand (Chang et al. 1994), video browsing (Zhong et al. 1996) and video editing (Meng and Chang 1996). There are some great technical challenges in improving access to archived visual information. First, current search tools are primitive. Typically, the IVSR system utilizes textual descriptions or keywords for querying for visual items. However, producing meaningful annotations for an entire archive of visual data requires great human effort. Any set of text descriptions cannot characterize the content of the images and videos sufficiently or consistently. Second, the enormity of the visual data prohibits the user from visually inspecting all but small portions of the archive at a time. Therefore, the ability to find the desired images and videos depends primarily on the capabilities of the query tools the system provides. Finally, traditional ISVR systems do not enable the user to retrieve items using queries of the type: "give me all images that look like this one." Rather, content-based visual query tools provide this type of enhanced operation.

1.2 Content-based Visual Query Systems

Content-based visual query (CBVQ) tools enhance the operation of IVSR systems by providing the means for conducting visual searches. The user may search for images in several ways, (1) by image example, (2) by sketch or (3) by features, such as color and texture. Thus far, research on CBVQ has fo-

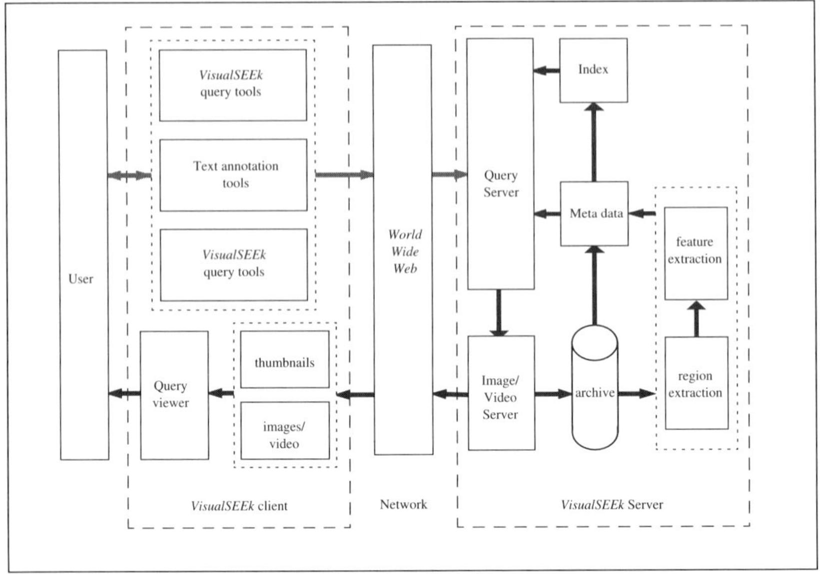

Figure 2. The VisualSEEk system.

cused on color, texture and shape features because these are most natural for the user and can be represented effectively by computer. For example, the IBM Query by Image Content (QBIC) project (Faloutsos et al. 1994) provides tools for querying by color, texture and shape. Other research systems such as MIT's Photobook system (Pentland et al. 1994) and the Virage system (Bach et al. 1996) also provide CBVQ tools for searching for images by color, texture and shape. However, these systems have neglected an important aspect of visual perception—spatial information and spatial relationships.

There are still many unresolved research issues in CBVQ, such as, (1) what visual features are best, (2) how should they be extracted, coded and compared, (3) what are the proper searching techniques and indexing structures and (4) how should the user best browse and search for images. Furthermore, particular applications require custom solutions. For example, searching through a medical image archive using medical artifacts requires a different approach and different visual features than a satellite image system using terrain features.

1.3 The VisualSEEk CBVQ System

The goal of the VisualSEEk project is to implement a CBVQ system that provides the means for efficient and effective retrieval of images and video (Chang et al. 1996). The VisualSEEk project has emphasized several unique

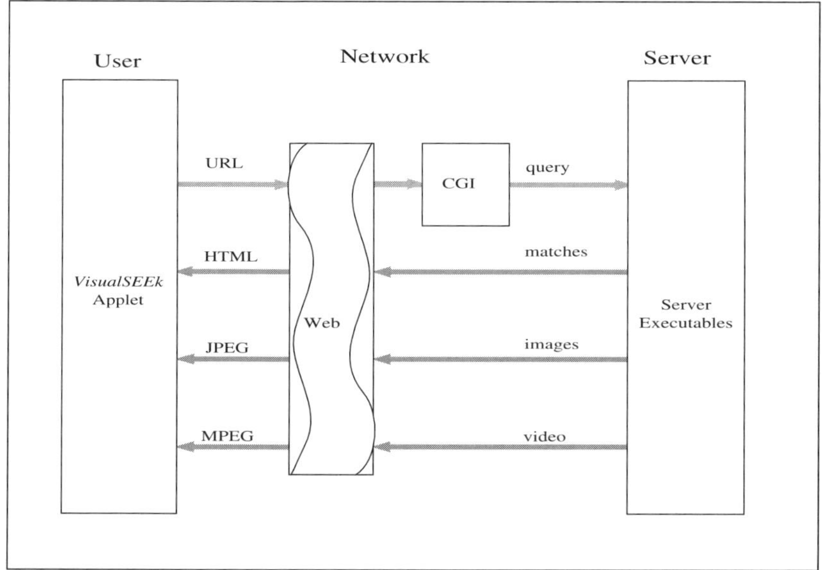

Figure 3. VisualSEEk system overview.

objectives in order to improve functionality: (1) automated extraction of localized regions and features (Smith and Chang 1996a) (2) querying by both
feature and spatial information (Smith and Chang 1996b), (3) extraction
from compressed data (Chang and Smith 1995), (4) fast indexing and retrieval and (5) highly functional user tools. We developed the VisualSEEk
client application in the Java language to allow for maximum functionality,
client platform independence and accessibility on the World Wide Web. Currently, the VisualSEEk system provides a test-bed of 12,000 color images.

2. System Requirements and Design

The overall system consists of several components: the VisualSEEk user
tools, the query server, the image and video retrieval server, the image and
video archive, the meta-data database and the index files, as illustrated in
figure 2.

2.1 System Architecture

The VisualSEEk system consists of three applications: (1) the client application, (2) the network and communication application, and (3) the server application, as illustrated in figure 3. The client application consists of a suite

of Java applets that execute within the world wide web browser. The VisualSEEk applet collects the query from the user and sends the query string to the server. The hypertext transfer protocol (HTTP) client-server system handles all communication across the World Wide Web. The common gateway interface (CGI) component of the HTTP executes the server program on the VisualSEEk query server machine.

2.2 User Application

The user application collects the query from the user and generates the query string. The query tools allow the selection of region properties and the assignment of the spatial layout of regions. For example, one tool coordinates the placement of the color regions on the query grid. Another allows for selection of color. The client application packages the user's query into the query string which it sends to the server.

2.3 Server Application

The server application receives the query string, executes the query and returns the results to the user. The server first parses the query string and processes the query's color selection. It converts the color parameters into a corresponding color in hue-saturation-value (HSV) color space. Next, it returns to the user a mock-up image that depicts the received query. Then, a query program finds the best matches to the user's query. This program produces hypertext markup language (HTML) code that displays the results of the query to the user. The HTML output includes thumbnail images to depict the images and videos found in the query. The output also indicates the distance scores for each matched item. When the user selects a thumbnail image the system retrieves the corresponding image or video from the image and video server. The system also allows the user to search again by image example using the returned images.

2.4 Color Region Queries

The user graphically constructs joint color/spatial queries using the VisualSEEk query tools illustrated in figure 4. The user sketches the regions, positions them on the query grid and assigns them properties of color, size and absolute location. The user may also assign boundaries for location and size of the regions. The spatial relationships between regions are diagrammed in VisualSEEk by connecting regions. In this way, the interface provides for construction of queries that include region features and combinations of both absolute and relative placement of the regions. For example, figure 5(a) depicts a query that specifies three regions—blue, green and light blue with no constraint on their spatial arrangement. Figure 5(b) illustrates the results of

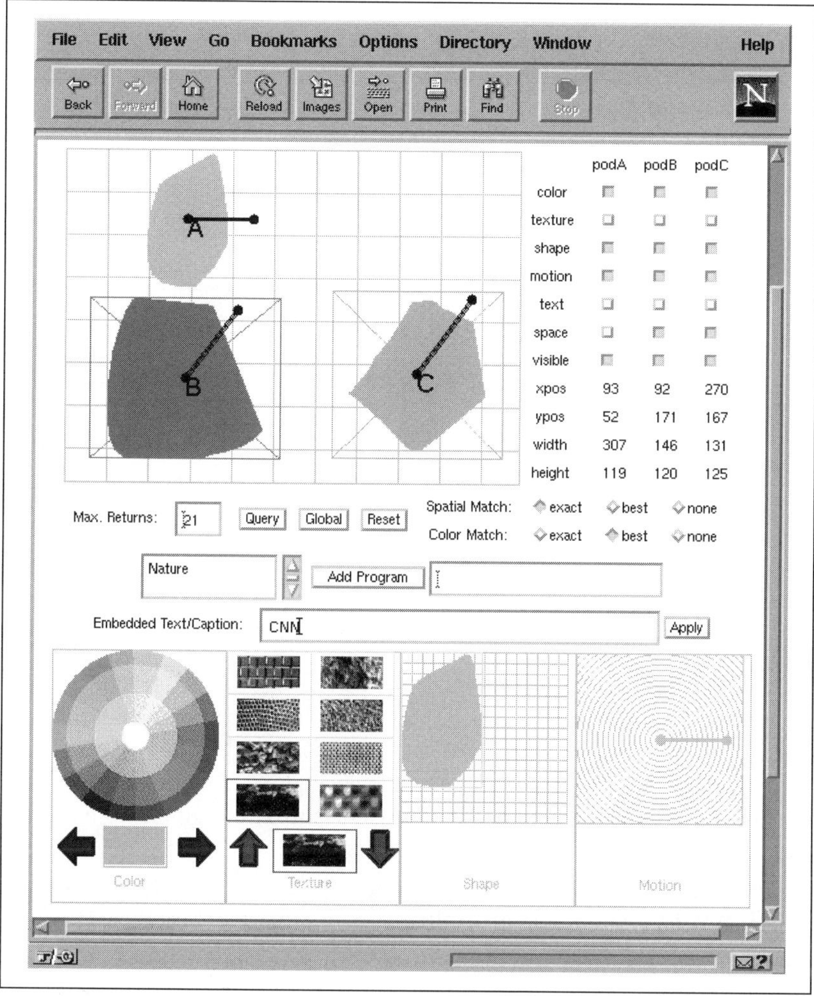

Figure 4 VisualSEEk Java user interface.

the query which has found images of underwater scenes and nature with blue skies and trees.

2.5 Give Me More Queries

After the system finds the matches and returns the thumbnail images, as in figure 5(b), the user has several options: (1) select items for full retrieval and viewing, (2) modify the query and try again and (3) select items for Give Me More queries. In a Give Me More query, VisualSEEk searches the database

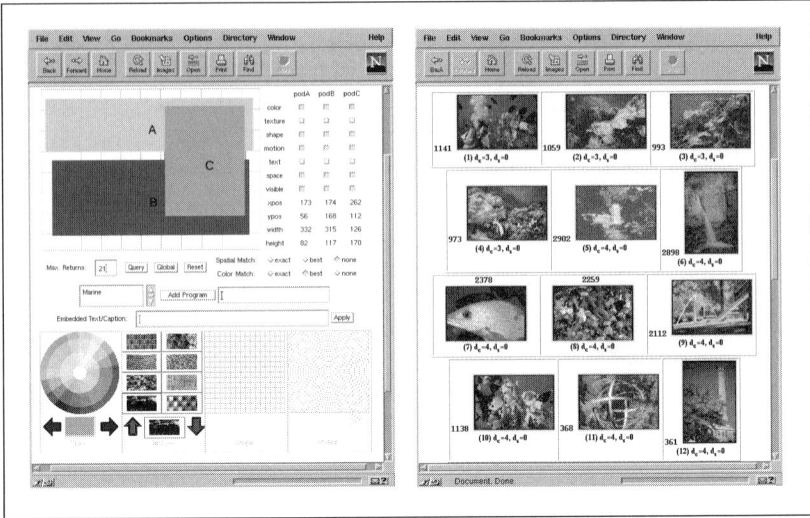

Figure 5. A sample query that specifies three colors.
(a) Query configuration in VisualSEEk. (b) Query results.

for the best matches to the selected item. The Give Me More query tools allow the user to select from several global similarity metrics such as: global color, color regions, global texture, and joint color and texture. Figure 6 illustrates an example Give Me More query using global color features of a selected image from figure 6(a). The images displayed in figure 6(b) have the most similar color content to the selected image.

2.6 Image and Video Annotation

The VisualSEEk system also provides tools for annotating scenes individually and in groups. The annotation tool, figure 7(a), allows the user to easily assign text to images and videos. The user adds new annotations by entering keywords into the entry box corresponding to the image or video. VisualSEEk also provides a system for the group annotation of images. By clustering items from the database by their visual features, the user may annotate them in groups, which significantly reduces the time and effort required to annotate the archive. For example, the first image, which depicts an ocean scene, see figure 7(a), is selected for "power annotation." The system searches the database for similar images and returns them to the user, figure 7(b). Many of the returned images have a similar subject to the selected image and also depict ocean scenes. The user may now assign the annotations, as appropriate, to the group of images.

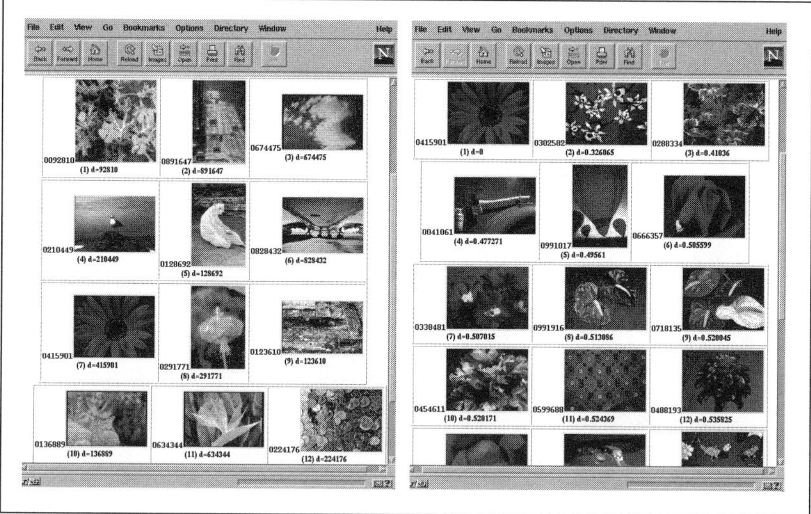

*Figure 6. Give me more query. (a—left) Images selected at random
from the database. (b—right) Results of a Give Me More
query using global color of the image in (a) third down on the left.*

2.7 Integrated Text/Image Feature Searching

Text-based searching is still an important component of CBVQ systems. Although text alone is not always sufficient, text-searching combined with CBVQ improves query capabilities. For example, given that some of the images and videos are annotated, a user may find some matches in a text-based search. If the text-based search is partially successful, the user can select some of the resulting matches to seed visual feature-based queries. For example, say that only two of the many images of lions from the database have been annotated with the keyword "lion." By conducting a text-based search using "lion," the system finds both of the matches, see figure 8(a). However, many images of lions remain in the archive and are not retrieved. By selecting one of the returned lion images and by issuing a Give Me More query based upon the visual features of the selected image, the system finds many of the remaining images of lions, see figure 8(b).

3. Querying Using Spatially Localized Color Regions

As discussed already, there are two approaches for querying by color: by regional color and by global color. Regional color corresponds to spatially localized colored regions within the scenes. Global color corresponds to the

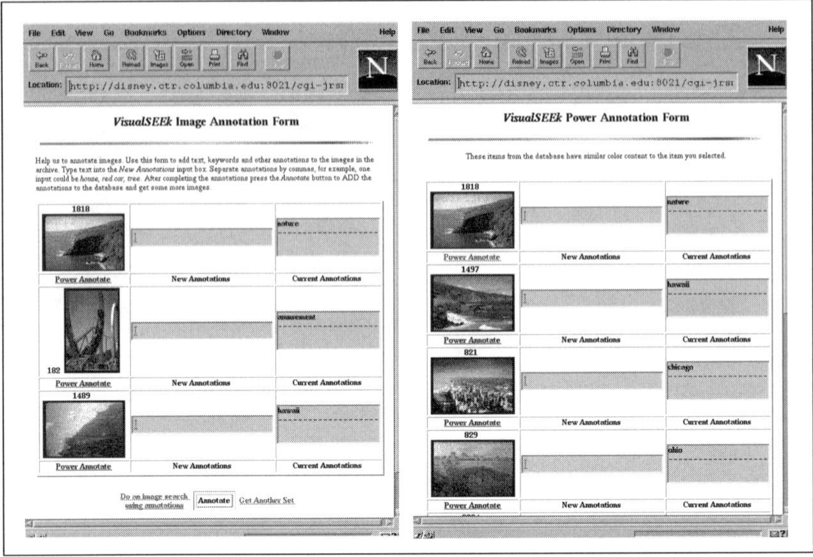

Figure 7. Annotation (a) individual image annotation.
(b) "Power" annotation allows for group annotation of similar images.

overall distribution of color within the entire scene. This next section describes the process for the automated extraction and query of spatially localized color regions, which uses color sets.

Color sets provide a compact and easily indexed representation of regional color content (Smith and Chang 1996b). The extraction and query of color sets is analogous the process of file inversion for search and retrieval of textual document (Witten et al. 1994). The goal is to efficiently index the color regions. A binary color set back-projection algorithm extracts the color regions automatically. In short, VisualSEEk extracts color regions in a process that (1) transforms, (2) quantizes and (3) filters the images and videos to emphasize prominent color regions. The back-projection algorithm extracts the prominent color regions, which the system represents and indexes by color set value.

3.1 Color Representation and Back-Projection

Color sets provide an efficient alternative to color histograms for representation of color information. The following paragraphs define color sets and explain their relationship to color histograms.

3.1.1 Color Set Representation of Color Regions. Three dimensions of color can be defined and measured. For example, each image point can be represented as a 3-D vector $v_c = (r,g,b)$ in the *RGB* color space. The transfor-

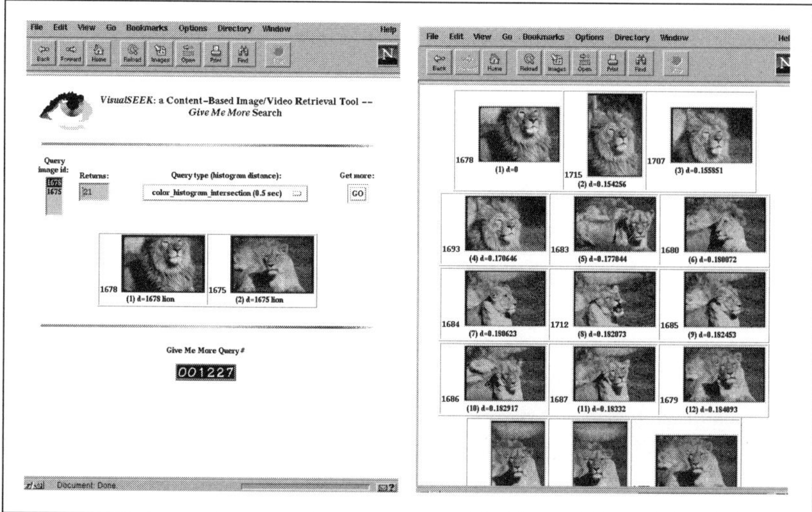

Figure 8. Integrated text/image-feature searching. (a) Text-based search using key-word "lion" yields only two matches. (b) Feature-based search using a lion image from (a) finds many images of lions.

mation T_c and quantization Q_c^M of the *RGB* color space reorganize and group the vectors v_c. The perceptually distinct colors are obtained by the sets of vectors that are mapped to different indices M as diagrammed in figure 9. We define color sets as follows: let B_c^M be the M dimensional binary space such that each axis in B_c^M corresponds to one unique index value m. A color set is a binary vector in B_c^M that corresponds to a selection of colors $\{m\}$.

3.1.2 Color Set Example. For example, let T_c transform *RGB* to *HSV* and let Q_c^M where $M = 8$ quantize the *HSV* color space to 2 hues, 2 saturations and 2 values. The quantizer Q_c^M assigns a unique index M to each quantized *HSV* color. Then, B_c^8 is the eight dimensional binary space whereby each axis in B_c^8 corresponds to one of the quantized *HSV* colors. A color set $\hat{c}$ contains a selection from the eight colors. For example, the color set $\hat{c} = [10010100]$ corresponds to the selection of three colors, $m = 7$, $m = 4$, and $m = 2$ from the quantized *HSV* color space. In the VisualSEEk application, we chose T_c to transform *RGB* to *HSV* because *HSV* provides a breakdown of color into its most natural components: hue, saturation and intensity.[1] We chose the quantization Q_c^M to provide $M = 166$ represented colors as illustrated in figure 10 (Smith and Chang 1996b).

3.1.3 Color Set Back-Projection. The process of region extraction requires several stages: color set iteration, back-projection, thresholding and labeling. The color set iteration procedure selects candidate color sets to back-project onto the image by considering the content of the image histogram and the

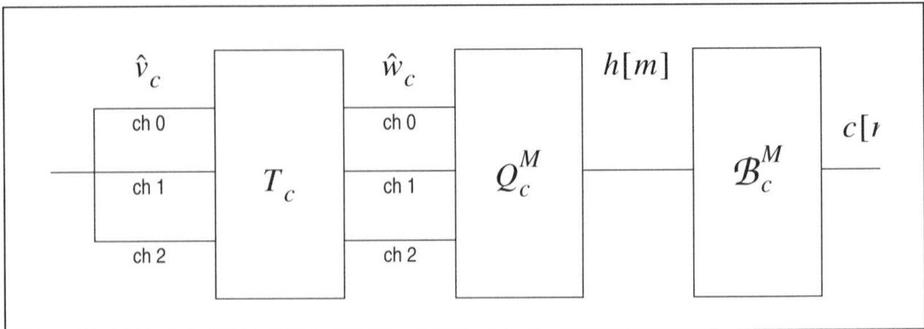

Figure 9. Generation of the binary color space from three color channels.

previously extracted color regions. The back-projection of a color set is accomplished as follows: given image $I[x,y]$ and binary color set $\hat{c}$, let $k = I[x,y]$, then generate bi-level image $B[x,y] = c[k]$. That is, $B[x,y]$ depicts the back-projection of color set $\hat{c}$. The bi-level image $B[x,y]$ is then filtered morphologically and analyzed to reveal spatially localized color regions (Smith and Chang 1996b).

3.1.4 Color Similarity. The similarity between any two colors $m_q = h_q,s_q,v_q)$ and $m_t = (h_t,s_t,v_t,)$ and is given by

$$a_{q,t} = 1 - \frac{[(v_q - v_t)^2 + (s_q \cos h_q - s_t \cos h_t)^2 + (s_q \sin h_q - s_t \sin h_t)^2]^{\frac{1}{2}}}{\sqrt{5}} \tag{1}$$

which is derived from the distance in the cylindrical *HSV* color space depicted in figure 10. Single color similarity is used within the computation of the distance between color distributions.

3.1.5 Color Histograms. A color histogram corresponds to a distribution of colors. By transforming the three color channels of image $I[x,y]$ using transformation T_c and quantization Q_c^M where $(\hat{v}_c)_{xy} = I_R[x,y], I_G[x,y], I_B[x,y])$ the single variable color histogram is given by, where X and Y are the width and height of the image, respectively,

$$h[m] = \frac{1}{XY} \sum_{x=0}^{X-1} \sum_{y=0}^{Y-1} \begin{cases} 1 \text{ if } Q_c^M T_c\left(\hat{v}_c\right)_{xy} = m \\ 0 \text{ otherwise} \end{cases} \tag{2}$$

3.1.6 Histogram Quadratic Distance. The QBIC project proposed the histogram quadratic distance for image retrieval (Niblack et al. 1993). It measures the weighted similarity between histograms, which provides more desirable matching than "like-bin" only comparisons. The quadratic distance between histograms ($\hat{h}_q$ and ($\hat{h}_t$ is given by

$$d_{q,t}^{hist} = (\hat{h}_q - \hat{h}_t)^t A (\hat{h}_q - \hat{h}_t), \tag{3}$$

where $A = [a_{ij}]$ and a_{ij} denotes the similarity of colors with indexes i and j. By

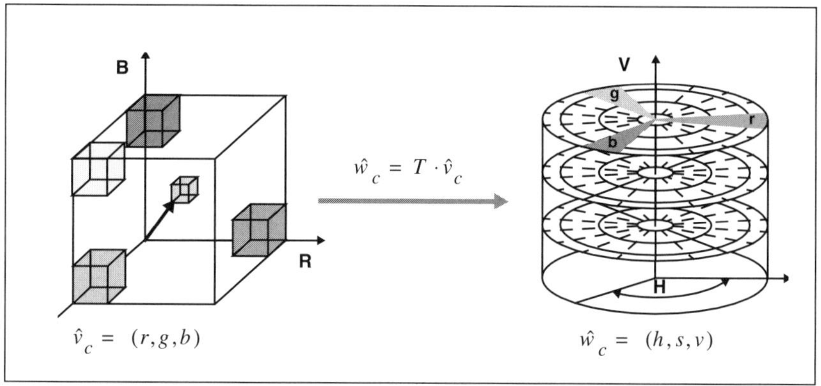

Figure 10. Transformation from RGB to HSV and quantization gives 18 hues, 3 saturations, 3 values and 4 grays = 166 colors.

defining color similarity in *HSV* color space, a_{ij} is given by eq. 1. Since the histogram quadratic distance computes the cross similarity between colors, it is computationally expensive. Therefore, large applications require other strategies, such as pre-filtering to avoid exhaustive search (Hafner et al. 1995).

3.1.7 Color Sets Versus Color Histograms. Color sets give only the selection of colors, whereas, a color histogram denotes the relative amounts of colors. A color set approximates a color histogram by thresholding the color histogram. For example, given threshold τ_m for color *m*, a color set is obtained from (see also figure 11),

$$c[m] = \begin{cases} 1 & if\ h[m] \geq \tau_m \\ 0 & otherwise \end{cases} \tag{4}$$

The color set indicates only those colors that are found above threshold levels. It works well to represent regional color since (1) T_c and Q_c^M have been derived to give a complete set of distinct colors and (2) the region extraction is based upon the dominant colors in the regions (Smith and Chang 1996b). A color that is not well represented in a region—for example, if it is below threshold τ_m— is ignored. One good choice of threshold τ_m is $\tau_m = 1/\sigma_m^2$ where σ_m^2 is the variance of color *m* in a random sample of images.

3.1.8 Color Set Distance. The histogram quadratic distance equation, Eq. 3, is also used for the distance between color sets. The distance between two color sets $\hat{c}_q$ and $\hat{c}_t$ is given by

$$d_{q,t}^{set} = (\hat{c}_q - \hat{c}_t)^t A (\hat{c}_q - \hat{c}_t). \tag{5}$$

However, given the binary nature of the color set representation, the computational complexity of the quadratic distance function can be reduced. We de-

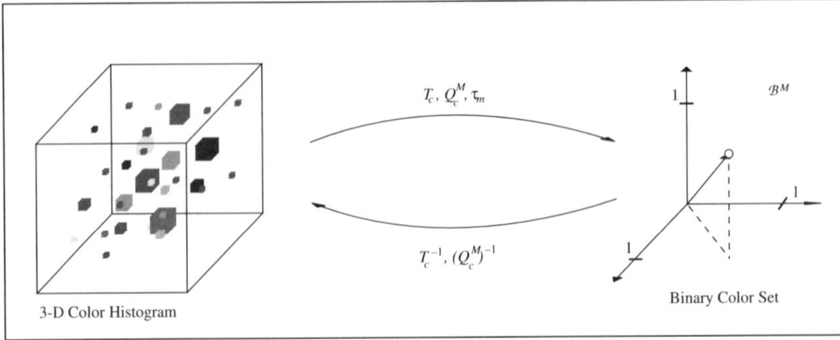

Figure 11. Relationship between 3-d color histogram and binary color sets.

compose the color set quadratic formula to provide for efficient computation and indexing. By defining $\mu_q = \hat{c}_q^t A \hat{c}_q$, $\mu_t = \hat{c}_t^t A \hat{c}_t$ and $\hat{R}_t = A\hat{c}_t$, and since A is symmetric, the color set quadratic distance is equivalent to

$$d_{q,t}^{set} = \mu_q + \mu_t - 2\hat{c}_q^t \hat{R}_t \tag{6}$$

Since $\hat{c}_q \in B^M$ ($\hat{c}_q$ is a binary vector),

$$d_{q,t}^{set} - \mu_q = \mu_t - 2 \sum_{\forall m \, where \, c_q[m]=1} R_t[m]. \tag{7}$$

That is, any query for the most similar color set to $\hat{c}_q$ may be easily processed by storing and indexing individually μ_t and $R_t[m]$, where $m \in 1 \dots M$. Notice also that μ_q is a constant of the query. The closest color set $\hat{c}_t$ is given as the one that minimizes

$$\mu_t - 2\sum_{\forall m \, where \, c_q[m]=1} R_t[m] .$$

4. Query Examples and Evaluation

In this section we discuss VisualSEEk, join content-based/spatial query examples, and the evaluation of color sets.

4.1 VisualSEEk Queries

We illustrate the power and flexibility of the VisualSEEk query system over non-spatial techniques in figure 12. In figure 12(a) (top left), a VisualSEEk query is diagrammed that specifies two regions (outer is orange and inner is yellow) and their spatial layout with the goal of retrieving images of sunsets. The best matches to the color/spatial query (left) have a similar arrangement of similarly colored regions. In figure 12(b), a typical sunset image is used

Figure 12. Sample "sunset" queries. (a) VisualSEEk query using diagrammed query at top left. (b) Color histogram query using image at top right. Best matches are listed from top to bottom.

(top right), and the best matches (right) are found that have the most similar color histograms to the query image. We see that the global color histogram query process gives the user little control in specifying the query and more readily returns images that are not desired.

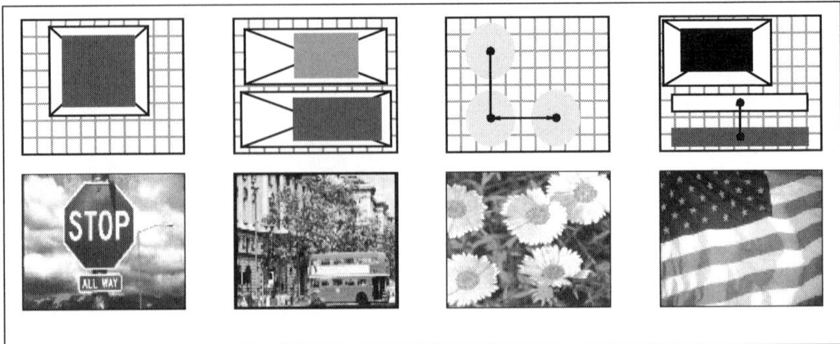

Figure 13. Example VisualSEEk queries. (a.) Single region with absolute locations. (b.) Two regions with absolute locations. (c.) Multiple regions with relative locations. (d.) Multiple regions with absolute and relative locations.

4.2 Joint Content-based/Spatial Query Examples

We now illustrate the range of color/spatial queries that are possible in VisualSEEk. In the first example, see figure 13(a), the query (top) specifies the absolute location of a single region. The retrieved image (bottom) has the best match in color and size to the query region. In figure 13(b), the query specifies two regions. The retrieved image has two color match regions located at the positions in the query image. In figure 13(c), the query specifies the spatial relationships of three regions. The retrieved image has three regions that best match the colors of the query regions and their spatial relationship satisfies that specified in the query. In figure 13(d), the query specifies both absolute and relative locations of regions. In this query, the match to the region positioned by absolute location (top left region in query image) considers both the color and location of this region. The match to the other regions (bottom two regions in query image) at first considers only the colors of these regions. In the last stage of the query, the spatial relationships of the regions are evaluated to determine the match.

4.3 Evaluation of Color Sets

In order to evaluate the impact of the loss of information in using color sets instead of color histograms, we compared their performance in retrieving images by global color content. This experiment does not evaluate the color/spatial query system, rather, it compares color sets directly to color histograms.

In an image database of 3,100 images, we measured the ability of color sets and color histograms to retrieve the 83 images of lions using an example

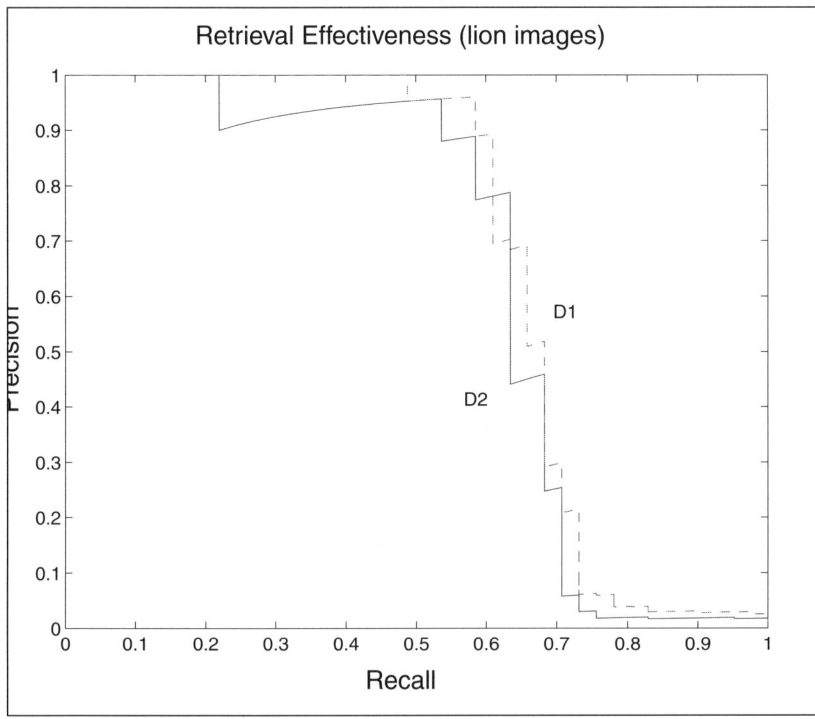

Figure 14. Retrieval of 83 lion images from a database of 3,100 images: D1= color histogram quadratic distance. D2= solor set quadratic distance.

lion image. Figure 14 depicts the retrieval effectiveness (Sparck Jones 1981) in the retrieval of the images of lions. The experiment shows that retrieval effectiveness degrades only slightly using color sets (D2) and the quadratic distance measure (Eq. 5) compared to color histograms (D1) using the quadratic distance function (Eq. 3). This indicates that the perceptually significant color information is retained in the color sets.

5. Summary and Future Work

This chapter presented the VisualSEEk content-based visual query system. VisualSEEk provides tools for querying for images by diagramming the spatial layout of color regions and by providing example images. VisualSEEk also provides tools for annotating images in the archive and for searching the archive using text. In future work we will extend many of the search capabilities of VisualSEEk to include other visual features such as texture, shape, embedded text and motion.

References

Bach, J. R.; Fuller, C.; Hampapur, A.; Horowitz, B.; Humphrey, R.; Jain, R. C.; and Shu, C. 1996. Virage Image Search Engine: An Open Framework For Image Management. In Proceedings, Symposium on Electronic Imaging: Science and Technology - Storage & Retrieval for Image and Video Databases IV., 76 - 87. San Jose, CA.: IS&T/SPIE.

Chang, S.-F.; Smith, J. R.; and Meng, J. 1996. Efficient Techniques for Feature-Based Image/Video Access and Manipulation. In Proceedings of the 33rd Annual Clinic on Library Applications of Data Processing: Digital Image Access and Retrieval, 40-49, eds. P. Bryan Heidorn and B. Sandore. Champaign, IL: University of Illinois Press.

Chang, S.-F.; and Smith, J. R. 1995. Extracting Multi-Dimensional Signal Features for Content-Based Visual Query. In Proceedings of Visual Communications and Image Processing '95, SPIE Vol. 2501, 995-1006, ed. Lance T. Wu, Bellingham, WA: The International Society for Optical Engineering.

Chang, S.-F.; Anastassiou, D.; Eleftheriadis, A.; Meng, J.; Paek, S.; and Smith, J. R. 1994. Development of Advanced Image/Video Servers in the Video on Demand Testbed. In Proceedings of the IEEE Workshop on Visual Signal Processing and Communications, 1-5, Piscataway, NJ.: IEEE.

Faloutsos, C.; Barber, R; Flickner, M.; Niblack, W.; Petkovic, D.; and Equitz, W. 1994. Efficient and Effective Querying by Image Content, Technical Report RJ9453 (83074), 1993, IBM Research Division, Almaden Research Center, San Jose, CA.

Hafner, J.; Sawhney, H. S.; Equitz, W.; and Flickner, M.; and Niblack, W. 1995. Efficient Color Histogram Indexing for Quadratic Form Distance Functions. *IEEE Transactions on Pattern Analysis and Machine Intelligence* 17(7): 729-736.

Meng, J.; and Chang, S.-F. 1996. Tools for Compressed-Domain Video Indexing and Editing. In Proceedings, Symposium on Electronic Imaging: Science and Technology—Storage & Retrieval for Image and Video Databases IV, 180-193. San Jose, CA.: IS&T/SPIE.

Niblack, W.; Barber, R.; Equitz, W.; Flickner, M.; Glasman, E.; Petkovic, D.; Yanker, P.; and Faloutsos, C. 1993. The QBIC project: Querying Images by Content Using Color, Texture and Shape. In Proceedings of Storage and Retrieval for Image and Video Databases, ed. W. Niblack, SPIE Vol. 1908, 173-187. Bellingham, WA: The International Society for Optical Engineering.

Pentland, A.; Picard, R. W.; and Sclaroff, S. 1994. Photobook: Tools for Content-Based Manipulation of Image Databases. In Twenty-third AIPR Workshop: Image and Information Systems: Applications and Opportunities, ed. Peter J. Costianes, SPIE Vol. 2368, 37-50. Bellingham, WA: The International Society for Optical Engineering.

Smith, J. R. and Chang, S.-F. 1996a. Automated Binary Texture Feature Sets for Image Retrieval. In Proceedings of the International Conference On Acoustic Speech and Signal Processing (ICASSP), 2241-2244, Atlanta, GA.: IEEE.

Smith, J. R.; and Chang, S.-F. 1996b. Tools and Techniques for Color Image Retrieval. In Proceedings, Symposium on Electronic Imaging: Science and Technology - Storage & Retrieval for Image and Video Databases IV, 426-437. San Jose, CA.: IS&T/SPIE.

Sparck Jones, K. 1981. *Information Retrieval Experiment.* London: Butterworth and Co.

Witten, I. H.; Moffat, A.; and Bell, T. C. 1994. *Managing Gigabytes: Compressing and Indexing Documents and Images*. New York: Van Nostrand Reinhold.

Zhong, D.; Zhang, H. J.; and Chang, S.-F. 1996. Clustering Methods For Video Browsing and Annotation. In Proceedings, Symposium on Electronic Imaging: Science and Technology - Storage & Retrieval for Image and Video Databases IV, 239-246. San Jose, CA.: IS&T/SPIE.

Chapter 3

Word Spotting: Indexing Handwritten Manuscripts

R. Manmatha and W. B. Croft
University of Massachusetts, Amherst

Abstract

There are many single author, handwritten historical manuscripts that would be useful to index. Examples include the early Presidential papers at the Library of Congress and the collected works of W. B. DuBois at the library of the University of Massachusetts. The standard technique for indexing documents is to scan them in, convert them to machine readable form (ASCII) using optical character recognition (OCR), and then index them using a text retrieval engine. However, OCR does not work well on handwriting. In this chapter an alternative scheme is proposed for indexing such texts. Each page of the document is segmented into words. The images of the words are then matched against each other to create equivalence class (each equivalence classes contains multiple instances of the same word). The user then provides ASCII equivalents for the most frequent equivalence classes.

This chapter addresses the matching aspects of this process. Due to variations in even a single person's handwriting, it is expected that the matching will be the most difficult step in the process. Two different techniques for matching words are discussed. The first method, based on Euclidean distance mapping, matches words assuming that the transformation between the words may be modeled by a translation (shift). The second method, based on an algorithm developed by Scott and Longuet-Higgins (1991), matches words assuming that the transformation between the words may be modelled by an affine transform. Experiments are shown demonstrating the feasibility of the approach for indexing handwriting.

1. Introduction

The explosion of information in today's society has led to a need for automated indexing. If the information is in machine readable form (ASCII), it can be indexed using text retrieval engines. However, much of today's information is multimedia in nature and in nondigital form (e.g., paper, analog video). A number of chapters in this collection discuss the problem of retrieving and indexing multimedia information. For example, Flickner et al. (this volume) discuss the QBIC system to query images based on attributes like color, texture and shape, while Jones et al. (this volume) discuss the problem of retrieving video mail by indexing on speech.

There is, however, a large amount of textual information on paper that needs to be indexed and retrieved efficiently. One solution for converting scanned paper documents into ASCII is to use optical character recognition (OCR). Existing OCR technology works well with good machine printed fonts against good clean backgrounds. It works poorly if the text is handwritten. We propose an alternative solution for indexing handwritten text when a large corpus of texts written by a single person exists.

Specifically the problem being addressed in this chapter is the indexing of historical manuscripts. These manuscripts are largely written in a single hand and most of them are unpublished. For example, even the collected works of well known people like W. E. B. Du Bois, the African American civil rights leader, and Margaret Sanger, a pioneer in birth control, are mostly unpublished. Both left a substantial amount of their work and correspondence written in their own hand. It is unlikely that all of this material will ever be published.

Such manuscripts are, however, valuable resources for scholars as well as others who wish to consult original source material. It would, therefore, be useful to index them to allow rapid perusal. Since conventional OCR and text retrieval engines cannot be used, this chapter proposes an alternative strategy for indexing such documents.

The indexing scheme proposed here also simplifies reading documents where the handwriting is hard to read. A scanned page from the correspondence of Erasmus Darwin Hudson (1809-1880), an anti-slavery organizer and pioneer orthopaedic surgeon, is shown in figure 1. This page is part of a letter from James S. Gibbons to Erasmus Hudson. The authors of this chapter are still unable to decipher some of the words on this page, although the indexing scheme suggested here did help in deciphering some of the other words.

Since the document is written by a single person, the assumption is that the variation in the word images will be small. The proposed solution will match the actual word images against each other to create equivalence classes. Each equivalence class will consist of multiple instances of the same word. Each word will have a link to the page it came from. The number of words in each equivalence class will be tabulated. Those classes with the largest numbers of words will probably be stopwords i.e. conjunctions like "and" or articles like "the." Classes containing stopwords are eliminated (since they are not very useful for indexing). A list is made of the remaining classes. This list is ordered occuring to the number of words contained in them. The user provides ASCII equivalents for a representative word in each

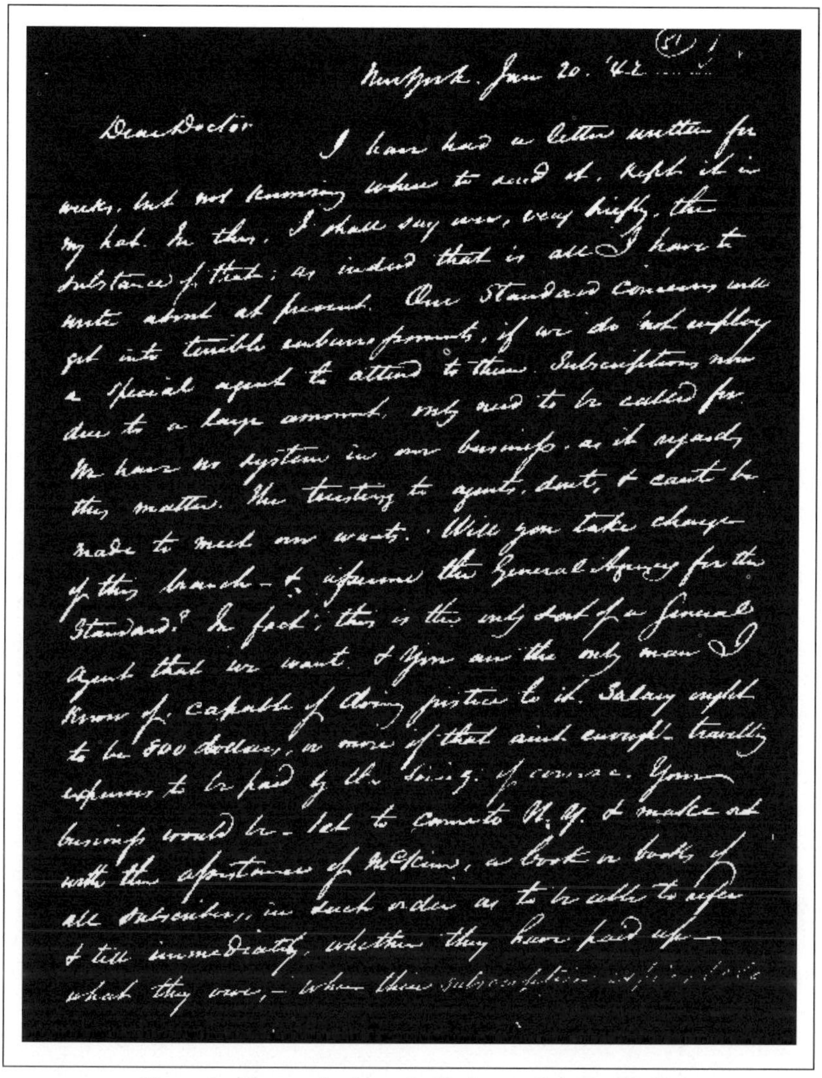

Figure 1. Manuscript from the Hudson collection (1842).

of the top *m* (say $m = 2000$) classes. The words in these classes can now be indexed. This technique will be called "word spotting" as it is analogous to "word spotting" in speech processing (Jones 1995).

The proposed solution completely avoids machine recognition of handwritten words as this is a difficult task (Mori 1992). Robustness is achieved compared to OCR systems for two reasons:

1. Matching is based on entire words. This is in contrast to conventional

OCR systems which essentially recognize characters rather than words.

2. Recognition is avoided. Instead a human is placed in the loop when ASCII equivalents of the words must be provided.

The present chapter deals with the first part of the problem where the scanned document is segmented into word images and the word images are matched against each other. The matching phase of the problem is expected to be the most difficult part of the problem. This is because unlike machine fonts, there is some variation in even a single person's handwriting. This variation is difficult to model.

In this chapter, two different matching techniques are discussed. The first models the transformation as a translation (i.e., shift) while the second models it as a general affine transformation.

2. Prior Work

The traditional approach to indexing documents involves first converting them to ASCII (Bokser 1992) and then using a text based retrieval engine (Salton 1989, Turtle 1992). Scanned documents can be converted into ASCII by first segmenting a page into words and then running them through an OCR (Bokser 1992). The OCR segments the words further into characters and then attempts to recognize the characters using statistical pattern classification (Bokser 1992, Mori 1992). This approach has been highly successful with good clean machine fonts against clean backgrounds. It has had much more limited success when handwriting is used. Character segmentation is much more difficult in the presence of handwriting and also because of the wide variability in handwriting. Not only is there variability between writers, but a given person's writing itself varies.

An approach similar to ours has been used to recognize words in documents which use machine fonts (Khoubyari 1993). The word images are compared against each other and divided into equivalence classes. The words within an equivalence class — all of which are presumably identical — are used to construct a noise-free version of the word. This word is then recognized using an OCR. Recognition rates are much higher than when the OCR is used directly (Khoubyari 1993).

Machine fonts have a number of advantages over handwriting. Multiple instances of a given word printed in the same font are identical except for noise. This situation does not hold for handwriting. Multiple instances of the same word on the same page by the same writer show variations. The variations are many and include scaling of the words with respect to each other, small changes in orientation, and changes in the lengths of descenders and ascenders.

In figure 2, the first two images are two instances of the same word from

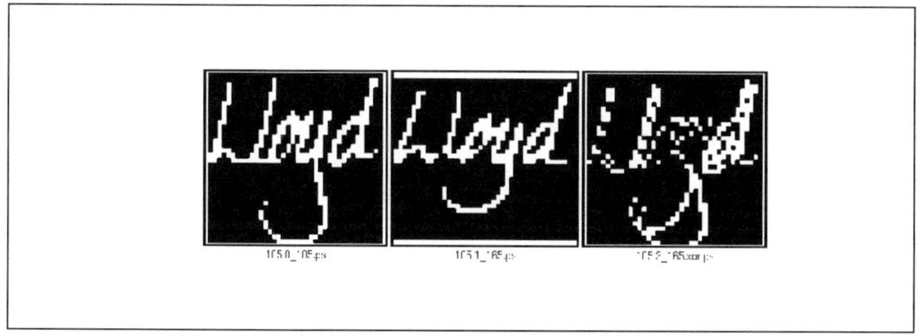

Figure 2. XOR of images.

the same document, written by the same writer. The third image which is the XOR image under optimal translation shows that the two words differ slightly. It is necessary to account for these variations.

3. Outline of Algorithm

Our processing approach is as follows:

1. A scanned greylevel image of the document is obtained.

2. The image is first reduced by half by Gaussian filtering and subsampling.

3. The reduced image is then binarized by thresholding the image (note the thresholding is done in such a way that the characters are white and the background black).

4. The binary image is now segmented into words. This is done by a process of smoothing and thresholding described later.

5. A given word image (i.e., the image of a word) is used as a template and matched against all the other word images. This is repeated for every word in the document. The matching is done in two phases. First, the number of words to be matched is pruned using the areas and aspect ratios of the word images (the word to be matched cannot have an area or aspect ratio which is too different from the template). Next, the actual matching is done by using a matching algorithm. Two different matching algorithms are attempted. One of them only accounts for translation shifts, while the other accounts for affine matches. The matching divides the word images into equivalence classes, each class ideally containing other instances of the same word.

6. Indexing is done as follows. For each equivalence class, the number of elements in it is counted. The top n equivalence classes are then determined from this list. The equivalence classes with the highest number of words (elements) are likely to be stopwords (i.e. conjunctions like

"and," "articles like "the," and prepositions like "of") and are therefore eliminated from further consideration. Let us assume that of the top n, m are left after the stopwords have been eliminated. The user then displays one member of each of these m equivalence classes and assigns their ASCII interpretation. These m words can now be indexed anywhere they appear in the document.

We now discuss these techniques in detail.

4. Word Segmentation

Since the purpose of this chapter is to demonstrate the feasibility of word spotting, a simple technique is used for segmenting words. The method works reasonably well on the images tested so far. It is expected that this technique will be improved with further use.

The technique assumes that a binary image of each page is available and further assumes that the words are white against a dark background (if it is otherwise in the original image, the image can be inverted). Since the spacing between adjacent characters in a word is smaller than the spacing between adjacent words, a new image is constructed using a smoothing and thresholding operation. If two white pixels are separated by less than a certain distance k, the intermediate pixels are made white. This is done in the horizontal direction, k_{horiz}. In the case of handwriting, this procedure also needs to be performed in the diagonal direction, k_{diag}, mainly to prevent descenders from breaking up. Note that each of these window operations may be viewed as a smoothing and thresholding operation or as a morphological closure operation. Connected components are now recovered from this image. A minimum bounding rectangle is now constructed using the connected components. The minimum bounding rectangles essentially give a segmentation of the page into words. Figure 3 shows an example. Certain errors do occur; for example the dot over the i is segmented as a separate word. This is ignored by requiring that word images have a minimum size. Other errors in segmentation may also occur because the writer left a large gap between parts of a word in one instance but did not do so when writing the word again. A number of algorithms exist in the literature for segmenting words from binary images (Wahl 1982, Wang 1989).

5. Determination of Equivalence Classes

The matching is done in a number of phases. First, the number of possible words that need to be matched is pruned by using the areas and aspect ratios of the words. Since the entire document is written by the same hand, it is expect-

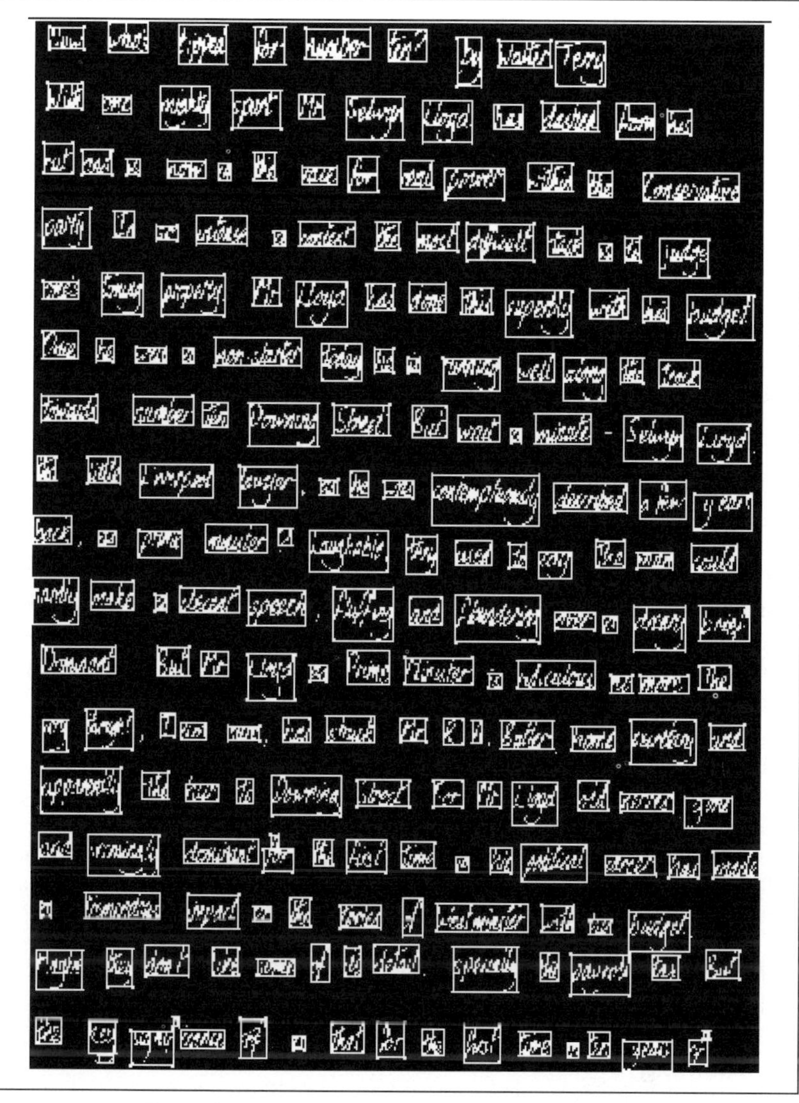

Figure 3. Page segmentation of the senior document.

ed that variations in size will be small. Thus the pruning can be done on the basis of the area of the word images and the aspect ratios of the word images.

5.1 Pruning

It is assumed that;

$$1/\alpha <= A_{word} / A_{template} <= \alpha.$$

where $A_{template}$ is the area of the template and A_{word} is the area of the word to be matched. It is also assumed that

$$1/\beta <= \text{Aspect}_{word} / \text{Aspect}_{template} <= \beta.$$

where $\text{Aspect}_{template}$ is the aspect ratio (width/height) of the template and Aspect_{word} is the aspect ratio of the word to be matched.

α and β should not be too small so that valid words are omitted, nor too large so that too many words are passed onto the matching phase. The average value of the area ratio and the ratio of aspect ratios determine a lower bound or minimum value for α and β. These average values may be determined statistically by sampling a small set of known documents.

The average of the area ratio over all matching words is computed as follows. Assume that all possible matches for every word are known. The area ratio is then computed for all pairs of matching words. If any of these numbers is less than one, that value is replaced by its inverse (taking the average directly would give a number close to 1.0). The average of the resulting area ratios is then taken.

It turns out that words with only one or two characters may have large area ratios and bias the results. However, most words with only one or two characters are stop words which are not useful for indexing. The average is, therefore, computed by considering words of length 3 or greater (alternatively, words of length 4 or greater could be used but the former gives a more conservative estimate).

The minimum value of β may be computed in the same manner. The actual values of α and β used are larger than the minimum values so that valid words may not be missed. There is considerable leeway in the choice of these parameters. In the experimental section it is shown that the minimum value of the average area ratio for the two documents used here is 1.20 and that the results do not differ significantly whether α is chosen to be 1.22 or 1.3.

Typical values of α used in the experiments range between 1.2 and 1.3 while typical values of β used in the experiments range between 1.4 and 1.7.

5.2 Matching

The template is then matched against the word of each image in the pruned list (actually the number of words to be matched can be further restricted by eliminating all words which have already been placed in equivalence classes). The matching function must satisfy two criteria :

1. It must produce a low match error for words which are similar to the template.

2. It must produce a high match error for words which are dissimilar.

Two matching algorithms have been investigated. The first algorithm, Euclidean Distance Mapping (EDM) (Danielsson 1980) is fast but assumes that no distortions have occured except for relative translation. This algorithm usually ranks the matched words in the correct order (i.e. valid words first, followed by invalid words) when the variations in words is not too large. Although, it returns the lowest errors for words which are similar to the template, it also returns low errors for words which are dissimilar to the template. The second algorithm by Scott and Longuet-Higgins (1991), referred to as SLH here, assumes an affine transformation between the words. It thus compensates for some of the variations in the words. It is shown in the experiments that the average precision for the SLH algorithm is much better than that for the EDM algorithm. As currently implemented, the SLH algorithm is much slower than the EDM algorithm. We expect to be able to speed up the SLH algorithm.

6. Using Euclidean Distance Mapping for Matching

This approach is similar to that used by Khoubyari (1993) to match machine generated fonts. Consider two images to be matched. There are three steps in the matching:

1. *Alignstep:* First the images are roughly aligned. In the vertical direction, this is done by aligning the baselines of the two images. The baseline is computed as follows. The difference in the number of white pixels between adjacent scan lines is computed. The point at which the difference is maximum is declared to be the baseline. The baseline computation is performed for both images, and the images then shifted so that they are aligned. In the horizontal direction, the images are aligned by making their left hand sides coincide. The alignment is, therefore, expected to be accurate in the vertical direction and not as good in the horizontal direction. This is borne out in practice.

2. *XORstep:* Next the XOR image is computed. This is done by XOR'ing corresponding pixels. An example of two images and the corresponding XOR image is shown in figure 2. A match error EXOR may be computed by finding the number of white pixels in the XOR image. The XOR image match error is in general not accurate enough for matching. Notice that XOR images may consist of either isolated pixels or pixels in a blob. The error measure computed above gives equal weight to both. However, an isolated pixel in the XOR image may be due to noise while a blob may be due to a major mismatch. Therefore, blobs should be given more weight. This can be done by using an Euclidean distance mapping.

3. *EDMstep:* An Euclidean distance mapping (Danilesson 1980) is computed from the XOR image by assigning to each white pixel in the

image its minimum distance to a black pixel. Thus a white pixel inside a blob will get a larger distance than an isolated white pixel. An error measure E_{EDM} can now be computed by adding up the distance measures for each pixel.

4. Although the approximate translation has been computed using step 1, this may not be accurate and may need to be fine-tuned. Thus steps 2 and 3 are repeated while sampling the translation space in both x and y. A minimum error measure E_{EDMmin} is computed over all the translation samples.

7. SLH Algorithm for Matching

The EDM algorithm does not discriminate well between good and bad matches. In addition, it fails when there is significant distortion in the words. This happened with the writing of Erasmus Hudson (figure 1). Thus a matching algorithm which models some of the variation is needed. A second matching algorithm (SLH) which models the distortion as an affine transformations was, therefore, investigated. Note that it is expected that the actual variation is much more complex.

An affine transform is a linear transformation between coordinate systems. In two dimensions, it is described by $\mathbf{r'} = \mathbf{Ar} + \mathbf{t}$ where $\mathbf{t}$ is a 2-D vector describing the translation, $\mathbf{A}$ is a 2 by 2 matrix which captures the deformation, $\mathbf{r'}$ and $\mathbf{r}$ are the coordinates of corresponding points in the two images between which the affine transformation must be recovered. An affine transform allows for the following deformations — scaling in both directions, shear in both directions and rotation.

The literature describes a number of algorithms to recover affine transforms (Bergen 1992, Gold 1994, Manmatha 1994a, Manmatha 1994b, Scott and Longuet-Higgins 1991, Szeliski 1994). A number of criteria restrict the choice of algorithms.

1. One of the requirements of the problem being considered here is that the algorithm must recover both the correspondence between images and the affine transform simultaneously.

2. Greylevel matching techniques are not necessarily appropriate for matching binary images.

These criteria restrict the choice of algorithm to those that operate on points. Scott and Longuet-Higgins (1991) proposed an algorithm to recover the correspondence between two sets of points I and J under an affine transform (actually the Scott and Longuet-Higgins algorithm does not require that the correspondence between the two sets of points be affine but only in the case of affine transforms has it been shown to recover the correct correspondence). This algorithm will now be described.

Two sets of points I and J are created as follows. Every white pixel in the first image is a member of the set I. Similarly, every white pixel in the second image is a member of set J. First, the centroids of the point sets are computed and the origins of the coordinate systems is set at the centroid. An adjacency matrix $\mathbf{G}$ is then computed. The entries G_{ij} are Gaussian weighted distances between a point i in set I and a point j in set J. Each entry G_{ij} is given by $G_{ij} = \exp(- r_{ij}^T r_{ij} / (2\ \sigma^2))$ where r_{ij} is the Euclidean distance between i and j. The matrix $\mathbf{G}$ is then diagonalized using singular value decomposition (SVD) to give $\mathbf{G} = \mathbf{T}\,\mathbf{D}\,\mathbf{U}$ where $\mathbf{D}$ is a diagonal matrix and $\mathbf{T}$ and $\mathbf{U}$ are orthogonal matrices. The diagonal entries in $\mathbf{D}$ are replaced by 1's to give an m by n matrix $\mathbf{E}$. The pairing matrix $\mathbf{P} = \mathbf{T}\,\mathbf{E}\,\mathbf{U}$ indicates the strength of the attraction between points i and j. Thus a correspondence between two points i and j is posited only if the entry P_{ij} is the greatest element in row i and the greatest element in column j. Intuitively $\mathbf{P}$ is the matrix which correlates best with the $\mathbf{G}$ matrix in the sense of maximizing the trace of $\mathbf{P}^T\mathbf{G}$. The transformation can then be computed using the recovered correspondence. Scott and Longuet-Higgins showed that if σ is chosen large enough, the method would compute the correspondence correctly for translations, scale changes (i.e. expansions, contractions) and shears. Here, as in intensity based algorithms, large values of σ are useful in recovering large translations. However, the method cannot be shown to compute the correct correspondence if a rotation is involved. In practice, small rotations can be handled most of the time. Note that some points will have no correspondence, i.e. what the algorithm returns is a one to one correspondence between some subset of I and some subset of J.

Given the (above) correspondence between point sets I and J, the affine transform can be computed in a straightforward manner. The correct affine transform $\mathbf{A},\mathbf{t}$ is that transform which minimizes the following least mean squares criterion: $E_{SLH} = \sum_v (I_v - \mathbf{A}J_v - \mathbf{t})^2$ where I_v, J_v are the (x,y) coordinates of point I_1 and J_1 respectively.

The values of $\mathbf{A},\mathbf{t}$ can be computed in closed form by minimizing the above expression (i.e. differentiating and setting it to zero). The values are then plugged back into the above equation to compute the error E_{SLH}. The error E_{SLH} is an estimate of how dissimilar two words are and the words can, therefore, be ranked according to it.

One disadvantage of computing the affine parameters is that in certain situations two very different words can give a low error rate E_{SLH} (this is similar to the fact that given enough parameters any continuous function can be fitted by a polynomial). If, however, the range of values of the affine parameters is constrained, this is unlikely to occur. It will, therefore, be assumed that the variation for valid words is not too large. This implies that if A_{11} and A_{22} are considerably different from 1, the word is probably not a valid match.

The affine matching algorithm is much more accurate than the Euclidean distance mapping technique. The current implementation of this technique is slow because of the need to compute the SVD of a large matrix (often the matrix may have a few hundred rows and columns). However, the **G** matrix is sparse (since the values of σ are low). The computation of the SVD can, therefore, be sped up by utilizing methods which compute the SVD of a sparse matrix quickly. This will be done in future implementations.

Note: The SLH algorithm assumes that pruning on the basis of the area and aspect ratio thresholds is performed.

8. Experiments

The performance of both techniques was tested on two handwritten pages, each written by a different writer. The first page was obtained from the DIMUND document server on the internet (see http://documents.cfar. umd.edu/resources/ database/handwriting.database.html) which was scanned by Andrew Senior (this page will be referred to as the Senior document). The handwriting on this page is fairly neat. The second page is from the Hudson archival collection from the library of the University of Massachusetts. The page used is a letter written by James S. Gibbons to Erasmus Darwin Hudson. The handwriting on this page is difficult to read and in fact the indexing technique helped in deciphering some of the words.

The experiments will show examples of how the matching techniques work. The experiments show rankings and match errors for a few selected words. Recall precision curves for both documents are also presented. The recall precision curves are generated by considering queries (templates) for which there is at least one other (besides itself) possible match in the document. All rankings were produced by matching the template with every word left in the pruned class. However, only a few of the matches are displayed in the figures and tables.

For page segmentation (see section 4), $k_{horiz} = 9$ and $k_{diag} = 3$ were chosen. The parameters were determined empirically by varying them and choosing one which gave the best segmentation. Table 1 shows the number of words in each document, the number of words which have length of 3 or more characters and a length of 4 or more characters.

Table 2 shows statistical information determined from the documents for the purpose of determining the thresholds for pruning. The numbers are calculated for words with three or more characters in them. This is done so that words with two characters or less (likely stopwords) do not skew the results.

The columns in table 2 list the average value of the area ratio and the average of the ratio of aspect ratios for words with three or more characters in the document.

The minimum value of the thresholds (α_{min} and β_{min}) for pruning may now be determined. They are obtained by finding the maximum over both docu-

Document	# of words	# of words of length >= 3	# of words of length >= 4
Senior	192	155	130
Hudson	153	113	101

Table 1. Number of words in each document.

Document	Avg. area ratio	Avg. ratio of aspect ratios
Senior	1.09	1.10
Hudson	1.20	1.15

Table 2. Statistical information for words with 3 or more characters.

ments of the averages of the area ratio and the ratio of aspect ratios. Using table 2, they are given by:

$$\alpha_{min} = 1.20, \ \beta_{min} = 1.15$$

The actual values used for α and β are much higher to allow for some variation. For the Euclidean Distance Matching technique, $\beta = 1.4$ was used for both documents. Note that this is so large compared to β_{min} that very few valid matches are likely to be eliminated. The EDM algorithm was tried with $\alpha = 1.22$ and 1.3. The experimental results in the following subsection show that both values of α give roughly the same results. There is, therefore, considerable leeway in choosing the pruning thresholds.

Since the current implementation of the SLH algorithm is slow, the EDM algorithm is first run, a threshold picked, and words which have a match error under this threshold are then processed by the SLH algorithm. The actual value of the threshold is not crucial. Before the EDM algorithm is run, the words are pruned as before using the area and aspect ratios. To ensure that the SLH algorithm did most of the matching and pruning, the thresholds were picked to be conservative. $\alpha = 1.4$ and $\beta = 1.7$ were chosen.

8.1 Experiments Using the EDM Algorithm.

The EDM algorithm was run on both documents. All experiments were conducted by matching the template with every word in the documents — Senior (192 words) and Hudson (153 words). The translations were sampled to within ± 4 pixels in the x direction and ± 1 pixel in the y direction. Increasing the translation sample space did not change the results.

Figure 4. Rankings for the template "Lloyd" using the EDM algorithm.

Token	Word	Area	E_{EDMmin}	X	Y
105	Lloyd	1360	0.000	0	0
70	Lloyd	1224	0.174	0	0
165	Lloyd	1230	0.175	-2	0
197	Lloyd	1400	0.194	4	0
239	Lloyd	1320	0.197	-3	0
21	Maybe	1147	0.199	-1	0
180	along	1156	0.200	1	0
215	party	1209	0.202	1	0
245	spurt	1170	0.205	-1	0
121	dreary	1435	0.206	3	0

*Table 3. Rankings and match errors for the template "Lloyd"
using the EDM algorithm.*

The figures below show examples of the rankings achieved. In these figures, the first word is the template. The template is followed by words ranked according to the error measure. A cut-off threshold is used to limit the number of words displayed. This threshold is common to all the experiments.

On the Senior document, the EDM algorithm does quite well (the average precision > 78%). This performance is to be expected because the handwriting is fairly neat. A typical example is shown in figure 4. In the figure, the first word is the template "Lloyd." The four other instances of "Lloyd" are ranked before any of the other words. Table 3 shows that the match error for

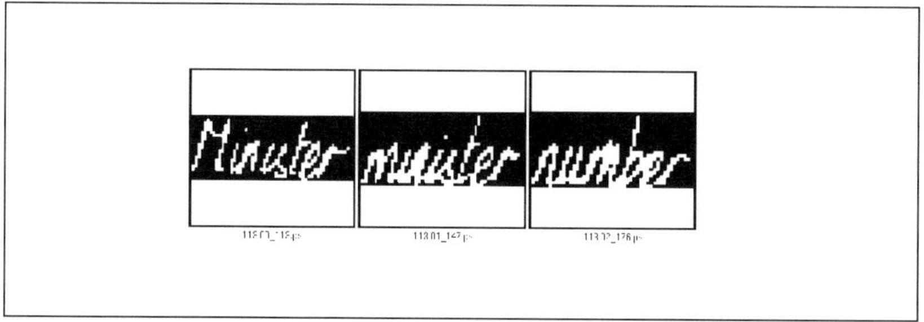

Figure 5. Rankings for the template "Minister" using the EDM algorithm.

Token	Word	Area	E_{EDM}	X	Y
113	Minister	1134	0.000	0	0
147	minister	1078	0.210	-1	0
176	number	1104	0.285	2	0

Table 4. Rankings and match errors for the template "Minister"
using the EDM algorithm.

the other instances of "Lloyd" is less than that for any other word. In the table, the first column lists the Token number, the second column gives a transcription of the word, the third column shows the area in pixels, the fourth gives the match error and the last two columns specify the translation in the x and y directions respectively. Note the significant change in area of the words.

In English, the first letter in a word is capitalized when the word begins a sentence and not otherwise (unless it is a proper noun). Thus it is desirable that the technique be relatively insensitive to this capitalization. Figure 5 and table 4 show an example of this. The word "minister" is the highest ranked word obtained for the template "Minister" inspite of the fact that "minister" begins with a lower case letter while "Minister" starts with an uppercase letter.

The algorithm performs poorly in one respect. It shows poor discrimination between valid words and invalid words. For example, in table 3 the last "Lloyd" has a match error of 0.197 while the next word in the ranking "Maybe" has a match error of 0.199. Thus it is difficult to discriminate between valid and invalid words using the error measure.

The performance of a retrieval algorithm is often evaluated in terms of its recall and precision. Recall is defined as the "proportion of relevant material actually retrieved in answer to a search request" (van Rijsbergen 1979) while precision is defined as the "proportion of retrieved material that is actually relevant" (van Rijsbergen 1979).

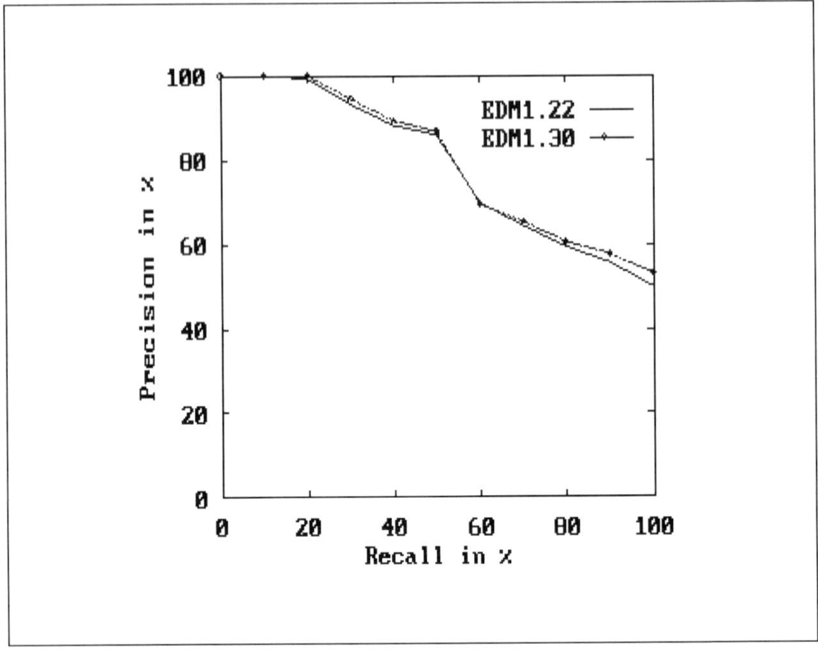

*Figure 6. Recall precision graph for the senior document
using the EDM algorithm.*

Figure 6 shows a graph of precision versus recall for the Senior document using the EDM algorithm. The plots were generated by using only words with more than 3 characters as queries. Only those words were used as queries for which there was at least one other instance of the word in the document. The number of queries was 59.

The two plots were generated using different values of the area pruning threshold ($\alpha = 1.22$ and $\alpha = 1.3$). Figure 6 shows that there is no significant difference in performance using either pruning threshold. The average precision using $\alpha = 1.22$ is 78.7% while for $\alpha = 1.3$ it is 79.7%.

The EDM algorithm was also tested on the Hudson document. Figure 7 shows the recall precision graph for the Hudson document. The average precision using $\alpha = 1.22$ was 56.1% while for $\alpha = 1.3$ it was 57.9%. The poorer performance on the Hudson document can be attributed to the handwriting. The handwriting in the Hudson collection (figure 1) is difficult to read even for humans looking at greyscale images at 300 dpi.

An example of failure from the Hudson collection is now shown. The word "Standard" from the Hudson collection was matched. Figure 8 and table 5 show the results of this matching. The performance is not very good.

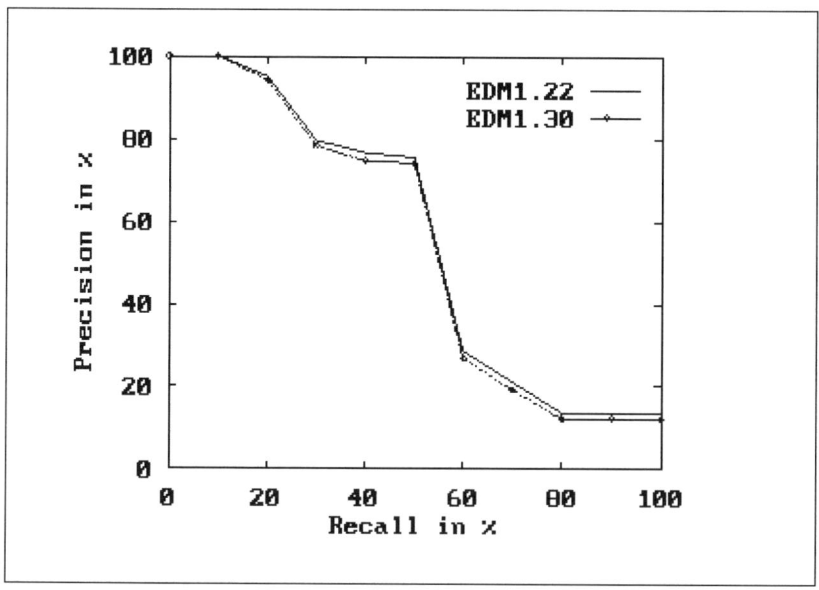

Figure 7. Recall precision graph for the Hudson document using the EDM algorithm.

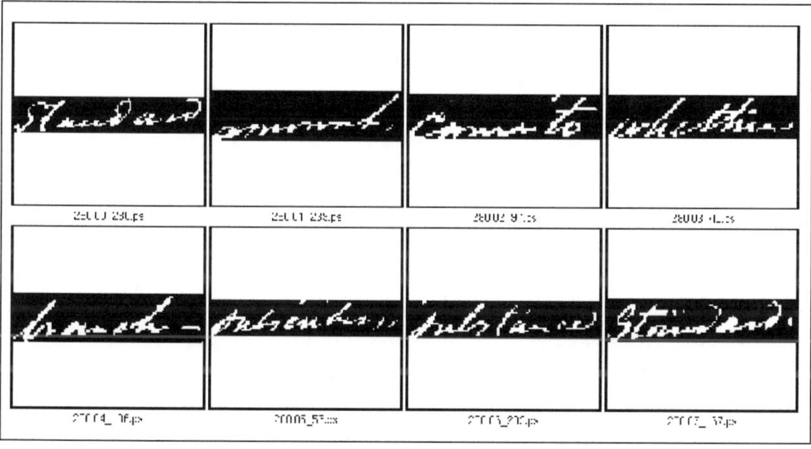

Figure 8. Rankings for the template "Standard" using the EDM algorithm.

The reason is that the words are written differently. In the template, there is a gap between the *"t"* and the *"a."* However, in the second example of "Standard" there is no gap. This implies that a technique which models some kind of distortion may be needed.

Token	Word	Area	E_{EDMmin}	X	Y
280	Standard	1530	0.000	0	0
239	comment	1722	0.203	-4	0
94	cometo	1241	0.212	1	0
45	whether	1258	0.212	1	0
186	branch	1743	0.218	0	0
56	subscribes	1900	0.228	-4	0
283	substances	1479	0.231	1	0
167	Standard	1440	0.231	1	0

Table 5. Rankings and match errors for the template "Standard" using the EDM algorithm.

Token	Word	Area	Pts.	E_{SLH}	A		T
105	Lloyd	1368	233	0.00	1.00 0.00	0.00 1.00	0.00 0.00
197	Lloyd	1400	199	1.302	0.96 0.01	-0.04 1.04	1.58 0.14
70	Lloyd	1224	176	1.356	0.94 0.03	0.09 0.92	-1.02 -1.38
165	Lloyd	1230	189	1.631	1.03 -0.01	0.05 0.87	-0.43 -2.60
239	Lloyd	1320	203	1.795	0.99 0.03	-0.05 1.07	1.44 2.21
157	lawyer	1518	185	3.393	0.96 0.05	-0.03 1.11	1.89 0.03
240	Selwyn	1564	188	3.673	0.94 0.05	0.06 1.05	-4.23 -0.75

Table 6. Rankings and match errors for the template "Lloyd" using the SLH algorithm.

8.2 Experiments Using the SLH Algorithm

Experiments were performed using the Senior document. Since the current version of the SLH algorithm is slow, the initial matches were pruned using the EDM algorithm and then the SLH algorithm run on the pruned subset.

To account for the large variations in the Hudson papers, the area threshold α was fixed at 1.4 and the aspect ratio threshold at 1.7. The value of σ depends on the expected translation. Since it is small, $\sigma = 2.0$. A lower value of $\sigma = 1.5$ yielded poorer results.

The matches for the template "Lloyd" are shown in table 6 whose successive columns indicate the Token Number, the transcription of the word, the area of the word image, the number of corresponding points recovered by the SLH algorithm, the match error E_{SLH} using the SLH algorithm, and the affine transform. The entries are ranked according to the match error, E_{SLH}. If either of A_{11} or A_{22} is less than 0.8 or greater than 1/0.8, that word is eliminated

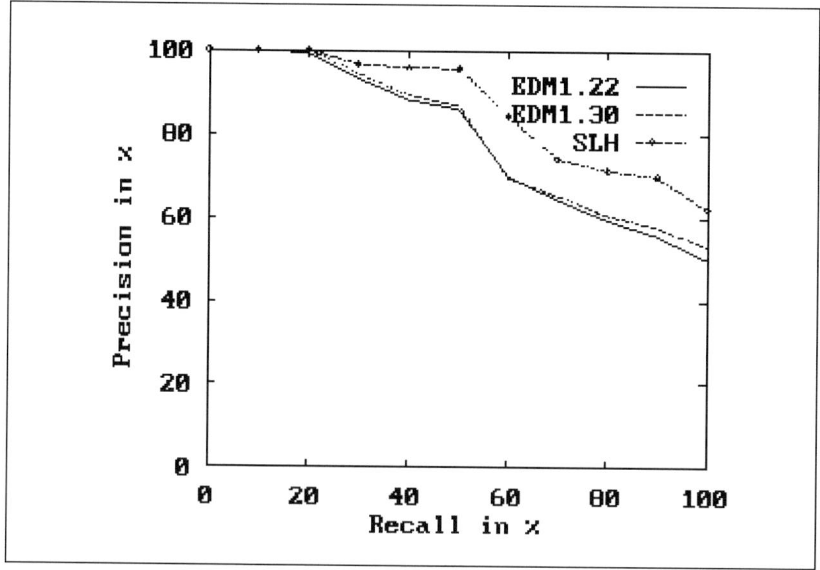

Figure 9. Recall precision graph for the SLH and the EDM Algorithms on the senior document.

from the rankings. A comparison with table 3 shows that the rankings change. This is not only true of the invalid words (for example the sixth entry in table 3 is "Maybe" while the sixth entry in table 6 is "lawyer") but is also true of the "Lloyd"s. Both tables rank instances of "Lloyd" ahead of other words. The technique also shows a much greater discrimination in match error — the match error for "lawyer" is almost double the match error for the fifth "Lloyd."

Figure 9 compares the recall and precision of the EDM algorithm and the SLH algorithm on the Senior document. Note the significant improvement in performance. As before, words with three or more characters of which there was at least one other instance were used as queries. For the SLH algorithm, the average precision came out to be 86.3% compared to 79.7% for the EDM algorithm.

The SLH algorithm was also run on the Hudson document (figure 1). This document is particularly difficult — the writing is hard for people to read.

Performance on templates like "they" is good as shown in table 7. Good discrimination between valid and invalid words is also obtained using the error measure, E_{ESH}. (In this particular case, the EDM algorithm also ranks correctly, but the discrimination is not so good).

Finally, we look at the word "Standard" which the EDM method did not rank correctly. The SLH method produces the correct ranking (see table 8) in

Token	Word	Area	Pts.	E_{SLH}	A		T
1	they	899	108	0.000	1.00	0.00	0.00
					0.00	1.00	0.00
43	they	891	97	0.636	0.92	0.05	-0.93
					0.05	1.01	1.62
156	only	775	85	3.172	0.89	-0.22	1.53
					0.03	1.20	-0.38
191	this?	696	83	8.466	0.97	-0.15	1.40
					-0.05	1.14	7.23

Table 7. Rankings and match errors for the template "they"
using the SLH algorithm.

Token	Word	Area	Pts.	E_{SLH}	A		T
280	Standard	1530	251	0.00	1.00	0.00	0.00
					0.00	1.00	0.00
167	Standard	1440	183	4.36	1.03	0.10	5.07
					-0.01	0.94	0.33
56	subscribers	1900	196	7.82	0.99	0.20	1.27
					0.00	0.94	-0.38
283	substance	1479	183	39.18	0.92	0.12	-1.39
					-0.02	0.82	1.02

Table 8. Rankings and match errors for the template "Standard"
using the SLH algorithm.

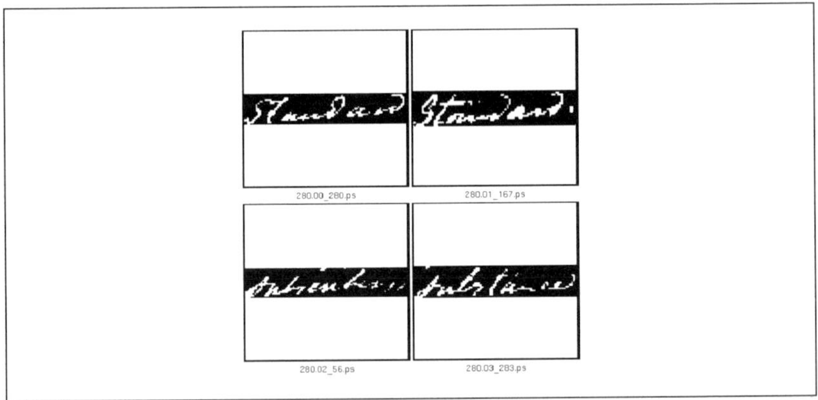

Figure 10. Rankings for the template "Standard" using the SLH algorithm.

spite of the significant distortions in the word (see figure 10). As discussed before, the first instance of "Standard" is written with additional gaps between the *"t"* and the *"a"* and the *"d"* and the *"a"* (visible in figure 10).

In summary, it is clear that the SLH algorithm ranks words correctly almost all the time. In some situations, the discrimination between valid and invalid words needs to be improved. Nevertheless, it seems to be a reasonable algorithm upon which to base wordspotting.

9. Conclusion

Our investigations demonstrate the feasibility of indexing handwritten words when there exists a corpus of words written by a single author. Two algorithms were used for ranking matches of handwritten words with a template. The first (EDM) based on Euclidean distance mapping does not account for any distortions and thus performs poorly when the handwriting is bad. The second (SLH) algorithm, based on an algorithm of Scott and Longuet-Higgins, almost always produces the correct rankings even if the handwriting is bad. Two areas need to be improved — speed and the discrimination between valid and invalid words.

Acknowledgements

This material is based on work supported by the Center for Intelligent Information Retrieval under the following grants: The National Science Foundation, Library of Congress and Department of Commerce under cooperative agreement number EEC-9209623; NSF contract number CDA 9502639; NRaD contract number N66001-94-D-6054; the United States Patent and Trademark Office and DARPA/ITO under ARPA order number D468, issued by ESC/AXS contract number F19628-95-C-0235; and NSF IRI-9619117. Any opinions, findings and conclusions or recommendations expressed in this material are the authors and do not necessarily reflect those of the sponsors.

Chengfeng Han and David Hirvone provided assistance with programming. Jonathan Lim and Bob Heller provided help with systems software. The page from the Hudson collection was scanned in and provided by Gail Giroux of the University of Massachusetts W. B. DuBois Library.

References

Bergen, J. R.; Anandan, P.; Hanna, K. J.; and Hingorani, R. 1992. Hierarchical Model-based Motion Estimation. In Proceedings of the 2nd European Conference on Computer Vision, 237-252. Santa Margherita Ligure, Italy. Volume 588 of *Lecture Notes in Computer Science*, ed. G. Sandini, Berlin: Springer-Verlag.

Bokser, M. 1992. Omnidocument Technologies. *Proceedings of the IEEE* 80(7): 1066-1078.

Danielsson, Per-Erik, 1980. Euclidean Distance Mapping. *Computer Graphics and Image Processing*. 14: 227-248.

Flickner, M.; Sawhney, H.; Niblack, W.; Ashley, J.; Huang, Q.; Dom, B.; Gorkani, M.; Hafner, J.; Lee, D.; Petkovic, D.; Steele, D.; and Yanker, P. 1997. Query by Image and Video Content: The QBIC System. In this volume.

Gold S.; Rangarjan, A.; Lu, C. P.; Pappu, S.; and Mjolsness, E. 1995. New Algorithms for 2d and 3d Point Matching: Pose Estimation and Correspondence. In Neural Information Processing Systems (NIPS), eds. G. Tesauro, D. Touretsky and T. Leen, Cambridge: MIT Press 7: 957-964.

Jones, G. J. F.; Foote J. T.; Sparck Jones K.; and Young, S. J. 1995. Video Mail Retrieval: The Effect of Word Spotting Accuracy on Precision. In *Proceedings of the International Conference on Acoustics, Speech and Signal Processing,*. (1): 309-316. Detroit: IJCAI.

Khoubyari, S. and Hull, J. J. 1993. Keyword Location in Noise Document Image. In *Proceedings of the Second Annual Symposium on Document Analysis and Information Retrieval*, 217-231. UNLV, Las Vegas, USA.

Manmatha, R. 1994a. Measuring the Affine Transform using Gaussian Filters.In *Proceedings of the 3rd European Conference on Computer Vision*, 159-164. Stockholm, Sweden. Volume 801 of *Lecture Notes in Computer Science*, ed J. O. Eklundh, Berlin: Springer-Verlag.

Manmatha, R. 1994b. A Framework for Recovering Affine Transforms using Points, Lines or Image Brightnesses. In *Proceedings of the IEEE Computer Vision and Pattern Recognition Conference*, 141-146. Seattle, USA.

Mori, S.; Suen, C. Y.; and Yamamoto, K. 1992. Historical Review of OCR Research and Development, *Proceedings o f the IEEE* 80(7): 1029-1058.

Salton, G. 1989. *Automatic Text Processing—the Transformation, Analysis and Retrieval of Information by Computer.* Reading, USA: Addison-Wesley.

Scott, G. L. and Longuet-Higgins, H. C. 1991. An Algorithm for Associating the Features of Two Patterns. *Proceedings of the Royal Society of London B* B244: 21-26.

Shapiro, L. S. and Brady, J. M. 1992. Feature-based Correspondence: An Eigenvector Approach. *Image and Vision Computing* 10: 283-288.

Szeliski, R. and Coughlan, J. 1994. Hierarchical Spline-based Image Registration. In *Proceedings of the IEEE Computer Vision and Pattern Recognition Conference*, 194-201. Seattle, USA.

Turtle, H. R. and Croft, W. B. 1992. A Comparison of Text Retrieval Models. *Computer Journal* 35(3): 279-290.

van Rijsbergen, C. J. 1979. *Information Retrieval.* London: Butterworths.

Wahl F.; Wong. K.; and Casey, R. 1982. Block Segmentation and Text Extraction in Mixed Text/Image Documents. *Computer Vision Graphics and Image Processing* 20: 375-390.

Wang D., and Srihari, S. N. 1989. Classification of Newschapter Image Blocks using Texture Analysis. *Computer Vision Graphics and Image Processing* 47: 327-352.

Chapter 4

Automatic Classification of Objects in Captioned Depictive Photographs for Retrieval

Neil C. Rowe and Brian Frew
U.S. Naval Postgraduate School

Abstract

We investigate the robust classification of objects within photographs in a large and varied picture library of natural photographs. We assume the photographs have captions describing and locating imprecisely some of the objects present in the picture, as is common in libraries. Our approach does not match to shape templates nor do full image picture understanding, neither of which works well for natural photographs where appearance varies considerably with lighting and perspective. Instead, we strike a robust compromise by statistically characterizing photograph regions with 17 key domain-independent parameters covering shape, color, texture, and contrast. We explored two ways to use the parameters to classify picture regions, case-based reasoning and a neural network, both of which require training. We found the neural network outperformed case-based reasoning, especially when caption information and a separate neuron inferring likelihood that a region was the "visual focus" of the picture were included. Then 25-category shape classification succeeded 48.1% of the time on a set of pictures randomly selected from a large picture library currently in use. Our work represents good progress on the difficult problem of retrieval by content from large real-world picture libraries.

1. Introduction

Increasing attention is being paid to retrieval from picture libraries. Picture captions are especially helpful in finding the right pictures for a user need (Srihari 1994). Our previous research in the MARIE project (Rowe 1994,

1996) proposed and confirmed by testing a theory of how captions refer to pictures. Rowe (1994) in particular identified linguistic clues that indicated whether a noun or verb in a caption was fully depicted, partially depicted, or definitely undepicted, and also inferred presence of supertypes from the presence of types, partial presence of wholes from the presence of parts, broad picture categories, and cases of the absence of things.

However, picture captions are rarely sufficient descriptions of a picture for all purposes because of space limitations and the unanticipated uses to which a picture can be put. For instance, for the MARIE-2 testbed of the picture library of the U.S. Navy air test facility NAWC-WD in China Lake, California, many pictures show airplanes, but the captions never describe the airplane-image size, something of great importance to someone wanting a good picture of an airplane. Other features important to users but rarely mentioned in the captions are orientations of objects, colors, the time of day, the illumination, and the identities of objects in the background; identities of objects are also sparingly provided in captions for complex scenes. If these features are to be queried in picture retrieval, they must be computed from the pictures, preferably during library setup. This requires guessing what "regions" of the picture (clusters of pixels of similar characteristics) represent, using the region's properties and general principles (like that man-made objects have many right angles). This sounds difficult, but there are clues from the caption and the intent of the photographer to present a clear photographic subject.

Previous work that does attempt content analysis of a wide variety of images generally make important simplifications of the task, assumptions impossible for large real-world picture libraries. Barber et al. (1994) analyzes a broad class of images and matches regions of the picture to ideals summarized by feature vectors, but requires user definition of the outlines of the shapes to be recognized. Smith and Chang (this volume) simplify the matching problem to colors and global spatial layout for finding pictures in a library; Flickner et al. (this volume) simplify it to colors and simple shape properties; Ogle and Stonebraker (1995) simplify it to colors; and Kato (1992) simplifies it to a few image properties. There is some good work on recognition of objects in artificial graphical images by Chuah et al. (this volume), engineering drawings and floor plans by Rabitti and Savino (1992), and aerial photographs by Choo et al. (1990). Robust recognition of objects in scenes observed by a mobile robot is addressed in Draper et al. (1989) and Strat (1992); both researchers used domain-dependent context-based inferences to infer identities of objects, using frame-like "schemas" in the first and frame-like "contexts" in the second.

Some image-understanding work requires detailed predefined models of what can be seen, (e.g. Lamdan and Wolfson 1988), but in most real-world picture libraries (including our testbed), far too many different objects appear to build models for all of them. There is a variety of work on "shape matching" where just the outline of a picture region is matched to an ideal outline (Scassellati et al. 1994, Rickman and Stonham 1993, Mehrotra and Gary 1995), but these methods do not work well for natural photographs where objects can appear in many orientations and lighting conditions: region color and texture are more helpful then. Similar problems of sensitivity to photographic conditions apply to two-dimensional strings for compact representation of spatial relationships in images in image databases (Chang et al. 1987).

So our work reported here differs from previous work in image-content analysis in that: (1) it is concerned with "natural" (real-world) images from photographs of three-dimensional objects, so pixel-by-pixel matching to templates will not work; (2) it is concerned with recognizing parts of a picture, not relating the parts; (3) it requires only minimal specialized domain knowledge or visual-object models, so it can handle a broad class of retrieval situations; (4) it does not require user input beyond a natural-language query; (5) it is fully implemented. We also focus on just image-content analysis, and our methods would just be one module in a multimedia-retrieval system like those described in this volume by Mani et al., Merialdo and Dubois (as an "agent"), and Griffioen, Yavatkar and Adams ("extraction of embedded semantic information").

2. Finding Regions in the Pictures

Our experiments used the MARIE-2 multimedia retrieval system we are developing. MARIE-2 is written in Quintus Prolog, like the programs reported in this chapter. Our experiments used a random sample of 127 pictures from the China Lake picture library of about 100,000 pictures. The library includes views of facilities, views of equipment, views of how equipment should be mounted on aircraft (since this a naval air test facility), views of tests, views of routine base activities, public relations photos, historical photos, and views of natural features of the area.

The originals were high-quality 8.5 x 11 inch color prints. The 127 selected for testing were digitized and reduced to approximately 100 by 100 colored pixels each, where each pixel was represented by 8-bit red, green, and blue values. We chose to work with this low level of resolution because it saves a great deal of space, enabling magnetic-disk storage of full libraries of such reduced images. The image resolution appeared sufficient for most browsing of the database, and in fact, many World Wide Web sites with image collections use such resolution on overview pages. However, considerable detail is lost at this resolution, preventing detailed image analysis such as that needed for classification of aircraft. Dithering was necessary to give best visual display for a fixed number of bits, although it complicates the subsequent image processing.

Figure 1. Example input picture.

Figure 1 shows an example picture we analyzed. It is shown here in black and white, but is stored and analyzed in our system in color. It has the caption: "Photovoltaic cell panels for generating power to ultimately operate a radar. Left to right: NASA employee and Richard Fulmer with the batteries and power inverter."

Our challenge was to process a wide variety of pictures in a robust way. We used mostly standard methods of pixel-level image processing from Ballard and Brown (1982) to find regions of homogeneous characteristics in the picture, using implementations adapted from the program in Seem and Rowe (1994). These were, in order: (1) image averaging; (2) color gradient thresholding; (3) clumping of the results into pixel regions; (4) computation of basic region properties; (5) merging of single-cell regions into adjacent regions; and (6) iterative merging of the remaining adjacent regions with similar characteristics. Figure 2 shows results of this processing on the example of figure 1, with the regions numbered for future reference. Because of its visual variety, this picture was of above-average difficulty for our software.

Image averaging of each square of four adjacent cells was done first to compensate for dithering. Then gradient thresholding was done, with a tight color gradient threshold so as to separate many pixel boundaries and avoid splitting regions later. Clumping was then done in a single pass, and the tight gradient meant on the order of 500-2000 initial regions were created for the 10,000-pixel pictures.

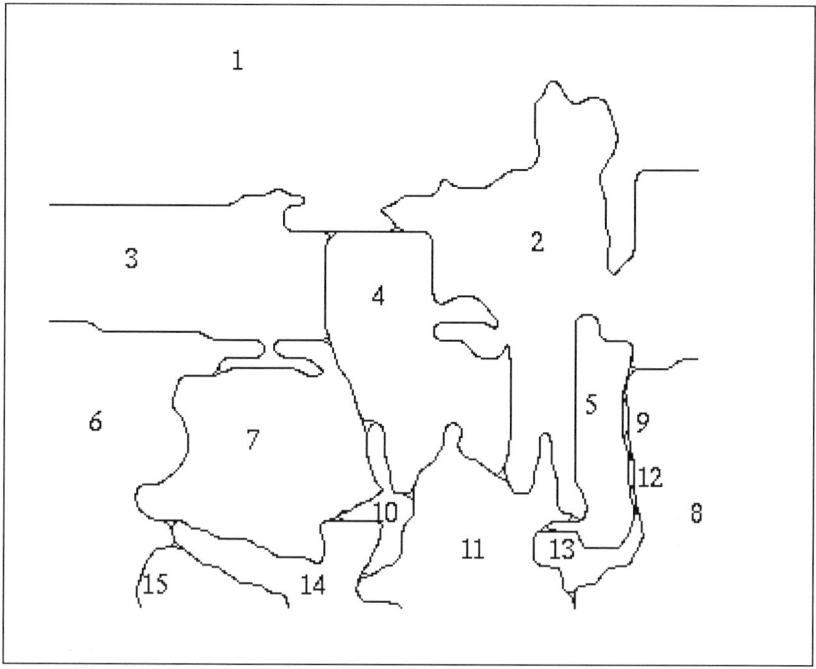

Figure 2. Regions found by our program for the picture in figure 1.

Next we computed 26 statistical properties of each region of the image, properties providing a good summary of the basic visual properties of the image regions. We chose these properties from study of the test library, observing that color and texture are often more important than shape in identifying many objects (like sky and terrain) in natural photographs. The region properties we used are listed in figure 3. They include geometric properties, brightness and color properties, and shape properties for the regions. Dimensions (statistics A – H and U) are measured in numbers of pixels; brightnesses (statistics K – Q and T) are computed with a 0-255 gray scale for each color; skews (statistics I – J) are proportional to the size of the box; diagonality (statistic V) is a fraction of the boundary length; curviness (statistics W) is in radians (and minus twice pi for closed curves); correlations (statistics R-S) run –1 to 1; and counts (statistics X and Y) are unadjusted. We did not compute statistics on linear features like Draper et al. (1989) because they appeared rarely important in pictures intended for depiction.

Next we merged single-cell regions into their neighbor regions in a best-first approach. Such merges were ranked by the weighted sum of the absolute differences in red, green, green and blue values (item (4) above) between the

Code	Explanation	Code	Explanation
A	region number	B	area in pixels
C	circumference in pixels	D	number of picture-boundary pixels
E	minimum x-coordinate	F	minimum y-coordinate
G	maximum x-coordinate	H	maximum y-coordinate
I	x-skew of center of mass from box center	J	y-skew of center of mass from box center
K	average red brightness	L	average green brightness
M	average blue brightness	N	standard deviation of red brightness
O	standard deviation of green brightness	P	standard deviation of blue brightness
Q	average brightness variation between adjacent cells	R	correlation of brightness with increasing x
S	correlation of brightness with increasing y	T	average strength of the region edge
U	smoothed-boundary length	V	smoothed-boundary diagonality
W	smoothed-boundary curviness	X	smoothed-boundary number of inflection points
Y	smoothed-boundary number of right angles	Z	whether boundary is open or closed

Figure 3. The twenty-six basic region statistics and their codes.

cell and the average of the other (merged-into) region; the weights were the reciprocals of the standard deviations (item (5) above) of the color values of the other region, a standard idea with distance calculation with normally-distributed random variables. Region properties were updated with each merge.

Finally, we did best-first merges of the remaining regions. After some experimentation, best performance was obtained when merges were ranked on the weighted sum of three factors: the average color difference between the regions (calculated and weighted as with single-cell merges), the absolute difference in the neighbor-brightness variation (item (6) above) over the regions (weighted by reciprocals of the standard deviations as the preceding), and the weighted decrease in density (computed from items (9) and (1) above) of the bounding boxes. The weighting on the last was twenty times the square root of the area of the larger merged region, the latter of which we found experimentally to be helpful in preventing accidental merges of small regions until more pixels could provide more accurate properties of them. The first merging factor modeled color similarity; the second, pixel-level textural similarity (to distinguish regions of same average color but markedly different uniformities); and the third, resulting-region compactness (to discriminate against creation of thin and curvy regions).

A maximum threshold defines the end of merging. However, if more than 30 regions remain, we judge that the picture analysis was too conservative, so the color-gradient and merge thresholds are increased and picture analysis is redone. Similarly, if no region touches the picture border, we judge that picture analysis was too liberal, decrease the thresholds, and redo. Again after each merge, properties of the new region were computed, using in part the properties of the merged regions.

Figure 4 shows the 26 basic statistics on the final set of regions computed for the picture in figure 1, the regions shown in figure 2. To understand the numbers, it is helpful to compare them for region 1 (the sky, represented by

A	1	2	3	4	5	6	7	8	9	10	11	12	13	14	15
B	3012	1099	689	574	214	675	626	346	5	75	437	5	74	191	118
C	162	231	136	128	70	92	125	45	5	52	88	5	45	79	30
D	162	21	13	0	0	47	0	48	0	0	29	0	0	19	25
E	1	57	1	48	85	1	16	90	98	50	53	99	83	22	16
F	1	16	28	33	42	43	45	47	51	54	54	57	63	65	68
G	110	110	48	78	99	37	57	110	98	62	89	99	101	60	41
H	37	64	48	61	67	74	69	74	55	70	74	61	72	74	74
I	0.04	0.58	0.55	0.12	0.69	0.79	0.32	0.87	0.77	0.03	0.31	0.79	0.64	0.23	0.53
J	0.61	0.01	0.01	0.23	0.48	0.52	0.53	0.65	0.41	0.68	0.78	0.58	0.82	0.86	0.92
K	580	434	445	540	229	655	252	618	408	455	327	370	424	585	398
L	600	295	399	521	36	666	107	597	278	343	170	255	311	520	312
M	808	358	559	677	80	834	200	774	391	416	246	357	408	605	408
N	45	96	48	51	31	45.7	70	28	34.0	69	63	37	95	59	125
O	55	111	65	76	44	61	92	42	33	79	85	50	131	75	173
P	61	120	79	115	51	66	111	46	18	81	101	68.0	180	76	177
Q	75	168	138	136	90	101	170	83	46	153	164	67	244	134	244
R	-0.26	-0.28	-.06	-.40	0.10	-.50	-.26	-.07	0	0.15	-.10	0	-.44	0.18	0.34
S	-0.62	-0.09	-.26	-.17	0.12	0.22	0.13	0.42	-.85	0.27	-.09	-.96	0.25	0.40	0.51
T	186	197	175	216	157	234	287	346	343	206	241	321	200	301	273
U	163	234	150	133	76	92	130	45	7.86	55	90	7.86	48	80	32
V	0.24	0.28	0.15	0.30	0.24	0.27	0.31	0.27	0.33	0.37	0.37	0.33	0.35	0.29	0.34
W	2.99	3.62	2.76	2.74	2.11	2.97	2.42	2.93	-.04	3.52	4.45	-.04	2.60	3.15	2.60
X	14	24	11	10	6	9	15	6	0	7	13	0	6	10	3
Y	3	5	0	2	1	0	0	0	0	0	1	0	2	1	0
Z	o	o	o	c	c	o	c	o	c	c	o	c	c	o	o

Figure 4. Statistics computed for the 15 regions of figure 2
(see figure 3 for explanation of the statistics codes).
Rows represent statistics and columns represent regions.

the second column from the left) and region 7 (the batteries and power inverter, the black area in the lower left, represented by the eighth column).
Region 1 has 3012 pixels (property B) to 626 for region 7. Region 1 has a
110 by 37 bounding rectangle (properties E   H) while region 7 has a smaller
30 by 13 one, consistent with the size difference. One significant difference
is that 162 of the region 1 pixels are on the edge of the picture (property D)
while none of the region 7 pixels are. Another is that region 1 brightness
(properties K – M) is considerably greater than region 7 brightness, especially in the blue as should be expected with sky. Two interesting things about
the brightness are that region 1 shows significant increasing brightness with
height in the picture (property S), as is typical of sky, and region 7 has
significant variation in its blue level (property P), apparently from the light
from the sky reflecting off different colors of the objects. Finally, the shape
properties (T – Z) are not too helpful because of the inaccuracies in the
boundaries, but the greater contrast of region 7's edge (property T) is useful.
(Note that pixels on the edge of the picture are excluded from region 1's
boundary since these do not characterize its shape.)

3. Classifying Regions

In this section we will discuss case-based and neural network methods of identifying regions, a neuron for focus identification, and using focus information to improve region identification.

3.1 Case-based Methods of Identifying Regions

One approach to region identification is to use human judgment to classify (label) some example regions and store these as cases for case-based retrieval. That then means for an unknown region, we find the case region with closest metric distance to the unknown's statistics, and assign the case's classification to the unknown. Our closeness metric was the square root of the weighted sum of the squares of the differences in 17 corresponding derived statistics between unknown region and case region. Weights were initially the reciprocals of the standard deviations of the statistic values over all cases; they were adjusted manually to improve performance. The 17 derived statistics are shown in figure 5. They were obtained by us manually: We examined pairs of regions in the library, developing meaningful concepts computed from the 26 basic region statistics to distinguish the pairs, until we had a set of derived properties we thought sufficient to distinguish any two regions in the pictures. They function as a feature space analogous to those used in the chapters in this collection by Blum et al. (characterization of sounds) and Manmatha et al. (characterization of handwritten words), but of necessarily greater dimensionality given the greater complexity of images.

We tested this approach with a case library of all the recognizable regions in a random subset of 64 of our 127 test pictures (containing 935 of the 1685 picture regions). We ran tests involving both 5 and 25 broad object classes that we developed from our experience (in both captions and pictures) with the database. The 5 classes used were being (living creature), equipment, gas (clouds, smoke, etc.), landscape, and structure (buildings, etc.); the 25 classes were airplane, airplane part, bomb, bomb part, building, building part, equipment, fire, flower, helicopter, helicopter part, horse, missile, missile part, mountain, pavement, person, person body part, rock, ship part, sky, tank, terrain, wall, and water. The intent of these classes was to provide a start of a visual taxonomy of the objects in the pictures, a start that could then be refined by caption information. While some of the 25 are domain-specific, they could be generalized for a more broadly applicable system.

To ensure a high-quality case library, we excluded from the cases the numerous unidentifiable small regions, a few unidentifiable larger regions, and some regions created by merging errors during pixel-level visual processing; these amounted to 605 of 1685 regions. For figure 2 for instance, we classified regions 3, 4, 5, 7, 10, and 11 as equipment; region 1 as sky; and re-

Code	Name	Definition	Case Weight
a	circularity	area/(circumference*circumference)	1.22
b	narrowness	height/width of bounding rectangle	0.31
c	marginality	1/(1+(circumference/number of border cells))	5.06
d	redness	average red brightness	0.005
e	greenness	average green brightness	0.004
f	blueness	average blue brightness	0.004
g	pixel texture	average brightness variation of adjacent cells	0.017
h	brightness trend	brightness correlation with x or y	4.47
i	symmetry	fractional skew of center of mass from bounding-rectangle center	3.24
j	contrast	average strength of the region edge	0.010
k	diagonality	smoothed-boundary diagonality	9.07
l	curviness	smoothed-boundary curviness	0.694
m	segments	smoothed-boundary number of inflection points	0.130
n	rectangularity	smoothed-boundary number of right angles	0.650
o	size	area in pixels	0.001
p	density	density of pixels in bounding rectangle	0.050
q	picture height	y-skew (unsigned) of center of mass within bounding rectangle	3.45

*Figure 5. Seventeen derived statistics used in classifying regions,
with their final weights used in case-based reasoning.*

gion 5 as a part of a person. Region 2 cannot be classified since the people were incorrectly merged into the fence in pixel-level processing; regions 9 and 12 cannot be classified since they are too small; and regions 6 and 8 cannot be classified because their color could mean either terrain or pavement.

With 5 classes, the percentage of correct identifications for the regions in the other half of the 127 pictures was 57.4%; with 25 categories, the percentage was 29.8%. For figure 2 and 25 classes, only one region was properly identified, region 1 as sky; 3 and 5 were identified as terrain, 4 as an airplane part, 7 as a helicopter part, 10 as a person part, and 11 as a flower. Of course, accuracy could be improved by increasing the number of cases.

Finding the best weights (the last column of figure 5) even for this level of performance required significant trial-and-error: 78 test runs on all 64 case pictures at 13 minutes of cpu time per run (1.39 seconds per region analysis), for a total of 17.1 hours, plus an additional ten hours spent analyzing the output. (These times are for Quintus Prolog in the default semi-compiled mode.) This tedious adjustment of weights is an important disadvantage of this approach.

3.2 Neural Network Methods of Identifying Regions

Neural networks have been successful at shape recognition (Rickman and Stonham 1993), and some evidence suggests that neural networks outperform case-based reasoning for text-retrieval tasks (Schutz, Hull and Pedersen 1995), so they should be considered for visual-region retrieval too. A simple neural network approach is to have a neuron for each region class c, taking

Statistic Code	Weight for "equipment"	Weight for "landscape"	Weight for "structure"	Weight for "being"	Weight for "gas"
a	5.42037	-6.97767	-1.94022	-0.175702	6.17973
b	4.26491	-8.3301	2.66959	2.55869	1.34759
c	-2.65447	-1.83798	7.46498	-3.76228	3.34481
d	-1.09679	0.809329	4.76544	2.73314	-4.60454
e	5.05693	5.958	-4.6198	3.70639	-7.52645
f	-2.14902	-4.8451	0.489836	-6.63653	15.7119
g	1.35821	-0.716794	3.14483	1.64459	-2.82619
h	0.518828	0.74166	0.849864	-0.039771	0.47357
i	1.19423	2.70491	-2.10099	1.60758	-0.775907
j	1.37304	1.35419	-0.781583	-0.625126	1.27464
k	0.780265	0.819155	-0.859497	1.71527	0.132284
l	0.357971	2.2851	-3.13827	0.713661	2.37169
m	1.17743	-0.37642	2.06484	-0.196143	-0.169705
n	0.0904502	0.113563	1.07907	0.491628	0.725293
o	-1.98266	4.27702	-2.03083	0.643991	1.59248
p	1.2905	0.138557	0.260798	0.0888679	0.725936
q	0.947604	1.28191	-0.05991	1.50196	-0.880632

Figure 6. Weights found by the neural network, without linguistic information, for connections between the 17 input region statistics and the 5 output region classifications.

as inputs the 17 derived region statistics for a particular region r, and providing as output the degree to which r has classification c. Then the classification associated with the largest output can be taken as r's classification. As in the standard approach (Wasserman 1989, chapter 3), inputs have weights to control their importance to each output, a linear sum is taken of the weighted inputs, and a nonlinear gain function (here a logarithm) is applied to the result; so the cth neuron computes $\log(Wca \cdot sa + Wcb \cdot sb + ... + Wcq \cdot sq)$ where the Wck denotes the weight on the derived statistic k and sk is the value of derived statistic k for the region.

The weights were initially 1. Adjustment of weights (feedback) was done only when the neuron for the correct classification did not have the highest output, and was computed by adding to each weight the product of these factors:

- the corresponding input value;
- the reciprocal of the standard deviation of that input value over all training cases, to normalize the input value;
- the ratio of the number of nonexamples of the neuron's class to the number of examples, to balance positive and negative feedback over the training examples;
- the output of the weight's neuron minus the output of the correct-classification neuron for the input, the error amount;
- a "learning speed" constant.

This means weights can range greater than 1 or less than 0, but they rarely went negative. We ran the training examples, as a set, through the neural net several hundred times.

We first tried such a single-level network. We obtained 67.1% accuracy (389/580) for 5 output classes, and 33.4% (194/580) for 25 output classes; only the first was significantly better than with case-based reasoning. In both cases it helped to turn off weight adjustment during testing. For figure 2 and 25 classes, the neural net got three regions correct: regions 1 (sky), 4 (equipment), and 10 (equipment); but it misidentified 2 and 5 as equipment, and 11 as terrain. Figure 6 shows the final weights for the 5 output classes found by the neural net after training. This performance was somewhat disappointing, so we looked for additional sources of information that would help the neurons.

3.3 A Neuron for Focus Identification

Pictures are not put in picture libraries unless they depict something well. This means that such pictures usually have a "visual focus," an image subject (or more formally, a region or set of regions of primary visual importance). This means the visual focus should generally be inferable from region properties, although photography is less precise than verbal description because photographs are sometimes taken in a hurry and do not provide the best possible view of the subject. When a picture is captioned, visual focus often corresponds to the linguistic focus (Grosz 1977) of the caption. From examination of a wide range of pictures depicting things, we identified six factors that contribute to the probability that a region in a picture is likely to be part of the visual focus:

- it is big;
- it is surrounded by a strong discontinuity in color or texture;
- it has a uniform color mix, though its brightness may vary;
- it does not touch the boundary of picture (with the exception of people's bodies when their faces are shown);
- its center of mass is close to the center of the photograph;
- its properties differ from those of any other region in the picture (with exceptions for some natural subjects like vegetation).

For figure 2 for instance, regions 1, 3, 6, 15, 11, 8, and 2 are unlikely to be foci by border touching, factor 4; the remaining regions, 7, 4, and 2 are the most likely to be foci by size, factor 1. Regions 4 and 7 are best on uniformity of color, factor 3, and region 4 is best on location of the center of mass, factor 5. Hence region 4 is most likely to be a subject of the picture; and indeed, it corresponds to the subject noun phrase of the first sentence of the caption, the linguistic focus.

Since the first five factors were used for region classification, it was easy to build and train a focus neuron on them. That is, a neuron computing

$\log(Wfo \cdot so + Wfj \cdot sj + Wfg \cdot sg + Wfc \cdot sc + Wfq \cdot sq)$ where s factors are from the 17 statistics and the weights are special focus-neuron weights. Regions that corresponded to caption word senses in one or more of the 25 object classes were assumed to be part of the visual focus, and the focus-neuron weights were given positive feedback for them, while other regions caused negative feedback. Word senses for the nouns in the captions were obtained by parsing with an improved version of the caption-parsing program described in Rowe (1996) which uses, among other things, the Wordnet thesaurus system to find superconcepts of word senses. We then mapped foci to the 25 region classes (taking also "instrumentality" for "equipment," "explosion" for "fire," "angiosperm" for "flower," "paved surface" for "pavement," "personnel" for "person," and "cloud" for "sky"). This simple way of using linguistic information did allow too many possible visual foci, but it is quick and easy to implement. The result was a 38.3% success rate (223/580) in focus identification for the set of test regions. This is not great, but is not bad without using the region-classification information of the last section, and is significantly better than random guessing since about 10% of the regions are foci.

3.4 Using Focus Information to Improve Region Identification

We then used the numerical output of the focus neuron to improve the region-classification neurons. For instance with our test library, being the visual focus should correlate negatively with being sky, since sky is rarely the subject of these photographs, but being the visual focus should correlate positively with being an aircraft, the main subject of the library. So for the region-class neuron for class c, when c is a superconcept for at least one caption word sense, we multiply the output of the region-class neuron by the output of the focus neuron to get a cumulative output. Otherwise, when c is not a superconcept for any caption word sense, we multiply by 0.5, a default value found to work well by experiment.

This approach improved the rate of success of the region-class neurons, again taking a success as when the greatest such neuron output corresponded to the correct classification of the corresponding region. We obtained a success rate of 48.1% (i.e., 48.1% of the regions were identified correctly) for the modified network on 25 classes, a significant improvement over the success rates both without the focus information and in case-based reasoning. In addition, the mistakes made were more intelligent, like confusing an aircraft region with a missile region rather than an aircraft with a sky region. To show what kind of mistakes were made, figure 7 shows the confusion matrix for 500 harder test regions, for the final state of the neural network after training with focus information. Rows represent classes chosen by the program, columns represent the correct classes drawn from the same set, and the entries

Class	1	2	3	4	5	6	7	8	9	10	11	12	13	14	15	16	17	18
1	0	2	0	0	0	0	0	0	0	0	0	0	0	0	0	0	0	0
2	0	41	0	0	2	0	3	0	13	0	0	1	19	12	11	8	0	0
3	0	0	1	0	0	0	0	0	3	0	0	0	1	0	0	0	0	0
4	0	1	0	0	0	0	0	0	0	0	0	0	0	0	0	0	0	0
5	0	0	0	0	0	0	0	0	0	0	0	0	0	0	0	0	0	0
6	0	1	0	0	0	0	0	0	1	0	0	0	0	0	0	2	0	1
7	1	1	0	0	0	0	0	0	0	0	0	0	2	0	0	0	0	0
8	0	0	0	0	0	0	1	0	0	0	0	1	0	0	0	0	0	0
9	0	24	1	0	0	0	0	0	73	1	0	2	9	3	9	9	1	0
10	0	0	0	0	0	0	0	0	2	2	0	0	0	1	1	0	0	0
11	0	0	0	0	0	0	0	0	2	0	0	0	0	0	2	0	0	0
12	0	8	0	0	1	0	0	0	4	0	0	0	0	2	2	3	0	0
13	0	6	0	1	0	1	1	0	15	0	0	0	14	3	12	0	0	0
14	0	3	0	0	0	0	0	0	10	0	0	0	10	23	6	0	0	0
15	0	12	0	0	4	2	1	0	3	2	0	0	2	7	27	0	2	5
16	0	2	0	0	0	0	0	0	4	0	0	1	2	1	1	0	0	0
17	0	3	0	0	0	0	0	0	0	0	0	0	0	1	0	0	0	1
18	0	3	0	0	0	0	1	0	3	0	0	0	2	0	0	1	1	7

Figure 7. Confusion matrix for 500 additional regions on the final version of the neural net with focus information, after training.

in the matrix are counts. Here class 1 = airplane, 2 = airplane part, 3 = helicopter part, 4 = bomb, 5 = bomb part, 6 = missile, 7 = missile part, 8 = tank part, 9 = equipment, 10 = building part, 11 = wall, 12 = mountain, 13 = pavement, 14 = terrain, 15 = sky, 16 = person part, 17 = smoke, and 18 = fire. (The remaining seven of the 25 classes are omitted from figure 7 since they occurred rarely, in only three events: sky was misidentified as water once, rock was misidentified as pavement once, and building was misidentified as sky once.) The counts show that human artifacts, like the first 11 classes, are easier to identify than natural objects, and that identification of people is very hard (apparently because of the widely varying body configurations and clothing colors). Note that these results were reached without any region-relationship constraints, which ought to significantly help. Running the neural net averaged 0.0852 seconds per region using semi-compiled Quintus Prolog.

4. Conclusions

We have attempted the difficult task of robust information retrieval of objects in a class of widely varying depictive natural photographs, using mostly domain-independent ideas. Content based access to these kinds of images has not been attempted before, so our results are difficult to compare with other systems. Like most information-retrieval methods, our methods are imperfect, but they may be sufficient for browsing. Our results suggest that traditional region-segmentation methods suffice for most regions in most natural photographs in a 100 by 100 pixel reduction, and that a simple neural net can correctly identify general object classes half the time. Results also suggest that a neural net is preferable to case-based reasoning for region classification. They also showed that the notion of visual focus helps in classification, as does as enumeration of objects mentioned in captions. In this we confirm the advantages of multimodal redundancy cited in Mani et al. and Hauptman and Witbrock (this volume). Our errors appear due to the small size of our training set (each region had to be manually identified), some inaccuracy of our segmentation, and our failure to exploit relationship constraints between regions, all of which are remediable with additional work. The largely domain-independent nature of our methods (albeit not in some of our defined classes) suggests scalability of our approach. Our work could provide a valuable component in the multimedia-retrieval systems discussed in this collection.

Acknowledgments

This work was sponsored by DARPA as part of the I3 Project under AO 8939, by the U.S. Army Artificial Intelligence Center, and by the U. S. Naval Postgraduate School under funds provided by the Chief for Naval Operations.

References

Ballard, D. and Brown, C. 1982. *Computer Vision*. Englewood Cliffs, New Jersey: Prentice-Hall.

Barber, R.; Flickner, M.; Hafner, J.; Niblack, W.; Petkovic, D.; Equitz, W.; and Faloutsos, C. 1994. Efficient and Effective Querying by Image Content. *Journal of Intelligent Information Systems*, 3(3-4): 231-262.

Blum, T.; Keislaer, D.; Wheaton, J.; and Wold, E. 1997. Audio Databases with Content-based Retrieval. In this volume.

Chang, S.; Shi, Q.; and Yan, C. 1987 (May). Iconic Indexing by 2-D Strings. In *IEEE Transactions on Pattern Analysis and Machine Intelligence*, 9: 413-428.

Choo, A.; Maeder, A.; and Pham, B. 1990. Image Segmentation for Complex Natural Scenes. *Image and Vision Computing*, 8(2): 155-163.

Draper, B.; Collins, R.; Brolio, J.; Hanson, A.; and Riseman, E. 1989. The Schema System. *International Journal of Computer Vision*, 2: 209-250.

Hauptmann, A. G. and Witbrock, M. 1997. Informedia: News-on-Demand Multimedia Information Acquisition and Retrieval. In this volume.

Kato, T. 1992. Database Architecture for Content-Based Image Retrieval. In Proceedings of SPIE, Image Storage and Retrieval Systems, 112-123, San Jose, Calif. 13-14 February.

Flickner, M.; Sawhney, H.; Niblack, W.; Ashley, J.; Huang, Q.; Dom, B.; Gorkani, M.; Hafner, J.; Lee, D.; Petkovic, D.; Steele, D.; and Yanker, P. 1995. Query by Image and Video Content: The QBIC System. *Computer,* 28(9): 23-32.

Flickner, M.; Sawhney, H.; Niblack, W.; Ashley, J.; Huang, Q.; Dom, B.; Gorkani, M.; Hafner, J.; Lee, D.; Petkovic, D.; Steele, D.; and Yanker, P. 1997. Query by

Image and Video Content: The QBIC System. In this volume.

Griffioen, J.; Yavatkar, R.; and Adams, R. A 1997. Framework for Developing Content-Based Analysis Systems. In this volume.

Grosz, B. 1977. The Representation and Use of Focus in a System for Understanding Dialogs. In Proceedings of the Fifth International Joint Conference on Artificial Intelligence, 67-76, Cambridge, Massachusetts. Los Altos, Calif.: William Kaufmann, Inc.

Lamdan, Y. and Wolfson, H. 1988. Geometric Hashing: a General and Efficient Model-Based Recognition Scheme. In Proceedings of the Second IEEE International Conference on Computer Vision, 238-249. Tampa, Florida.

Manmatha, R.; and Croft, W. 1997. Word Spotting: Indexing Handwritten Archives. In this volume.

Mani, I.; House, D.; Maybury, M.; and Green, M. 1997. Towards Content-Based Browsing of Broadcast News Video. In this volume.

Mehrotra, R. and Gary, J. 1995. Similar-Shape Retrieval in Shape Data Management. *Computer*, 28 (9): 57-62.

Mérialdo, B. and Dubois, F. 1997. An Agent-based Architecture for Content-Based Multimedia Browsing. In this volume.

Ogle, V. and Stonebraker, M. 1995. Chabot: Retrieval from a Relational Database of Images. *Computer*, 28(9): 40-48.

Rabitti, F. and Savino, P. 1992. Automatic Image Indexation to Support Content-Based Retrieval. *Information Processing and Management*, 28(5): 547-565.

Rickman, R. and Stonham, J. 1993. Similarity Retrieval from Image Databases—Neural Networks Can Deliver. In Proceedings of SPIE, Storage and Retrieval for Image and Video Databases, 1908:85-94. San Jose, Calif. 2-3 February.

Rowe, N. 1994. Inferring Depictions in Natural-Language Captions for Efficient Access to Picture Data. *Information Processing and Management*, 30(3): 379-388.

Rowe, N., 1996. Using Local Optimality Criteria for Efficient Information Retrieval with Redundant Information Filters. *ACM Transactions on Information Systems*, 14(2):138-174.

Scassellati, B.; Alexopoulos, S.; and Flickner, M. 1994. Retrieving Images by 2D Shape: A Comparison of Computation Methods with Human Perceptual Judgments. In Proceedings of SPIE, Storage and Retrieval for Image and Video Databases II, 2185:2-14, San Jose, Calif., 7-8 February.

Schutz, H.; Hull, D. and Pedersen, J. 1995. A Comparison of Document Representations and Classifiers for the Routing Problem. In Proceedings of Eighteenth International Conference on Research and Development in Information Retrieval, 229-237. Seattle, Washington: ACM SIGIR.

Seem, D. and Rowe, N. 1994. Shape Correlation of Low-Frequency Underwater Sounds. *Journal of the Acoustical Society of America*, 90(5): 2099-2103.

Smith, J.R; and Chang S. 1997. Querying by Color Regions Using the VisualSEEk Content-Based Visual Query System

Srihari, R. 1994-1995. Use of Captions and Other Collateral Text in Understanding Photographs. *Artificial Intelligence Review*, 8(5-6), 409-430.

Strat, T. 1992. *Natural Object Recognition*. New York: Springer-Verlag.

Wasserman, P. 1989. *Neural Computing*. New York: Van Nostrand Reinhold.

Content-based Graphics and Audio Retrieval

The chapters in this second section focus on intelligent multimedia information retrieval systems for graphics and audio. Techniques in this area will become increasingly important as access to on-line information sources and multimedia collections (including graphics and audio) becomes more prevalent.

The first chapter considers content-based access to graphics. Mei Chuah, Steven Roth, and Stephan Kerpedjiev, (Carnegie Mellon University) describe their system, SageBook, with enables search for and customization of stored data graphics. Their chapter describes data-graphic query, representation (i.e., content description), indexing, search, and adaptation. Queries are formulated via a graphical direct-manipulation interface (called SageBrush) by selecting and arranging spaces (e.g., charts, tables), objects contained within those spaces (e.g., marks, bars), and object properties (e.g., color, size, shape, position). In addition, retrieved data-graphics can be manually adapted. SageBook maintains an internal representation of the syntax and semantics of data-graphics, which includes spatial relationships between objects, relationships between data-domains (e.g., interval, 2D coordinate), and the various graphic and data attributes. Search is performed both on graphical and data properties, with three and four alternative search strategies, respectively, to enable varying degrees of match relaxation. Just as in large text and imagery collections, several data-graphic grouping techniques based on data and graphical properties were designed to enable clustering for browsing large collections. Finally, SageBook provides automatic adaptation techniques which can modify the retrieved graphic (e.g., eliminating graphical elements that do not match the specified query).

Just as users will need content-based access to graphics, they also will require content based access to non-speech audio (e.g., for audio clip art). In the second chapter, Thom Blum, Douglas Keislar, James Wheaton, and Erling Wold (Muscle Fish, Berkeley, CA) describe a user-extensible sound classification and retrieval system that draws from several disciplines, including signal processing, psychoacoustics, speech recognition, computer music, and multimedia databases. Just as several authors in section one of this collection use visual feature vectors to index and match images, Blum et al. use a vector of directly measurable acoustic features (e.g., duration, loudness, pitch, brightness) to index sounds, enabling search for sounds within specified feature ranges. For example, their SoundFisher system supports such complex content queries as "Find all AIFF encoded files with animal or human vocal sounds that are similar to goose sounds without regard to duration or amplitude." The system can also be trained by example, so that perceptual properties (e.g., "scratchiness" or "buzziness") that are more indirectly related to acoustic features, can be specified and retrieved. Performance of their Sound-Fisher system is illustrated on a database of 400 widely ranging sound files (e.g., captured from nature, animals, instruments, speech). The authors outline additional requirements identified by their system development, including the need for sound displays, sound synthesis (a kind of query formulation/refinement tool), sound separation, and matching of trajectories of features over time. As experienced in Roth et al.'s research, sound grouping and sound browsing techniques will become important as sound collections grow.

Chapter 5

Sketching, Searching, and Customizing Visualizations: A Content-based Approach to Design Retrieval

Mei C. Chuah, Steven F. Roth, and Stephan Kerpedjiev
School of Computer Science, Carnegie Mellon University

Abstract

We present new techniques for retrieval of data-graphics and a system, SageBook, that employs these techniques to facilitate the process of visualization design. Design is an important activity in many different disciplines, including engineering, science, and business, but current systems provide little support for non-expert users to design new graphics for use in data analysis. SageBook's approach is to provide expertise through the retrieval and reuse of previously successful designs. The design task places new demands on retrieval technology because it requires not only a good search engine but also effective tools to pose queries, browse results, and adapt previous designs for reuse. Despite our focus on data-graphic design, the concepts presented can be transferred to other design activities.

1. Introduction

This chapter will discuss retrieval as it relates to the problem of graphic design, an important activity in many disciplines and tasks. Graphics are used by analysts in many domains to analyze trends, detect patterns and anomalies, and answer focused questions. Data analyses are also performed by statisticians to identify relationships or detect problem areas. These activities are classified as exploratory data analysis (Tukey 1977). In addition to analysis, graphics are useful for succinctly and clearly communicating information to others in presentations. Whether for analysis or presentation, the success of these tasks depends on the ability of people to design effective graphics of their data quickly.

In the area of visualization design, the last decade saw significant progress in developing intelligent tools that help users construct data-graphics (e.g., Mackinley 1986, Roth and Mattis 1990, Casner 1991). A common feature of these systems is their ability to generate graphics that integrate multidimensional data. Most commercial applications, including popular spreadsheet systems, produce only simple graphics that tend to isolate data attributes in separate charts. In contrast, these intelligent systems integrate multiple attributes into one graphic using a variety of composition techniques: multiparameter graphical objects, space alignment, and grapheme clustering.

Another major problem that has been addressed only recently in the SAGE research is providing users with an interface that helps them design custom visualizations (Roth et al. 1994). This research stresses the need for a combination of user-controlled interactive design tools and automatic design mechanisms. Their assumption is that design is inherently a dual process of constructing or assembling graphic elements into composites in a bottom-up fashion, as well as a process of considering previous examples that might be relevant to current needs. Thus, these processes suggest complementary tools for specifying graphics constructively and browsing previously created graphics to reapply them.

To support these processes, two tools were created. SageBrush is a tool with which users sketch their design ideas; the intelligent design engine of SAGE then converts this sketch into a data-graphic. Moreover, the sketch may be incomplete, in which case SAGE attempts to complete the graphic by selecting and composing additional graphical elements and properties. Although the interactive graphic design techniques supported by SageBrush are useful when people know the graphic they wish to create, it is still necessary to provide them with alternative graphics when they are unsure how to visualize data and need to browse through design alternatives. To provide this type of design support, we developed another tool called SageBook. It is closely integrated within the SAGE system and provides retrieval capabilities that help users extract relevant visualization designs and adapt them to their needs. The major processes occurring in SageBook are shown in figure 1.

Central in the retrieval and reuse process shown in figure 1 is a library (store) of visualization designs. This storage infrastructure is expressive in such a way that it accommodates important design elements and supports easy conversion of existing designs into its internal storage language. In figure 1, the rectangles labeled "internal structure" represent designs or queries in the internal language. Users can query the stored designs based on their current tasks and data. Query interfaces help users communicate to the

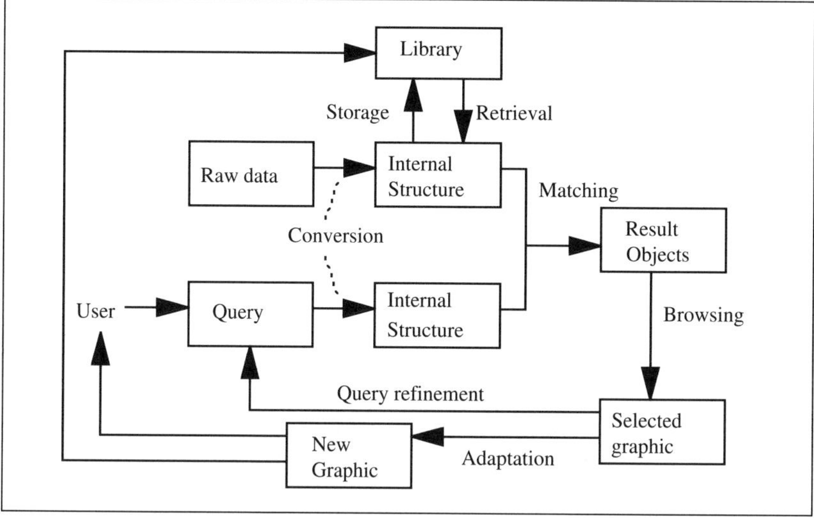

Figure 1. The retrieval and reuse process for designs.

system the types of designs that are desired. Therefore, the interface should closely match the users' mental model of design elements in the intended domain. Before matching a query with library entries, the system converts that query to the system's internal storage language in a way similar to the conversion of the original designs.

The internal description of the query is then used to retrieve library entries. There are two types of retrieval algorithms based on *exact* and *similarity* matching. Exact matching returns designs that fulfill all the criteria specified in the query, while similarity matches are less stringent and may return designs that contain enough, but not all, of the query elements. In design, one important use of graphic libraries is for getting new ideas from past successes. Since exact matching would severely limit the number and types of designs retrieved, it is critical to be able to retrieve designs based on some similarity measure. Similarity matching, however, can result in a large number of hits, especially when the library is well-populated. In order to effectively process the search results, users need tools that can help them organize the retrieved graphics. For example, users should be able to quickly browse through the retrieved graphics, collect them across multiple search sessions, and group them according to their importance, the data stored, or the graphical elements used. Finally, after selecting some designs from the library, users need to adapt these objects for current use. This might involve integration, addition and deletion of elements, altering the attributes used, or even completely redesigning the graphic.

In summary, there are five components of the retrieval and reuse process:

query, storage, search, browse, and adaptation. These components are all important to understanding the difficulties involved in supporting the retrieval and reuse process in the design domain:

Need for integration with other activities. The retrieval activity is usually not performed in isolation. In design domains, users retrieve information to get ideas or for integration into new designs. These tasks require not only the retrieval of objects but also the manipulation of those objects. To be a useful appliance for a designer, the retrieval process must occur seamlessly coupled with other tools. They need to be able to search libraries in the midst of other activities and make use of retrieved artifacts in their design workspaces. This includes tasks of querying, retrieving, browsing, and integrating. Most current retrieval systems only provide support for a very narrow part of these processes.

Designs are complex artifacts. Users' expectations from a retrieval system vary with the domains and tasks of interest. As it has been pointed out in (Griffioen et al., this volume), the retrieval process is domain-dependent because users need to search based on semantic content or embedded information. Hence, in order to effectively support the retrieval of designs, it is crucial to identify and represent the critical elements of a design within the system. Because designs are usually complex, it is difficult to capture all the properties of interest to the users.

Support for non-expert users. Most retrieval systems assume a certain level of user expertise and provide little support for users who are not experts or have little computer experience. In the case of data-graphic design, many of the users are analysts, planners and decision makers who lack design knowledge. In addition, design tasks often require a fair amount of computer experience because users need to manipulate the objects retrieved. To solve these problems, intelligent support should be provided in the form of design assistance or critiquing.

The communication problem. It is often difficult for users to convey their intentions to the system. This is especially true when specifying spatial or temporal structure. In order to improve the usability of retrieval systems, users must be able to communicate easily with the system, and support should be provided for articulating and refining queries and for understanding search results. Support should also be provided to allow smooth transitions between the different activities associated with the retrieval and reuse process in design.

In this chapter we present a content-based[1] retrieval system, SageBook, that addresses all of the above issues in the domain of data-graphic design. Although our work focuses on data-graphic retrieval, the concepts and techniques developed, as well as the tasks supported, can be generalized and applied to other design domains. SageBook provides the following functionalities to support graphic design:

Visual and context sensitive workspace for retrieving data. SageBook provides a visual workspace for storing and managing sets of data. Each data set incorporated within a graphic becomes a first-class object, retrievable based on cues relevant to users, such as visual appearance and data characteristics. Once retrieved, these objects can be browsed or interactively organized into groups.

A library of visualizations. When users are unsure about how to design a data-graphic, they can use SageBook as a library of examples, both for ways to visualize their data and to learn the design capabilities of the system. SageBook can be searched or browsed for prior data-graphics that have particular data or graphical characteristics. For example, one can retrieve all charts that have networks embedded in them to see how the lines and nodes can be embellished with additional graphical objects.

A tool for rapidly considering alternative graphic designs. Data-graphics can be created through a constructive process of selecting and arranging graphical elements (Roth et al. 1994). However, even when users are skillful graphic designers or use an automatic presentation system (e.g., APT (Mackinley 1986), SAGE (Roth et al. 1994), or BOZ (Casner 1991)), it can be very time consuming to generate many different data graphics that express the same data set in order to choose the most effective one. Even expert designers often need ideas when working with new data sets, perhaps ideas accumulated as a result of other users' successful attempts to visualize similar data. SageBook can quickly display a large number of browsable graphics, all related to a user's data set. Of course, this assumes that a portfolio of graphics has been accumulated over a sufficiently large range of data-types and graphic styles to provide a variety.

A tool for customization of prior designs. After a set of data-graphics is retrieved, users may request that one of them be used to create an analogous graphic for their new data (i.e., reuse the design of the graphic for a new data set). Users may also modify the designs from retrieved graphics. Thus even though a prior graphic design may not exactly match a user's goals, the parts of the design that do can be reused; those parts that do not match can be removed or altered. SageBook allows users to combine graphic design elements from several previously created data-graphics.

Current data-graphic design tools, particularly those provided with spreadsheets, do not support design retrieval. As a result, previous designs can only be retrieved by memorizing file names or exhaustively looking through all the data-graphic files. SageBook addresses this issue by providing users with support for storing data-graphics, formulating queries, retrieving, browsing and adapting data-graphics to suit current tasks. In the following sections, we will discuss how each of the five sub-tasks in the design retrieval process are supported by SageBook.

2. Query Interface

Users must be able to easily communicate their search requests to the system. Effective query interfaces will have a direct mapping from the user's model of the objects to be retrieved to the query expressions in the interface model. Current query interfaces can be divided into five categories: command language, direct manipulation, keyword, query by example, and sketch.

To use a command language (Chang, Lee and Dow 1992, Rabitti and Savino 1992), users are required to learn the primitives and the syntax of the query language. Such languages are usually robust but difficult to learn and use.

Direct manipulation queries are created by manipulating widgets, menus, and objects. These interfaces are easy to learn but are less robust than command languages. This is because users can only make queries that have already been predefined. There is not much opportunity for formulating the complex queries that are possible with a command query language. Recently, Papantonakis and King (1995) developed Gql, a visual language whose expressive power is comparable to that of SQL. They also reported that a small-scale experiment had shown time decrease for formulating queries compared to text input. However, this type of language still requires that users develop a complete mental model of a language of the complexity of SQL, which increases learning time. An alternative approach (Young and Shneiderman 1993) exploits the metaphor of water flowing through filters for creating Boolean queries. An experiment has shown that there is a significant difference in the total number of correct queries favoring the Filter/Flow approach to text only SQL interfaces.

Keyword queries have long been used in retrieval systems. Keywords have the advantage that they require no learning time. Users simply enter a sequence of words and the system does the matching based on those words. However, keywords suffer from not being able to convey more complex relationships (e.g. spatial relationships among objects). In addition there may be mismatches between user-generated keywords and system keywords (Borgman et al. 1988). Many current systems complement image analysis with keyword matching to increase precision and recall (Kato 1992; Smith and Chang, this volume; Rowe and Frew, this volume).

Query by example (Kato 1992; Holt and Hartwick 1994) is a powerful query method. It has very low learning time because users simply have to select an example object that represents what is required and submit it as the query. Employing this method, users can convey complex queries because the example object submitted is capable of representing as much semantic and syntactic information as any other object in the database. However, this method may be problematic when users cannot find an example image that is a good representation of what is desired. In such cases, users may have to look exhaustively through the library to find a suitable example. For this reason, this method is typically used in query refinement.

Sketch queries are most common for retrieving images. There are two types of sketch queries: *free-hand sketch* (Holt and Hartwick 1994, Nishiyama 1994) and object manipulation sketch. In free-hand sketching, users freely draw the query using a mouse, pen or other input device. There is no limitation on the set of permissible object types. The sketch is then analyzed, and important features are extracted (e.g., spatial relationships and shapes) and used for matching. Even though users may freely sketch many different types of objects, the system will only be able to understand the forms that are representable within its internal language. In object manipulation sketching interfaces, users construct sketches from available primitive objects, usually arranged in palettes. Although this method seems to be more limiting than free-hand, the fact that it does not need image analysis makes it much more efficient. In addition, users are guaranteed that all elements in the sketch will be fully understood by the system and that there won't be any error in interpretation. Object manipulation sketch interfaces are usually appropriate for systems that address focused domains.

2.1 SageBook Query Interface

SageBook allows users to query the system based on graphical properties and/or data properties of the stored images. Users form queries through an object manipulation interface called SageBrush (figure 1). It provides a palette of spaces and graphemes as well as a view of the data, from which users create sketches of graphical elements or select subsets of data attributes. Sketches are constructed by simple drag-and-drop operations. For example, to create the sketch in figure 1, the user dragged a chart space from the top palette to the working area, dragged a line, a mark, and a text grapheme from the left palette to the area inside the chart, and "opened" the line grapheme by clicking on it, so that all graphical properties pertinent to lines get visualized as icons (in the case of lines, four positional properties, color and line thickness are relevant). The user might have further specified this sketch by dragging data attributes to these property icons. Any data attribute mapped to a graphical property gets interpreted as a directive for encoding that attribute by that property. In this case, the *average temperature* data attribute has been assigned to the color of the line. The sketch and the set of attributes at the bottom represent a query, which SageBook matches with the entries in the design library, returning the graphics that fulfill the graphical and/or data constraints specified by the user. Query interface details are provided in (Chuah et al. 1995).

Unlike command language queries, users do not need to know a complex vocabulary for describing content. Instead of learning the terms that the sys-

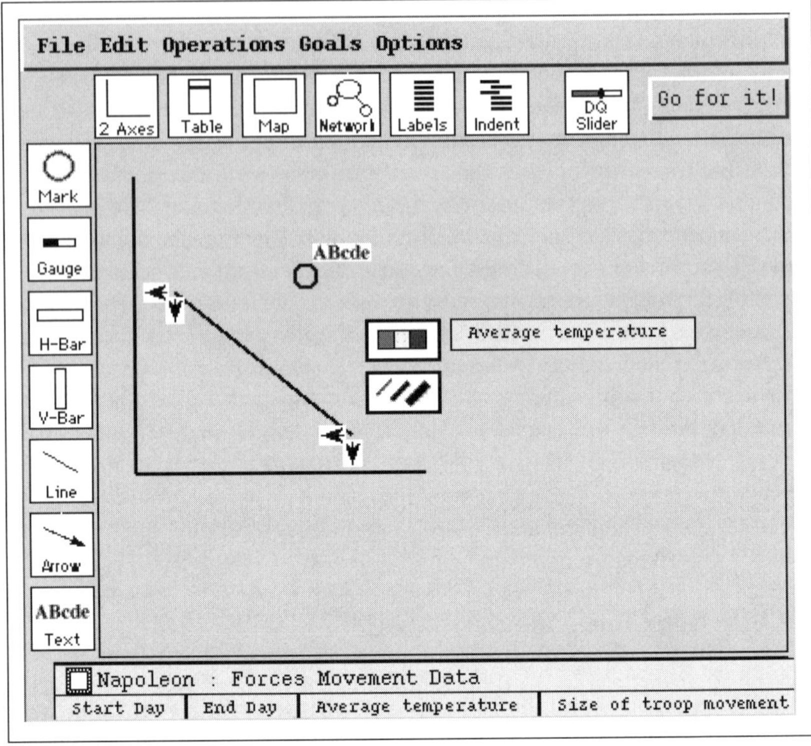

Figure 2. SageBrush: The SageBook query interface. The space and grapheme palettes are located at the top and to the left of the interface, the data area is at the bottom, and the sketch is constructed in the middle of the interface.

tem uses internally to refer to axes, map spaces, interval bars, gauges, indented text, etc., SageBrush enables users to select and arrange spaces (e.g., charts and tables), the objects contained within those spaces (e.g., marks and bars), and the objects' properties (e.g., color, size, shape and position). Likewise, users do not have to learn the terms for describing the characteristics of data, such as scale of measurement (nominal, ordinal, and quantitative), or the relationships among data attributes (functional dependency, interval, and 2D coordinate). Instead, they just select some or all the attributes listed in the SageBrush data area. In addition to serving as a query interface, SageBrush can also be used to construct data-graphics and to manually adapt retrieved data-graphics. Because of SageBrush's multiple functionality, any data-graphic that can be constructed can also be queried.

SageBook uses object manipulation sketching because it supports a focused domain, in which all the primitive objects can be identified and made available to the user. An object manipulation sketching interface is more accurate, simpler and requires less processing. In addition to the object manipulation interface, SageBook supports query by example. Users can query the graphic library either by giving a graphic example, a data example, or both. Since we are complementing this method with a sketching interface, users can just sketch what they want when no examples are available.

Once a query has been formed and submitted, it is translated into a language (design-directives) that is understood by the system components. When users select a data set or construct a graphical query, the system extracts the characteristics of each selected data attribute and graphical element and then reformulates the query in terms of underlying data and graphical properties.

SageBook does require data objects to be characterized when the data is first created. This characterization must be provided by database creators (e.g., in the form of relation schemes), by analysis modules that examine data values, or by modules that acquire this information from users interactively. However, once data is characterized and stored, users need not be aware of the characteristics or the language that is used to describe them.

3. Storage

The storage of objects has two main components: *storage vocabulary* and *method of translation*. Storage vocabulary refers to how objects are represented and determines which criteria can be used for matching. In principle, graphics could be stored in raw format (e.g., a bitmap, a video sequence, raw text) or in a formal language. The advantage of using a language is that less storage space is required and the search is more efficient. In addition, language representations have richer expressiveness and explicitly show relationships and structures that are implicit in images. Finally, language representations are easier for the system to manipulate. Typically, the disadvantages of using formal representations are that information may be lost in the translation from raw format to formal language and that the translation may introduce errors. The types of languages used in current systems include: low-level object attributes (Rowe and Frew, this volume; Pentland, Picard and Sclaroff 1994), entity-attribute-relation language (Hibler et al. 1992), and object-oriented language (Griffioen, Yavatkar and Adams, this volume; Halin and Mouaddib 1992).

Method of translation refers to how the raw formats are translated into the internal language of the system. Objects that are stored in raw form do not need a method of translation. Current methods include: object analysis, spatial and temporal parsing, model descriptions, and manual translation. Object analysis involves generating object properties and structure by using low level processing routines. For example, histogram distributions and segmentation fall under this category. Object analysis techniques (Rowe and Frew, this volume; Pentland, Picard and Sclaroff 1994) are general (i.e., domain independent) but are not able to produce higher level semantic content such as object relationships and other embedded information. Temporal and spatial parsing (Lakin 1986) retrieve object structure and relationships by using the location and temporal occurrence of those objects. Such techniques produce more structure and semantics than the previous method but require domain knowledge. Model descriptions refer to systems that have access to the full object descriptions. This information is usually not available unless the search objects were created electronically as well-defined models. Some examples include computer modeled scenes and CAD models. Finally, manual translation requires a person to annotate the search objects with relevant descriptions. This method is general and can produce complex semantic information; however, it requires a significant amount of human effort and may be inconsistent. Automatic indexing, when possible, is preferable to manual methods because the object library can be easily populated, maintained and organized for efficient search.

Yet another element of storage is its *organization,* which is extremely important for very large document bases. A poor organization may make the search time prohibitively high. Frequently used instruments for storage organization are indexing, hashing, and clustering. Indexing ensures direct access to the objects that have a given value specified in the query. Hashing organizes the documents according to the values of a hash function which may combine the values of different attributes. Clustering puts similar objects in continuous areas. Depending on the type of objects and methods of retrieval, one method of organization may be preferable to others. SageBook uses hashing and indexing techniques.

3.1 SageBook Storage Vocabulary

SageBook uses an expressive object-oriented vocabulary for describing the graphical and data relationships contained in data-graphics so they can be searched by content. The objects represented in the language are reflected in the query interface. This enables SageBook to translate user requests accurately and unambiguously (i.e. without vocabulary mismatches). Preliminary user tests show that users can construct queries with very little learning time, which indicates that the query interface and the vocabulary model correspond well with the user expectations.

A common data and graphic representation is used by all the modules of our system. This vocabulary is capable of expressing the syntax and semantics of data-graphic designs, and characterizing the data contained within them. It is able to express the spatial relationships among graphical objects, the characteristics and relationships among data-attributes. Most other retrieval sys-

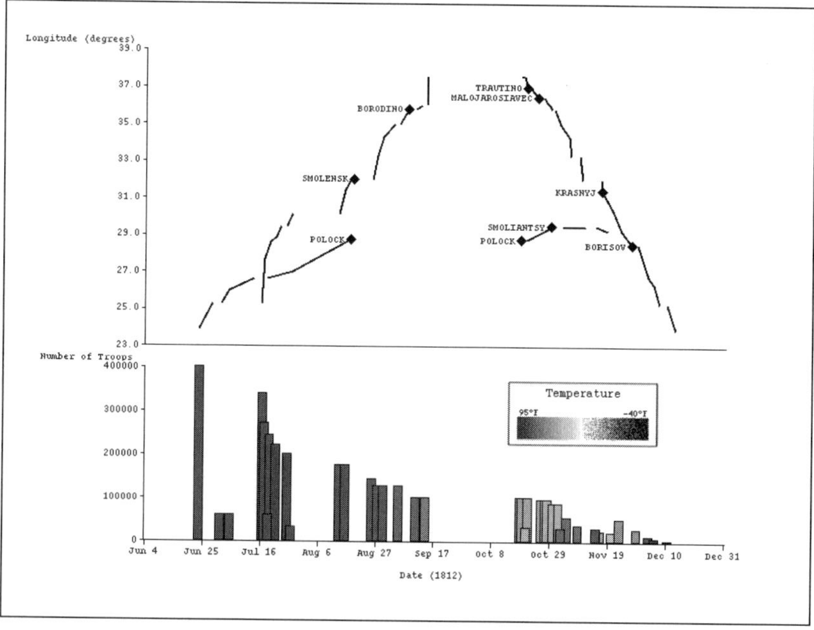

Figure 3. A two-space SAGE graphic.

tems do not provide such a detailed and expressive internal language.

3.1.1 Data Representation. The data characterization language expresses scales of measurement (nominal, quantitative, ordinal), structural relationships among data (e.g., between the endpoints of ranges and between the two attributes of a geographic 2D coordinate), and dependencies among attributes (e.g., whether each person has one or more birthdates, residences, children). We describe some examples in Section 4.2.2. A detailed description of the data characterization used in SageBook can be found in (Roth and Mattis 1990).

3.1.2 Graphic Representation. The internal representation describes each data-graphic as a design-specification, which contains one or more related spaces. Spaces can be related by being aligned, either vertically or horizontally. Spaces can only be aligned when the data types represented by the common axis are consistent. For example, *cost-of-labor* and *cost-of-materials* are two consistent attributes because both express dollar amounts. However, *person-weight* and *person-height* are not consistent attributes because weight is expressed in pounds while height is expressed in inches. In figure 3, which shows a data-graphic from Napoleon's 1812 march on Russia, the spaces are vertically aligned by the common data type date. The *x*-positions of the lines and marks in the upper chart and the bars in the lower chart all encode dates and therefore can be portrayed with a common axis.

Each space represents groupings of graphical elements that are positioned according to a single layout discipline. There are many types of layout disciplines; map, chart, table, and network are the most common ones. The graphical elements contained within a space are *graphemes*. Examples of graphemes are marks, bars, text, lines, and gauges. Each grapheme uses different properties to encode data. Some of these attributes may be used to encode attributes, to distinguish different relations shown in the same space, or to convey a relation to another grapheme. For example, the data graphic in Figure 3 presents spatial, temporal and quantitative data. The positions of the labels are relative to the positions of the marks, which encode the *east-west-location* and *date-of-battle* attributes. Graphical attributes not encoding attributes or relations have default values (e.g., the size and the shape of the marks).

Figure 4 expresses the data-graphic in figure 3 in terms of its constituents. The data-graphic contains two vertically aligned spaces, both of whose layout discipline is chart. Within the first space there are three sets of graphemes: a line, mark and label. The line position, the mark position, and the text lettering all encode data values, while the text position is relative to the position of the mark. The second space contains a set of bar graphemes using x-position, length and color to encode data.

Thus, the *content description* language specifies classes of objects, the spatial relations among spaces and among graphemes, the graphical properties of objects, and the way they are assigned to data.

3.2 SageBook Method of Translation

The data-graphic descriptions used by SageBook get generated when the data-graphics are first created by SAGE, an automatic presentation system (Roth and Mattis 1990). When a SAGE data-graphic is saved, a description of it is stored in conjunction with an image reduced in size for rapid viewing (a large image is generated as requested from the description). This description is later used by SageBook during the search process. Because the same description is used to generate the data-graphic, the stored representation contains at least as much information as the graphic. This is not true in other retrieval systems where the stored representation contains only a small subset of the object information and inconsistencies may exist between the stored representation and the object itself. The disadvantage of SageBook, however, is that only graphics created by the SAGE system can be stored. It is possible that, by using spatial parsing techniques (Lakin 1986) and domain knowledge, we can analyze general data-graphics and encode them into our language. Information on the graphical elements (e.g., spatial relationships) can be derived from visual processing, and other information such as data properties and relationships can be obtained from the database. Note that this is

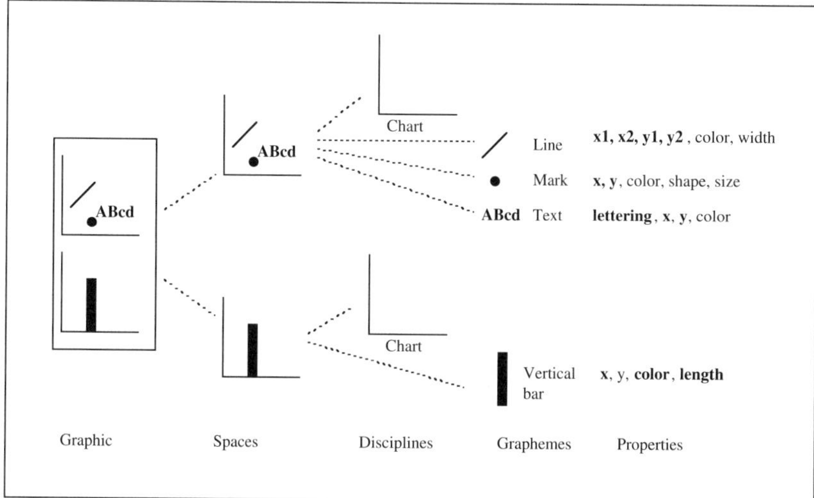

Figure 4. Constituents of the data-graphics in figure 3 (the graphical properties that encode data attributes or are relative to others are printed in bold)

not a big change to the current system as it only affects the conversion methods from raw images to the system internal structure (cf. figure 1), which is a small part of the system.

4. Search

Search is the process of matching stored objects with user queries. There are three main issues in search: the match criteria, the type of search and similarity model, and finally, matching objects that have multiple types of data. The match criteria used in search depend on the storage vocabulary (presented in the previous section). Depending on the expressiveness of that language, the match can be simply based on keywords or might instead match object structure, relationships, and attributes. The richness of vocabulary in SageBook allows the matching algorithm to not only retrieve objects based on their properties but also on object structure and relationships among objects.

There are two classes of search - exact search and similarity search. Exact search will return only those objects that exactly match all of the constraints specified in the query whereas similarity search will return a set of objects that meet some similarity metric but may not conform to all the specifications of the query. Garber and Grunes (1992) showed that similarity matching is important and useful. The problem with it however is coming up with a good metric for judging similarity. How different attributes of the stored objects should be weighed in the similarity algorithm is based on a user's perception of which attributes, relationships and elements are more important. Current methods for determining similarity include neural networks, case-based reasoning and other uses of domain knowledge. Both neural nets and case-based reasoning require users to train the system on a set of examples. In fact Rowe and Frew (this volume) show that even though results are promising, they are still inaccurate and require a significant amount of training. In SageBook, the different similarity matching algorithms are based on specific knowledge of graphic design.

Another issue in search algorithms is how to deal with objects that contain data of different types. For example, in video there is an image stream, a text stream, and an audio stream. To effectively search for such objects, we need to not only process each data type individually but also combine their results. Combining the results from processing each data type improves search accuracy and enables users to convey constraints based on more than one type of data. Mérialdo and Dubois (this volume) present a method for combining results of various data types through the use of agents. Similarly, in SageBook, support is provided for users to search based on either graphical elements or data content.

4.1 SageBook Match Criteria

The search strategies in SageBook are based on the structural properties of the graphical and data elements in a data-graphic. The storage vocabulary enables matching on semantic content and relationships among objects. SageBook's match criteria recognize positional relationships (including clusters, alignment and containment), graphical properties (e.g., color, shape, size), and data mappings (i.e. the assignment of graphical properties to data attributes). The search algorithm is able to make fine distinctions in graphics, for example the differences between figures 5 and 6. Figure 5 shows a datagraphic of project-management data. The interval bars indicate the time spans of activities of different types. Their y-position and color properties encode the *work-type* and *status* attributes, respectively. Associated with each bar is a circle whose size encodes the cost of the operation. Note that circle positions do not encode any data attributes. Figure 6 shows house sale data. It also contains interval bars which show the *selling-price/asking-price* range for house sales, and a set of circles whose x-positions indicate the *agency-estimate* attribute. The color of the bars encodes the house neighborhood. Note that the interval bars and the marks in figure 6, unlike in figure 5, are not attached to each other positionally. Therefore, it is necessary for search techniques to be sensitive to the subtle difference in the relation between the circle and bars in the two figures.

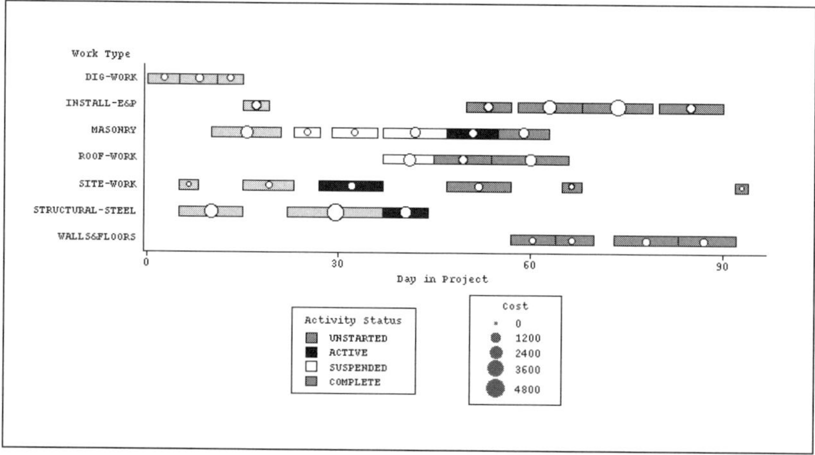

Figure 5. Data-graphic using interval bars and a mark associated with each bar.

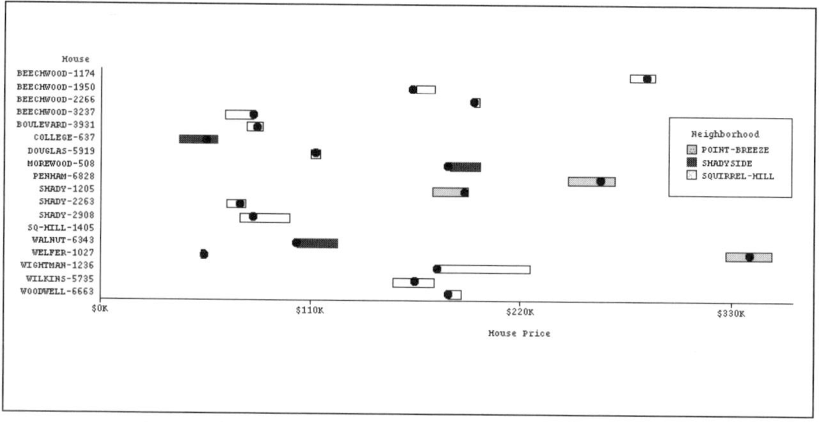

*Figure 6. A Data-graphic using interval bars and marks
whose x-positions encode a data attribute.*

4.2 SageBook Exact and Similarity Search

SageBook provides matching based on both graphical elements and data attributes. There are several alternative match strategies which provide different degrees of relaxation on the search criteria based on the degree of overlap between the library data-graphic and the user query. Each retrieves a different number of data-graphics depending on its degree of relaxation.

A typical reason for relaxation is to find compromises if no entries match the query exactly. Additionally, similarity-based relaxation finds items that are equally desirable but would otherwise not match because of insignificant feature differences. Most importantly, supporting data-graphic design suggests an additional function of relaxation: giving users ideas for how to integrate additional graphical elements and properties with partial designs they have created. The latter answers questions like: "How can additional *graphemes* be added to the space I've created and integrated with the graphemes I've already included?" "How have previous data-graphics used additional properties of these objects?" and "How can other *spaces* or *graphemes* be substituted for the ones I've selected to express the same data?" Enabling users to answer questions like these motivated the choice of match criteria that evolved in SageBook. Finally, our choice of criteria reflected the fact that it was easy for users (or the system) to remove extra *spaces, graphemes* and *properties* when the design is adapted for new data. In the future, we intend to extend the model by taking user tasks into account and providing matches based on task specifications.

4.2.1 Graphical Matching. *Close Graphical Matching.* This strategy searches for pictures that have the same number of spaces as the query. Figure 7 shows a graphical query and the data-graphics returned for that query. For rhetorical purposes, we have drawn a black border around the seven data graphics that are retrieved by the close matching process. All these data-graphics only contain one space because the query only has one space.

For a space in the query to match a space in a library data-graphic, the layout disciplines of both spaces must be identical. However, the library data-graphic space may have more graphemes in it as long as the ones specified in the query match graphemes in the library data-graphic space. For two graphemes to match, they must be of the same class (i.e. bars, lines, marks) as well as use the same properties (i.e. color, shape, size, width) to encode data. In figure 7, all the data-graphics returned by this search strategy have a space of type chart, consistent with the query. Furthermore, all the charts in the resulting data-graphics contain graphemes of type *horizontal interval bar.* Note also that only the positional properties of the bar were specified in the query. If additional properties were specified, these must also be present in the retrieved data-graphic. The retrieved data-graphics may contain grapheme properties not contained in the query.

Subset Graphical Matching. Subset graphical matching is more inclusive than close graphical matching. In subset matching the data-graphics may have more spaces and graphemes than the query as long as all the spaces in the query match some unique space in the library data-graphic. The data-graphics shown in the grid in figure 7 are returned by subset graphical matching. The matches returned are sorted according to their degree of similarity to the query, based on the match criteria. For example, in figure 7 all one-space matches are shown first, followed by the two-space matches and so on.

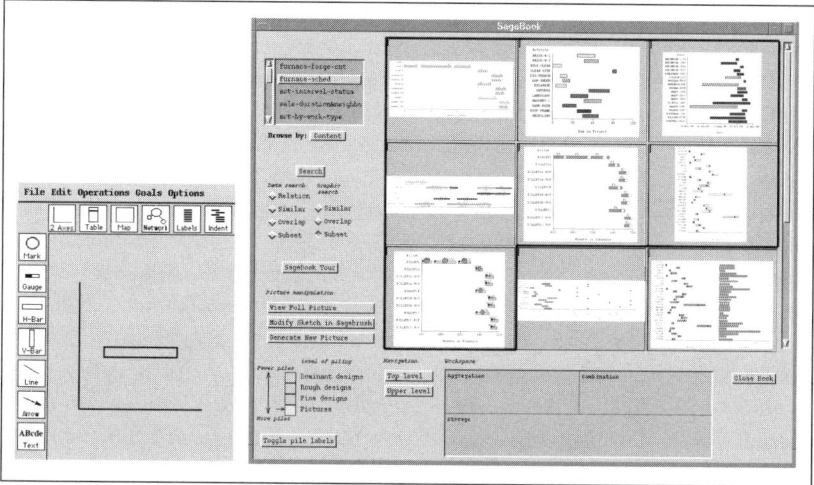

Figure 7. A graphical query and the data-graphics returned by SageBook.

The subset matching idea is similar to the process of a library search. First, the user enters a query, and a super-set of data-graphics is returned. Each data-graphic in the set contains all the elements specified in the query and may contain more. To narrow down the choices presented by subset match- ing, the user may have to add some additional constraints to the query. Alter- natively, the user may browse through the data-graphics and pick one based on other criteria. Even though the data-graphic retrieved by subset matching may contain more spaces than the user desires, the unwanted spaces can easi- ly be edited out of the data-graphic by using SageBrush.

Overlap Graphical Matching. Subset matching may sometimes exclude data-graphics that are useful but fall slightly short of meeting the match crite- ria (which requires each space of the query to match with at least one space in the library data-graphic). Thus, in addition to a strict subset search, we im- plemented a match strategy that sets upper and lower bounds around the number of spaces in the query that must match a space in the library data- graphic. The lower and upper bounds are set to be a percentage decrement and increment of the total number of spaces in the query.

4.2.2 Data Matching. *Data-Relation Matching.* Relation matching retrieves all previously saved data-graphics that have all of the desired relations specified in the query. By relation we are referring to the name of the relation scheme in relational database terms. This matching strategy is useful for re- trieving sets of daily or weekly data from the same database and redisplaying them consistently. This also suggests an additional use for data-graphic re- trieval - searching for information (rather than just graphic displays) stored in graphic media. For example, the house-sales relation might be used to construct many displays over time.

Close Data Matching. This strategy enables users to find graphics that contain data that have similar characteristics to their current working set. Given a list of attributes and their properties, the close data matching algorithm tries to find a mapping from attributes in the query to attributes in prior data-graphics. For an attribute in the query to match an attribute in a library data-graphic, the two attributes must have the same data-type (nominal, ordinal, quantitative) and frame of reference (quantitative/valuation, coordinate), as well as participate in the same kinds of functional-dependencies and complex types. Figure 8 shows an example of this data-matching process. In figure 8, *Activity* matched *HouseID* because both are nominal data-types and both are functionally independent. Materials-cost matched *Number-of-Rooms* because both are quantitative data-types and have the same frame of reference (quantitative/valuation). *Start-Date* and *End-Date* match *Date-on-Market* and *Date-Sold* because they have the same frame-of-reference (Coordinate) and belong to the same complex-type (Interval Type). The close data match process must also ensure that the number of attributes in the query and the library data-graphic are the same and that every attribute in the query matches some unique attribute in the library data-graphic. In figure 8, the query and library data-graphic satisfy both of these criteria.

Unlike the relation matching strategy which requires the query and the library data-graphic to contain identical relation names, the close data matching strategy only requires that the attributes have similar data characteristics. Thus, this search strategy is not a keyword search but a search based on the similarity of characteristics and relationships of the data.

Subset Data Matching. The idea behind subset data matching is very similar to that of subset graphical matching. Subset matching is like close data matching, except that instead of requiring a bijective (i.e. one-to-one and onto) mapping of attributes between the query and the saved data-graphics, subset matching allows the saved data-graphics to have more attributes than the query as long as each attribute in the query has similar characteristics with some attribute in the data-graphic.

Data-overlap Matching. As with graphical matching, a variant of the data-subset matching strategy was created that sets upper and lower bounds around the number of data-attributes that must match instead of a strict subset rule.

4.2.3 Manual Search. Users may also manually search through the library. This is necessary in the cases where the user is uncertain how to form a query or unsure what to look for. Manual search is also useful when the user is unfamiliar with the contents of the library and wants to quickly get an idea of what data-graphics are available.

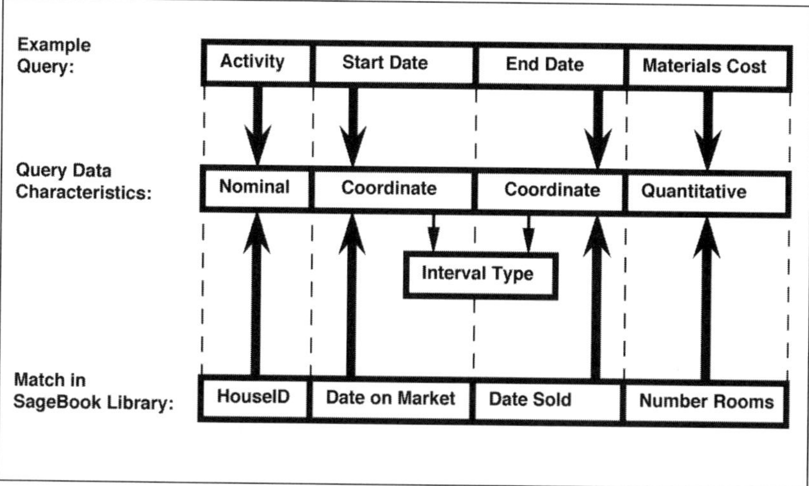

Figure 8. Close data matching process.

SageBook provides two different library browsing facilities that support manual search. First, users may organize and browse data-graphics through a folder system. This facility allows users to easily navigate through directories and view data-graphic files in the same grid used for visualizing the results of a search (figure 7). In addition to supporting manual search, this file navigation interface is also useful when a user knows the exact location or filename of the data-graphic of interest. The file navigation interface provided is similar to those seen on Macintosh interfaces.

The second facility provided to support manual search is a book tour. The tour facility in SageBook includes all of the library data-graphics in a book-like structure. The book consists of chapters, sections, and subsections, which serve to provide a hierarchical categorization to the data-graphics. More detail is provided in the next section on browsing.

5. Browsing

If the library contains many objects, some queries may retrieve a large set of items. In such cases, the cognitive load placed on the user to browse through the retrieved objects would be significant. In order to deal with large retrieval sets, it is necessary for the system to provide tools to help users browse search results quickly and effectively. Browsing is also useful in those cases where the user simply wants to navigate through the library. Such cases arise when the user is unsure of the kinds of graphics contained in a library, when the user is unable to formulate a query, or when the user simply wants to go through many alternatives to get ideas. Despite its importance, browsing is rarely supported in retrieval systems. Many systems provide a sorted list of objects to the user, making it difficult for users to identify categories or to determine general features and distributions of the result set.

Some browsing methods include sorted lists, visualization of results (Pu and Faltings 1995; Hibino and Rundensteiner, this volume) and structuring the results, for example, through the use of hierarchies and piles (Chuah et al. 1995, Ballay 1994). The sorted list has no structure apart from being ordered according to match scores. This technique is useful when the user is only interested in individual results and not on overall properties of the result set. One big disadvantage is that when match scores are uniformly high or low for a large set of graphics, the sorted list does not provide any useful structure within that set.

Another browsing method involves 2D or 3D visualization of results. This method is very useful for seeing overall distributions of the results and detecting groups that are significantly different. A problem with this method however is that it is not always clear which attributes of the retrieved objects should be viewed or how to compute a numeric score based on similarity. Finally, browsing can be facilitated by organizing the search results in hierarchical or other structures. Pu and Faltings (1995) indicated that categorization is a useful method for supporting browsing. As in the previous case, however, this technique suffers from the uncertainty of what are good attributes to use as the organizing structures.

5.1 SageBook Browsing

To support browsing, we developed a scrollable, grid-like interface that enables multiple data-graphics to be viewed at once (figure 7). Our recent work has explored ways to enhance browsing efficiency by grouping similar data-graphics into a stack in one cell of the grid. Thus the retrieval in figure 7 can be compressed to three stacks as shown in figure 9. The number of data-graphics in a stack is indicated by the length of a black bar at the top of each cell. For example, the first stack in figure 9 clearly contains more graphics than the others. The expand operation can be used to distribute members of any stack into a new grid. An interesting challenge has been to develop effective grouping strategies (i.e. similarity criteria) for organizing a large number of data-graphics into a small number of meaningful stacks. The formal representation of data-graphics provides a framework for regrouping strategies, as it did for graphic and data queries.

We are experimenting with three levels of granularity for grouping graphics: *fine design, rough design*, and *dominant design*. Since SageBook's pur-

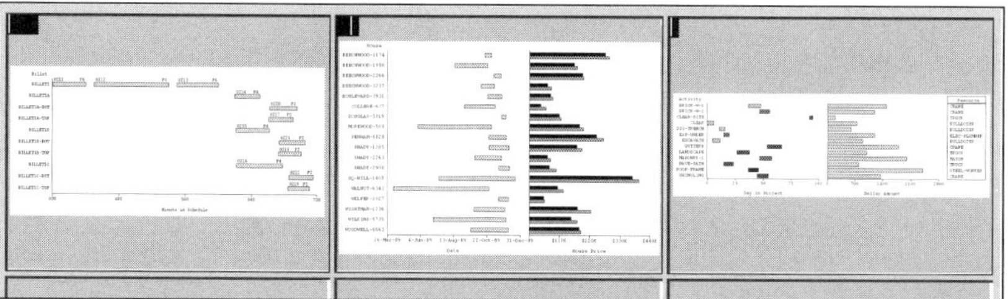

Figure 9. A grid of stacks.

pose is primarily to help users get design ideas, these levels are intended to increase the design differences between stacks by grouping similar data-graphics together. *Fine design* includes together those data-graphics that have the same number and types of spaces, number and types of graphemes within each space and properties of graphemes. Effectively, these are cases in which the same design was saved for different data. Viewing the same design with multiple data sets can often bring out striking differences in how effective it is for different contexts.

The *rough design* method differentiates data-graphics based on the space types and grapheme types, and not on the properties of those graphemes. This method is similar to the fine-design criteria except that graphemes may use different properties and the number of each grapheme type in a space may differ. For example, data-graphics like the ones in figures 5 and 6 would be stored in the same stack regardless of the properties of the graphemes that were used (e.g., circle size). In addition, this also groups bar charts with one, two or more bars per axis element in the same stack or maps with points containing a single label or multiple labels in the same stack. The intent of this type of grouping is to group together graphics that share basic design elements that differ mainly in the number and properties of graphemes they contain. For example, bar charts containing a single bar per independent variable would be included with charts containing two or more bars. Charts that contain bars with superimposed circles would be differentiated from charts that have bars with text labels because they emphasize different design relationships.

Finally the *dominant design* method further relaxes the constraints on the data-graphics that go into the same pile. It requires that the data-graphics that are grouped into one pile have the same spaces and each space has the same *dominant* grapheme. The dominant grapheme is the most salient grapheme in a particular space. For example, lines or bars are dominant when they are combined with marks. This technique was developed when it was discovered that users frequently searched for use of particular graphemes and had biases

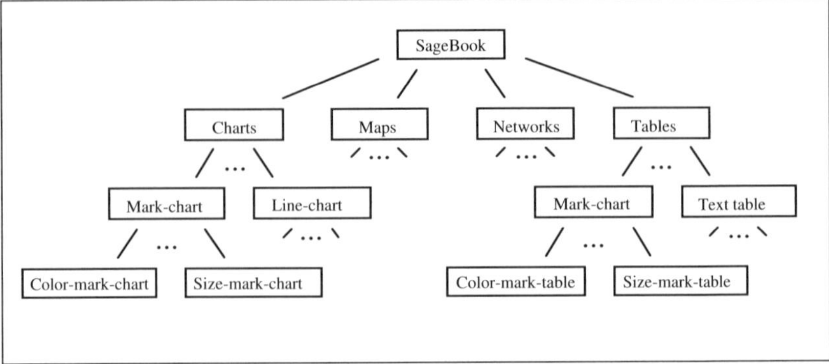

Figure 10. The book organization.

as to which graphemes were primary or secondary.

We have found that these methods significantly lower the number of data-graphic piles that are shown to the user at any one time. For example, the retrieval of 15 graphics for the horizontal interval bar query (9 of them are shown on the grid in figure 7) was compressed to 3 dominant grapheme stacks (figure 9). The degree of reduction will depend greatly on the nature of the library. Libraries created by individuals who store many examples of the same graphic will show much different savings from libraries specifically constructed to maximize differences among graphics to provide many design alternatives.

Another metaphor for browsing is that of a *book*. Search results are organized into a book organized into chapters, subchapters and sections based on a classification scheme. Users can browse this book at any level, including individual graphics. Part of the browsing hierarchy is shown in figure 10. At the first level, data-graphics are divided according to the space disciplines they contain, namely charts, maps, tables, etc. In a study conducted by Lohse (Lohse et al. 1994), these were the main categorizations picked by the users. The next level in the hierarchy separates out data-graphics by grapheme class within the same space type. This is the next most salient feature. Data-graphics that have multiple grapheme classes will be present in multiple piles, enabling people to access them from different perspectives. Finally, we classify the data-graphics according to the properties used. Note that, as before, if a data-graphic is using two different properties, it will be classified under two different sections in the hierarchy.

The browsing interface also provides a workspace where collections of data-graphics can be stored and manipulated by users. This can be achieved by dragging individual or piles of data-graphics into the workspace. Within the workspace, users may organize their retrievals into new piles by merging, differentiating, and intersecting sets of graphics designs.

6. Adaptation

The most important assumption of SageBook is that graphics are retrieved to support design. Therefore, while the quality of the retrieved set is important, what is equally important is how easily an element of this set can be modified to create the desired design. Relatedly, the use of *similarity* search strategies opens up the possibility that some of the graphics retrieved may not fully conform to what the user desires. In addition, users may sometimes need to edit the results to combine multiple retrieved objects. To support these tasks, retrieval systems that support design need to provide tools that facilitate adaptation of retrieved objects. Most systems do not support adaptation, and the few that support it usually only provide manual editing capabilities. The adaptation process, however, may sometimes be complex and inexperienced users or designers may have trouble articulating desired effects. SageBook provides users with automatic adaptation as well as manual editing capabilities. The automatic adaptation facility alters prior designs to suit current data and design preferences.

6.1 SageBook Adaptation Support

To support adaptation, our system provides manual adaptation capabilities with SageBrush and automatic adaptation capabilities through SageBook. The automatic adaptation module maps data-attributes in the query to data-attributes in the retrieved data-graphic based on their similar data characteristics. This mapping process can produce two types of inconsistencies: (1) The retrieved data-graphic has more graphical elements than necessary to express the data-attributes in the query. This can result from a *subset* query that retrieved a graphic portraying more data attributes than were in the query. (2) The graphical elements in the retrieved graphic do not express some of the data-attributes in the query. This can happen when an *overlap query* retrieves a graphic that does not satisfy all the query attributes. It is possible for both inconsistencies to occur simultaneously.

In the first case, the adaptation module will discard extra graphical elements in the retrieved data-graphic. The module first discards any extra properties of graphemes (e.g., discarding the use of color or size). If discarding these properties results in a grapheme that would have no properties mapped to data, then the grapheme itself is discarded. Finally, if a space contains no remaining graphemes, it is discarded as well. The progressive removal of unnecessary graphical elements preserves the most salient features for possible reuse. During adaptation, we assume that the user would want to change the retrieved design as little as possible when there are still data attributes to be expressed. Because a space is a very salient design feature, it will be very noticeable to the user when the adaptation module deletes a space from the de-

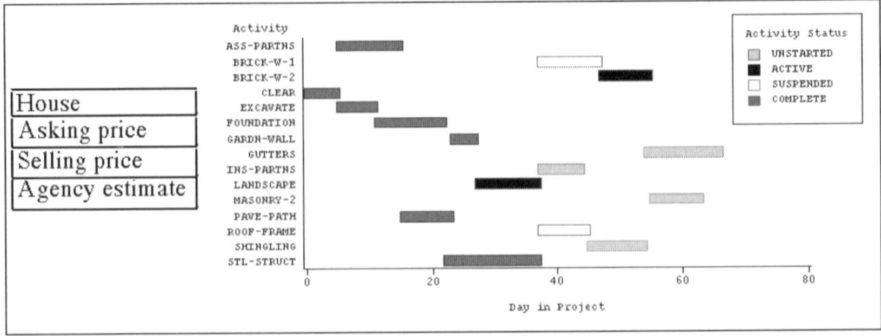

Figure 11. A data query and an example data-graphic returned by that query.

sign. Similarly, removing graphemes is more salient than not using some of their properties. In the second case, when there are data attributes that are not expressible by the graphic, SAGE will search for an additional design to express them.

Figure 11 shows a data query for attributes of house sales and an example retrieved graphic that shows attributes of construction project activities. The graphic was retrieved because the *start-* and *end-date* interval in the graphic matches the *asking-price/selling-price* range in the query, and the activity-name attribute matches the *house* attribute. However, the activity status attribute, expressed by the color of the bar, does not match the agency estimate attribute (the latter is a quantity, dollar amount, while the former is a set of four nominal values). Since the search criterion was overlap, the graphic was retrieved even though these two do not match.

To adapt figure 11, the color property is first discarded because it does not match any data. Then, the adaptation module sends the query data and partially completed graphic to SAGE to search for an additional design element to complete it. Figure 12 shows the new data-graphic.

SAGE encoded *agency-estimate* by using the x-position of a new mark grapheme. Position is an effective property for representing attributes and is preferred over size, shape, color, text lettering, etc. However, the positional properties of the bars are already used, so SAGE added a new grapheme to the chart space. In this case, the additional attribute was a dollar-amount and could be expressed relative to the same x-axis as the other dollar-amounts. Otherwise, SAGE would have to choose between adding another chart aligned to the right of this one or using text labels on the bars to express the agency estimate. In general, SAGE can generate multiple alternatives from which a user can choose. We have encoded a knowledge base of design techniques within SAGE that can complete partial design specifications or create graphics when no specifications are provided (Roth et al. 1994).

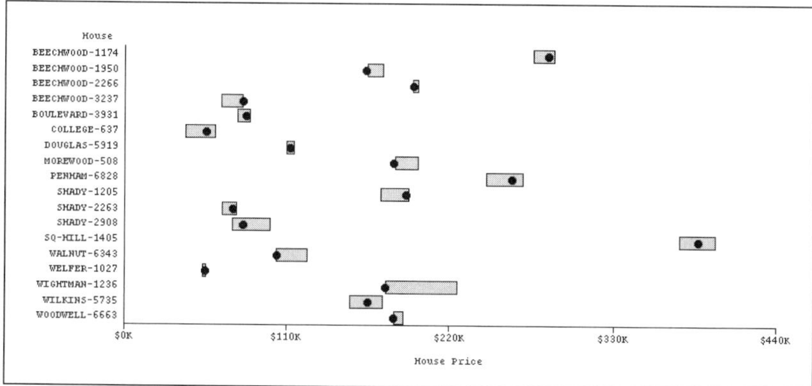

Figure 12. A new data graphic generated from the query and the data-graphic design in figure 11 after automatic adaptation.

7. Evaluation

Common evaluation measures such as precision and recall have been used to indicate the performance of a retrieval system. Generally, performance is affected by three classes of errors depending on which part of the system they are produced (cf. figure 1): interface errors (that affect query construction and adaptation), translation errors (i.e. from query to internal representation), and retrieval errors (that occur in search and match steps).

Interface errors are user-system communication problems that might occur when users are unable to accurately convey their queries or adapt retrieved objects for their current goals using the SageBrush interface. In principle, these errors may occur as the result of poor editing tools. As a result of iterative interface improvements based on preliminary user tests interface errors have been reduced to insignificant levels. The main remaining weakness is the potential for users to specify complex spatial relationships among graphemes that are not yet accurately interpreted by the system (e.g., the arrangement of several text labels around a bar in a chart). Problems like these indicate incompleteness in the representation language and greater flexibility in the interface than is supported by the representation. It can be solved by extending the language or constraining the interface. Related problems can occur in manual adaptation.

Translation errors occur during the conversion of raw objects and queries into the system's internal representation. They usually occur when the internal structure is very high level because complex embedded semantic information has to be derived. For example, translation errors are especially problematic for image retrieval systems where high-level semantic information embedded in the image needs to be extracted accurately (Griffioen et al., this volume).

SageBook does not have translation errors because the query interface is tightly coupled with the internal representation. SageBook has access to the model descriptions of the data-graphics as generated by SAGE during graphics creation. These storage descriptions contain at least as much information as the data-graphic itself; therefore, there are no inconsistencies between the generated data-graphic and their stored descriptions.

Retrieval errors fall into two categories: structural errors and relevance errors. Structural errors occur when the match criteria does not coincide well with user expectations. Since the user's model is usually at a high semantic level, these errors tend to occur when the internal representation is at a very low level. For example, if the representation contained image properties such as object outlines, then objects that users perceive as structurally identical might not be correctly matched due to orientation and scale differences. Pentland, Picard and Sclaroff (1994) described such matching errors. Sage-Book has few structural errors because of closeness of the query language to the system representation.

The other type of retrieval errors are *relevance errors*. The concept of relevance reflects the degree of utility of the retrieved objects for users and the tasks they perform. For example, if a user can easily adapt a visualization from the library to his or her data, then we can assume that that visualization has been relevant to that user. However, since designs are so task oriented, just creating a new visualization from an old design may not be sufficient for judging design relevance: the new visualization might be appropriate for some tasks and not others (e.g., viewing correlations vs. making comparisons between pairs of values). Conversely, a library design may not be directly adaptable to a new visualization but it may contain just one element that is valuable for the user. By using this element, one might be able to solve a difficult design problem. In the latter case, even though the user would discard a major part of the original design, it still should be considered relevant. These characteristics of designs make the evaluation of our retrieval and automatic adaptation techniques difficult and perhaps suggests that traditional information retrieval evaluation methods may be insufficient. New research must create an evaluation procedure for judging the relevance of designs that is based on the following:

- A method of assigning a degree of relevance based on measures of the ease and completeness of the supported design task (including feedback from users on the value of the retrieval set for the tasks)
- Well populated libraries collected from naturally occurring samples
- A corpus of naturally occurring data analysis tasks to be performed with the search task

8. Conclusion and Future Work

We have presented querying, storing, searching, browsing, and adaptation techniques pertaining to the retrieval and reuse of graphic designs. We also describe an implemented system, SageBook, that employs these techniques. The following types of retrieval components are essential for this domain:

- A common vocabulary for representing data-graphics designs
- An object manipulation querying interface (like SageBrush)
- Graphic- and data-matching strategies that support different levels of similarity between queries and designs
- A visual interface for presenting the results of the retrieval and flexible browsing at different levels of aggregation
- Automatic and manual adaptation of retrieved designs for new data.

Preliminary experience with SageBook suggests that these features ensure very few interface, translation and structural errors. Positive evaluation of relevance errors depends both on methods for assessing tasks, as well as encoding task properties in the query and search process (i.e. enabling users to express the tasks they wish to perform with retrieved graphics). Future work includes performing comprehensive user testing and incorporating SageBook as a design support tool within an extensive information exploration environment called Visage (Roth et al. 1996).

Acknowledgments

The authors would like to acknowledge the contributions of Mark Derthick, John Kolojejchick and Joseph Mattis to the research, implementation and preparation of this chapter. This work was supported by DARPA and Army Research Lab.

Note

1. By the content of data-graphics, we mean their graphical properties (graphical objects, properties and relations), how they encode data attributes (i.e. their mapping to data) and the abstract characteristics of data relevant to design. We are not refering to the meaning or interpretation of the data values contained in graphics.

References

Ballay, J. M. 1994. Designing Workscape: An interdisciplinary Experience. In Proceedings CHI'94 Human Factors in Computer Systems, 10-15. Boston, MA: ACM.

Borgman, C. L.; Belkin, N. J.; Croft, W. B.; Lesk, M. E.; and Landauer, T. K. 1988. Retrieval Systems for the Information Seeker: Can the Role of the Intermediary Be Automated? In Proceedings CHI'88 Human Factors in Computing Systems, 51-53. ACM.

Casner, S. M. 1991. A Task-Analytic Approach to the Automated Design of Information Graphic Presentations. *ACM Transactions on Graphics* 10(2): 111-151.

Chang, S. K.; Lee, C. M.; and Dow, C. R. 1992. A 2D-String Matching Algorithm for Conceptual Pictorial Queries. In Image Storage and Retrieval Systems, Proc. SPIE, eds. A. A. Jamberdino and W. Niblack, 47-58.

Chuah, M. C.; Roth, S. F.; Mattis, J.; Kolojejchick, J.; and Juarez, O. 1995. Sage-Book: Searching Data Graphics by Content. In Proceedings CHI'95 Human Factors in Computing Systems, 338-345. Denver, CO: ACM.

Garber, S. R. and Grunes, M. B. 1992. The Art of Search: A Study of Art Directors. In Proceedings CHI'92 Human Factors in Computer Systems, 157-163. Monterey, CA: ACM.

Griffioen, J.; Yavatkar, R.; and Adams, R. A 1997. Framework for Developing Content-Based Analysis Systems. In this volume.

Halin, G.; and Mouaddib, N. 1992. An Object Oriented Approach to Design a Content-based Image Retrieval Model. In Image Storage and Retrieval Systems, Proc. SPIE, eds., A. A. Jamberdino and W. Niblack, 100-111.

Hibino, S. and Rundensteiner, E. 1997. Interactive Visualizations for Temporal Analysis: Application to CSCW Multimedia Data. In this volume.

Hibler, J. N. D.; Leung, C. H. C; Mannock, K. L.; and Mwara, N. K. 1992. A System for Content-based Storage and Retrieval in an Image Database. In Image Storage and Retrieval Systems, Proc. SPIE, Jamberdino, eds. A. A. and W. Niblack, 80-92.

Holt, B. and Hartwick, L. 1994. Visual Image Retrieval for Applications in Art and Art History. In Storage and Retrieval for Image and Video Databases II, Proc. SPIE, eds. W. Niblack and R. C. Jain, 70-81.

Kato, T. 1992. Database Architecture for Content-based Image Retrieval. In Storage and Retrieval for Image and Video Databases II, Proc. SPIE, eds. W. Niblack and R. C. Jain, 112-123.

Lakin, F. 1986. Spatial Parsing for Visual Languages. In Visual Languages, eds. S. K. Chang, T. Ichikawa, and P. A. Ligomendes, 35-85. New York: Plenum Press.

Lohse G. L.; Biolsi, K.; Walker, N.; and Reuter, H. H. 1994. A Classification of Visual Representations. *Communications of the ACM* 37(12): 36-49.

Mackinlay, J. D. 1986. Automating the Design of Graphical Presentations of Relational Information. *ACM Transactions on Graphics* 5(2): 110-141.

Mérialdo, B. and Dubois, F. 1997. An Agent-based Architecture for Content-Based Multimedia Browsing. In this volume.

Nishiyama H.; Kin, S.; Yokoyama, T.; and Matsushita Y. 1994. An Image Retrieval System Considering Subjective Perception. In Proceedings CHI'94 Human Factors in Computing Systems, 30-36. Boston, MA: ACM.

Papantonakis, A.; and King, P. J. 1995. Syntax and Semantics of Gql, a Graphical Query Language. *Journal of Visual Languages and Computing*, 6(1): 3-25.

Pentland, A.; Picard, R. W.; and Sclaroff, S. 1994. Content-based manipulation of Image Databases. In Storage and Retrieval for Image and Video Databases II, Proc. SPIE, eds. W. Niblack and R. C. Jain, 34-47.

Pu, P. and Faltings, B. 1995. Multimedia Systems for Design. In Working notes of the IJCAI-95 Workshop on Intelligent Multimedia Information Retrieval, ed. M. Maybury, 134-145. August 19, 1995, Montreal, Canada.

Rabitti, F. and Savino, P. 1992. Querying Semantic Image Databases In Image Storage and Retrieval Systems, Proc. SPIE, eds. A. A. Jamberdino and W. Niblack, 69-78.

Roth, S. F.; Lucas, P.; Senn, J. A.; Gomberg, C. C.; Burks, M. B.; Stroffolino P. J.; Kolojejchick, J. A.; and Dunmire, C. 1996. Visage: A User Interface Environment for Exploring Information. In Proceedings IEEE InfoVis'96, San Francisco, CA. Forthcoming.

Roth, S. F.; Kolojejchick J.; Mattis J.; and Goldstein J. 1994. Interactive Graphic Design Using Automatic Presentation Knowledge. In Proceedings CHI'94 Human Factors in Computing Systems, 112-117. Boston, MA: ACM.

Roth, S. F.; and Mattis J. 1990 Data Characterization for Intelligent Graphics Presentation. In Proceedings SIGCHI'90 Human Factors in Computing Systems, 193-200. Seattle, WA: ACM.

Rowe, N. C. and Frew, B. 1997. Automatic Retrieval of Objects in Captioned Depictive Photographs. In this volume.

Smith, J. R.; and Chang, S.-F. 1997. Querying by Color Regions Using the VisualSEEk Content-Based Visual Query System. In this volume.

Tukey, J. W. 1977. Exploratory Data Analysis. Addison-Wesley Pub. Co., Reading, MA.

Young, D. and Shneiderman, B. 1993. A Graphical Filter/Flow Representation of Boolean Queries: A Prototype Implementation and Development. *Journal of American Society of Information Science* 44(6): 327-339.

Chapter 6

Audio Databases with Content-Based Retrieval

Thom Blum, Douglas Keislar, James Wheaton, and Erling Wold
Muscle Fish LLC

Abstract

Despite vast research and development efforts in such diverse domains as digital signal processing, psychoacoustics, speech recognition, computer music, and multimedia databases, there is a paucity of literature that addresses the issue of automatic classification of sounds. Many audio and multimedia applications would benefit from the ability to classify and search for audio based on the characteristics of the audio rather than by resorting exclusively to keywords. This chapter describes an audio analysis, search, and classification engine which reduces sounds to perceptual and acoustic attributes. Sounds can then be searched or retrieved by any one or a combination of the attributes, by specifying previously learned classes based on these attributes, or by selecting or entering reference sounds and asking the engine to retrieve sounds that are similar (or dissimilar) to them. After surveying some related research, we examine this engine and describe a specific application for browsing sounds in a database.

1. Introduction

The rapid increase in speed and capacity of computers and networks has allowed the inclusion of audio as a data type in many modern computer applications. For example, multimedia databases or file systems can easily have thousands of audio recordings. These could be anything from a library of sound effects to the soundtrack portion of an archive of news footage. Such sound libraries often are poorly indexed or named to begin with. Even if a previous user has assigned keywords or indices to the data, these are often highly subjective and may be useless to another person. To search for a particular sound or class of sound (e.g., applause, or music, or the speech of a particular speaker) can be a daunting task. When, on occasion, an audio data type is incorporated into today's software architectures, it is usually treated as an opaque collection of bytes with only the most primitive attributes attached, for example, name, file format, sampling rate and so on.

Anyone who has ever attempted to describe the perceived features of a sound knows of the difficulties. Words are woefully inadequate to convey the essence of a sound, and there is no all-encompassing standard for sound classification. No two listeners will propose the same descriptions for every sound. This being the case, people often resort to describing sound by using one of the following methods, all of which we have incorporated into our engine and sound browser application.

Simile: saying one sound is like another sound or a group of sounds in terms of some characteristics. For example, "like the sound of a herd of elephants." A simpler example would be to say that it belongs to the class of speech sounds or the class of applause sounds, where the system has previously been trained on other sounds in this class.

Acoustic/perceptual attributes: describing the sounds in terms of commonly understood physical characteristics, such as brightness, pitch and loudness.

Subjective attributes: describing the sounds using personal descriptive language. This requires training the system (in our case, by example) to understand the meaning of these descriptive terms. For example, a user might be looking for a "shimmering" sound.

Onomatopoeia: making a sound similar in some quality to the sound you are looking for. For example, the user could making a buzzing sound to find bees or electrical hum.

In a content-based sound retrieval application, all of the methods described above could be used in combination with traditional keyword and text queries.

To accomplish these methods of audio content-based retrieval, we first reduce a sound to a small set of parameters using various analysis techniques. Secondly, we use statistical techniques over the parameter space to accomplish the classification and retrieval.

While the specific analysis algorithms we use for audio differ from those found in image or video analysis systems, the general techniques employed bear some resemblance to non-audio content-based retrieval systems, for example, the Query by Image Content (QBIC) system (Flickner et al., this volume).

This chapter is divided into three sections. In the first section, we will offer a brief historical perspective by reviewing some related research, mostly in the areas of computer music and digital audio signal processing. Next, we will present our analysis and classification algorithms and show examples of some results produced by algorithms. Finally, we will examine a few of the features of our multiplatform sound browser application, SoundFisher, currently under development.

2. Previous Research

During the last four decades, numerous attempts have been made to develop taxonomies of sounds, including musical and environmental sounds (Schaeffer 1966, Schafer 1980, Vertegaal and Bonis 1994). This interest of musicians and psychologists has shed some light on the analysis and classification of sound, be it by objective or subjective measures.

Sounds are traditionally described by their pitch, loudness, duration, and timbre. The first three of these perceptual attributes are well-understood and fairly easily measured. Timbre, on the other hand, is a somewhat ill-defined attribute that encompasses all the distinctive qualities of a sound other than its pitch, loudness, and duration. The effort to discover the components of timbre underlies much of the previous psychoacoustic research that is relevant to content-based audio retrieval.

Salient components of timbre include the amplitude envelope, harmonicity, and spectral envelope. The attack portions of a tone are often essential for identifying the timbre. Timbres with similar spectral energy distributions (as measured by the centroid of the spectrum) tend to be judged as perceptually similar. However, research has shown that the time-varying spectrum of a single musical instrument tone cannot generally be treated as a "fingerprint" identifying the instrument, because there is too much variation across the instrument's range of pitches, and across its range of dynamic levels (Grey 1977, Gordon and Grey 1978).

In the early 1980s, various researchers discussed or prototyped algorithms capable of extracting audio and musical structure from a sound (Buxton et al. 1981; Chafe et al. 1982; Foster et al. 1982). The goal was to allow queries such as "find the first occurrence of the note G-sharp." These algorithms were tuned to specific musical constructs and were not appropriate for all sounds. Unfortunately, this work was terminated prematurely.

The Intuitive Sound Editing Environment (ISEE) is a recent software package for controlling MIDI (Musical Instrument Digital Interface) synthesizers (Vertegaal and Bonis 1994) using a small number of orthogonal, device-independent timbral parameters. The parameters are "overtones" (harmonicity), "brightness" (spectral energy distribution), "articulation" (control of spectral transients and persistent noise), and "envelope" (the speed of the amplitude envelope). These parameters could also be applied to the analysis of digital audio, an approach that would bear some similarity to the analysis techniques presented in this chapter.

For speech recordings, it is possible to use speech recognition systems to convert the audio to text and then use normal text-based search and retrieval techniques (Shäuble et al. 1995). There are numerous examples of this process described in other chapters of the present publication (Hauptmann et al., this volume; Mérialdo and Dubois, this volume). The specific methods of audio analysis, training, and classification described in this chapter are not intended to provide traditional speech recognition capabilities, however, as discussed in the following sections, they are effective for automating tasks such as distinguishing speech and non-speech sounds or female and male speakers.

There has been work done on the indexing of audio databases using neural nets (Feiten and Günzel 1994). Although they had some success with their method, it has several problems from our point of view. One, while the neural nets report similarities between sounds, it is very hard to "look inside" the net after it is trained or while it is in operation to determine how well the training worked or what aspects of the sounds are similar to each other. It is difficult for the user to specify which features of the sound are important and which to ignore.

3. Analysis and Retrieval Engine

In this section of the chapter, we present a general paradigm and specific techniques for analyzing audio signals in a way that facilitates content-based retrieval.

3.1 Introduction to the Analysis Technique

By content-based retrieval of audio, one can mean a variety of things. At the lowest level, one could retrieve a sound by specifying the exact numbers in an excerpt of the sound's sampled data. This is analogous to an exact text search and is just as simple to implement in the audio domain. At the next higher level of abstraction, the retrieval would match any sound containing the given excerpt, regardless of the data's sample rate, quantization, compression and so on. This is analogous to a fuzzy text search and can be implemented using correlation techniques. At the next level, the query might involve acoustic features that can be measured directly as well as perceptual (subjective) properties of the sound (Keislar et al. 1995; Blum et al. 1995). Above this, one can ask for speech content or musical content.

It is the "sound" level—acoustic and perceptual properties—with which we are most concerned here. Some of the aural (perceptual) properties of a sound, such as pitch, loudness, and brightness, correspond closely to measurable features of the audio signal, making it logical to provide fields for these properties in the audio database record. However, other aural properties (for instance, "scratchiness") are more indirectly related to easily measured acoustic features of the sound. Some of these properties may even have different meanings for different users.

We first measure a variety of acoustic features of each sound. This set of N features is represented as an N-vector. In text databases, the resolution of queries typically requires matching and comparing strings. In an audio database, we would like to match and compare the aural properties as described above. For example, we would like to ask for all the sounds similar to a given sound or that have more or less of a given property. To guarantee that this is possible, sounds which differ in the aural property should map to different regions of the N-space. If this were not satisfied, the database could not distinguish between sounds with different values for this property. Note that this approach is similar to the "feature-vector" approach currently used in content-based retrieval of images, although the actual features used are very different (Zhang et al., this volume).

Since we cannot know the complete list of aural properties that users may wish to specify, it is impossible to guarantee that our choice of acoustic features will meet these constraints. However, we can make sure that we can meet these constraints for many useful aural properties.

3.2 Acoustic Features

The following aspects of sound are currently analyzed:

Loudness is approximated by the signal's RMS level in decibels, which is calculated by taking a series of windowed frames of the sound and computing the square root of the sum of the squares of the windowed sample values. (This method does not account for the frequency response of the human ear; if desired, the necessary equalization can be added by applying the Fletcher-Munson equal-loudness contours.) The human ear can hear over a 120 decibel range. Our software produces estimates over a 100 decibel range given 16-bit audio recordings.

Pitch is estimated by taking a series of short-time Fourier spectra. For each of these frames, the frequencies and amplitudes of the peaks are measured and an approximate greatest common divisor algorithm is used to calculate an estimate of the pitch. We store the pitch as a log frequency. The pitch algorithm also returns a pitch confidence value which can be used to weight the pitch in later calculations. A perfect young human ear can hear frequencies in the 20Hz to 20kHz range. Our software can measure pitches in the range of 50Hz to about 10kHz.

Brightness is computed as the centroid of the short-time Fourier magnitude spectra, again stored as a log frequency. It is a measure of the higher-frequency content of the signal. As an example, putting your hand over your mouth as you speak reduces the brightness of the speech sound as well as the loudness. This feature varies over the same range as the pitch, although it cannot be less than the pitch estimate at any given instant.

Bandwidth is computed as the magnitude-weighted average of the differences between the spectral components and the centroid. As examples, a single sine wave has a bandwidth of 0 and ideal white noise has an infinite bandwidth.

Harmonicity distinguishes between harmonic spectra (e.g., vowels and most musical sounds), inharmonic spectra (e.g., metallic sounds), and noise (spectra that vary randomly in frequency and time). It is computed by measuring the deviation of the sound's line spectrum from a perfectly harmonic spectrum. This is currently an optional feature and is not used in the examples that follow. It is normalized to lie in a range from 0 to 1.

All the above aspects of sound vary over time. The trajectory in time is computed during the analysis but not stored as such in the database. However, for each of these trajectories, several features *are* computed and stored. These include the average value, the variance of the value over the trajectory, and the autocorrelation of the trajectory at a small lag. Autocorrelation is a measure of the smoothness of the trajectory. It can distinguish between a pitch glissando and a wildly varying pitch (for example), which the simple variance measure cannot. The average, variance, and autocorrelation computations are weighted by the amplitude trajectory so that the perceptually important sections of the sound are emphasized. In addition to the above features, the duration of the sound is stored. The feature vector thus consists of the duration plus the parameters just mentioned (average, variance, and autocorrelation) for each of the aspects of sound given above. Figure 1 shows a plot of the raw trajectories of loudness, brightness, bandwidth, and pitch for a recording of male laughter. Figure 2 shows the same for a recording of a single violin pizzicato (plucked) tone.

After the statistical analyses, the resulting analysis records contain the values in table 1.

The sets of numbers in table 1 are the only information used in content-based classification and retrieval of these sounds. The differences between the sets of numbers capture some of the essential differences between the sounds, notably the time-varying nature of the laughter compared to the violin pizzicato.

3.3 Training the System

It is possible to specify a sound directly by submitting constraints on the values of the *N*-vector described above directly to the system. For example, the user can ask for sounds in a certain range of pitch or brightness; however, it is also possible to train the system by example. In this case, the user selects examples of sounds which demonstrate the property the user wishes to train, for example, "scratchiness."

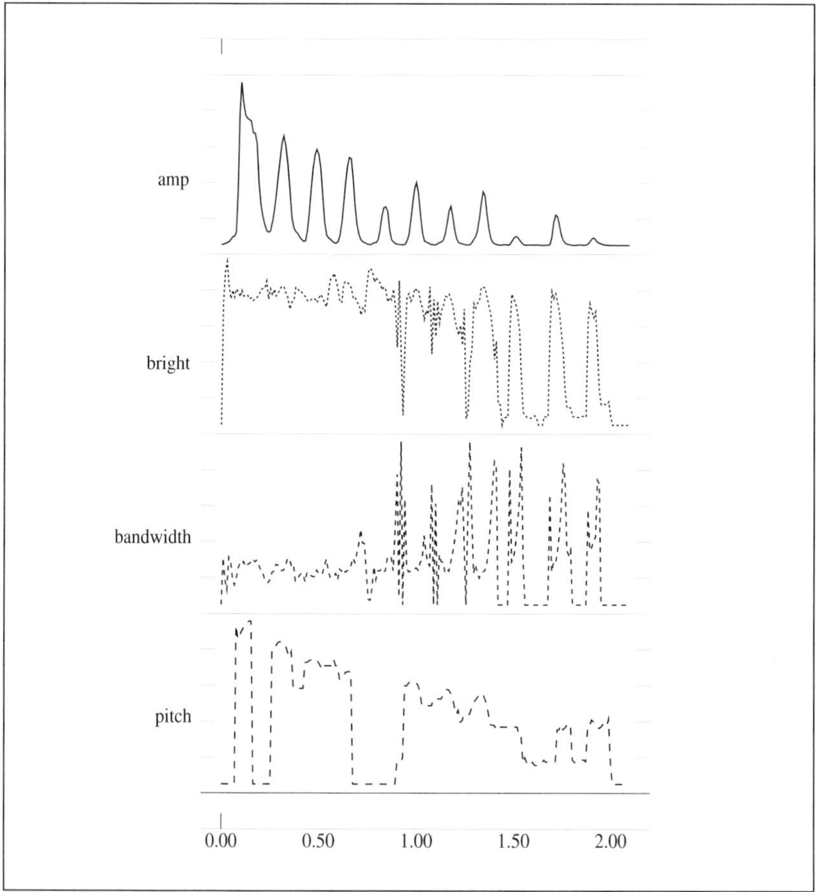

Figure 1. Young male laughter.

For each sound that has been entered into the database, the N-vector, which we represent as a, is computed. When the user supplies a set of example sounds for training, the mean vector μ and the covariance matrix R for the a vectors in each class are calculated. The mean and covariance are given by:

$$\mu = (1/M) \sum_{j} a[j]$$
$$R = (1/M) \sum_{j} (a[j]-\mu)(a[j]-\mu)^T$$

where M is the number of sounds in the summation. In practice, one can ignore the off-diagonal elements of R if the feature vector elements are reasonably independent of each other. This simplification can yield significant sav-

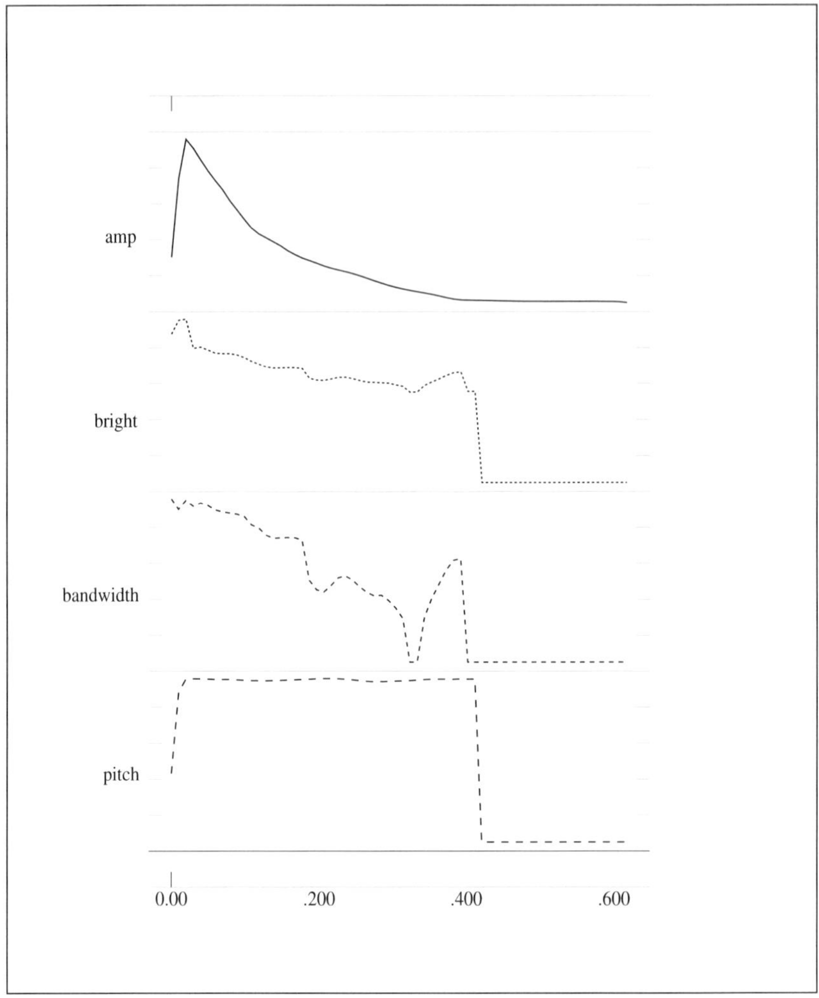

Figure 2. Violin pizzicato.

ings in computation time. The mean and covariance together become the system's model of the perceptual property being trained by the user.

3.4   Classifying Sounds

When a new sound needs to be classified, a distance measure is calculated from the new sound's a vector and the model above. We use a weighted L_2 or Euclidean distance:

$$D = ((a\text{-}\mu)^T R^{-1} (a\text{-}\mu))^{1/2}$$

	Male Laughter	*Violin Pizzicato*
duration	2.12571	0.617143
loudnessMean	-54.4112	-49.9793
loudnessVariance	221.451	171.052
loudnessAutocorrelation	0.938929	0.967417
pitchMean	4.21221	4.30498
pitchVariance	0.151228	0.0170136
pitchAutocorrelation	0.524042	0.0934027
brightnessMean	5.78007	4.639240
brightnessVariance	0.0817046	0.142973
brightnessAutocorrelation	0.690073	0.606832
bandwidthMean	0.272099	0.425949
bandwidthVariance	0.0169697	0.00404443
bandwidthAutocorrelation	0.519198	0.680038

Table 1. Analysis records.

Again, the off-diagonal elements of R can be ignored for faster computation. Also, simpler measures, such as an L_1 or Manhattan distance, could be used if computation time is a problem. The distance is compared to a threshold to determine whether the sound is "in" or "out" of the class. If there are several mutually exclusive classes, the sound is placed in the class to which it is closest, i.e., for which it has the smallest value of D.

If it is known *a priori* that some acoustic features are unimportant for the class, these can be ignored or given a lower weight in the computation of D. For example, if the class models some timbral aspect of the sounds, the duration and average pitch of the sounds can usually be ignored.

We also define a likelihood value L based on the normal distribution and given by

$$L = exp(-D^2/2)$$

This value can be interpreted as "how much" of the defining property for the class the new sound has.

3.5 Retrieving Sounds

It is now possible to select or sort or classify sounds from a database using the distance measure. Some example queries are:

- Retrieve the "scratchy" sounds. That is, retrieve all the sounds which have a high likelihood of being in the "scratchy" class.
- Retrieve the top twenty "scratchy" sounds.
- Retrieve all the sounds which are less "scratchy" than a given sound.
- Sort the given set of sounds by how "scratchy" they are.

- Classify a given set of sounds into the following set of classes.

For small databases, it is easiest to compute the distance measure(s) for all the sounds in the database and then to choose the sounds that match the desired result. For large databases, this can be too expensive. To speed up the search, we index (sort) the sounds in the database by all the acoustic features. This allows us to quickly retrieve any desired hyper-rectangle of sounds in the database by requesting all the sounds whose feature values fall in a set of desired ranges. Requesting such hyper-rectangles allows a much more efficient search. This technique has the advantage that it can be implemented on top the very efficient index-based search algorithms in existing commercial databases.

As an example, consider a query to retrieve the top M sounds in a class. If the database has M_0 sounds total, we first ask for all the sounds in a hyper-rectangle which is centered around the mean μ and has volume V such that

$$V/V_0 = M/M_0$$

where V_0 is the volume of the hyper-rectangle surrounding the entire database. The extent of the hyper-rectangle in each dimension is proportional to the standard deviation of the class in that dimension.

We then compute the distance measure for all the sounds returned and return the closest M sounds. If we did not get enough sounds to match the query from this first attempt, we increase the volume by the ratio of the number requested to the number found and try again.

Note that the above discussion is a simplification of our current algorithm, which asks for bigger volumes to begin with to correct for two factors. First, for our distance measure, we really want a hypersphere of volume V, which means we want the hyper-rectangle which circumscribes this sphere and, secondly, the distribution of sounds in the feature space is not perfectly regular. If we assume some reasonable distribution of the sounds in the database, we can easily compute how much larger V has to be to achieve some desired confidence level that the search will be successful.

3.6 Quality Measures

The magnitude of the covariance matrix R is a measure of the compactness of the class. This can be reported to the user as a quality measure of the classification. For example, if the dimensions of R are similar to the dimensions of the database, this class would not be useful as a discriminator, since all the sounds would fall into it. Similarly, the system can detect other irregularities in the training set, such as outliers or bimodality.

The size of the covariance matrix in each dimension is a measure of the importance of the particular dimension to the class. From this, the user can see if a particular feature is too important or not important enough. For example, if all the sounds in the training set happen to have a very similar duration, the classification process will rank this feature highly, even though it may be irrelevant. If this is the case, the user can tell the system to ignore duration or weight it differently, or the user can try to improve the training set. Similarly, the system can report to the user the components of the computed distance measure. Again, this is a means by which the user can diagnose possible problems in the class description.

Note that all of these measures would be difficult to derive from a non-statistical model such as a neural network.

3.7 Segmentation

The discussion above deals with the case where each sound is a single gestalt. Some examples of this would be single short sounds, such as a door slam, or longer sounds which are of uniform texture, such as a recording of rain on cement. Recordings which contain many different events need to be segmented before using the features above. Segmentation is accomplished by applying the acoustic analyses, described above, to the signal and looking for transitions (sudden changes in the measured attributes). The transitions define segments of the signal, which can then be treated like individual sounds. For example, a recording of a concert could be automatically scanned for applause sounds to determine the boundaries between musical pieces. Similarly, a video-audio recording of a sporting event could be scanned for the loudest crowd cheers to determine when a significant "play" or point had been made. If spatial cues were preserved in the recording, it would be possible to determine, directly from the sound which team had scored the point. Likewise, after training the system to recognize a certain speaker, a recording could be segmented and scanned for all the sections where that speaker was talking. Examples of this kind offer inspiration and justification for continued research in cross-channel analysis and interaction (Mérialdo and Dubois, this volume).

3.8 Extensibility

The architecture of the software for the analysis engine should be extensible, allowing a user to "plug in" new analysis algorithms. The results of these analyses would be added to the database record and used along with the existing attributes. The acoustic attributes we have chosen are intended to be generally useful for a wide range of sounds. They may not be the best for all applications. For example, if the entire universe of sounds consisted of female speech, it would be appropriate to add specific analysis algorithms for speech and speaker recognition.

3.9 Performance

We have used the above algorithms at Muscle Fish on a test sound database that contains about 400 sound files. These sound files were culled from various sound effects and musical instrument sampler libraries. There are a wide variety of sounds represented, including those from animals, machines, musical instruments, speech and nature. The sounds vary in duration from less than a second to about 15 seconds.

A number of classes were made by running the classification algorithm on some reasonably similar sets of sounds. These classes were then used to re-order the sounds in the database by their likelihood of membership in the class (similarity). The following shows the results of this process for several sound sets. These examples show the character of the process and the fuzzy nature of the retrieval.

3.9.1 Example 1: Laughter. For this example, all of the recordings of laughter in the database except two were used in creating the class. Figure 3 shows a plot of the class membership likelihood values (the Y-axis) for all of the sound files in the test database. Each vertical strip along the X-axis is a user-defined category (the directory in which the sound resides). The highest returned likelihoods are for the laughing sounds, including the two that were not placed in the original training set, as well as one of the animal recordings. This animal recording is of a chicken coop and has strong similarities in sound to the laughter recordings, consisting of a number of strong sound bursts.

3.9.2 Example 2: Female Speech. Our test database contains a number of very short recordings of a group of female and male speakers. For this example, the female spoken phrase "tear gas" was used. Figure 4 shows a plot of the similarity (likelihood) of each of the sound files in the test database to this sound using a default value for the covariance matrix R. The highest likelihoods are for the other female speech recordings, with the male speech recordings following close behind.

3.9.3 Example 3: Oboe Tone. Our test database has a large number of musical instrument sounds. In this example, all of the single-tone oboe recordings except for three were used to generate the class. Figure 5 again shows a likelihood plot. The oboe recordings have the highest likelihood overall, including the three left out of the training set. The high likelihood alto trombone sound is, in fact, a very oboe-like alto trombone recording. It is a high-pitched tone on the alto trombone and has a reedy quality.

4. Database Record

Any audio database or, equivalently, a filesystem designed to work with large numbers of audio files, would benefit from content-based capabilities. Both of these require that the audio data be represented or supplemented by a data record or object which points to the sound and adds the necessary analysis

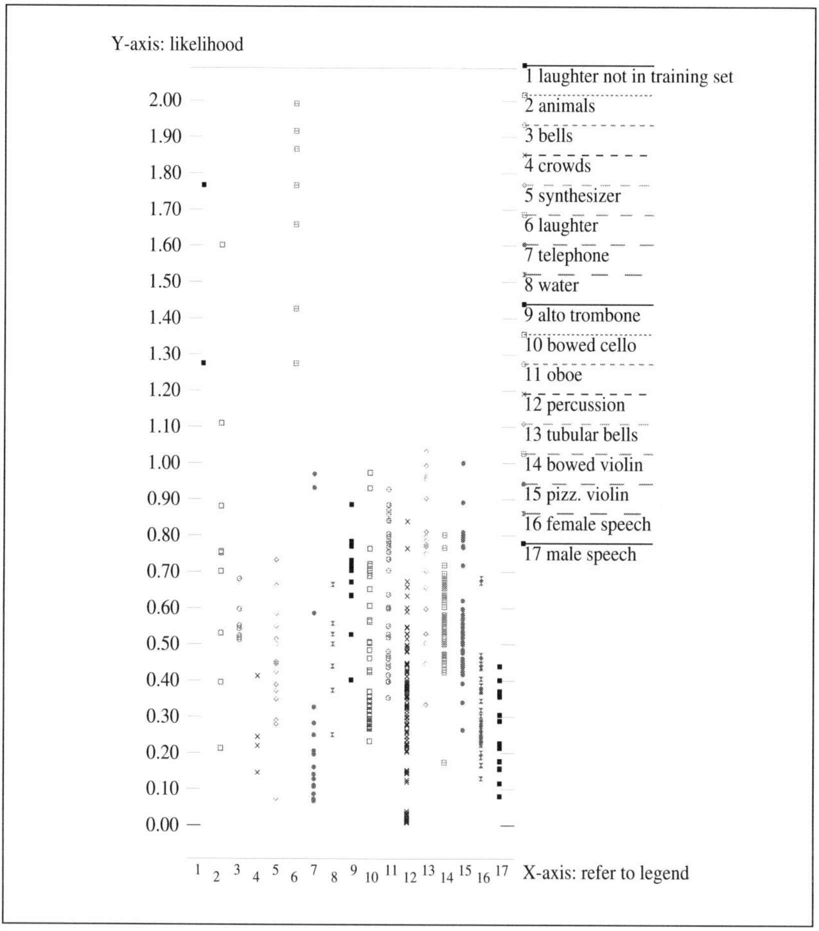

Y-axis: likelihood

Figure 3. Reordering all sounds by similarity to laughter class.

data. When a new sound is added to the database (or filesystem), the analyses presented in the previous section are run on the sound and a new database record or object is formed with this supplemental information.

After the sound is analyzed, the database record is filled with the results. The record contains the following fields, holding the *analyzed feature vector*:

- duration
- loudness (mean, variance, autocorrelation)
- brightness (mean, variance, autocorrelation)
- pitch (mean, variance, autocorrelation)
- bandwidth (mean, variance, autocorrelation)

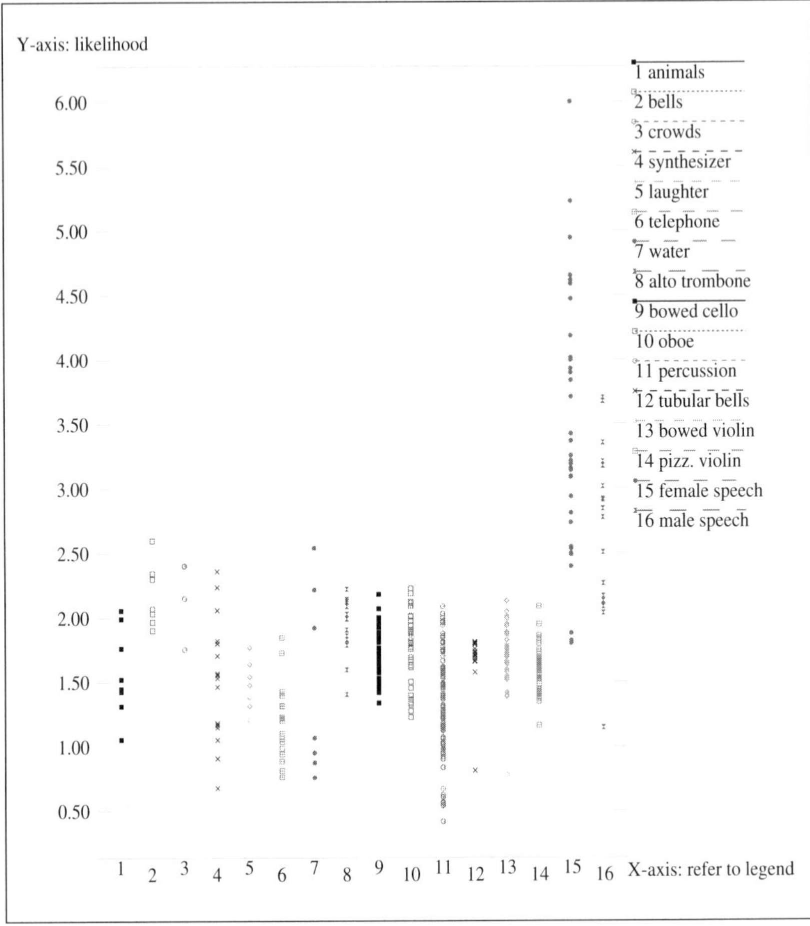

Figure 4. Reordering all sounds by similarity to female "teargas" speech example.

The process of adding a sound to the database also automatically fills in some *sound file attributes*:

- filename
- format (e.g., AIFF, AU, SoundDesigner II, WAV, etc.)
- filesize
- number of channels
- sample rate
- sample size (i.e., bits per sample)
- creation date
- analysis date

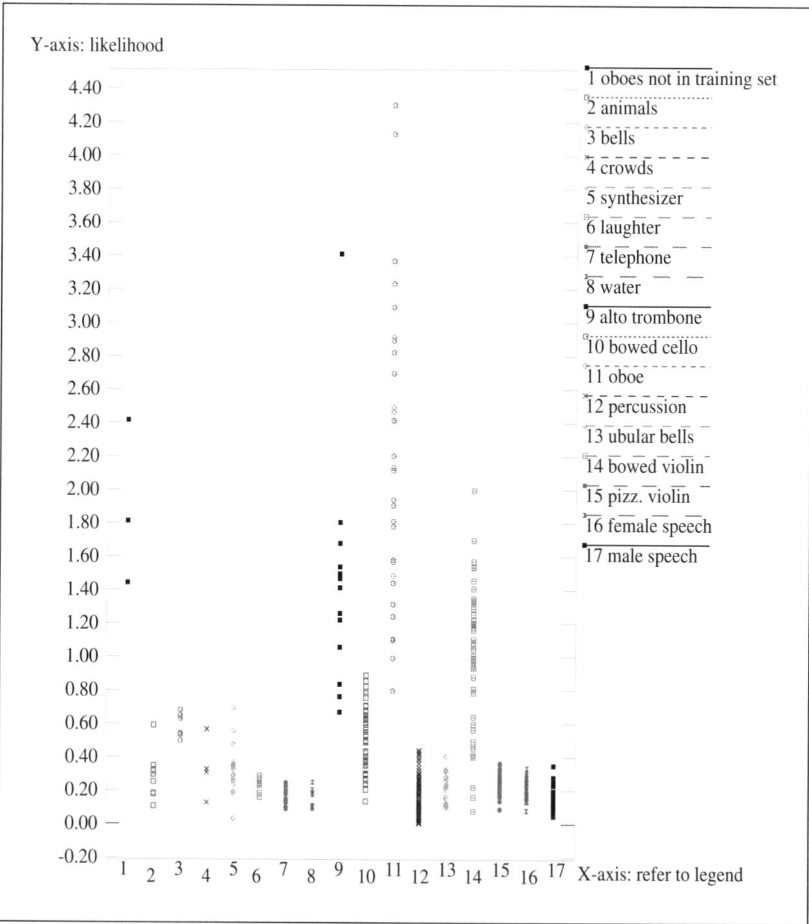

Figure 5. Reordering all sounds by similarity to oboe class.

Despite the advantages offered by content-based retrieval, users of an audio database may also want to store textual descriptions of sounds. Therefore, our database record contains slots for the following *user-defined attributes:*

- *keywords*
- *comments*

Together, this information constitutes a complete record for each sound entered into the database or, alternatively, audio-aware filesystem.

Any user of the database can form an audio class. Audio classes are formed by presenting a set of training sounds to the classification algorithm of the last section. The object returned by the algorithm contains a list of the sounds and the resulting statistical information. This class can be private to the user or could be made available to all users of the database. The kinds of classes which would be useful depend on the application area. For example, a user who was doing automatic segmentation of sports and news footage might develop classes which allow the recognition of various audience sounds (applause, cheering, jeering), referees' whistles, close-miked speech, etc.

The database should support the queries which were described in the last section in combination with more standard queries on the keywords, sampling rate and so on.

5. A Content-based Audio Database Browser

At Muscle Fish, we are currently developing a graphical browser as a front-end to an audio database. We call this application SoundFisher. Space limitations here prevent us from going into a detailed analysis of all of the application's features. This description will focus primarily on using SoundFisher to build and submit various types of queries to the database.

5.1 Overview of the Browser

SoundFisher's user interface contains a typical menu bar permitting the user to access the application's features. Examples of some of these features include opening an existing database, creating a new database, navigating to and from previous queries of the current session, viewing or modifying the sounds' database records, playing selected sounds and launching an external waveform editor.

There are two panels within the main SoundFisher window. The top panel contains elements enabling a user to build and submit a query, and the bottom panel initially contains a list-view of all the sounds in the currently opened database. The bottom panel is relatively passive and is used for two purposes: (1) to display all or some of the current database, ordered according to the search results of a query; (2) optionally, to select training sounds to be used in a query. The user can also reorder, or "filter," the fields (i.e., columns) of this panel.

5.2 Constructing Queries

The top panel in SoundFisher permits the user to build various types of queries, including query-by-example, field-value queries, weighted queries, and combined queries (mixtures of the preceding types). A query, once constructed, can be named, saved, and reused as an element of a subsequent query, which in turn can be named, saved, and reused and so on; this is one method in SoundFisher of refining a search.

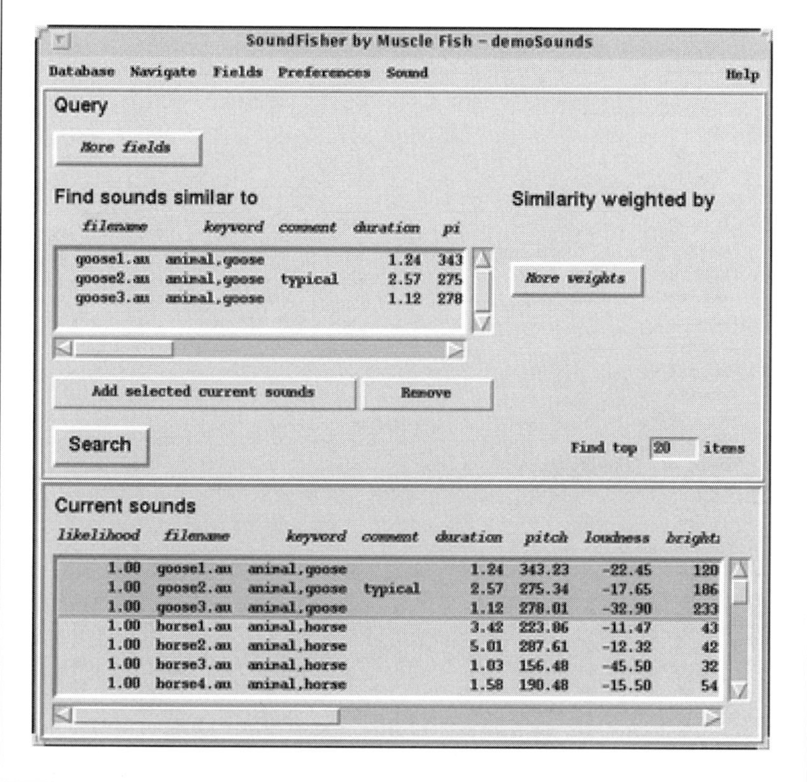

Figure 6. Query-by-example in SoundFisher.

5.2.1 Query-by-example. Figure 6 presents the construction of a simple query-by-example. The goal of this query is to train the browser on a particular class of sounds. The user has selected three sounds of geese from the open database, "demoSounds," and added them to the training set which is displayed in the query panel's list-view labeled *Find sounds similar to*. This comprises a complete query. If the user were to press the *Search* button at this point, SoundFisher, using the training, classification, and retrieval algorithms described in the previous sections, would compute a perceptual model, μ and R, of the training sounds and display in the bottom panel the 20 sounds with the smallest distance measure, D, from that model. If the user desired, this query could be saved and given a name (for example "goose-like"). It could then be reused as an element in more complex queries within either the current or subsequent browsing sessions.

5.2.2 Field-value and Weighted Queries. Pressing the button labeled *More fields* in the query panel (refer to figure 6) allows a user to add new con-

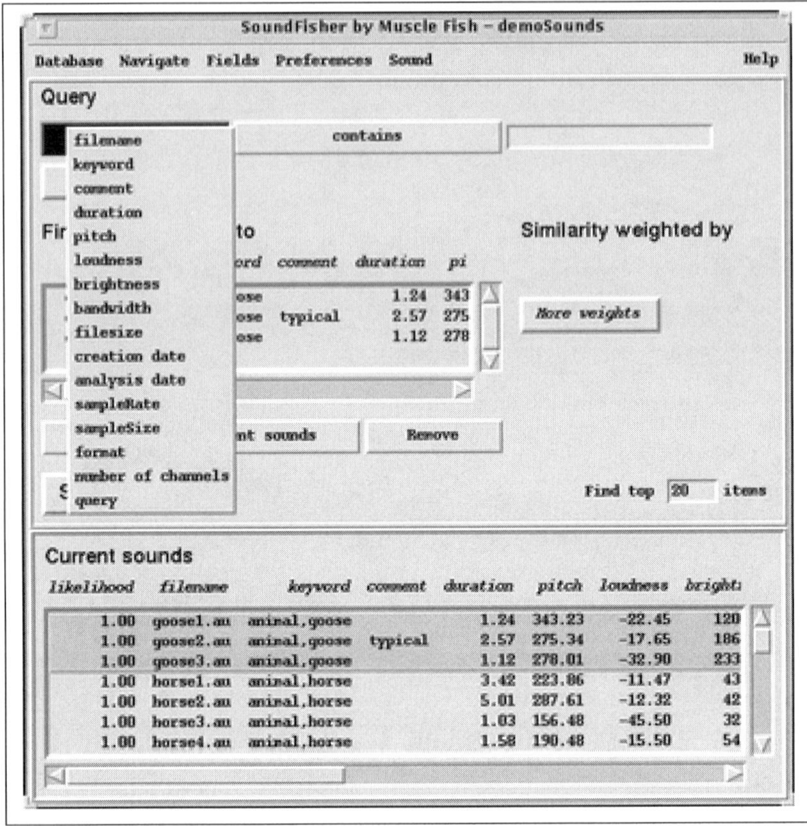

Figure 7. Adding a new constraint-row in SoundFisher.

straints, or terms, to the query being constructed. *More fields* creates a new "constraint row," containing three graphical components. The components, from left to right, include: a field menu-button, for selecting a field or attribute; an operator menu-button, with a constraint operator appropriate to the selected field; and either a text-entry field, a menu-button, or a slider, to set the value of the selected field.

Figure 7 presents the query panel with a newly added constraint row. The field's menu is displayed. Notice that this menu allows the user to select any item from the database record, which is described in the previous section. In addition, the last item in this menu permits the reuse of a previously saved query.

Figure 8 presents a fairly complicated query combining all three types mentioned above—query-by-example, field-value and weighted queries.

This query attempts to find human vocal or animal sounds that might

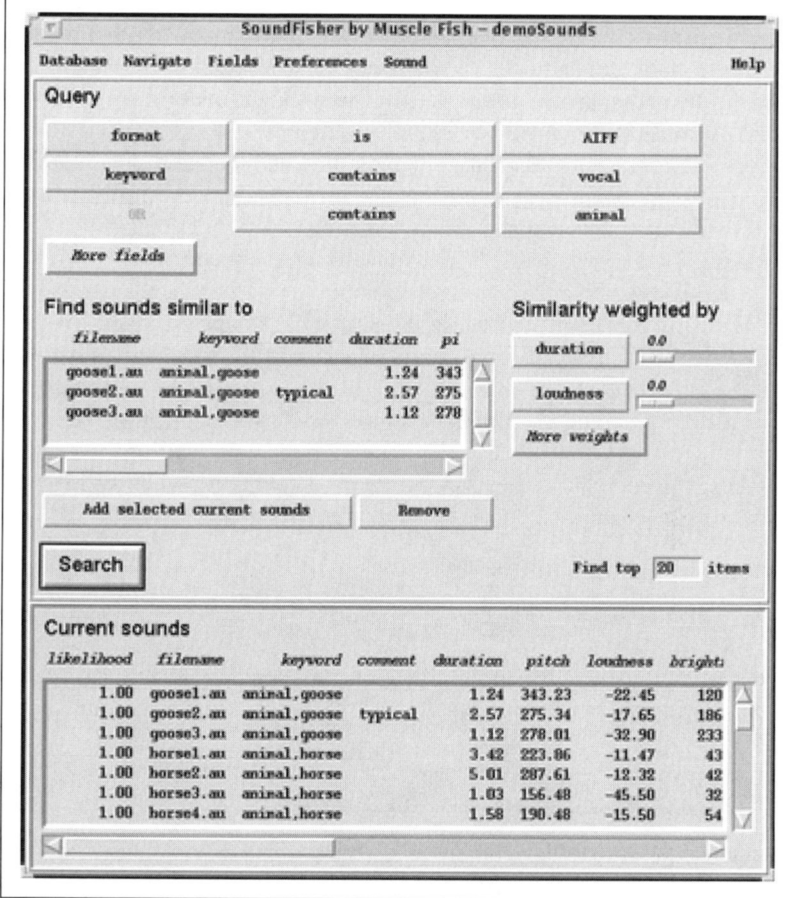

Figure 8. A mixed query in SoundFisher.

blend well with the goose-like sounds of the previous example; the user is, perhaps, trying to design a new composite sound effect. Constraint rows, as described above, have been added to form this query. It will search the open database for AIFF-format sounds containing the keyword of "animal" or "vocal" and that are similar to the goose sounds. The query will disregard duration and amplitude. Although it not shown here, the *Navigate* menu allows the user to choose whether a search runs over the entire open database or is limited to the list of *Current Sounds*. The latter choice is another way for the user to iteratively refine searches.

Successive constraint rows are *and*'ed together. The or operator in the above query is accessible from the application's *Fields* menu and can be applied to values within a given field. Although this query language has limits, it is sufficient for a majority of sound-browsing tasks, and it does not require the user to learn (or hand-enter) a complicated query syntax.

Using the button labeled *More weights*, shown in the query panel in Figure 8, the user is able to adjust the similarity weightings of any attribute in the analyzed feature vector. By setting the duration and loudness sliders in this example to zero, the user is telling the browser to ignore those attributes during the similarity calculation (see section 3.4 on Classifying sounds).

Although not shown in this figure, some of the query component operators are fuzzy. For example, the user can constrain the pitch to be approximately 100 Hz. This constraint will cause the system to compute a likelihood (or similarity) for each sound equal to the inverse of the distance between that sound's pitch feature and 100 Hz. This likelihood is used as a multiplier against the likelihood computed from the similarity calculation, or other parts of the query that yield fuzzy results. Note that *and*'ing two fuzzy searches is accomplished by multiplying the likelihoods, while *or*'ing two fuzzy searches requires adding the likelihoods.

6. Future Directions

In this section we explore future directions in alternative sound and search displays, general phrase-level content-based retrieval, source separation, and sound synthesis.

6.1 Alternative Sound and Search Displays

It would be useful to develop some alternative methods of displaying the sounds or the search results. Perhaps in the case of an audio browser, displaying text strings in list-views is not the most elucidating means of depiction. Although our browser permits the user to audition sounds, this can be a very time-consuming process, especially when a search results in many sounds. A sonic analog to a key-frame or thumbnail image would be helpful, particularly one which offers comparable space-time reductions while preserving the perceptual gestalt. Waveform and spectral displays are sometimes useful, but only to the highly trained eye (and ear). Visual displays of the n-dimensional search space, similar to those discussed by David Wessel (Wessel 1979), would be appropriate for browsers of large sound databases.

6.2 General Phrase-level Content-based Retrieval

Our current set of acoustic features is targeted toward short or single-gestalt sounds. Matching sets of our features as trajectories in time or matching segmented sequences of single-gestalt sounds would allow phrase-level content of audio to be stored and retrieved. As with all media search, a fuzzy match is what is desired.

6.3 Source Separation

In our current system, simultaneously sounding sources are treated as a single ensemble. We make no attempt to separate them. Source separation is a difficult task. Approaches to separating simultaneous sounds typically involve either Gestalt psychology (McAdams 1993) or non-perceptual signal-processing techniques (Moorer 1977, Wold 1987). For musical applications, polyphonic pitch-tracking has been studied for many years, but might well be an intractable problem in the general case.

6.4 Sound Synthesis

Sound synthesis could assist a user in making content-based queries to an audio database. When the user was unsure what values to use, the synthesis feature would create sound prototypes that matched the current set of values as they were manipulated by the user. The user could refine the synthesized example until it bore enough similarity to the desired sort of sound.

It would also be very helpful, in some cases, if the user could prototype desired sounds using their voice, and then conduct searches on the database for the sounds that closely match the prototype.

7. Conclusion

This chapter has outlined some of the main features of our audio analysis, classification, and search engines. The technique is based on analyzing the acoustic features of the audio and reducing these to a few statistical values. The analyzed features are relatively straightforward but suffice to describe a relatively large universe of sounds. More analyses could be added to handle specific problem domains.

We have described our GUI-based sound browser, emphasizing its various kinds of queries. And, we have presented examples that show the efficacy of fuzzy searches on audio databases. The results of these searches are sometimes surprising in that they cross semantic boundaries, but aurally the results are reasonable.

This is work in progress. Further implementation and testing of the system will reveal whether the chosen acoustic features are sufficient or excessive for usefully analyzing and classifying most sounds. We believe, however, that the basic approach presented here works well for a wide variety of audio database applications.

We invite readers with Internet access to visit our web site at www.musclefish.com for an interactive demonstration of our audio content-based retrieval system.

Acknowledgments

We would like to thank Mark T. Maybury (The MITRE Corporation) and the anonymous referees of this chapter for their helpful comments and suggestions. We would also like to acknowledge Stephen Smoliar and Hong Zhang (Institute of Systems Science, Singapore) and Michael Olson and Chuck O'Neill (Informix Software, Inc.) for encouraging our efforts, offering insightful feedbacks, and helping us to embed our technologies into an Informix Data Blade® module.

References

Blum, T.; Keislar, D.; Wheaton, J.; and Wold, E. 1995. Audio Databases with Content-Based Retrieval. In Notes from International Joint Conference on Artificial Intelligence Workshop on Intelligent Multimedia Information Retrieval, 71-92, ed. M. T. Maybury, Montreal, Quebec, Canada.

Buxton, W.; Patel, S.; Reeves, W.; and Baecker, R. 1981. Scope in Interactive Score Editors. In *Computer Music Journal* 5(3): 50-56.

Feiten, B. and Günzel, S. 1994. Automatic Indexing of a Sound Database Using Self-Organizing Neural Nets. *Computer Music Journal* 18(3): 53-65.

Flickner, M.; Sawhney, H.; Niblack, W.; Ashley, J.; Huang, Q.; Dom, B.; Gorkani, M.; Hafner, J.; Lee, D.; Petkovic, D.; Steele, D.; and Yanker, P. 1997. Query by Image and Video Content: The QBIC System. In this volume.

Foster, S.; Schloss W.; and Rockmore, A. J. 1982. Towards an Intelligent Editor of Digital Audio: Signal Processing Methods. *Computer Music Journal* 6(1): 42-51.

Grey, J. M. 1977. Multidimensional Perceptual Scaling of Musical Timbres. *Journal of the Acoustical Society of America* 61:1270-1277.

Gordon., J .W., and Grey, J. M. 1978. Perception of Spectral Modifications on Orchestral Instrument Tones. *Computer Music Journal* 2(1): 24-31.

Hauptmann, A. G. and Witbrock, M. 1997. Informedia: News-on-Demand Multimedia Information Acquisition and Retrieval. In this volume.

Keislar, D.; Blum, T.; Wheaton, J.; and Wold, E. 1995. Audio Analysis for Content-Based Retrieval. In Proceedings of the International Computer Music Conference, 199-202, San Francisco: International Computer Music Association.

McAdams, S. 1993. Recognition of Sound Sources and Events. In *Thinking in Sound: The Cognitive Psychology of Human Audition*, eds. S. McAdams and E. Bigand, 146-198, Oxford: Clarendon Press.

Mérialdo, B. and Dubois, F. 1997. An Agent-based Architecture for Content-Based Multimedia Browsing. In this volume.

Moorer, J. A. 1977. On the Transcription of Musical Sound by Computer. *Computer Music Journal* 1(4): 32-38.

Schaeffer, P. 1966. solfge des objets. In *Trait des objets musicaux*, 584-587. 2nd ed. Paris: Seuil.

Schafer, R. M. 1980. Classification. In *The Tuning of the World: Toward a Theory of Soundscape Design*, 133-150. Philadelphia, Pennsylvania: University of Pennsylvania Press.

Schäble, P. and M. Wechsler. 1995. First Experiences with a System for Content Based Retrieval of Information from Speech Recordings. In Notes from International Joint Conference on Artificial Intelligence Workshop on Intelligent Multimedia Information Retrieval, 59-70, ed. M. T. Maybury, Montreal, Quebec, Canada

Vertegaal, R. and E. Bonis. 1994. ISEE: An Intuitive Sound Editing Environment. *Computer Music Journal* 18(2): 21-29.

Wessel, D. L. 1979. Timbre Space as a Musical Control Structure. *Computer Music Journal* 3(2): 45-52.

Wold, E. 1987. Nonlinear Parameter Estimation of Acoustic Models. Ph.D. diss., University of California at Berkeley, California.

Zhang, H.J.; Low, C.Y.; Smoliar, S. and Wu, J.H., 1997. Video Parsing, Retrieval and Browsing: An Integrated and Content-based Solution. In this volume.

Content-based Retrieval of Video

Increasing amounts of video from a broad range of sources (e.g., broadcast networks, video archives, surveillance cameras) has given rise to a requirement for more effective and efficient video browsing, search, and retrieval that goes beyond the program level, sequential access provided by analog video cassette recorders. Initial algorithm development has focused on the automatic indexing of visual features of fixed and moving imagery which can be used as a means for retrieving similar images without the burden of manual indexing. More recently, researchers have attempted to extract higher level semantic meaning from underlying video images. Chapters in this third section of this book report advances in a range of content-based indexing techniques that enable new forms of interaction with video. The fourth section complements this by focusing on processing of the audio and closed caption channels of video to enable similar functionality.

In the first chapter, HongJiang Zhang, Chien Yong Low, Stephen W. Smoliar and JianHua Wu (Institute of Systems Science, National University of Singapore) describe their video parsing algorithms which, like QBIC (described in the first chapter of this collection), are founded on visual feature processing, but also take advantage of content-dependent processing, such as the classification of news images into anchor or reporter shots. They include the ability to detect both rapid and gradual shot transitions (e.g., fades, wipes, dissolves), camera motion (e.g., pan, tilt, zoom) using motion vectors, and extraction of keyframes from camera shots using color and motion information. The latter enables heuristics, such as abstracting a zoom shot using the first, last, and middle frames. They report shot segmentation accuracy of over 95% on widely varying video sources, and report key frame performance that rivals human extraction. They demonstrate the use of visual features and shot-level semantics derived from camera operation and motion analysis to support content based browsing and retrieval of video, including partially specified queries and hierarchical shot browsing.

Just as Zhang et al. aim to provide more sophisticated video search and browsing tools by getting at the (e.g., anchor/reporter) structure of video, in the second chapter Phillipe Aigrain, Philippe Joly, and Véronique Longueville (Institut de Recherche en Informatique de Toulouse) describe a rule-based method for automatically obtaining video macrostructure. In contrast to Zhang et al.'s approach, however, Aigraine et al. aim to avoid content-specific models (e.g., of anchor or reporter scenes) to provide genre independent indexing. Even given effective techniques for shot transition detection and classification, Aigraine et al. argue that a higher level structure of video is required to deal with the resultant hundreds of shot sequences per hour of video. Examples of this video macrostructure include shot sequences constituting a narrative unit or shot sequences sharing the same setting. In Aigraine et al.'s approach these are identified using local (in time) clues, such as transition effects (e.g., a fade out or fade to black is a shot boundary, shots surrounded by gradual transitions are likely important), shot repetition (e.g., color distribution discontinuity indicates a possible break), music onset, and editing rhythm. Macrostructure not only supports segmentation, but also guides keyframe selection (e.g., an effective summary of a zoom includes the first, last, and middle shots, as in Zhang et al.). In an empirical test on a limited set of documents, the authors demonstrate the independence of their rule set from video genre (e.g., broadcast news, documentary).

In the third and final chapter of the section, Alex Pentland (MIT Media Lab) builds on research in feature based image processing to create more semantic object recognizers, such as processes that recognize body parts in video and that track heads, hands and feet. Alex further builds on these to recognize more complex behaviors (e.g., body gestures, facial expressions). Using the output of his face finder, preliminary experiments on facial expression classification (e.g., anger, surprise, smile) result in high accuracy on small databases. Descriptions of application to sign language and driver intention prediction are also presented.

These three chapters contribute important approaches and solutions to the challenges of representing, processing, and retrieving video data. Moreover, collectively, these early systems point to future applications which will include content based video browsing, retrieval, and automated presentation design.

Chapter 7

Video Parsing, Retrieval and Browsing: An Integrated and Content-Based Solution

HongJiang Zhang, Chien Yong Low, Stephen W. Smoliar and JianHua Wu, Institute of Systems Science, National University of Singapore

Abstract

This chapter presents an integrated solution for computer assisted video parsing and content-based video retrieval and browsing. The uniqueness and effectiveness of this solution lies in its use of video content information provided by a parsing process driven by visual feature analysis. More specifically, parsing will temporally segment and abstract a video source, based on low-level image analyses; then retrieval and browsing of video will be based on key-frames selected during abstraction and spatial-temporal variations of visual features, as well as some shot-level semantics derived from camera operation and motion analysis. These processes, as well as video retrieval and browsing tools, are presented in detail as functions of an integrated system. Also, experimental results on automatic key-frame detection are given.

1. Introduction

Interfaces to multimedia information systems, such as video on demand (VOD), are in general very weak in interactive functionality (even if some are very visually appealing). Selection rarely involves anything better than keywords; and any manipulation of the video itself is limited to the lowest level of VCR control. The problem is that, from the point of view of content, the resources managed by such systems are *unstructured*. The source material is not subject to any structural analysis (parsing) and therefore can be neither indexed nor accessed on the basis of structural properties. Fundamentally, such a system is a database which must support extended capabilities for retrieval (for the user) and insertion (for the system manager). Parsing is the primary extension which serves insertion, while retrieval must exploit parsing results. In addition, because of the subjective nature of the source material, retrieval must be supplemented by capabilities for browsing.

Our use of the term "parsing" differs slightly from linguistic conventions. We see it as encompassing two tasks: *temporal segmentation* of a video program into elemental units, and *content extraction* from those units, based on both video and audio semantic primitives (Zhang and Smoliar 1994). Many effective algorithms are now available for temporal segmentation (Nagasaka and Tanaka 1991, Zhang et al. 1993). However, fully automated content extraction is a much more difficult task, requiring both signal analysis and knowledge representation techniques; so human assistance is still needed. We thus feel the most fruitful research approach is to concentrate on *facilitating tools,* using low-level visual features. Such tools are clearly feasible and research in this direction should ultimately lead to an intelligent video parsing system (Swanberg et al. 1993, Zhang et al. 1994, Zhang et al. 1995a).

Retrieval and browsing require that the source material first be effectively *indexed*. While most previous research in indexing has been text-based (Davis 1993, Rowe et al. 1994), content based indexing of video with visual features is still a research problem. Visual features can be divided into two levels: low-level image features, and semantic features based on objects and events. To date automation of low-level feature indexing (Faloutsos et al. 1994; Pentland et al. 1994; Gong et al., 1994; Flickner et al., this volume) has been far more successful than that of semantic indexing (Davis 1993). Perhaps the biggest problem with indexing video using the low-level image features of every frame is its enormous volume, but a viable solution seems to be to index representative key-frames (O'Connor 1991) extracted from the video sources.

While we tend to think of indexing supporting retrieval, *browsing* is equally significant for video source material. By "browsing" we mean an informal perusal of content which may lack any specific goal or focus. The task of browsing is actually very intimately related to retrieval. On the one hand, if a query is too general, browsing is the best way to *examine the results*. This should provide some indication of *why* the query was poorly expressed; so browsing also serves as an aid to *formulating queries*, making it easier for the user to "just ask around" in the process of figuring out the most appropriate query to pose (Zhang et al. 1995b).

Unfortunately, the only major technological precedent for video browsing is the VCR (even available in "soft" form for computer viewing), with its support for sequential fast forward and reverse play. Browsing a video this way is a matter of skipping frames: the faster the play speed, the larger the skip factor. The "content-based" browser of Arman et al. (1994) takes this approach, but a uniform skip factor really does not account for video content. Furthermore, there is always the danger that some skipped frames may contain the content of greatest interest. A *truly* content-based approach to video browsing should be based on some level of analysis of the actual image content, rather than simply providing a more sophisticated view of temporal context. However, few published research efforts (Zhang et al. 1995a; Flickner et al., this volume; Aigraine et al., this volume; Pentland, this volume) have discussed how parsing results may be applied to support more powerful browsing tools.

This chapter presents our work on developing an integrated system for parsing, retrieval, and browsing based on three levels of automated content analysis. What makes our solution effective is its use of the content information represented by the visual feature extracted video parsing processes. There are three processes in our solution which capture different levels of content information. The first is temporal segmentation. At the second level each segment is abstracted into key-frames, based on a simple analysis of content variation which yields results far more useful than sub-sampling at a fixed rate. Finally, visual features, such as color and texture, are used to represent the content of key-frames. In addition, variations among key-frames from the same shot are calculated and integrated with information about camera operation and object motion to provide event-based cues. Indexing is then supported by a clustering process which classifies key-frames into different visual categories; this categorization may also support manual user annotation. These results facilitate retrieval and browsing in a variety of ways. Retrieval may be based on not only the annotated index but also low-level image features of key-frames and temporal variation, object motion and camera operation features of segments. The key-frames enable browsing with a fast forward/backward player, a hierarchical time-space viewer, and cluster-based clip windows.

This chapter is organized as follows: section 2 presents our approaches to video parsing, including a brief summary of temporal segmentation and a detailed discussion of key-frame extraction. Section 3 reviews the visual features of key-frames used in content representation. The resulting approach to retrieval and browsing is then presented in detail in section 4. Finally, section 5 offers concluding remarks and a brief view of our current and future work.

2. Video Parsing: Segmentation and Abstraction

In this section we present our approaches to video parsing, including a brief summary of temporal segmentation and a detailed discussion of key-frame extraction.

2.1 Temporal Segmentation and Camera Operation Detection

The basic unit of video to be represented or indexed is usually assumed to be a single camera shot, consisting of one or more frames generated and recorded contiguously and representing a continuous action in time and space. Thus, temporal segmentation is the problem of detecting boundaries between consecutive camera shots. The general approach to the solution has been the definition of a suitable *quantitative* difference metric which represents significant *qualitative* differences between frames. Our own system detects not only simple camera breaks but also gradual transitions implemented by special effects such as fades, wipes, and dissolves (Zhang et al. 1993).

For compressed video data, it would be advantageous to segment it directly, saving on the computational cost of decompression and lowering the overall magnitude of the data to be processed. Also, elements of a compressed representation, such as DCT coefficients and motion vectors in JPEG and MPEG data streams, are useful features for effective content comparison (Zhang et al. 1994, Yeo and Liu 1995). Our experiments have shown that proper use of both DCT coefficients and motion vectors can achieve both fast processing speed and very high segmentation accuracy (Zhang et al. 1994).

To obtain motion features of video, our system also identifies frames involving camera operations, such as panning, tilting, and zooming, as false positives, and dominant object motions. The simple and effective approach in our system analyzes the characteristic patterns of motion vectors (Zhang et al. 1993). An alternative approach, implemented in our system, is to examine spatio-temporal slices of video sequences (Adelson and Bergen 1985). These images also provide characteristic patterns for camera operation, and they may be used for abstraction and representation of shot content (Zhang et al. 1995b).

2.2 Automated Video Abstraction: Key-Frame Extraction

Even when videos are compressed, it is rarely feasible or desirable to index and/or store all frames for retrieval purposes. Instead, an abstraction process is necessary, which may be effectively applied at the individual segment level. We view abstraction as a problem of mapping an entire segment to some small number of representative images, usually called *key-frames*. An index may be constructed from key-frames, and retrieval queries may be directed at key-frames, which can subsequently be displayed for browsing purposes. Also, if storage space is limited, only these key-frames need to be maintained on-line. These techniques will be discussed at greater length in the sequel.

Key-frames are still images which best represent the content of the video sequence in an abstracted manner, and may be either extracted or reconstructed from original video data. Key-frames are frequently used to supplement the text of a video log (O'Connor 1991), but there has been little progress in identifying them automatically. The challenge is that the extraction of key-frames needs to be automatic and content based so that they maintain the important content of the video while removing all redundancy. In theory semantic primitives of video, such as interesting objects, actions and events should be used. However, because such general semantic analysis is not currently feasible, we have to rely on low-level image features and other readily available information instead. Based on these constraints, we have developed a US Patented, robust key-frame extraction technique which utilizes information computed by the parsing processes:

- *Color features:* The basic representation of the color of a video frame is a histogram of the distribution of color components. Also, average brightness, color moments (including mean), and dominant color are used. Our specific mathematical definitions will be presented in section 3. If compressed data are used, these features may be calculated from DCT coefficients of video frames (Yeo and Liu 1995).

- *Motion:* Dominant motion components resulting from camera operations and large moving objects are the most important source of information, since motion is the major indicator of content change. For instance, a zoom shot is usually best abstracted by three frames—the first, the last, and one in the middle. When MPEG video is used, motion vectors from B and P frames can be directly extracted for motion analysis.

In our implementation, the key-frame extraction process is integrated with the processes of segmentation. Each time a new shot is identified, the key-frame extraction process is invoked, using parameters already computed during segmentation. Certain heuristics are also applied, such as the decision to use the first frame of every shot as a key-frame. In addition users can adjust several parameters to control the density of key-frames in each shot. The default is that at least two key-frames will be selected for each shot; and, in the simplest case, they could be the first and last frames of the shot. The process is faster with compressed video data, and real time extraction can be achieved.

2.3 Experimental Results

The performance of various temporal segmentation systems has been discussed elsewhere (Nagasaka and Tanaka 1991, Zhang et al. 1993, Zhang and Smoliar 1994, Yeo and Liu 1995) and will not be repeated here. Table 1 summarizes key-frame extraction results obtained from four test sets, which represent the effectiveness of the techniques described in section 2.2 in abstracting different types of video material. The first test was based on two "stock footage" videos consisting of unedited raw shots of various lengths, covering a wide range of scenes and objects. "Singapore," the second test set, is trav-

Video	Length (sec.)	N_d	N_m	N_f	N_k
Stock footage 1	451.8	35	1	1	116
Stock footage 2	1210.7	78	1	5	271
Singapore	173.8	31	1	0	71
Dance	2109.1	90	17	4	205

Table 1. Video segmentation and key-frame extraction results.
N_d: number of shots correctly detected; N_m: number of shots missed by the detection algorithm; N_f: false detection of shot boundaries; N_k: number of key-frames extracted.

elogue material from an elaborately produced documentary which draws upon a variety of sophisticated editing effects. Finally, the "Dance" video is the entirety of *Changing Steps*, a "dance for television" containing shots with fast moving objects (dancers), complex and fast changing lighting and camera operations, and highly imaginative editing effects, many of which are far less conventional than those in "Singapore." We feel that these four source videos are representative of both the content material and style of presentation that one will generally find in professionally produced television and film.

Because key-frame extraction takes place at the segment level, segmentation results are also listed in table 1. Furthermore, because it is hard to quantitatively measure the accuracy of key-frame extraction (even human selection can be subjective), only the number of key-frames extracted for each test is given. Table 1 shows that segmentation performs with an accuracy of over 95% (counting both missing and false detection as errors) in the first three tests. The dance video yields the lowest accuracy, due to the elaborate production technique, and can be considered the lowest achievable accuracy of the segmentation techniques. For all segments which were correctly detected, key-frames were correctly extracted, yielding an average of between two and three key-frames per shot, which tends to be a suitable abstraction ratio. In addition the test results demonstrate that camera operations (both panning and zooming) have been properly abstracted by the key-frames detected.

It is also worth observing that, particularly in the "Dance" example, key-frame extraction actually compensated for segmentation errors. That is, in many of the cases where a shot boundary was missed, one or more additional key-frames were detected to represent the material in the missed shot. In other words, key-frame detection is more robust than shot boundary detection.

To systematically evaluate the effectiveness and accuracy of our key-frame extraction system, we conducted a user trial comparing automatic extraction with human identification of key-frames from the two stock footage videos listed in table 1, which were provided by the Singapore Broadcasting Corporation (Now the Television Corporation of Singapore). Members of the Singapore Broadcasting Corporation Film/Videotape Library staff were instructed to identify key-frames from these source tapes, on the basis of which they then evaluated the results of our system. Our system did not miss any of the key-frames selected by the librarians. The only difficulty was that our results were more "generous," extracting more key-frames than were selected manually; but this discrepancy has been remedied by providing user control of the density of frames selected. On the other hand the librarians agreed that our automatic extraction was more objective (our system always tried to identify at least one key-frame per shot), while they sometimes tended to ignore certain shots which they felt were not important.

3. Shot Content Representation and Similarity Measures

After partitioning and abstraction, the next step is to identify and compute *representation primitives*, based on which the content shot can be indexed, compared, and classified. Ideally these should be semantic primitives that a user can employ to define "interesting" or "significant" events. However, such an ideal solution is not feasible; therefore our representation primitives are based on information accessible through the techniques described in section 2. The resulting representation is divided into two parts: primitives based on key-frames and those based on temporal variation and motion information. These parts complement each other and can be used either separately or together.

3.1 Representation of Shot Content Based on Key-frame Features

Following the techniques used in image database systems (Faloutsos et al. 1994, Pentland et al. 1994, Gong et al. 1994), key-frames are represented by properties of color, texture, shape, and edge features, each of which will now be reviewed.

3.1.1 Color Features. Color has excellent discrimination power in image retrieval systems. It is very rare that two images of totally different objects will have similar colors (Swain and Balllard 1991). Our representation primitives for color features include mean brightness, color histogram, dominant colors, and statistical moments.

Color Histogram: A histogram of the distribution of color intensities is a quantitative representation which is especially useful for textured images which are not well served by segmentation techniques. Also, color histograms are invariant under translation and rotation about the view axis and change only slowly under change of angle of view, change in scale, and occlusion (Swain and Balllard 1991). We have chosen the Munsell space to define color histograms because it is close to human perception of colors (Ioka 1989). As in QBIC (Flickner et al., this volume), we have quantized the color space into 64 "super-cells" using a standard minimum sum of squares clustering algorithm (Faloutsos et al. 1994). A 64-bin color histogram is then calculated for each key-frame where each bin is assigned the normalized count of the number of pixels that fall in its corresponding supercell.

The distance between two color histograms, I and Q, each consisting of N bins, is quantified by the following metric:

$$D_{his}^2(I, Q) = \sum_i^N \sum_j^N a_{ij} (I_i - Q_i)(I_j - Q_j) \tag{1}$$

where the matrix a_{ij} represents the similarity between the colors corresponding to bins i and j, respectively. This matrix needs to be determined from human visual perception studies, and we have derived it using the method of Gorkani and Picard (1994). Notice that if a_{ij} is the identity matrix, then this measure becomes Euclidean distance.

Dominant Colors: Because, in most images, a small number of color ranges capture the majority of pixels, these dominant colors can be used to construct an approximate representation of color distribution. These dominant colors can be easily identified from color histograms of key-frames. Experiments have shown that using only a few dominant colors will not degrade the performance of color image matching (Swain and Balllard 1991, Gong et al. 1994). In fact, performance may even be enhanced, since histogram bins which are too small are likely to be noise, thus distorting similarity computations. Our current implementation is based on twenty dominant colors, corresponding to the histogram bins that contain the maximum numbers of pixels.

Color Moments: Because a probability distribution is uniquely characterized by its moments, following (Stricker and Orengo 1995) we also represent a color distribution by its first three moments:

$$\mu_i = \frac{1}{N} \sum_{j=1}^N p_{ij} \tag{2}$$

$$\sigma_i = \left(\frac{1}{N} \sum_{j=1}^N (p_{ij} - \mu_i)^2 \right)^{\frac{1}{2}} \tag{3}$$

$$s_i = \left(\frac{1}{N} \sum_{j=1}^N (p_{ij} - \mu_i)^3 \right)^{\frac{1}{3}} \tag{4}$$

where p_{ij} is the value of the i-th color component of the j-th image pixel. The first order moment, m_i, defines the average intensity of each color component; the second and third moments, s_i and s_i, respectively, define the variance and skewness.

Using these three moments, distance may be computed as follows (Stricker and Orengo 1995):

$$D_{mom}(I,Q) = \sum_{i-1}^{r} \left(w_{i1} \mid \mu_i(I) - \mu_i(Q) \mid + w_{i2} \mid \sigma_i(I) - \sigma_i(Q) \mid + w_{i3} \mid s_i(I) - s_i(Q) \mid \right) \quad (5)$$

where r is the number of color components and the w_{ij} weights the contributions of the different moments for each color component. As we use only a small set of moments, it is possible for two qualitatively different color images to have a D_{mom} value of 0. Nevertheless, experimental evidence has shown that this measure is more robust in matching color images than color histograms (Stricker and Orengo 1995).

Mean brightness: This number reflects the overall lighting conditions, and is defined similar to and can be derived from (2).

3.1.2 Texture Features. Texture has long been recognized as being as important a property of images as is color, if not more so, since textural information can be conveyed as readily with gray-level images as it can in color. Nevertheless, there is an extremely wide variety of opinion concerned with just what texture is and how it may be quantitatively represented (Tuceryan and Jain 1993). Among all these alternatives we have chosen two models which are both popular and effective in image retrieval: Tamura features (Tamura et al. 1979) and the Simultaneous Auto-regressive (SAR) model (Mao and Jain 1992).

Tamura Features: The Tamura features are *contrast, directionality,* and *coarseness,* which were introduced as a quantification of psychological attributes. Coarseness is a measure of the granularity of the texture. It is derived from moving averages computed over windows of different sizes; one of these sizes gives an optimum fit in both the horizontal and vertical directions and is used to calculate the coarseness metric. Directionality is computed from distributions of magnitude and direction of gradient at all pixels. The quantification of contrast is based on the statistical distribution of pixel intensities (Tamura et al. 1979).

SAR Model: Given an image of gray-level pixels, the SAR model provides a description of each pixel in terms of its neighboring pixels. For an $M \times M$ textured image, the intensity of a pixel at position $s = (s_1, s_2)$, $s_1, s_2 = 1, ..., M$, can be given by

$$g(s) = \mu + \sum_{r \in D} \theta(r) g(s + r) + \in (s) \quad (6)$$

The parameters for this model are as follows: m is a bias value which depends on the mean gray-level of the entire image; q is a set of model parameters which characterize the dependence of pixel s on its neighbors r; D is the set of neighbors; $e(s)$ is an independent Gaussian random variable with zero mean whose variance s^2 models the noise level. The effectiveness of the SAR model depends on the quality of estimates for q and s, which are usually determined by either least squares or maximum likelihood estimation.

Our implementation uses the multiresolution SAR (MRSAR) model (Mao and Jain 1992) which describes textures at different resolutions in order to model different granularities. Images are represented by a multiresolution Gaussian pyramid obtained by low-pass filtering and subsampling operators applied at several successive levels. We have chosen four levels of resolution, and the collection of model parameters at each level is used as the texture features of each image.

Similarity: For either model texture is represented quantitatively as a feature vector X. For the SAR model the distance between two such vectors is given by the Mahalanobis function:

$$D_{Mahal} = \left(X^1 - X^2\right)^T C^{-1}\left(X^1 - X^2\right) \tag{7}$$

C is the covariance matrix which models pairwise relationships among the individual model features. Because the Tamura features are almost uncorrelated, the following simplified Mahalanobis function may be used instead:

$$D_{simp} = \sum_{i=1}^{J} \frac{\left(x_j^1 - x_j^2\right)^2}{c_j} \tag{8}$$

3.1.3 Shape Features. Dominant objects in key-frames represent important semantic content and are best represented by their shapes, if they can be identified by either automatic or semi-automatic spatial segmentation algorithms. In our implementation dominant objects in key-frames are obtained by a color-based segmentation algorithm (Gong et al. 1994) and an interactive outlining algorithm (Daneels et al. 1993). In comparing similarity between shapes, cumulative turning angles are used, because they provide a measure closer to human perception of shapes than algebraic moments or parameteric curves (Arkin et al. 1991). This metric also provides: 1) invariance under translation, rotation and scaling, 2) invariance with respect to convex and non-convex polygons, and 3) relatively easy computation.

3.1.4 Edge Features. Edges derived from an image using a technique such as a Sobel filter provide good cues for content: humans can easily identify some objects from their edge maps. We have derived such binary edge maps as a representation of key-frames. Two images can then be compared by calculating a correlation between their edge maps (Kato et al. 1992). Key frames can also be retrieved based on such a similarity measure. However, these comparisons are limited by their dependency on image resolution, size, and orientation.

3.2 Temporal Features for Representation of Shot Content

Key frames utilize only spatial information and ignore the temporal nature of a video to a large extent. With such a representation only it will be difficult to support event-based classification and retrieval. An example is that frame-to-frame differences can be used to classify news video clips into anchorperson shots and news shots (Zhang et al. 1995a). We shall now review some of the temporal features we are currently using to represent temporal characteristics at shot level.

Camera operations: We have already discussed the detection of camera operations, including panning, tilting, and zooming, by analyzing either motion fields or spatio-temporal images; this information provides a useful representation of temporal content for each shot.

Temporal variation of brightness and colors: They are represented by the mean and variance of average brightness and a few dominant colors calculated over all frames in a shot.

Salient stills: Salient stills are images that are constructed from the content of all the frames in a shot, which capture both the content and context of the entire shot (Teodosio and Bender 1993). However, constructing salient stills requires sophisticated motion analysis and segmentation and is computationally expensive. Though we are currently working on improving the accuracy and speed of constructing salient stills, we are not ready to integrate this representation into our current system.

Other features: Other temporal features for representing video content include global orientation parameters of spatio-temporal images and object motions. The spatio-temporal global orientation parameters calculated using steerable orientation filters provide additional information about motion in each shot and can be used to classify shots. Developing algorithms for moving object detection, tracking, and description is a longer-term research effort.

4. Content-based Retrieval and Browsing

Once a scheme for representation of video content has been established, tools for content-based retrieval and browsing can be built upon that representation; a set of such tools of our system will now be reviewed.

4.1 Content-Based Retrieval of Video Shots

With the representation and similarity measures described in section 3, querying a video database to retrieve shots can be performed based on key-frame features, temporal shot features, or a combination of the two. The retrieval system we are building supports retrieval as a more interactive process than is provided by simply formulating and processing conventional queries, providing fewer constraints on the possibilities the user may wish to explore. The query process is still iterative, with the system accepting feedback to narrow or reformulate searches or change its link-following behavior, and to refine any queries that are given.

4.1.1 Key-Frame-Based Retrieval. Once a video has been abstracted to key-frames, search becomes a matter of identifying those key-frames from the database which are similar to the query, according to the similarities defined in section 3. To accommodate different user requests, three basic query approaches are supported: query by template manipulation, query by object feature specification, and query by visual examples. Also, the user can specify a particular feature set to be used for a retrieval.

Query by visual templates is based on the assumption that a user often wants to retrieve key-frame images which consist of some known color patterns, such as a sunny sky, sea, beach, lawn, or forest. These pre-defined templates are stored and displayed as color texture maps and can be selected by the user to form a query, as shown in figure 1(a). The color distribution of a selected template can also be manipulated: the color manipulator consists of three scalars, corresponding to red, green, and blue intensities, and a display of up to 20 significant colors in the selected template, in descending order of contribution to the template image. The user can modify the red, green, and blue content of any selection to approximate more closely what he/she has in mind. The manipulation is performed in real time, meaning that the user is able to see changes in the template color while making adjustments.

As shown in figure 1(b), it is not necessary that the entire area of the target image be filled by templates: images can be retrieved based on matching only those regions for which templates have been specified. For example, one can form a query by selecting a sky and a green area template and place them in the regions as shown in figure 1(b). This partially specified query resulted in the five best histogram-based matches displayed in figure 1(c).

Once a key-frame has been identified, the user may view its associated video clip by clicking the "Video" button in the "Retrieved Images" window. This initiates a video player, as shown in figure 1(d), which is cued by the location of the key-frame. That frame may also be used to derive a hierarchical display, as will be seen in figure 3, in which the key-frames are elements of the lowest level. Retrieval may thus be followed by browsing as a means to examine the broader context of the retrieved key-frame. On the other hand a query can also be initiated from browsing. Thus, a user may select an image while browsing and offer it as a query: a request to find all key-frames which resemble that image.

4.1.2 Shot-Based Retrieval. Entire shots can also be retrieved based on their temporal features. Queries such as "find all shots with a camera panning at 10∞/second" can be easily satisfied based on temporal representations. It is

Figure 1. Key-frame-based query of video database.
(a) Template panel with color template selection and color manipulation tools;
(b) Composed template image which forms a query;
(c) Retrieved key-frames based on color similarity to the query.

also possible to combine temporal and key-frame features in a single query, such as "query by example". Figure 2 shows an example of such a query using an anchorperson shot, shown in figure 2(a), where retrieval is based on average colors, color histograms, and their temporal variations. This is, in fact, a general technique for distinguishing anchor-person shots from news shots.

4.2. Content-based Video Browsing

As we pointed out earlier, the uniqueness of our browsing tools lies in their

Figure 1(d). A player to browse a shot represented by a key-frame retrieval.

use of the content information obtained from video parsing including segment boundaries, camera operations, and key-frames. Our browsing tools support two different approaches to accessing video source data: *sequential* access and *random* access. In addition, these tools accommodate two levels of granularity—overview and detail—along with an effective bridge between the two levels.

Sequential access browsing takes place through the VCR-like interface illustrated in figure 1(d). Overview granularity is achieved by playing only the extracted key-frames at a selected rate. Detailed granularity is provided by normal viewing, with frame-by-frame single stepping; and this approach is further enhanced to "freeze" the display each time a key-frame is reached. Finally, viewing at both levels of granularity is supported in the reverse, as well as forward, direction.

Figure 2a. Query formed by this example anchorperson shot.

The hierarchical browser is designed to provide random access to any point in a given video: a video sequence is spread in space and represented by frame icons which function rather like a light table of slides (Zhang et al. 1995b). In other words the display space is traded for time to provide a rapid overview of the content of a long video (Mills et al. 1992). As shown in figure 3, at the top of the hierarchy, a whole video is represented by five key-frames, each corresponding to a segment consisting of an equal number of consecutive camera shots. Any one of these segments may then be subdivided to create the next level of the hierarchy. As we descend through the hierarchy, our attention focuses on smaller groups of shots, single shots, the representative frames of a specific shot, and finally a sequence of frames represented by a key-frame. We can then move to more detailed granularity by opening the first type of video player to view sequentially any particular segment of video selected from this browser at any level of the hierarchy.

As we pointed out earlier, another advantage to using key-frames in

Figure 2b. Shot-based video retrieval.
Retrieved shots represented by their key-frames from the video database
based on their similarity to the query example in terms of shot features.

browsing is that we are able to browse the video content down to the key-frame level without necessarily storing the entire video. This is particularly advantageous if our storage space is limited. Such a feature is very useful not only in video databases and information systems but also to support previewing in VOD systems. What is particularly important is that the network load for transmitting small numbers of static images is far less than that required for transmitting video; and, because the images are static, quality of service is no longer such a critical constraint. Through the hierarchical browser, one may also identify a specific sequence of the video which is all that one may wish to "demand." Thus, the browser not only reduces network load during browsing but may also reduce the need for network services when the time comes to request the actual video.

The browsing tools presented above are basically *programs* or *clips* based. That is, video programs or clips are loaded into the browser either from a list of names specified by retrieval result, a database index or a user. As shown in figure 3, the only criteria used to select the representative icons displayed at the top level of the hierarchy is time: they are the first key-frame of the first shot among all shots represented. In other words, the shots at the high levels are grouped only according to their sequential relations not their content. As a result, though random access is provided, a user has to browse down to the second or third level to get a sense of content of all shots in a group. This is less a problem if the browsing is launched from retrieval result such as shown in figure 1 and figure 2, but it will not be very convenient when we use it to browse raw video data or parsing results.

To support *class-based* browsing, we have been working on clustering algorithms using the same content representation as used in retrieval. Two types of algorithms, ISODATA partitioning and hierarchical clustering (Duda

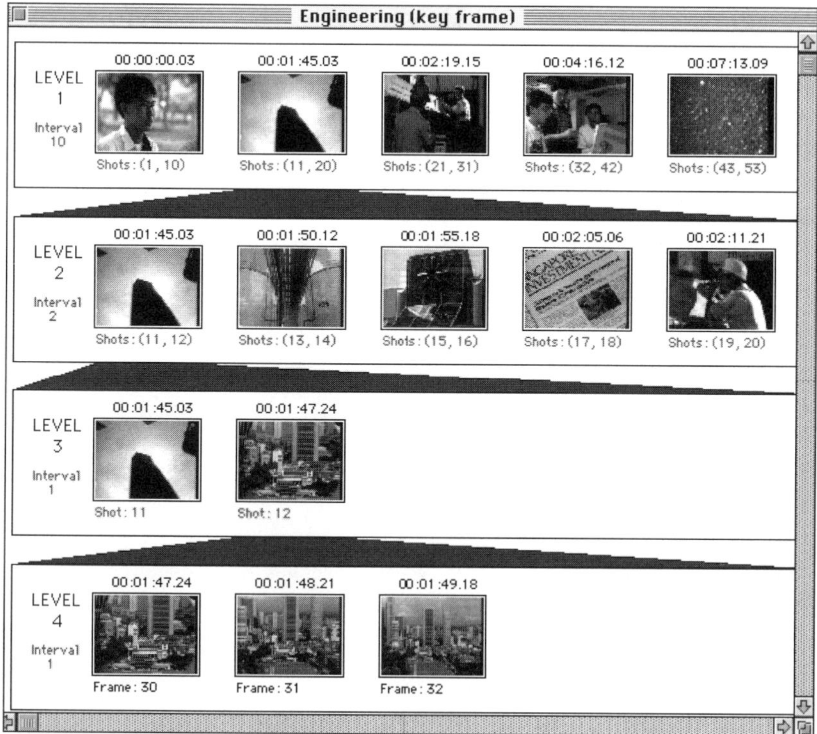

Figure 3. Key-frame-based hierarchical video browser.

and Hart 1973), have been used for this task. With such clustering processes, when a list of video programs or clips are provided, the parsing system will use either key-frame and/or shot features to cluster shots into classes, each of which consists of shots of similar content. After such clustering, each class of shots can be represented by an icon, which can then be displayed at the high levels of hierarchical browser. As a result, a user can know roughly the content of each calls of shots even without moving down to lower levels of the hierarchy. Such clustering is also useful in index building and computer-assisted video content annotation. We are currently working on integrating this into our system.

5. Concluding Remarks and Future Work

In this chapter we have presented an overview of our work in developing an integrated and content-based solution for computer-assisted video parsing, abstraction, retrieval and browsing. The most important feature of our approach is its use of low-level visual features as a representation of video content and its automatic abstraction process. Such a representation and extracted key-frames, together with spatio-temporal features and some semantic primitives derived at shot level, can then be used to facilitate indexing, retrieval and browsing. Experimental results and usability studies have shown that such a solution is effective and feasible and will be useful in many multimedia applications, though traditional text-based indexing and retrieval tools will still be part of the integrated system.

We are now working on more robust algorithms to extract event-based features. Case studies on parsing and indexing news broadcasts have already allowed us to support queries such as "find me all interview shots in a news program" (Zhang et al. 1995a). An important extension of our work is to incorporate audio analysis and text parsing into both video parsing and content representation (Bender and Chesnais 1988, Hauptmann et al., Jones et al., Mani et al., and Takeshita et al., this volume).

References

Aigraine, P.; Joly, P.; and Longueville, V. 1997. Medium Knowledge-Based Macro-Segmentation of Video into Sequences. In this volume.

Adelson, E. H. and Bergen, J. R. 1985. Spatiotemporal Energy Models for the Perception of Motion. *Journal of the Optical Society of America* A 2 (2): 284-299.

Arkin, E. M.; Chew, L. P.; Huttenlocher, D. P.; Kedem, K.; and Mitchell, J. S. B. 1991. An Efficiently Computable Metric for Comparing Polygonal Shapes. *IEEE Transactions on Pattern Analysis and Machine Intelligence* 13(3): 209-216.

Arman, F.; Depommier, R.; Hsu, A.; and Chiu, M.-Y. 1994. Content-based Browsing of Video Sequences. In Proceedings of the Second ACM International Multimedia Conference, 97-104, August, San Francisco, CA: ACM.

Bender, W. and Chesnais, P. 1988. Network Plus. In Proceedings of SPIE Electronic Imaging Device and Systems Symposium, Vol. 900, 81-86, Los Angeles, CA, January.

Daneels, D.; Van Campenhout, D.; Niblack, W.; Equitz, W.; Barber, R.; Bellon, E.; Firens, F. 1993. Interactive Outlining: An Improved Approach Using Active Geometry Features, Proceedings of IS&T/SPIE. Conference on Storage and Retrieval for Image and Video Databases II, 226-233, San Jose, CA, February.

Davis, M. 1993. Media Streams: An Iconic Visual Language for Video Annotation. In Proceedings of IEEE Symposium on Visual Languages, 196-202, Bergen, Norway: IEEE.

Duda, R. and Hart, P. 1973. *Pattern Recognition and Scene Analysis*. New York: Wiley.

Faloutsos, C.; Barber, R.; Flickner, M.; Hafner, J.; Niblack, W.; Petkovic, D.; and Equitz, W. 1994. Efficient and EffectiveQuerying by Image Content. *Journal of Intelligent Information Systems* 3: 231-262.

Flickner, M.; Sawhney, H.; Niblack, W.; Ashley, J.; Huang, Q.; Dom, B.; Gorkani, M.; Hafner, J.; Lee, D.; Petkovic, D.; Steele, D.; and Yanker, P. 1997. Query by Image and Video Content: The QBIC System. In this volume.

Gong, Y.; Zhang, H. J.; Chuan, H. C.; and Sakauchi, M., 1994. An Image Database System with Content Capturing and Fast Image Indexing Abilities. In Proceedings of the First IEEE International Conference on Multimedia Computing and Systems, 121-130, May, Boston, MA: IEEE Computer Society Press.

Gorkani, M. and Picard, R. 1994. Texture Orientation for Sorting Photos at a Glance. In Proceedings of the 12th International Conference on Pattern Recognition, I: 459-464. Jerusalem, Israel: IEEE Computer Society Press, October.

Hauptmann, A. G. and Witbrock, M. 1997. Informedia: News-on-Demand Multimedia Information Acquisition and Retrieval. In this volume.

Ioka, M. 1989. A Method Of Defining the Similarity of Images on the Basis Of Color Information, Technical Report RT-0030, IBM Tokyo Research Laboratory.

Jones, G. J. F.; Foote, J. Sparck Jones, K.; and Young, S. 1997. The Video Mail Retrieval Project: Experiences in Retrieving Spoken Documents. In this volume.

Kato, T.; Kurita, T.; Otsu, N.; and Hirata K. 1992. A Sketch Retrieval Method for Full Color Image Database: Query by Visual Example. In Proceedings of the 11th International Conference on Pattern Recognition, 530-533, Amsterdam, Holland: IEEE Computer Society Press.

Mao, J. and Jain, A. K. 1992. Texture Classification and Segmentation Using Multiresolution Simultaneous Autoregressive Models. *Pattern Recognition* 25(2): 173-188.

Mani, I.; House, D.; Maybury, M.; and Green, M. 1997. Towards Content-Based Browsing of Broadcast News Video. In this volume.

Mills, M.; Cohen, J.; and Wong, Y. Y. 1992. A Magnifier Tool for Video Data. In Proceedings of Human Factors in Computing Systems (CHI '92), 93-98. Monterey, CA: ACM.

Miyahara, M. and Yoshida, Y. 1988. Mathematical Transform of (R,G,B) Color Data to Munsell (H,V,C) Color Data. In Proceedings of SPIE Visual Communication and Image Processing 1001: 650-657, Boston, MA: SPIE.

Nagasaka A. and Tanaka, Y. 1991. Automatic Video Indexing and Full-Video Search for Object Appearances. In *Visual Database Systems II*, eds. E. Knuth and L. M. Wegner, 119-133. Amsterdam: North-Holland.

O'Connor, B. C. 1991. Selecting Key Frames of Moving Image Documents: A Digital Environment for Analysis and Navigation. *Microcomputers for Information Management* 8(2): 119-133.

Pentland, A.; Picard, R. W.; and Scarloff, S. 1994. Photobook: Tools for Content-Based Manipulation of Image Databases. In Proceedings of the IS&T/SPIE Conference on Storage and Retrieval for Image and Video Databases II, 34-47. San Jose, CA.

Pentland, A. 1997. Machine Understanding of Human Behavior. In this volume.

Rowe, L. A.; Boreczky, J. S.; and Eads, C. A. 1994. Indexes for User Access to Large Video Databases. In Proceedings of the IS&T/SPIE Conference on Storage and Retrieval for Image and Video Databases II, 150-161, San Jose, CA.

Stricker M. and Orengo, M. 1995. Similarity of Color Images. In Proceedings of the IS&T/SPIE Conference on Storage and Retrieval for Image and Video Databases III, 381-392, San Jose, CA, February.

Swain M. J. and Balllard, D. H. 1991. Color Indexing. *International Journal of Com-*

puter Vision 7(1): 11-32.

Swanberg, D.; Shu C.-F; and Jain, R. 1993. Knowledge Guided Parsing in Video Databases. In Proceedings of the IS&T/SPIE Conference on Storage and Retrieval for Image and Video Databases, 13-24. San Jose, CA February.

Takeshita, A.; Inoue, T.; and K. Tanaka. 1997. Topic Based Multimedia Structuring. In this volume.

Tamura, H.; Mori, S.; and Yamawaki, T. 1979. Texture Features Corresponding to Visual Perception. *IEEE Transactions on Systems Man, and Cybernetics* 6(4): 460-473.

Teodosio, L. and Bender, W. 1993. Salient Video Stills: Content and Context Preserved. In Proceedings of the First ACM International Multimedia Conference, 39-46. Anaheim, CA, August.

Tuceryan, M. and Jain, A. K. 1993. Texture Analysis. In *Handbook of Pattern Recognition and Computer Vision*, eds. C. H. Chen; L. F. Pau; and P. S. P. Wang, 235-276. Singapore: World Scientific.

Yeo, B.-L. and Liu, B. 1995. Rapid Scene Analysis on Compressed Video. *IEEE Transactions on Circuits and Systems for Video Technology*, to appear.

Zhang, H. J.; Kankanhalli, A.; and Smoliar, S. W. 1993. Automatic Partitioning of Full-motion Video. *Multimedia Systems* 1(1): 10-28.

Zhang, H. J. and Smoliar, S. W. 1994. Developing Power Tools for Video Indexing and Retrieval. In Proceedings of the IS&T/SPIE Conference on Storage and Retrieval for Image and Video Databases II, 140-149, San Jose, CA, February.

Zhang, H. J.; Low, C. Y.; Gong, Y.; and Smoliar, S. W., 1994. Video Parsing Using Compressed Data. In Proceedings of the IS&T/SPIE Conference on Image and Video Processing II, 142-149. San Jose, CA, Feburuary.

Zhang, H. J.; Tan, S. Y.; S. W. Smoliar; and Y. Gong, 1995a. Automatic Parsing and Indexing of News Video. *Multimedia Systems* 2(6): 256-266.

Zhang, H. J.; Smoliar, S. W.; and Wu, J. H. 1995b. Content-Based Video Browsing Tools. In Proceedings of the IS&T/SPIE Conference on Multimedia Computing and Networking, 389-398. San Jose, CA, February.

Zhang H. J. and Ho, W. C. 1995. Video Sequence Parsing. Technical Report, Institute of Systems Science, National University of Singapore.

Medium Knowledge-Based Macro-Segmentation of Video into Sequences

Philippe Aigrain, Philippe Joly, and Véronique Longueville
Institut de Recherche en Informatique de Toulouse,
Université Paul Sabatier

Abstract

Efficient and reliable methods for the segmentation of the image part of a video into shots have been proposed. In actual motion picture or video documents, there can often be 500 to 1000 shots per hour. Thus, if one wants to enable quick browsing of the video contents, quick positioning in the document for interactive viewing, or if one wants to automatically construct abstracts of the document, it is necessary to find more macroscopic time objects, for instance larger sequences constituting a narrative unit or sharing the same setting. In this chapter, we present a method for obtaining automatically such a macro-segmentation in sequences. This method is based on the application of rules expressing the local (in time) clues which are given by the medium contents to enable identification of more macroscopical changes. We describe how the results from these rules can be combined to obtain a macro-segmentation, and to extract particularly important representative images. We give arguments for the choice of such a general purpose medium-based approach compared to approaches based on modelling specific types of contents, and present results from its automatic application to a limited sample of documents.

1. Introduction

Efficient and reliable methods have been presented for shot change detection in video, even when it occurs through gradual transition effects such as wipes and dissolves (see for instance Zhang et al. 1994, Arman et al. 1993, Aigrain and

Joly 1994a, Meng et al. 1995). These methods can operate on an analog video source or on a compressed digital video M-JPEG or MPEG file.) Using representative image icons for each shot (Ueda 1991; Tonomura 1991; Koechlin 1992; Aigrain and Joly 1992; Nagasaka and Tanaka 1992; Pentland, this volume) one can build browsing user interfaces or automatic story-boards (Aigrain and Joly 1994b, Aigrain et al. 1995b). However, since there can be a large number of shots in a lengthy video document (500 to 1000 shots per hour are common values), it is necessary to build a more macroscopic segmentation of the video contents, which can be used in hierarchical browsers (Cherfaoui and Bertin 1994, Zhang et al. 1995b) or for direct positioning in a time-line oriented browser (Aigrain et al. 1995a). Automatic construction of such a macro-segmentation is a relatively difficult problem. Motivation for doing it automatically lies in the fact that human macro-segmentation can not be done reliably by only accessing representative images for one shot and thus requires access to the full video contents which is time-consuming. HongJiang Zhang, Yihong Gong and Stephen Smoliar have proposed a method for the automatic macro-segmentation of news programs (Zhang et al. 1993, Zhang et al. 1994). This method is based on a specialized model for this type of program, using recognition of particular types of shots (anchor person, anchor person with insert, interview, etc) and rules on the possible global temporal organization of the news program. More recently Minerva Yeung et al. (1995) have proposed a technique for structuring the complete contents of a video in a directed graph, whose nodes are clusters of similar shots, and whose edges represent temporal relations between shot clusters: there is an edge between cluster $C1$ and cluster $C2$ if some shot in $C2$ immediately follows some shot in $C1$. This type of macro-structuration is very interesting, but being based only on shot image similarity, it does not capture a wide category of sequence change clues coming from transition effects, soundtrack contents change, or editing rhythm. Moreover, it does not build a linear macro-segmentation suitable for hierarchical browsers.

In this chapter we propose a general-purpose method for macro-segmentation of video, which uses more general media-knowledge-based rules. These rules exploit the existence of temporally local clues of macroscopic change. Section 2 presents the local rules and their application, and gives some justification for their efficiency. Section 3 describes our method for combining the results from applying the local rules in order to produce a global representation and segmentation. Section 4 presents preliminary results from the automatic application of our method to a limited set of documents.

2. Local Rules for Sequence Construction

It is well known that in a temporal medium, local clues need to be given to the viewer or listener in order to help him or her identify macroscopic change. In the field of music, such local rules have for instance been identified by Franz Lerdahl and Ray Jackendoff (1983) in their pioneering attempt to formalize human segmentation in listening to music and Carolyn Drake and Caroline Palmer (1994) have confirmed that actual performers emphasize macroscopical changes in both timing and accent. In motion picture and video, there are a wide range of possible temporally local clues for macroscopic changes, from use of special transition effects, modification of soundtrack, change of editing rhythm, and modifications of the type of images due to change in settings or to special effects. Such clues are used by the viewer/listener in collaboration with its global semantic understanding of action or narration. Of course, our method will use only the local clues, and will lack the global understanding. One further difficulty is that there is a wide range of variation regarding which clues are used depending on directors, producers, and types of programs. Nonetheless we claim that the rules themselves are sufficiently medium-invariant to enable automatic segmentation if the analysis process combines several types of rules in a sufficiently adaptative way.

2.1 Context

We will assume as input of our algorithm a set of shots S_1, S_2, ... S_n, with corresponding durations T_1, T_2, ... T_n, representative images R_1, R_2, ... R_n, and introductory transition effects E_1, E_2, ... E_n. We will also denote the second image of each shot by SEC_1, SEC_2, ... SEC_n, and the penultimate image of each shot by PEN_1, PEN_2, ... PEN_n. The thresholds and constants used by the rules have been empirically determined. They are convenient in most cases. They can be adjusted to be more efficient on particular kinds of video documents (news, or talkshows or films...).

2.2 Transition Effect Rules

Transition effects TI are noted by the letter C for a cut transition and G for a gradual transition effect (dissolves and fades, various types of wipes). The complete list of transition effects can thus be viewed as a word on the alphabet {C,G}. Transition effect rules are based on recognition of subwords which are of the form: $C^i G^j C^k$

We have the following rules (see figure 1):

Rule 1. If $i > 2$, $j = 1$, $k > 2$ then it is likely that there is a sequence limit at the beginning of the G transition effect. If the gradual transition effect is a fade out or a fade through black, then a sequence limit can be assumed. For other gradual effects it can be either a sequence limit or an indication that the next shot is an important shot.

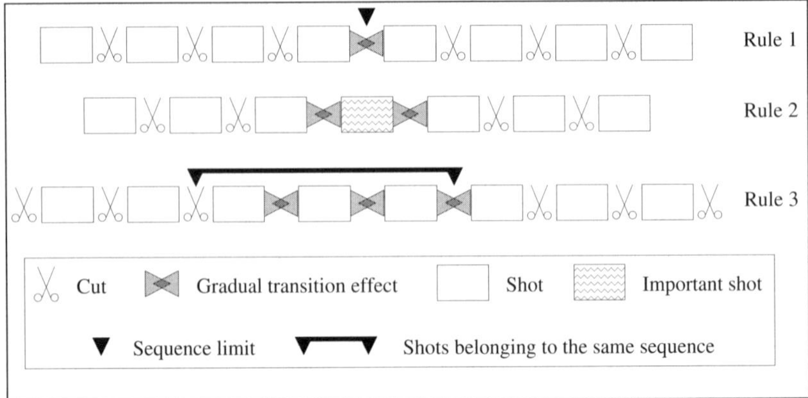

Figure 1. Transition effect rules.

Rule 2. If $i > 2$, $j = 2$, $k > 2$, $Sm+1$ is the shot surrounded by gradual transition effects, then it is likely that $Sm+1$ is an important shot in a sequence (whose limits cannot be known from this rule)

Rule 3. If $i > 2$, $j > 2$, $k > 2$, and Sm is the shot introduced by the first gradual transition effect, and $Sm+j$ is the shot introduced by the last gradual transition effect, then there is a sequence which begins at most 2 shots before Sm, and which ends at the end of $Sm+j-1$.

Rule 3 is very reliable. On the contrary it is not easy to reliably distinguish between cases where rule 1 or rule 2 apply, for the following reasons:

- In some cases, gradual transition detection may not be reliable enough, in particular when an insert is brought up or turned off on part of the screen through a dissolve. In those cases one of two gradual transitions may be missed and rule 1 applied instead of rule 2.

- An insert is sometimes brought up through a dissolve but turned off "cut": applying rule 1 in that case may be erroneous.

This gives more evidence for not interpreting always single gradual transition effects as sequence limits (except for the special case of transitions through a black screen).

2.3 Shot Repetition Rules

Let us assume that $D(i,j)$ is a dissimilarity measure between images i and j and K a threshold such that $D(i,j) < K$ is equivalent to i and j belong to similar shots. The shot repetition rule is as follows (see figure 2) :

Rule 4. If $D(PEN_i, SEC_{i+j}) < K$ and $1 < j < 4$, then S_i and S_{i+j} belong to the same sequence

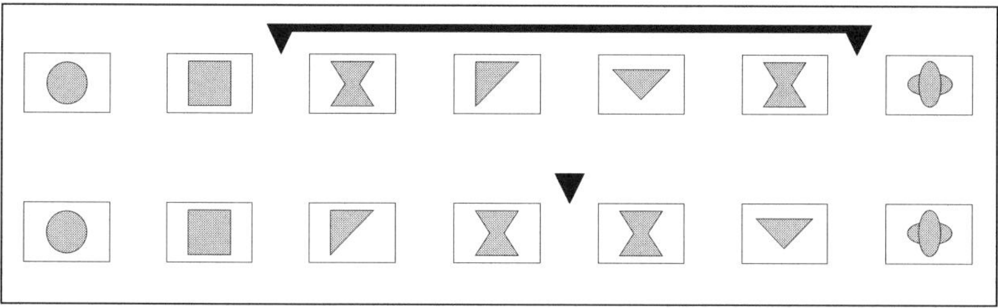

Figure 2. Shot repetition rules.

Rule 5. If $D(PEN_i, SEC_{i+j}) < K$ and $j = 1$, then there is a sequence limit between S_i and S_{i+j}.

These rules express the fact that if a shot is repeated at a distance of no less than 2 shots and no more than 3 shots, then there has been no sequence break. On the contrary, if two very similar shots occur in immediate succession, this is likely to indicate a sequence change. Repeated applications of rule 4 results in the recognition of field/counter-field or interview type sequences. Only the compound result of repeated application of rule 4 is kept: the limits of the segment in which shot repetition occurs and the indices of repeated shots (for later use in selecting representative images for sequences). The precise limits of the sequence are not known, but they lie almost always in a 2-shot neighborhood before the beginning of shot repetition and after the last shot repetition. This rule is not reliable in some cases: in some TV shows, short term shot repetition may occur across sequence boundaries, for instance for the shot of the anchorperson. Thus, a rule leading to inference of a sequence break during a shot repetition sequence will be given precedence (see section 3). Rule 5 is problematic: is there is a false detection of shot change, it will assume that there is a sequence break at this point. We suggest to use rule 5 only for feature films and eventually for sport casts, and only if shot change detection is very reliable.

In our system, the dissimilarity measure used for detection of shot repetition is the same measure used for cut shot change detection (Aigrain and Joly 1994a) (proportion of pixels in pixel-to-pixel difference between low resolution normalized luminance images which have an absolute value greater than $0.45 * a$, where a is the number of grey levels). The threshold used is of course different of the threshold used for cut detection: we use $K = 0.08$ for shot repetition detection instead of $K \times 0.04$ for cut detection[1].

2.4 Contiguous Shot Setting Similarity Rule

This rule applies only for color video. Let us assume that $D2(i,j)$ is a dissimilarity measure between images i and j and $K2$ a threshold such that from

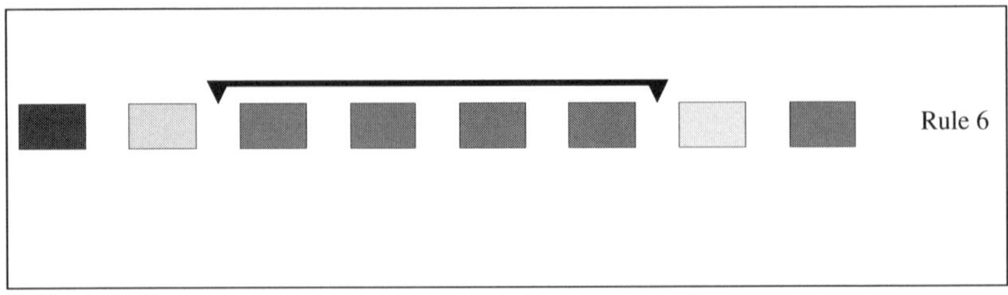

Figure 3. Contiguous shot setting similarity rule.

$D2(R_i, R_{i+1}) < K2$ it follows that S_i and S_{i+1} are (consecutive) shots filmed in the same setting (eventually with different camera position, angle and focus). The contiguous shot setting similarity rule is as follows (see figure 3):

Rule 6. If $[S_i \ldots S_{i+k}]$ are consecutive shots such that $k > 2$, $\forall$ "j, $0 < j < k-1$, $D2(R_{i+j}, R_{i+j+1}) < K2$, $D2(R_{i-1}, R_i) \geq K2$ and $D2(R_{i+k}, R_{i+k+1}) \geq K2$ then $[S_i \ldots S_{i+k}]$ is a sequence.

We use a dissimilarity measure based on the distributions of hue and saturation in the (low resolution) color representative images for two shots. Each pixel is considered as a 2D-vector in the hue-saturation discus (a complex number in the unit disc), and we compute mean $m(i)$ and standard deviation $\sigma(i)$ of the distribution of vectors in image i. Our dissimilarity measure is defined by $D2(i,j) = \|m(i) - m(j)\| + |\sigma(i) - \sigma(j)|$ and the threshold as $K2 = 0.10$

Rule 6 produces remarkably reliable information about sequence continuity when one uses the above-proposed measure, but of course the fact that no continuity is detected does not mean that there is a sequence break: a close shot in the middle of a sequence will for instance interrupt the detection of setting continuity.

2.5 Editing Rhythm

Editing ("montage") rhythm is a powerful tool for the structuration of viewer perception (Villain 1991, Vanoye and Goliot-Lété 1992). We propose to detect editing rhythm changes through order 2 auto-regressive modelling of shot durations. We will predict the duration of a shot by:

$$PRED(n) = a\, T_{n-1} + b\, T_{n-2}$$

the coefficients a and b being estimated in a 10-shot sliding window.

Rule 7. If $T_n > (2.0 * PRED(n))$ or $T_n < (PRED(n) / 2.0)$ then it is likely that S_n is an important (distinguished) shot in a sequence

A change in editing rhythm has to be relatively important to be significant: a change will be detected only if the shot is twice longer or twice shorter than predicted from the model (see figure 4).

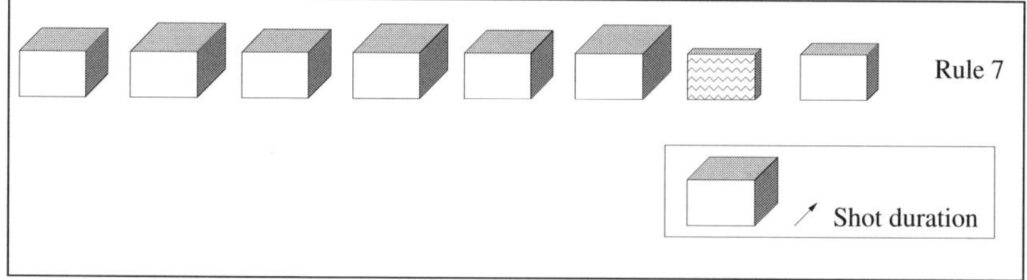

Figure 4. Editing rythm.

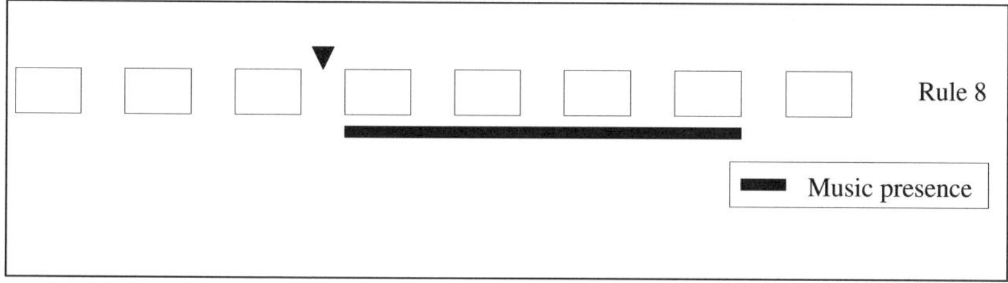

Figure 5. Soundtrack rule.

2.6 Soundtrack Rule

Rule 8. If there is no music during 30 seconds and music appears in the sound-track, then there is a sequence limit at the beginning of the music

This rule can only be applied if one has a music detector. Mike Hawley (1993) proposes such a detector which is reliable enough for this type of large time scale detection. We use a different and unpublished detector. Soundtrack contains very significant information about sequence change, but rule 8 is the only rule we have been able to define which can be applied in an homogeneous and reliable way (see figure 5).

From applying the local rules, we obtain incomplete and possibly contra-dictory knowledge about sequence limits in the video. The following section explains how one can infer a macro-segmentation and its representation from this data.

2.7 Camera Work Rule

This rule applies only when camera work information is available, and rarely applies even in this case (see figure 6).

Rule 9. If there is a succession of 3 or more simple shots with the same camera work (other than still shot) then they belong to the same sequence.

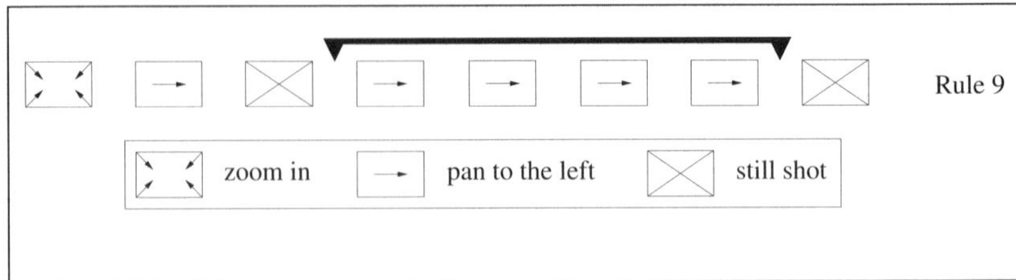

Figure 6. Camera work rule.

3. Obtaining a Macro-Segmentation and Sequence Representation from the Combined Results of the Local Rules

The combined application of all rules on a video document leads to the following data:

- A set of sequence breaks (precise limits of sequences) produced by rules 1, 5 and 8.
- A set of segments $[S_i,S_j]$ which are inferred to belong to the same sequence but with imprecise knowledge on the sequence limits outside of the $[S_i,S_j]$ range. Each segment is labelled by the rule (3, 4, 6 or 9) which has lead to infer its existence.
- A set of "distinguished" shots from rule 2 and 7.

In order to derive a macro-segmentation from this data, we propose the following steps:

- *Merging*: recognition of compatible starting points and ending points for various segments and break points, and merging of the corresponding data.
- *Precedence*: treatment of conflicts between breakpoints and segments and overlap between segments by use of precedence rules.
- *Hole filling*: adding segments for parts of the video document which are not covered by any segment.
- *Choice of representative images*: this choice depends on the rule label for the sequence.

3.1 Merging

Three different types of merging are done in this step:

Merging Between break points:

- Any simultaneous break points are merged, and given the labels of all rules having produced them (see figure 7).
- Any rule 8 break point can be merged with any break point produced by another rule if the rule 8 break occurs in the previous or next shot

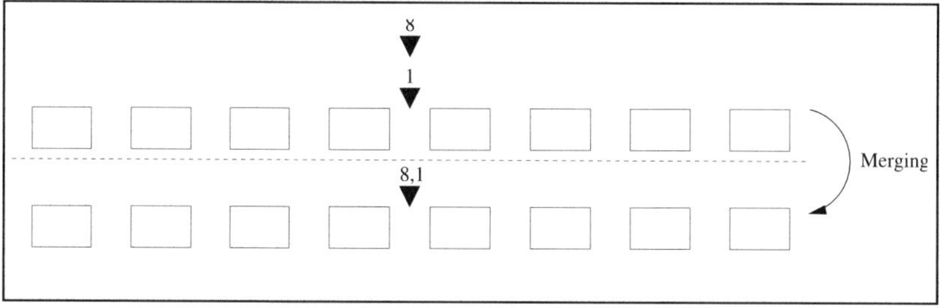

*Figure 7. Merging simultaneous breakpoint (the same sequence limit is
produced by the rules 1 and 8. The breakpoint label is {1,8}).*

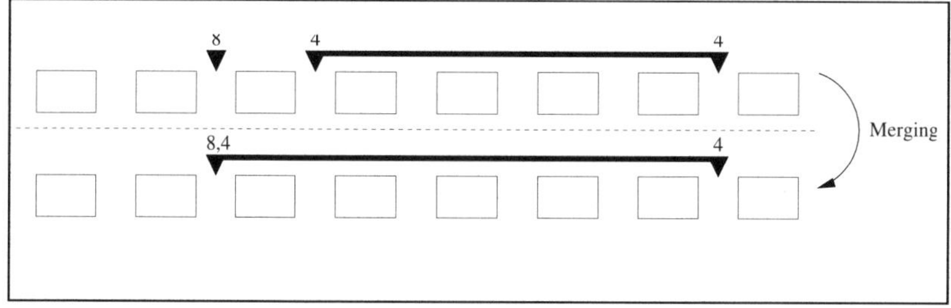

*Figure 8. Merging a segment starting point with a neighboring breakpoint
(The breakpoint identified by the rule 8 is moved to the limit
produced by the rule 4. The breakpoint label is {4,8}.)*

of the other break point. A single break point is then created, with the
time value of the break point not labelled by rule 8. The break point is
given the labels of all rules which have produced the merged data.

Merging between a break point and a segment limit: a rule 3 starting point,
or rule 4, 6 or 9 starting or ending point can be merged with a rule 1, 5, 8 or
multi-labelled break point, if the break point is in the compatible neighborhood of the segment (see figure 8). The compatible neighborhood is defined
as follows:

- at most −2 shots for a starting point for any segment producing rule,
- at most +2 shots for an ending point for any segment producing rule except for rule 3.

The starting point or ending point of the segment is adjusted to coincide
with the break point. This process cannot be repeated (a segment cannot be
adjusted several times to be merged with different break points).

Merging between segments limits: rule 3 starting points, or rules 4, 6, or 9
starting or ending points can be merged if their respective compatible neighborhoods intersect. The limit points are adjusted to the first shot change in
the intersection (see figure 9).

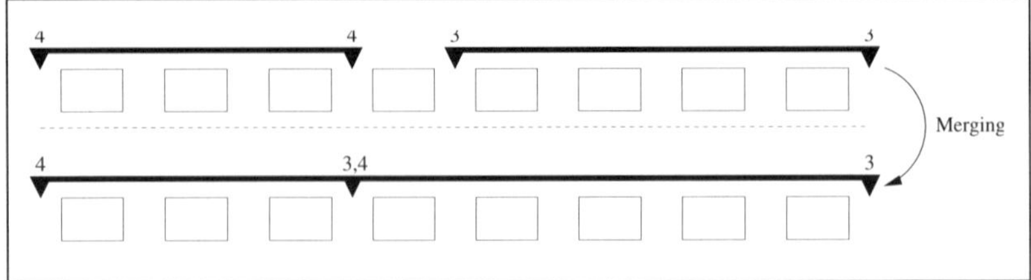

Figure 9. Merging between segments limits:
The segment 4 ending point and the segment 3 starting point are
merged on the first limit (segment 4 ending point).

3.2 Precedence

At this step the following modifications to the data (segment, break points and labels) produced after merging take place:

- If a rule 4 or 6 segment conflicts with a rule 1 or 8 breakpoint, it is split in two segments at this breakpoint. The first segment is labelled as the original segment, the second segment is labelled with both its original label and the breakpoint label.

- Finally, a segmentation is produced by taking the intersection of all remaining segments, and labelling each produced segment by all labels of segments which contain it before the intersection.

The special treatment of segments produced by rules 4 and 6 takes into account the fact that these rules are not perfectly reliable, while still making it possible to benefit from them when no other rule applies. No special treatment for confusion between rule 1 break points (single gradual transition effects) and 2 distinguished images is necessary. If an insert is incorrectly recognized as a rule 1 break point, over-segmentation may occur, but we will be careful to select the first shot after the break point as a representative image for the sequence. Thus, the fact that the image is particularly important will not be lost.

3.3 Hole Filling

We then introduce a last rule:

Rule 10. Any maximally connected time segment which does not overlap with segments produced by the previous steps is merged with the previous segment[3] if it lasts 1 or 2 shots, and this merging does not conflict with a detected breakpoint, or is taken as a segment of its own labelled as unknown type, if it lasts more than 2 shots.

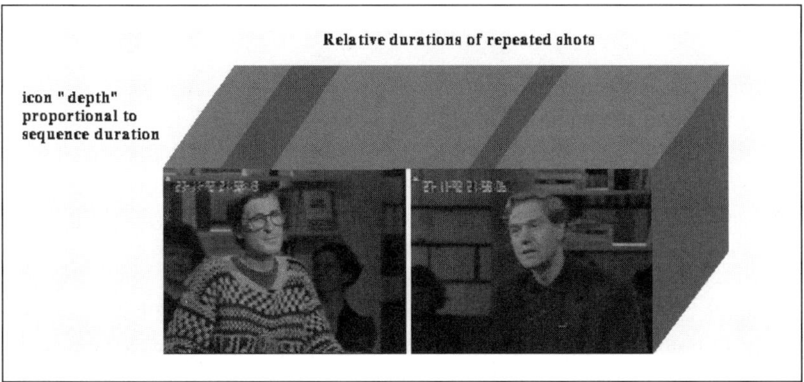

Figure 10. Possible sequence icon for 66 sec, 5-shot repetition sequence. (The width of stripes on "top" of the icon represent the relative duration of each repeated shot: note that not only it is obvious that this is an interview sequence, but the screen time for each locutor is also immediately visible.)

The special treatment of 1 or 2 shots "holes" is necessary to avoid over-segmentation.

3.4 Visual Representation for the Macro-Segmentation

We now have obtained a partition of the full document in segments which are likely to constitute sequences. We propose to represent each sequence by an icon containing one or two representative images, and whose pseudo-3D depth represents the sequence duration (see figure 10). The representative images are selected as follows (the first of the rules listed below whose conditions are met is applied):

- If the sequence labels contain 1 then the representative image of the first shot after the gradual transition effect is selected.

- If the sequence labels contain 4 (shot repetition) then the representative images of the first occurences of the 2 most frequently repeated shots in the segment are selected. A special case is made when there is a rule 2 or 7 distinguished image in the sequence: we then select the most frequently repeated image and the distinguished image.

- If a rule 2 or 7 distinguished image exists in the segment then it is selected as representative image for the sequence.

- In all other cases the middle shot representative image is selected if the sequence length is less than 20 shots; the representative images of the shots situated at 1/3 and 2/3 of the sequence are selected if the sequence length is more than 20 shots.

4. Status of Our Work, Results and Conclusion

The rules presented in section 2 have been derived from intensive analysis of video documents, readings in film theory, and discussion with film and video directors, teachers, critics and analysts. They have been refined through evaluation of their application. As of now, we have implemented them in an integrated software system and tested their application on a single documentary video (produced from film) and extracts of TV news shows. It is evident that much further work will have to be done before our method can be proved to be generally applicable. The measures and thresholds for rule 4, 6 and 7 have been extensively tested but may still need some limited adjustment. It may be that the method does not produce meaningful results on some types of documents for which a model-based approach is preferable (sports television for instance).

We nonetheless think that a convincing case can be made for the interest of applying media-perception-based rules. Figure 11 displays the results from our automatic segmentation and choice of representative images for a documentary video. We consider documentary videos as difficult cases for macro-segmentation (compared to feature films or live TV) because in many cases the information about topic change is in the semantic contents of the speech soundtrack, and the viewer is assumed to be attentive (contrary to live TV for which a "zapping" viewer is assumed). Only systematic comparison with manually produced segmentations can provide a convincing evaluation for macro-segmentation methods. We plan to do such an evaluation in the future, as well as comparison with methods combining video analysis with close caption analysis (when close captions are available).

In the example presented in figure 11, the segmentation is very good. Figure 12 shows a frame of each shot of the first 2 sequences (produced by rule 6) and of the beginning of the third one (produced by rule 8). The 6th and 7th sequences ("cheese making") should only be one sequence, as well as the 16th and 17th sequences ("bear tamers"). They have been segmented in 2 because of the failure of rule 6 to detect continuity where it is broken by one shot with a different setting. Another continuity rule using texture-based object detection could probably fix this. Apart from this problem, all detected sequences actually correspond to content units: there are many sequences because the documentary movie presents many different facets of a region in succession. The choice of representative shots for one sequence is not always optimal: it is very good when shot repetition and distinguished shots have been detected, but random in other cases.

Acknowledgements

This research was conducted under support from the French Ministère de la Culture et de la Francophonie.

*Figure 11. Automatic segmentation and choice of
representative images for documentary video.*

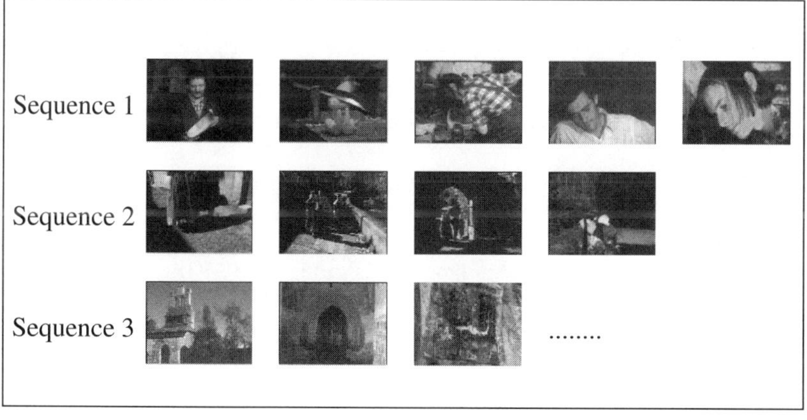

*Figure 12. Segmentations and choice of representative images for the
video "Ariège" (94 shot-15 minutes documentary).*

Notes

1 In our method for shot change detection, the threshold is adaptive, but more or less it remains close to 0.04.

2 With the next segment if there is no previous segment.

References

Aigrain, P. and Joly, P. 1992. Une Approche de l'Analyse de l'Image Animée. *Dossiers de l'Audiovisuel* 45: 82-85.

Aigrain, P. and Joly, P. 1994a. The Automatic Real-Time Analysis of Film Editing and Transition Effects and its Applications. *Computers & Graphics* 18(1): 93-103. January-February.

Aigrain, P. and Joly, P. 1994b. Discrete Visual Manipulation User Interfaces for Video. In Proceedings of RIAO'94 Conference, Vol 2: 12-17, New-York: CID, October.

Aigrain, P.; Joly, P.; Lepain, P. and Longueville, V. 1995a. Representation-Based User Interfaces for the Audiovisual Library of Year 2000. In Proceedings of the IS&T/SPIE'95 Multimedia Computing and Networking. 2417: 35-45, San Jose. February.

Aigrain, P.; Joly, P.; and Longueville, V. 1995b. Medium-Knowledge-Based Macro-Segmentation of Video into Sequences. In Working notes from the IJCAI-95 Workshop on Intelligent Multimedia Information Retrieval, 5-16, ed. M. Maybury. Montréal, August.

Arman, F.; and Hsu, A.; and Chiu, M. Y. 1993. Feature Management for Large Video Databases. SPIE Vol. 1908: 2-12.

Cherfaoui, M. and Bertin, C. 1994. Two-stage Strategy for Indexing and Presenting Video. In Proceedings of SPIE'94 Conference on Storage and Retrieval for Video Databases 2185: 174-184. San Jose, CA. February.

Drake, C. and Palmer, C. 1994. Accent Structures in Music Performance. In *Music Perception* 10(3): 343-378.

Hawley, M. 1993. Structure Out of Sound. PhD Diss. MIT Media Laboratory. Cambridge, MA.

Koechlinl, O. 1992. Les Nouvelles Interfaces de l'Audiovisuel. *Dossiers de l'Audiovisuel* 45: 98-100.

Lerdahl, F. and Jackendoff, R. 1983. *A Generative Theory of Tonal Music*. Cambridge, MA: MIT Press.

Meng, J.; Juan, Y.; and Chang, S.F. 1995. Scene Change Detection in a MPEG Compressed Video Sequence. In IS&T Proceedings of the SPIE'95 Digital Video Compression: Algorithm and Technologies. 2419: 14-25. San Jose, CA. February.

Nagasaka, A. and Tanaka, Y. 1992. Automatic Video Indexing and Full-Search for Video Appearances. In *Visual Database Systems II*, eds. E. Knuth and I. M. Wegener, 113-127. Amsterdam: Elsevier Science Publishers.

Pentland, A. 1997. Machine Understanding of Human Behavior. In this volume.

Tonomura, Y. 1991. Video Handling Based on Structured Information for Hypermedia Systems. In Proceedings of the International Conference on Multimedia Information Systems, 333-344. January. Singapore: ACM.

Ueda, H.; Miyatake, T.; and Yoshisawa, S. 1991. Impact: An interactive Natural-motion-picture Dedicated Multimedia Authoring System. In Proceedings of INTERCHI, 343-350. New York: ACM.

Vanoye, F. and Goliot-Lété, A. 1992. *Précis d'analyse Filmique*. Paris: Nathan.

Villain, D. 1991. *Le Montage au Cinéma*. Collection Essais. Paris: Cahiers du Cinéma.

Yeung, M. M.; Yeo, B.L.; Wolf, W.; and Liu, B. 1995. Video Browsing using Clustering and Scene Transitions on Compressed Sequences. In Proceedings of IS&T SPIE'95 Multimedia Computing and Networking. 2417: 399-413, San Jose, CA. February.

Zhang, H.J.; Kankanhalli, A.; and Smoliar, S. 1993. Automatic Partitioning of Full-Motion Video. *Multimedia Systems* 1(1): 1-28.

Zhang, H.J.; Gong, Y.; and Smoliar, S. 1994. Automatic Parsing of News Video. In Proceedings of IEEE Conference on Multimedia Computing and Systems, 45-54. May 14-19 Boston, MA.

Zhang, H.J.; Smoliar, S. W.; and Wu, J. H. 1995a. Content-Based Video Browsing Tools. In Proceedings of the IS&T/SPIE'95 Multimedia Computing and Networking, 2417: 389-398. San Jose, CA. February.

Zhang, H.J.; Tan, S. Y.; Smoliar, S. W; and Yihong, G. 1995b. Automatic Parsing and Indexing of News Video. *Multimedia Systems* 2(6): 256-265.

Chapter 9

Machine Understanding of Human Behavior in Video

Alex Pentland, Perceptual Computing Section,
The Media Laboratory, Massachusetts Institute of Technology

Abstract

This chapter describes progress toward building computer systems that can analyze and understand human behavior using video information. I will describe methods for 3-D tracking of heads, hands, and feet, recognition of hand and body gestures, face recognition, and interpretation of facial expression.

1. Introduction

During the last few years research on the topic of image databases has blossomed. The key conceptual breakthough was the idea of content-based indexing, allowing images and audio to be searched directly rather than relying on keyword annotation. Pioneering efforts such as the IBM Query-By-Image-Content (Faloutsos et al. 1994; Flickner et al.,this volume) system, the ISS system developed in Singapore (Smoliar and Zhang 1994; Zhang et al.,this volume), and my Photobook project (Pentland et al. 1994, 1996) demonstrated that such search was both possible and useful, and the idea has since been the topic of dozens of workshops and special journal issues. There has also been some commercial success with this technology. Much of the QBIC and Photobook technology are now available in the IBM Ultimedia Manager system (http://www.ibm.com) and the Virage Engine (http://www.virage.com). Consequently content-based indexing is now widely available on a variety of platforms and as an option within several traditional database systems.

The one area which has most noticeably lagged behind, however, is related to human behavior in video. Most video is about people, and the identity and behavior of the people in the video are the most important element of the video's content. I believe that the correct way to approach the problem of understanding human behavior in video is to focus on answering questions such as who, what, when, where, and why, just as writers are taught to do. The answer to these questions allow one to classify the current situation. Once a computer has the ability to know who, what, when, where, and why, then simple statistical learning methods are probably sufficient for the computer to determine what aspects of the situation are significant, and to answer a wide variety of useful questions (Bajcsy 1988, Barwise and Perry 1986).

In the following sections of this chapter I will describe how standard 2-D processing modules (Ballard and Brown 1982, Rosenfeld 1969) can be extended to obtain building blocks to answer the "wwwww" questions. Although the building blocks described here are limited in comparison to human abilities, and only cover a scattering of human behavior, I believe that they are the first steps down a path to a fairly general ability to interpret human behavior as seen in video data.

Because of the broad scope of the work I will cover in this chapter, I do not have the space to also fully describe related research or to present all of the technical details. Readers are referred to the other papers in this book, and to our referenced papers, for such information.

1.1 The Modeling and Estimation Framework

The general theoretical approach I have taken is maximum *a posteriori* (MAP) interpretation on very low-level, 2-D representations of regions of the image data. The appearance of a target class Ω, e.g., the probability distribution function $P(x|\Omega)$ of its image-level features $\mathbf{x}$, can be characterized by use of a low-dimensional parametric appearance model. Once such a probability distribution function (PDF) has been learned, it is straightforward to use it in a MAP estimator in order to detect and recognize target classes. This is the same approach as used in the Photobook system. Behavior recognition is accomplished in a similar manner; these parametric appearance models are tracked over time, and their time evolution $P(\mathbf{x}(t)|\Omega)$ characterized probabilistically to obtain a *spatiotemporal behavior model*. Incoming spatiotemporal data can then be compared to the spatiotemporal PDF of each of the various behavior models using elastic matching methods such as dynamic time warping (Darrell and Pentland 1993) or hidden Markov modeling (Starner and Pentland 1995).

The use of parametric appearance models to characterize the PDF of an object's appearance in the image is related to the idea of view-based representation, as advocated by Ullman and Basri (1991) and Poggio and Edelman (1990). As originally developed, the idea of view-based recognition was to accurately describe the spatial structure of the target object by interpolating between various views. However in order to describe natural objects such as faces or hands, I have found it necessary to extend the notion of "view" to include characterizing the range of geometric and feature variation, as well as the likelihood associated with such variation.

This approach is typified by my face recognition research (Turk and Pentland 1991, Moghaddam and Pentland 1995), which uses linear combinations of eigenvectors to describe a *space* of target appearances, and then characterize the PDF of the targets appearance within that space. This method has been shown to be very powerful for detection and recognition of human faces, hands, and facial expressions (Moghaddam and Pentland 1995). Other researchers have used extensions of this basic method to recognize industrial objects and household items (Murase and Nayar 1994). Another variation on this approach is to use linear combinations of examples rather than eigenvectors; this type of appearance modeling has demonstrated a power similar to that of the eigenvector-based methods (Darrell and Pentland 1993, Jones and Poggio 1995), although it necessarily has a lower efficiency.

1.2 The Computer Architecture

Sensing and interpretation of human movement is accomplished by a modular computer architecture, which can be configured in a variety of ways, as more or less interpretation capability is required. The basic element is an SGI Indy computer; these computers are connected by video, audio, and ethernet networks. This allows each computer to independently access whatever portion of the audiovisual input it needs, to share control information among the other computers. Normally each computer is dedicated to perform only one type of interpretation. For instance, if video tracking, audio input, and gesture interpretation capabilities were desired, then three computers would be used, one for each task.

2. Building Blocks

The following sections will briefly describe each of a set of programs that can find, track, and interpret human behavior (Pentland 1996). In order of description, the modules are:

- Pfinder, a real-time program that tracks the user, and recognizes a basic set of hand gestures and body postures
- The face processor, an interactive-time program that recognizes human faces

- The expression processor, an interactive-time program that uses motion-energy templates to classify people's facial expressions
- Behavior recognition, real-time systems that examine users' movements in order to determine what they are doing

For additional detail the reader should examine the numerous papers, technical reports, interactive demos, and computer code available at our web site.[1]

2.1 Pfinder

Pfinder ("person finder") is a real-time system for tracking and interpretation of people. It runs at 10Hz on a standard SGI Indy computer, and has performed reliably on thousands of people in many different physical locations (Azarbayejani et al. 1996, Maes et al. 1995, Pentland 1996, Wren et al. 1995). The system uses a multi-class statistical model of color and shape to segment a person from a background scene, and then to find and track people's head and hands in a wide range of viewing conditions. It incorporates *a priori* knowledge about people primarily to bootstrap itself and to recover from errors.

In order to present a concise description of Pfinder, I will only describe its representations and operation in the "steady state" case, where it is tracking a person moving around an office environment, neglecting the problems of initially learning a person's description.

2.1.1 Modeling The Person. Pfinder models the human as a connected set of 2-D *blobs,* a representation originally developed (Pentland 1976) for application to multi-spectral satellite (MSS) imagery. The PDF of each blob is characterized by the *joint* distribution of spatial (x,y) and color features. Color is expressed in the YUV space, which is a simple approximation to human color sensitivity.

We define $\mathbf{m}_k$ to be the mean (x, y, Y, U, V) of blob k, and $\mathbf{K}_k$ to be the covariance of that blob's distribution. The mean of a blob expresses the concept "color a at location b," while the covariance expresses how the color and brightness of the blob changes across its surface. For instance, the blob statistics can express that one side is brighter than the other (perhaps due to illumination from the side), or that the color changes from top to bottom (perhaps due to light reflected from the floor).

Each blob also has associated with it a *support map* that indicates exactly which image pixels are members of a particular blob. Since the individual support maps indicate which image pixels are members of that particular blob, the aggregate support map $s(x, y)$ over all the blobs represents the segmentation of the image into spatial/color classes.

In video data, the statistics of each blob are recursively updated to combine information contained in previous video frames with measurements obtained from the current image. Because the detailed dynamics of each blob are unknown, we use approximate models derived from experience with a wide range of users. For instance, blobs that are near the center of mass have substantial inertia, whereas blobs toward the extremities can move much faster.

2.1.2 Modeling The Scene. It is assumed that the majority of the time Pfinder will be processing a scene that consists of a relatively static situation such as an office, and a single moving person. Consequently, it is appropriate to use different types of model for the scene and for the person.

The surrounding scene is modeled as a texture surface, as in QuickTime VR. However each point on this texture surface has associated with it both a mean color value and a distribution about that mean. The color distribution of each pixel is modeled by a Gaussian distribution with a full covariance matrix. Thus, for instance, a fluttering white curtain in front of a black wall will have a color covariance that is very elongated in the luminance direction, but narrow in the chrominance directions. In each frame visible pixels have their statistics recursively updated using a simple adaptive filter. This allows us to compensate for changes in lighting and even for object movement. For instance, if a person moves a book it causes the texture map to change in both the locations where the book was, and where it now is. By tracking the person we can know that these areas, although changed, are still part of the texture model and thus update their statistics to the new value. The updating process is done recursively, and even large changes in illumination can be substantially compensated within two or three seconds.

2.1.3 The Steady-State Analysis Loop. Given a person model and a scene model, Pfinder then acquires a new image, interprets it, and updates the scene and person models. To accomplish this there are several steps:

1. First, predict the appearance of the person in the new image using the current state of our model. This is accomplished using a set of Kalman filters with simple Newtonian dynamics that operate on each blob's spatial statistics.

2. Next, for each image pixel, measure the likelihood that it is a member of each of the blob models and the scene model. Self-shadowing and cast shadows are a particular difficulty in measuring this likelihood; this is addressed by normalizing the hue and saturation by the overall brightness.

3. Resolve these pixel-by-pixel likelihoods into a support map, indicating for each pixel whether it is part of one of the blobs or of the background scene. Spatial priors and connectivity constraints are used to accomplish this resolution.

4. Update the statistical models for each blob and for the background scene; also update the dynamic models of the blobs.

Figure 1. Analysis of a person in video data.
The frame on the left is the video input (n.b. color image shown here in black and white for printing purposes), the center frame shows the support map s(x,y) which segments the person into blobs, and the frame on the right showing a person model reconstructed from blob statistics alone (with contour shape ignored).

For some applications Pfinder's 2-D information must be processed to recover 3-D geometry. For a single calibrated camera this can be accomplished by backprojecting the 2-D image information to produce 3-D position estimates using the assumption that the person is standing on a planar floor. When two or more cameras are available, the hand, head, etc., blobs can be matched to obtain 3-D estimates via triangulation.

Figure 1 illustrates Pfinder's operation. At the left is the original video frame (shown in black and white rather than the original color). In the middle is the resulting segmentation into head, hands, feet, shirt, and pants. At the right are one-standard-deviation ellipses illustrating the statistical blob descriptions formed for the head, hands, feet, shirt, and pants. Note that despite having the hands either in front of the face or the body a correct description is still obtained. For additional detail see references (Azarbayejani et al. 1996, Wren et al. 1995, Pentland 1996).

2.2 Face Recognition

Once the rough location of the person's head is known, one can attempt to recognize their face. As with Pfinder, a maximum *a posteriori* (MAP) approach is applied to this problem. This has been accomplished by developing a method for determining the probability distribution function for face images within a low-dimensional eigenspace. Knowledge of this distribution then allows the face and face features to be precisely located, and compared along meaningful dimensions. The following gives a brief description of this system; for additional detail see (Moghaddam and Pentland 1995).

2.2.1 Face and Feature Detection. The standard detection paradigm in image processing is that of normalized correlation or template matching. However this approach is only optimal in the simplistic case of a *determinis-*

tic signal embedded in white Gaussian noise. When we begin to consider a target *class* detection problem—*e.g*, finding a generic human face or a human hand in a scene—we must incorporate the underlying probability distribution of the object of interest. Subspace or eigenspace methods, such as the KLT and PCA, are particularly well-suited to such a task.

In particular, the eigenspace formulation leads to a powerful alternative to standard detection techniques such as template matching or normalized correlation. The reconstruction error (or residual) of the KLT expansion is an effective indicator of a match. The residual error is easily computed using the projection coefficients and the original signal energy. This detection strategy is equivalent to matching with a linear combination of *eigentemplates* and allows for a greater range of distortions in the input signal (including lighting, and moderate rotation and scale). Some of the low-order eigentemplates for a human face are shown in figure 3a. In a statistical signal detection framework, the use of eigentemplates has been shown to be orders of magnitude better than standard matched filtering (Moghaddam and Pentland 1995).

Using this approach the target detection problem can be reformulated from the point of view of a MAP estimation problem. In particular, given the visual field, estimate the position (and scale) of the subimage which is most representative of a specific target class Ω. Computationally this is achieved by sliding an *m*-by-*n* observation window throughout the image and at each location computing the *likelihood* that the given observation $\mathbf{x}$ is an instance of the target class Ω—*i.e*, $P(\mathbf{x}|\Omega)$. After this probability map is computed, the location corresponding to the highest likelihood can be selected as the MAP estimate of the target location.

2.2.2 The Face Processor. This MAP-based face finder has been employed as the basic building block of an automatic face recognition system. The function of the face finder is to very precisely locate the face, since Pfinder produces only low-resolution estimates of head location. The block diagram of the face finder system is shown in figure 2; it consists of a two-stage object detection and alignment stage, a contrast normalization stage, a feature extraction stage, followed by recognition (and, optionally, facial coding.) Figure 2b-e illustrates the operation of the detection and alignment stage on a natural image containing a human face.

The first step in this process is illustrated in figure 2c where the MAP estimate of the position and scale of the face are indicated by the cross-hairs and bounding box. Once these regions have been identified, the estimated scale and position are used to normalize for translation and scale, yielding a standard "head-in-the-box" format image (figure 2d). A second feature detection stage operates at this fixed scale to estimate the position of 4 facial features: the left and right eyes, the tip of the nose and the center of the mouth (figure 2e). Once the facial features have been detected, the face image is warped to

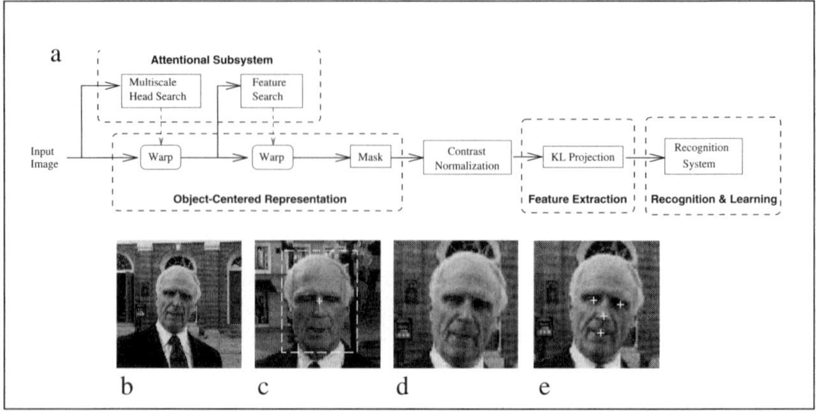

Figure 2. (a) The face processing system, (b) original image, (c) position and scale estimate, (d) normalized head image, (e) position of facial features.

align the geometry and shape of the face with that of a canonical model. Then the facial region is extracted (by applying a fixed mask) and subsequently normalized for contrast. This geometrically aligned and normalized image is then projected onto the set of eigenfaces shown in figure 3a.

The projection coefficients obtained by comparison of the normalized face and the eigenfaces form a feature vector which accurately describes the appearance of the face. This feature vector can therefore be used for facial recognition, as well as for facial image coding. Figure 3b shows a typical result when using the eigenface feature vector for face recognition. The image in the upper left is the one to be recognized and the remainder are the most similar faces in the database (ranked by facial similarity, left to right, top to bottom). The top three matches in this case are images of the same person taken a month apart and at different scales. Typical recognition accuracies are near 100%, even for large databases.

2.3 Expression Recognition

Once the face and its features have been accurately located, one can begin to analyze its motion to determine the facial expression. This can be done by using spatio-temporal motion-energy templates of the whole face (Essa and Pentland 1994, 1995). For each facial expression, the corresponding template expresses the *peak amount* and *direction* of motion that one would expect to see at each point on the face. Figures 4a–4d show Irfan Essa making two expressions (surprise and smile) and the corresponding motion-energy template descriptions. Figures 4a and 4c show expressions of smile and surprise, and 4b and 4d show the corresponding spatio-temporal motion energy pattern. Figures 4e – 4i show spatio-temporal motion-energy templates for various expressions.

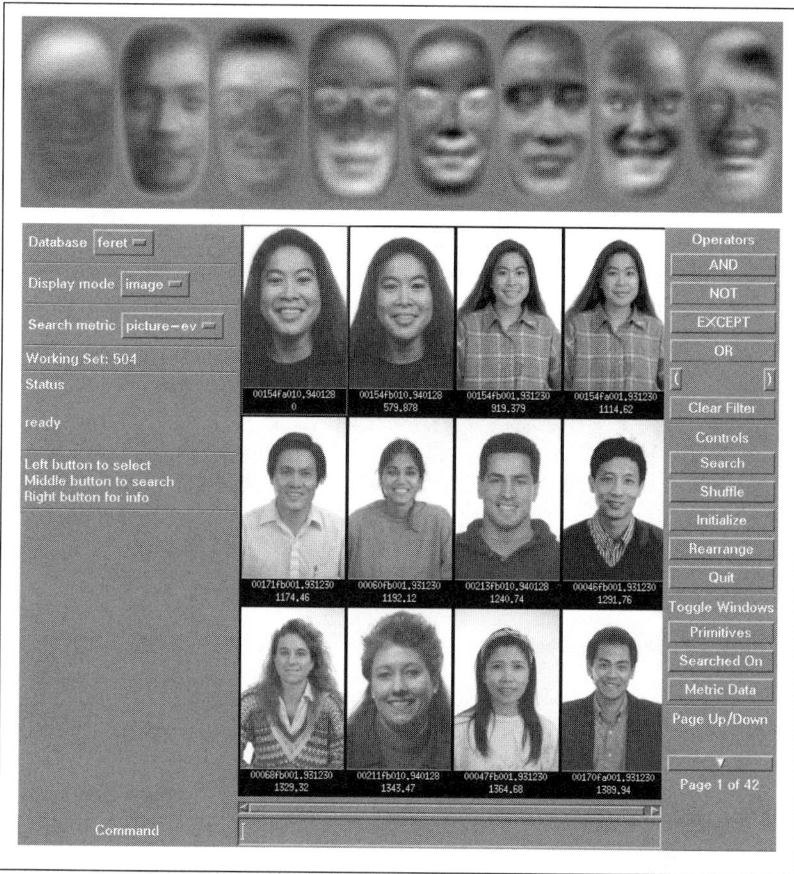

Figure 3. (a—top) The First 8 Eigenfaces. (b—bottom) Searching for similar faces in a database, using the photobook image database tool (Pentland et al. 1996).

These simple, biologically plausible motion energy "templates" can be used for expression recognition by comparing the motion-energy observed for a particular face to the "average" template for each expression. Figures 4e – 4i show the motion-energy templates for several expressions. To classify an expression one compares the observed facial motion energy with each of these motion energy templates, and then picks the expression with the most similar pattern of motion. This method of expression recognition has been applied to a database of 52 image sequences of 8 subjects making various expressions. In each image sequence the motion energy was measured, compared to each of the templates, and the expression classified, generating the confusion matrix shown in Table 1. This table shows just one incorrect

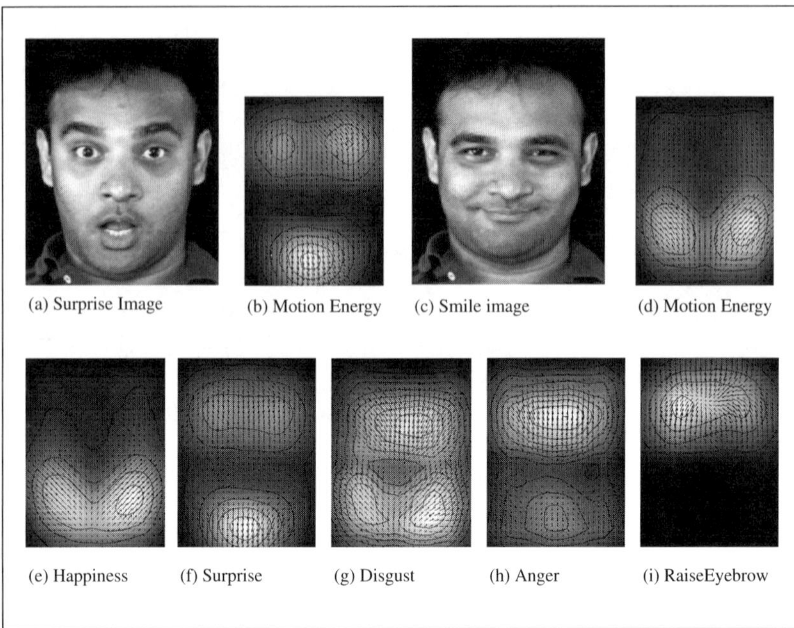

Figure 4. Determining expressions from video sequences.

classification, giving an overall recognition rate of 98.0%. For additional details see references (Essa and Pentland 1994, 1995).

2.4 Recognizing Human Behaviors

Work on recognizing body position, face, and expression are only the first steps toward understanding human behavior. To make computers really useful, these basic perceptual functions need to be integrated with higher-level models of human behavior, so that we can begin to understand what the person is *doing*.

A general approach to interpreting human behavior is to directly extend the MAP techniques used for recognition of face, expression, and body pose. That is, to track the 2-D parametric appearance models over time, and then probabilistically characterize the time evolution of their parameters. This approach produces the PDF of the behavior as both a function of time and 2-D appearance. Behaviors can then be recognized by comparing them to these learned models using MAP methods. To obtain high-accuracy behavior recognition, one must use an elastic spatio-temporal matching technique such as dynamic time warping (Darrell and Pentland 1993) or hidden Markov modeling (Starner and Pentland 1995).

To recognize particular gestures or behaviors, for instance, the person is

Expressions	Smile	Surprise	Anger	Disgust	Raise Brow
Template					
Smile	12	0	0	0	0
Surprise	0	10	0	0	0
Anger	0	0	9	0	0
Disgust	0	0	1	10	0
Raise Brow	0	0	0	0	8
Success	100%	100%	100%	100%	100%

Table 1. Results of facial expression recognition using spatio-temporal motion energy templates. This result is on based on 12 image sequences of smile, 10 image sequences of surprise, anger, disgust, and raise eyebrow. Success rate for each expression is shown in the bottom row. Overall recognition rate is 98.0%.

modeled as a Markov device, with internal mental states that have their own particular distribution of appearance and inter-state transition probabilities. Because the internal states of a human are not directly observable, they must be determined through an indirect estimation process, using the person's movement and vocalizations as measurements. One efficient and robust method of accomplishing this is to use the Viterbi recognition methods developed for use with Hidden Markov Models (HMMs).

This general approach is similar to that taken by the speech recognition community. The difference is that here internal state is not thought of as being just words or sentences; the internal states can also be actions or intentions. Moreover, the input is not just audio filter banks but can also include facial appearance, body movement, and vocal characteristics such as pitch to infer the user's internal state. Two good example applications that employ this approach to behavior recognition are reading American Sign Language (ASL) (Starner and Pentland 1995), and interpreting automobile driver's behavior (Pentland and Liu 1995).

The ASL reader is a real-time system that performs high accuracy classification of a forty-word subset of ASL using only the hand measurements provided by Pfinder (e.g., hand position, orientation, and width/height ratio). Thad Starner is shown using this system in figure 5a. The accurate classification performance of this system is particularly impressive because

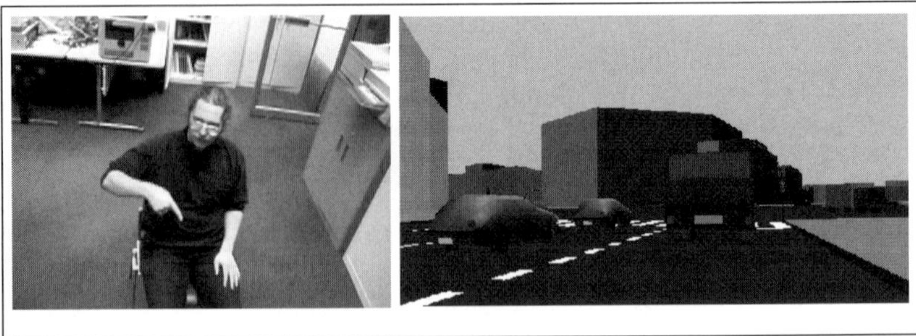

Figure 5a—left: Real-time reading of American sign language
(with Thad Starner doing the signing).
Figure 5b—right: Real-time classification of driver's actions in a driving simulator.

in ASL the hand movements are rapid and continuous, and exhibit large coarticulation effect.

The second system interprets people's actions while driving a car (Pentland and Liu 1995). In this system the driver's hand and leg motions were observed while driving in the Nissan Cambridge Basic Research Lab's driving simulator (see figure 5b). These observations are used to classify the driver's action as quickly as possible. Note that it is possible to estimate the same underlying variables (steering and acceleration) from the trajectory of the car, making possible classification of driver behavior from video of the car on the roadway. The goal is to develop safer cars by knowing what action the driver is beginning to execute, and responding appropriately.

This system is very accurate at identifying which driving maneuver the driver is beginning to execute (e.g., passing, turning, stopping, or lane changing). A recognition accuracy of 95.24 $\pm$3.1 % was obtained at 0.5 seconds after of the beginning each maneuver ... long before the major, functional parts of the maneuver were executed. This experiment shows that driver's execute *preparatory* movements that are reliable indicators of which maneuver they are beginning to execute, and that we can use hidden Markov models to quickly recognize and classify these driving maneuvers.

3. Conclusion

I have argued that understanding human behavior in video primarily requires the ability to correctly classify the situation, and that normally relatively little more is required to determine which elements are important, or to answer user's questions about the video's content.

To explore this idea, I have focused on answering the who, what, where, when, and why questions with respect to human behavior. By developing computer vision tools that answer these questions, and coupling them to a simple interpretation rules, it has proven possible to obtain real-time interpretation of simple human behaviors in office-like environments and in automobiles.

Although the interpretation tools we have developed do not have human-level performance or breadth, they have proven to be both useful and reliable enough for video interpretation applications such as human-computer interfaces and video security monitoring. These results are encouraging enough for me to believe that in the near future similar methods will be able to interpret human behavior in more complex environments, such as stores, city streets, and business meetings.

Acknowledgments

This research was supported by ONR, ARL, and ARPA under the MURI and FERET contracts, and by BT (British Telecom) and Texas Instruments. Portions of an earlier version of this chapter appeared in *Scientific American* 274(4) and were presented at the Image Understanding Workshop.

Note

1. Papers and technical reports on all aspects of this technology are available at http://www-white.media.mit.edu/vismod or by anonymous FTP from whitechapel.media.mit.edu.

Bibliography

Azarbayejani, A.; Wren, C.; and Pentland, A. 1996. Real-Time 3-D Tracking of the Human Body. ImageCom 96, 20-22. Bordeaux, France. Also, see Technical Report 374.

Bajcsy, R. 1988. Active Perception, *Proceedings IEEE* 76(8): 996-1005.

Ballard, D. and Brown, C. 1983 *Computer Vision*. Englewood: Prentice-Hall

Barwise, J. and Perry, J. 1986. *Situation Semantics*. Cambridge, MA: MIT Press.

Darrell, T. and Pentland, A. 1993. Space-Time Gestures. In IEEE Conference on Vision and Pattern Recognition, 335 340. New York, NY: IEEE. June.

Essa, I. and Pentland, A. 1994. A Vision System for Observing and.Extracting Facial Action Parameters, IEEE Conference on Computer Vision and Pattern Recognition, 76-83, Seattle, WA., June 1994.

Essa, I. and Pentland, A. 1995. Facial Expression Recognition Using a Dynamic Model and Motion Energy. In International Conference on Computer Vision, 360-367. Cambridge, MA, June 20-23 1995. IEEE Press.

Faloutsos, C.; Barber, R.; Flickner, M.; Hafner, J.; Niblack, W.; Petkovic, D.; and Equitz, W. 1994. Efficient and Effective Querying by Image Content. *Journal of Intelligent Information Systems* 1(3): 231–262.

Flickner, M.; Sawhney, H.; Niblack, W.; Ashley, J.; Huang, Q.; Dom, B.; Gorkani, M.; Hafner, J.; Lee, D.; Petkovic, D.; Steele, D.; and Yanker, P. Query by Image and

Video Content: The QBIC System. In this volume.

Jones, M. and Poggio, T. 1995. Model-Based Matching of Line Drawings by Linear Combinations of Prototypes. International Conference on Computer Vision, 531-536. Cambridge, MA, June 20-23 1995. IEEE Press.

Maes P. 1991. *Designing Autonomous Agents: Theory and Practice from Biology to Engineering and Back.*, ed. Maes, Cambridge, MA: Bradford Books/MIT Press.

Maes, P.; Blumburg, B.; Darrell, T.; and Pentland, A., 1995. The ALIVE System: Full-body Interaction with Autonomous Agents. In Proceedings of Computer Animation 95, 102-110. Geneva, Switzerland, May 24. IEEE Press.

Moghaddam, B. and Pentland, A. 1995. Probabalistic Visual Learning for Object Detection. International Conference on Computer Vision, 786-793. Cambridge, MA, June 20-23. IEEE Press.

Murase, H. and Nayar, S., 1994. Visual Learning and Recognition of 3-D Objects from Appearance. *International Journal of Computer Vision* 14(1): 5-24.

Pentland, A. 1976. Classification By Clustering. In Proceedings of the Symposium On Machine Processing Of Remotely Sensed Data, 101-103. June 1976, IEEE Computer Society Press No. 76.

Pentland, A. and Liu, A., 1995. Toward Augmented Control Systems. In Proceedings of IEEE Intelligent Vehicle Symposium '95, 350-355. September 25-26, Detroit, MI.

Pentland, A.; Picard, R.; Davenport, G.; and Haase, K. 1994. Video and Image Semantics: Advanced Tools for Telecommunications. *IEEE Multimedia* 1(2): 73-75.

Pentland, A.; Picard, R.; and Sclaroff, S. 1996. Photobook: Tools for Content-Based Manipulation of Image Databases. *International Journal of Computer Vision* 18(3):233-154.

Pentland, A. 1996. Smart Rooms, Smart Clothes. *Scientific American* 274(4): 68-76. April.

Poggio, T. and Edelman, S. 1990. A Network that Learns to Recognize Three-dimensional Objects. *Nature* (343):263-266.

Rosenfeld, A. 1969. *Picture Processing by Computer*. New York, New York: Academic Press.

Smoliar, S. and Zhang, H. 1994. Content-Based Video Indexing and Retrieval. *IEEE Multimedia* 1(1): 62–72.

Turk, M. and Pentland, A. 1991. Eigenfaces for Recognition. *Journal of Cognitive Neuroscience* 3(1): 71–86.

Starner, T. and Pentland, A. 1995. Visual Recognition of American Sign Language Using Hidden Markov Models. In Proceedings of the International Workshop on Automatic Face- and Gesture-Recognition, 189-154. Zurich, Switzerland: University of Zurich MultiMedia Laboratory, June 26-28.

Ullman, S.; and Basri, R., 1991. Recognition by Linear Combinations of Models, IEEE Trans. Pattern Analysis and Machine Vision, 13:992-1006.

Wren, C.; Azarbayejani, A.; Darrell, T.; and Pentland, A., 1995. Pfinder: Real-Time Tracking of the Human Body," SPIE Conference on Real-Time Image Processing, Philadelphia, PA.

Zhang, H. J.; Low, C. Y.; Smoliar, S.; and JianHua Wu, J.H. 1997. Video Parsing, Retrieval and Browsing: An Integrated and Content-Based Solution. In this volume.

Speech and Language Processing for Video Retrieval

Video is a complex artifact including coordinated streams of imagery, audio and sometimes text. The chapters in this section specifically focus on processing the linguistic (spoken and written) channels of video, in some cases in addition to image processing, in order to index video to support content-based browsing and search. The first two chapters focus primarily on speech processing, the last two on (closed caption) language processing.

In the first chapter, Gareth Jones, Jonathan Foote, Karen Sparck Jones, and Steve Young (Cambridge University, England) summarize the Video Mail Retrieval (VMR) project which aims to develop spoken document retrieval. By marrying speech recognition with information retrieval, the authors draw from the wealth of research in these two fields, including such important ideas as corpus-based training and evaluation using precision and recall metrics. The authors present a comparative evaluation of speech and text retrieval. Using standard information retrieval evaluation techniques, their speaker-dependent techniques retain approximately 95% of the performance of retrieval of text transcripts, speaker independent techniques about 75%. As the authors discuss, system scalability remains a significant challenge. For example, whereas even the best speech recognition systems have on the order of 100,000 words in an electronic lexicon, text lexicons include upwards of 500,0000 vocabulary words. Another significant challenge was that this project, like many others, had no annotated video mail corpus that could be utilized to benchmark results and had to engage the expensive and time consuming process of developing such a corpus to support evaluation.

Alex Hauptmann and Michael Witbrock (Carnegie Mellon University) also investigate large vocabulary, continuous speaker independent broadcast news transcription in the second chapter. They describe their video library creation and exploration system, Informedia^{TM}. As in Aigraine et al.'s approach in the previous section, Informedia exploits multiple streams of information from the video (imagery, audio, text transcripts) to index the material, transcribing spoken language audio using CMU's Sphynx-II system. This enables a user to use spoken language query (e.g., "Tell me what's happening with White Water" which results in a list of hits from broadcast news video (e.g., ABC, McNeil-Lehrer News Hour), which is followed by a "video paragraph" presentation. The authors claim that even with transcription error rates of 60%, there remains sufficient material to support effective indexing, which is based on word frequencies. Image processing includes the use of optical vector flow analysis to detect edit classes and camera motion (e.g., pan, zoom), resulting in 95% shot detection accuracy. Results of individual streams are then integrated (e.g., correlating low signal to noise ratio areas with detected shots).

The last two chapters in this section assume a linguistic source (e.g., transcribed speech, closed captions), and turn to the issue of segmenting and clustering topics or stories within broadcast news to support content based news browsing. Inderjeet Mani, David House, Mark Maybury, and Morgan Green (The MITRE Corporation) report methods that detect, segment, and label stories in broadcast news to support content based browsing of sources such as CNN Prime News, ABC World News, and the Jim Lehrer News Hour. They compare two language processing methods — discourse cues and thesaurus-based subject classification — and measure their performance using modified information retrieval metrics of precision and recall, reporting segmentation accuracy above 90% for several sources. They measure how information from other channels (e.g., classification of speakers using speaker identification techniques) can improve topic segmentation performance. In subsequent work (Maybury et al. 1997), multichannel processing is reported which improves segmentation performance by exploiting cross channel redundancy.

Atsushi Takeshita, Takafumi Inoue, and Kazuo Tanaka (NTT Human Interface Lab) similarly aim to provide topic structured access to video. They report language processing algorithms which exploit both discourse markers (e.g., topic markers such as "ni tsuite" (with regard to) and "wa" (as for)) and lexical distributions to create hierarchical topic structures, called "semantic based skim structures." Using these language processing methods, they report 60% accuracy in topic classification. Moreover, by exploiting these topic structures to index into selected video keyframes, they report a 36% reduction in keyframes selected for inclusion in multimedia summaries over cut-detection based video keyframe extraction. Results were nearly equivalent when compared to human performance. The efforts in this section, particularly those in which machine learning is applied, yield the requirement for video corpora and associated metrics and methods which can be used to test and evaluate progress.

Chapter 10

The Video Mail Retrieval Project: Experiences in Retrieving Spoken Documents

Gareth Jones, Jonathan Foote, Karen Spärck Jones, and Steve Young, University of Cambridge

Abstract

This chapter outlines the Video Mail Retrieval (VMR) project at Cambridge University. The goal of the VMR project is to develop an application for the retrieval of spoken documents in multimedia systems. Spoken documents pose a particular problem for retrieval since the contents are unknown. The VMR project seeks to address this problem by combining state-of-the-art speech recognition with established document retrieval technologies to provide an effective and efficient retrieval tool. Experimental results with a small spoken message collection show that retrieval precision is somewhat dependent on the generality of the acoustic modeling used. For speaker-dependent acoustic modeling retrieval performance is around 95% of that observed when text transcriptions of the same files are used. However, even with incorporation of completely open-user speaker-independent acoustic models, retrieval performance of about 75% of text can be obtained.

1. Introduction

This chapter discusses work to date on the Video Mail Retrieval (VMR) project at Cambridge University. Our objective is to develop a novel multimedia application for the retrieval of spoken documents. The project seeks to combine state-of-the-art speech recognition and document retrieval technologies for spoken message retrieval, envisaged as one function among many provided on a workstation equipped with multimedia video facilities.

The work described here focuses on analysis of the audio stream since this is where nearly all information of practical interest is found in our application. In the video mail environment the vast majority of messages are just "talking head" images from a small pool of users viewed against static backgrounds. While image analysis may be employed to identify the speaker, this can also be inferred from the audio stream or most easily from the text header of the mail message. Messages are typically short and on an individual topic, thus complex topic segmentation algorithms are not required and the retrieval documents are the individual messages.

The chapter outlines the problems involved in retrieval of video mail, specific strategies being deployed to overcome these, the current system implementation, and the design and results of our retrieval tests to date. We demonstrate that the straightforward probabilistic methods established for text retrieval can be naturally extended to the speech domain; and also that current speech recognition technology can support good message retrieval performance.

Section 2 presents background details of the VMR project: to provide a context for the subsequent discussion of the distinctive problems to be overcome in speech retrieval, and to motivate our own approach. Section 3 describes the specific objectives of the VMR project and outlines the project strategy, and section 4 considers problems encountered in spoken document retrieval. Details of our experimental investigations to date are given in section 5. Finally, section 6 comments on our work to date and summaries our planned future research.

2. Background

Recent years have seen a rapid expansion in the availability of multimedia applications, including video conferencing, and video and audio mail. Using these systems can create large archives of material which can pose significant problems since the data is expensive to store and unwieldy to access. A particular problem is that users are unable to find particular stored documents since, unlike text, there is no simple content-based way to search for an individual reference. Manual search of an archive by listening is significantly more time consuming than a similar search of a text archive since audio browsing is much less efficient than visual browsing.

Little work has been reported in the area of spoken document retrieval. Schäuble and others (Glavitsch et al. 1994) have proposed a system for spoken document retrieval based on predefined acoustic units, and have considered the effect of term occurrence errors of semantic and acoustic origin, but only by simulation. Their most recent work has included some real speech document retrieval results (Wechsler and Schäuble 1995). However, there are significant differences between this work and that reported here and hence it cannot be compared directly.

The VMR project is addressing these problems in multimedia retrieval and browsing by developing a system to retrieve stored video mail messages using voice indexing. A specific goal of the project is to develop a useful retrieval application for the Medusa multimedia environment installed at Olivetti Research Ltd in Cambridge (Wray et al. 1994).

3. VMR Project Objectives and Strategy

The VMR project goals should be evident from the preceding sections. The primary research issue is how to integrate text retrieval methods with automated speech recognition technology. However, the final objective is to develop a practical spoken document retrieval system for the ORL Medusa environment. A usable tool must rapidly provide robust high retrieval performance using a practical amount of computation and storage. Because speech recognition is computationally expensive, the only practical way to achieve this is to index spoken documents at the time they are added to the archive. To retrieve documents, the pre-computed indexes can then be rapidly searched to find potentially relevant documents. Identifying potentially relevant documents is only part of the solution; the user must be able to select and play back any desired document. Since audio and video consume orders of magnitude more storage than text, this is a non-trivial problem in itself. Further, it is inefficient to play back entire documents when just a small portion is of interest. A truly useful retrieval application should give the user the ability to identify and play back potentially interesting portions of individual messages. Finally, a useful application should be well-integrated into the environment in which it is to be used, in our case Medusa.

3.1 Project Strategy

The VMR project has three phases that encompass progressively less restricted and more realistic conditions for spoken document retrieval. In Stages 1 and 2 (the work reported here) searching depends only on a fixed keyword vocabulary, known in advance of search time. Stage 1 assumed a closed speaker community responsible for all messages. Speech recognition was restricted to locating instances of the fixed keyword set in acoustically clean speech from a known speaker from a set of 15 speakers. In addition, all speakers provided sufficient examples of their speech so that specialized models could be built. Though this is clearly unrealistic in the long run, it did provide a benchmark for performance in later, less favorable conditions.

Stage 2 relaxed the requirement that the speaker's identity be known in advance. In addition, more sophisticated retrieval strategies were implemented and additional evaluation material used.

Key results from Stages 1 and 2 are described later in this chapter. An obvious drawback of this approach is that the fixed keyword must be know in advance of recognition. Further, since speech recognition is a computationally expensive task requiring on the order of real-time response, it must be done in advance of retrieval. Hence the indexing vocabulary must be specified before retrieval as well. Stage 3 of the VMR project, where research is ongoing, extends the search term vocabulary from the small set of known keywords to a potentially open search term vocabulary.

An integral part of each stage is the development of the general user interface and ultimately the integration into the ORL Medusa system.

4. Problems in Spoken Document Retrieval

In this section we consider problems encountered in spoken document retrieval.

4.1 Speech Document Indexing Issues

Attempts to retrieve spoken documents encounter similar problems to those associated with text document retrieval but there are further important issues which must be considered. Most obvious among these is that the contents of spoken documents are unknown and hence the initial phase must perform an indexing operation using speech recognition. This speech recognition phase may be carried out in one of two basic ways. Either the speech recognition system may attempt to perform a full transcription of the contents of the documents using a large vocabulary recognizer or recognition may be restricted to a limited and, hopefully, useful set of indexing terms (or *keywords*) selected *a priori*. The recognition used in the Stages 1 and 2 of the VMR project is of the second type. In both of these approaches the indexing vocabulary is limited to that of the recognizer. Large vocabulary systems are now available with vocabularies approaching 100,000 words but this should be compared to the 500,000 word vocabularies encountered in text retrieval systems. Many words, particularly proper nouns, cannot be recognized correctly by either recognition system since they are outside the domain of its vocabulary. This creates a significant search problem which does not exist in text based systems where new document terms are merely added into the inverted file structure.

Additionally, speech recognition is inherently not completely reliable. Even the very best systems will make recognition errors often arising from variable pronunciation or events outside its domain. The recognizer typically maps out-of-vocabulary words to something in its existing vocabulary, which will inevitably result in a recognition error. Short words are more susceptible to recognition errors than longer ones, both because of their inherent greater confusability and the greater tendency to poor articulation. Actual recognition performance is dependent on these and many other factors. Of particular significance is the level degree of spontaneity in the speech, for example the amount of disfluency, the formality of the linguistic structure, and the clarity of articulation. The effect of these factors is evidenced by the difference in recognition performance between formal dictation where over 90% of the words can often be recognized correctly and informal conversational speech where performance may fall to less than 40%. In any case it is important to realize that good text search terms may not be as useful in the speech domain because of their acoustic properties.

4.2 Comparison with Text Information Retrieval

There are some similarities between term identification for text and spoken document retrieval. For example, in the text case there may be *false alarms* on search terms with multiple senses. If one of these terms is present in a query it will match any occurrence in a document regardless of the sense used in each case. This has been shown to have minimal effect on retrieval effectiveness except for very short queries (Sanderson 1994), but is nevertheless a real issue. Also, there may be *misses* on search terms which occur in the documents as synonyms of a query term; although of course there are techniques designed to overcome this problem. Finally there may be query-document term matching errors arising from spelling errors in the documents or query, or inappropriate term stemming.

These problems are also potentially present in spoken document retrieval. However, there are two additional sources of potential error similar in effect to those just described. Acoustic false alarms which occur when the speech recognizer hypotheses the presence of a term when none is actually present, and acoustic misses where the occurrence of a term is not detected by the recognizer.

All these sources of search error may be offset by adding more search terms to the query.

5. Experimental Investigations

This section outlines experimental strategies on the VMR project. The following subsections describe the experimental message archive, acoustic training data for the speech recognition component, indexing of spoken documents via word spotting, retrieval testing and our prototype video mail retrieval application.

5.1 Message Archive

A particular problem which we encountered was the lack of real video mail data for experimental use. Thus we had to engage in a serious collection construction exercise for our initial retrieval test data. Our first message set, VMR1, was designed to satisfy requirements of both document retrieval and the speech recognition. From the document retrieval perspective the database had to consist of messages with the same general properties as could be expected in real video mail messages. But in order to meet the specification for Stage 1 of the project, it also had to consist of messages making natural use of a set of fixed search keywords. At the same time the corpus should have the sort of message similarities and differences that pose challenges for recall and precision typical of expected VMR situations. Messages should also have similar acoustic properties and speaking styles to those found in an operational system, and be of comparable length.

A key issue for system assessment is to evaluate the performance of the speech recognition component and to investigate the extent to which word recognition accuracy affects retrieval performance. For this reason all messages were orthographically transcribed, including marking of pauses, disfluencies, and extraneous noises. This detailed transcription can only be done manually and is very expensive to carry out. For this reason the VMR1 archive is a very small collection from the retrieval point of view. In order for this small database to be viable for retrieval research it had to be carefully structured.

5.1.1 The VMR1 Message Corpus. The structure of the VMR1 archive was derived as follows. Messages were sought on *topics* within a set of *topic categories*. Associated with each category was a set of *keywords* drawn from a small fixed keyword *vocabulary* from which all search terms used in Stages 1 and 2 of the project must be taken. In addition, since the keyword vocabulary is not very large, a set of *other-words* were provided for each category as further prompting and potential search vocabulary. The messages were prompted by using *scenarios* which stimulated the speaker to talk on a topic within a category without constraining them to produce messages strictly tied to pre-specified topics. The prompt for each message consisted of the scenario and the keywords and other-words for the category. Speakers were asked to favor the use of the listed keywords and other-words, but not at the expense of construction of realistic messages. They were also not restricted to the keywords precisely as shown to them but could use them in variant word forms: for example the keyword *mail* might be used in the forms *mailed, mails* or *mailing*. The speakers were not shown a complete list of the keywords available, but only those relevant to the current category. However, they were free to use any keyword in any message. The collected messages varied in their individual topics but are clustered around the prompting categories.

The total keyword vocabulary was 35 words, along with a total of 31 related other-words. The keywords were selected manually and contained a mixture of longer more easily recognized words and shorter monosyllabic words. The full list of 35 keywords used was:

> active assess badge camera date display document find indigo interface keyword locate location mail manage meeting message microphone network output Pandora plan project rank retrieve score search sensor spotting staff time video windows word workstation

A total of 10 topic categories were defined and a keyword subset associated with each one. The categories were chosen to reflect the anticipated messages of a particular user community, the staff associated with the VMR project. The 10 categories were:

> spotting document output retrieval windows management badge Pandora schedule equipment

Keywords were assigned manually to the categories as being representative of the topics defined within the category. For example, for the category schedule the following assignment was made:

> schedule -> manage project meeting plan

Five message prompt scenarios were generated for each category. Fifteen evenly distributed sets of four categories were formed. Each category group was assigned to a knowledgeable speaker. The speaker then recorded a message in response to each prompt, giving a total of 20 messages for each speaker, and a total of 300 in the VMR1 archive.

The average message length was approximately one minute, giving a total message archive of around five hours. The average number of fixed keywords per message was about seven. A detailed description of VMR1 is contained in Jones et al. (1994).

5.2 Speech Training Data

Speech recognition systems require acoustic data for the training of recognition models. In Stages 1 and 2 of the VMR project training data was required for fixed keyword models, background models for non-keyword speech, and a model for silence. In Stage 1 individual models were needed for each speaker, and so separate training data had to be collected for each model set. In Stage 2 general acoustic recognition models were trained to recognize any speaker (The speaker-independent system developed here was trained primarily for native British English speakers.). This requires a large set of training data collected from many different speakers.

5.2.1 Data Stage 1 Training. Each speaker provided the following speech training data:

- 77 read sentences ("r" data): sentences containing keywords, constructed such that each keyword occurred a minimum of five times.

- 170 isolated keywords ("i" data): 5 occurrences of each of the 35 keywords spoken in isolation.
- 150 read sentences ("z" data): phonetically-rich sentences from the TIMIT corpus (Lamel et al. 1986).

There were a total of about 5 hours of spoken training data collected from the same 15 speakers who generated the experimental message set.

5.2.2 Stage 2 Training Data. For this stage the WSJCAM0 British English spoken corpus was used. This consists of spoken sentences taken from the Wall Street Journal. Data was collected for 100 British English speakers with equal numbers of male and female speakers drawn from a variety of age groups and regional backgrounds. The corpus contains a total of around 12 hours of spoken data. WSJCAM0 was collected at Cambridge University Engineering Department and further details are contained in (Robinson et al. 1995).

5.2.3 Recording Environment. All speech data was recorded in parallel at 16kHz using both the desk microphone from the Medusa system and a Sennheiser HMD 414 close-talking microphone (as used in many current speech recognition systems). The former represents the operational system and latter functions as an experimental control. The speech recordings were made in a quiet environment.

5.3 Word Spotting

Automatically detecting fixed keywords in unconstrained speech is termed "word spotting" (Rose and Paul 1990, Wilcox and Bush 1992); this technology is the basis of the speech recognition in Stages 1 and 2 of the VMR project. The best-performing word spotters are based on hidden Markov model (HMM) methods, used in successful continuous-speech recognition (Rabiner 1989). A hidden Markov model is a state-based statistical representation of a speech event, typically a word or subword. Different states model differing characteristic speech sounds. A typical subword unit is the phone (sometimes referred to as a phoneme). All words are built from a phone sequence drawn from the set of around 45 distinct phones. Phones vary somewhat with context, i.e. the phones which precede recognition can be achieved by modeling this variation.

There exist efficient algorithms for both training HMM parameters and finding the most likely model sequence given unknown speech input. The HTK tool set developed at Cambridge University (Young et al. 1993) is a powerful and flexible set of software tools for developing HMM applications such as the keyword spotting system presented here.

5.3.1 Word Modeling. *Stage 1 models:* Whole-word speaker-dependent key-

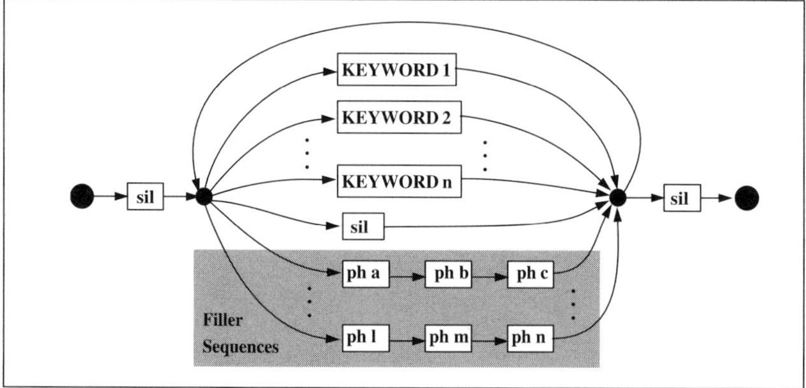

Figure 1. Speaker-dependent keyword recognition network.

words models and phone filler models were constructed for each of the 15 speakers, using the HTK tool set. Each keyword model was trained with the 10 occurrences of the word in the training data. Filler phones models to represent non-keyword speech were trained on the remaining data. The Stage 1 keyword recognition network is shown in figure 1. The filler models here were monophones, phone models which are independent of context. All examples of these phones occurring in the filler training data are used to train a single HMM model of each phone.

Stage 2 models: A set of speaker-independent keyword models were formed using the WSJCAM0 data (Robinson et al. 1995). The keyword models were built using word-internal triphone HMMs. Word-internal triphones model phone context within words, but do not take into account phonetic variation arising from interaction with the previous or following word. These were generalized using a tree-based clustering technique (Young et al. 1994). This training method enables all possible triphones, biphones and monophones to be modeled. Given such a model set, a particular keyword may be easily modeled by concatenating the appropriate sequence of subword models (obtained from a phonetic dictionary). Biphones are used at the beginning and end of the keyword, while triphones model the internal structure. For example, the keyword "find" is represented by the model sequence f+ay f-ay+n ay-n+d n-d. Non-keyword speech is modeled by an unconstrained network of monophones. The Stage 2 keyword recognition network is shown in figure 2.

5.3.2 Keyword Recognition. The speech recognition is performed using the Viterbi algorithm, a standard technique for HMM based speech recognition (Rabiner 1989). The Viterbi algorithm combines the HMM model parameters and spoken data to calculate the most likely state sequence of the HMM models in the recognition vocabulary. The output is the corresponding HMM model sequence.

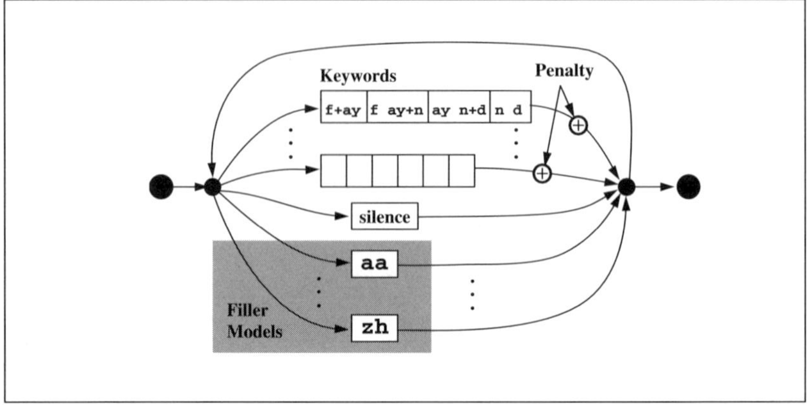

Figure 2. Speaker-independent keyword recognition network.

Word spotting is done with a two-pass recognition procedure (Rose and Paul 1990). First, the Viterbi decoding is performed on a network of just the filler models, yielding a time-aligned sequence of the maximum-likelihood filler monophones and their associated log-likelihood scores. Secondly, another Viterbi decoding pass is done using the appropriate full network (as shown in figures 1 and 2). Putative keyword hits are rescored by normalizing each hypothesis score by the average filler score over the keyword interval. This procedures helps take into account variation in hypothesis score arising from changes in speaking style or background conditions.

In the Stage 1 system, it was necessary to tune the filler models so that they did not match an undue number of keywords. This problem arose because of the limited training data available for the whole-word keyword models. A satisfactory solution was to introduce filler models of common 3-phone sequences (not contained within any of the keywords) by concatenating three monophone models, and adjusting the word transition penalty to penalize the filler sequences (which must be traversed in groups of three).

A similar problem was observed in the Stage 2 system; however, in this case there were too many false alarms. A solution was to introduce a separate transition penalty to the keyword models as shown in figure 2. It is observed that increasing this penalty dramatically reduces the number of false alarms, while only mildly impacting the number of correctly identified keywords. The net effect is similar to, but better than, increasing a cut-off threshold on keyword scores, such that those with low scores are ignored.

5.3.3 Recognition Results. An accepted figure-of-merit (FOM) for word spotting is defined as the average percentage of correctly detected keywords as a threshold on the putative keyword scores is varied from one to ten false

	Data set	
	head (%)	desk (%)
Dependent	81.2	76.4
Independent	69.9	55.9

Table 1. Average figure-of-merit for the different model sets.

alarms per keyword per hour. The keyword spotting output was scored by comparing it against time aligned manual text transcriptions of the documents. A putative hit is counted as a hit if it overlaps more than half of an occurrence of this keyword in the text transcription. Exact time aligned boundaries of the transcriptions and word spotting output are unlikely to be the same. Word boundaries in the text transcription are determined manually by the transcriber and those from the word spotter are calculated stochastically in the Viterbi decoder. In the speech recognition the Viterbi decoder must form the optimal state sequence for the acoustic data using only available models. Inevitably this optimal fit will slightly distort the word boundaries. The FOM for model sets in the Stage 1 and 2 word spotting systems are shown in table 1, averaged across both the 15 speakers and the 35 keywords. FOMs for the speaker-independent models are taken at the best experimentally-determined transition penalty value.

5.3.4 Speaker Adaptation. VMR1 is realistic in that it contains speakers with non-British accents. For example, one of our speakers is a native American. This is problematic when using models trained exclusively on British English speakers since the model parameters will not well represent the acoustic content of the speech of these speakers. In an attempt to ameliorate this problem, and increase word spotting performance in general, speaker adaptation was investigated. In this procedure a small amount of "adaptation" data is used to generate a modified HMM model set which better represents the speech of the individual speaker. The approach chosen was maximum-likelihoods linear regression because it has been shown to improve recognition with a comparatively small amount of adaptation data (Leggetter and Woodland 1995). This method involves adapting only some of the model parameters (the means of the HMM Gaussian mixtures) to increase the likelihood of the adaptation data given the models. Varying amounts of the VMR Stage 1 training corpus were used as enrollment data for speaker-adaptation experiments.

Word spotting performance using speaker adaptation is shown in table 2. The *R13* row used 13 utterances of enrollment data containing in all 2 occur-

<table>
<tr><td></td><td colspan="2">Data set</td></tr>
<tr><td></td><td>head (%)</td><td>desk (%)</td></tr>
<tr><td>R13</td><td>77.1</td><td>57.8</td></tr>
<tr><td>R75</td><td>80.5</td><td>65.5</td></tr>
</table>

*Table 2. Average figure-of-merit for the different
model sets after speaker adaptation.*

rences of each keyword. The *R75* row used the full 75 "r" sentences from the
Stage 1 training material, containing 5 utterances of each keyword. Adaptation does not uniformly improve performance for all speakers. However the
average increase is substantial, and is particularly dramatic for our American
English speaker. As shown in table 2 using a small amount of enrollment
data improved the FOM performance substantially.

This type of speaker adaptation is referred to as *supervised* since the correct
transcription of the enrollment data is known by the recognizer. In operation
this requires an operator to speak some given enrollment text in advance of
message recognition, so that models can be suitably adapted. This may not be
possible in practice for the VMR system since it is quite probable that there
will be no opportunity to gather the enrollment material for messages from a
new speaker. We hope to investigate *unsupervised* adaptation where the parameters are modified without use of *a priori* transcriptions.

Further details of our word spotting systems and corresponding experimental results are contained in (Jones et al. 1995a, Foote et al. 1995).

5.4 Retrieval Message

5.4.1 Requests and Relevance Assessments. Our retrieval tests so far have
used VMR1 with two different request sets defining two retrieval test collections, VMR1a and VMR1b. The primary purpose of these tests has been to
establish that spoken document retrieval is feasible and viable.

VMR1a Queries were formed from the message prompts used in the
database recording. To reduce variations in word form, query words were
suffix stripped to stems using the standard Porter algorithm (Porter 1980).
Queries were formed from the prompts by selecting those stems also found
in a keyword stem list. For example, given the prompt:

> Your current project is lagging behind schedule. Send a message pointing this
> out to the other project management staff. Suggest some days and times over the

next week when you would be willing to hold a meeting to discuss the situation.

the following query was obtained:

project messag project manag staff time meet

To obtain relevance assessments, the 6 recorded messages generated in response to each prompt were assumed relevant to the query constructed from that prompt. The 24 other messages in the same category were assumed to be not relevant, even though they are quite likely to contain similar keywords.

VMR1b This is a more realistic set of requests and relevance assessments, collected from the user community that supplied the database messages. A total of 50 requests were collected, 5 for each of the 10 categories used in message collection. These were gathered from 10 users, each of whom generated 5 requests and corresponding relevance assessments. This was achieved by forming 10 unique sets of 5 categories, and assigning each to a user knowledgeable about the categories in that set. For each category a text prompt was formed by combining information given in the 5 message prompts associated with the category.

Users were shown the prompt for the category and asked to compose a natural language request from the information given in the prompt. Users were asked that their request include at least one of the keywords associated with the category.

As for VMR1a, request words were suffix-stripped using the Porter algorithm and search queries were formed by selecting the keyword stems. For example, given the request:

In what ways can the windows interface of a workstation be personalized.

the following query was obtained:

window interfac workstat

Ideally, the relevance of all archived messages should be assessed; however this is not practical even for our 300 message archive. A suitable assessment subset was formed by combining the 30 messages in the category to which the original message prompt belonged, plus 5 messages from outside the category having the highest query-message scores (computed using collection frequency weighting (see section 5.4.2) on the VMR1 document archive). Subjects were presented with the transcription of each potentially relevant document in random order and asked to mark it as "relevant", "partially relevant", or "not relevant". The average number of highly relevant documents was 10.8, while 17.2 were judged highly or partially relevant. The following sections report results only for the highly relevant relevance set. A full description of the VMR1b naturalistic request set is contained in (Jones et al. 1995b).

Apart from the greater realism, the main difference between VMR1a and VMR1b is that there were far fewer terms per query for the latter, an average of 2.6 distinct terms, against an average of 4.6 for VMR1a.

5.4.2 Query-Document Matching. Document retrieval experiments compared three forms of document scoring: *unweighted (uw)* term matching, *collection frequency weighting (cfw)*, and *combined weight (cw)* which takes into account several factors. The unweighted score is simply the sum of matching terms occurring in both the query and the document. The collection frequency is conventional inverse document frequency weighting, computed as:

$$cfw(i) = \log \frac{N}{n(i)},$$

where *cfw(i)* is the cfw weight of term *i*, *N* is the total number of documents and *n(i)* is the number of documents in which term *i* appears. The combined weight incorporates cfw, within-document term frequency, and normalized document length. The cw weight was defined in (Robertson and Spärck Jones 1994) and derived in (Robertson and Walker 1994): the cw scheme reflects the City University work for TREC (Robertson et al. 1995). The cw weight for each term in each document is calculated as follows:

$$cw(i,j) = \log \frac{cfw(i) * tf(i,j) * (K+!)}{K * ndl(j) * tf(i,j)}$$

where *cw(i,j)* represents the cw weight of term *i* in document *j*, *tf(i,j)* is the frequency of *i* in *j*, and *ndl(j)* the normalized document length. *ndl(j)* is calculated as:

$$ndl(j) = \log \frac{dl(j)}{\text{Average } dl \text{ for all documents}},$$

where *dl(j)* is the total length of *j*. The combined weight constant *K* has to be tuned empirically: after testing we set *K = 1* .

5.4.3 Calibration via Text Retrieval. Retrieval performance for speech documents can be expected to suffer degradation relative to text documents due to either misses or false alarms. The degradation can be measured, when transcribed texts are available, by comparing performance for spoken word spotting results with that for the transcriptions. We used our transcribed corpus to provide us with this performance standard.

A particular problem with word spotting is that unrelated acoustic events will often resemble valid keywords. For example, the last part of "hello Kate" is acoustically quite similar to the keyword "locate." Because even the most accurate acoustic models cannot discriminate between homophones, the output of an ideal word spotter that reports all keyword phone sequences provides a more legitimate standard of comparison than text. We simulated this ideal 'phonetic text' performance by scanning phonetic transcriptions of the messages for phone sequences that match those of a keyword.

Table 3 shows retrieval performance for the standard transcribed messages (*text*) and for the ideal phonetic text (*phonetic*) with collection VMR1a and Table 4 shows that for VMR1b. It can be seen that introducing cfw weighting

		Text			Phonetic		
Wt Scheme		uw	cfw	cw	uw	cfw	cw
Prec.	5 docs	.26	.30	.30	.25	.29	.31
	10 docs	.22	.25	.27	.22	.24	.27
	15 docs	.19	.21	.24	.19	.21	.23
	20 docs	.17	.19	.21	.17	.18	.20
Av Prec.		.29	.33	.36	.28	.32	.35

Table 3. VMR1a text and phonetic text retrieval performance.

		Text			Phonetic		
Wt Scheme		uw	cfw	cw	uw	cfw	cw
Prec.	5 docs	.34	.35	.34	.34	.35	.35
	10 docs	.28	.31	.29	.29	.32	.31
	15 docs	.26	.30	.30	.26	.30	.30
	20 docs	.24	.28	.28	.25	.28	.28
Av Prec.		.30	.33	.35	.30	.34	.36

Table 4. VMR1b text and phonetic text retrieval performance.

gives a substantial improvement in performance over the unweighted case, and cw in turn does better than cfw. For VMR1a the text transcription performs better than the phonetic reference; however the opposite is true for VMR1b. We attribute this phenomenon to stemming inconsistencies between the text transcription and phonetic data. VMR1b in particular is sensitive to this effect due to its very short queries. Due to the small size of the message collection absolute values and observed differences must be treated with caution.

5.4.4 Spoken Message Retrieval Performance. As described previously, the word spotter outputs a list of putative keyword hits and associated acoustic scores. It is found that acoustic false alarms frequently score worse then true hits, and hence a score threshold can be applied to remove most of the false alarms. Clearly, it is desirable to choose an operating threshold that optimizes retrieval performance in trading false alarms against 'pseudo'-misses, i.e. hits with scores below the threshold (this question is discussed in more detail in Jones et al. 1995a). Tables 5, 6 and 7 show spoken document retrieval performance for the three investigated weighting schemes and the different word spotting models at the best *a posteriori* threshold. In practice, an *a priori* fixed threshold would be used in an operational system. For simplicity, only aver-

VMR1a		Avg. Prec.	Text (%)	Phon. (%)		VMR1b		Avg. Prec.	Text (%)	Phon. (%)
Text		.293	100.0	—		Text		.296	100.0	—
Phonetic		.279	95.2	100.0		Phonetic		.302	102.0	100.0
Head	Depen	.259	88.4	93.8		Head	Depen	.265	89.5	87.7
	Indep	.241	82.4	86.5			Indep	.249	84.0	82.2
	R13	.234	80.1	84.0			R13	.245	82.9	81.2
	R75	.256	87.6	91.9			R75	.270	91.1	89.2
Desk	Depen	.241	82.3	86.4		Desk	Depen	.254	85.8	84.1
	Indep	.184	62.8	65.9			Indep	.214	72.3	70.8
	R13	.172	58.6	61.5			R13	.203	68.6	67.1
	R75	.181	61.9	64.9			R75	.234	79.2	77.5

Table 5. Retrieval performance with uw scheme.

VMR1a		Avg. Prec.	Text (%)	Phon. (%)		VMR1b		Avg. Prec.	Text (%)	Phon. (%)
Text		.332	100.0	—		Text		.332	100.0	—
Phonetic		.317	95.5	100.0		Phonetic		.339	102.1	100.0
Head	Depen	.295	88.8	93.1		Head	Depen	.312	94.0	92.0
	Indep	.263	79.2	83.0			Indep	.287	86.4	84.7
	R13	.274	82.5	86.4			R13	.283	85.2	83.5
	R75	.294	88.6	92.7			R75	.307	92.5	90.6
Desk	Depen	.283	85.2	89.3		Desk	Depen	.296	89.2	87.3
	Indep	.219	66.0	69.1			Indep	.249	75.0	73.5
	R13	.211	63.4	66.5			R13	.251	75.5	73.8
	R75	.227	71.6	76.3			R75	.276	83.1	81.2

Table 6. Retrieval performance with cfw scheme.

VMR1a		Avg. Prec.	Text (%)	Phon. (%)		VMR1b		Avg. Prec.	Text (%)	Phon. (%)
Text		.358	100.0	—		Text		.346	100.0	—
Phonetic		.349	97.5	100.0		Phonetic		.355	102.6	100.0
Head	Depen	.316	88.3	90.5		Head	Depen	.330	95.4	93.0
	Indep	.300	83.8	86.0			Indep	.309	89.3	87.0
	R13	.324	90.5	92.8			R13	.303	87.6	85.4
	R75	.338	94.4	96.8			R75	.335	96.8	94.4
Desk	Depen	.299	83.5	85.7		Desk	Depen	.315	91.0	88.7
	Indep	.275	76.8	78.8			Indep	.265	76.6	74.6
	R13	.243	67.8	69.5			R13	.271	78.5	76.5
	R75	.266	74.4	76.3			R75	.295	85.3	83.1

Table 7. Retrieval performance with cw scheme.

age precision values are shown in these tables. It is found that precision at the cutoff values shown in tables 3 and 4 follow similar relative performance trends to the average precision observed for different acoustic model sets.

It can be seen from these tables that speaker-dependent models produce

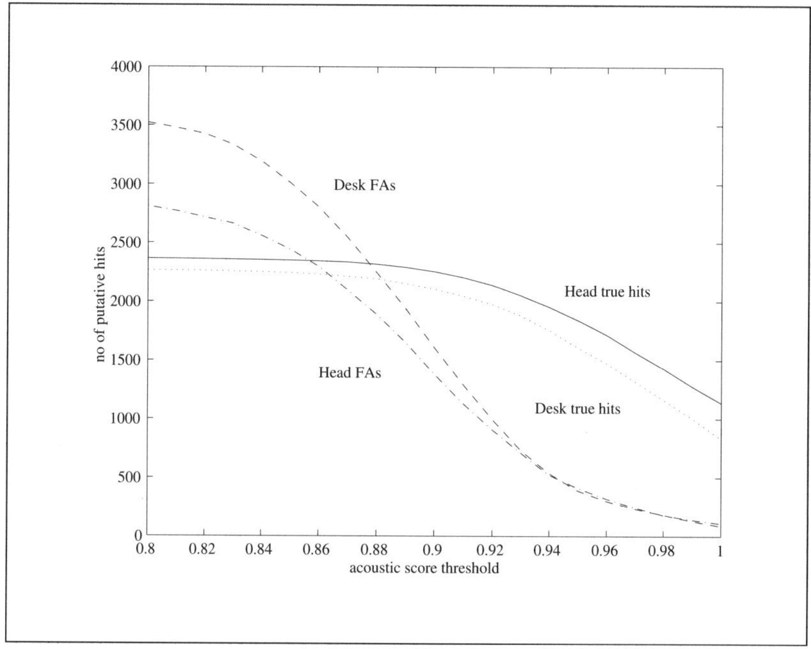

Figure 3. Number of putative hits versus threshold
for speaker-dependent models.

the best overall retrieval performance values. This was anticipated from the superior word spotting FOM discussed earlier. Also, supervised speaker adaptation can significantly improve retrieval performance. In some cases, speaker adapted models using R75 adaptation data achieve superior retrieval performance to speaker-dependent models. The reason for this is not clear, however, it is important to remember that the document set here is very small. Performance trends for the different weighting schemes are similar to those observed for the text standards, with cw again producing the best performance. Note not only does cw give the best absolute values but performance relative to the text standards is improved as well.

Figure 3 illustrates the effect of increasing score threshold on the number of true hits and false alarms for speaker-dependent head and desk microphone models. Figure 4 shows spoken document retrieval performance for VMR1a and VMR1b using speaker-dependent head-microphone models at different acoustic thresholds for uw, cfw and cw schemes. These figures show that the performance trends observed for the a posteriori best performance thresholds are consistent across the different threshold levels. Also, significantly, as well as achieving the best retrieval performance in absolute

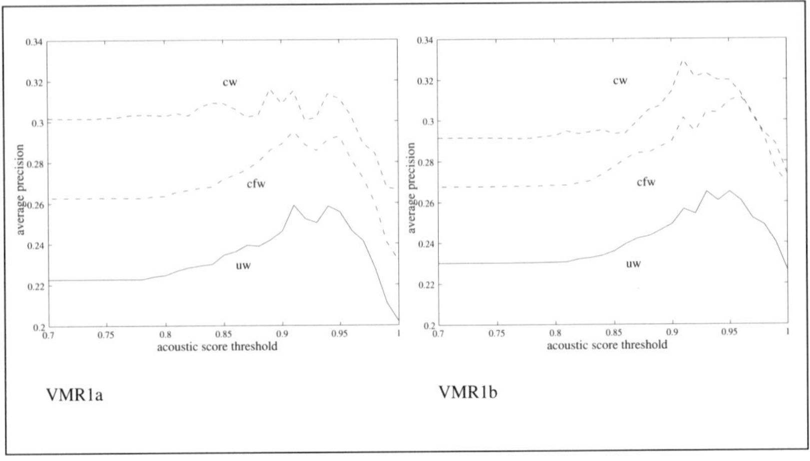

Figure 4. Average retrieval performance versus threshold for speaker-dependent head-microphone models.

terms, the cw scheme is also less sensitive to the choice of threshold than the other schemes. This trend is more pronounced with the VMR1a results which is probably due to their longer average query length.

Figure 5 shows that increasing the keyword transition penalty (shown in figure 2) dramatically reduces the number of false alarms, while only mildly impacting the number of correctly identified keywords. Figure 6 shows the effect of keyword score thresholding for word spotting output from systems with different keyword transition penalties. It can be seen that there is little difference between the best retrieval performance at the optimal a posteriori threshold. However, the system with fewest false alarms prior to the use of thresholding (transition penalty 100) not only exhibits the best available individual retrieval performance, but is also less sensitive to variation in the acoustic score threshold.

5.4.5 Retrieval Results Summary. In summary, the following general points can be made:

- Term weighting schemes developed for text retrieval transfer well to the retrieval of spoken documents.
- Spoken document retrieval performance of between 75% and 95% of that achieved with text transcriptions can be obtained depending on the generality of the acoustic recognition models.
- Unsurprisingly, spoken document retrieval performance is adversely affected by degradation in word spotting performance.

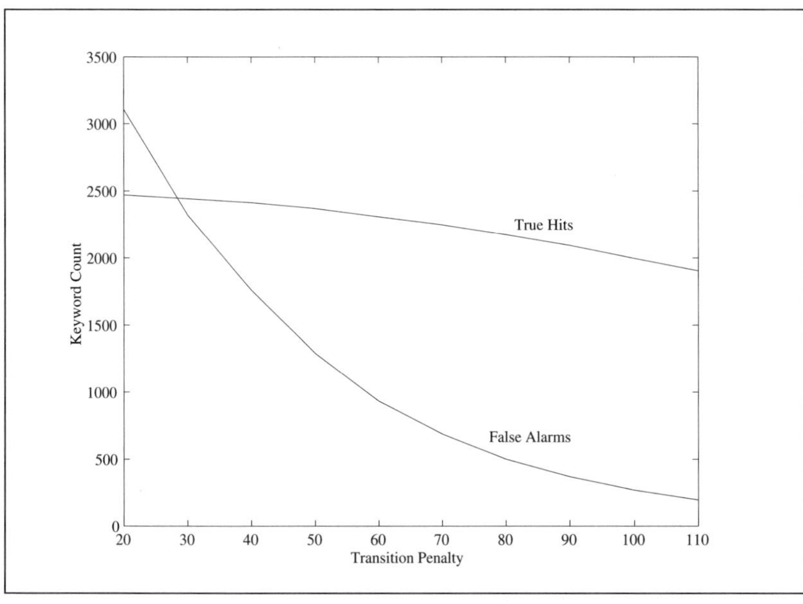

Figure 5. False alarms vs. keyword transition penalty (r75 models)

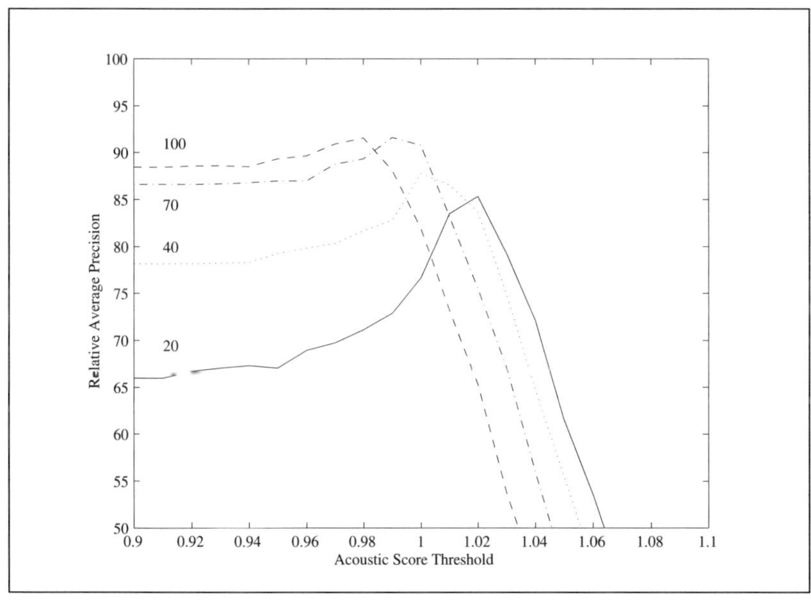

Figure 6. Relative average precision vs. keyword score threshold for vmr1a using (r75 models) with keyword transition penalty set to 20, 30, 70 and 100.

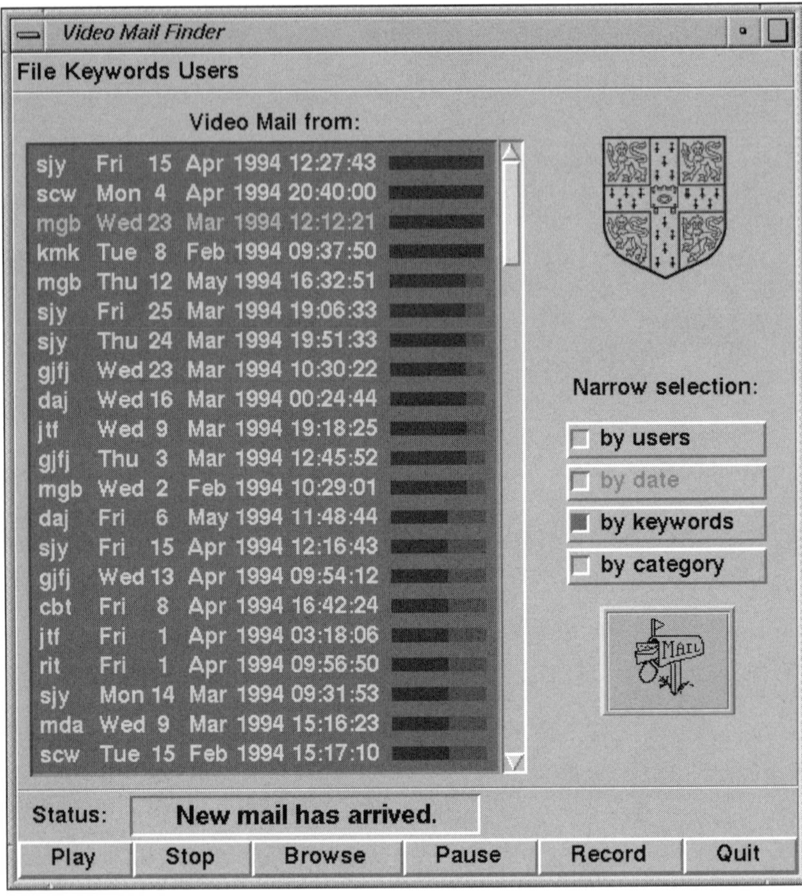

Figure 7. Video mail user interface application.

5.5 User Interface

We have developed a prototype VMR application that integrates keyword spotting, information retrieval, and video capture/playback capabilities. The audio soundtrack of each message (whether from an existing archive or received as new mail) is passed to the acoustic word spotter. This computes a sequence of putative keyword hits, which is added to an index containing all putative hits for all messages, along with mail header information and pointers to the message data (for playback). Because the computationally-intensive word spotting phase is done off-line (as messages are added to the archive), retrieval of archived messages is nearly instantaneous.

The VMR user interface is shown in figure 7. The interface shows a scrollable list of all available messages in the user's video mail archive. Various controls let the user "narrow" the list, for example, by displaying only those messages from a particular user or received after a particular time. Unsetting a constraint restores the messages hidden by that constraint; multiple constraints can be active at one time, giving the messages selected by a boolean conjunction of the constraints. With no constraints, messages are ranked by origination date, such that the most recently received document is displayed at the top of the list. When the user inputs a search query the retrieval engine computes the resulting score for each message. The interface then displays a list of messages ranked by score, with the scores shown as bar graphs. Messages with identical scores are ranked by date.

To review an individual message, a "video browser" can be activated. The browser, shown in figure 8, graphically represents the message as a dark horizontal bar, with putative keyword hits displayed as lighter regions. Time runs from left to right, and keyword hits are displayed proportionally to when they occur in a message; for example, keywords at the beginning appear on the left side of the bar. The brightness of a keyword region is proportional to the score computed by the word spotter, so that more likely hits appear brighter and stand out. Portions of the video message can be selected for playback by dragging over part of the bar; this enables the user to selectively audition regions of interest rather than the entire message. Analysis of the video stream could be used to identify scene changes arising either from movement in front of the camera or switching to an alternative camera. The browser could then be augmented with "thumbnail" images to show the positions of these changes. A more sophisticated content-based multimedia browsing tool of this type, for broadcast news recordings, is described by Mérialdo and Dubois in this volume. However, as stated in the introduction these additional indexing features are likely to be of limited practical utility in the video mail domain.

A more detailed discussion of the complete VMR retrieval system is contained in Brown et al. (1994).

6. Conclusions and Future Work

The results obtained in the VMR project so far suggest that spoken document retrieval is a feasible proposition. Retrieval performance of between 75% and 90% of text has been achieved for indexing via word spotting, though so far only in limited and relatively favorable circumstances. Of course, the ultimate evaluation is whether users find the retrieval tool useful in day-to-day operation.

Current work is concentrated on completing the last phase, Stage 3, of the VMR project. System development is focused on greater integration with the ORL Medusa system, and on enhancing the user interface, hopefully making

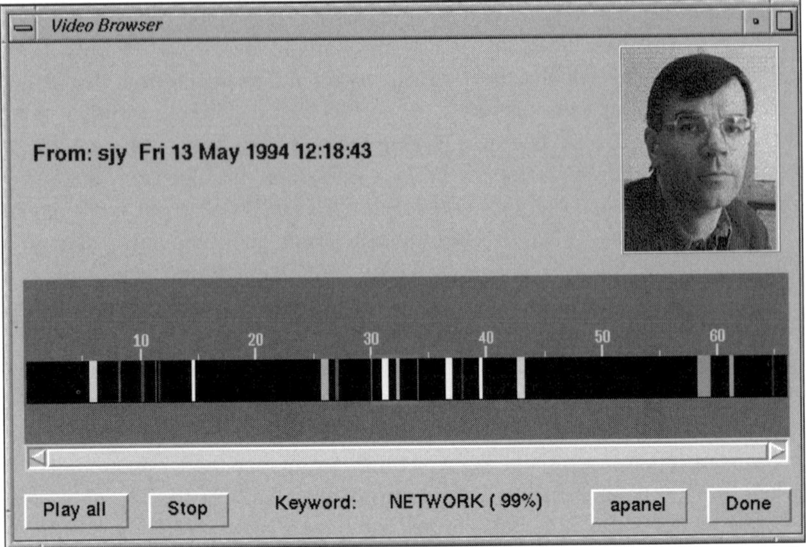

Figure 8. Prototype mail browser.

use of feedback from real users. The final Stage 3 system will use an open vocabulary retrieval system indexed via the phone lattice method developed by James and Young (1994). An alternative indexing method under investigation is the use of large vocabulary recognition to generate a transcription. Current results reported in Jones et al. (1996ab) indicate that each of these techniques, though errorful, can be used successfully for retrieval in isolation, and that they can be more effectively used in combination.

Further directions for this work include the development of a system for the automated retrieval of broadcast TV news. An operational system has been developed for use with Medusa and initial results from retrieval experiments using text subtitles to index the data are very encouraging (Brown et al. 1995). We intend to extend this to indexing using speech recognition in the near future. As evidenced by several chapters in this volume, broadcast news is becoming a major domain for multimedia research. In particular our work on news retrieval bears many similarities to the Informedia project at Carnegie Mellon University. The news domain is a particularly interesting area for multimedia retrieval research since many possible sources of indexing information are available. News broadcasts provide a rich field for research in several areas including speech recognition, image processing, topic segmentation and matching, and text summarization. But much investigation is required to develop systems that combine all this available information for effective document retrieval and browsing. One current research program in this area is described by Mani et al. (this volume).

Acknowledgements

This project is supported by the UK DTI Grant IED4/1/5804 and EPSRC Grant GR/H87629. Olivetti Research Limited is an industrial partner of the VMR project and we are indebted to them for the use of the Medusa system. We wish to thank Julian Odell for the baseline triphone models, and Chris Leggetter and Phil Woodland for the speaker-adaptation software.

A version of this text appeared under the title "Video Mail Retrieval using Voice: An Overview of the Stage 2 System" in the proceedings of the MIRO workshop, University of Glasgow, 1995. Details of the VMR project are contained in the project web page from which copies of VMR publications can be obtained (http://svr-www.eng.cam.ac.uk/Research/Projects/Video_Mail_Retrieval_Voice/).

References

Brown, M. G.; Foote, J. T.; Jones, G. J. F.; Spärck Jones, K.; and Young, S. J. 1994. Video Mail Retrieval Using Voice: An Overview Of The Cambridge/Olivetti Retrieval System. In Proceedings of the ACM Multimedia 94 Workshop on Multimedia Database Management Systems, 47–55, San Francisco, CA: ACM Press. October.

Brown, M. G.; Foote, J. T.; Jones, G. J. F.; Spärck Jones, K.; and Young, S. J. 1995. Automatic Content-Based Retrieval Of Broadcast News. In Proceedings of ACM Multimedia 95, 35–43, San Francisco, CA: ACM Press. November.

Foote, J. T.; Jones, G. J. F.; Spärck Jones, K.; and Young, S. J. 1995. Talker-Independent Keyword Spotting for Information Retrieval. In Proceedings of Eurospeech 95, 3: 2145–2148, Madrid, Spain. ESCA.

Glavitsch, U.; Schäuble, P.; and Wechsler, M. 1994. Metadata for Integrating Speech Documents in a Text Retrieval System. *SIGMOD* Record 23(4): 57–63, December.

James, D. A. and Young, S. J. 1994. A Fast Lattice-based Approach to Vocabulary Independent Wordspotting. In Proceedings of ICASSP 94, I: 377–380, Adelaide, Australia: IEEE.

Jones, G. J. F.; Foote, J. T.; Spärck Jones, K.; and Young, S. J. 1994. VMR Report On Keyword Definition and Data Collection. Technical Report 335, Cambridge University Computer Laboratory, May.

Jones, G. J. F.; Foote, J. T.; Spärck Jones, K.; and Young, S. J. 1995a. Video Mail Retrieval: The Effect Of Word Spotting Accuracy On Precision. In Proceedings of ICASSP 95, Vol I, 309–312, Detroit, MI. IEEE, May.

Jones, G. J. F.; Foote, J. T.; and Spärck Jones, K. 1995b. Video Mail Retrieval Using Voice: Report on Collection of Naturalistic Requests and Relevance Assessments. Technical Report 402, Cambridge University Computer Laboratory, April.

Jones, G. J. F.; Foote, J. T.; Spärck Jones, K.; and Young, S. J 1996a. Robust Talker-Independent Audio Document Retrieval. In Proceedings of ICASSP 96, I: 311–314, Atlanta, GA: IEEE, April.

Jones, G. J. F.; Foote, J. T.; Spärck Jones, K.; and Young, S. J. 1996b. Retrieving Spoken Documents by Combining Multiple Index Sources. In Proceedings of SIGIR 96, 30-38, Zürich, Switzerland, August. ACM.

Lamel, L. F.; Kassel, H. K.; and Seneff, S. 1986. Speech Database Development: Design and Analysis of the Acoustic-Phonetic Corpus. In Proceedings of DARPA Speech Recognition Workshop, 26–32.

Leggetter, C. J. and Woodland, P. C. 1995. Flexible Speaker Adaptation For Large Vocabulary Speech Recognition. In Proceedings of Eurospeech '95, 1155 - 1158. September. Madrid, Spain: ESCA.

Porter, M. F. 1980. An Algorithm for Suffix Stripping. *Program* 14(3): 130–137, July.

Rabiner, L. R. 1989. A Tutorial on Hidden Markov Models and Selected Applications in Speech Recognition. In Proceedings of IEEE, 77(2): 257–286, February.

Robertson, S. E. and Spärck Jones, K. 1994. Simple, proven approaches to text retrieval. Technical Report 356, Cambridge University Computer Laboratory, December.

Robertson, S. E. and Walker, S. 1994. Some Simple Effective Approximations to the 2–Poisson Model for Probabilistic Weighted Retrieval. In Proceedings of SIGIR 94, 232–241, Dublin, Ireland: ACM, Spinger-Verlag.

Robertson, S. E.; Walker, S.; Jones, S.; Hancock-Beaulieu, M. M.; and Gatford, M. 1995. Okapi at TREC-3. In The Third Text REtrieval Conference (TREC-3), NIST Spec Pub 500-225, ed. D. K. Harman, 109–126, Gaithersberg, MD: NIST

Robinson, T.; Fransen, J.; Pye, D.; Foote, J.; and Renals, S. 1995. WSJCAM0: A British English Speech Corpus for Large Vocabulary Continuous Speech Recognition. In Proceedings of ICASSP 95, 81–84, Detroit, MI: IEEE. May.

Rose, R. C. and Paul, D. B. 1990. A Hidden Markov Model Based Keyword Recognition System. In Proceedings of ICASSP 90, 129–132. Albuquerque, NM: IEEE.

Sanderson, M. 1994. Word Sense Disambiguation and Information Retrieval. In Proceedings SIGIR 94, 142-151. Dublin, Ireland: ACM, Springer-Verlag.

Wechsler, M. and Schäuble, P. 1995. Indexing Methods for a Speech Retrieval System. In Proceedings of the MIRO Workshop, ed. C. J. van Rijsbergen, University of Glasgow, Scotland: Springer-Verlag, September.

Wilcox, L. D. and Bush, M. A. 1992. Training and Search Algorithms For An Interactive Wordspotting System. In Proceedings of ICASSP 92, volume II, 97–100, San Francisco, CA. IEEE.

Wray, S.; Glauert, T.; and Hopper, A. 1994. The Medusa Applications Environment. In Proceedings IEEE International Conference on Multimedia Computing and Systems, 265–273, Boston, MA. IEEE. May.

Young, S. J.; Odell, J. J.; and Woodland, P. C. 1994. Tree-Based State Tying For High Accuracy Acoustic Modeling. In Proceedings of ARPA Spoken Language Technology Workshop, 286 - 291. March. Plainsboro, NJ: Morgan Kaufmann.

Young, S. J.; Woodland, P. C.; and Byrne, W. J. 1993. HTK: Hidden Markov Model Toolkit V1.5. Entropic Research Laboratories, Washington, DC.

Chapter 11

Informedia: News-on-Demand Multimedia Information Acquisition and Retrieval

Alexander G. Hauptmann and Michael J. Witbrock
School of Computer Science, Carnegie Mellon University

Abstract

In theory, speech recognition technology can make any spoken words in video or audio media subject to text indexing, search and retrieval. This chapter describes the News-on-Demand application created within the Informedia™ Digital Video Library project and discusses how speech recognition is used for transcript creation from video, time alignment of closed-captioned transcripts, a speech query interface, and audio paragraph segmentation. Our results show that speech recognition accuracy varies dramatically depending on the quality and type of data used, but the system is quite useable with only moderate speech recognition accuracy.

1. What is Informedia: News-on-Demand

The Informedia™ digital video library project (Informedia 19995, Wactlar et al. 1996) at Carnegie Mellon University is creating a digital library in which text, image, video and audio data are available for full content retrieval. News-on-Demand is an application within Informedia which monitors news from TV, radio and text sources and allows the user to retrieve news stories of interest.

This chapter gives a brief overview of the Informedia digital video library project (Christel et al. 1994ab, Stevens et al. 1994, Informedia 1995) followed by a detailed description of the News-on-Demand application (Hauptmann et al. 1995). Both the automated library creation process for News-on-

Demand and the news library exploration process will be explained. We show how speech recognition fits into the various digital news library processing steps. Results are presented for speech recognition on actual broadcast news data. Finally we discuss some active areas of research relevant to the multimedia information acquisition and retrieval problem.

1.1 An Overview of the Informedia Digital Video Library Project

Vast digital libraries of information will soon become available on the World Wide Web as a result of emerging multimedia computing technologies. However, it is not enough simply to store and play back information as many commercial video-on-demand services apparently intend to do. New technology is needed to organize and search these vast data collections, retrieve the most relevant selections, and permit them to be effectively reused.

Through the integration of technologies from the fields of natural language understanding, image processing, speech recognition and video compression, the Informedia project (Christel et al. 1994a) allows a user to explore multimedia data in depth as well as in breadth. The Informedia digital video library project goes far beyond the current paradigm of video-on-demand, where a user can select one video from a limited set and view that video after a delay of perhaps a few minutes. The computer adds no substantial benefit to this video-on-demand model over a VCR with each video on a tape; the user remains a passive observer of someone else's produced material. By contrast, the Informedia Project segments hours of video into logical pieces and indexes these pieces according to their raw content (dialog, images, narration). The users can actively explore the information by finding sections of content relevant to their search, rather than by following someone else's path through the material (as one does when using the current generation of educational CD-ROMs) or by viewing a large chunk of pre-produced material (as with video on demand). Through the active, dynamic exploration supported by a deep, rich library and the indexing and retrieval capabilities of the computer, the user is more motivated and may learn more from the data set. Using such a library, a large body of video material can be searched with very little effort.

Users are able to explore Informedia libraries through an interface that allows them to search using typed or spoken natural language queries, to select relevant documents retrieved from the library and to play or display the material on their PC workstations. The library retrieval system can effectively process natural spoken queries and deliver relevant video data in small video paragraphs, based on information associated with the video during library creation. Video and other data may be explored in depth for related content. During retrieval based on keyword searches by a user, only the query-relevant video segments are displayed.

The Informedia project is developing new technologies and embedding them in a video library system primarily for use in education and training. The Informedia project will establish an on-line digital video library consisting of over 1000 hours of video material. In order to be able to process this volume of data, practical, effective and efficient tools are essential.

In the United States, schools and industry together spend between $400 and $600 billion per year on education and training, an activity that is 93% labor-intensive, with little change in teacher productivity ratios since the 1800s. The new digital video library technology will bring about a revolutionary improvement in the way education and training are delivered and received.

The initial Informedia testbed system has been installed in a K-12 school, where students use the Informedia System to explore multimedia data for educational purposes. We plan to extend this testbed to other Pittsburgh schools. During library creation for the testbed, video material obtained from our Informedia Project Partners such as WQED/Pittsburgh and the British Open University is used. Our project plan calls for four testbed installations with users ranging from grade school children to university faculty. In addition, we will provide networked access to the primary testbed, and export portions of the system and data to other sites for their local exploration and experimentation.

The user tests will be conducted at Carnegie Mellon University, the Winchester Thurston School in Pittsburgh, the Fairfax County (VA) public school system, and with the Open University in the UK. Users will be of many different types, as we test the practicality of the concept of multimedia library search and the usability of the user interface for various age and interest groups.

Universal access to large amounts of low-cost digital information and entertainment will significantly affect the conduct of business, professional, and personal activity. The initial impact of the Informedia project's activity will be by enabling broad accessibility and reuse of existing video materials (e.g., documentaries, news, vocational, training) previously generated for public broadcast, public and professional education, and vocational, military and business training.

1.2 The Informedia: News-on-Demand Application

One compelling application branch of the Informedia project is the indexing and retrieval of television, radio and text news. The Informedia: News-on-Demand application (Hauptmann and Smith 1995) is an innovative example of indexing and searching broadcast news video and news radio material by its text content. News-on-Demand is a fully-automatic system that monitors TV, radio and text news and allows selective retrieval of news stories based on spoken queries. The user may choose among the retrieved stories and play back the news stories of interest. The system runs on a Pentium PC using MPEG-I video compression. Speech recognition is currently done on a separate platform using the Sphinx-II continuous speech recognition system (CMU-Speech 1995).

The News-on-Demand application forces us to consider the limits of what can be done automatically and in limited time. Since news events happen daily, it is not feasible to process, segment and label news through manual or "human-assisted" methods. Immediate availability of the library information is important, as is continuous updating of the contents.

Unlike other Informedia prototypes which are designed to be educational testbeds, the News-on-Demand system is fully automated. While the educational testbed prototypes' library is developed using computer-assisted methods that require human post-processing, the News-on-Demand system is fully automatic. We are forced, therefore, to fully exploit the potential of computer speech recognition without the benefit of human corrections and editing.

While our work is centered around processing news stories from TV broadcasts, the system exemplifies an approach that can make any video, audio or text data accessible. Similar methods can be used to index and search other streamed multimedia data by content for other Informedia applications.

Currently, TV and radio news is broadcast at particular times, and if a person is not in front of a TV or radio at that time, the information becomes virtually inaccessible. There is simply not enough time to scan through tapes of yesterday's news for relevant stories. Even when it is possible to watch when the news is being broadcast, the viewer must spend the time required to view all the stories in a news show, since broadcasts do not provide the ability to select which stories to skip and which to pursue in more detail.

Furthermore, a person can only attend to one news channel at a time. Similar or related information broadcast on another news channel at the same time cannot easily be viewed. In contrast, text news on a topic is generally available in overwhelming quantities but cannot provide the comprehensive visual and audio information available in radio and video material.

The solution is to compress, digitally store and analyze news broadcasts on the computer. All information is made accessible through interactive queries. These queries allow the user to retrieve relevant segments from all the news programs that carried stories on the topic of interest. Each individual news story is indexed based on a text transcript. All news information becomes accessible through interactive queries at the user's convenience, permitting the retrieval of relevant news stories from all the networks and news sources that covered the topic of interest. An outline of the system is given in figure 1.

Most other attempts at solving the news retrieval problem by providing

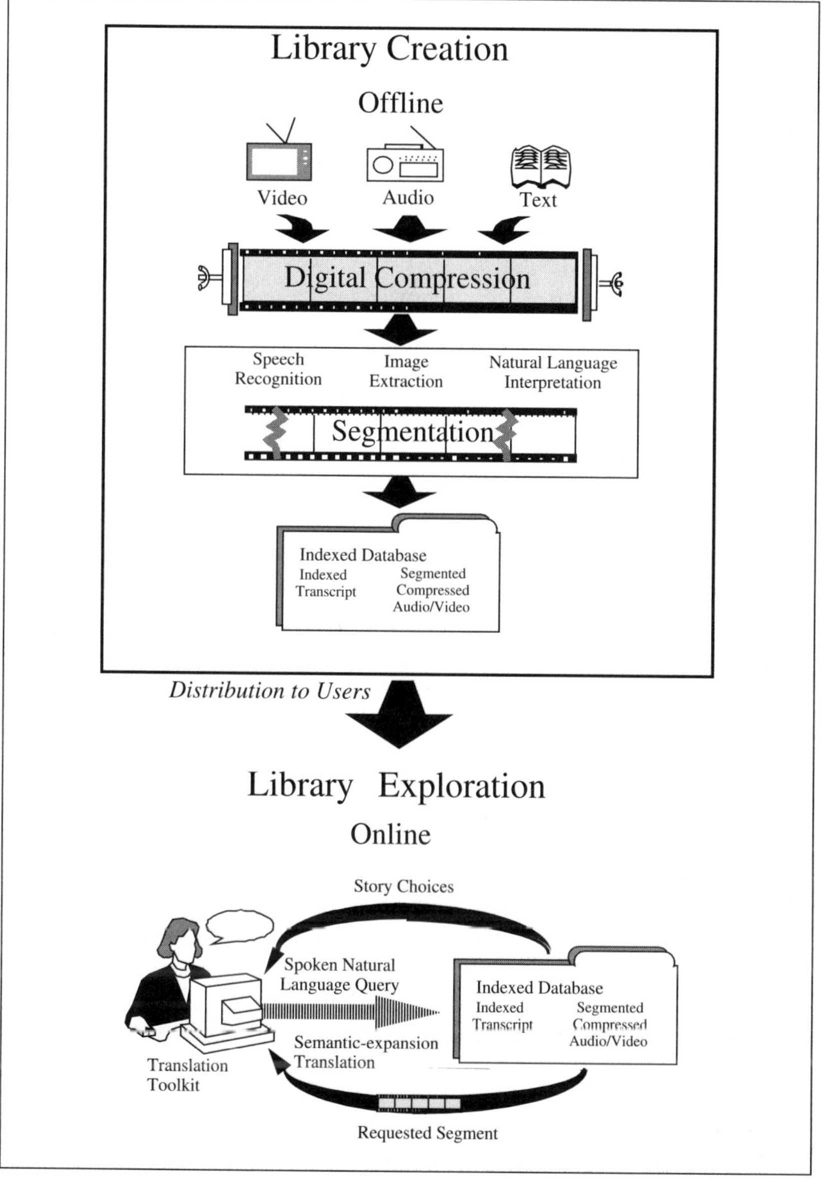

Figure 1. Overview of the News-On-Demand system.

news databases have restricted the data to text material only. Video-on-demand allows a user to select, and pay for, a complete program, but does not allow for selective retrieval. The closest approximation to News-on-Demand can be found in the "CNN-AT-WORK" system offered to businesses by a

CNN/Intel cooperation. At the heart of the CNN-AT-WORK solution is a digitizer that encodes the video into INDEO format compression format and transmits it to workstations over a local area network. Users can store headlines together with video clips and retrieve them at a later date. However, this service depends entirely on the separately transmitted "headlines" and does not include other news sources than CNN. In addition, CNN-AT-WORK does not feature an integrated multimodal query interface (CNN-AT-WORK 1995).

Preliminary investigation into the use of speech recognition for analysis of a news story was carried out by Schäuble and Wechsler (1995). Without a powerful speech recognizer, their approach used a phonetic engine that transformed the spoken content of the news stories into a, possibly errorful, phoneme string. The query was also transformed into a phoneme string and the database searched for the best approximate match. Errors in recognition and word prefix and suffix differences did not prevent the operation of the system since these errors scattered evenly over all documents allowing the well-matching search scores to dominate the retrieval.

Another news processing system that includes video materials is the MEDUSA system (Brown et al. 1995). The MEDUSA news broadcast application can digitize and record news video and teletext transcriptions, which are equivalent to closed-captions. Instead of segmenting the news into stories, the system uses overlapping windows of adjacent text lines for indexing and retrieval. During retrieval the system responds to typed requests by returning an ordered list of the most relevant news broadcasts. Query words are stripped of suffixes before search and the relevance ranking takes word frequency in the segment and over all the corpus into account, as well as the ability of words to discriminate between stories. Within a news broadcast, it is up to the user to select and play a region, using information provided by the system about the position of the matched keywords. The focus of MEDUSA is in the system architecture and the information retrieval component. No image processing and no speech recognition is performed.

Other projects that seek to index and retrieve from video news sources include the Conceptually Indexed Video project at Sun (Woods 1996), which is attempting to build conceptual taxonomies of query terms to improve the quality of returned stories, and the VISION system at the University of Kansas which, while similar in aim to Informedia, is concentrating on the problems of compressing video data and delivering it over the Internet. It is also distinguished by its stated concentration on the use of pre-existing, mature, domain independent indexing technologies (Li et al. 1996).

The Broadcast News Navigator (BNN) system (Maybury et al. 1996; Mani et al., this volume) has concentrated on the automatic segmentation of stories from news broadcasts using discourse structure. While a great deal of success has been achieved so far using heuristics based on stereotypical features of particular shows (e.g. "still to come on the News Hour tonight..."), the longer term objective is to use multi-stream analysis of such features as speaker change detection, scene changes, appearance of music and so forth to achieve reliable and robust story segmentation. The system also aims to provide a deeper level of understanding of story content than is provided by simple full text search, by extracting and identifying, for example, all the named entities in a story.

The Informedia project, in as much as it involves the indexing of non-textual data, also bears similarities to projects such as QBIC (Flickner et al. 1995, this volume), which applies both automatic image characterization and hand-annotation to images, and supports their retrieval using image similarity. One of the more interesting features of the QBIC system is that it allows query by demonstration, with the user sketching the features desired in the retrieved image. A similar effort, which also encompasses some video material, is the Photobook system (Pentland et al. 1994). Photobook employs relatively sophisticated statistical characterizations of selected image features, such as faces, shapes and textures, to support accurate retrieval by image similarity. A final example of an image retrieval system is Chabot (Ogle and Stonebraker 1995), a part of the Berkeley digital library project. This system includes an element of cross-modal operation, allowing users to search simultaneously in pre-existing annotations and color content characterizations of a large set of landscape images. This allows searches for objects such as "yellow flowers," that might not have been easily identified from the annotations or image qualities alone.

1.3 Component Technologies

There are three broad categories of technologies we can bring to bear to create and search a digital video library built from broadcast video and audio materials (Hauptmann and Smith 1995):

Text processing looks at the textual (ASCII) representation of the words that were spoken, and at other text annotations that may be derived from the transcript, from the production notes, or from closed-captioning that is sometimes broadcast with the news stories. Text analysis can work on an existing transcript to help segment the text into paragraphs (Mauldin 1989). An analysis of keyword prominence allows us to identify important sections in the transcript. Other more sophisticated language based criteria are under investigation. We currently use two main techniques for text analysis:

- If we have a complete time-aligned transcript available from the closed-captioning or from a human-generated transcription, we can exploit "structural" text markers such as caption punctuation to identify news story boundaries.

- To rank the contents of news segments, we use the well-known TFIDF (term frequency, inverse document frequency) weighting scheme to identify critical keywords and their relative importance for the video document (Salton and McGill 1983).

Image analysis looks at the images in the video stream. Image analysis is primarily used for the identification of scene breaks and to select static frame icons that are representative of a scene. Primitive image features based on image statistics, such as color histograms, are used for indexing, matching and segmenting images (Zhang et al. 1995). The following two techniques are currently implemented in our News-on-Demand production system:

- Using *color histogram analysis,* video is segmented into scenes through the use of comparative difference measures. Images with small histogram disparity are considered to be relatively similar. By detecting significant changes in the weighted color histogram of successive frames, image sequences can be separated into individual scenes. A comparison between cumulative distributions is used as a difference measure. This result is passed through a high pass filter to further isolate peaks and an empirical threshold is used to select only those regions where scene breaks occur.

- Optical flow analysis is an important method of visual segmentation and description based on interpreting camera motion. We can identify camera motion as a pan or zoom by examining the geometric properties of the optical flow vectors. Using the Lucas-Kanade (Lucas and Kanade 1981) gradient descent method for measuring optical flow, we can track individual regions from one frame to the next. By measuring the velocity of individual regions over time, a motion representation of the scene is created. Sudden, widespread changes in this flow suggest random motion, and therefore, new scenes. Optical flow changes also occur during gradual transitions between images such as fades or special effects.

Only regions of low ambiguity are selected for tracking. Trackable regions are found by searching the entire image for sub-windows whose gradient derivatives exhibit relatively similar eigenvalues. In order to accurately track a region over large areas, a multi-resolution structure is used. With this structure we can track regions across many pixels and reduce the time needed for computation. When optical flow is minimal the frames are suitable for use in an iconic frame representation.

These techniques work well when scene changes are abrupt, however, camera motion and gradual transitions can severely affect the scene segmentation accuracy of the system. When changes are gradual, we combine the optical flow results with histogram analysis. This allows for segmentation under conditions that do not involve sudden changes in image content.

Speech analysis provides the basis for analyzing the audio component of the news broadcast. To transcribe the content of the video material, we use the Sphinx-II speech recognition engine, a large-vocabulary, speaker-independent, continuous speech recognizer created at Carnegie Mellon (CMU-Speech 1995; Hwang et al. 1994). Sphinx-II uses senonic semi-continuous hidden Markov models (HMMs) to model between-word context-dependent phones. The system uses four types of codebooks: mel-frequency cepstral coefficients, first cepstral differences, second cepstral differences, and power and its first and second differences. Twenty-seven phone classes are identified, and a set of four VQ codebooks is trained for each phone class. Cepstral vectors are normalized using an utterance-based cepstral mean value. The semi-continuous observation probability is computed using a variable-sized mixture of the top Gaussian distributions from each phone-dependent codebook.

The recognizer processes an utterance in four steps:

1. A forward time-synchronous pass using between-word senonic semi-continuous acoustic models with phone-dependent codebooks and a bigram language model is performed. This produces a set of possible word occurrences, with each word occurrence having one start time and multiple possible end times.

2. A backward pass using the same system configuration is then performed, resulting in multiple possible begin times for each end time predicted in the first pass.

3. An A* algorithm is used to generate the set of N-best hypotheses for the utterance from the results of the forward and backward passes. Any language model can be applied in this pass — the default is a trigram language model. This approximate A* algorithm is not guaranteed to produce the best-scoring hypothesis first.

4. The best-scoring hypothesis is selected from among the N-best list produced. This hypothesis is output as the recognizer's result.

The language model consists of words with probabilities, bigrams or trigrams which arc word pairs or triplets respectively with conditional probabilities for the last word given the previous word or word-pair. Normally, a word trigram is used to predict the next words for the recognizer. However, a back-off procedure allows the next word predicted from only the current word, using bigram probabilities, at a penalty. A word may also occur independently of context, based only on its individual probability, with another larger back-off penalty. Our current largest and most accurate language model was constructed from a corpus of news stories from the Wall Street Journal collected from 1989 to 1994, and from the Associated Press news service stories from 1988 to 1990. Only trigrams that were encountered more than once were included in the model, but the most frequent 58800 words in the corpus, and their bigrams, were all included (Rudnicky 1995).

Acoustic signal analysis is used to identify segment boundaries of paragraph size. We can detect transitions between speakers and topics which are marked by silence or low energy areas in the acoustic signal. To detect breaks between utterances we use a Signal to Noise ratio (SNR) computation. This algorithm computes the power of digitized speech samples where each si is a pre-emphasized sample of speech gathered over a twenty millisecond frame. A low power level indicates that there is little active speech occurring in the frame. Segmentation breaks between utterances are set at the point of minimum power after smoothing over a one second window. To prevent unusually long segments, we force the system to place at least one break within each thirty seconds. This algorithm seems to be fairly robust in segmenting speech at silences or speaker changes. An empirical evaluation of the algorithm is in progress.

We can distinguish two distinct phases during News-On-Demand processing: library creation and library exploration. Library creation deals with the accumulation of information, transcription, segmentation and indexing. Library exploration concerns the interaction between the system and the user trying to retrieve selections in the database. The following section illustrates how the different technologies interact in the creation of a multimedia digital news library.

2. What is Informedia: News-on-Demand

Unlike other Informedia prototypes (Christel et al. 1994ab) which are designed to be testbeds for educational uses of the system, News-on-Demand focuses on the research goal of finding rapid and fully automatic methods for the creation of an indexed digital video library. While the educational content of the other Informedia prototypes allows time for careful computer-assisted human editing, the short-lived nature of news requires library creation and update for News-on-Demand to be completely automatic. In our early work on the Informedia digital video library, all segmentation was done by hand. Due to the time constraints of continuous daily news coverage and the volume of data, we are now using fully automatic news library creation methods.

The following steps are performed during library creation by a set of cooperating scripts and programs:

1. Digitize the video and audio data using MPEG-I compression format.
2. Create a time-aligned transcript from closed-captioning or from speech recognition output.
3. Segment shows at story boundaries.
4. Segment images by finding scene breaks and select key frames for each scene
5. Index all stories for access using the Informedia client program.

In more detail, these steps proceed as follows:

1. Our current library creation process starts with a raw digitized video tape. Generally, the videos in the Informedia: News-on-Demand Library are half-hour news shows selected from amongst the evening news broadcasts. Radio news shows such as "All Things Considered" or the news broadcasts from the Voice of America are also compressed and incorporated into the library. Using inexpensive off-the-shelf PC-based hardware we can compress video and audio to about 520 Mbytes/hour of video in MPEG-I format. The audio-only data is compressed to about 80 Mbytes/hour.

2. The audio portion of the signal is extracted and fed through the speech analysis routines, which produce a transcript of the spoken text. A subset of the news stories also have closed-captioning text available. However, the closed-captioned data, if available, may lag up to twenty-five seconds behind the actual words spoken. This problem, and general inaccuracies in transcription, are especially glaring when the broadcast is ``live''. In News-on-Demand we use speech recognition in conjunction with closed-captioning, when available, to improve the time-alignment of the transcripts. To create a time-aligned transcript from closed-captioned text, the speech recognizer output is aligned against the closed-caption transcript words using an orthographic distance measure with a standard dynamic programming algorithm. Through this alignment each word in the closed-captioned transcript is assigned an accurate time marker derived from the corresponding word in the speech recognition output.

   For the news broadcasts that are not closed-captioned, we use a transcript generated exclusively by the speech recognition system. The vocabulary and language model used here approximate a "general American news" language model. It was based on a large corpus of North American business news from 1987 to 1994 (Rudnicky 1995). In addition, transcripts or closed-captioning text may be obtainable for the video data. If there is a text transcript available during library creation, speech recognition helps create a time-aligned transcript of the spoken words as well as segmenting the broadcast into paragraphs. The library index needs very specific information about the start and end of each spoken word, in order to select the relevant video "paragraph" to retrieve and to find individual words within the story.

3. To allow efficient access to the relevant content of the news data, we need to break up the broadcasts into small pieces or news stories. To answer a user query by showing an entire half-hour long news show is rarely a reasonable response. Initially, the speech signal is analyzed for low energy sections that indicate acoustic "paragraphs" by the presence of silence. This is the first pass at segmentation; if a closed-captioned

text transcript is available, we also use structural markers such as punctuation and paragraph boundaries to identify news stories. If only a speech recognition generated transcript is available, the acoustically determined paragraph boundaries identified using silence detection are used.

4. Image analysis is primarily used for the identification of breaks between scenes and for the identification of a single static frame icon that is representative of a scene. Primitive image features based on image statistics, such as color histograms, and their time functions, are computed and used for indexing, matching and segmenting images.

The Informedia library creation phase uses three different levels of segmentation for a video. The largest segment type consists of a "news story"—a series of related scenes with a common content. The system needs to determine the beginning and ending of an individual news story. In the ideal case, a news story starts at the natural boundary of the relevant content and ends wherever the video moves to a different context.

The second level of segmentation identifies an individual scene of video within the news story. Segment breaks produced by image processing are examined along with the boundaries identified by the speech and natural language processing of the transcript, and an improved set of segment boundaries are heuristically derived to partition the news story into scenes.

Finally, within a single scene we also need to be able to select a representative, characteristic *frame icon* for static display. Such a single frame is displayed as the representative for the whole video segment. This is used in a static display showing the results of a user query. Showing frame icons allows the user to look simultaneously at a static representation of multiple video paragraphs and to obtain some information about their content and possible relevance to the user's query, before selecting any one paragraph to be played. In choosing a static icon representative of a video clip, we rely exclusively on the image data. The paragraph bounds are determined by the transcript and keywords. Within the paragraph the most prominent keywords identify the most prominent scene. The scene boundaries are determined by color histogram differences and optical flow analysis. Within the scene we select the key frame icon using optical flow analysis.

5. The keywords and their corresponding paragraph locations in the video are indexed for inclusion in the Informedia library catalogue. An inverted index is created using the Pursuit search engine (Mauldin 1989). To obtain video clips that are candidate matches to a user's query, the system searches for keywords from the query in the recognition transcript.

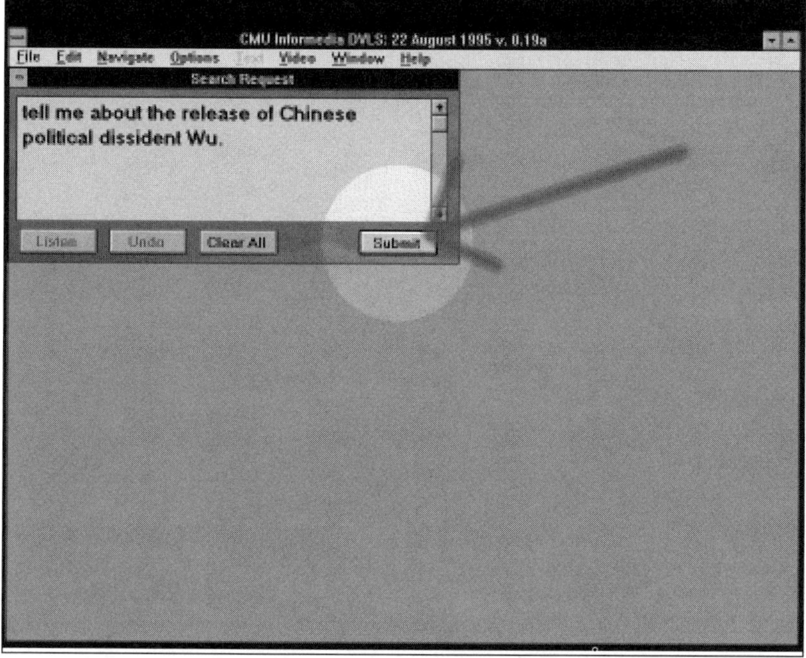

Figure 2. User submitting spoken query to the database search engine.

When a match is found and selected by the user, the surrounding video paragraph is returned.

3. Library Exploration

Library exploration concerns the interaction between the system and the user trying to retrieve news material in the database.

During library exploration the user generally goes through the following procedure, where steps may be repeated or skipped:

1. The user speaks a query to the system. If the query was misrecognized, the user may repeat or edit it by hand (see figure 2).

2. The query is submitted and the database is searched for matches.

3. The user selects among the news stories returned as results, possibly refining the query first (see figure 3).

4. A result story is selected for display (see figures 4 and 5).

Figure 3. Display of best three icons matching the query.
The left result icon is a book, indicating a text source.
The middle icon is a radio, indicating and audio-only source.
The right, highlighted, icon is a key frame from a video news story.
The user selects the "filmstrip" button at the bottom of the right icon.

3.1. Speaking a Query

Users are able to explore the Informedia library through an interface that allows them to search the library using typed or spoken natural language queries, select relevant documents retrieved from the library and play or display the material on their PC workstations. The current interface for the Informedia system is very simple. There are four buttons and a query text window. The text window shows the result of the speech recognition and can be edited by selecting portions of the text and typing.

The LISTEN button must be held pressed while the user is speaking. Pushing the LISTEN button starts the recognition process and releasing the button signals the end of the query. In the future we hope to include a continuous listening mode, with the computer deciding when it is being spoken to, enabling us to eliminate this button.

The SUBMIT button sends the text that is currently in the query text window to the search retrieval component, which then returns the relevant matches.

The CLEAR button erases all text from the text query window.

The UNDO button erases just the last recognized utterance from the query text window. All earlier utterances are still part of the current query until they are erased with a CLEAR.

This simple interface seems sufficiently simple and intuitive to learn. However we are currently experimenting with even fewer buttons, where undo becomes unnecessary, or is replaced by a voice command, and every query is immediately submitted, eliminating the need for the separate submit button.

This library retrieval system can effectively process natural spoken queries. During library exploration, the Sphinx-II speech recognition allows a user to query the system by voice, simplifying the interface by making the interaction more direct. The integration of speech with the interface enhances access to the stored video data by allowing more immediate and direct entry of queries.

During library exploration, the Sphinx-II (Hwang et al. 1994) speech recognition system allows a user to query the system by voice, simplifying the interface by making the interaction more direct. The integration of speech with the interface enhances access to the stored video data by allowing more immediate and direct entry of queries. The language model used during exploration is similar to that in (Rudnicky 1995) but emphasizes key phrases frequently used in queries such as "How about," "Tell me about," "Is there anything about," etc. In the future we plan to limit the language model to only those words found in the actual library data, making the language model more efficient and smaller.

3.2 Submitting a Query

Figure 2 shows the user making the query "tell me about the release of Chinese political dissident Wu." The words "tell," "me," "about," "the," and "of" have been eliminated from the query as stop-words. The stop-words are function words selected from the most frequent query words. The keywords "release," "Chinese," "political," "dissident" and "Wu" are used for the query. The query also looks for words with the same stems derived from a Houghton-Mifflin electronic dictionary of word roots (e.g., dissident and dissidents). Retrieval is done using an inverted index of the entire transcripts of all news stories, and each indexed story is ranked by relevance based on the frequency of the keywords occurring within the news stories.

3.3 Selecting Among the Returned Query Results

Figure 3 shows the results of the query display through 3 types of icons. A book icon indicates that the result is from a text source. The middle icon indicates a radio only source. The right icon shows the key frame for a video story. The most relevant words from early in each story are displayed at the

Figure 4. The filmstrip view displays the full news story with one key icon for each scene. Moving the cursor over the red marks the system places on the scene icon shows where the search query words were spoken in the scene.

top of each icon. The user wants to find out more about the video story and clicks on the filmstrip button below the right thumbnail poster frame icon. Figure 4 shows the resulting filmstrip view. In this view, one key-frame thumbnail icon is displayed for each scene in the news story, as determined by the image analysis. Moving the mouse over the scene displays the key-words that were matched within the scene. The location of these words is also marked. These features help the user select among the returned results, and deliver relevant data about the video in the library in a compact format, using information embedded with the video during library creation.

3.4. Playing or Displaying a Story

Once the user has made a choice, and clicked on a story icon to play, the matching news story is displayed in the video window on the right half of the screen. Figure 5 also shows each word being highlighted as it is spoken. The transcript can be displayed below the video window, and automatically scrolls in sequence with the video.

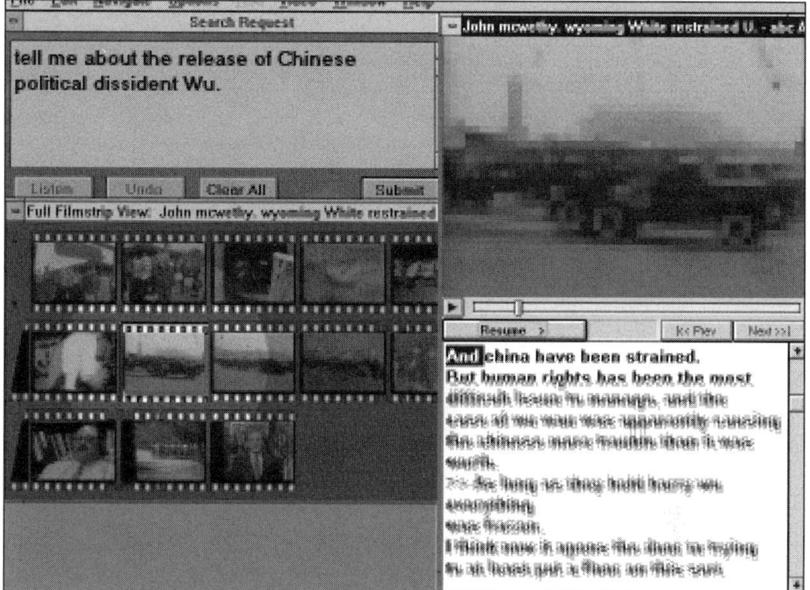

Figure 5. The user now plays the news story from the chosen scene.
A text transcript is displayed below the video on the right side.
Each text word is highlighted as it is spoken.

4. News-on-Demand: Speech Recognition Facts and Results

Table 1 shows the results of testing recognition accuracy on a variety of video data. The results on our data show that the type of speech and the environment in which it was created dramatically alter the speech recognition accuracy.

4.1 Speech Benchmark Evaluation

The basic reference point is the standard speech evaluation data which is used to benchmark speech recognition systems with large vocabularies between 5– and 60–thousand words. The recognition systems are carefully tuned to this evaluation and the results can be considered close to optimal for the current state of speech recognition research. In these evaluations, we typically see word error rates ranging from eight to twelve percent depending on the test set. Note that word error rate is defined as the sum of insertions, substitutions and deletions. This value can be larger than one hundred percent and is regarded as a better measure of recognizer accuracy than the number

Type of Speech Data	Word Error Rate = Insertions + Deletions + Substitutions
1) Speech benchmark evaluation	~ 8% - 12%
2) News text spoken in lab	~ 10%- 17%
3) Narrator recorded in TV studio	~ 20%
4) C-Span	~ 40%
5) Dialog in documentary video	~ 50% - 65%
6) Evening News (30 min)	~ 65%
7) Complete 1-hour documentary	~ 75%
8) Commercials	~ 85%

Table 1. Speech recognition results.

of words correct. (i.e. words correct = 100% - deletions - substitutions).

4.2 News Text Spoken in Lab

Taking a transcript of TV broadcast data with an average reader and re-recording it in a speech lab under good acoustic conditions, with a close-talking microphone shows an estimate of word error rate between ten and seventeen percent for speech recognition systems that were not tuned for the specific language and domain in question.

4.3 Narrator Recorded in TV Studio

Speech that has been recorded by a professional narrator in a TV studio and that does not include any music or other noise gives us an error rate of around twenty percent. Part of the increased error rate is due to poor segmentation of utterances leaving the speech recognizer unable to tell where an utterance started or ended. This problem was not present in the lab recorded data. Different microphones and environmental acoustics also contribute to the higher error rate.

4.4 C-Span

Speech recognition on C-Span broadcast data shows a doubling of the word error rate to forty percent. While speakers in this data are mostly constant and always close to the microphone, other noises and verbal interruptions degrade the accuracy of the recognition.

4.5 Dialog in Documentary Video

The dialog portions of broadcast documentary videos yielded recognition word error rates of fifty to sixty-five percent, depending on the video data.

The signal for these sections contains many more environmental noises as well as speech recorded outdoors.

4.6 Evening News

The evening news was recognized with sixty five percent overall error rate. This rate includes recognition accuracy for commercials and introductions as well as the actual news program.

4.7 Complete One-Hour Documenary

A full one-hour documentary video including commercials and music raised the word error rate to seventy-five percent.

4.8 Commercials

Worst of all were commercials, which were recognized with an eighty-five percent error rate due to the large amounts of music in the audio channel as well as the unusual speech characteristics, and singing, contained in the spoken portion.

4.9 Recognition Results

While these recognition results seem dismaying at first glance, they merely represent a first attempt at quantifying the usefulness of speech recognition for broadcast video and audio material. Fortunately speech recognition does not have to be perfect to be useful in the Informedia digital video library.

The transcript generated by Sphinx-II recognition need not be viewed by users, but can be hidden. However, the words in the transcript are time-aligned with the video for subsequent retrieval. Because, generally, only the timing information from the speech recognition output is used directly, errors in recognition are not directly visible to users and our system can tolerate higher error rates than those that would be required to produce a human-readable transcript.

5. Issues for Future Research

The research issues are split into five broad areas: data delivery, user interfaces, image understanding, natural language processing and speech recognition.

There are two main data delivery issues: How can we address the problem of huge storage requirements of the MPEG-I encoded video data accumulated through daily news broadcasts? An hour of video takes up about half a gigabyte of disk space. To populate the news on demand library we need to investigate how much data is necessary for the index to be kept current and when the data can be "forgotten." The data could be degraded to lower quality video at fewer frames per second, and lower resolution. We could also eliminate the video entirely and save only the audio portion. Finally we could retain only the text transcript without audio or video.

The second data delivery issue concerns the transmission of the video news story to a remote user. Essentially, we need to provide fast enough networks to allow MPEG-I bit rates to be transmitted continuously, and servers that can keep up with this demand for many simultaneous users.

The user interface issues deal with the way users explore the library once it is available. Can the user intuitively navigate the space of features and options provided in the Informedia: News-on-Demand interface? What other features should the system provide to allow users to obtain the information they are looking for? We plan to move the system to a testbed deployment so that we can gain design insights from users and investigate various interface design alternatives.

Natural language processing research for News-on-Demand has to provide acceptable segmentation of the news broadcasts into stories. We also want to generate more meaningful short summaries of the news stories in natural sounding English. Natural language processing also has a role in query matching for optimal retrieval from the story texts. Finally, the system would greatly improve if queries could be parsed to separate out dates, major concepts and types of news sources.

Image processing research (Hauptmann and Smith 1995) is continuing to refine the identification of cuts in the video for scene segmentation. Within a scene and within a story, image processing gives us a key frame to represent that scene or story. The choice of a single key frame to best represent a whole scene is a subject of active research. In the longer term, we plan to add text detection and OCR capabilities for reading captions and text off the screen background. In the future, we also hope to include comprehensive similarity-based image matching in the retrieval features available to a user. An initial implementation of image matching is included in a current version of the system.

Speech recognition helps create a time-aligned transcript of the spoken words. While the use of a speech recognizer for transcribing all the audio data into text is a simple concept, we must consider the accuracy of the recognition system. Speech recognition is inherently error prone, and the magnitude of the error rate will determine whether the system is usable or useless. Thus recognizer accuracy is the critical factor in any attempt to use speech recognition for the digital video library. There are a many speech research issues that have been brought to light while studying this data and the uses of speech recognition in the News-on-Demand Library.

When the speech recognizer does not find a trigram (word triple) probability recorded in the language model for the current hypothesized word triplet, it uses bigrams in the language model, although with a probability penalty. Similarly, when an appropriate bigram cannot be found in the language model, individual word probabilities are used, again with a penalty. There were between one and four percent of the spoken words missing from the transcription lexicon. Since each missed word gives rise on average to one and a half to two word errors, this alone accounts for two to eight percent of the error rate. The word pairs (bigrams) in the language model were also inadequate. Depending on the data set, anywhere from eight to fifteen percent of the word pairs were not present in our language model. The trigram coverage gap was quite large. Between seventy and eighty percent of the trigrams in the data were not in the language model — these triples would consequently be recognized with a much lower probability.

By itself, the video library's unlimited vocabulary degrades recognition rate. However, several innovative techniques can be exploited to reduce errors. The use of program-specific information, such as topic-based lexicons and interest-ranked word lists can be added to the information sources employed by the recognizer. Word hypotheses can be improved by using adaptive, "long-distance" language models, and we can use a multi-pass recognition approach that considers multi-sentence contexts. Recent research at CMU in long distance language models indicates twenty to thirty percent improvement in accuracy may be realized by dynamically adapting the vocabulary based on words that have recently been observed in prior utterances.

In addition, most broadcast video programs have significant amounts of descriptive text available. These include early descriptions of the program design called treatments, working scripts, abstracts describing the program, and captions. Words that are likely to appear in the daily news can be obtained from many other sources of news such as the on-line wire services. In combination, these resources can provide valuable additions to dictionaries used by the recognizer. We are exploring the use of these sources of information in our current research.

Speech recognizers are very sensitive to different microphones and to the different environmental conditions in which their acoustic models were trained. Even microphone placement is a factor in recognizer accuracy. Much of the degradation of speech accuracy in the results of Table 1 between the lab and the broadcast data, using identical words, can be attributed to microphone and environment noise. We are actively looking at noise compensation techniques and microphone independence to ameliorate this problem. The use of stereo data from the left and right broadcast channel may also help in reducing the drop in accuracy due to environmental noise.

Perhaps the greatest benefit of speech recognition comes from alignment to existing transcripts or closed-captioning text. The speech recognizer is run independently and the result is matched using a forced text alignment against the transcript. Even though the recognition accuracy may only provide one correct word in five, this is sufficient to allow the system to accurately find the boundaries of the story paragraphs, and the time at which the words were spoken within those boundaries.

Of course, a fully automated system like News-on-Demand will inevitably make errors. We distinguish five types of errors, all of which are subjects of active research aimed at improving the system:

1. False segmentation of stories. This happens when we incorrectly identify the beginning and end of a video paragraph associated with a single news story. Incorrect segmentation is usually due to inaccurate transcription, either from errors in the closed-captioning itself, errors in processing the closed-captioning text into stories, or errors in the segmentation based on the speech transcription.

2. False words in transcripts. Errors in the transcript are either the result of faulty speech recognition or errors in the closed-captioned text. The result is the appearance of incorrect words in stories and consequent errors in the index and in retrieval.

3. False synchronization. Occasionally words are retrieved that were actually spoken elsewhere in the video. This is generally due to closed-captioning mismatched with the speech recognition.

4. Incorrectly recognized queries. This is the result of an incorrect speech recognition during the library exploration. The user can edit and correct query recognition errors by typing, or simply repeat or rephrase the query.

5. Incorrect set of stories returned for a query. The prevalence of this type of error is measured through information recall and precision. The user might get stories that are not relevant to the query or miss relevant stories. Some of these errors are caused by previously mentioned problems, and others are the result of shortcomings in the processing of the query into retrieval keywords.

6. Conclusions

Despite the drawbacks of a fully automated system, the benefits of News-on-Demand are very dramatic. With News-on-Demand, we can navigate the complex information space of news stories, without the linear access constraint that normally makes this process so time consuming. Thus Informedia News-on-Demand provides a new dimension in information access to video and audio material. In the future, we plan to add OCR capabilities for reading headlines and image processing for visual scene segmentation to the News-on-Demand system.

Speech recognition is not a panacea for retrieval from video libraries. There is no "listening typewriter." However even speech recognition with reasonable accuracy can be used to great effect in making accessible data that would otherwise be completely unavailable. Especially in conjunction with the use of transcripts or closed-captioning, speech recognition even at high error rates is tremendously useful in the digital video library creation process. For queries, the ability to quickly correct and edit spoken commands makes the spoken query interface quite usable. Despite the drawbacks of errors in the system, the benefits of speech recognition are very dramatic.

Universal access to digitally processed news will significantly affect the conduct of business, professional, and personal activity. The initial impact of News-on-Demand will be on the broad accessibility and reuse of all standard news materials, including TV, radio and text, previously generated for broadcast or publication.

The greatest societal impact of the Informedia project is anticipated in K-12 education. The Informedia Digital Video Library represents a critical step toward an educational future that we can hardly recognize today. Ready access to multimedia resources will bring to the paradigm of "books, blackboards, and classrooms" the energy, vitality, and intimacy of "entertainment" television and video games. The persistent and pervasive impact of such capabilities can help to revolutionize education as we've known it, making it as engaging and powerful as the television students have come to love.

Acknowledgments

This material is based upon work supported by the National Science Foundation under Cooperative Agreement No. IRI-9411299. Any opinions, findings, and conclusions or recommendations expressed in this material are those of the authors and do not necessarily reflect the views of the National Science Foundation.

We would like to thank Michael Smith for his help with News-on-Demand image processing, Mike Christel for the Informedia library interface and Ravi Mosur for the fbs6/fbs8 Sphinx-II implementation. We are also indebted to all the members of the Informedia Project under Howard Wactlar for helping to digitize and record the data as well as the CMU Speech Group under Raj Reddy for all their support.

References

Brown, M. G.; Foote, J. T.; Jones, G. J. F.; Sparck Jones, K.; and Young, S. J. 1995. Automatic Content-based Retrieval of Broadcast News. In Proceedings of ACM Multimedia, 35-43. San Francisco: ACM.

Christel, M.; Stevens, S. and Wactlar, H. 1994a. Informedia Digital Video Library,

Proceedings of the Second ACM International Conference on Multimedia, Video Program, 480-481. New York: ACM.

Christel, M.; Kanade, T. ; Mauldin, M. ; Reddy, R. ; Sirbu, M. ; Stevens, S. ; and Wactlar, H. 1994b. Informedia Digital Video Library. *Communications of the ACM* 38(4): 57-58.

CNN-AT-WORK. 1995. Cable News Network/Intel CNN at Work - Live News on your Networked PC Product Information. http://www.intel.com/comm-net/cnn_work/index.html.

Flickner, M.; Sawhney, H.; Niblack, W.; Ashley, J.; Huang, Q.; Dom, B.; Gorkani, M.; Hafner, J.; Lee, D.; Petkovic, D.; Steele, D.; and Yanker, P. 1995. Query by Image and Video Content: The QBIC System. *IEEE Computer* 28(9): 23-31. Also in this volume.

Hauptmann, A. G.; Witbrock, M. J.; Rudnicky, A.; and Reed, S. 1995. Speech for Multimedia Information Retrieval. In Proceedings of User Interface Software Technology (UIST-95), Pittsburgh, PA: ACM. In press.

Hauptmann, A. G. and Smith, M. 1995. Text, Speech, and Vision for Video Segmentation: The Informedia Project. AAAI Fall 1995 Symposium on Computational Models for Integrating Language and Vision, 90-95. Cambridge, MA: MIT.

Hwang, M.; Rosenfeld, R.; Thayer, E.; Mosur, R.; Chase, L.; Weide, R.; Huang, X.; and Alleva, F. 1994. Improving Speech Recognition Performance via Phone-Dependent VQ Codebooks and Adaptive Language Models in SPHINX-II. In Proceedings of IEEE International Conference on Acoustics, Speech and Signal Processing (ICASSP-94), Vol I: 549-552.

Informedia. 1995. http://www.informedia.cs.cmu.edu/

Lucas, B. D. and Kanade, T. 1981. An Iterative Technique of Image Registration and Its Application to Stereo. In Proceedings of the 7th International Joint Conference on Artificial Intelligence (IJCAI), 674-679. Los Altos, CA: William Kaufmann.

Li, W.; Gauch, S.; Gauch, J.; and Pua, K. M. 1996. VISION: A Digital Video Library. In Proceedings of Digital Libraries '96: 1st ACM International Conference on Research and Development in Digital Libraries, 17-27. Bethesda, MD: ACM.

Mani, I.; House, D.; Maybury, M.; and Green, M. 1997. Towards Content-Based Browsing of Broadcast News Video. In this volume.

Mauldin, M. 1989. Information Retrieval by Text Skimming. Ph.D. diss., Carnegie Mellon University. Revised edition published as Mauldin, M. 1991. Conceptual Information Retrieval: A Case Study in Adaptive Partial Parsing, Boston: Kluwer.

Maybury, M.; Merlino, A.; and Rayson, J. 1996. Segmentation, Content Extraction and Visualization of Broadcast News Video Using Multistream Analysis. Draft Manuscript.

Ogle, V. and Stonebraker, M. September 1995 Chabot: Retrieval from a Relational Database of Images. *IEEE Computer* 28(9): 40-48.

Pentland, A.; Picard, R.; Sclaroff, S. 1994. Photobook: Tools for Content-Base Manipulation of Image Databases. In Proceedings of SPIE Conference on Storage and Retrieval of Image and Video Databases II, 34-47 (SPIE paper 2185-05) San Jose, CA: SPIE.

Rudnicky, A. 1995. Language Modeling with Limited Domain Data. In Proceedings of the 1995 ARPA Workshop on Spoken Language Technology, 66–69, San Mateo, CA.

CMU-Speech. 1995. http://www.speech.cs.cmu.edu/speecH/

Salton, G. and McGill, M. J. 1983. Introduction to Modern Information Retrieval. In McGraw-Hill Computer Science Series. New York: McGraw-Hill.

Schäuble, P. and Wechsler, M. 1995. First Experiences with a System for Content Based Retrieval of Information from Speech Recordings. In Working notes of IJCAI-95 Workshop on Intelligent Multimedia Information Retrieval, 59-69, ed. M. T. Maybury. Montreal: IJCAI.

Stevens, S.; Christel, M.; and Wactlar, H. 1994. Informedia: Improving Access to Digital Video. *Interactions* 1: 67-71.

Wactlar, H. D.; Kanade, T.; Smith, M.A.; and Stevens, S.M. 1996. Intelligent Access to Digital Video: Informedia Project. *IEEE Computer* 29(5): 46-52.

Woods, W. 1996. Conceptually Indexed Video: Enhanced Storage and Retrieval. Unpublished manuscript. http://www.sun.com/960201/cover/video.html

Zhang, H.; Low, C.; and Smoliar, S. 1995. Video Parsing and Indexing of Compressed Data. *Multimedia Tools and Applications* (1): 89-111.

Chapter 12

Towards Content-Based Browsing of Broadcast News Video

Inderjeet Mani, David House, Mark Maybury, The MITRE Corporation; Morgan Green, School of Computer Science, Carnegie Mellon University

Abstract

This chapter reports on investigations to create a content-based information retrieval system for broadcast news video. We report results from experiments investigating the automated segmentation of video using linguistic analysis of the closed-caption text, comparing a subject classification approach with one based on discourse cues. We discuss how this work might be extended to support more sophisticated multimedia browsing/visualization, information extraction, and (multimedia) summarization.

1. Introduction

Content-based access to video is fundamental to a number of applications including video mail, video teleconference archiving, and on-line information services (e.g., broadcast news search, personalized electronic newspapers, encyclopedia creation and access). The advent of digital video affords the opportunity for rapid network or broadcast delivery and direct access to content tailored to individual goals and interests. Unfortunately, manual indexing of video content remains time consuming, costly, often inaccurate, and inconsistent. Automatic indexing of videos has been lacking, in part because of the complexity of image understanding and/or spoken language understanding. At the same time, we see increasing demand for mechanisms to support the annotation, browsing, search, visualization, and summarization of video. In addition, continued research on content-based video browsing could promise new applications such as customized television, interactive radio, and content-based multimedia authoring tools.

This chapter reports on investigations to create a content-based information retrieval system for broadcast news video. Our focus has been to develop techniques that can automatically segment, label, and summarize broadcast news video to support searching and browsing of long video segments. This chapter describes techniques which exploit the information in the closed-captioned text which accompanies many news broadcasts. This closed-captioning is generated by human operators, and was originally intended for the benefit of the hearing impaired. Before describing this further, we will first explain some of the issues in dealing with and exploiting different video data streams.

Video is a complex artifact that includes multiple, simultaneous streams of information: video, audio, and (increasingly) closed captioned text. Each of the different media streams shown in figure 1 have their own relative advantages and disadvantages with respect to the goal of content-based video access. As shown in figure 1, text is a rich information source, and can be easier to process than speech. On the other hand, the presence of errors, incompleteness, and relatively unstructured form present challenges.

Our work demonstrates how language processing can be successfully applied to automatically segment transcripts and the associated video to support content-based browsing and access. We report results from experiments investigating the automated segmentation of video using linguistic analysis of closed-captioned text, comparing a subject classification approach and one based on discourse cues. In addition, we describe an embodiment of these techniques in a content-based information retrieval system for on-line news on the World Wide Web, the IDD News Browser (Mani et al. 1995, Bloedorn et al. 1996). In this system, which is in use at MITRE, a user can query various Internet news collections, which are usually drawn from Internet newspaper and USENET feeds. These result in matches in the form of personalized newspapers, which provide multiple views of the information space in terms of summary-level features. The user controls the length, depth, and degree of abstraction in the summary, whether collections are to be sorted or clustered hierarchically based on content, whether the summary is to be connected text, a template, or a more fragmentary thumbnail sketch (e.g., salient entities, words, phrases, headlines), whether the summary should be sensitive to a particular user query, etc. The techniques developed here were used to extend the IDD News Browser to handle broadcast news video.

2. The Broadcast News Data and Associated Problems

The data we have experimented with consists of roughly a week's worth of broadcast news (7/15/91 to 7/23/91) from major network news programs

Stream	Information Content	Processing Challenges	Summary
Graphic/ Image/ Video	- Camera angle, focus, motion - Object shape, size, color, location - Motion over time - Faces and postures (expressions), non-verbal communication - Efficient/reliable shot change detection (both rapid and gradual transitions, e.g., wipe/fade) - Editing rhythm in video indicative of content	- Image/video segmentation complex and computationally expensive - Overgeneration of shots, storyboards (500-1000 shots) - Image stream segmentation typically yields flat structure, need hierarchy - Gradual transitions, noisy signals decrease transition detection/content analysis - Segmentation (within, across frames)	key frame key clip
Text	- Discourse segmentation/ structure - Easier to process closed-captioned (CC) text than speech - CC highly correlated with speech/imagery stream - Prominent keyword/meanings can indicate content	- CC text often absent - Errorful, incomplete, unstructured - Ambiguous or vague language	key word key phrase key sentence key paragraph key topic event
Spoken Language	- Intonation and pitch can indicate speaker, gender, importance, emotional state, intention - Energy level can be used to indicate speaker/scene shift	- Continuous, large vocabulary, speaker independence, noisy environments - Word boundaries - Recognition errors - false positives, recall errors - Limited vocabulary, languages	sound bite
Non Speech Audio	- Music indicator of segment onset, mood	- Acoustic properties non-variable but perceptual/intentional descriptions vary	

Figure 1. Characteristics of multimedia streams.

(CNN Prime News, PBS' MacNeil Lehrer News Hour, ABC World News Tonight, ABC Nightline and CBS Evening News). One characteristic that emerges from this data is that even in this relatively small collection (seventeen and one-half hours) there are multiple stories related to the same subject. As is evident from the example in figure 2, the closed-caption text associated with our news video is in upper case and contains typographical errors, omissions, and commissions. Figure 2 also marks cues that mark boundaries of individual stories or reports. Our ability to recognize and exploit these cues automatically, while remaining robust to noise in the data, is discussed in section 3.2 (Story Segmentation).

If we examine the structure of an evening news broadcast (figure 3), we see that the broadcast consists of a number of segments, which provide either a segue function such as a summary or preview (usually reported by a news anchor), or else constitute reports or interviews. Further, each segment has some informative label, or *topic*. It is this kind of table of contents that we strive to automatically generate. Of course, the table of contents could be even more detailed, revealing how different topics are introduced and elaborated through each sentence of a report or interview. In general, we refer to the decomposition of a news broadcast into arbitrarily fine segments dealing with particular topics as *topic segmentation* (discussed in section 3.1). On the other hand, we refer to the decomposition of a news broadcast into segments associated with a distinct program unit, such as an interview involving an an-

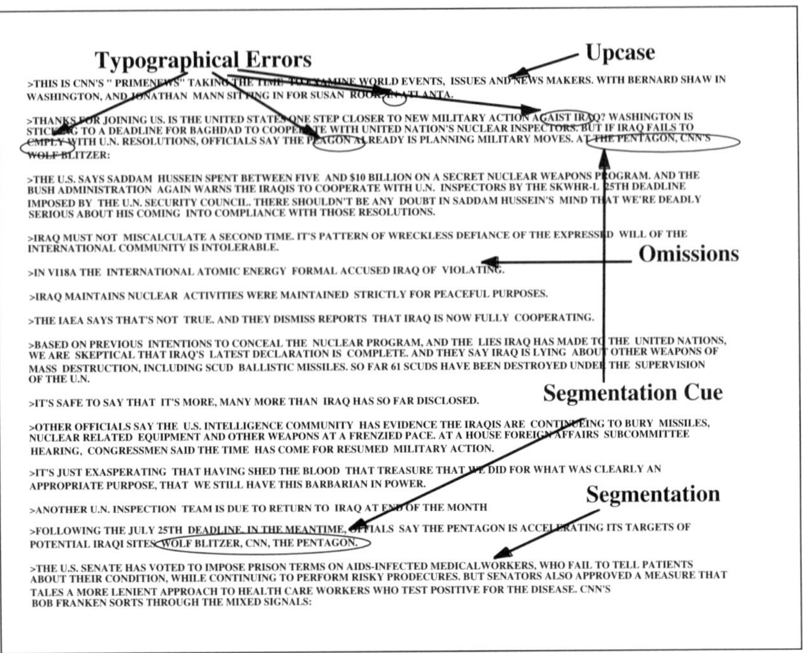

Figure 2. Closed-captioned example
(CNN Prime News, July 18, 1991).

chor or a reporter, or a report from a reporter, as *story segmentation* (discussed in section 3.2). Note that a story segmentation may in fact correspond to a fairly coarse topic segmentation. As will become more evident, while both problems present challenges, the problem of topic segmentation (which is of considerable interest to research on text summarization) is more complex than the problem of story segmentation.

3. Topic and Story Segmentation

In this section, we discuss topic segmentation, story segmentation, and entity extraction.

3.1 Topic Segmentation

The challenge of being able to elicit a topic segmentation for unrestricted news broadcasts is a substantial one. A topic may be brought up initially, and then returned to eventually while other related topics (including more specialized topics) are discussed. A passage or dialog may have multiple threads of topics. In general, we may think of a topic as a locus of some distinct infor-

<pre>
Overview
Middle East Peace Process
Iraq
Coming Up
Economic Summit
Census
Coming Up
Bank merger, loans
Tax on junk food
Coming Up
Yugoslavia
China, Natural Disasters
Russian/US joint talk show
Coming Up
Health Care, AIDS
Alzheimer's Drug
Environment
        Environment, train derailment
        Environment, INDIANA DUNES NATIONAL LAKESHORE
        Environment, recycling
Sports
        bike racing
        baseball
Economics, G-7
Weather
</pre>

Figure 3. Manually generated video table of contents
(CNN Prime News,[1] 15 August 1991).

mation content. The problem of discovering topics can then be viewed as one of tracking changes in information content to identify major unit boundaries, and then clustering together similar units as instances of common topics. Techniques for detecting transitions in information content are obviously of interest in segmentation of other media, such as imagery, audio, and video. In particular, fully overlapped analysis windows techniques have been explored in computer vision as well (e.g., (Schalkoff 1989)). Adjacent windows are compared for similarity, with dissimilarity being indicative of a boundary.

An interesting application of such a technique to topic identification is found in the work of Hearst (1994), who presented an algorithm (TextTiling) for partitioning expository texts into coherent multi-paragraph discourse units. The algorithm divides the text into units of a fixed length (e.g., 20 words). Adjacent blocks of units (e.g., 6 units) are compared for similarity based on the traditional cosine measure of similarity. The weight of a term is the frequency of the term in the block. In essence, two blocks are similar if they have many terms in common. The similarity scores are then plotted against gaps between units or blocks. The resulting gaps are then sorted by how large a positive change in similarity occurs (towards a local maximum) on either side of the gap (i.e., compute the sum of the change on each side), with the system assigning boundaries to the gaps with the largest similarity change (i.e., above some threshold, and so as to avoid very close adjacent boundaries). (For more details, see (Hearst 1994)).

In our approach, we attempted to extend Hearst's algorithm to simultaneously provide a labeling of topic structure. To achieve this, instead of using term overlap as a similarity measure, we decided to use a labeled subject classification from a thesaurus. Assuming that one could associate terms in a document with subjects in a thesaurus, one could hypothesize that as topics change, the associated thesaural subjects change as well. We also speculated that this might be more effective than term overlap in certain cases, namely when the terms do not overlap but do belong to similar subject classes. One could thus apply the overall analysis window approach, but computing inter-block similarity in terms of thesaural subjects instead of term repetition.

One well-known problem which arises here is that of word-sense disambiguation, in this case deciding which of several thesaurus categories are the most likely ones for a term and for larger units of text. We decided to apply here the approach used by the Subject Field Coder (SFC) (Liddy and Myaeng 1992, Liddy and Paik 1992) (from TextWise, Inc.), which produces a vector representation of a text's subject categories, based on a thesaurus of 124 subject categories. Text summaries are represented by vectors in 124-dimensional space, with each vector's projection along a given dimension corresponding to the salience in the text of that subject category. The overall vector is built up from sentence-level vectors, which are constructed by combining the evidence from local context (e.g., unambiguous words) with evidence from large-scale statistics (e.g., pairwise correlations of subject categories)[2]. Thus, our similarity measure is based on cosine similarity between subject vectors in 124-dimensional subject space. The similarity Sim(X, Y) between two subject vectors X and Y is defined as the angle between the two vectors[3], where a smaller angle means more similarity:

$$Sim(\mathbf{X}, \mathbf{Y}) = \left(\frac{180}{\pi}\right) acos \frac{\mathbf{X} * \mathbf{Y}}{\sqrt{(\mathbf{X} * \mathbf{X})(\mathbf{Y} * \mathbf{Y})}}$$

where $\mathbf{X} * \mathbf{Y}$ is the inner product of vectors $\mathbf{X}$ and $\mathbf{Y}$

The similarity score is then normalized to range from 0 (least similar) to 100 (most similar). Figure 4 shows the normalized similarity scores plotted at block gaps, for one night of the McNeil-Lehrer News Hour. The true starting and ending boundaries for segments in the broadcast (labeled summary, segue, recap, Saddam Hussein, Philippines, Gorbachev, and CIA) were assigned manually, based on story segments. Thus, while these are story segments, they served the function of coarse topic segments. (Note that, in general, it is easier to judge the boundaries of story segments like this than topic segments). The system used these similarity scores to compute boundaries

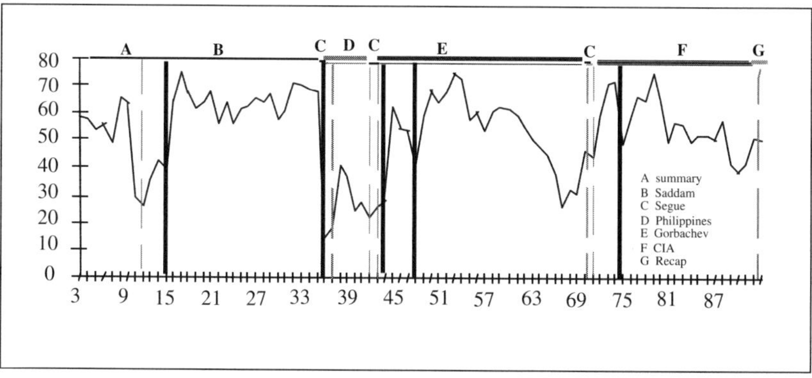

Figure 4. Automatic topic segmentation (McNeil-Lehrer, July 16, 1991).
Graph plots similarity in subject space (y-axis) at block gaps (x-axis).
Dark vertical lines are system generated boundaries.
Horizontal lines and light vertical dashed lines indicate true boundaries.

based on the 'largest similarity change' calculation described above.

How well did the system perform? The system misjudged the start of the Saddam Hussein topic by 3 block gaps (it guessed block gap 14 instead of 11), was correct about the end of that topic and the segue into the next (Phillipines), and overshot the end of Phillipines and the start of Gorbachev by one block gap (block gap 43 instead of 41 and 42). It also misjudged the end of Gorbachev by 5 blocks. Given the current block size of 1200 lines, the error can be rather pronounced. In all, the system missed three boundaries (out of 8), and offered one boundary which wasn't there. Allowing for partial matches (a rather generous assumption), then the *precision* would be (#correct system boundaries/ #system boundaries) = 4/5 or 0.80, and *recall* would be (# correct system boundaries / # true boundaries) = 4/8 or 0.50.

An obvious issue here is the block size. A block size of less than 1000 lines led to very low similarity scores. The 1200-line block size is in general too large to permit segmentation of segues from other topics, since they often lie within the same block. In the future, we hope to use a more recent version of the SFC, which is less sensitive to block size. Also, the heuristic of avoiding very close adjacent boundaries does not make sense for segues, which are often very short. Finally, we note that the system mistook a local minimum (block gap 14) for a global minimum, while there was in fact a global minimum at the "true" boundary (block gap 11). This suggests that the largest similarity change filter is not always appropriate. We therefore intend to explore algorithms which adjust the block size automatically and which use other methods of sorting local minima. Finally, we need to investigate whether a different similarity metric (e.g., a cosine similarity metric using word-frequency, rather than thesaurus based similarity) would work better.

Block Gap	Best Subject of RHS Block	"True" Label
14	War&Military	Saddam Hussein
43	Government	Phillipines
47	Politics	Gorbachev
74	Business&Economics	CIA

Figure 5. Comparison of system-generated and human-generated topic labels (McNeil-Lehrer, July 16, 1991).

We also examined the labels of each system generated segment, by finding the best subject of the block to the right of the block gap. The results are shown in figure 5. The data in figure 5 suggest correctly that there is a predominance of war/military usage in the Saddam Hussein segment. This inference is clearly one of the strengths of the SFC approach. However, the manually generated labels (in themselves highly subjective) emphasize the names of peoples and places. For this broadcast, these latter labels appear to be more informative. This suggests the applicability of combining subject labels with name tagging-based labels, and perhaps using the distribution of names in some way in the segmentation. We discuss name tagging in section 3.3.

Recognizing that conclusive results require evaluation on a large corpus, our experiment in video topic segmentation suggests that, while potentially quite powerful from the standpoint of automatic labeled segmentation, this approach does not as yet perform as accurately as desired. The next section describes an approach which is far more restricted in scope. It does only story segmentation, not topic segmentation, but achieves more satisfactory results.

3.2 Story Segmentation

Part of the task of a TV news anchor involves introducing news stories from reporters, interviewing, promising more news, and offering commentary and observations. In order to do this, they employ various discourse cues. Based on a manual analysis of three different nightly news broadcasts (CNN, ABC, and McNeil-Lehrer) these can be grouped into four categories. Here is an example from CNN Prime News:

Program Begin/End
- THIS IS CNN'S " PRIMENEWS" TAKING THE TIME TO EXAMINE WORLD EVENTS, ISSUES AND NEWS MAKERS WITH BERNARD SHAW IN WASHINGTON, AND SUSAN ROOK IN ATLANTA
- THANK YOU FOR JOINING US. I'M SUSAN ROOK IN ATLANTA.
- I'M BERNARD SHAW IN WASHINGTON. NEXT ON CNN, LARRY KING LIVE. LARRY, WHO'S ON TONIGHT
- THAT'S ITS FOR PRIME NEWS. IN WASHINGTON I'M BERNARD SHAW. SUSAN AND I WILL BE BACK IN ONE HOUR WITH WORLDNEWS. AND IN ATLANTA, I'M SUSAN ROOK.

Start of Segment

- IN NEWS AFFECTING OUR ENVIRONMENT,
- IN BASEBALL NEWS,
- IN OUR EARTH MATTERS SEGMENT,
- IT'S TIME FOR WEATHER. HERE'S KAREN MCGINNIS.
- CNN'S WOLF BLITZER HAS MORE
- CNN'S JEFF FLOCK REPORT
- NOW "PRIMENEWS" CONTINUES WITH SUSAN ROOK.
- "PRIMENEWS" CONTINUES WITH RALPH WENGE.

Cataphora

- UP NEXT ON PRIME NEWS: IT'S THE PLACE TO BE, IF YOU BELIEVE IN
- COMING UP ON " PRIMENEWS",
- COMING UP NEXT ON PRIME NEWS;
- STILL TO COME: (3)
- WHEN PRIME NEWS RETURNS,
- AHEAD ON "PRIMENEWS",
- STILL AHEAD ON PRIME NEWS:

Segment End

- CHARLES BIERBAUER WITH THE PRESIDENT IN LONDON.
- WOLF BLITZER, CNN, THE PENTAGON
- JEFF LEVINE, CNN, AT JOHN HOPKINS IN BALTIMORE
- JILL DOUGHERTY FOR CNN, CHICAGO.
- BOB FRANKEN, CNN, CAPITOL HILL.

The anchor usually 'hands off' to the reporter during Segment Start, with the reporter signing off during Segment End. However, the patterns for Segment Start show a great deal of variability. In contrast, there are only a small number of Segment End patterns, involving the reporter signing off.

Another source of information regarding story segmentation are cues introduced by the operators who generate the closed-caption text. In particular, the sequence >> is used to indicate change of speaker, and >>> to indicate change of story. However, these cues (especially >>>) aren't always present. Also, techniques which rely on operator cues could not be expected to work in the future on automatic transcriptions of audio, where no human intermediary may be involved in generating the text (though >> cues could perhaps be inserted by a speaker identification program). Rather than rely on operator cues, we decided to develop a segmentation program which would exploit the discourse cues to automatically identify reporter and anchor segments. The approach we took was to catch the sign off, modeling only the segment end patterns, in particular catching the reporter's name. Using this name, the start of segment can also be identified. The identification of start and end of segment allows for the segmentation of broadcasts into individual news stories, anchor segments, and reporter segments, as well as identification of the reporter's name.

To study how general the patterns were across genres, we implemented the above discourse-cue approach with the ABC patterns, making only minor modifications for CNN and McNeil-Lehrer. We then used the earlier hand tagging of the story boundaries. We also hand-tagged changes of speaker for ABC news. Then, we measured the accuracy of the system's identification of story boundaries against the human's. Precision and recall were calculated as follows:

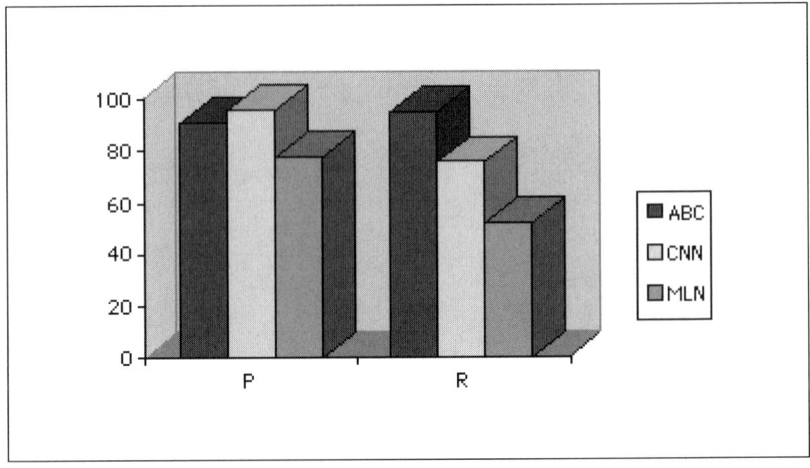

Figure 6. Precision (P) and recall (R) for automatic story segmentation for one week of three nightly news broadcasts.

precision = # correct program tags / # program tags.
Recall = # correct program tags / # hand tags.

Figure 6 shows our results for the entire week's broadcasts for three news sources, plotted in terms of precision and recall at a single threshold. As can be seen from figure 6, the program is quite successful at both ABC and CNN story segmentation, and somewhat less so on McNeil-Lehrer (MNL). An error analysis on McNeil-Lehrer suggested that MNL-specific transitions, e.g., "Robin.", "Goodnight Jim," had not been coded. If we added these two patterns in, we estimate the recall would go up to about 75%.

The algorithm also provides identification of the reporters' and anchors' names. While we did not count these in our evaluation, it should be obvious that since the segmentation is based on matching the reporter's name (extracted during the Segment End) to identify Segment Start, if the segmentation is correct, it is likely to involve a correct identification of the reporter's name. The anchor's name(s) is caught by modeling Program Begin/End, and this too is relatively simple to catch.

In terms of exploiting multiple data streams, we should note that on CNN we found 13 missed handoffs and signoffs for which there were no textual cues. There were visual cues, however. This suggests that analysis of the video stream could make a contribution towards improving recall. Our analysis also suggests that if we used such discourse-based heuristics to identify change of speaker, the recall for ABC news would be only around 51%, in other words, we would miss roughly half the changes of speaker. This means such an approach will not work in general for identifying change of speaker.

In short, the discourse-cue based approach performs far more satisfactorily than the earlier topic segmentation approach for story segmentation. It does beg the question, however, as to whether and how the patterns associated with these cues could be acquired automatically for a given news source, rather than being encoded by hand. While it is less general, in terms of providing only anchor segment/ reporter segment structuring (in contrast to more fine-structured topic analysis), such a segmentation can be quite useful. section 4, in fact, demonstrates how effective this can be in video retrieval.

3.3 Entity Extraction

As indicated in previous sections, name tagging has a useful role to play in video retrieval. To date, MITRE has developed several algorithms to extract entities such as people, organizations, and places from text. The Alembic name tagger (Aberdeen et al. 1995) identifies names based on Eric Brill's rule-sequence learning approach (Brill 1994). The name tagger is driven by a sequence of phrase-finding rules. These rules can either change the label of a phrase, grow its boundaries, or create new phrases. For example, a rule may change the label of a phrase from *:none* to *:person* if the phrase is bordered on its left by another phrase with a *:title* label. A particularly attractive feature of this approach is that it works also on upper case text, and is trainable, applying the same general error-reduction learning approach designed by Eric Brill for generating part-of-speech rules to the problem of learning phrase identification rules. The name tagger was successfully fielded in the 1995 Message Understanding Conference (MUC-6).

Our work in performing entity extraction for use in video retrieval is still at an early stage. So far, we have used the name tagger as is on the closed-captioned sources, but have not as yet formally evaluated its performance. Obviously, considerable human effort is required (even though it could be machine-assisted) to create a reasonably sized test set for the closed-captioned sources. At this point we can offer only anecdotal evidence that while there were numerous errors, it does not fare altogether badly (an example is shown in the next section). We expect substantial gains from being able to retrain it on upper case text. Empirical results are forthcoming (Maybury et al. 1997).

4. Embodiment: Extending the IDD
News Browser to Broadcast Video

The techniques described in the previous section can be leveraged to build a powerful content-based video browsing capability. We now describe extensions to the IDD News Browser to handle broadcast news video. As mentioned earlier, using the IDD News Browser, a user can query various Inter-

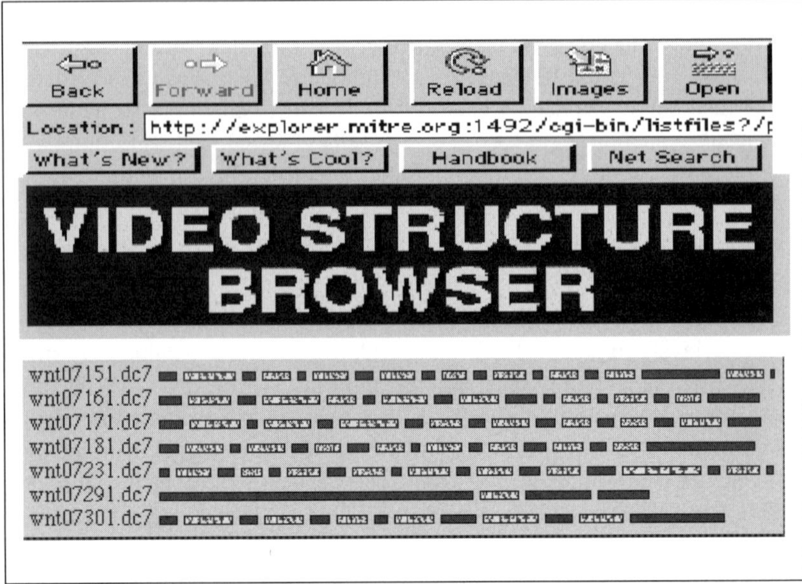

*Figure 7. Story segmentation of ABC world news tonight newscasts.
(Dark segments are anchor segments, light segments are reporter segments.)*

net news collections to generate matches in the form of personalized newspapers, which provide multiple views of the information space in terms of summary-level features. Using the tools in the IDD system, we were able to very quickly extend it to video.

Figure 7 shows the IDD Video Structure Browser page. This view allows the user to easily see the anchor, reporter, and interview segments, which were automatically tagged using the approach in section 3.2. For each broadcast name, a different-colored bar appears for each segment type, with the lengths of these bars corresponding to the durations of the associated video clips. (Both filenames and bars can be clicked on to see text or video.)

Figure 8 shows an interface for searching. Here the user has typed in the search terms "AIDS" to be run against different sources. (The search engine used here is WAIS 2.0, one of many search engines that the IDD News Browser uses locally or over the World Wide Web). The hits resulting from submitting the HTML search form are shown on the right: 2 ABC (World News Tonight) broadcasts and 4 CNN broadcasts, sorted by relevance. The icon to the right of the name is that of a video clip for the broadcast. To align the text and the video, timestamp tags were inserted into the closed-captioned transcripts. Given a timestamp tag, the system automatically generates a hyperlink to the video frame associated with that timestamp.

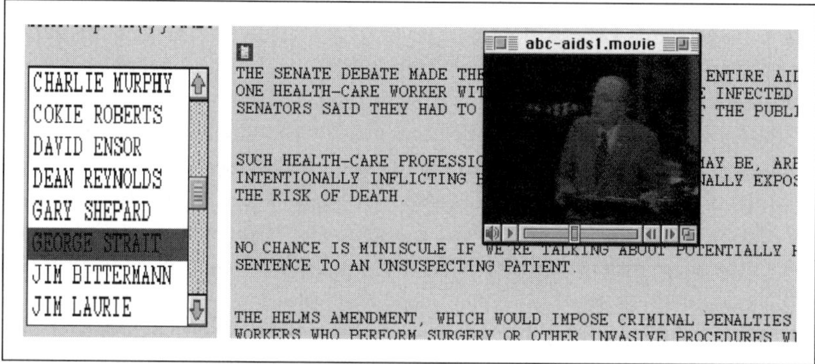

Figure 8. Searching for terms in TV news.

*Figure 9. Search and retrieval of video for a report
(ABC World News Tonight, July 18, 1991).*

Figure 9 shows the user searching by reporter name. Here again, the reporter name menu was generated automatically from the reporter name tags generated by the story segmentation tagger described in section 3.2. Selecting one or more reporters retrieves broadcasts associated with that reporter, as shown in figure 9. Here the text associated with the broadcast is shown (a discussion of the Helms Amendment, having to do with governmental AIDS policy) with a hyperlink to the reporter, as well as an icon for a video clip for that particular section of the broadcast. Clicking on the icon retrieves the video (the video snapshot shown is of Senator Jesse Helms). The video here is displayed using Movie Player, a Quicktime movie player on the Macintosh. The video clips were encoded in both Quicktime and MPEG.

Figure 10 shows the ability to browse names in a broadcast, using the output of the MUC-6 name tagger. Clicking on a name allows one to go to the video clip nearest the name in the text. The system also provides video access via menus of all names found in the broadcasts.

GOOD EVENING. LEADING THE NEWS THIS TUESDAY, ECONOMIC SUMMIT LEADERS CLEARED THE WAY FOR WORLD BANK AND OTHER ECONOMIC HELP FOR THE *SOVIET UNION*. THEY ALSO SAID SANCTIONS AGAINST *IRAQ* SHOULD BE MAINTAINED. AND IN THIS COUNTRY, *FEDERAL RESERVE* CHAIRMAN *GREENSPAN* SAID THE *FED* HAS STOPPED TRYING TO LOWER INTEREST RATES. WE'LL HAVE THE DETAILS IN OUR NEWS SUMMARY IN A MOMENT. ROBIN.

AFTER THE NEWS SUMMARY, DEFENSE SECRETARY *DICK CHENEY* DISCUSSES THE NEW WARNINGS TO *SADDAM HUSSEIN*. FROM *MOSCOW*, *CHARLES KRAUSE* HAS A POLITICAL PROFILE OF *MIKHAIL GORBACHEV* AS HE MEETS WESTERN LEADERS.

Figure 10. Browsing names in a broadcast
(McNeil Lehrer News Hour, July 16, 1991).

5. Related Work

There have been a variety of systems built which nicely complement the work on content-based video retrieval described here, and some of these are now identified. Researchers at the NTT Human Interface Lab in Japan are also researching the application of language processing to video analysis. Taniguchi et al. (1995) have utilized language processing techniques to create structure in video, for example, using topic markers such as "ex ni tsuite" (with regard to) and "wa" (as for), subject/object markers, and frequency measures to extract discourse structures from transcripts, which are then used to provide topic-oriented browsers for video. Takeshita et al. (this volume) extract topic structures from text, using these to select from among time-synchronized images segmented from a video stream, to produce topic-based multimedia "skim" structures, which contain some summary-level information. Their techniques exploit syntactic analysis and the presence of topic markers in the text. It is an open question as to how well such techniques would work on English closed-captioned news sources. Unlike their work, the topic segmentation techniques described here do not create nested topic structures, but as indicated below, we expect to investigate clustering of topics.

Shahraray and Gibbon (1995) also describe a World Wide Web-based interface for retrieving video frames. In addition, they too identify names in closed-caption text, and (as with many such systems, e.g., (Bender and Chesnais 1988, Brown et al. 1995; Hauptmann and Witbrock, this volume)) index words in the text. Although there are striking similarities, there are some significant differences as well. Their emphasis is on the automatic generation of hypermedia documents, with a particular focus on video sampling. Our emphasis is on text segmentation and summarization, neither of which is performed by their system. There are also some differences in the use of name tagging: our name tagger classifies different kinds of names without performing case-conversion; it is also trainable, and has been evaluated in the Message Understanding Conference (Aberdeen et al. 1995, MUC-6).

The Informedia™ project (Hauptmann and Smith 1995) at Carnegie Mellon University is focused on a video library creation and exploration system. Hauptmann and Witbrock (this volume) describe the methods used in the In-formedia: News-on-Demand system for indexing and retrieval of news from TV, radio, or text news sources. Their main focus is on indexing and retrieval of text generated by automatic speech recognition using CMU's Sphynx-II system. The authors indicate that even at high word error rates, the output of speech recognition may contain enough information to be useful for indexing and retrieval. They note some interesting differences in the word error rate based on the type of data, for example the recognizer fares poorly on the evening news, but somewhat better on C-Span. Given that their system does not as yet carry out much detailed analysis of the text, it would be interesting to test the techniques described in our chapter on these different types of speech recognition data, preliminary results of which are reported in May-bury et al. (1997).

Brown et al. (1995) describe various multimedia information retrieval ex-periments on the accompanying teletext of video news broadcasts. In their approach, automatic segmentation is carried out using fixed-length overlap-ping segments. Compared with manual segmentation, however, their use of this segmentation technique results in less accurate segment retrieval. While it seems likely that our entity extraction techniques would carry over to these (BBC1) news broadcasts, it would be worthwhile discovering whether the segmentation approaches described here would apply as well.

Finally, researchers at the University of Singapore (Zhang et al. 1995, this volume) have developed video parsing algorithms for broadcast news. This approach utilizes models of expected video frames (e.g., news anchors sitting at desks with graphics in typical locations) to detect and then classify shots as anchor shots versus story shots. In application to three Singapore broad-cast news programs, the algorithms achieve higher than 90% accuracy.

6. Conclusions

We have described our experiments investigating the automated segmenta-tion of video using linguistic analysis, comparing a subject classification ap-proach to context with one based on discourse cues. The latter approach was found to work better for story segmentation, while the former suggested pos-sibilities for fine-structured labeled topic segmentation. We also indicated some of our first steps in applying entity extraction, in the form of name identification, to the text data stream. We suggested that continued work on entity extraction might also improve the labeled topic segmentation. In addi-tion, we described an embodiment of these techniques in a content-based in-formation retrieval system for broadcast video.

There are two natural extensions to this work, as we see it. While previous work has primarily focused on single data stream analysis (e.g., the image, audio, or closed-captioned streams of a video), researchers are now beginning to investigate cross-channel analysis. We believe that collaborative research with other groups will greatly further progress on attempting to leverage multiple streams. In particular, our work on closed-captioned text can be extended to transcribed speech as well. We can expect also that speaker identification and/or change of speaker segmentation carried out on the audio (e.g., (Wilcox et al. 1994)) could be combined with our techniques applied to the text to get more detailed segmentation information.

A second and related direction is to exploit more powerful summarization techniques. We have developed mechanisms to automatically summarize structured and semi-structured information sources using condensation and content selection techniques, including information aggregation and abstraction as well as intention-based summarization (Maybury 1995b, Mani 1995). We are now redesigning the topic identification algorithm (including having the system adjust the block size, and using word frequency in the similarity metric) with a view towards embedding it in a topic clustering algorithm, which will provide labeled topic summaries for news articles for use with the IDD News Browser. We believe there is great promise in applying these same mechanisms to the linguistic sources associated with video, as well as investigating aggregation and abstraction of the video itself. As figure 1 illustrated, analysis of particular streams can result in summaries of varying kinds (e.g., key frames, words, phrases, sound bites). In contrast to text summarization, content analysis can occur in a stream different than that in which content selection and/or condensation (abstraction or aggregation) occurs. Thus, whereas image understanding may remain computationally intractable, heuristic approaches to linguistic stream analysis (including spoken language and closed captions), such as the ones we have illustrated here, can be used to select appropriate audio and/or video. This also raises the opportunity for automated generation of multimedia summaries (Maybury 1994; Takeshita et al. 1996, this volume), in which a combination of video, audio, and text may remain the most efficient and effective means of summarization. This remains an open research issue.

Notes

1. Copyright © Cable News Network.

2. An earlier version of the SFC, which used subject codes from Longman's Dictionary of Contemporary English (LDOCE), was tested on 166 sentences from the Wall Street Journal (1638 words). It gave the right category on 87% of the words (Liddy and Myaeng 92).

3. We used the angle between vectors instead of the Tanimoto similarity measure built into the SFC.

Acknowledgments

We are grateful to Richard MacMillan, who as local custodian of the Subject Field Coder, provided us with the interfaces we needed. We also acknowledge Debora Ercolini who helped get things started by creating an initial mockup application of a video browser. This work was funded under MITRE Sponsored Research.

References

Aberdeen, J.; Burger, J.; Day, D.; Hirschman, L.; Robinson, P.; and Vilain, M. 1995. Description of the Alembic System Used for MUC-6. In Proceedings of the Sixth Message Understanding Conference, 141-155. Advanced Research Projects Agency Information Technology Office, Columbia, MD, 6-8 November.

Bender, W. and Chesnais, P. 1988. Network Plus. In Proceeedings SPIE Electronic Imaging, Devices and Systems Symposium, 900: 81-86.

Bloedorn, E.; Mani, I.; and MacMillan, T. R. 1996. Representational Issues in Machine Learning of User Profiles. In Proceedings of 14th National Conference on Artificial Intelligence (AAAI-96), 433-438. Portland, Oregon, August 4-8, 1996. Menlo Park, CA: AAAI.

Brill, E. 1994. Some Advances in Rule-Based Part of Speech Tagging. In Proceedings of 12th National Conference on Artificial Intelligence (AAAI-94), 722-727, Menlo Park, CA: AAAI.

Brown, M. G.; Foote, J. T.; Jones, G.J.F.; Sparck-Jones, K.; and Young, S.J. 1995. Automatic Content-Based Retrieval of Broadcast News. In ACM Multimedia 95, 35-43, San Francisco, CA: ACM.

Hauptman, A. and Smith, M. 1995. Text, Speech, and Vision for Video Segmentation: The Informedia Project. In Maybury, M., ed. Working notes of IJCAI-95 Workshop on Intelligent Multimedia Information Retrieval, 17-22. Montreal, August 19, 1995.

Hauptmann, A. G. and Witbrock, M. J. 1997. Informedia: News-on-Demand Multimedia Acquisition and Retrieval. In this volume.

Hearst, M. 1994. Multi-Paragraph Segmentation of Expository Text, Proceedings of the 32nd Annual Meeting of the Association of Computational Linguistics (ACL-94). Las Cruces, New Mexico, 1994.

Liddy, E. and Myaeng, S. 1992. DR-LINK's Linguistic-Conceptual Approach to Document Detection. In Proceedings of the First Text Retrieval Conference, 113-129. Washington D. C.: National Institute of Standards and Technology.

Liddy, E. and W. Paik 1992. Statistically Guided Word-Sense Disambiguation. In Proceedings of the AAAI Fall Symposium Series: Probabilistic Approaches to Natural Language, 98-107. Menlo Park, CA: AAAI.

Mani, M. and MacMillan, T. R. 1995. Identifying Unknown Proper Names in Newswire Text. In *Corpus Processing for Lexical Acquisition*, ed. B. Boguraev and J. Pustejovsky, 41-59. Cambridge, MA: MIT Press.

Mani, I.; House, D.; and Bloedorn, E. 1995. The Intelligent Document Detection News Browser, Technical Note, MITRE Corporation, 1995. Not in Public Domain.

Mani, I. 1995. Very Large Scale Text Summarization. Technical Note, MITRE Corporation. Not in Public Domain.

Maybury, M. T., ed. 1993. *Intelligent Multimedia Interfaces*, Cambridge, MA: AAAI/MIT Press.

Maybury, M. T. 1994. Knowledge Based Multimedia: The Future of Expert Systems and Multimedia. *International Journal of Expert Systems with Applications*. Special issue on Expert Systems Integration with Multimedia Technologies. 7(3):387-396. ed. J. Ragusa.

Maybury, M. T. 1995a. Research in Multimedia Parsing and Generation. *Artificial Intelligence Review: Special Issue on the Integration of Natural Language and Vision Processing* 9(2-3): 103-127, ed. P. McKevitt.

Maybury, M. T. 1995b. Generating Summaries from Event Data. *International Journal of Information Processing and Management: Special Issue on Text Summarization*. 31(5): 735-751.

Maybury, M. T.; Merlino, A.; Morey, D.; and Rayson, J. 1997. Capturing, Analyzing and Browsing Broadcast News. Technical note. The MITRE Corporation.

MUC-6, Proceedings of the Sixth Message Understanding Conference. Advanced Research Projects Agency Information Technology Office, Columbia, MD, 6-8 November, 1995.

Schalkoff, R. J. 1989. *Digital Image Processing and Computer Vision*, New York, NY: John Wiley & Sons.

Shahraray, B. and Gibbon, D. 1995. Automatic Authoring of Hypermedia Documents of Video Programs. In Proceedings of ACM Multimedia 95, 401-409. San Francisco: ACM.

Takeshita, A.; Inoue, T.; and K. Tanaka. 1997. Topic Based Multimedia Structuring. In this volume.

Taniguchi, Y.; Akutsu, A.; Tonomura, Y. and Hamada, H. 1995. An Intuitive and Efficient Access Interface to Real-time Incoming Video based on Automatic Indexing. In Proceedings of ACM Multimedia 95, 25-34. San Francisco: ACM.

Wilcox, L. D.; Chen, F. R.; Kimber, D. G.; Balasubramanian, V. 1994. Segmentation of Speech Using Speaker Identification. In *Proceedings of the International Conference on Acoustics, Speech and Signal Processing*, Adelaide, Australia, April, 1994.

Zhang, H.J.; Low, C. Y.; Smoliar, S. W. and Wu J., 1997. Video Parsing, Retrieval, and Browsing: An Integrated and Content-Based Solution. In this volume.

Chapter 13

Topic-based Multimedia Structuring

*Atsushi Takeshita, NTT Hokkaido Business Communications;
Takafumi Inoue and Kazuo Tanaka, NTT Human Interface
Laboratories*

Abstract

This chapter proposes a new method for aiding people in comprehending the outline of
targeted multimedia data. This method, called "topic-based multimedia structuring,"
combines "topic structures" extracted from texts and images extracted from a video
stream, and creates semantic-based multimedia skim structures. A new method for extracting monologue topic structures is also proposed. This extraction method is based
on knowledge about linguistic phenomena concerning topic expansion. Through this
method, robust and practical extraction is achieved. The effectiveness of the extraction
method is shown. A multimedia method that combines the results of text and video
analysis is also proposed. This combination method creates topic-based representatives
and groups as the semantic-based multimedia skim structures. The descriptive power
of these skim structures is richer than that of topic structures alone or that of images
alone. The effectiveness of combining multiple media is discussed.

1. Introduction

One of the greatest benefits of multimedia data is its rich and descriptive
power. Video is the main component of multimedia data, which means that
copious amounts of video will be created. The major problem is information
overload, i.e., people cannot grasp the contents of a video instantaneously
and cannot select relevant video streams from video libraries. This is because
video is a dynamic medium whose description changes as time progresses
and each video contains a large volume of information.

Current video processing technologies reduce the volume of information
by transforming the dynamic medium of video into the static medium of images, that is, a video stream is segmented and a representative image is ex-

tracted from each segment (Tonomura et al. 1994, Arman 1994, Gabbe et al. 1994). Although representative images enable users to view the contents of a video at a glance, this method does not address the overload problem because the number of extracted representative images is too great. To address the overload problem, extraction methods for macro structure of multimedia data are proposed. These methods are classified into three approaches. The first one provides an environment where users can perform macro segmentation and annotation by themselves (Aigrain and Joly 1994). The second one uses single medium processing. Aigrain (this volume) uses primarily video processing, and Mani et al. (this volume) text processing. The third one employs multistream processing, e.g., video and text processing (Hauptmann and Smith 1995; Hauptmann and Whitbrock, this volume; Shahraray and Gibbon 1995).

This chapter proposes a new method called "topic-based multimedia structuring" which belongs to the multistream approach. By combining the results of text and video processing, this method creates semantic-based multimedia skim structures. The text processing unit extracts "topic structures" from texts such as closed captions. The video processing unit extracts representative images from the video stream and the multimedia combination unit creates the multimedia skim structures. Compared with other multistream approaches, our method is very simple, and creates a very compact representation for skimming.

In this chapter, we first explain the basic idea behind topic-based multimedia structuring. Second, a practical and robust approach for topic structure extraction is proposed and evaluated. This approach is based on knowledge about linguistic phenomena concerned with topic expansion. Finally, a method for multimedia combination is proposed, and its effectiveness is discussed.

2. Topic-based Multimedia Structuring

In this section we discuss the basis and outline for topic-based multimedia structuring.

2.1 Basis for Topic-based Multimedia Structuring

Our goal is to create effective and semantic-based multimedia skim structures from targeted multimedia data. Although text, video, image, and audio media are included in multimedia data, text is the only media supporting general and automatic semantic analysis. Therefore, it is essential to extract semantic-based skim structures from texts in topic-based multimedia structuring.

(1-1) Tsuushin sa-bisu ga samagawari shitekite masu ga, (1-2) *.
(2-1) Mazu, iroirona shinki sa-bisu ga arimashite, (2-2) haba hiroku riyou sarete imasu.
(3-1) NCC ni taikousuru tame ni, (3-2) sa-bisu A ga sakunen kaishi sare mashita.
(4-1) Kore wa *, (4-2) *.
(5-1) Tsugi ni, juurai kara no sa-bisu ni tsuite desu ga, (5-2) *.
(6-1) Kore wa *, (6-2) *, (6-3) *.
(7-1) Sa-bisu B wa 10 nen mae ni hajimari mashita ga (7-2) imadewa riyousha suu ga heri (7-3) kosuto mo * (7-4) * (7-5) *.

(a) In Japanese

(1-1) Telecommunication services have become varied , (1-2) *.
(2-1) To begin with, various new services are provided, (2-2) and are widely used.
(3-1) In order to compete with NCC, (3-2) service-A was put into use last year.
(4-1) This is *, (4-2) *.
(5-1) Next, regarding existing services, (5-2) *.
(6-1) This is *, (6-2) *, (6-3) *.
(7-1) As for service B, it started ten years ago, (7-2) however the number of users has been decreasing, (7-3) while the service cost has been * (7-4) * (7-5) *.

(b) In English

Figure 1. Telecommunication monologue.

We selected "topic structures" as the semantic-based skim structures. This is because topic structures help users grasp an outline of the targeted text, and these structures can be easily synchronized with other dynamic media such as video. Topic structures consist of topics and topic scopes. The topic scopes can be nested, and the nesting structure can be used to derive topic levels.

Figure 1 shows a Japanese monologue transcript and the English translation. In this monologue, each simple sentence, which includes only one predicate, is numbered, and some of them are abbreviated for simplicity, as indicated by "*" in the text.

Figure 2 shows the topic structures manually extracted from the monologue in figure 1. In figure 2, the topic levels are indicated in angle brackets, and each topic is accompanied by an English translation. For example, the first topic "tsuushin sa-bisu (telecommunication services)" is level 1, and its scope covers simple sentences (1-1) to (7-5).

```
<1> tsuushin sa-bisu                        [scope=(1-1) - (7-5)]
   (telecommunication services)
      <2>    iroiro na shinki sa-bisu       [scope=(2-1) - (4-2)]
      (various new services)
         <3>         sa-bisu A (service-A)  [scope=(3-1) - (4-2)]
      <2>    juurai kara no sa-bisu         [scope=(5-1) - (7-5)]
      (existing services)
         <3>         sa-bisu B (service-B)  [scope=(7-1) - (7-5)]
```

Figure 2. A topic structure example.

Although it is difficult to extract skim-based structures via video processing, cut-based skim structures can be extracted. Figure 3 shows an output of a video segmentation system called "paper video" (Tonomura et al. 1994). The system accepts a video stream as an input, detects cut changes in the stream to achieve video stream segmentation, and extracts a representative image from each segment. The output of the system is a series of images, and is not based on semantic structures.

The basic idea of topic-based structuring is that multimedia skim structures should be created so as to reflect the topic structures. This is achieved by combining topic structures from texts, with non-semantic skim structures extracted from a video stream. An example of the topic-based multimedia skim structures is the group of three images in figure 3 which is labeled "rocket."

2.2 Outline of Topic-based Multimedia Structuring

Figure 4 outlines topic-based multimedia structuring. Captioned video data is input into the structuring process. First, two stream analyses are performed: a cut-based video segmentation system extracts representative images from the video stream, and SkimViewer extracts topic structures from a video caption or a video transcript.

The second step combines multiple media, i.e., the topic structures and the images are combined into new topic-based skim structures. Two types of topic-based multimedia skim structures are created: semantically representative images labeled with the corresponding topics and groups, each of which has a topic as a label and images related to that topic. The topics make the images and groups richer in descriptive power.

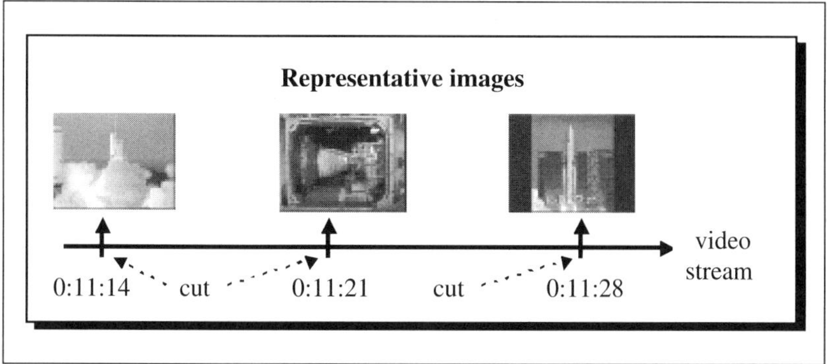

Figure 3. Output of video segmentation.

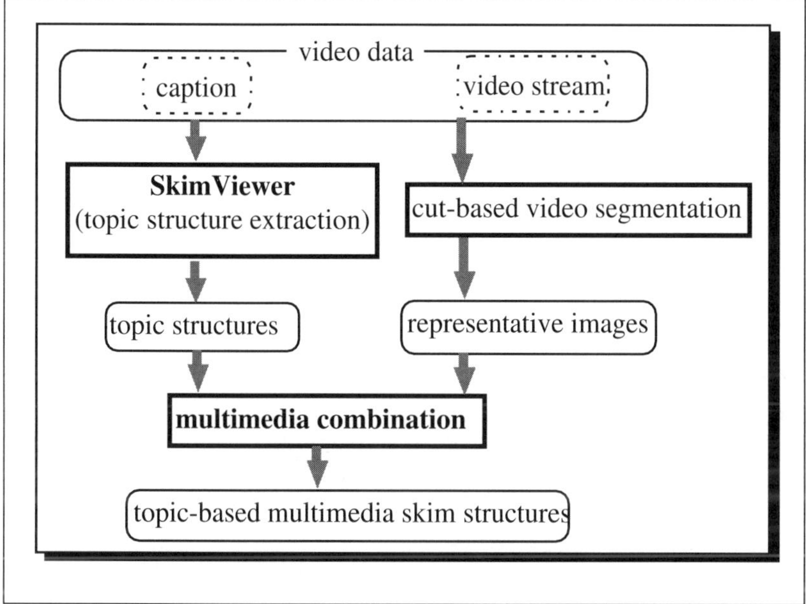

Figure 4. Outline of topic-based multimedia structuring.

3. Extracting Topic Structures from Monologue Transcripts

In this section, we discuss an approach and outline to topic structure extraction, extracting global and local topics from monologues, unifying global and local topics, and an experimental evaluation of topic structure extraction.

3.1 An Approach to Topic Structure Extraction

Text structure extraction methods have been proposed in the field of text processing (Cohen 1987, Morris 1991, Kurohashi and Nagao 1994). These are based on the idea of "cohesion," i.e., they try to recognize semantic aggregations of sentences. They commonly need thesauruses or knowledge-bases for calculating the degree of cohesion between adjacent sentences. Therefore, their applicable domains are very restricted. As our target covers a wide variety of domains, the traditional cohesion-based methods are not suitable for our purpose. The statistical method by Hearst and Plaunt (1993) and Hearst (1994) does not use either thesauruses or knowledge-bases. It uses term repetition for cohesion analysis, and can be applied to a variety of domains. However, it can only divide texts into segments and cannot recognize topics and their nest structures.

This chapter proposes a new approach based not on cohesion, but on the hypothesis that topic structures are fundamental for natural language communication. Therefore, linguistic phenomena such as clues and behavior are commonly observed in communicating topic structures. Our approach uses knowledge about such phenomena and enables robust and domain-independent processing. We developed a topic structure extraction system called "SkimViewer" which incorporates three modes. One mode is for written texts. The other two are for spoken transcripts: monologue and dialogue. The dialogue mode is described in Takeshita (1992). This chapter focuses on the monologue mode.

3.2 Outline of Topic Structure Extraction

Figure 5 shows an outline of skim structure extraction. Two kinds of topic structures are treated: global and local topics. The global topics are indicated explicitly by linguistic clues. The clues include cue phrases such as "first." Local topics are not accompanied by such clues. The extraction process consists of three steps: extracting global and local topics, and unifying them. Each extraction step has three substeps: identifying topic introducing parts (TIPs), identifying the topic in each TIP, and identifying its scope.

The topic extraction uses knowledge about linguistic phenomena. There are six linguistic phenomena for monologue topic extraction.

1. The first phenomena involves cue phrases such as "mazu (first)" and "tsugi ni (next)." These indicate not only the introduction of a topic but also a topic nest relation.

2. The second involves topic continuation expressions such as "kore wa (this is)" and "kono kekka (as a result)." These show that no new topic is introduced.

3. The third involves topic markers such as "ni tuite (with regard to)" and

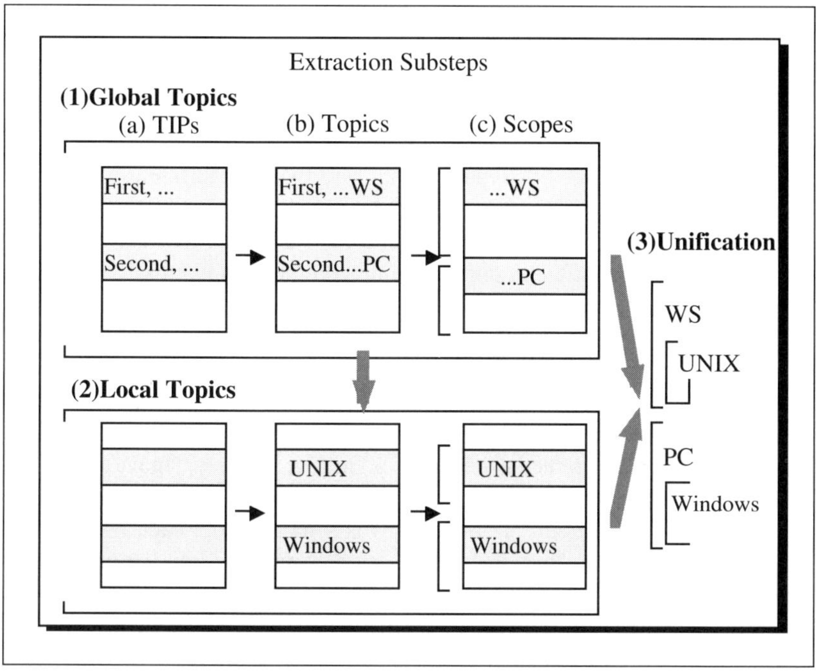

Figure 5. Outline of topic structure extraction.

"ga (subject marker)." In Japanese, grammatical functions such as subjects and objects are indicated by post-positional expressions.

4. The fourth phenomenon is sentence length. When a new topic is introduced, sentence length tends to increase because a speaker uses a longer explanation to communicate the topic to the audience. In addition to sentence length, topic extraction also uses block length. A block is an aggregation of sentences connected by topic continuation expressions.

5. The fifth phenomenon involves preview descriptions. When introducing a significant topic, a speaker explains subtopics which will be described. Therefore, noun phrases appearing in these preview descriptions are likely to be subtopics. A monologue title also works as a preview description.

6. The sixth phenomenon involves interrogative expressions such as "tazuneru (ask a question)" and example expressions such as "tatoeba (for example)." These tend to present a subtopic.

3.3 Extracting Global Topics from Monologues

Although the following explanation uses the simple monologue in figure 1, our method can accept complex and real-world data.

3.3.1 Identifying Global Topic Introducing Parts (TIPs). First, TIP candidates are detected. At the beginning of a monologue, a topic must be introduced. Except for the beginning of a monologue, the only linguistic phenomenon indicating an introduction of a global topic is cue phrases. These cue phrases are classified into three types: nest start (NS), topic change (TC), and nest end (NE). The NS type includes "mazu (first, to begin with)," the TC type includes "tsugi ni (next)," and "dai ni ni (second)," and the NE type includes "saigo ni (finally)." SkimViewer knows 6 NS, 37 TC, and 2 NE cue phrases. In contrast with cue phrases, topic continuation expressions such as "kore wa (this is)" show that no new topic is introduced. SkimViewer has 5 topic continuation expressions. Thus, the following is detected as TIP candidates: a) a sentence which contains a cue phrase, but whose first simple sentence has no topic continuation expression, and b) the first sentence in the monologue. In figure 1, sentence (1) is detected as a TIP candidate. Sentence (2) and (5) are also detected because of the cue phrases "mazu (to begin with)" and "tsugi ni (next)."

Next, a prominent noun phrase (P-NP) is selected from each simple sentence according to predetermined P-NP marker priority: *explicit markers > implicit markers*. The explicit markers are used only for indicating P-NPs, while implicit markers indicate case such as subjects and objects. Explicit markers include "ni tsuite" and "wa" in Japanese, meaning "with regard to" and "as for" in English. Implicit markers include the subject marker "ga" and the object marker "wo." In English, case is indicated by word order, e.g., subjects precede verbs. Therefore, instead of implicit markers, the result of syntactic analysis is used. SkimViewer knows 41 explicit and 14 implicit markers.

In figure 1, "tsuushin sa-bisu (telecommunication services)" in (1-1), "iroiro na shinki sa-bisu (various new services)" in (2-1), "sa-bisu A (service-A)" in (3-2) and "riyousha suu (the number of the users)" in (7-2) are indicated by the subject marker "ga," and "juurai kara no sa-bisu (existing services)" in (5-1) by the explicit marker "ni tsuite (regarding)," and "sa-bisu B (service-B)" in (7-1) by the explicit marker "wa (as for)."

Finally, global topic cost is calculated for each P-NP, a topic presentation type is identified for each TIP candidate, and each candidate is validated. In order to have a cost of 1, a P-NP must be an explicit marker, including a proper noun, or be part of the monologue title. P-NPs not satisfying these conditions are assigned a cost of 2. These cost assignments are based on interview results with subjects of a manual topic extraction experiment.

If a TIP candidate has two P-NPs with a cost of 1, the topic presentation is recognized as being "gradual," e.g., a global topic is followed by a more detailed one. Otherwise, the type is recognized as being a "lump," e.g., even a complex topic is presented as a lump. If a TIP candidate is a gradual type, the end of the TIP is corrected to the end of the simple sentence including the first P-NP with a cost of 1, and the candidate is validated. If the candidate is a lump type, the candidate is validated without any correction. These TIPs also work as preview descriptions.

In figure 1, the presentation type of the TIP candidate in sentence (1) is "lump" because the cost of "tsuushin sa-bisu (telecommunication services)" is 1, and this is the only P-NP in the sentence. The candidate is validated as a TIP without any correction. The TIP candidates at (2) and at (5) are also identified as being "lumps" and are validated as TIPs.

3.3.2 Identifying Global Topics, Levels, and Scopes. The P-NP with the lowest cost in each TIP is identified as a topic. If the TIP includes more than one P-NP with an equally low cost, the earliest one is selected. In figure 1, "tsuushin sa-bisu (telecommunication services)" in (1-1) is identified as the topic in the first TIP. "Iroiro na shinki sa-bisu (various new services)" in (2-1) and "juurai kara no sa-bisu (existing services)" in (5-1) are also identified as topics.

The level of the first topic is 1 and according to cue phrases, these levels change. If the current cue phrase is an NS type, the level increases by 1, i.e., more details are given. If the current cue phrase is a TC or NE type, and the previous one is an NS or TC type, the level does not change. If the current phrase is a TC or NE type, and the previous one is an NE type, the level decreases by 1, i.e., something new is introduced. The scope of the topic is taken from the beginning of its TIP to the end of the sentence just before the earliest topic whose level is equal to or less than the current topic's level. In figure 1, the level of the topic "tsuushin sa-bisu (telecommunication services)" is 1, that of "iroiro na shinki sa-bisu (various new services)" is 2, and that of "juurai kara no sa-bisu (existing services)" is 2. Therefore, topic scopes are (1-1) to (7-5), (2-1) to (4-2), and (5-1) to (7-5).

3.4 Extracting Local Topics from Monologues

In this section, we discuss identifying local topic introducing parts and identifying local topics, levels, and scopes.

3.4.1 Identifying Local Topic Introducing Parts (TIPs). First, each sentence satisfying the all of the following condition is detected as a TIP candidate. We use sentence length to identify TIPs.

- The number of simple sentences in the sentence is equal to or more than the predefined value, *sent-size*.

- No lump-type global topics are extracted from the sentence.

- The sentence is the first sentence in a block which is an aggregation of sentences connected by topic continuation expressions, and the number of simple sentences in the block is equal to or more than the predefined value, *block-size*.

Two parameters *sent-size* and *block-size* are used based on interview results with subjects of a manual topic extraction experiment.

Next, local topic costs are calculated for P-NPs in the TIP candidates. P-NPs with a cost of 1 are those that accompany interrogative or example expressions such as "tazuneru (ask a question)" or "tatoeba (for example)." A P-NP including a proper noun, indicated by an explicit marker, or included in the previous preview description, i.e., in the previous global topic TIP, is assigned a cost of 2. Other P-NPs are assigned a cost of 3. These cost assignments are based on interview results with subjects of a manual topic structure extraction experiment.

Finally, the TIP candidates with a P-NP with a cost of 2 or less are validated as TIPs. In figure 1, sentences (3) and (7) are detected as TIP candidates. The costs of "sa-bisu A (service-A)" in (3-2) and "sa-bisu B (service-B)" in (7-1) are both 2, and that of "riyousha suu (the number of users)" in (7-2) is 3. Therefore, if *sent-size = 2* and *block-size = 4*, both candidates are validated as TIPs.

3.4.2 Identifying Local Topics, Levels, and Scopes. First, local topics are selected using the same rule as that for global topics. In figure 1, "sa-bisu A (service-A)" in (3-1) and "sa-bisu B (service-B)" in (7-2) are selected as topics.

Next, topic levels are assigned using a simple rule: 1 is added to the maximum global topic level for a particular sentence. This rule is based on the hypothesis that speakers can achieve accurate topic expansion and tend to keep discussing the same thing. In figure 1, topic levels of both local topics are assigned 3.

Finally, the scope is defined as running from the beginning of the TIP to the end of the sentence just before the earliest local or global TIP beginning after the current TIP. In figure 1, the scope of "sa-bisu A (service-A)" is from (3-1) to (4-2), and that of "sa-bisu B (service-B)" is from (7-1) to (7-5).

3.5 Unifying Global and Local Topics

Global and local topics are unified to achieve complete topic structures, and topic duplication is considered. Assume topic-A precedes topic-B, and both are the same. If topic-A is a parent of topic-B, or they have the same level and are adjacent, topic duplication is detected. If duplication is detected, topic structure extraction is performed again in the same way as the previous extraction except that topic-B is removed from the P-NPs. Otherwise, the topic extraction is terminated. The entire topic structure of figure 1 is shown in figure 2.

3.6 Experimental Evaluation of Topic Structure Extraction

Manually extracted topic structures were used in the experiments. In this kind of experimental evaluation, objectivity must be taken into consideration, i.e., topic structures may differ from user to user. Hearst (1994) discusses text segmentation by human readers. In this paper, segment boundaries by 7 readers were compared. If 3 out of 7 readers judge a point to be a segment boundary, the point is regarded as a "true" boundary.

However, creating "true" topic structures is a much more difficult task than performing such a simple comparison. For example, even if topic-A extracted by a reader and topic-B extracted by another reader differ, the meaning may be the same. Therefore, we had two readers cooperate with each other in creating "true" topic structures: 1) the first reader extracted topic structures, 2) the second reader checked the topic structures, and 3) both readers discussed any disagreement and then the "true" topic structure was decided. Although this does not guarantee complete objectivity, it seems to be the best and the most realistic method.

To measure agreement between the "true" topic structures and those from SkimViewer, we calculated precision and recall ratios. If the system topics are "S," true topics "T," and their intersection "I," the precision ratio is "I/S" and the recall ratio is "I/T."

TV news manuscripts were used as the monologues. Half the data, 63 monologues with 2,942 simple sentences, were used for refining parameter values of *sent-size* and *block-size* so as to maximize the sum of precision and recall ratios of topic scopes. The result of this refinement is that *sent-size = 4* and *block-size = 4*. By coincidence, the condition in which the *block-size* is always satisfied is when the condition of *sent-size* is satisfied.

The remaining data, 64 monologues with 3,182 simple sentences, were used in the evaluation. The precision and recall ratios for topics were 57.6% and 61.3%, and those for scope were 61.8% and 58.5%. Distribution of precision and recall ratios are also important: out of 64 sets of evaluation data, there are 10 sets of data whose topic precision and recall ratios are more than 80%, 24 data sets more than 60%, and 3 data sets less than 30%. The precision and recall ratios for TIPs, i.e., segmentation, are 63.4% and 63.9%.

Thus, the topic structures output by SkimViewer have some extraction error. However, even if the topic structures are not correct, people can easily spot the inaccuracies and hypothesize the correct structures. A prominent extraction error is the misinterpretation of a cue phrase. For example, the word "next" is not always a cue to a topic change. In the sentence "The next train will arrive soon," "next" is not a cue. The system has a rule for this, but not all instances are interpreted correctly.

Although quantitative evaluations were performed on the above-mentioned data, other real-world texts were applied to SkimViewer, and the system's robustness and effectiveness were validated. In our laboratory, SkimViewer is used as a browsing interface for text databases such as minutes of Congress and lecture manuscripts.

4. Multimedia Combination

In this section, we discuss multimedia combination algorithms, including two-stream synchornization,topic-based representative creation, and topic-based group creation, and the outline of our experiments.

4.1 Multimedia Combination Algorithm

Multimedia combination consists of three steps. The first step is called two-stream synchronization. It synchronizes topic structures as output by SkimViewer, with images extracted by a video segmentation system from the video sequence. The second and the third steps are called topic-based representative and group creation. They create different types of topic-based multimedia skim structures.

4.1.1 Two-stream Synchronization. Each image has a time stamp because each image in a video stream is provided with the time stamp in advance. Each topic is given the time span of the sentence in which the topic appears. This time span is an approximation of the time span for the topic itself, but the accuracy is sufficient for our purposes. This is because many sentences are very short, e.g., from 3 to 8 seconds.

Figure 6 shows an example of synchronization. The upper part of the time line indicates the image positions. Each image is numbered and the time stamps are abbreviated. The lower part shows the time spans of sentences from which topics were extracted. For example, the sentence for the "ladder car" topic starts at 0:16:21 and ends at 0:16:25.

In this synchronization, we assume that we have precise information on the timing of the captions. But this is not generally the case. In many cases, captions and video soundtracks are not perfectly synchronized. The InfoMedia project analyzes the soundtrack by a word spotting technique to put time stamps on closed-captions (Hauptmann and Whitbrock, this volume). This is future work for us.

4.1.2 Topic-based Representative Creation. The basic idea of the topic-based representative creation is that a truly representative image should have a corresponding topic. However, the image and the topic do not always appear simultaneously. In most cases, there is a time-lag between each topic and the corresponding image. Therefore, the time-lag must be incorporated into this creation process. The following describes the creation process. Each topic is assigned no more than one topic-based representative image.

1. If a sentence introducing a topic includes one or more images, the image appearing first is selected. The image is called the topic-based representative.

2. If a topic introducing sentence includes no image, but if an image lies

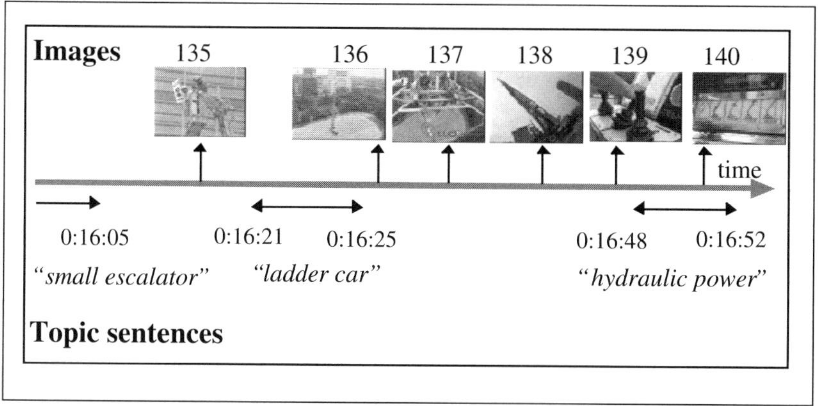

Figure 6. Example of two-stream synchronization.

within the period of **delta** seconds before or after the sentence, it is selected. **Delta** indicates the time-lag. At present, the value of **delta** is arbitrarily defined: **delta** = *5 seconds*. If the span includes two or more images, the one nearest the sentence is selected. If two images are equally near to the sentence, the one coming before the sentence is selected. The selected image is the topic-based representative.

3) If a topic is not assigned a topic-based representative by the first two rules, the topic is removed from the topic structures.

In figure 6, image No. 140 is selected, and the image with topic "hydraulic power" is output as a topic-based representative because of the above mentioned step 1. If the time stamps of image No. 135 and No. 136 are 0:16:16 and 0:16:28 respectively, No. 136 is selected, and, together with the topic "ladder car," it is output as a topic-based representative because of step 2. Figure 7 shows the topic based representative interface of our topic-based multimedia structuring system. Each topic is numbered in section format. According to the numbers, the topic "hydraulic power" is a subtopic of "ladder car."

4.1.3 Topic-based Group Creation. The basic idea of creating topic-based groups is that images in the same topic scope pertain to the corresponding topic and should be grouped. A group is created for each topic-based representative. Let the current topic introducing sentence be S1, the next topic introducing sentence be S2, the start time of S1 be *start(S1)*, and the end time of S2 be *end(S2)*.

First, topic-based time segment boundaries are calculated using the rule shown below. Second, groups are created according to the boundaries, i.e., images in the same time segment are grouped, and the corresponding topic is taken as the label for that group.

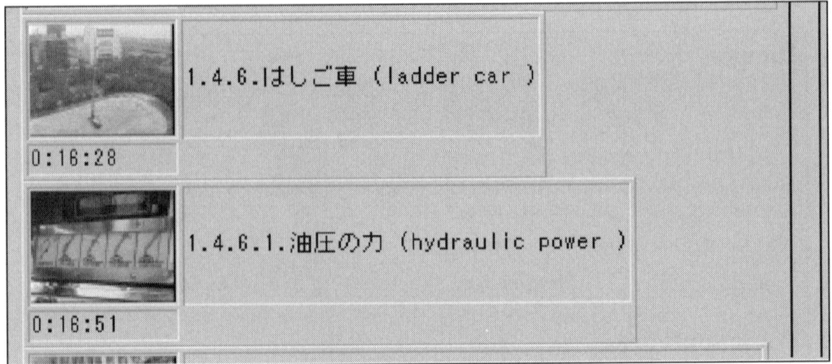

Figure 7. A topic-based representative interface.

1. If *start*(*S2*) – *end*(*S1*) >= **delta** * 2, the position **delta** seconds before *start*(*S2*) is selected as a boundary.

2. If *start*(*S2*) – *end*(*S1*) < **delta** * 2, the position between *end*(*S1*) and *start*(*S2*) is selected as a boundary. There is an exception however: if the topic-based representative image of *S2* is included in *S1*, the boundary is set 1 second before the time of the topic-based representative image.

Assume that **delta** = *5* seconds. In figure 6, 0:16:16 and 0:16:43 are selected as the time segment boundaries because of rule 1. Therefore, the time segment for the "ladder car" topic runs from 0:16:16 to 0:16:42. If the time stamps of images No. 135, 138, and 139 are 0:16:16, 0:16:42 and 0:16:46 respectively, the group comprising No. 135, 136, 137, and 138 labeled "ladder car" is output as a topic-based group.

Figure 8 shows the topic-based group interface of our system. Similar to the topic-based representative interface, each topic is numbered. The group for the topic "ladder car" includes four images, and that for "hydraulic power" includes two images. Images outlined in bold lines have ones of topic-based representatives.

4.2 Experiment and Discussion

First, the outline of our experiments is described. Our system performed topic-based multimedia structuring on four educational video streams on scientific themes. Each stream is about 20 minutes long. In this experiment, transcribing and providing each sentence with a time span was performed manually. This is because captioned TV programs are limited in number in Japan. However, they will increase in popularity because captions are useful to the hearing impaired, and to those people studying foreign languages.

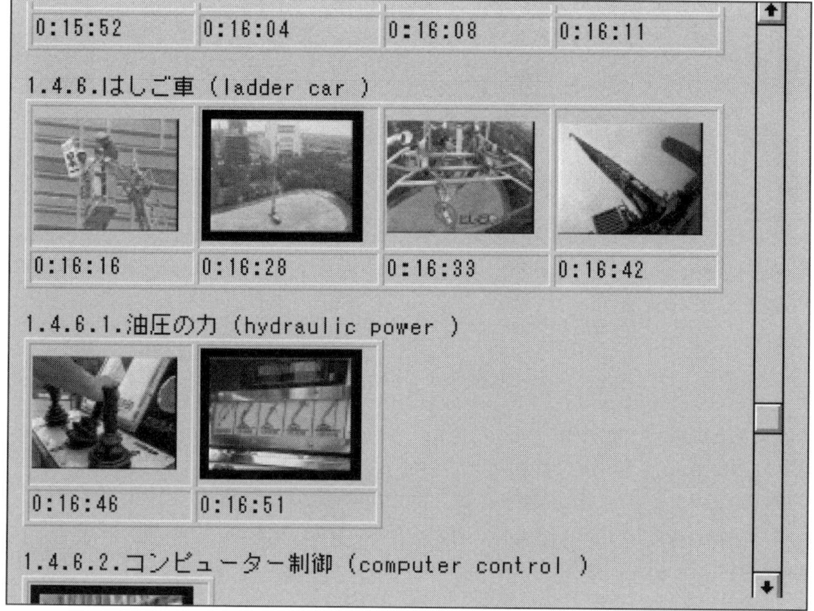

Figure 8. Topic-based group interface.

SkimViewer extracted 232 topics in total from the four transcriptions. For cut-based video segmentation, we used "Paper Video" (Tonomura et al. 1994). Paper Video accepts a video stream as input, detects cut changes in the stream to achieve video stream segmentation, and extracts a representative image from each segment. The output of Paper Video is a series of images, and is not based on semantic structures. From the four video streams, Paper Video extracted a total of 533 representative images.

Second, the action of topic-based representative creation was examined. Under the condition that *delta* = *5 seconds*, 191 topic-based representatives were created from the four video transcriptions and streams. The reduction ratio of the images is 191 / 533 = 35.8%. This indicates that the topic-based representative creation makes browsing easy and effortless. Furthermore, combining topics and images makes the topic-based scenes richer in descriptive power. The topic-based representatives in figure 7 are easier to understand than the topics or images by themselves.

Third, topic-based group creation was examined. A total of 191 groups were created. 62 groups contain only one scene, i.e., about a third of all groups are just topic-based representatives. Groups containing from two to four images are frequently created: 96 groups. A few groups contain 8 or more images: 6 groups.

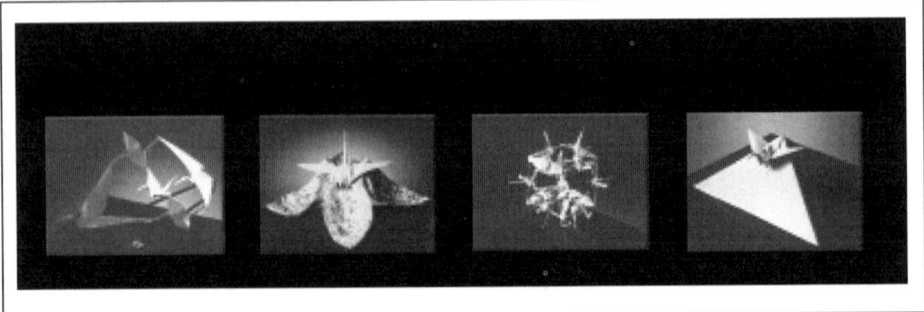

Figure 9. A part of a topic-based group pertaining to
"origami cranes" in "records for smallest things."

Figure 9 shows part of a topic-based group. Users may be unable to understand what the images are about if the topics were not given. The topic structures definitely help comprehension. The topic assigned to the group is "origami cranes," and the topic is a subtopic of the topic "records for smallest things." From this topic structure, users can assume that the images are concerned with "very small origami cranes." Figure 10 shows another topic-based group. In contrast with the topic for the group in figure 9, this group's topic "largest engines in Japan" is inappropriate. If only the topic is shown to users, the users may be unable to understand the precise meaning. Instead of the topic, images help comprehension of what this group concerns. The images suggest that the group concerns rockets. Therefore, users can assume that the group is about a very large-scale rocket engine.

Fourth, inappropriate topic-based skim structures should be discussed. In topic-based representatives and groups, not every image matches the given topic because a video stream is not always concerned with what is discussed in its caption. For example, some parts of a video stream show only the reporter's face. Although video segmentation methods are not useful in this case, topics can aid in user skimming.

Another inappropriate skim structure is a group which contains one or more images which should be included in the next or in the previous group. Although users can assume true group boundaries and there is no problem in practical use, such groups make skimming troublesome. To reduce the number of inappropriate groups, accuracy of topic structure extraction, especially TIP extraction, must be improved. In order to accomplish this, it seems to be effective to combine our topic structure extraction approach with other approaches such as Hearst's (1994) statistical method.

Finally, for which types of video documents does our method achieve good results? Skim Viewer is good at informative language passages because it is based on linguistic phenomena in communicating information. Therefore, topic-based multimedia structuring is suitable for informative video

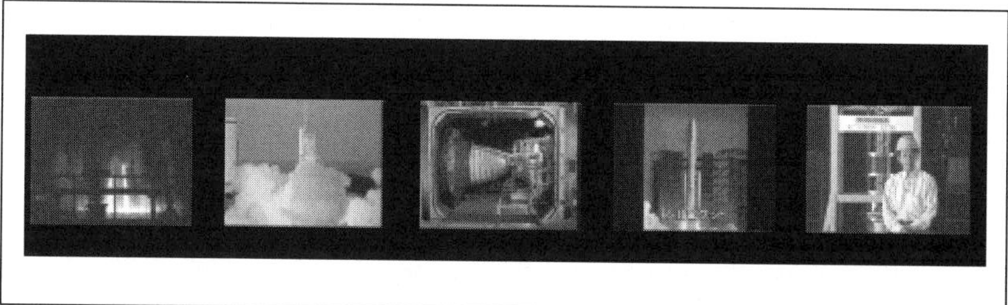

Figure 10. A topic-based group pertaining to "largest engines in Japan."

documents such as educational programs, TV news, documentaries, and lectures. On the contrary, our method is poor at amusement and entertainment video documents. For example, topic-based skim structures for movies may be meaningless.

5. Comparison with Related Work

The most significant characteristic of topic-based structuring is its use of multiple streams, e.g. text and video. As mentioned in section 1, there have been few multistream approaches to the creation of skim structures.

Shahraray and Gibbon (1995) proposed a method for automatic generation of hypermedia documents by text and video analysis. Their system takes a video stream accompanied by closed caption information, and creates skim structures consisting of representative images and the corresponding text segments. Each text segment contains 1 or more sentences. Compared with this approach, the biggest merit of our method is compactness of the created skim structures. The topic-based multimedia skim structures consist of representative images and noun phrases representing topics, and therefore enables more effective browsing.

In their InfoMedia Project, Hauptmann and Whitbrock (this volume) extract representative images and keywords from a captioned video stream. But their system does not generate a multimedia representation for skimming. Our method is superior in that topic-based multimedia skim structures are semantic-based, and are easy for users to understand.

Mani et al. (this volume) proposes an approach to content-based information browsing system for broadcast news video using automated text segmentation technique. They investigated two types of automated segmentation for closed-caption texts: a subject classification approach to context and an approach based on discourse cues. The former approach also extracts a topic for each segment. Their system provides an access interface to video streams using segmented texts and topics. However, video streams are an add-on and are not used for processing while our method achieves multistream processing.

Aigrain and Joly (1994) describes a simple software tool called "Video-script." It uses sequence-shot level video segmentation to provide an environment where users can easily enter shot-by-shot transcription and annotation, i.e., where users can manually create multimedia skim structures consisting of representative images and texts. In comparison with this approach, the automatic generation of multimedia skim structures is the principal merit of our method.

6. Conclusion

This chapter has proposed a new method for helping people grasp the outlines of targeted multimedia data. The method, called "topic-based multimedia structuring," combines the results of text and video analysis and creates semantic-based multimedia skim structures.

A new topic structure extraction method for text analysis was proposed. The extraction method is based on knowledge about linguistic phenomena concerning topic expansion and achieves robust and practical extraction. The effectiveness of the extraction method was shown by comparing manually obtained and system obtained topics. The system's level of accuracy is nearly as high as that of a person.

A method for combining the two streams of results, i.e., text and video, was proposed. The method synchronizes the topic structures and images extracted by video segmentation and creates topic-based representatives and groups as semantic-based multimedia skim structures. The effectiveness of the method was discussed.

Acknowledgments

The authors give special thanks to "TV Asahi" for allowing us to use their video streams. We also acknowledge SUGIZAKI, Masayuki for many helpful discussions.

References

Arman, F.; Depommier, R.; Hsu, A.; and Chiu, M-Y. 1994. Content-based Browsing of Video Sequences. In Proceedings of Second ACM Multimedia 94, 97-103. 15-20 October. San Francisco.

Aigrain, P. and Joly, P. 1994. Discrete Visual Manipulation User Interface for Video. In Proceedings of RIAO'94 Workshop on Multimedia Information Representation and Retrieval, Vol. 2: 12-17.

Aigrain, P.; Joly, P. and Longueville, V. 1997. Medium Knowledge-Based Macro-Segmentation of Video into Sequences. In this volume.

Cohen, R. 1987. Analyzing the Structure of Argumentative Discourse. *Computational Linguistics* 13: 11-24.

Gabbe, J. D.; Ginsberg, A.; and Robinson, B. S. 1994. Towards Intelligent Recognition of Multimedia Episodes in Real-Time Applications. In Proceedings of Second ACM Multimedia 94, 227-236. San Francisco, CA, 15-20 October.

Harn, U. 1992. On Text Coherence Parsing. In Proceedings of Fourteenth International Conference on Computational Linguistics (COLING-92), 25-31. Nante, France, 23-28 July.

Hauptmann, A. G. and Smith, M. A. 1995. Text, Speech and Vision for Video Segmentation. Presented at the IJCAI-95 Workshop on Intelligent Multimedia Information Retrieval. Montréal, Canada.

Hauptmann, A. G. and Whitbrock, M. J. 1997. Informedia: News-on-Demand Multimedia Information Acquisition and Retrieval. In this volume.

Hearst, M. A. and Plaunt, C. 1993. Subtopic Structuring for Full-length Document Access. In 60th International ACM SIGIR Conference, 59-68. Pittsburg, PA, 27 June - 1 July.

Hearst, M. A. 1994. Multi-paragraph Segmentation of Expository Text. In 32nd Annual Meeting the Association for Computational Linguistics (ACL-94), 9-16. New Mexico, 27-30 June.

Kurohashi, S. and Nagao, M. 1994. Automatic Detection of Discourse Structure by Checking Surface Information in Sentences. In 50th International Conference on Computational Linguistics (COLING-94), 1123-1127. Kyoto, Japan.

Morris, J. and Hirst, G. 1991. Lexical Cohesion Computed by Thesaural Relations as an Indicator of the Structure of Text. *Computational Linguistics* 13: 21-48.

Mani, I.; House, D.; Maybury, M. and Green, M. 1997. Towards Content-Based Browsing of Broadcast News Video. In this volume.

Shahraray, B. and Gibbon, D. C. 1995. Automated Authoring of Hypermedia Documents of Video Programs. In Proceedings of Third ACM Multimedia 95, 401-409. San Francisco, CA.

Takeshita, A. 1992. Recognizing Topics Through the use of Interaction Structures. In Proceedings of Fourteenth International Conference on Computaional Linguistics (COLING-92), 1064-1068. Nante, France

Tonomura, Y.; Akutsu, A.; Taniguchi, Y.; and Suzuki, G. Fall 1994. Structured Video Computing. *IEEE Multimedia* 1(3): 34-43.

Architectures and Tools

The chapters in this fifth section focus on the architectures required to support multimedia information processing. In the first chapter of this section, Bernard Mérialdo and Florence Dubois (Instiut Eurécom, France) describe a generic tool to develop and experiment with agents that detect complex events in multimedia streams by combining information extracted by simpler agents. Consider a query such as "Find me all video segments in which person X is talking about topic Y". This would require a face location, identification, and movement agent, as well as a speaker identification, word spotting, and possibly caption understanding agent. Agents must interact in a variety of ways, including succession (e.g., a face location agent provides recognized regions to a face identification agent), validation (e.g., video and audio agents might confirm that a speaker is talking), and composition (e.g., we know X is talking about Y if we combine output from a face or speaker identification algorithm together with output from a speech transcription and/or closed caption agent). Mérialdo and Dubois describe a Multimedia Flow Browser and related Agent Editor that enables users to both visualize agent interactions and combine existing agents into new agents. A broadcast news example is used to illustrate the system.

The second chapter by James Griffioen, Rajendra Yavatkar, and Robert Adams (University of Kentucky) similarly investigates architectures for integrating multiple algorithms. The authors describe MOODS, a framework for developing content-based analysis systems. A key issue in engineering these systems is the tradeoff between processing and storage, for example, precomputing computationally expensive operations prior to user query. The authors illustrate the application of their framework to the rapid creation of image understanding systems in two domains: music note recognition and analysis of ancient Beowulf manuscripts (e.g., to support letterform identification used by paleographers to analyze differences in writing styles). Thus, whereas the focus of this chapter is on software architecture, this work is related to Manmatha and Croft's investigation into indexing handwritten manuscripts reported in the first section of the collection.

In the previous two sections we saw tools that support indexing and query of video by visual and linguistic content. In the last chapter of this section, Stacie Hibino and Elke Rundensteiner (University of Michigan) present a direct manipulation paradigm to interactively query, filter, and browse data in order to discover and analyze temporal relationships and trends. The authors present the multimedia visual information seeking (MMVIS) environment which supports the analysis of the temporal structure of video documents, and report its successful application in a case study based on video data from computer supported collaborative work. The chapter investigates how to temporally analyze annotations (that capture the extracted content of a video) using a direct-manipulation and feedback environment. This work is related to Pentland's chapter in section one which addresses understanding human behavior in video, however, here the focus is on temporal analysis from video content.

Each of these chapters points to architectural requirements and potential solutions for managing multimedia information. Collectively, the chapters point to a need for more effective tool integration, visualization and analysis support environments.

Chapter 14

An Agent-based Architecture for Content-Based Multimedia Browsing

Bernard Mérialdo and Florence Dubois, Institut Eurécom

Abstract

The automatic analysis of the content of multimedia documents requires combination of information coming from various data types (e.g., audio, video, text). In this chapter, we propose an architecture that describes agents for processing flows of information. These agents can be applied to elementary data types (e.g., audio, video), but also to the results produced by other agents. The architecture includes a Multimedia Flow Browser, which is able to display simultaneously visual representations of the various information flows produced by agents, and an Agent Editor, which provides a graphical interface to create new agents by combining existing agents. The architecture is open, so that it is possible to add new data types (and the procedures to visualize them) and new agents. A simulated example is presented to show the possible use of this tool in an application based on television broadcast news recordings.

1. Introduction

A multimedia application mixes speech, audio, image, video and text processing and navigation, in order to offer an improved and transparent interface and provide a communication that is as natural as possible. The traditional functions that can be performed on a multimedia document mainly use its syntactic structure and not its semantic content: operations such as cut-and-paste, play-back, go-to, fast-forward and rewind are only possible on indices such as byte count and time stamp. More elaborate operations such as a search for a particular event or generate a summary of the document require an analysis of the contents of the document. This is a very difficult task because of the variety and complexity of the recognition techniques that are involved (speech recognition, image analysis, natural language understanding).

Hence there is a need for tools which facilitate the development, experimentation, combination and integration of various indexing techniques.

As an example, suppose that we are interested in a given topic in a television news recording. If we don't know the time where the presentation of this topic took place, we must playback the whole recording (even if at higher speed) to find the desired spot, thus consuming time. If an automatic system is able to detect, for example, events such as *"Mister X is talking about topic Y,"* then it will be possible to directly access the appropriate location. This event can be detected using information extracted from different components of the recording. For example, face recognition on the video part can be used to detect the presence of Mister X (another possibility would be speaker identification on the audio channel), word spotting on the audio part can identify the utterance of word Y, and captions could be searched for certain string patterns.

We propose an architecture which facilitates the creation of and experimentation with such detectors. They are built as a combination of agents. Some agents will process elementary data types (e.g., audio, video), whereas some agents will combine the results obtained by other agents to create complex detectors. A first tool, the Multimedia Flow Browser, allows us to visualize simultaneously the original data and the results of the processing by different agents. A second tool, the Agent Editor, provides a graphical interface to easily construct new agents as the combination of existing agents. These tools are extensible, and it is possible to incorporate new visualization procedures for new data types, and new agents in the agent library. This architecture is inspired from the image processing Khoros software (Konstantinides and Rasure 1994).

The chapter is organized in the following way. Section 2 presents related research conducted in video indexing and retrieval. Section 3 gives an example of an application of the Browser. Section 4 gives a general overview of the architecture; we present the Browser, the different types of visualization that it currently provides, the search features that are available, and describe the Agent Editor. Conclusions are presented in section 5.

2. Related Work

A major issue in multimedia document processing is the construction of indices that are representative of the content of the document. This involves pattern recognition techniques, including speech, image and natural language processing, analysis and understanding. Such techniques have been extensively studied for a long time, however, for the most part, each media was studied in isolation. With the development of multimedia technologies and the wider usage of multimedia documents such as video recordings, a strong emphasis has emerged on the intelligent processing of multimedia documents.

Because text indices are easier to manipulate, many approaches use techniques derived from textual Information Retrieval (IR) (Salton 1989), by processing either the textual component of the document (for example the caption of a picture (Ogle and Stonebreaker 1995)), or textual annotations that have been manually added to the document (Weber and Poon 1994). Although it is harder to define indices in non-textual data, such indices are potentially so useful that many projects tackle this difficult problem. Using speech recognition techniques such as word spotting, it is possible to detect the utterance of keywords in the audio component so that information retrieval techniques can be used. The Video Mail project (Brown et al. 1994; Jones et al., this volume) at Cambridge University is an example of this approach. Schauble and Wechsler (1995) use specific techniques to handle the problem of inaccurate keyword recognition. Blum et al. (this volume) use specially computed parameters to handle an audio database of sounds. Other approaches exploit the image component of the document, for example by computing and comparing textures. This is the case of the QBIC (Query by Image Content) Project at IBM (Flickner et al. 1995, this volume), and the PhotoBook Project at MIT (Pentland et al. 1993). Many approaches analyze the video component, where the basic operation is a segmentation of the video into consecutive shots using a cut detection algorithm (Arman 1994, Benedetti et al. 1995). This step often is followed by a more elaborate processing such as macro-segmentation (Aigrain et al., this volume) or parsing (Zhang et al. 1995, this volume).

While many projects use indices from a single media to process multimedia documents, some efforts combine indices from a variety of different media, such as the multimedia episodes defined in Gabbe et al. (1994). Srihari (1995) combines natural language processing and image understanding to create an automatic indexing system for captioned pictures of people; Rowe and Frew (this volume) use a related approach.

Because of the potential interest of users, broadcast news are the subject of many investigations to create, manipulate and process indices allowing intelligent processing such as filtering and retrieval. Examples of such systems are presented in Brown et al. (1995), Hauptman and Witbrock (this volume), Mani et al. (this volume).

Finally, multi-agent systems are the focus of a great interest in the field of Artificial Intelligence (Levis 1993) because they facilitate the implementation of complex behaviors. In particular, the coordination between agents, the information they exchange, the protocols they should use, are extensively studied.

3. An Example of an Application

Assume that you want to know if a given topic has been discussed in yesterday's TV news. You can get the recording and process it with agents that are available in our architecture. For example, you might start by using a word spotting agent to locate the relevant utterances in the audio part. The Multimedia Flow Browser will allow you to visualize the video and audio part, together with the results of the word spotting agent. The resulting display will be similar to the one shown in figure 1.

Suppose now that you want to detect a complex event such as when "Person X is talking about topic Y." This can be accomplished with a complex agent built by combining simpler agents, such as a:

- Face Location (FL) agent: takes a video as input and produces a list of regions in the image that are classified as faces of people;
- Face Identification (FI) agent: takes as input an excerpt of the video which has been recognized as a human face and identifies the person (with reference to a given database);
- Face Movement (FM) agent: takes an extract of the video which has been recognized as a human face and checks if the person is currently speaking or not (for example by analyzing lip movement);
- Speaker Identification (SI) agent: takes as input an audio signal and determines the instants where a given speaker (from a set of known speakers) is talking;
- Word Spotting (WS) agent: takes as input an audio signal and determines the instants where certain words (from a predefined vocabulary) are pronounced;
- Caption Word (CW) agent: takes as input a text stream (words with time stamps) and determines the instants at which certain words appear.

Assuming that X is a particular person, and that topic Y is illustrated by a keyword, a possible structure of such a system is indicated in figure 2.

The video part of the recording is analyzed by the Face Location agent to detect face locations, which are then identified by the Face Identification agent. At the same time, the Face Movement agent will detect when the person is talking. The combination of the identity of the person and its lip movement gives an indication of the event "*X is talking*" based on the video source. In parallel, the Speaker Identification agent analyses the audio signal to detect when "*X is talking.*" The video and audio information are then combined to formulate an evidence for "*X is talking.*" Similar operations occur with other agents. This example shows that there are three different ways by which simple agents can be combined together:

- *Succession:* when the output of one or several agents are used as input

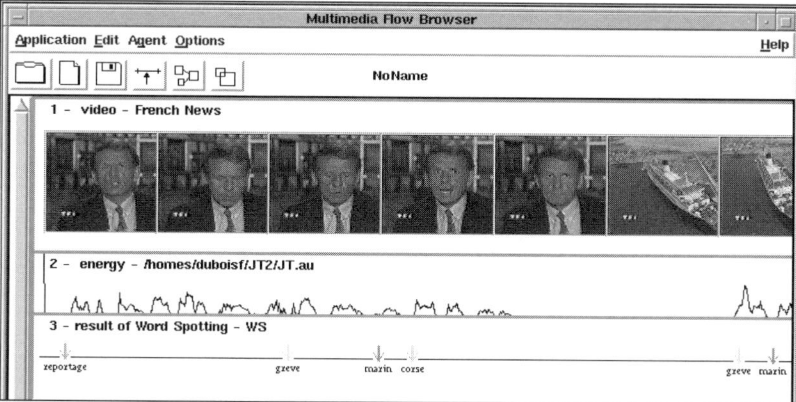

Figure 1. An example of an application using a word spotting agent.

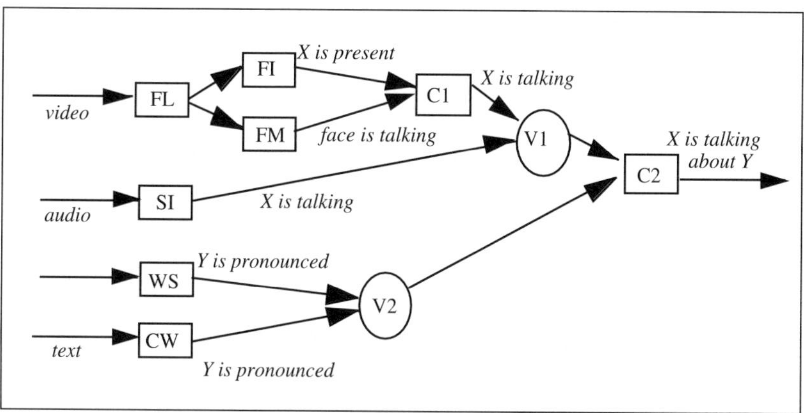

*Figure 2. A multi-agent architecture for detecting the complex event
"person x is talking about topic Y."*

to another agent. This is the case when the Face Location agent provides information to the Face Identification agent;

- *Validation:* when several agents provide information about the same event, and that their advice have to be combined in a single hypothesis. This is the case when we want to combine the output of the video and audio identification agents;

- *Composition:* when the hypotheses formulated by various agents have to be combined to form a more complex hypothesis. This is the case when we combine the information "X is talking" with the information "word Y is being pronounced."

Complex agents can be built with the *Agent Editor*, which offers a graphi-

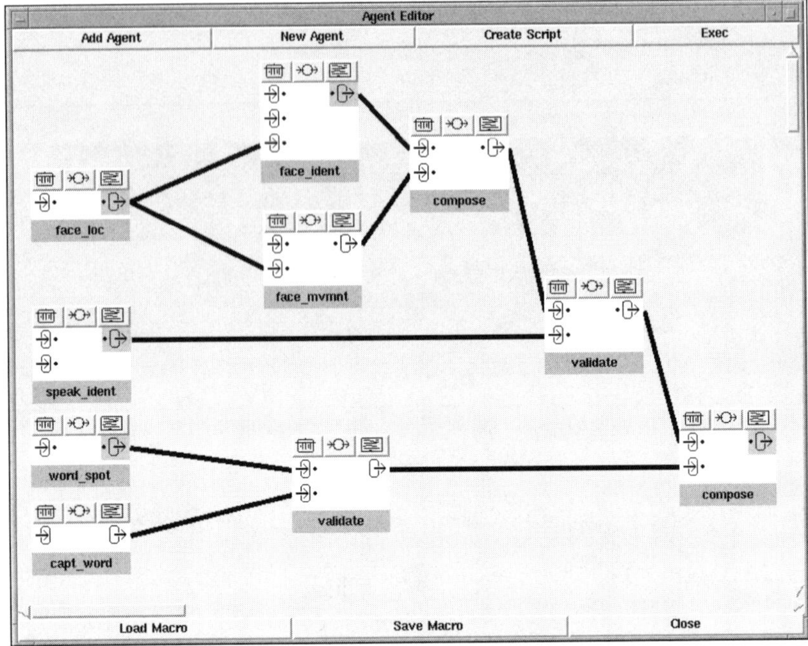

Figure 3. Construction of the architecture with the agent editor.

cal interface to select and link together simple agents. Figure 3 contains an example of the display when creating the complex agent previously described. The Browser can then be used to display some of the flows computed by the various agents, as shown in figure 4.

4. The Multimedia Flow Browser

The role of the Multimedia Flow Browser is to simultaneously visualize several flows of data. Those flows might be of various data types, either continuous (such as audio, video) or discrete (events characterized by an instant or an interval, such as captions), but we assume that they are all related to the same timeline. They might have been either recorded from external sources (audio, video), or have been produced as the result of the processing of other flows by agents.

4.1 Visualization Formats

The Browser provides a number of visualization formats for the standard data types. When the user wants to visualize a data flow, he can choose

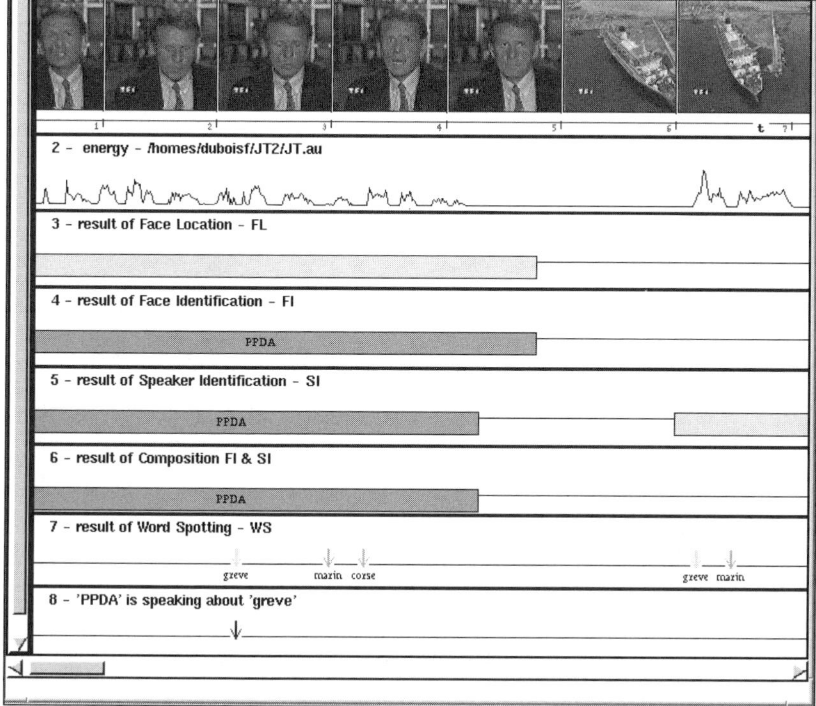

Figure 4. Results visualized on main window of multimedia flow browser.

among the formats that are available and choose which flows he wants to display on the Browser. Depending on the format that has been chosen, some computation will be performed by the Browser to compose the visualization window from the data flow. We give some examples of visualization formats that are currently implemented in the Browser.

A video flow can be represented as a sequence of consecutive images. These images can be placed either at regular time intervals or at each new cut detected (using a cut detection algorithm). A comparison of these formats is given in figure 5.

The audio flow can be displayed as signal or energy (the energy is automatically computed from the signal). An example is provided in figure 6.

Representation of discrete flows is also possible. We have defined a few data types (and file formats) for describing such flows which contain text labels associated with either time spots or time interval definitions. Several visualization formats are provided to visualize these data types. They are constructed using arrows or boxes (to indicate starting and ending time) located on a timeline, text labels, and eventually colors to differentiate different la-

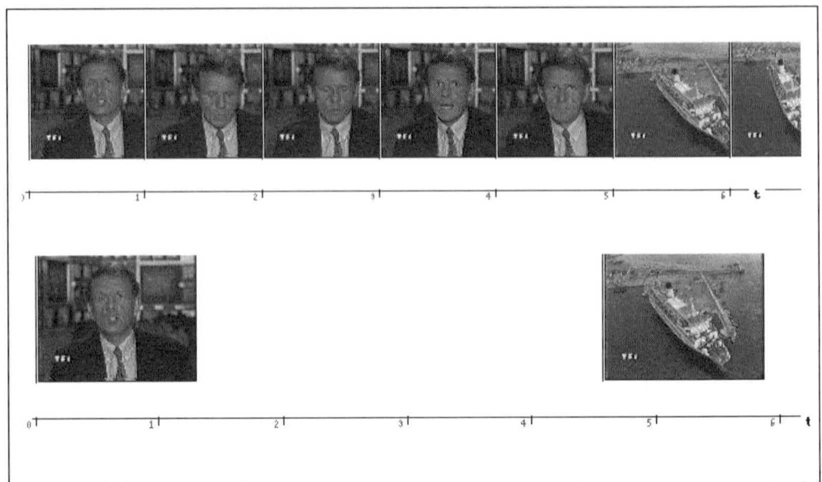

Figure 5. Representation of video flows.

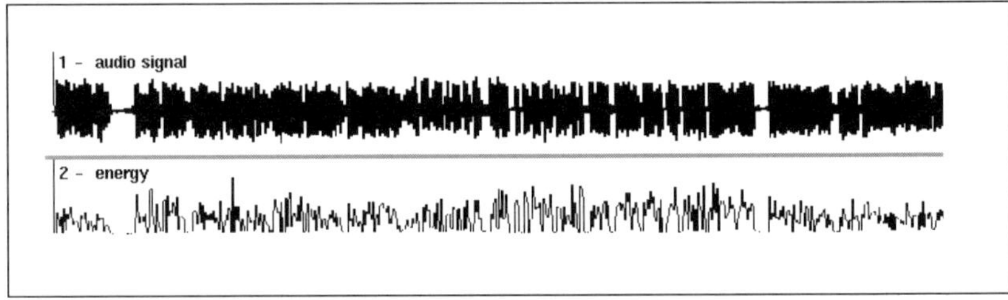

Figure 6. Representation of audio flows.

bels. Examples illustrating these possibilities are provided in figure 7.

The Browser has been designed so that it is easy to add new data types, new visualization formats, and the procedures that are needed to implement them. When creating new agents, it is preferable to use an existing data type, for example, a word spotting agent can produce a data flow composed of time-stamped text labels. In the case where no existing data type is suitable, for example, if we want to visualize the Fourier transforms of images, new visualization procedures will have to be written and added to the Browser.

The first function of the Browser is visualization. The user can select the data flows he wants to see, choose the visualization formats that will present these flows, and move the cursor on the time axis to explore the contents of these flows. He can also directly provide the time he wants to visualize. However these operations use only the syntactic structure of the data (perhaps with the exception of the cut detection algorithm for the video). We

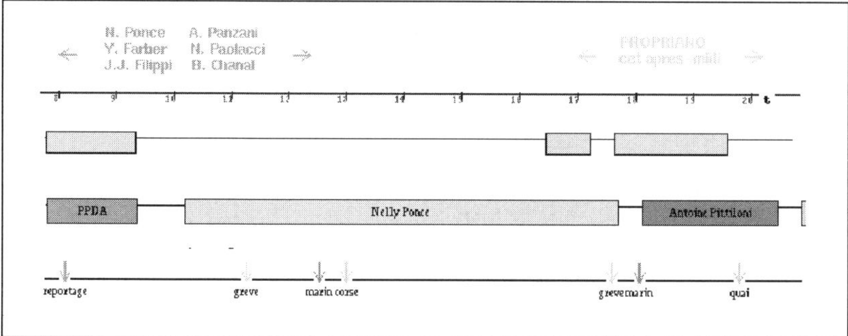

Figure 7. Representation of discrete events.

now describe other functions of the Browser that rely more on the content of the document.

4.2 Search and Indices

The Browser also provides Search and Index functions. The Search function is given a pattern by the user, searches for the next occurrence of this pattern in the data and positions the time cursor at the first instance found. The Index function displays an ordered list of possible patterns for a data flow, together with indications on the number and position of the occurrences of these patterns in the data.

Each data type has its own implementation of the Search and Index functions (we currently do not allow complex searches combining several data types to be performed; rather, we would create a new agent for this combination and search the data flow produced by this agent). It is also possible to have several implementations of a single data type, if the data contained in the flow can be observed from different perspectives. For certain data types, these implementations are straightforward. For example, data flows containing time-stamped text labels (like captions), can be easily searched for certain keywords in the text, or for certain constraints on the duration of the time interval. For other data types, the definition of patterns is more difficult. For example, how to define patterns that can be used to describe an image in a video is far from obvious.

Similar problems arise in the implementation of the Index function. Not only should we define the patterns that have to appear in the Index, but we should also define an ordering on these patterns to build the index. In the case of time-stamped labels, the patterns might be the labels themselves, listed in order of occurrence. Figure 8 is an example of an index created from the results of a word spotting agent. In the case of video, we can provide a list of different images appearing in the video (images that are only slightly

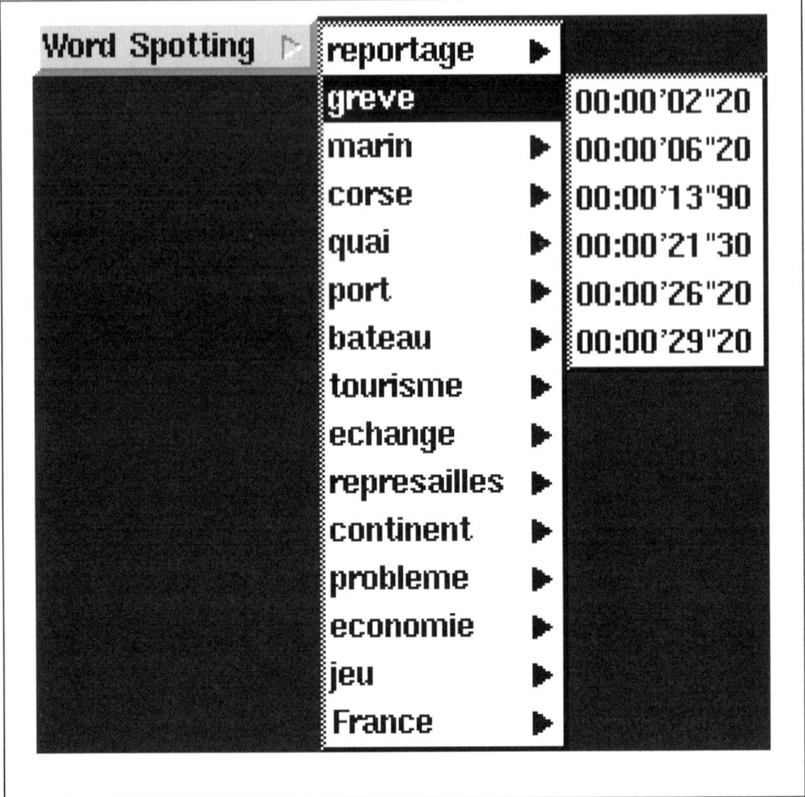

Figure 8. Example of indices resulting from word spotting.

different are considered identical), sorted by decreasing number of occurrences.

4.3 The Agent Editor

Agents process one or several input data flows and provide their results as one or several output data flows. Agents can be of two types: simple or complex. Simple agents are stand-alone procedures (such as word-spotting). The architecture provides conventions for defining their input and output parameters. Complex agents are combinations of simple or complex agents. They are created using the Agent Editor which provides a graphical interface to select and link agents together. The user will select the agents he wants to use in the library of available agents, and they will appear as boxes in the graphical interface with slots indicating the possible input and output flows. To connect agents together, he will then link the output to certain agents to the

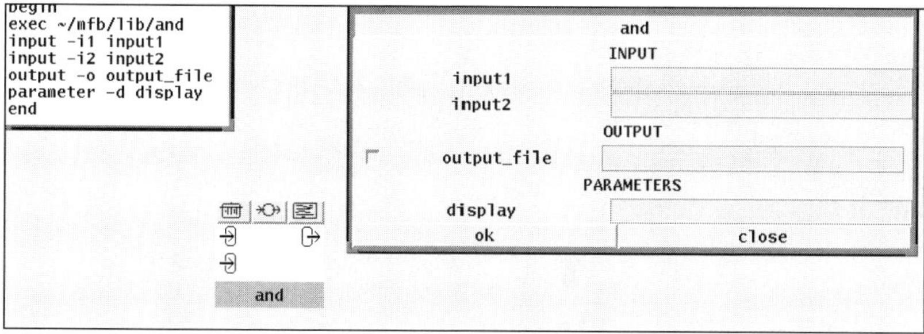

Figure 9. Agent representation.

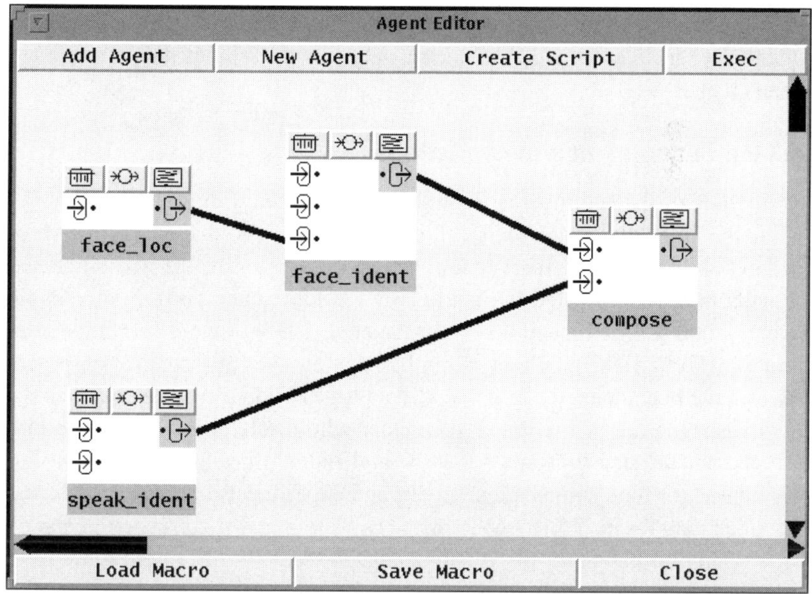

Figure 10. Example of combination of agents with the agent editor tool.

input of the adequate agents by drawing lines from/to the corresponding boxes.

Once they are created, complex agents are included in the library of available agents, and can be modified or reused to build other agents.

The Agent Editor and the Browser are linked together. It is possible to call the Agent Editor from the Browser to display or modify an existing agent or to create a new one. It is also possible to select intermediate data flows that will be visualized in the Browser window. The Browser is able to run agents to construct new data flows. Before running an agent, the user has to define the data flows that will be used as input, and the output flows that he wants to

Data type	Visualization format	Search procedure	Index procedure
video	images at fixed rate images at cuts	image similarity	list of different images
audio	signal energy graph	amplitude or energy threshold	*none*
text label	arrows, boxes	keyword search	list of keywords

Table 1. Experiment summary.

visualize. If the agent is a simple one, the Browser will simply start the corresponding program with the adequate parameters. If the agent is a complex one, the Browser will decompose it into simpler agents that it will call sequentially, so that an agent is started only when its input data flows have been created.

4.3 Implementation and Limitations

Prototypes of the Multimedia Browser and the Agent Editor have been built using the Tcl/Tk language/toolkit (Ousterhout 1994), so that adding new procedures is easy. In the first version, the processing of agents was simulated (results files were created by hand or by random generation). Some simple agents, such as face recognition (Clergue et al. 1995) or word spotting (Gelin and Wellekens 1996), are now being built. A number of visualization procedures have been defined for the basic data types (video as sequence of shots, audio as signal or energy graphs), together with results indicating labeled intervals, and labeled time spots. Search and Index procedures have been implemented for time-stamped text labels, and experiments are being conducted on video data flows. Table 1 contains a brief summary of our experiments.

A strong limitation of this version is that it assumes that all the flows have the same timeline, so that when using the Browser, all the visualization windows are updated simultaneously. This restricts the usage of the Browser to a single "document." The user interface is designed for experimentation by agent developers, so that it is not appropriate for the potential end-user of such agents.

Another limitation is that there is currently no synchronization mechanism between the agents when they process data. When a complex agent is applied on some data, the simple agents are simply ordered and called one after each other, so that an agent is called when the flows that it should process are available. Ideally, we could think of a more elaborate strategy where the results found by certain agents would influence the processing of others, so that, for example an agent does not look for a face on the video when nobody is talking on the audio.

5. Conclusion

The Multimedia Flow Browser and the Agent Editor are research tools that are currently being developed. They facilitate the experimentation of agents which analyze the contents of multimedia documents to detect the occurrence of complex events. They have been designed with an open architecture that allows us to easily include new features such as adding a new data types, new visualization formats, new agents, or new indexing schemes.

The development of the Browser raises a number of issues concerning the processing of various data types, for example, the possible ways to implement search and index functions on non-textual data types. Our intention is to build a basic library of agents that users will be able to extend and combine to fulfill their needs. We are currently starting to use the tool to experiment on real-life situations, such as TV news indexing.

References

Arman, F.; Depommier, R.; Hsu, A.; and Chiu, M-Y. 1994. Content-based Browsing of Video Sequences, ACM Multimedia Conference, 97-103, October 1994.

Aigrain, P.; Joly, P.; and Longueville, V. 1997. Medium Knowledge-based Macro-segmentation of Video into Sequences. In this volume.

Benedetti, G.; Bodin, B.; Lhuisset, F.; Martineau, O.; and Merialdo, B. 1995. A Structured Video Browsing Tool. In *Engineering for Human-Computer Interaction*, eds. L. J. Bass and C. Unger, 17-26. London: Chapman and Hall.

Blum, T.; Keislaer, D.; Wheaton, J.; and Wold, E. 1997. Audio Databases with Content-based Retrieval. In this volume.

Brown, M.; Foote, J.; Jones, G.; Sparck-Jones, K.; and Young, S. 1994. Video Mail Retrieval by Voice: An Overview of the Cambridge/Olivetti Retrieval System. ACM Multimedia Conference, Workshop on Multimedia Database Management Systems, 47-55, October 1994.

Brown, M.; Foote, J.; Jones, G.; Sparck-Jones, K.; and Young, S. 1995. Automatic Content-based Retrieval of Broadcast News. ACM Multimedia Conference, 35-43, November 1995.

Clergue, E.; Goldberg, M.; Madrane, N.; and Merialdo, B. 1995. Automatic Face and Gestual Recognition for Video Indexing. IWAFGR95 Workshop, 110-115. 26-28 June 1995. Zurich, Switzerland.

Flickner, M.; Sawhney, H.; Niblack, W.; Ashley, J.; Huang, Q.; Dom, B.; Gorkani, M.; Hafner, J.; Lee, D.; Petkovic, D.; Steele, D.; and Yanker, P. 1997. Query by Image and Video Content: The QBIC System. In this volume.

Gabbe, J. D.; Ginsberg, A.; and Robinson, B. S. 1994. Towards Intelligent Recognition of Multimedia Episodes in Real-time Applications. In ACM Multimedia Conference, 227-235. October 1994. San Francisco: ACM Press.

Gelin, P. and Wellekens, C. 1996. Keyword Spotting for Video Soundtrack Indexing. In Proceedings of the IEEE ICASSP-96. Atlanta, GA. IEEE.

Hauptmann, A. G. and Witbrock, M. J. 1997. Informedia: News-on-Demand Multimedia Information Acquisition and Retrieval. In this volume.

Jones, G. J. F.; Foote, J.; Sparck-Jones, K.; and Young, S. 1997. The Video Mail Retrieval Project: Experiences in Retrieving Spoken Documents. In this volume.

Konstantinides, K. and Rasure, J. R. 1994. The Khoros Software Development Environment for Image and Signal Processing. *IEEE Transactions on Image Processing* 3(3): 243-52.

Levis, A. H. 1993. Modeling and Design of Artificial Intelligence Systems. In *An Introduction to Intelligent and Autonomous Control*. eds. P. J. Antsaklis and K. M. Passino, 109-127. Boston, MA: Kluwer Academic Publishers.

Mani, I.; House, D.; Maybury, M. and Green, M. 1997. Towards Content-Based Browsing of Broadcast News Video. In this volume.

Ogle, V. and Stonebreaker, M. 1995. Chabot: Retrieval from a Relational Database of Images. *IEEE Computer* 28(9):40-48, September.

Ousterhout, J. K. 1994. Tcl and the Tk toolkit. Reading, MA: Addison-Wesley.

Pentland, A.; Picard, R.; and S. Sclaroff. 1993. Photobook: Tools for Content-base Manipulation of Image Databases. MIT Media Lab TR #255.

Rowe, N. C. and Frew, B. 1997. Automatic Retrieval of Objects in Captioned Depictive Photographs. In this volume.

Salton, G. 1989. Automatic Text Processing. Reading, MA: Addison-Wesley.

Schauble, P. and Wechsler, M. 1995. First Experiences with a System for Content-based Retrieval of Information from Speech Recordings. In Working notes of the IJCAI-95 Workshop on Intelligent Multimedia Information Retrieval, ed. M. Maybury, 59-69, Montreal, Canada: IJCAI.

Srihari, R. K. 1995. Automatic Indexing and Content-based Retrieval of Captioned Images. *IEEE Computer* 28(9):49-56, September.

Weber, K. and Poon, A. 1994. Marquee: A Tool for Real-time Video Logging. In Proceedings of ACM CHI'94 Conference on Human Factors in Computing Systems, volume 2 of PAPER ABSTRACTS: Multimedia in Use, 203.

Zhang, H. J.; Tan, S. Y.; Smoliar, S.; and Yihong, G. 1995. Automatic Parsing and Indexing of News Video. *Multimedia Systems* 2:256-266.

Zhang, H. J.; Low, C. Y.; Smoliar, S. 1997. and JianHua, W. Video Parsing, Retrieval and Browsing: An Integrated and Content-based Solution. In this volume.

Chapter 15

A Framework for Developing Content-based Retrieval Systems

James Griffioen, Raj Yavatkar, and Robert Adams
Department of Computer Science, University of Kentucky

Abstract

Conventional multimedia content-based retrieval tools provide capabilities to search for features in multimedia data. However, multimedia data, unlike alpha-numeric data, is used primarily to convey conceptual information that is evident when the data is taken as a whole. Future content-based retrieval systems should support access to both the content of the data and the concepts portrayed by the data. In addition, they must support queries on content that has not yet been discovered.

We are investigating a new model for managing multimedia data called *MOODS*. MOODS takes a new approach to the design of information management systems by incorporating the ability to directly model and manipulate multimedia data objects with the ability to extract both the basic and high-level semantic concepts contained in the data. MOODS is a framework for building content-based retrieval applications that provide automatic access to the full semantic content of multimedia. MOODS incorporates a knowledge base for modeling and representing the high-level semantic concepts that cannot be identified through processing alone. Undiscovered semantic content is automatically identified (processed) on-demand in response to user requests for the data. By adding rules to the knowledge base, completely new user-specific concepts and content automatically become searchable.

1. Introduction

Computers are quite adept at manipulating and retrieving alpha-numeric data consisting of numbers and characters. However, recent hardware and software advances have created a wide variety of new data types, generally referred to as multimedia data, that have almost no similarities to alpha-numeric data, and are not currently supported like alpha-numeric data. Specifically, we want to be able to search, modify, and manipulate multimedia data much like current applications are able to search, modify and manipulate alpha-numeric data. Unfortunately, multimedia data is not directly searchable. In its raw form multimedia data is relatively meaningless from the computer's perspective. To search multimedia, it is first necessary to identify the semantic content of the data and represent it in a way that is meaningful and can be manipulated by computers.

A major limitation of current multimedia systems is that they only provide access to the "features" of the data, such as shapes, colors, and textures. However, users really want to know what the multimedia data contains. That is, users are interested in what the features represent (dogs, cats, cars, etc.) The features themselves are only hints or clues to help identify the "real" information content that users want to access and manipulate.

To make multimedia data truly useful, content-based search tools need to go beyond the initial step of identifying *recognized components* in the data (e.g., dog, car, or person). Multimedia data, particularly visual data, portrays high-level conceptual information that is obtained by viewing all the components of the data as a whole. For example, users should be able to ask for pictures containing U.S. Presidents. The concept of President is something that must be inferred from the recognized components and definitions about what, or who, a "President" is. Such conceptual content is domain and user specific and thus requires domain-specific descriptions. The definition of U.S. Presidents could be as simple as a list of the current and former Presidents, or could be as complex as a rule built out of other domain-specific concepts such as "vip," "politician," "commander-in-chief," "air-force-one," or "political event." A content-based retrieval system must support this type of high-level *conceptual content* that can only be derived from the recognized components.

To support this type of powerful content-based retrieval, a multimedia system must address several issues. First, the system must support a configurable processing component that can automatically identify semantic content. It must include the ability to map from *features* (colors, shapes, textures) to *recognized components* (dog, car, Joe Smith). Automatic identification of content typically requires a sequence of processing operations. The sequence usually begins with simple processing operations, such as contrast-enhancement, noise-removal, or edge-detection, and finishes with domain-specific identification routines. The processing component must support transformation sequences.

Second, a content-based retrieval system must provide a mechanism for expressing high-level conceptual ideas and definitions. The knowledge base must be integrated with the processing component to allow access to the recognized components of the data. Because conceptual information is domain and user dependent, the knowledge base must support multiple views of the data and allow the views to evolve or change over time.

Third, the amount of information that can be recognized is virtually limitless. Consequently, it is prohibitively expensive to process all multimedia data for all content. Thus, a content-based multimedia query system must be able to efficiently identify semantic content on demand.

Finally, users need to be able to modify and manipulate the multimedia data or its content. Once queries have returned information, users often need to modify the information to suit their particular needs, such as cropping regions from an image, or isolating scenes in a video.

We are investigating a new model for managing multimedia data called *MOODS*. MOODS takes a new approach to the design of information management systems by incorporating the ability to directly model and manipulate multimedia data objects with the ability to extract both the basic and high-level semantic content contained in the data. The MOODS data model supports a new semantic object-oriented approach that provides the required processing and manipulation capabilities while tracking the semantic meaning (content) of data at all times. MOODS addresses the above-mentioned issues by providing processing paths that represent sequences of operations required for automatic processing of multimedia data. MOODS also supports dynamic application of processing sequences to discover content on demand. A knowledge base is used to represent high-level conceptual information. MOODS incorporates an interactive interface to allow users to manipulate and modify data to suit their needs. Finally, MOODS provides an intelligent database that ties all the components together.

2. The MOODS Multimedia Data Model

The goal of our research is to design a framework for developing content-based multimedia retrieval tools. The retrieval tools must treat embedded content as first-class entities that can be queried and manipulated. The system should allow experts in a particular application domain to quickly construct a content-based retrieval application that supports automatic processing to extract content, on-demand processing to limit initial computation and data storage costs, semantic queries, and user or domain-specific views of the semantic content. The framework must also provide support for a wide variety of multimedia data types. Although we will focus on image data in this chapter, our techniques can be applied to other multimedia types as well.

Unlike conventional database systems which either support standard alpha-numeric data or limited-access multimedia data (e.g., simple storage, retrieval, and display), MOODS allows full access to and manipulation of the semantic content found in multimedia data. To achieve this, MOODS combines a database management system with a multimedia data processing system that allows users to access and manipulate embedded semantic informa-

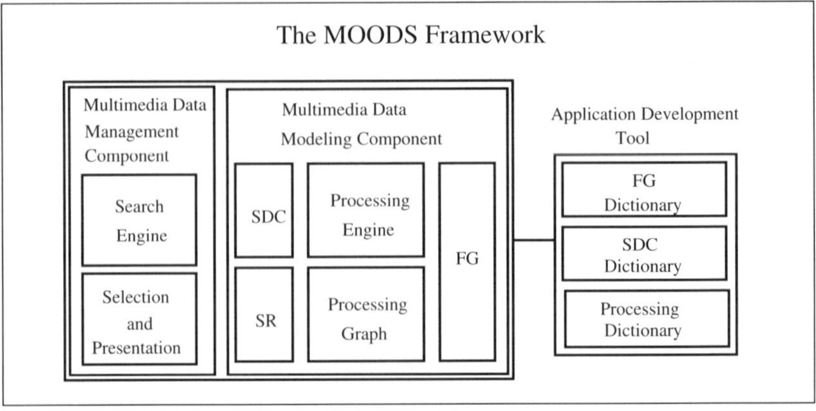

Figure 1. Overview of the MOODS system.

tion. Not only does the resulting system support interactive queries and re-trievals, but it also provides functionality to automatically and interactively extract new semantic content, reinterpret previously extracted semantic content, and define new data interpretations and data models.

Figure 1 illustrates the components of the MOODS system. The system consists of two main components: a *database* component and a *data modeling* component. An auxiliary *application development tool* aids in the construction of modeling systems and facilitates reuse of functions.

The *data modeling* component distinguishes MOODS from conventional data management systems by providing the capability to automatically and dynamically (on-demand) extract embedded information from stored data. Expert users configure the processing engine by defining processing paths specific to their application domains. Once constructed, the processing engine can automatically extract semantic content of interest to the user or domain. Alternatively, users may decide to use the engine to refine or further manipulate data returned from a search. The ability to process data dynamically (on-demand) is important because it reduces data storage requirements without limiting the amount of potentially accessible information. Conventional database systems that employ static processing schemes limit the potential information that can be accessed.

The data modeling system consists of five components. The types of known semantic information are represented by a set of semantic data classes (SDC). For instance, in a music manuscript domain, we may have a semantic class that indicates a treble clef is contained (has been identified) in the image. Other states such as note, key, and title would also exist to represent other knowable information. A set of function groups (FG) defines the logical operations that can be applied to the data, such as "edge detection" or "texture analysis." The processing graph defines the transformations that a data item may legally undergo over its lifetime. A runtime processing engine allows users to interactively apply functions to extract and identify embedded information. Finally, a set of semantic inference rules (SR) describes the logical relationship between the various semantic data classes and express high-level conceptual ideas.

The *database* component is tightly integrated with the semantic processing system. After the processing engine has identified the important semantic content, the semantic information is automatically entered and becomes available to the database for searching or browsing via conventional database techniques. The transfer of information from the modeling system to the database means that any new information identified (or reinterpreted) by the modeling system will be made available to the user. Using the dynamic processing capabilities of the processing engine, the database also supports efficient queries for information that has not yet been extracted or has only been partially extracted. For example, a query for a "Chevrolet Camaro" may be satisfied by locating all data items that contain a car and analyzing them further to determine the car's model. The database also makes use of the semantic inference rules to resolve queries for higher-level conceptual ideas or facts that require more sophisticated descriptions. For example, using the content information and registration information for an image, inference rules may be able to locate images of the NCAA 1996 championship basketball game (even though this fact is not readily available from any single semantic component in an image). In both of the previous cases, the database dynamically invokes the services of the modeling system to locate the desired information.

The *application development* system is an auxiliary tool that aids in the development of new data modeling systems. It maintains a complete database of all known (previously defined) function groups, semantic classes, semantic relationship models, and processing graphs. The tool allows users to construct new data models by defining their own semantic classes, relationships, and graphs, or by modifying, incorporating, or combining existing structures.

3. Multimedia Processing Engine

This section describes the two major components of the data modeling system, namely *semantic data classes* and the *processing graph*.

The data modeling system supports a new abstraction called *semantic data objects* which differs from conventional objects. Conventional objects consist of data along with methods that operate on the data. A conventional object abstracts some data structure or service (e.g., stack, file, or print service). Applying a method may change the data in an object, but it does not change the abstraction exported by the object. MOODS supports semantic data objects which differ from conventional objects in that they also contain a *semantic description*. The purpose of the semantic description is to record the currently known semantic content of the data for the purposes of search and retrieval. The current semantic information also defines the set of applicable methods. For example, it makes no sense to threshold a black and white image or to apply segmentation to an edge-detected image. Methods are only applicable if the semantic information they work on is present in the object.

Applying a method to an object typically changes both the content of the object and the known semantic information. Changes to the semantic information mean that the applicable methods will also change. Consequently, semantic data objects are an effective way to define the semantics at each step of the typical transformation process. For example, once a car has been identified in an image, the object can be processed further to classify the car's model. The processing operations used to identify a particular type of car are not available in the initial object, but once a car has been identified, identifying the car's model makes sense. Likewise, methods may be removed from an object once they are no longer applicable.

The *processing graph* provides the links between semantic objects needed to define a transformation process. Each node in the graph represents a semantic state (class). Arcs between nodes represent the transformation that results from applying a method to an object in that class.

Figure 2 illustrates an example processing graph. Processing begins with transformations such as contrast enhancement, edge detection, segmentation, shape analysis, etc., until domain-specific content is found—in this case, car and car model.

The processing paths represented by the graph do not define how to extract semantic content. To extract content from a specific image, a specific processing path tailored to the image must be used. Defining an appropriate path involves defining the arcs to be traversed and defining the parameters to be used in the methods on the path so that content can be identified. The parameters are typically defined interactively. Users interactively apply methods and analyze the results. If the results are not satisfactory, the method is reapplied to the data with different parameter values. Once the results are acceptable, processing continues. Once a path and specific parameters have been defined, the path can be replayed automatically on similar data to extract its semantic content.

Because of the vast amount of potentially identifiable content in multimedia data, it is unreasonable to assume that every data object can been processed for all semantic content. What is needed is an intelligent method of

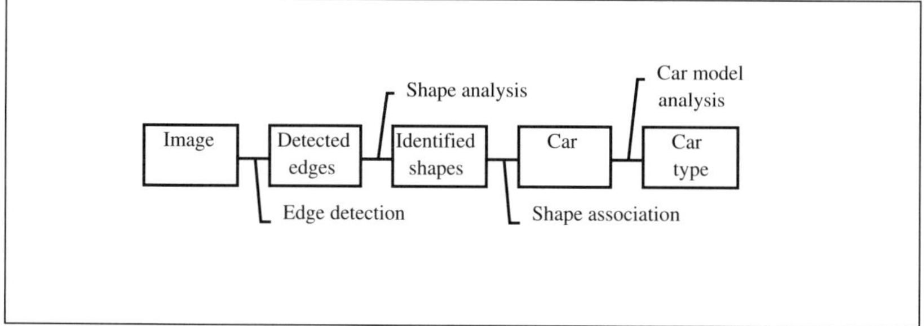

Figure 2. An example of a simple processing path.

delaying the processing of data until the specific content is actually needed. On the other hand, some semantic states in the processing graph are so basic or frequently requested that they should be automatically identified for all data. To support automatic identification of these basic states while delaying all other processing, MOODS allows users to define sections of a processing path that should be run automatically (the "pre-processing" component), and sections that should be delayed (the "search-processing" component), depending on the importance of the state and the cost of reaching the state. The pre-processing path component is applied automatically to new data as it is entered into the system. The search-processing path component is applied to data only when necessary, as described in the next section.

4. Inference Rules and Content-Based Queries

Semantic processing allows us to identify features of the data and their associated meaning. However, content identification only solves part of the content-based retrieval problem. In order to search for conceptual content we need a way to derive high-level meaning from the identified content.
MOODS provides a method of identifying complicated semantic information that cannot be gained from processing alone. MOODS allows users to create a knowledge base of *inference rules* which MOODS uses to conclude the existence of high-level semantic information. Inference rules are written in a logic language, currently Prolog, that describes the complex relationships between semantic features. In its simplest form, an inference rule is a semantic alias, such as: dog ↔ canine. This rule states that dog and canine are identical terms and searches for "dog" should look for "canine" as well.

Inference rules can also define high-level semantic concepts from more basic semantic content. For example, the rule

> NCAA_Championship_Game ← 1996 & Basketball & Kentucky_Uniform & Syracuse_Uniform

allows MOODS to assign the semantic label NCAA_Championship_Game to objects where this derived information is not otherwise available. The right-hand side of inference rules can be any logic expression.

The number of rules and types of rules in a system typically depend on the particular application domain addressed by the system. For simple, well-defined domains, the set of rules may be small. However, for complex domains like medicine, the set of rules may be quite large. The domain expert typically provides an initial set of rules that provides enough semantic information for users to identify common semantic concepts. As users find they cannot identify information important to them, they define new user-specific rules to supplement the current rule set and identify user-specific content.

Given an inference rule base and processed data where the content has been identified, users can begin issuing content-based queries. If the database contains objects matching the user's query, the objects are returned. Current database systems would quit at this point. However, because the MOODS database component is closely tied to the processing engine, MOODS is capable of searching for information not currently found in the database.

There are two ways of locating the desired information if it does not exist in the database. The first method is called *dynamic processing*. Given semantic processing paths, we locate the desired semantic states and begin processing data in an attempt to push data to the desired state. To restrict the amount of data that needs to be processed on-demand, MOODS uses a proximity range and the dynamic portion of the processing path to limit the search and focus processing. The second method for locating information on-demand is to examine the inference rule base for provable rules. Note that examination of the inference rules may trigger other queries which may cause additional dynamic processing. For example, if the user searches for "Chevy Camaro" in figure 2, and no objects in the database have that label, MOODS would process some objects further to determine if they actually contain a Chevy Camaro or not. Good candidates for processing would be those objects already identified as containing a car.

Coupling the database with the processing engine means that the system has the ability to learn new information based on the semantic processing graph, dynamic processing, and the inference rules. Consequently, the set of information that can be queried is significantly larger than the amount of information stored in the database. The ability to search for information that has not yet been found represents a significant and necessary departure from standard database practice, and results in increased query power while limiting storage costs. Given the limitless amount of domain-specific content extractable from a single piece of data, such functionality is mandatory.

5. Prototype Systems

To evaluate our design, we have developed a prototype framework called MOODS that aids in the development of content-based multimedia retrieval systems. We have used the MOODS framework to implement several application-specific content-based retrieval tools.

The MOODS framework consists of a database for storage and retrieval of multimedia objects, and a visual runtime interface (X-Windows Tcl/Tk) to the processing engine that allows users to define processing graphs and generate paths through the graphs. The framework also incorporates a Prolog engine for capturing high-level semantic concepts. The prototype includes a library of processing operations useful to a large number of application domains. The MOODS framework requires no special features from the database beyond storage and retrieval of large objects. We have used a number of database systems ranging from simple flat files to complex multimedia databases such as Illustra. Queries that cannot be answered by the standard database are passed to the Prolog interpreter or processing engine.

Defining processing graphs is accomplished via a new language. The MOODS language is an extension of C++ that allows definitions of semantic objects. It permits experts to define the data and semantic processing stages the data may traverse over its lifetime. From this specification, the MOODS compiler automatically constructs a retrieval application that incorporates the functionality of the database, knowledge base, and library of processing operations.

MOODS includes a graphical user interface that helps users push semantic data through the various processing stages at runtime, creating processing paths. The user interface displays the stages the data has already traversed and allows the user to interactively direct further processing. Backtracking can be achieved easily by clicking on earlier states. Our experience shows that users are rarely satisfied with their first choice of parameters and make heavy use of backtracking.

5.1 Music Note Recognition Example

To illustrate the power of the MOODS framework, we begin with a simple example taken from the domain of music manuscript analysis. The goal of the system is to identify the features (noteheads, stems, tails, etc.) in digitized manuscripts and assign a semantic meaning to them. Using the MOODS framework we define the transformations from one semantic state to another in terms of the functions given in figure 3. The semantic states and legal processing paths are shown in figure 4.

The processing graph and semantic classes shown in figure 4 can be coded in a few lines of the MOODS semantic object programming language. Be-

Enhancement Functions: *neighborhood averaging, median filtering,* and *histogram modification* to clean up the image for further processing
Erode: erode an image using *disk, horizontal* line, or *vertical line* erosion
Dilate: dilate an image using *disk, horizontal* line, or *vertical line* dilation
Difference: compute the pixel differences between two images resulting in a bitmap image with differences marked by "1"
Union: merge two images into a single image
Domain Dependent Labeling: this set of functions process the results of previous stages to label the image objects detected (e.g., notes, staff, etc.)

Figure 3. Transformations methods used on music manuscript.

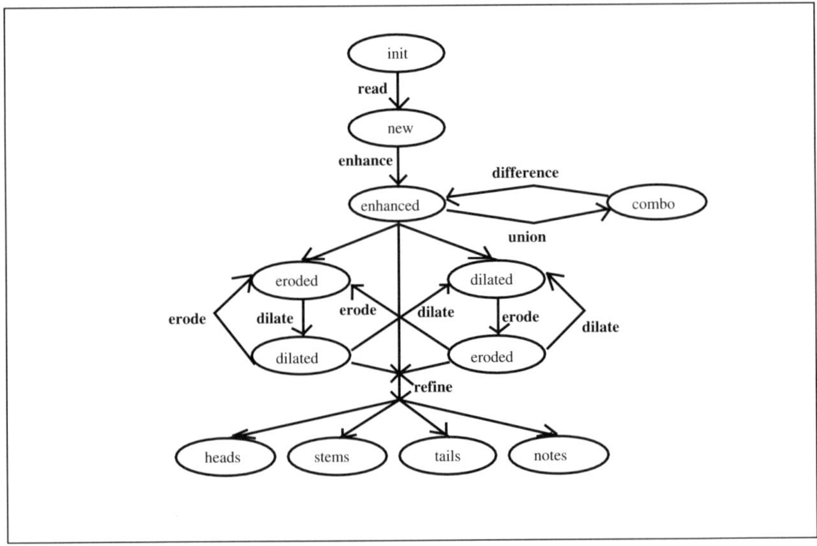

Figure 4. The semantic stages a music manuscript may traverse over its lifetime.

cause the global set of function groups already contains the necessary image processing functions, the user only needs to specify the semantic processing steps. Usually, the existing set of functions suffices for most domains. However, if a new user-specific processing function is required, it may be added by writing the function in C/C++ (except for a special function header). The specification is then compiled into an executable module that can be applied to the images stored in the database. Consider the portion of music shown in figure 5(a). Given this image, a user might interactively define the series of processing steps shown in figure 6 at runtime, to extract the notes and their components (note heads, stems, and tails).

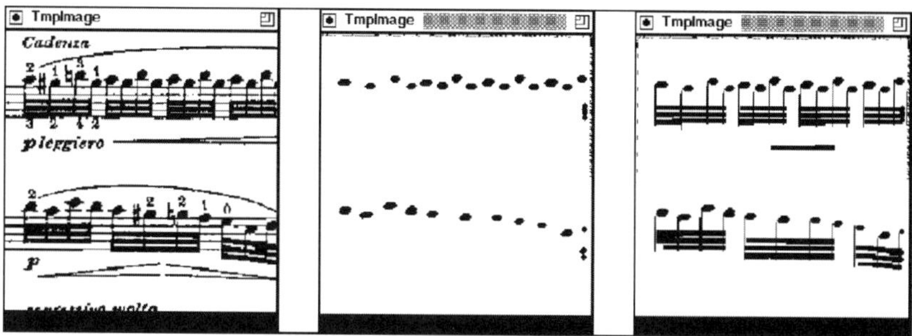

Figure 5. (a—left) The original image before processing,
(b—center) The noteheads extracted by step 8,
(c—right) The final image after the union in step 12.

Using the defined path, other portions of the manuscript or similar manuscripts can be automatically processed. Figures 5(b) and 5(c) depict the images at various stages of the processing sequence. The database, now equipped with access to the extracted semantic information and a processing graph, is ready to respond to queries and apply additional processing if necessary.

5.2 Beowulf Example

We have also used the system to implement a paleographic tool for analyzing ancient manuscripts, in particular, the Beowulf manuscript. Identification of *letterforms* allows paleographers to analyze the differences in writing styles, and gives clues to the authorship of manuscript pages.

Figure 7(a) shows a segment of a page from the manuscript. The goal is to identify and highlight various letterforms that appear, such as "æ" or "ea," and ultimately derive information about authorship.

The prototype uses image correlation routines, along with sample letterforms to match the sample with the letters in the manuscript. The parameters to the correlation routines allow the user to vary the sensitivity of the match. Once the letterforms have been identified, they are extracted and scaled for fine-tuned analysis. The processing steps used to identify the letterforms are given in figure 8.

Figure 7(b) shows the manuscript page after Æ forms have been identified. The results are then added back into the database for retrieval by other paleographers. If another paleographer is unhappy with the results, they can return to the processing engine to refine the data themselves. To express high-

1. Read in the original image.
2. Apply a noise removal function to generate an enhanced image.
3. Apply a series of erosion/dilation functions to extract note stems.
4. Apply a series of erosion/dilation functions to extract note tails.
5. Apply a series of erosions/dilations to extract the staff and the note tails.
6. Create a combined object containing the enhanced image and the image of staff and note tails.
7. Calculate the difference between the two images, creating a new image without the staff and tails.
8. Apply a series of erosion/dilation functions to isolate the note heads.
9. Create a combined object containing note heads and stems.
10. Union the note heads and stems into a single image of notes with stems.
11. Create a combined object containing note heads/stems and tails.
12. Union note heads/stems with tails to obtain a single image containing complete notes.

Figure 6. Processing sequence for music manuscripts.

er-level concepts such as authorship, the inference rule-base would include rules such as:

multiple_scribes <- (caroline & 1st_recto) & (insular & 1st_verso)
caroline <- caroline_A | caroline_S | caroline_G
insular <- insular_A | insular_S | insular_G

These rules capture the concept that the folio was transcribed by two or more scribes based on identification of two different methods of writing letters (caroline or insular). Subsequent searches for "multiple-scribes" would invoke the inference rule engine and possibly the processing engine.

6. Experience

Our attention thus far has been focused on the design of a framework for implementing multimedia applications. In terms of actual usability, our experience constructing example applications indicates that the framework meets our objectives. Both the music and paleography applications were implemented in less than an hour using existing image processing routines. Because the user interface, database, common image processing routines and complex data interactions are automatically handled by MOODS, the application developer can focus on the overall design of the system and the processing stages needed to identify the desired content.

In both examples, the processing graph that describes the legal transformation process consists of approximately 80 lines of MOODS code. This code would normally be written just once by a domain expert. General users would then process the data using the interactive interface. Definition of processing paths through the graph occurs interactively, allowing the user to backtrack and start over if they are unhappy with the results. In both of our

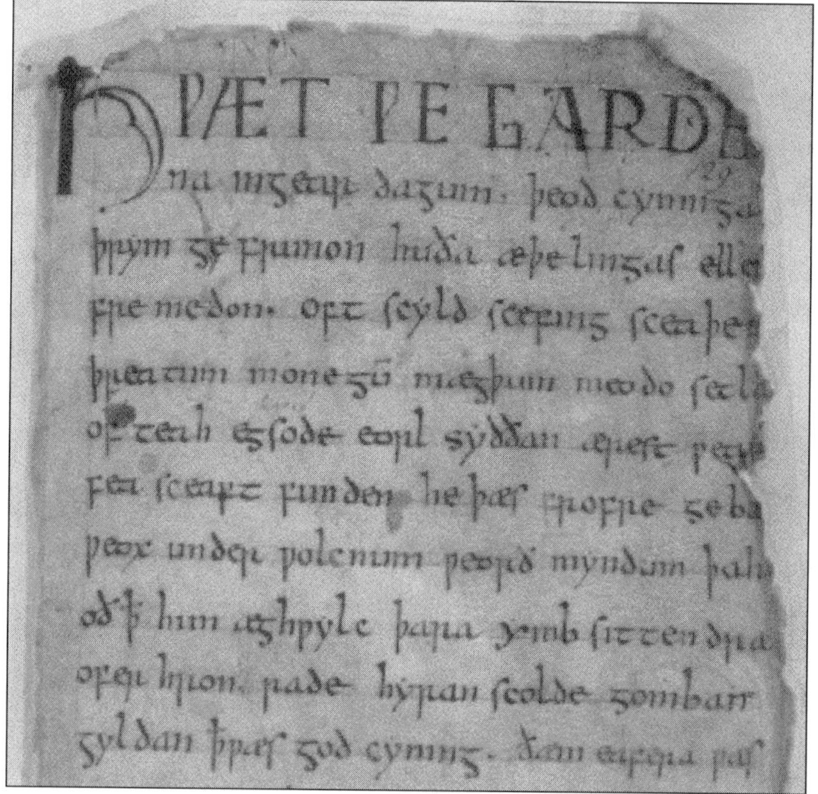

Figure 7. (a) A portion of a manuscript page from Beowulf,

examples, the processing paths were defined by novice users in less than an hour. Once the processing paths were defined, additional pages of the music manuscript or folios from the Beowulf manuscript were automatically processed and added to the database.

In the event that a specialized processing function is required, the application programmer would need to write the code in standard C or C++ and then add the appropriate MOODS header information to turn the function into a MOODS processing operation. Because the majority of the code is written in a standard programming language, it is very easy to add new functionality to the MOODS system.

From a user's standpoint, the interactive visual user interface for manipulating objects is easy to use and comes naturally to most computer users. Fur-

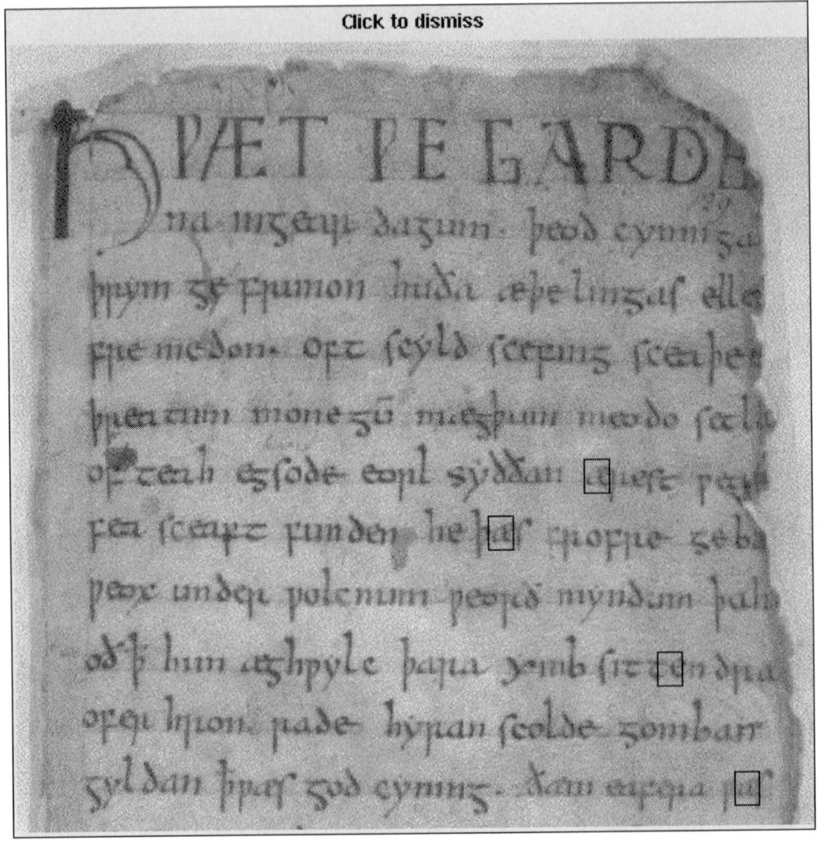

Figure 7 (b) The manuscript page after æ's are identified.

thermore, searching the database for images containing specific content is equally easy via the use of a conventional database query language.

7. Related Work

Most systems that attempt to manage semantic information are limited by either their inability to identify a wide range of semantic types or their reliance on specialized database systems.

Several systems are limited in the types of semantic content they can identify. The Virtual Video Browser (Little 1994, Little 1994 and Carriera 1995) allows users to annotate videos with several types of semantic tags, but provides no easy way of extending the semantics. Similarly, the system devel-

read: reads a manuscript page from the disk
correlation: matches a sample letterform against the letters of the page
threshold: filters out matches that have a low confidence factor
expand/refine: extracts and scales the matching letterforms from the manuscript page

Figure 8. Operations for processing Beowulf manuscript pages.

oped by Chuah et al. (this volume), allows users to query for graphs and charts that match the user's specification via similarity matching. Although appropriate for restricted data formats like graphs and charts, similarity matching is inappropriate for more "free-form" data formats. The QBIC system (Lee 1994; Niblack et al., this volume) allows queries for image features, but has no provision for categorizing features in a domain-dependent fashion. Other management systems, such as those developed by Oomoto (1993), Hjelsvold (1993), and Smoliar (1994), allow a variety of content to be identified, however all identification must be done manually. Systems such as DEDAL from Baudin (1994a, 1994b, 1993a, 1994b), and Media Streams by Davis (1994), require the user to learn a specialized query language. Mérialdo and Dubois (this volume) create processing sequences (called flows) by linking together agents that identify features in the multimedia similar to our processing graphs. Related to our Beowulf example, Manmatha and Croft (this volume) have developed a handwriting analysis system, although their approach is strictly limited to that domain.

Illustra (1994) is an object-oriented database that supports both image management and manipulation via DataBlades (a collection of primitive image processing routines). Illustra does not provide any kind of framework for applying these functions. Consequently, users are free to apply any function to any object, regardless of the outcome. Similarly, Khoros, from the University of New Mexico (1993), provides the user with an enormous selection of image processing capabilities with little or no control of how the user applies those capabilities. Khoros is only a processing system and lacks a database or search engine.

8. Conclusions

Future multimedia content-based retrieval systems must address the following issues. First, they must provide access to *recognized content* (such as dog, cat, car), not just the "features" such as colors, textures, or shapes. Second they must allow access to conceptual information because multimedia conveys conceptual information not just primitive features. And third, a content-based retrieval system should be adaptable to provide access to any content or concept, not just a few simple concepts predefined by the system.

We have designed and implemented a framework for building content-based retrieval systems that addresses the issues mentioned above. The system introduces a new semantic object model, semantic processing system, and a closely coupled database used to drive the processing engine and service queries. The framework provides automatic and demand-driven processing to identify semantic content along with the capability of identifying conceptual information.

We have implemented two example content-based retrieval applications to demonstrate the power and ease of developing content-based retrieval applications using the framework. Developing a content-based retrieval application typically involves defining semantic states, linking them together via methods selected from the function dictionary, and defining knowledge-base rules to express conceptual information. The framework uses this specification to create the desired system automatically.

Bibliography

Baudin, C.; Kedar, S.; and Pell, B. 1994a. Increasing Levels of Assistance in Refinement of Knowledge-Based Retrieval Systems, Technical Report FIA-94-08, NASA Ames Research Center.

Baudin, C.; Pell, B.; and Kedar, S. 1994b. Using Induction to Refine Information Retrieval Strategies, Technical Report FIA-94-08, NASA Ames Research Center, AI Research Branch.

Baudin, C.; Kedar, S.; Underwood, J.; and Baya, V. 1993a. Question-based Acquisition of Conceptual Indices for Multimedia Design Documentation, Technical Report FIA-93-22, NASA Ames Research Center, AI Research Branch.

Baudin, C.; Underwood, J.; and Baya, V. 1993b. Using Device Models to Facilitate the Retrieval of Multimedia Design Information, Technical Report FIA-93-21, NASA Ames Research Center, AI Research Branch.

Carriera, M.; Casebolt, J.; Desriers, G.; and Little, T., 1995. A Capture-Time Indexing Scheme and Authoring Tool for Digital Audio and Video. In Proceedings of IS&T/SPIE Symposium on Electronic Imaging: Science & Technology, 227-236. San Jose, CA: The International Society for Optical Engineering.

Chuah, M.; Roth, S.; and Kolojejchick, J. 1997. Sketching, Searching, and Customizing Visualizations: A Content-based Approach to Design Retrieval. In this volume.

Davis, M. 1994. Media Streams: Representing Video for Retrieval and Repurposing. In Proceedings of ACM Multimedia '94, 464-465. San Francisco, CA: ACM Multimedia.

Flickner, M.; Sawhney, H.; Niblack, W.; Ashley, J.; Huang, Q.; Dom, B.; Gorkani, M.; Hafner, J.; Lee, D.; Petkovic, D.; Steele, D.; and Yanker, P. 1997. Query by Image and Video Content: The QBIC System. In this volume.

Hjelsvold, R. 1993. Sharing and Reuse of Video Information. In Proceedings of ACM Multimedia '93, 283-293. San Francisco, CA: ACM Multimedia.

Illustra 1994. *Illustra Information System User's Guide.*

Lee, D.; Flickner, M.; Barber, R.; Hafner, J.; Niblack, W.; and Petovic, D. 1994. Indexing for Complex Queries on a Query-By-Content Image Database. In Proceedings of International Conference on Pattern Recognition '94, 189-200.

Little, T.; and Venkatesh, D. 1994. Prospects for Interactive Video-on-Demand. *IEEE Multimedia*, Fall 1994: 1(3): 14-24.

Little, T.; Ahanger, G.; Folz, R.; Gibbon, J.; Reeve, F.; Schelleng, D.; and Venkatesh, D. 1993. A Digital On-Demand Video Service Supporting Content-Based Queries. In Proceedings of ACM Multimedia '93, 76-88. San Francisco, CA: ACM Multimedia.

Manmatha, R.; and Croft, W. 1997. Word Spotting: Indexing Handwritten Archives. In this volume.

Mérialdo, B. and Dubois, F. 1997. A Generic Tool for Content-Based Multimedia Browsing. In this volume.

Oomoto, E.; and Tanaka, K. 1993. OVID: Design and Implementation of a Video-Object Database System. *IEEE Transactions on Knowledge and Data Engineering*, August 1993, 629-643.

Smoliar, S.; and Zhang, H. 1994. Content-Based Video Indexing and Retrieval. *IEEE Multimedia*, Summer 1994, 1(2): 62-72

University of New Mexico, Department of Electrical and Computer Engineering 1994. *Khoros Systems User's Manual.*

Yoshitaka, A.; Kishida, S.; Hirakawa, M.; and Ichikawa, T. 1994. Knowledge-Assisted Content-Based Retrieval for Multimedia Databases. *IEEE Multimedia*, Winter 1994: 1(4): 74-92.

Chapter 16

Interactive Visualizations for Temporal Analysis: Application to CSCW Multimedia Data

Stacie Hibino, EE and Computer Science Department, The University of Michigan, and Elke A. Rundensteiner, Department of Computer Science, Worcester Polytechnic Institute

Abstract

Although multimedia data is commonly collected by various researchers for a variety of purposes, previous support for specifying temporal queries and analyzing such data for temporal trends has been limited. In this chapter, we present a new paradigm for temporal analysis—one where users *browse* the data in search of temporal trends and relationships by using simple mouse manipulations to incrementally pose temporal queries within an integrated MultiMedia Visual Information Seeking (MMVIS) environment. In MMVIS, our specialized temporal visual query language (TVQL) not only allows users to pose specific temporal queries based on strict relationships (e.g., when A events start at the same time as B events), but also to relax the constraints to explore *similar* relationships (e.g., when A events start within a few seconds of B events). The temporal visualization (TViz) of results highlights the strengths of temporal relationships by *clustering* them together rather than distributing the display of them over time in a timeline format. TViz is dynamically updated *as* users manipulate the TVQL query filters. In this chapter, we present a case study using our approach to temporally analyze video data collected as part of a CSCW study. This case study illustrates how our approach simplifies the process of examining temporal trends and complements traditional timelines and statistical analyses. It also indicates how we could enhance intelligent multimedia information retrieval through supporting the analysis of temporal structure of multimedia documents.

1. Introduction

The Need for Temporal Analysis. Temporal data is commonly collected by various researchers for different purposes. User interface evaluators collect video data and logfiles, doctors review cardiology diagrams, sports analysts collect team and individual statistics, etc. Previous support for analyzing such temporal data has primarily focused on the use of variations of timelines (e.g., Harrison et al. 1994), the use of statistical methods (e.g., Markov analysis), and/or the analysis of temporal sequences (e.g., Sanderson et al. 1994) rather than analysis of any type of temporal relationship—sequential, parallel, or overlapping. New paradigms are needed to analyze and explore *temporal relationships* between various events in these multimedia documents. In our work, we provide a solution to this temporal analysis problem, with special focus on analyzing video.

Moving Towards an Object-Level of Video Analysis. Current research in *bit-level* video analysis is making significant advances towards efficiently automating the identification and indexing of objects and events occurring within a video (e.g., Hauptman and Witbrock, this volume; Mani et al. this volume; Zhang et al. 1995). Even when events need to be subjectively coded according to interpretation, tools are available for doing so at a speed proportional to the time required for real-time playback (Weber and Poon 1994). Now that we can efficiently abstract atomic objects and events, we can thus move on to a more complex, *object-level* of video analysis—one where we can analyze *relationships* between objects and events. In our research, we are examining this object-level of video analysis. In particular, we are exploring issues related to supporting:

- *Direct queries* over a video (collection) based on specific temporal relationships (e.g., when do events of type A temporally occur during events of type B?)

- *Analysis* of these relationships between such events (e.g., *how often* do A events occur during B events?),

- *Browsing* and exploring variations on these relationships (e.g., *comparing* results of different analyses, such as how often do A and B events start at the same time? versus how often does A occur any time during B?)

Chapter Overview. This chapter is divided into five additional sections. In section 2, we describe the details of our new exploratory paradigm for temporal analysis. In section 3, we present the case study of applying this approach to real video data. This is followed by an evaluation in section 4. In section 5, we discuss related work, and in section 6, we present our conclusions.

2. Temporal Explorations with Interactive Visualizations

In this section, we describe the details of our new exploratory paradigm for temporal analysis.

2.1 A New Paradigm for Temporal Analysis

In our new paradigm for temporal analysis, users can temporally *explore* data in search of *temporal relationships* and trends. While this approach builds on existing work by Ahlberg and Shneiderman (1994) in Visual Information Seeking (VIS), we go beyond the scope of the original VIS and focus on exploiting a particular dimension, namely the temporal one, for the purpose of video analysis. Similar to VIS, users in our MultiMedia VIS (MMVIS) can browse a database of information through direct manipulation of buttons and sliders. This use of dynamic query (DQ) filters provides us with an easy-to-use *visual* paradigm for developing and posing questions. A visualization of the results is dynamically updated as users adjust a query filter. Users thus incrementally specify and refine queries and can see the direct correlation between adjusting parameter values and corresponding changes to the display of results.

More specifically, MMVIS provides an *exploratory approach to temporal analysis*, consisting of the following user process:

1. Select subsets of the data via subset query palettes.

2. Query for temporal relationships between subsets via specialized temporal query filters (TVQL).

3. Review visualization (TViz) of results for temporal trends.

4. Customize visualization for further clarification, if desired, and go to 3.

5. Go to 2 to incrementally adjust temporal query or to 1 to select new subsets.

In MMVIS, each *subset query palette* includes a multi-select listbox for each type of annotation characteristic (i.e., name, action, receiver, and category). Sample subset selection palettes are included as part of figures 4 and 6. TVQL and TViz form the primary core of MMVIS and are summarized below. A more detailed description can be found elsewhere (Hibino and Rundensteiner 1996a, 1996b).

Note that the underlying database of our MMVIS system stores a collection of video annotations that abstract *atomic* objects and events in the video data[1]. While we provide primitive support for creating annotations manually within MMVIS as part of our tool suite, users can import events that have been automatically indexed by bit-level video analysis systems.

2.2 Temporal Visual Query Language (TVQL)

Specifying Primitive and Neighborhood Temporal Queries. Given two events A1 (⊶) and B1 (▄▄▄) with nonzero duration, Allen (1983) has defined thirteen possible primitive temporal relationships between them (see figure 1). Note that one endpoint relationship between two events may pose a constraint on one or more of the others. Besides analyzing these primitive rela-

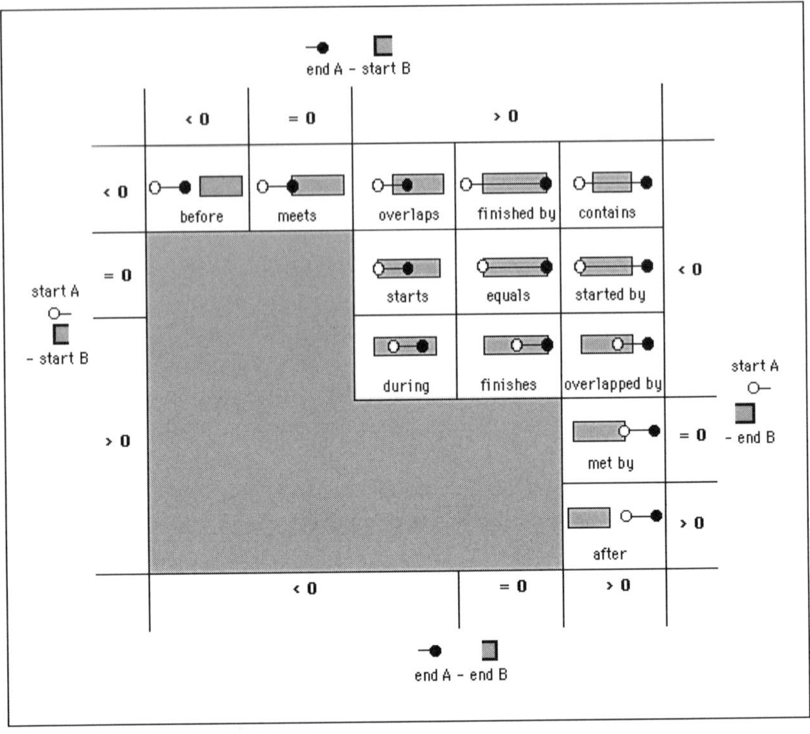

*Figure 1. Relationships between temporal primitives and the
four defining endpoint difference relations.*

tionships, it is also desirable to specify combinations of the primitives (e.g.,
to look at situations where events start at the same time but may end at different times, corresponding to combining the *starts, started by,* and *equals*
primitives). Rather than forcing users to explicitly specify a number of complex disjunctions and conjunctions for combining the temporal primitives, we
propose an alternative approach based on the principle of *temporal neighborhoods* (Freska 1992).

Two primitive temporal relationships between two events are defined to be
(*conceptual*) *neighbors* if a continuous change (e.g., shortening, lengthening,
or moving of the duration of the events) to the events can be used to transform either relation to the other [without passing through an additional primitive temporal relationship]. Thus, the "before" ( ) and "meets"
( ) relations *are* neighbors, because we can move the ending
point of A from before the start of B to its start without specifying any additional primitive relationship. In contrast to specifying arbitrary combinations

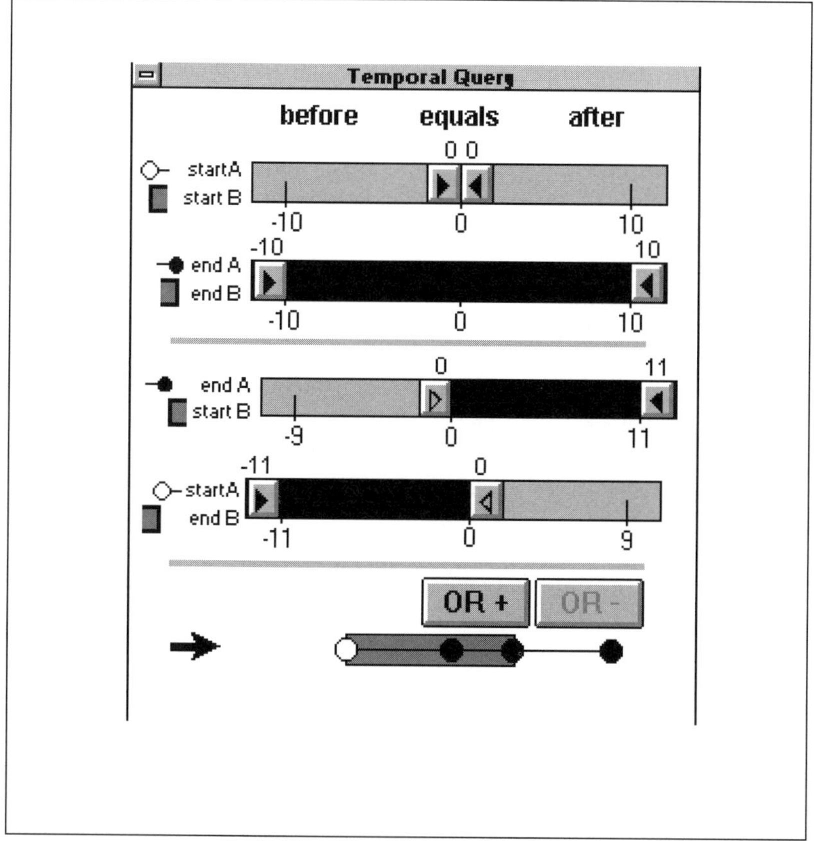

Figure 2. TVQL palette.

of the primitives, this notion of temporal neighborhoods supports users in selecting *similar* primitives (i.e. equivalent to selecting a series of adjacent
cells such as a row, column, or grid from figure 1).

TVQL Description. While a complete specification of our temporal visual
query language (TVQL) can be found elsewhere (see Hibino and Rundensteiner 1996b), we review its basic principles here as needed for the remainder of this chapter. Using a temporal query filter for each of the defining endpoint difference relationships described above (figure 1), we can define a
temporal query interface capable of specifying not only all individual temporal *primitives*, but also *temporal neighborhoods*. This allows users not only
to browse for temporal relationships between two subsets, but to do so in a
temporally continuous manner.

The TVQL palette (figure 2) has three primary components: the temporal query filters (i.e. sliders for specifying temporal parameters), disjunctive OR+ and OR- buttons for combining discontinuous temporal primitives or neighbors (e.g., to specify a query such as (A *meets* B) OR (A is *met by* B)), and a dynamic temporal diagram that visually displays the qualitative semantics of the specified query. The temporal DQ filters are used to examine *quantitative* ranges for the endpoint relationships, such as *startA-startB* set to 0 in the top DQ filter. They are also intelligently bound to one another to prevent the specification of invalid queries. As users adjust one query filter, the other filters are automatically updated accordingly. In figure 2, the user only has to set the filter thumbs of the top *startA-startB* query filter to 0. The second filter is unaffected, but the bottom two filters are automatically constrained. The underlying framework of the temporal endpoint relationships and their interactions are used to derive these automated constraints (Hibino and Rundensteiner 1995, 1996b). Note that a filled or open arrow thumb of a DQ filter indicates when the endpoint of a range is included or excluded respectively.

To enhance the TVQL user interface, we have incorporated qualitative descriptive labels along the top and side and our dynamic temporal diagrams along the bottom of the palette. The labels allow users to "read" the relationship specified and the diagrams provide visual confirmation of the temporal primitive(s) specified (though not quantitative values as given by the filters). If subset A specified person P1 and subset B specified all Plan design rationales, then figure 2 illustrates how users could ask the query "show me how often person P1 starts at the same time as a Plan starts." The descriptive labels can be used to "read" the top query filter as "start A equals start B." The relationship between the temporal ending points is unconstrained as indicated by the selection of all values in the second (i.e. *endA-endB*) query filter. This is also reflected in the temporal diagram, which indicates that the end of A (represented by a filled circle) is before, equal to, or after the end of B.

The power of TVQL is that it allows users to incrementally specify queries by sliding both within and between the specification of temporal primitives and within and between temporal neighborhoods. For example, suppose we want to see when person P1 finishes speaking up to five seconds before a Plan starts (i.e. when A events occur *before* B events by up to five seconds). In order to specify the *before* (   ) temporal primitive, we want endA to be before startB. Thus, we would adjust the third (endA-startB) DQ filter of TVQL to select a range of values less than zero and greater than or equal to -5. Now, by simply sliding the left thumb of the endA-startB filter, we could easily compare when P1 finishes speaking up to five, four, three, etc. seconds before a Plan. By setting the right thumb of the endA-startB filter to include zero, we can add the *meets* (   ) relationships to the temporal query. By sliding the right thumb past zero, we can add the *over-*

laps (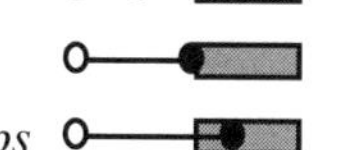) temporal relationship (i.e., indicating when P1 starts a Plan after finishing another design rationale). These simple mouse manipulations thus illustrate how we can slide from specifying:

- Only the before temporal primitive
- To the temporal neighborhood of *before* or *meets*
- To the temporal neighborhood of *before, meets, or overlaps*

When coupled with a visualization of results, TVQL can thus be used to temporally *browse* the data without any particular temporal query in mind. The TVQL temporal diagram is dynamically updated as users manipulate the sliders, thereby enabling them to simply slide the DQ filter thumbs back and forth until an interesting result appears, and then use the temporal diagram to identify the type of temporal query specified. Thus, the power of TVQL is that it can be used to 1) specify particular temporal queries (primitives or neighborhoods), 2) browse (i.e. slide within and between) temporal relationships of different types of events, and 3) move seamlessly between querying and browsing.

2.3 Temporal Visualization of Results (TViz)

TViz, presented in the main MMVIS window, is used to abstract, highlight, and compare the relative frequency of the temporal relationships (specified by TVQL) between selected subsets. That is, as a TVQL query is incrementally refined, MMVIS processes changes in the query and passes newly retrieved information to TViz, where the visualization of results is dynamically updated. Thus, in contrast to a text-based tabular display of results, TViz provides a visual abstraction of the answer set and how it changes as queries are refined. TViz is a variation of the visualizations used by Olson et al. (1995) to describe temporal sequences.

The Main MMVIS Window. The main MMVIS window (figure 3) is divided into three areas: the primary *visualization area* containing icons representing the various types of annotations in the database, the *key* below the visualization area to indicate the color-coded data subsets, and the *visualization options* in the lower right of the window to allow users to customize their view.

Visualization of the Selected Event Subsets. In our temporal visualization (TViz), selected subsets are visually highlighted with transparent overlays in the main MMVIS window—subset A is indicated with yellow circles and subset B with blue squares. Figure 4 presents an example where the user has set Subset A to all types of annotations and Subset B to none. By doing so, the user can use the visualization options to gain an overall big picture comparing the relative *frequency, average duration,* or *total duration* of all types of events (visually indicated by the relative sizes of the transparent circular

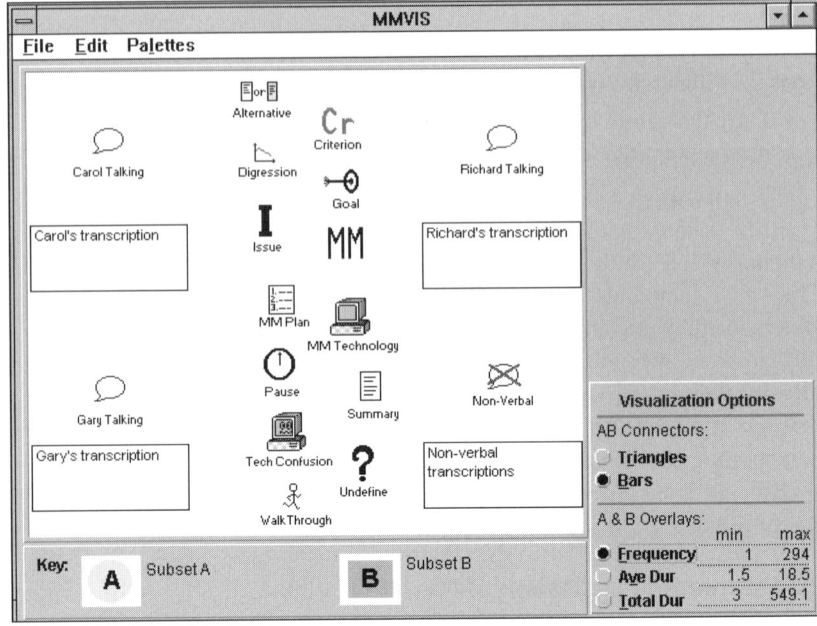

Figure 3. The Main MMVIS window.

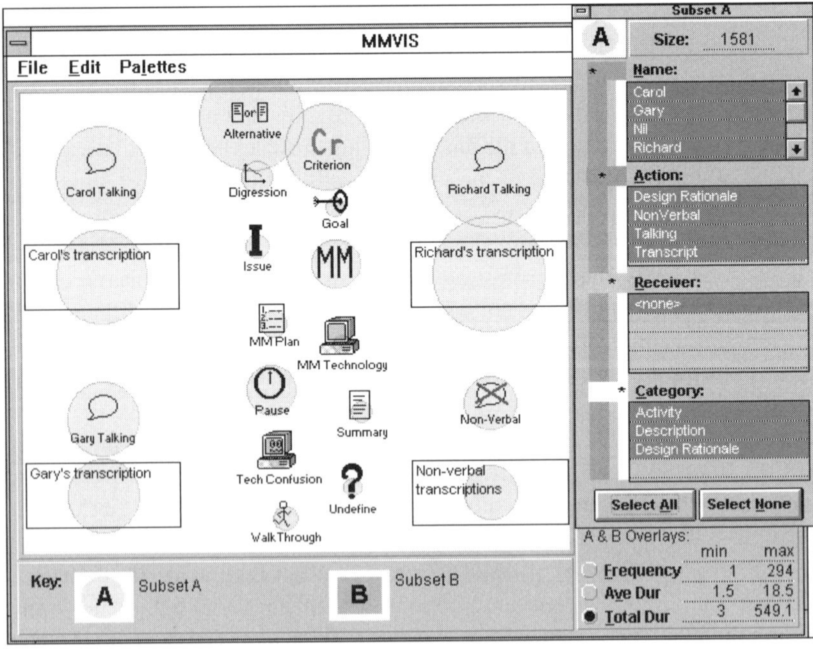

Figure 4. Visualization of selected subsets.

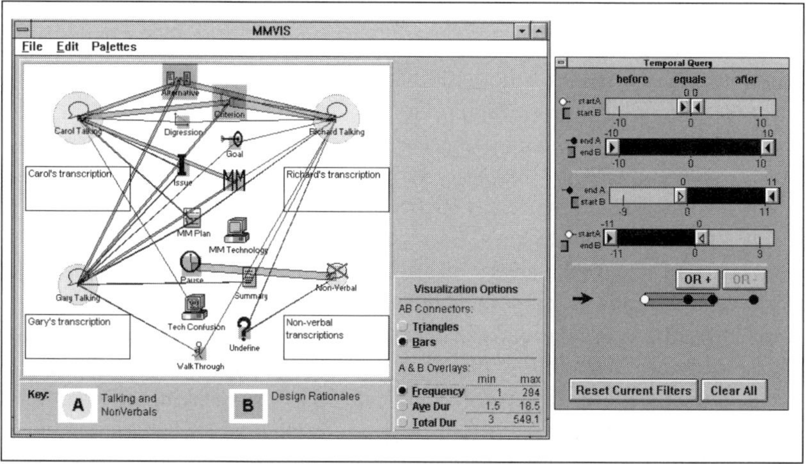

Figure 5. Sample TViz (left) resulting from temporal query (right palette).

overlays). In figure 4, for example, we can see, that the *total duration* that Richard speaks is longer than that of Carol or Gary.

Visualization of the Temporal Relationships. Once users have selected A and B subsets, they can then use TVQL to specify a temporal query. As they manipulate the temporal filters, they see connectors between the centers of A and B events appear and disappear, grow and shrink, thereby indicating the existence and strength of the temporal relationship currently specified. The base width of the connector denotes the relative frequency that the temporal relationship occurs. Figure 5 shows the TViz for the *all starts* temporal query, where events start at the same time but may end at the same or different times. The thick bar between NonVerbal and Pause indicates that these types of events frequently start at the same time. The temporal relationship connectors are also user-customizable, being viewable as triangles (to reinforce the direction from A to B) or bars. Figure 5 shows the view by *bars*.

3. CSCW Case Study: Temporally Exploring Real Data

In this section we present the case study of applying our approach to real video data.

3.1 Description of the Data Set

The sample data set is based on video collected during a computer-supported cooperative work (CSCW) study (Olson et al. 1995). During the session, three subjects worked together in a simulated design meeting to draft the initial requirements for an automatic post office. Subjects worked from remote locations using a shared editor, and had two-way video links to each of the other subjects. This video setup provided a virtual conference where the subjects could both see and hear one another. The final video data is a composite of the three subjects. In this case, subject 1 ("Carol") was recorded in the upper left quadrant, subject 2 ("Richard") in the upper right, and subject 3 ("Gary") in the lower left.

In terms of temporal analysis, the original researchers worked on identifying potential trends in temporal sequences of different types of events (e.g., to see "if subjects are currently discussing an Alternative for design, are they likely to immediately follow that with Criteria for that alternative?"). Each event in the database was coded to indicate who was speaking or what nonverbal action was taking place (e.g., a pause or laughter), what was said or a description of the nonverbal, and the starting and ending times of the event. Events were also coded as one of the following thirteen design rationales (DRs): Issue, Alternative, Criterion, Meeting Management (MM), MM Plan, Summary, Digression, Goal, Walkthrough, Pause, MM Technology, Technology Confusion, and Undefined (see Olson et al. 1996). In our case study, we used the CSCW video data to examine temporal relationships between people speaking and the DRs taking place (e.g., to see whether a Digression is always initiated by one person) and we re-coded the data to separate this information out. While the original data was purely sequential, the re-coded data introduced temporal overlaps.

3.2 Using Subset Event Visualizations for an Overview of the Data

In order to examine the interactions between people speaking and the design rationales taking place, we can set subset A to NonVerbal and Talking annotations and subset B to Design Rationales. The corresponding annotations are highlighted in the main visualization area. Using the visualization display options for "A&B Overlays," we can compare relative frequency, average duration, and total duration of different events.

In figure 6a, we can compare the relative frequency of events while in figure 6b, we can view differences in average duration. (In section 2.3, figure 4 showed relative total duration.) The contrasting sizes of the individual overlays within the same, and between different, visualization views provide temporal information that can be used as part of the temporal analysis (e.g., while figure 6a shows that Alternatives and Criteria occur more frequently than Digressions, figure 6b indicates that Digressions have a longer average duration).

3.3 Using Relationship Visualizations for Temporal Analysis

Once subsets have been formed, we can specify temporal queries and review

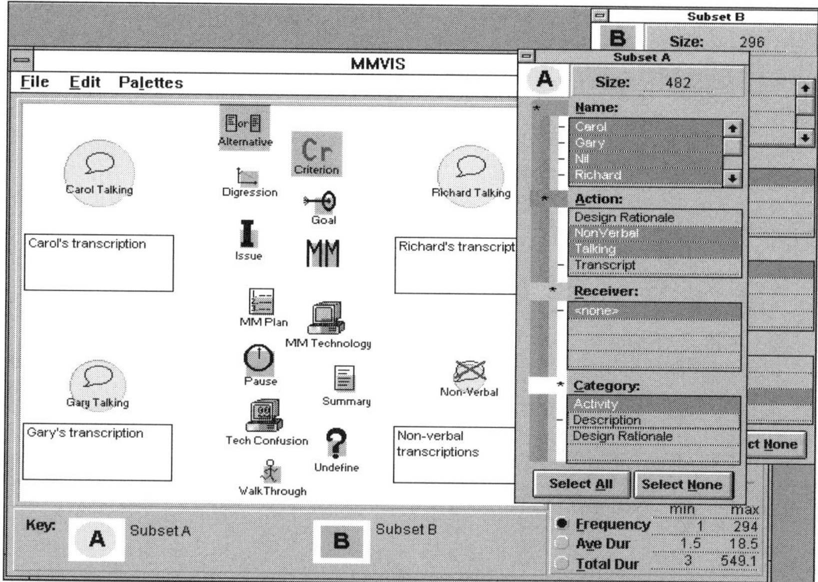

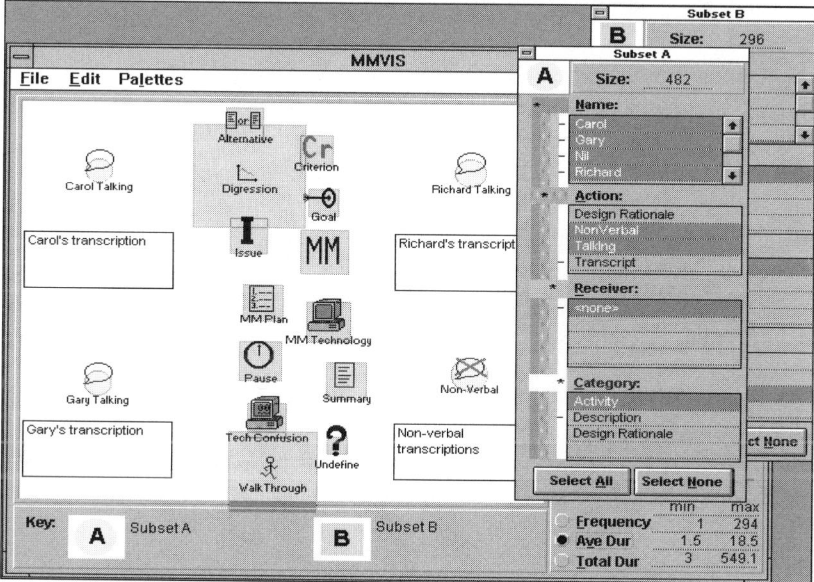

Figure 6. Selecting multiple subsets. (6a—top) View of subsets by relative frequency. (6b—bottom) View of subsets by average duration.
In this example, subset A (indicated by circular overlays) is used to select talking and nonverbal events while subset b (indicated by square overlays) highlights design rationales. The visualization options allow users to customize the overview visualization (e.g., to constrast (a) relative frequency with (b) average duration).

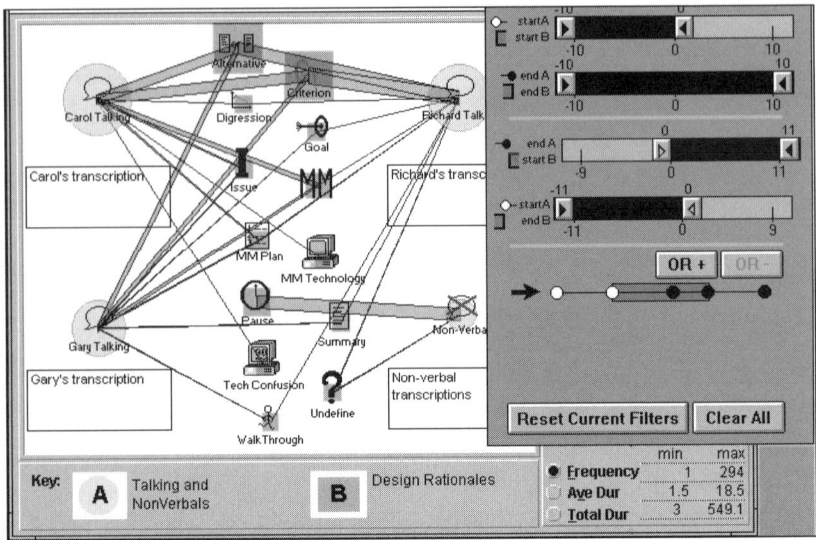

*Figure 7. Examining temporal relationships. In this example, the user
is querying for talking and nonverbal events which* initiate *DRs.*

the temporal visualizations for temporal analysis. In this section, we present
a sample scenario to illustrate how a researcher might use our MMVIS environment to temporally explore the case study data.

As we begin analyzing the interaction between people speaking and the
DRs, we might first want to see who or what tends to start a DR. We could
begin by asking a query such as when do activities (i.e., Talking and NonVerbal events) *start* at the same time as DRs (see figure 5). However, even more
interesting is to examine who or what *initiates* (i.e. starts at the same time or
before) a DR. We can easily modify a *starts* TVQL query to an *initiates* one
by simply dragging the left thumb of the top (startA-startB) query filter from
its middle (i.e. "equals") position to the left, thereby setting "startA before or
equal to startB" (figure 7).

Now that we have seen an overview of when A events *initiate* B events,
we might be interested in seeing when A events *end* B events (see figure 8).
For example, we may want to see who ends a Digression. We note, however,
that when someone stops talking at the same time as a DR, they don't necessarily "cause" the DR to end (e.g., Richard may be the last one to participate
in a Digression rather than the one who initiates a context switch from a Digression to some other DR).

One way to examine such *context switching* is illustrated in figure 9. In
this scenario, a context switch can occur when someone participates in one
DR and finishes talking *after* that DR ends (thereby starting the next DR,

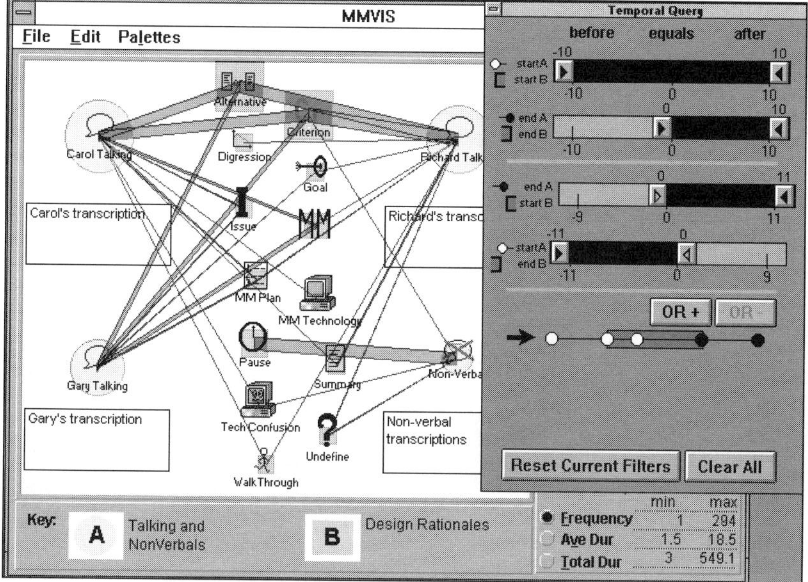

*Figure 8. Visualization of the frequency in which a person talking
or a nonverbal temporally ends a DR.*

since DRs occur one-by-one in sequence), or when someone or something
(i.e., such as silence, a NonVerbal action) starts at the same time that the current DR ends. We can update the *ends* temporal query to the *context switching* situation in two simple mouse manipulations to the TVQL query filters
(compare the top two query filters in figure 8 to those in figure 9), and we
can also watch the visualization change *as* we manipulate the query filters.
By comparing the visualizations in figures 8 and 9, we see that there is a difference between the *ends* and *context switching* temporal relationships.
These are just a few examples of temporal interactions between activities and
DRs that we can study. We could continue exploring the data in this fashion,
looking for other temporal trends.

3.4 Results of Temporal Analysis

In this subsection, we present a series of observations that can be obtained
from reviewing visualizations in figures 6 to 9. This provides us with some
feedback on the capability of our proposed paradigm for temporal analysis.

Frequency vs. Average Duration Versus Total Duration. Figure 6 illustrates how even simple display options can provide information about the relationship between the frequency and duration of different types of events.
Using this two-part figure, we can draw several conclusions.

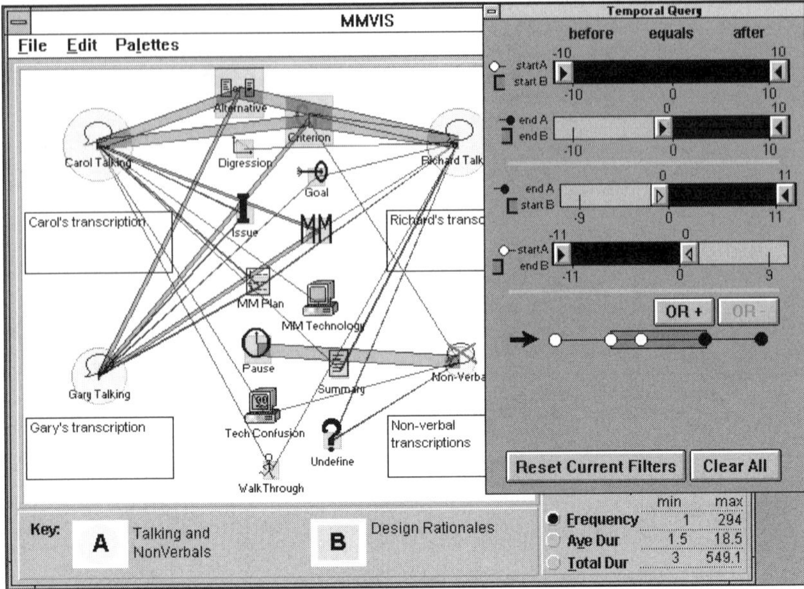

Figure 9. Visualization of the frequency in which talking or nonverbal events temporally start a new DR (i.e. which actions lead to a context switch).

Based on the *frequency* visualization (figure 6a) (frequency counts range from 1 to 294), we see among other observations that:

- Subjects talk with similar frequency, but Gary speaks the least frequently.
- NonVerbals occur less often than any one person talks.
- Alternatives and Criteria occur most frequently, followed by Pauses, Meeting Management, and other DRs.
- Carol and Richard appear to talk with similar but slightly higher frequency than that of Alternatives and Criteria.

Based on the *average duration* visualization (figure 6b) (average duration (aveDur) ranges from 1.5 to 18.5 seconds), we see the following:

- Average duration of NonVerbals is greater than any of the Talking events.
- Each person talks with about the same aveDur.
- Digressions have the largest aveDur, followed by Walkthroughs. Undefined and possibly Goals have the smallest aveDur. All remaining DRs have similar aveDurs which are greater than the aveDur of Undefined and less than aveDur of WalkThrough.

By comparing and contrasting parts (a) and (b) of figure 6, we find for example:

- Digressions do not occur very often, but when they do occur, they last, on average, longer than other DRs. A similar situation is true for Walk-Throughs.

- Although Alternatives and Criteria occur with the highest frequency, they do not occur with the highest aveDur.

- The total time that Gary speaks is less than Carol or Richard. This is indicated by the fact that Gary speaks with the smallest frequency but a similar aveDur. It is also verifiable by the Total Duration display option (see figure 4).

These results lead us to some interesting observations, some of which are desirable and expected and some of which could lead to more in-depth analysis. For example, the low frequency of Digressions indicates that the subjects tended to stay on task (a desirable result). However, the larger average duration of Digressions indicates that when they do become distracted or go off-track, then more time is wasted until they get back on track. In order to confirm that the Digressions did *not* overpower the rest of the DRs in general, it is important to have the option to view the subset highlighters by total duration. This view was shown in figure 4, and does indeed show that the total duration of Digressions is *not* the largest when compared to the other DRs.

In terms of Talking and NonVerbal events, the low frequency of the Non-Verbals indicates that the subjects were talking more frequently than not talking (another probably desirable result). In addition, we see that Carol seems to speak with the largest frequency, but with slightly smaller average duration. Although it is not obvious whether her frequency and average duration is significantly different from those of the other subjects, it is a curious result. By examining Carol's transcripts, we see that she frequently uses short words and utterances of acknowledgment and encouragement, such as "uh-huh" or "ok." It would be interesting to see if such a trend is correlated with female versus male subjects.

Frequency and average duration of Talking events could provide information about which person, if any, emerged as a leader of the simulated design meeting, even though no leader was appointed in the study. For example, one might expect a leader to generate lots of ideas and thus talk a lot. However, another sign of leadership can be the ability to listen (i.e. speak less frequently) and to facilitate and focus the direction of the meeting rather than spend a lot of time presenting ideas. Since Gary seems to speak the most infrequently, it would be interesting to see if he takes on a facilitator role. One way to answer such a question is to analyze Gary's participation in Digressions. That is, does Gary participate in Digressions? Does he initiate them? Does he frequently speak right after a Digression (i.e., does he move the discussion away from the Digression and back on track)? We can easily examine these and similar types of questions with our temporal analysis tools. Our tools thus allow researchers to embark on a much more detailed analysis of human behavior in a meeting setting, if so desired.

Relationships between Actions and Design Rationales. figures 7 to 9 illustrate three different types of temporal relationships (corresponding to initiates, ends, and context switching) between Talking/NonVerbal actions and the thirteen DRs. Using these figures, we can identify various temporal trends, some of which are listed below:

Based on figure 7 (*initiates* temporal relationships), we see that:

- Carol never initiates a Goal, Summary, or WalkThrough.
- Carol is the only one who initiates MM Technology and Technology Confusion.
- Richard never initiates an Issue.
- Gary never initiates a Digression.
- Carol initiates Meeting Management (MM) the most, while Richard initiates it the least frequently.
- A Pause is only initiated via a NonVerbal action.
- The strongest relationships are Talking/Alternative, Talking/Criterion, and NonVerbal/Pause pairs.

Although Carol strongly initiates Meeting Management (MM), the first four results indicate that she is probably not someone who acts as the leader of the design meeting. Gary's potential as a leader increases with the fact that he does not initiate a Digression and does initiate MM more than Richard. We expect NonVerbals to be highly correlated with a Pause, since silence is a NonVerbal event that would be categorized as a Pause in the design meeting.

Based on figure 8 (*ends* temporal relationship), we see that:

- Carol never ends with or after a Goal.
- Only Carol ends with or after MM Technology.
- Only Richard ends with or after a Digression.
- Gary does not end with or after over half of the DRs.

Combined with the results of figure 7, these results suggest that Carol is not very likely to participate in a Goal while Richard participates at both the start and end of a Digression (possibly an indication that he is easily distracted, though it may also indicate that while he starts a Digression, he does help in ending it). Gary's initiative nature, indicated by the fact that he initiates more DRs than he finishes, adds more weight to his potential to be the emergent leader of the group.

Based on figure 9 (*context switching* temporal relationship), we see that:

- Richard is the only one who does *not* move the discussion off of a Digression.

- Richard appears to initiate switching from Alternatives and Criteria the most.
- NonVerbals initiate context switching from several of the DRs, including Digressions and Technology Confusion.

Gary's potential as a leader over Richard is strengthened even more by the fact that he helps direct the discussion away from a Digression while Richard does not. The utility of NonVerbal events to context switching indicates the importance of silence during meetings.

4. Evaluation and Discussion

In this section, we use the above results to compare and contrast our interactive visualization approach to timelines and statistically-based approaches.

MMVIS vs. Timelines. Figure 10 presents a timeline of events of the first four minutes of the twenty-five minute CSCW video data evaluated in our above MMVIS examples. In contrast to the timeline format, our temporal visualizations *cluster* the occurrences of events that occur over a time period of the video, rather than displaying them sequentially. This allows us to more easily highlight the relationships between different types of events. In the timeline format, not only are the occurrences of events spread out, but the temporal relationships are also distributed. This distribution effect could make it more difficult to compare lots of relationships over time as well as to isolate the non-existence of a relationship. For example, in figure 9, we only need to make one examination to see if there is a link between Richard Talking and Digression. Since no link exists, we can infer that Richard never provides a context switch from a Digression to another DR. Using the timeline in figure 10, however, we need to scan through all Digressions or all instances of Richard Talking or some subset of the highlighted regions in order to derive the same conclusions.

Although the timeline could be filtered to only show the Richard Talking and Digression events that meet the context switching situation, this would not allow us to compare *all* context switching situations. In general, (unfiltered) timelines are limited in that they (1) are less compact than TViz, (2) require users to do more work by looking across rows and making their own deductions about relationships, and (3) inhibit users from directly making relative comparisons such as temporal relationships between different types of event pairs (e.g., comparison between (Gary, Digression) and (Richard, Digression) event pairs). Note that we are not proposing our exploratory approach as a replacement to timeline-based approaches, but rather as a *complement* to these approaches. In fact, timelines are just another type of visualization—only less compact and summarized than the ones we propose.

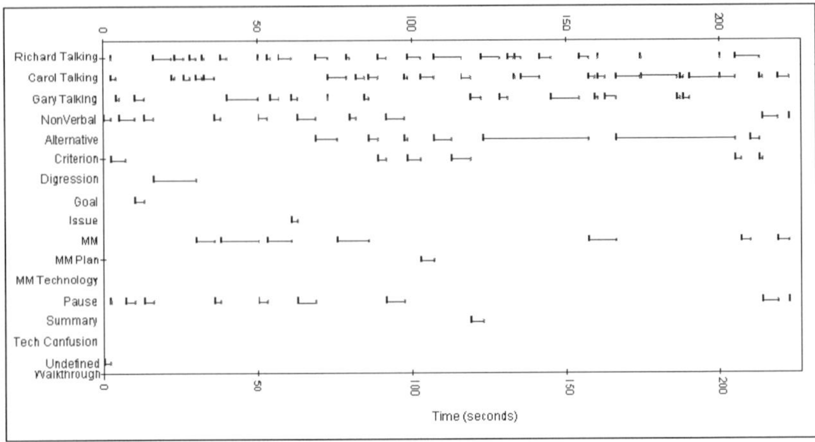

Figure 10. Timeline view of the first four minutes of the cscw video events.

MMVIS vs. Statistics. The exploratory and interactive nature of our approach provides two powerful techniques not possible with statistical approaches: 1) users can use TVQL to *temporally explore* the data *without intentionally* stating a particular temporal relationship, and 2) users can see the *intermediate* query results as well as the final ones (since the visualization is updated *as* they manipulate the temporal filters). Users can explore temporal relationships by simply sliding the temporal query filter thumbs back and forth, in any order, and watching the visualization as it is being dynamically updated. They can continue in this fashion until an interesting visualization appears, and then use the descriptive labels and temporal diagram to identify what type of temporal relationship was specified. This approach could lead users to discover and explore temporal relationships that they might not have examined otherwise. Even when users have specific initial and final temporal queries in mind, the ability to see the intermediate results can similarly focus their analysis efforts in ways they had not initially intended.

In contrast, most statistically-based approaches are less flexible, requiring users to specify the desired temporal relationships *before* calculations are made. Statistically-based approaches can complement our approach, however, by providing a means to test for statistical significance, once the types of temporal relationships of interest have been identified.

Potential of MMVIS as a New Paradigm for IMMIR. Text-based information retrieval (T-IR) systems support users in forming a "model" document to retrieve (e.g., using a list of desired keywords and synonyms, the frequency or density of terms, the distribution of terms, etc.). In addition, many T-IR systems are further enhanced with ranking mechanisms—either ranking by the system (e.g., Callan et al. 1992) or ranking by the user for relevance feedback (e.g., Salton and Buckley 1990). In order to consider the various types of content- and structure-based information to form a model and to retrieve and rank similar documents, T-IR systems must be able to *analyze* documents in the collection.

While much progress is being made in IMMIR for locating objects, less work has been done to use the *structure* of multimedia (MM) documents for IMMIR. The *temporal structure* abstracted via subset selection and temporal queries within MMVIS could be directly used to form a model of the temporal structure of MM documents to retrieve. In this way, our temporal analysis approach is a right step towards more sophisticated IMMIR approaches.

For example, consider the scenario where the CSCW video used in our case study is one in a series of videos on design meetings. Suppose we wanted to know how many of these videos have events (e.g., design rationales (DRs), talking and nonverbal events) with temporal frequency similar to the case study video. We could use the subset selection palettes to select these events and view A&B Overlays by *frequency* (see figure 6a). We could then use this visualization as a model of the temporal frequency of events, and pose a query such as "find all documents with similar temporal frequency density." Rather than displaying a text-based list of results, the system could provide visual thumbnail overviews of the "view by frequency" visualization for each of the retrieved documents. The results could be further enhanced by rank ordering the retrieved documents (e.g., documents with the same relative structure of frequency such as Alternatives and Criteria occurring more frequently than other DRs, Digressions occurring with relatively smaller frequency, etc. would be ranked fairly high). While the above discussion is based on *frequency*, the *average duration* and *total duration* views of subset selection could be similarly used in an IMMIR query.

Although recent IMMIR approaches are taking temporal relationships into consideration (e.g., "find all video clips where Dan Rather is speaking about politics" (Mérialdo and Dubois, this volume)), these approaches could be further enhanced with TVQL and its support for specifying temporal neighborhoods, fuzzifying temporal queries, etc. More importantly, the combination of TVQL and MMVIS allows us to take a more sophisticated look at the structure of temporal relationships. For example, if we used figure 7 as a model representing who or what initiates a DR, then rather than getting a set of video clips such as Carol initiating a Digression, Richard initiating a Digression, etc., we would get a longer video document including these clips and meeting other constraints (e.g., that Gary does *not* initiate a Digression). Again, the retrieved results could be presented as rank-ordered, thumbnail overviews to visually and numerically indicate the relative match between individual documents and the query specified.

5. Related Work

While many bit-level video (BLV) analysis systems are beginning to support the specification of temporal constraints for information retrieval, such constraints are typically limited to simple sequences or intersections of temporal overlaps. For example, many researchers are focusing their efforts on BLV analysis of news broadcast video (e.g., see other chapters in this volume—Hauptman and Witbrock, Mani et al., and Mérialdo and Dubois). Many of these systems support queries such as "find all video clips where person P1 is talking about topic T1." When P1 talking is indexed separately from topic T1, this query represents the set of non-empty "intersection" video clips of P1 talking and topic T1 events. By incorporating TVQL, BLV analysis systems would have a more flexible interface for specifying temporal constraints. This would enable them to pose queries such as "find all video clips where person P1 *initiates* topic T1."

Work by Carroll et al. (1994) has also examined design rationale using video data, but their work has focused on retrieving video clips based on keyword matches rather than analyzing relationships between events. In order to meet the needs of temporal analysis, our work has focused more on retrieving information on temporal relationships rather than accessing video clips based on these relationships. While using our annotations to obtain direct access to the underlying video would be trivial to implement from a technical point of view, the difficulty is in providing such access in a meaningful manner. Consider the above query to "find all video clips where person P1 initiates topic T1." Based on this query, we could retrieve any number of different combinations of P1 talking and topic T1 (e.g., we could retrieve clips that meet the temporal constraints but include: only P1 talking, only topic T1, or only the intersection of P1 and T1). Thus, while TVQL provides more flexibility in specifying sophisticated temporal constraints, it introduces new issues related to retrieving segments from the underlying document.

Other extensions to dynamic query filters and VIS have been explored (e.g., Fishkin and Stone 1995, Goldstein and Roth 1994), but these extensions primarily focus on aggregation extensions to the interface. While these aggregation techniques could be incorporated into our system to enhance the formation of subsets, they do not address the temporal and relative exploratory needs of video analysis. Our TVQL and MMVIS environment represent significant extensions to VIS, tailoring the paradigm for temporal analysis.

Variations of timelines have been used for various purposes such as Gantt charts, timelines for video analysis, calendar visualizations (e.g., Mackinlay et al. 1991), etc. Although *Timelines* (see Harrison et al. 1994) provides support for coloring subsets of events, it does not incorporate tools for examining temporal relationships between these subsets. Instead, the users are left to scrolling through a timeline and using colors to look for temporal patterns in the video data. While parallel timelines are useful for examining the occurrence and sequence of events over time, they have limited utility for temporal analysis. Rather than placing the burden of looking for temporal trends on the user, we provide direct support for examining temporal trends within MMVIS through integrating our TVQL with our TViz. The power of MMVIS is not just that users can specify relative temporal queries, but that they can *incrementally refine* their queries and immediately see the corresponding changes to the visualization of retrieved results *as* they make refinements. A previous usability study by Ahlberg et al. (1992) on DQ filters and the VIS paradigm provides further evidence supporting the utility of this paradigm for trend analysis.

Although much work has been conducted in the area of video annotation and analysis (e.g., Davis 1993, Harrison et al. 1994, Mackay 1989, Roschelle et al. 1990, Sanderson et al. 1994), this work has been limited in one or more of the following ways: 1) the work has focused more on novel approaches to creating annotations rather than analyzing them; 2) the temporal analysis hinges on *pre-coding* relationships rather than coding atomic information and searching or discovering temporal relationships (i.e., users can search for events, but they cannot search for *relationships* between events without previously identifying and explicitly annotating the relationships themselves); 3) visual presentations of the annotations are restricted to text- and timeline-based displays; 4) analysis is limited to temporal sequences rather than supporting all types of temporal relationships.

6. Conclusion

In this chapter, we presented a new paradigm for temporal analysis in which users can *temporally browse* data within an integrated MultiMedia Visual Information Seeking (MMVIS) environment. In MMVIS, specialized subset and temporal query filters (i.e., our Temporal Visual Query Language, TVQL) are coupled with a user-tailorable visualization of temporal relationships (TViz). TVQL provides a direct-manipulation interface for incrementally specifying and updating temporal queries and TViz is *dynamically* updated *as* users directly adjust the temporal filters, thus allowing users to browse the data in a temporally continuous manner. This interactive, exploratory technique for temporal analysis complements other timeline- and statistically-based approaches by providing a temporally clustered view of relationships and by focusing the direction of statistical analysis. We discussed the potential of MMVIS as a new paradigm for retrieving multimedia information based on temporal relationships between various events. This notion of taking temporal structure into consideration for retrieving MM documents is a novel approach to IMMIR which to our knowledge has not yet been explored.

We applied MMVIS to the temporal analysis of sample CSCW video data. This case study illustrated how our approach can be used to examine and identify temporal trends and how *different* types of temporal relationships (e.g., sequences and overlaps) can be easily explored within MMVIS. The MMVIS approach is generally applicable to any spatio-temporal data set (even if applied only to video data in this case study). Finally, our TVQL interface can enhance existing bit-level video analysis systems by providing a more flexible interface for specifying sophisticated temporal constraints.

Acknowledgments

This work was supported in part by a University of Michigan Rackham Fellowship, NSF NYI #94-57609, and equipment support from AT&T. Special thanks to Judy Olson for permission to use the sample data set.

Note

1. Our video annotations are formally described elsewhere along with the justification for processing video annotations rather than the raw video frames (see Hibino and Rundensteiner (1996b)).

References

Ahlberg, C. and Shneiderman, B. 1994. Visual Information Seeking: Tight Coupling of Dynamic Query Filters with Starfield Displays. In Proceedings of CHI '94, 313-317. New York, NY: ACM Press.

Ahlberg, C.; Williamson, C.; and Shneiderman, B. 1992. Dynamic Queries for Information Exploration: An Implementation and Evaluation. In Proceedings of CHI '92, 619-626. New York, NY: ACM Press.

Allen, J. F. 1983. Maintaining Knowledge About Temporal Intervals. *Communications of the ACM* 26(11): 832-843.

Callan, J. P.; Croft, W. B.; and Harding, S.M. 1992. The Inquiry Retrieval System. In DEXA 3: Proceedings of the Third International Conference on Database and Expert Systems Applications, 83-87. Berlin: Springer Verlag.

Carroll, J. M.; Alpert, S.; Karat, J.; Van Deusen, M.; and Rosson, M.B. 1994. Raison d'Etre: Capturing Design History and Rationale in Multimedia Narratives. In Proceedings of CHI '94, 192-197. New York, NY: ACM Press.

Davis, M. 1993. Media Streams: An Iconic Language for Video Annotation. *Telektronikk 4.93: Cyberspace* 89(4): 59-71.

Fishkin, K. and Stone, M.C. 1995. Enhanced Dynamic Queries via Movable Filters. In Proceedings of CHI '95, 415-420. New York, NY: ACM Press.

Freksa, C. 1992. Temporal Reasoning Based on Semi-Intervals. *Artificial Intelligence* 54(1): 199-227.

Goldstein, J. and Roth, S. 1994. Using Aggregation and Dynamic Queries for Exploring Large Data Sets. In Proceedings of CHI '94, 23-29. New York, NY: ACM Press.

Harrison, B.L.; Owen, R.; and Baecker, R.M. 1994. Timelines: An Interactive System for the Collection of Visualization of Temporal Data. In Proceedings of Graphics Interface '94, 141-148. Toronto: Canadian Information Processing Society.

Hauptman, A. G. and Witbrock, M. J. 1997. Informedia: News-on-Demand Multimedia Information Acquisition. In this volume.

Hibino, S. and Rundensteiner, E. 1996a. MMVIS: Design and Implementation of a MultiMedia Visual Information Seeking Environment. In *Proceedings of ACM Multimedia '96,* 75-86. New York: ACM Press.

Hibino, S. and Rundensteiner, E. 1996b. A Visual Multimedia Query Language for Temporal Analysis of Video Data. In *Multimedia Database Systems: Design and Implementation Strategies,* eds. K. Nwosu, B. Thuraisingham, and P.B. Berra, 123-159. Norwell, MA: Kluwer Academic Publishers.

Hibino, S. and Rundensteiner, E. 1995. A Visual Query Language for Identifying Temporal Trends in Video Data. In Proceedings of the 1995 International Workshop on Multi-Media Database Management Systems, 74-81. Los Alamitos, CA: IEEE Society Press.

Mackay, W. E. 1989. EVA: An Experimental Video Annotator for Symbolic Analysis of Video Data. *SIGCHI Bulletin* 21(2): 68-71.

Mackinlay, J. D.; Robertson, G. G.; and Card, S.K. 1991. The Perspective Wall: Detail and Context Smoothly Integrated. In Proceedings of CHI '91, 173-179. New York, NY: ACM Press.

Mani, I.; House, D.; Maybury, M.; and Green, M. 1997. Towards Content-Based Browsing of Broadcast News Video. In this volume.

Mérialdo, B. and Dubois, F. 1997. An Agent-based Architecture for Content-Based Multimedia Browsing. In this volume.

Olson, G. M.; Olson, J. S.; Storrosten, M.; Carter, M.; Herbsleb, J.; and Rueter, H. 1996. The Structure of Activity During Design Meetings. In *Design Rationale: Concepts, Techniques, and Use*, eds. T. Moran and J. Carroll. Mahwah, NJ: Lawrence Erlbaum Associates.

Olson, J.; Olson, G.; and Meader, D. 1995. What Mix of Audio and Video is Important for Remote Work. In Proceedings of CHI '95, 362-368. New York, NY: ACM Press.

Roschelle, J.; Pea, R.; and Trigg, R. 1990. VIDEONOTER: A Tool for Exploratory Analysis, Research Report, IRL90-0021, Institute for Research on Learning, Palo Alto, CA.

Salton, G. and Buckley, C. 1990. Improving Retrieval Performance by Relevance Feedback. *JASIS* 41(4): 288-297.

Sanderson, P.; Scott, J.; Johnston, T.; Mainzer, J.; Watanabe, L.; and James, J. 1994. MacSHAPA and the Enterprise of Exploratory Sequential Data Analysis (ESDA). *International Journal of Human-Computer Studies* 41: 633-681.

Weber, K. and Poon, A. 1994. Marquee: A Tool for Real-Time Video Logging. In Proceedings of CHI '94, 58-64. New York: ACM Press.

Zhang, H.J.; Low, C.; Smoliar, S.; and Zhong, D. 1995. Video Parsing, Retrieval, and Browsing: An Integrated and Content-Based Solution. In Proceedings of ACM Multimedia '95, 15-24. New York, NY: ACM Press.

Intelligent Hypermedia

Whereas the previous sections have focused primarily on indexing of and content extraction from multimedia data, the chapters in this sixth section address improving access to our global information web, making interaction both more helpful and personalized. The first two chapters address the use of user models to adapt hypertext and hypermedia; the last two chapters address the use of discourse models to manage multimedia interaction.

The first chapter by Alfred Kobsa, Andreas Nill, and Josef Fink (GMD FIT, Germany) describes the use of the user modeling shell, BGP-MS, to enable an adaptive hypertext client, KN-AHS. The user modeling shell thus acts as a common facility for representation of user beliefs and goals, as well as interests, preferences, and abilities (including possible handicaps). The authors present arguments supporting the need for adapting hypertext to the user's state of knowledge, describe how this is accomplished, and illustrate its application.

In the second chapter, in the context of a hypermedia hospital documentation system, Julita Vassileva (Federal Armed Forces University, Munich) argues that user needs are often imprecise, ambiguous, or unknown, particularly when dealing with novice users. She presents user adaptive, task-based interface hierarchies (e.g., a diagnosis task includes clinical observations and laboratory tests) which adapt to the different browsing and search strategies based on individual user models as well as user classes (e.g., nurse, doctor, administrator, students) which may have related location and rank attributes. Media preferences may be associated with particular users or with users classes (e.g., show trend graphics to a doctor, tabular measurements to a nurse), enabling customized interaction. Also, based on the user model, their system provides task hierarchy views for novices and semantic entity menus for experts. Moreover, users can actually cut and paste tasks to design their own custom task hierarchy. In controlled evaluations, both expert and novice users were able to complete tasks faster and more accurately using a task-based hypertext interface (although experts also utilized the semantic entity interface).

Just as explicit models of user attributes and knowledge enables personalizing interaction which can improve performance, so too models of discourse enable systems to explicitly track and react to user actions, the primary focus of the last two chapters of this section.

In the third chapter, Oliviero Stock, Carlo Strapparava, and Massimo Zancanaro (Instituto per la Ricerca Scientifica e Technologica, Italy) argue for information access and exploration that extends beyond hypertext browsing and query to a richer interactive context (e.g., integrated hypertext, natural language, and gestures) in which multimodal interaction is managed (i.e., interpreted, disambiguated) using communicative actions. The authors present a model of attentional state used to represent part of the context of a communicative act. Whereas their art domain knowledge base remains handcrafted, the development of multimedia extraction techniques presented in earlier sections could enable the automated creation of future systems which are as sophisticated as the described AlFresco art exploration system.

The final chapter of the section, authored by Adelheit Stein, Jon Atle Gulla, Adrian Müller, and Ulrich Thiel (GMD, Integrated Publication and Information Systems Institute, Darmstadt, Germany), similarly addresses communicative actions to manage multimedia information access. However, the authors characterize the primary information exploration tasks as 1) clarification of vague information needs, 2) selection of appropriate search strategies, and 3) relevancy assessment. Both the retrieval engine and the dialogue manager of their prototype MIRACLE system employ abductive reasoning to interpret ambiguous queries and to maintain coherent dialogue. With limited multimedia indexing and query interpretation facilities, active support of user information need satisfaction (via an "intelligent mediator agent") will remain an important facility as we move toward conversational interaction for semantic access to multimedia information.

Chapter 17

Adaptive Hypertext and Hypermedia Clients of the User Modeling System BGP-MS

Alfred Kobsa, Andreas Nill, and Josef Fink,
German National Research Center for Information Technology
Institute for Applied Information Technology (GMD FIT)

Abstract

This chapter[1] first describes the hypertext system KN-AHS which adapts to users' presumed domain knowledge, and discusses the support that the user modeling shell system BGP-MS can provide for this adaptation. The aim of constructing KN-AHS was to demonstrate the feasibility of user modeling with BGP-MS in a "normal" hardware and software environment that is frequently found in the workplace. Basic hypertext concepts will be introduced and reasons given for why hypertext should adapt to the current user (especially to his/her state of knowledge). A brief overview of those representation and inference components of BGP-MS that are used by KN-AHS will be provided, followed by a description of its adaptive user interface. The interaction between the adaptive hypertext system and the user modeling system will be investigated in detail based on a possible dialog with a user. The inter-process communication between KN-AHS and BGP-MS will then be described and related work discussed. A final section discusses recent research that extends the approach of KN-AHS to a hypermedia information system in the World Wide Web which additionally adapts its presentation to users' interests, preferences and abilities (including possible handicaps).

1. Hypertext and Adaptive Hypertext

In this first section, we discuss hypertext and two major problems that arise when working with hypertext systems.

1.1 Hypertext

Hypertext consists of any number of objects[2] that can be linked with one another in a network structure. Therefore, hypertext is not necessarily read in linear (i.e., sequential) order like conventional text, but can be read in a non-linear order by navigating within the hypertext node network. This non-linear linkage of objects represents the basic characteristic of hypertext (cf. Seyer 1991, Kuhlen 1991). Hypertext obviously follows the browsing paradigm of information access (like in (Pu and Faltings 1995; Vassileva, this volume)) rather than the information retrieval paradigm (Flickner et al., this volume; Stock et al., this volume).

Gaining information in a non-linear form is not new (see e.g. information search in encyclopedias). Unlike print media, however, the representation of information in electronic form allows the user to directly and comfortably traverse contextual connections. Hypertext has therefore been able to enjoy an increased importance in the last few years, especially as a basis for on-line information and help systems.

The user-friendliness of many hypertext systems is rooted in their usage of intuitively understandable direct-manipulative interfaces (cf. Kuhlen 1991, Shneiderman and Kearsly 1989). The user has the possibility of directly manipulating graphical objects with a pointer (e.g. a mouse) without having to use complicated commands. The effect of these actions can be seen immediately on the screen. Direct manipulation can be used, for example, to reach a different node from the node currently shown on the screen. The usual graphical objects used in such navigating operations include mouse-sensitive text passages (hotwords) or buttons (more on this in Section 3). Other important hypertext components are glossaries, indices, and graphical representations of the hypertext structure, which all offer important meta-information about the basic text objects. Recent research supplements associative navigation by controlled navigation and by search techniques from the field of Information Retrieval, in order to increase the search efficiency (cf. Kuhlen 1991).

1.2 Adaptive Hypertext

Two major problems arise when working with hypertext systems (see e.g. Brusilovsky 1996):

Orientation and navigation problems: When navigating in hypertext, users are frequently uncertain as to how to reach their goals. Since users can choose any course within hypertext, they run the risk of losing their orientation. Navigation aids that take users' goals into account may be helpful. (Kaplan et al. 1993) showed empirically that navigation suggestions based on knowledge about the objectives and the navigation behavior of previous users as well as the goals of the current user can significantly accelerate the current user's search for information.

Comprehension problems: Since hypertext is frequently read by users with differing knowledge and experience levels, it may at the same time be too difficult and too detailed for laypersons, and too redundant for experts. (Boyle and Encarnacion 1993) showed empirically that an automatic adaptation of hypertext to the user's state of knowledge significantly improves text understanding as well as partially improving search speed.

The system KN-AHS[3] deals with the second problem and adapts hypertext objects to the current user's state of knowledge. In contrast to other adaptive hypertext systems, the realization of KN-AHS took advantage of existing software products. TOOLBOOK (Asymetrix 1989), a widely available hypertext shell system, offers a powerful tool for the implementation of the hypertext and its user interface, and the user modeling shell system BGP-MS provides a wide variety of representation and inference possibilities that ensure flexible adaptation. Both tools run as independent software systems on a PC platform and interact via inter-process communication.

2. User Modeling Using BGP-MS

Over the last few years, researchers have developed several so-called "user modeling shell systems," since programming user modeling components in application systems is very time-consuming. These shell systems make integrated mechanisms and methods available which are often needed in user modeling systems.

One of these shells is BGP-MS[4], which is currently under development. From the perspective of the application system, BGP-MS can be regarded as a "black box" that receives information about the user and answers questions posed by the application system concerning current assumptions about the user. In order to realize its adaptive dialog behavior that is oriented to the user's state of knowledge, KN-AHS utilizes certain services of BGP-MS. The following sections will gradually present the BGP-MS components that are used, and explain their functionality with regard to the adaptation of hypertext by means of examples[5].

2.1 Communication Between the Application and BGP-MS

The user modeling component of KN-AHS is not integrated into the application (as is the case for user modeling components in virtually all other user-adaptive systems), but is rather an independent process that communicates with the application. Observations based on user actions will be reported to BGP-MS by the hypertext system (cf. figure 1, part a). The application can ask BGP-MS questions about the user (b) and BGP-MS can in return report its current assumptions concerning the user (c).

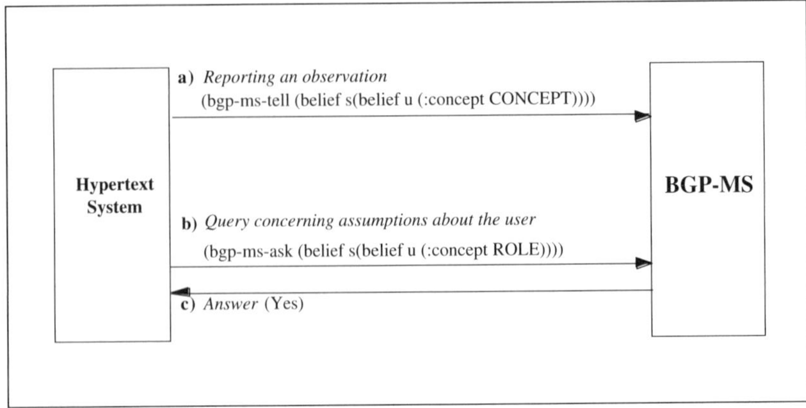

Figure 1. Communication between the application and BGP-MS.

2.2 Partitions for Collecting Different Types of Assumptions

BGP-MS utilizes the partition mechanism SB-PART (Scherer 1990), which allows different types of assumptions about the user to be represented simultaneously, but still separately. These assumptions include, for example, assumptions concerning the user's knowledge or goals, assumptions concerning application-relevant characteristics of user subgroups (so-called "stereotypes"), or the domain knowledge of the user modeling component.

Partitions can be ordered in an inheritance hierarchy, where subordinate partitions inherit the contents of superordinate ones. Figure 2 shows a simple partition hierarchy, as is currently used in our adaptive hypertext. The depicted partitions can be divided into three groups:

The *individual user model* consists of the partitions SBUB (System Believes User Believes), which contains BGP-MS's assumptions about the user's knowledge, and SB¬UB, which contains BGP-MS's assumptions about what the user does not know.

The *stereotypes* for user subgroups are ordered hierarchically. We assume for our application that the stereotype "any person" is available, which includes only general information, i.e. knowledge available to any user. All other stereotypes include typical characteristics of users with various fields of specialization, namely hypertext users, PC users, and computer science students[6]. They inherit the contents from the general stereotype.

The *domain knowledge* in BGP-MS, which is included in the partition SB (= System Believes).

2.3 Stereotype Mechanisms

BGP-MS allows the user model developer to define so-called "stereotypes"

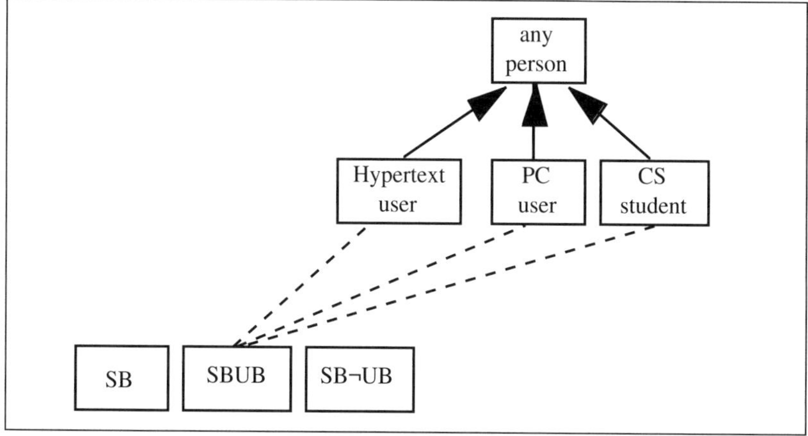

Figure 2: Partition hierarchy in SB-PART.

that contain application-relevant characteristics of user subgroups. The programmer can also define the conditions under which a user will be assigned to these subgroups, and those under which an existing assignment should be withdrawn. BGP-MS contains a stereotype managing mechanism that analyzes observations received from the application and checks the activation and retraction conditions of all stereotypes. It will then enter inheritance links between the individual user model and those stereotypes that become active, and delete links to stereotypes that become deactivated. More than one stereotype can be active at the same time, if allowed by the user model programmer. He/she can also define the frequency of stereotype revision.

The broken lines in figure 2 represent the possible inheritance relationships with the stereotypes hypertext user, PC user and CS student. Since only "positive knowledge" is contained in the stercotypes of KN-AHS at the time being, a connection to SB¬UB is not possible. Several stereotypes can be active simultaneously, since the readers (such as all authors of this chapter) can be both hypertext and PC users. On the other hand, an existing connection can be withdrawn if observations are made that meet the retraction conditions of the stereotype.

2.4 Representing Domain Knowledge in BGP-MS

So far we have described the organization of system knowledge, user assumptions and pre-defined stereotypes using separate partitions and inheritance links. Now we take a closer look at the contents of individual partitions and their representation. One of the knowledge representation languages used within partitions is SB-ONE (Profitlich 1989, Kobsa 1991), which belongs to the family of KL-ONE type languages. The following simplified

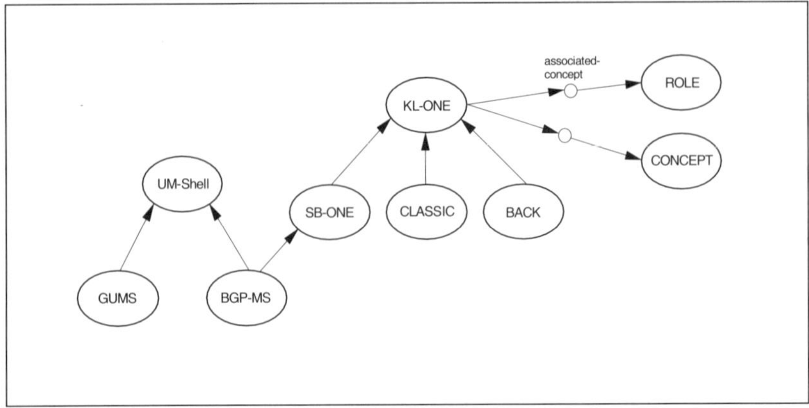

Figure 3. Detail of the concept hierarchy in the partition 'system believes' (SB).

description of the language elements is sufficient for this chapter.

The two most important representational elements in KL-ONE type languages are concepts (depicted as ovals in figure 3) and role relationships between concepts (depicted as small circles). For the purposes of KN-AHS, two types of concepts are distinguished: field concepts, which represent small fields of knowledge, and terminological concepts, which represent technical terms. In figure 3, UM-Shell, GUMS, BGP-MS, KL-ONE, SB-ONE, CLASSIC, and BACK are field concepts. "ROLE" and "CONCEPT" are terminological concepts. The role "associated-concept" (the only role used in KN-AHS) defines the relationship between fields and their associated terminology.

Super- and subordinations are also found for concepts, where the subordinated concept inherits all role relationships of the superordinated concept. The field concepts "SB-ONE" and BGP-MS in figure 3 inherit all roles of the field concept "KL-ONE," and thereby all associated terminological concepts.

2.5 User Model Acquisition and Inferences

Messages that an application communicates to BGP-MS may express various types of information about the user's knowledge. KN-AHS only takes assumptions about the user's conceptual knowledge into account when adapting hypertext documents. Its messages to BGP-MS are therefore restricted to information on whether the user is familiar or unfamiliar with certain concepts. These "primary assumptions" about the user become entered into the partitions SBUB and SB¬UB, respectively. Primary assumptions will be compared with all stereotype activation and deactivation conditions in regular pre-set intervals. As an effect, inheritance links between stereotype partitions and the partition SBUB may be entered or erased.

The user model developer may also define inference rules that become executed after each new entry into the individual user model. The inferences used in KN-AHS are based on domain knowledge that is represented in SB. They take sub- and superfield relationships and the "associated-concept" relationship between fields and their respective terminology into account, and comprise the following rules:

A. Sub- and Superfield Relationships

1. If a minimum percentage P1 of direct subfields of a field were reported to be known/unknown, then all its subfields are known/unknown.

2. If a minimum percentage P2 of direct subfields of a field were reported to be known/unknown (where P1 can be different from P2), then the superfield is also known/unknown.

B. Relationships between Fields and their Respective Terminology

1. If a minimum percentage P3 of the terminological concepts of a field were reported to be known/unknown, then all terminological concepts of the field are known/unknown.

2. If a minimum percentage P4 of the terminological concepts of a field were reported to be known/unknown (where P3 can be different from P4), then the field is also known/unknown.

Conflicts can arise between the observations made by the application and assumptions inferred in BGP-MS. If this is the case, then the inferred assumptions will have a lower priority and will be discarded from the partition. Dependency management between premises and consequences will not be able to be considered until sometime in the future.

3. The Adaptive Hypertext System KN-AHS

In this section, we will first describe the functionality of the user interface of KN-AHS. We will focus especially on reviewing the direct-manipulative actions that are available to the user. Then the assumptions will be described that KN-AHS draws about the user and reports to BGP-MS, as well as the kind of hypertext adaptation that it performs after consulting BGP-MS on the presumable conceptual knowledge of the user. Finally, the adaptive behavior of KN-AHS as well as its interaction with BGP-MS will be illustrated by an example of a possible user dialog.

3.1 The User Interface

Figure 4 shows an example of the user interface of KN-AHS. Special attention was paid to awakening interest and curiosity, and to stimulate users to navigate through the hypertext. It was also important that the interface

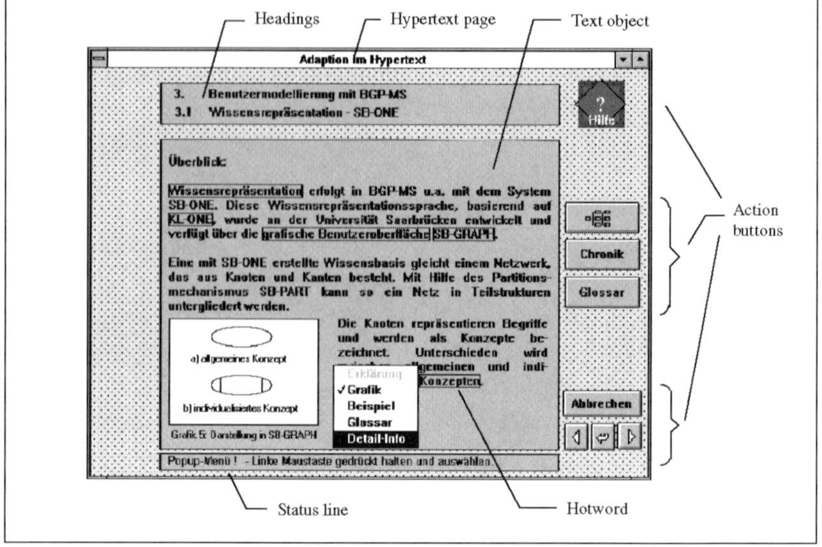

Figure 4. Selecting additional information on a hotword.

should be largely self-explanatory. Users should be able to correctly predict the outcome of each possible action. This is especially important if assumptions about their knowledge are formed on the basis of their actions.

In a simplified form, the hyperdocument can be divided into four areas:

Headings: This box informs the users of their whereabouts (i.e., the current chapter).

Text object: This area is the core of the hypertext page. The reader can receive information in the form of text and graphics (a vertical scroll bar will be automatically inserted if the text object is longer than a screen page). So-called "hotwords" can be found within this area, i.e. mouse-sensitive text passages such as the boxed text elements Wissensrepräsentation (knowledge representation), KL-ONE, Konzepten (concepts) etc. The actions that the user can perform on these hotwords will be described further below.

Status line: The status line is located on the lower screen edge below the text object. It offers the user additional information about possible actions for each hotword.

Action buttons: These are found on the right side of the screen. Starting here, the user can "jump" to other areas within the hypertext, for example (from top to bottom) to a context-sensitive help text, to a graphically represented table of contents, to the dialog history, (which includes a list of the already-viewed text objects to which the user can return on demand), and to the glossary, which is context-independent.

Other buttons are also available that enable the reader to jump to a previ-

Menu entry	Effect
Erklärung (Explanation)	Additional information which explains the hotword *in context* will be inserted near the hotword to ensure a terminologically supportive effect. In some cases the hotword may also become replaced by a simpler term or expression.
Grafik (Graphic)	A graphic appears which should illustrate the hotword.
Beispiel (Example)	An example will be shown that should clarify the hotword.
Glossar (Glossary)	The page of the glossary that contains the hotword will be displayed. A context-independent definition or description of the hotword can be found there.
Detail-Info (Detailed information)	Additional details related to the hotword will be inserted near the hotword.

Table 1. Effects of the options in the hotword pop-up menu.

ous or following page, as well as to the front-runner page of the one depicted on the screen.

When the user moves the mouse cursor across a hotword, the form of the mouse cursor indicates the available actions for the hotword. The user may (a) jump to another text object that provides detailed information on the hotword; or (b) request additional information with a pop-up menu, namely an explanation, a graphic, an example, a glossary definition, or additional details. Table 1 lists in greater detail the additional information that is available in KN-AHS via this pop-up menu. An example can be found in figure 4, where the user clicked on the hotword "Konzepten." Some kinds of additional information may not be available for a hotword; the respective menu entries then turn to grey in the pop-up menu (like "Erklärung" in figure 4).

3.2 Drawing Assumptions About the User

KN-AHS draws assumptions about the user's knowledge based on two information sources: namely an initial interview, and some of the hypertext actions which the user may perform.

In the initial interview, questions are posed to the user that refer to his membership in clearly separable user subgroups (like "computer science student"), and his exposure to PCs, hypertexts, etc. The user's replies become communicated to BGP-MS, which can activate initial stereotypes for the user (see Section 2.3). If the user decides to skip this interview, BGP-MS will only activate the "any person" stereotype.

Certain actions that the user may perform afterwards in the hypertext give rise to assumptions about his familiarity with individual concepts:

- If the user requests an explanation, a graphic, an example or a glossary definition for a hotword, then he is assumed to be unfamiliar with this hotword.

- If the user unselects an explanation, a graphic, an example or a glossary definition for a hotword, then he is assumed to be familiar with this hotword.

- If the user requests additional details for a hotword, then he is assumed to be familiar with this hotword.

With each hotword for which more information can be requested, the corresponding SB-ONE concept that represents this technical term in BGP-MS is associated. When KN-AHS draws an assumption about the user's familiarity with a hotword, KN-AHS notifies BGP-MS that the corresponding concept is known or unknown to the user. An example can be found in figure 1, in which KN-AHS informs BGP-MS that the user is familiar with the concept CONCEPT after it made the assumption that the user is familiar with the hotword "Konzepten" since he requested additional details for it.

BGP-MS is also equipped with a component that draws assumptions about the user based on the user's actions (Pohl et al. 1994). Instead of drawing assumptions itself and communicating them to BGP-MS, KN-AHS could therefore also inform BGP-MS about the actions that the user performed, and let BGP-MS draw the assumptions. However, since the concept names in BGP-MS must be anyway known to KN-AHS in order that it can ask BGP-MS about the user's familiarity with them (see Section 3.3), this option was not chosen in order to avoid redundancy.

3.3 Adapting the Document to the User's Conceptual Knowledge

When the user switches to a new text object, KN-AHS aims at adapting it to the user's presumed conceptual knowledge. For each hotword in the new text object, it asks BGP-MS about the user's familiarity with the corresponding SB-ONE concept. The hotword is then treated in the following way:

- If the user is unfamiliar with the associated concept, an explanation gets automatically added to the hotword. (The very same adaptation would take place if the user had selected the "explanation" entry in the pop-up menu for this hotword). Also, an icon that symbolizes an available graphic for the hotword is placed near the hotword.

- If the user is familiar with the hotword, more details are automatically added after the hotword.

- If no information is available from BGP-MS concerning the user's familiarity with the hotword, then the hotword is not changed.

Possibly icons that signal the availability of examples and glossary information may be added in the future for hotwords that are unknown to the user. However, this may raise the danger of the hypertext becoming visually overloaded on the terminal screen.

3.4 An Example of an Adaptation Step

In this section we present an example that shows how adaptation in hypertext can be performed based on reader actions. We will specifically concentrate on the interplay between hypertext components and the user modeling system.

The user in figure 4 would like to learn more about the hotword "Konzept" and asks for "Detail-Info" (detailed information). The displayed screen page will be expanded and the desired information will be shown. Because of this user action, the hypertext application reports to BGP-MS that the user is familiar with the associated concept CONCEPT (see Section 2.4). BGP-MS enters the term in the partition SBUB. Assume now that BGP-MS contains the following inference rule (which was defined by the user model developer at design time):

"If 50% of the terminological concepts of a field were reported to be known/unknown, then all terminological concepts of the field are known/unknown" (see b1 in Section 2.5).

This rule will fire for the field KL-ONE, and the terminological concept ROLE will also be entered into SBUB (and marked as having been inferred).

Figure 5 shows another text object that the reader could possibly encounter later in the hypertext session. Detailed information for the hotword "Rollen" is already provided, even though the user did not explicitly request more information. How did that happen? Before switching pages the hypertext system asked BGP-MS whether or not the user was familiar with the expandable hotwords shown on the newly requested page. BGP-MS checked the individual user model and informed the hypertext application[7]. The concept "ROLE" was reported as known (i.e., included in SBUB), and the hotword "Rollen" was therefore automatically supplemented by detailed information.

4. Discussion and Related Work

The aim of the work on KN-AHS was to demonstrate the feasibility of user modeling with BGP-MS in a "normal" hardware and software environment that is frequently used in the workplace. The basic architecture that we described—where application and user modeling system are independent processes that communicate via inter-process communication—is quite unique. Only Orwant (1995) proposes a related framework (which is however located on the level of a computer network).

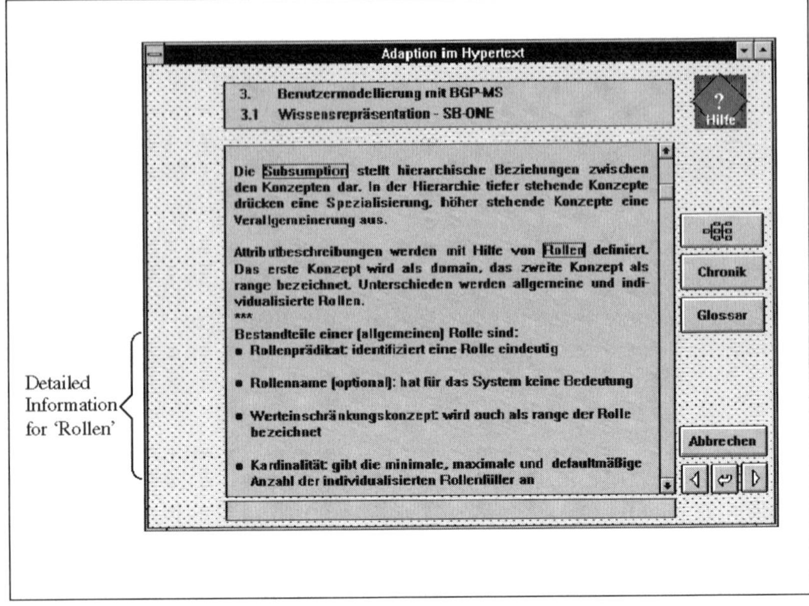

Figure 5. Automatic addition of detailed information for the hotword "Rolle."

Some work already exists in the area of adaptive hypertext documents. The system that seems most closely related to KN-AHS is MetaDoc (Boyle and Encarnacion 1994). It is also PC based and uses adaptation techniques that are similar to those in KN-AHS. Both its hypertext and its user-modeling component are "self-made." In comparison to MetaDoc, KN-AHS clearly profits from the greater expressiveness of the BGP-MS user modeling shell, which allows for the representation of hierarchically structured knowledge domains (instead of MetaDoc's flat "concept islands"), for inferences based on this hierarchy of knowledge domains, for more complex stereotype hierarchies than those of MetaDoc, and for more flexible stereotype activation rules. The adaptive range of KN-AHS goes somewhat beyond MetaDoc in that also graphics (and in the future possibly examples) become automatically included in the hypertext. A minor but noteworthy difference is that KN-AHS will only adapt the hypertext when the user switches to a *new* text object; it will never change a hotword in the current text as a result of an action that the user performed on a different hotword in the current text object since this seems to violate the constancy principle of software ergonomics.

Other related systems are ANATOM-TUTOR (Beaumont 1994) and HYP-ADAPTER (Böcker et al. 1990, Hohl et. al. 1996), which present hypertext-based tutorials on anatomy and Common Lisp, respectively. Both systems use self-made hypertext components. ANATOM-TUTOR contains a self-made user modeling component, while HYPADAPTER employs the MODUS user modeling shell (Schwab 1989), which is functionally included. Both systems are active tutorial systems and not only hypertext browsers like KN-AHS. They therefore have additional adaptive characteristics (e.g., HYPADAPTER exploits the user model for topic selection and presentation) and additional sources of information about the user (e.g., ANATOM-TUTOR receives information about the user through a quiz). The adaptation of hypertext contents consists in adding or omitting information based on the assumptions about the user's knowledge (and also the user's preferences and learner type in the case of HYPADAPTER).

5. Hardware and Software Environment

KN-AHS has been implemented under MS-DOS 6.2 and MS WINDOWS 3.1 on a PC platform. TOOLBOOK 1.5, a popular hypertext shell system from Asymetrix Corporation has been used to construct the hypertext. The BGP-MS user modeling shell was developed (and will be further enhanced) in Common Lisp on SUN workstations. The relevant parts were ported to Golden Common Lisp 4.3, which also runs under MS WINDOWS.

The communication between the hypertext system and BGP-MS was realized using the InterProcess Communication System KN-IPCMS[8]. The current PC version exploits the DDE functionality[9] that is also supported by TOOLBOOK and Golden Common Lisp. KN-IPCMS is a platform-independent message-oriented communication protocol that allows both for synchronous and asynchronous communication. In the interaction between KN-AHS and BGP-MS, observations made by KN-AHS will be transferred asynchronously. This means that KN-AHS and BGP-MS run concurrently, i.e. the user model management will largely be performed while the user is reading the current text object. Questions posed to BGP-MS will however be handled synchronously and will have priority over incoming observations.

6. From KN-AHS to AVANTI

The experiences gained from KN-AHS are currently leading to the development of a new system, AVANTI, which differs from KN-AHS in several important ways:

- While KN-AHS was a local application (with the hypertext and the user modeling system being communicating processes on the same computer), AVANTI should primarily run in a networked environment.

- While KN-AHS was a single-user application, AVANTI will service many users at the same time on the World Wide Web.

- While KN-AHS was a hypertext system enhanced by graphics, AVANTI will support multimedia.

- While KN-AHS stored all information in the hypertext pages, AVANTI will access external information from distributed multimedia databases and integrate it into the hypermedia pages.

- While KN-AHS only took the users' knowledge into account when adapting its presentation, AVANTI will additionally respect users' interests, preferences (e.g., about media—cf. Horacek this volume), and abilities (including possible handicaps such as sensory disabilities which hinder or prevent the perception of certain modalities).

- While KN-AHS adapted the presented information through local replacements and additions only, AVANTI will additionally re-position information units in WWW pages, highlight them, and also provide navigation support.

- While KN-AHS adhered exclusively to the browsing paradigm, AVANTI will also provide limited facilities for querying databases directly.

This wider perspective of adaptation has a number of fundamental consequences for BGP-MS, in particular the following:

- While BGP-MS so far has communicated with applications through inter-process communication only, it will become a network-wide service in the future that is addressable via KQML (Finin et al. 1993, Kobsa et al. 1996), a high-level communication language and protocol which is independent of the hardware and software platform, the network, and the programming language.

- While an instance of BGP-MS so far could only model a single user at a time, it will be able to communicate concurrently with multiple applications in the future and model several users in parallel.

- While the current version of BGP-MS can only represent one modal operator at a time (i.e. either "user believes," or "user wants," or "user can," or "user prefers"), the new version will support the simultaneous usage of all these operators.

- A new architecture based on interoperable objects like the Object Management Architecture (OMG 1991, 1994) will be investigated which would allow BGP-MS to be flexibly distributed over the traditional boundaries of computers and platforms, more easily accessed and functionally enhanced by application programmers, and configured on the level of user modeling services (Fink 1996).

Figure 6 shows the architecture of the AVANTI system (AVANTI). The Information Resource Control Structure (IRCS) contains HTML pages that

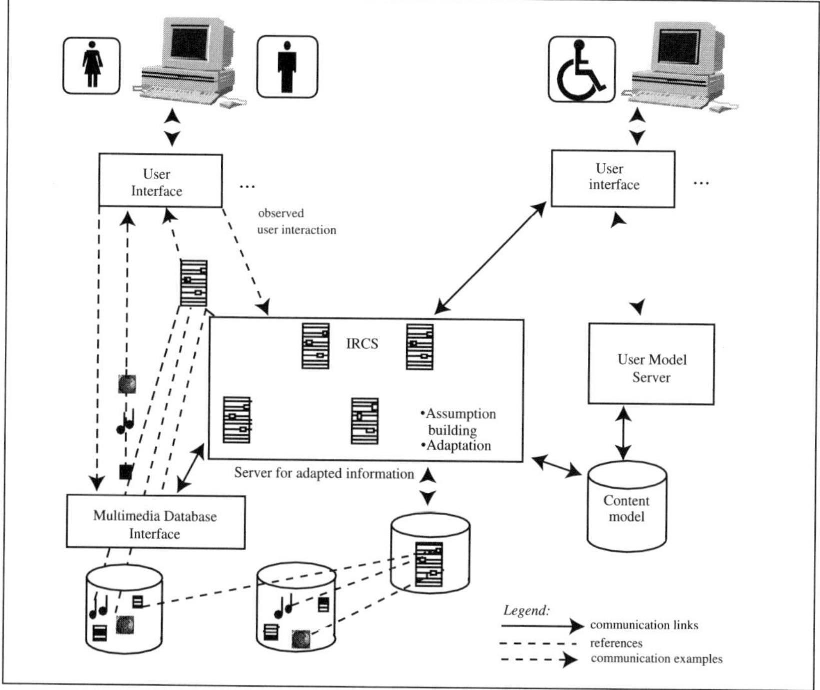

Figure 6. Architecture of AVANTI.

include numerous references to distributed multimedia databases, and executable parts that adapt each page to the user's needs as modeled in a network-wide BGP-MS-based user modeling server. The adaptations can be performed on the side of the server for adapted information, but also by the user interface if it is capable of executing program code. As was the case for KN-AIIS, a content model of the multimedia data (comparable to the one in Stock, this volume) and the user modeling server are being consulted in the adaptation process. The technical abilities of the user interface and the user terminal as well as the available network bandwidth will also be taken into account.

Acknowledgments

The work described here has been supported by the German Science Foundation (Grant Ko-1044), the University of Konstanz (Grant AFF 17/92), and the Commission of the European Union (Project ACTS AVANTI).

Notes

1. This is a revised and considerably updated version of Kobsa et al. (1994).

2. The objects in a hypertext base are not only text documents but can also include non-textual data (tables, graphs, animation, etc.). The term "hypermedia" is commonly used if an audiovisual component is involved.

3. KN-AHS stands for KoNstanz Adaptive Hypertext System.

4. BGP-MS stands for Belief, Goal and Plan Maintenance System (Kobsa 1990).

5. A more comprehensive description of BGP-MS can be found in (Kobsa & Pohl 1995) and (BGP-MS).

6. This type of stereotype hierarchy—a kernel with several specializations—has been investigated several times in connection with the use of UNIX commands (Hanson et al. 1984, Sutcliffe and Old 1987). The model is also referred to as "lettuce model" because of its graphical form in Venn diagrams (Kobsa 1990).

7. Possible answers are "known" or "unknown" (if the corresponding concept is included in SBUB or SBÿUB) as well as "no statement possible" (if neither is the case).

8. KN-IPCMS stands for Konstanz InterProcess Communication Management System

9. DDE (Dynamic Data Exchange) is a communication protocol under MS WINDOWS that defines how WINDOWS applications can exchange messages and data, and helps application programs communicate with one another, as long as they can support DDE as well

References

Asymetrix Corporation 1989. *Using TOOLBOOK®: A Guide to Building and Working with Books* (Version 1.5). Washington.

AVANTI Home Page. http://zeus.gmd.de/projech/avanti.html

Beaumont, I. 1994. User Modelling in the Interactive Anatomy Tutoring System ANATOM-TUTOR. *User Modeling and User-Adapted Interaction* 4(1): 21-45.

BGP-MS. BGP-MS Home Page. http://zeus.gmd.de/projects/bgp-ms.html/ (includes the software).

Boyle, C. and Encarnacion, A. O. 1994. An Adaptive Hypertext Reading System. *User Modeling and User-Adapted Interaction* 4(1): 1-19.

Böcker, H.-D.; Hohl, H.; Schwab, Th. 1990. "ψπADAPTεδ": Individualizing Hypertext. In Proceedings of Human-Computer Interaction—INTERACT '90, eds. D. Diaper et al., 931-936. Amsterdam, The Netherlands: North-Holland.

Brusilovsky, P. 1996. Methods and Techniques of Adaptive Hypermedia. *User Modeling and User-Adapted Interaction* 6(2-3): 87-129.

Finin, T. W; Weber, J.; Widerhold, G.; Genesereth, M.; Fritzson, R.; McKay, D.; McGuire, J.; Pelavin, R.; Shapiro, S.; Beck, C. 1993. Specification of the KQML Agent-Communication Language. http://www.cs.umbc.edu/kqml/papers/kqmlspec.ps

Fink, J. 1996. A Flexible and Open Architecture for the User Modeling Shell System BGP-MS. In Proceedings of the Fifth International Conference on User Modeling, 237-239. Kailua-Kona, HI: User Modeling, Inc.

Hanson, S. J.; Kraut, R. E.; Farber, J. M. 1984. Interface Design and Multivariate

Analysis of UNIX Command Use. *ACM Transactions on Office Information Systems* 2(1):42-57.

Hohl, H.; Böcker, H.-D.; Gunzenhäuser, D., 1996: Hypadapter: An Adaptive Hypertext System for Exploratory Learning and Programming. *User Modeling and User-Adapted Interaction* 6(2-3): 131-156.

Horacek, H. 1997. Empirical Evidence for the Need of Intelligent Methods in Multi-Media Information Retrieval. In this volume.

Kaplan, C.; Fenwick, J.; and Chen, J. 1993: Adaptive Hypertext Navigation Based on User Goals and Context. *User Modeling and User-Adapted Interaction* 3(3): 193-220.

Kobsa, A. 1990. Modeling the User's Conceptual Knowledge in BGP-MS, a User Modeling Shell System. *Computational Intelligence* 6(4): 193-208.

Kobsa, A. 1991. Utilizing Knowledge: The Components of the SB-ONE Knowledge Representation Workbench. In *Principles of Semantic Networks: Exploration in the Representation of Knowledge,* ed. J. Sowa, 457-486. San Mateo, CA: Morgan Kaufmann.

Kobsa, A.; Müller, D.; and Nill, A. 1994. KN-AHS: An Adaptive Hypertext Client of the User Modeling System BGP-MS. In Proceedings of the Fourth International Conference on User Modeling, 99-105. Hyannis, MA: User Modeling Inc.

Kobsa, A. and Pohl, W. 1995. The User Modeling Shell BGP-MS. *User Modeling and User-Adapted Interaction* 4(2), 59-106.

Kobsa, A.; Fink, J.; and Pohl, W. 1996. A Standard for the Performatives in the Communication between Applications and User Modeling Systems (draft). http://zeus.gmd.de/~kobsa/rfc.ps

Kuhlen, R. 1991. *Hypertext. Ein nicht-lineares Medium zwischen Buch und Wissensbank.* Berlin: Springer.

OMG 1991. The Common Object Request Broker: Architecture and Specification. Object Management Group.

OMG 1994. Object Models. Object Management Group.

Orwant, J. 1995. Heterogenous Learning in the Doppelgänger User Modeling System. *User Modeling and User-Adapted Interaction* 4(2): 107-130.

Pohl, W.; Kobsa, A.; and Kutter, O. 1994. User Model Acquisition Heuristics Based on Dialog Acts. WIS Report 6, Dept. of Information Science, University of Konstanz, Germany.

Flickner, M.; Sawhney, H.; Niblack, W.; Ashley, J.; Huang, Q.; Dom, B.; Gorkani, M.; Hafner, J.; Lee, D.; Petkovic, D.; Steele, D.; and Yanker, P. 1997. Query by Image and Video Content: The QBIC System. In this volume.

Profitlich, H. J. 1989. SB-ONE: Ein Wissensrepräsentationssystem basierend auf KL-ONE. Master's Thesis, Dept. of Computer Science, University of Saarbrücken, Germany.

Pu, P. and Faltings, B. 1995. Multimedia Systems for Design. Presented at the IJCAI-95 Workshop on Intelligent Multimedia Information Retrieval, August 19, 1995, Montreal, Canada.

Scherer, J. 1990. SB-PART: Ein Partitionsmechanismus für die Wissensrepräsentationssprache SB-ONE. Master Thesis, Dept. of Computer Science, University of Saarbrücken, Germany.

Schwab, T. 1989. Methoden zur Dialog- und Benutzermodellierung in Adaptiven

Computersystemen. Ph.D. diss., Dept. of Computer Science, University of Stuttgart, Germany.

Seyer, P.C. 1991. *Understanding Hypertext: Concepts and Applications.* Blue Ridge Summit, PA: Windcrest Books.

Shneiderman, B. and Kearsley, G. 1989. *Hypertext hands-on! An Introduction to a New Way of Organizing and Accessing Information.* Reading, MA: Addison-Wesley.

Stock, O.; Strapparava, C.; and Zancanaro, M. 1997. Explorations in an Environment for Natural Language MultiModal Information Access. In this volume.

Sutcliffe, A. G.; Old, A. C. 1987: Do Users Know They Have User Models? Some Experiences in the Practice of User Modeling. In Proceedings of Human-Computer Interaction: INTERACT'87, eds. H.-J. Bullinger and B. Shackel, 35-41. Amsterdam, The Netherlands: North-Holland.

Vassileva, J. 1997. Ensuring a Task-based Individualized Interface for Hypermedia Information Retrieval by User Modeling. In this volume.

Chapter 18

Ensuring a Task-based Individualized Interface for Hypermedia Information Retrieval through User Modeling

Julita Vassileva
Federal Armed Forces University—Munich

Abstract

The popularity of office documentation systems is growing with the increasing application of hypermedia techniques and the integration of traditional search techniques with browsing. With the growth of information contained in such systems as well as with the increasing variety of media used for presenting information it becomes more difficult for the user to search effectively for needed information. Browsing in a large hyperspace always entails risk of "getting lost." Formulating queries requires that the user is able and willing to describe in advance the information she is searching for, which is often not possible. In order to support effective user search in a large office documentation system I have developed a user adaptive task-based interface. It adapts to differences in browsing methods and to the search strategies of users with different levels of experience and in different user classes. The interface ensures a level of adaptability according to the media-preferences of individual users. In order to support the user's learning of the system, the adaptive interface provides a smooth transition between the options for search for novice-users and expert users. This interface has been implemented and tested in a hypermedia documentation system for hospitals.

1. Introduction

Increasingly office documentation systems incorporate hypermedia and are integrating traditional search techniques with browsing. The main cognitive

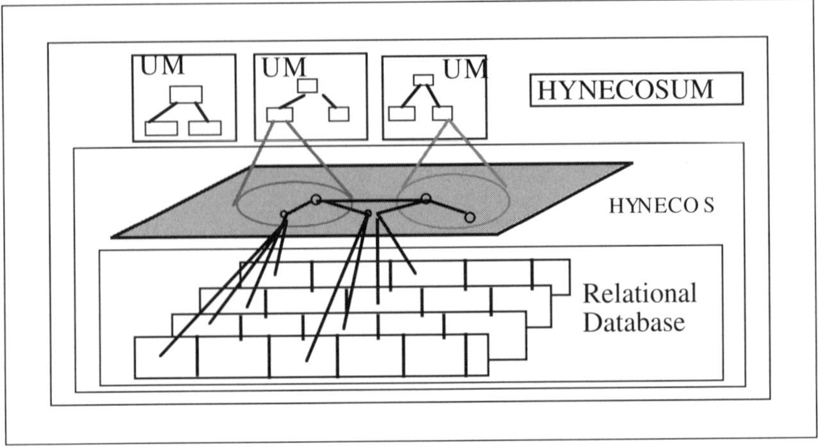

Figure 1. History and architecture of HYNECOSUM.

advantage of supporting both searching and browsing is that users are often better able to recognize the information they want than to characterize it in advance. Disadvantages of browsing include the ease of getting lost in a complex network of nodes representing documents and concepts (Conklin 1987) and that browsing is usually less effective than other, for example, query-based search strategies. With the growth of information contained in office documentation systems and the increasing variety of media used for presenting information it is becoming more difficult for the user to search effectively for needed information.

One way of coping with this problem is by creating a user-adaptive interface which supports search and browsing. In order to adapt to an individual user, the system has to keep some information about her. A user model is an explicitly represented collection of data about the user which allows the system to adapt its options to the needs of the user. The intensive development in the field of user modeling during the last decade (Kobsa and Pohl 1994) makes it possible to consider it as a practical approach for ensuring user-adapted information access in a hypermedia information system.

My work evolved in an industrial project for creating a large hypermedia documentation system for hospitals. The project started informally in 1991 with the creation of a small relational data-base (dBase) with hospital information at the University Orthopedics Clinic of Heidelberg. However, this system was not well accepted by the hospital staff and hardly ever used.

Two years later the dBase information system was integrated into HYNECOS (HYpertext Navigation on the Electronic patient reCord on the Orthopedic ward Section), work done at Siemens ZFE within the ESPRIT

Project No. 6532 HIFI (Hypertext Interface For Information). The goal of the project was to demonstrate the applicability of the Hypertext Design Model HDM (Grazotto et al. 1991) for design of hypertext-based information systems from relational databases. HYNECOS contains textual and imagery data about patients (administrative data, reports, x-rays, photos, etc.), hospital staff (names, photos, telephones and shift-information about all staff members), a medical encyclopedia containing text, images and videos about diseases and therapies, and the location of the wards (room-plans, beds-location, occupancy etc.). HYNECOS was implemented in ToolBook 3.0 and runs under Windows 3.10 and Windows 95.

During the third phase of the system's development, user modeling techniques were applied to achieve user support for more effective information retrieval. The resulting system, HYNECOSUM (see figure 1), ensures retrieval support for users with different levels of experience, adaptability and a simple way of data protection. This last phase of HYNECOSUM's development and testing has been carried out entirely at the Federal Armed Forces University in Munich.

The main idea in HYNECOSUM is to use task-hierarchies as a basis for defining "views" (analogous to database views) over the large information space and in this way to reduce the risk of users getting lost in browsing. By observing the work of users with earlier versions of the system I came to the conclusion that the users with different levels of experience organize their search in different ways. That is why I model the individual level of experience in order to support a smooth transition in the search options provided by the interface to novice-users and to expert users. In this way the interface performs a simple teaching function.

2. Characteristics of the Application

In this section I answer the questions: why browsing and not queries? Why user-adaptive support for browing? To what user features does the system adapt? I also discuss adapting the starting points for browsing to the current task, adapting the search strategy to the user's level of experience, how to model the user, and how to update the user model.

2.1 Why Browsing and not Queries?

One of the important characteristics of the application is that the users are not searching for new information, but for familiar standard forms. Actually, query-based retrieval should have been the most effective way to retrieve this kind of information. However, a query-based information system using a relational data-base (dBase) developed four years ago at the clinic was not well

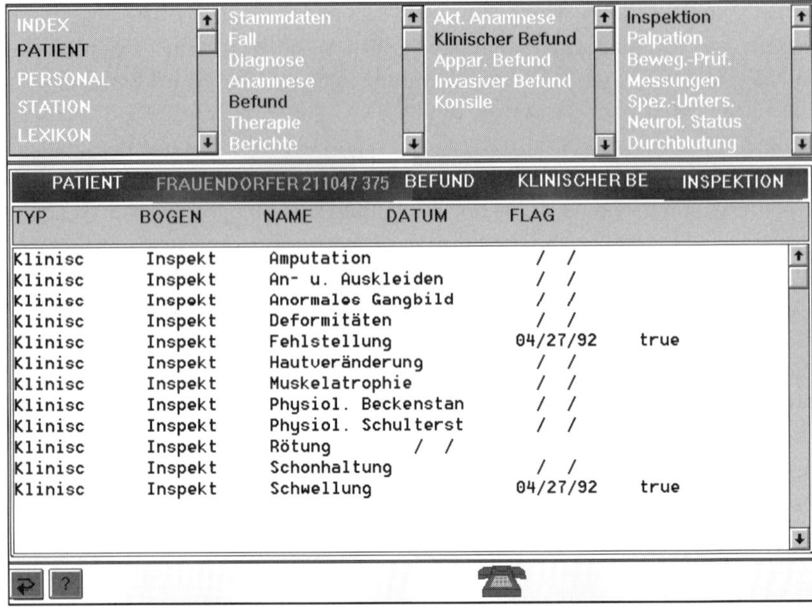

Figure 2. The semantic classification-based interface of HYNECOS.

accepted by the hospital staff and hardly ever used. One reason appears to be that personnel in hospitals typically browse paper folders of documents, they do not formulate search queries. In contrast to the dBase-version of the information system, HYNECOS supports browsing, with the advantage of using fast access-options (direct queries) provided by the underlying relational database for search by name, diagnosis, room, bed, therapy, etc. The interface between the user and the hypermedia is implemented as a set of menus corresponding to this semantic classification (see figure 2).

2.2 Why User-Adaptive Support for Browsing?

The HYNECOS interface, however, caused difficulties for the test group of inexperienced users. The reason was that they did not know how the entity[2], they were searching for had been classified and how to select the appropriate category from the menus. It became clear that the interface had to be designed in a different way to support users who were inexperienced in working with the system. That is why the most important requirement for **HYNECOSUM** was to ensure adaptation of the browsing and search options to the individual user's needs. There are three main approaches for adapting hypermedia information retrieval to the needs of the user (Brusilovsky 1996). The first one is to adapt the *presentation of the hypermedia nodes*, for example, by increasing the amount of details, adding explanations to the presentation of nodes (Böcker et al. 1990, Beaumont 1994, Boyle and Encarnacion 1994, Kobsa et al. this volume). This type of adaptation is not applied in HYNECOSUM since during the requirements analysis I did not find enough evidence that the user preferences for a specific way of presentation of information depend on their level of experience.

Another approach is to provide appropriate *starting points* for navigation. Several approaches (Böcker et al. 1990, Brusilovsky et al. 1993) use adaptive selection of starting points for navigation, depending on the user's state of knowledge, and then provide local orientation support by suggesting links which will be promising to follow (having in mind a specific goal node). In this application the approach makes sense because the number of starting points for browsing influences the cognitive load of the user and in this way can make her selection of a link harder or easier.

Restricting browsing to small portions of the hyperspace is an approach to adaptive hypermedia *navigation*. This is typical for educational hypertexts which try to focus the student's attention on a certain topic (lesson) reducing the risk that the user gets lost. The approach is also relevant for this application since limiting the browsing space for novice users can protect them from getting lost.

2.3 To What User Features Does the System Adapt?

After observing the work of the hospital staff at the outpatient's department and at one ward I found out that their interests in information were comparatively short-term and strongly dependent on their current tasks. That is why I decided that it would be advantageous to use a *task model* as a basis for user modeling and for organization of the user's interaction with the system.

Tasks are often used for representing context in office information systems (Croft 1984). In general, task-based interfaces to software systems have proven to be very effective (Rasmussen et al. 1994, Fischer 1995). In most approaches (Thompson and Croft 1989, Brajnik et al. 1990, Kok 1991, Hoppe 1992, Kaplan et al. 1993, Mathé and Chen 1996) the information obtained from the user (or the observation of her behavior) is used not only to change the indexing of information with respect to tasks, but also to infer and modify the task model in the UM. However, in the medical domain most tasks arise from scheduled meetings and activities and are therefore well defined in time and have well defined information needs. The comparatively smaller number and dynamics of the tasks distinguishes the domain of this application from other information retrieval applications. It is, therefore, justified to acquire the task model using traditional knowledge acquisition methods, like those described in (Rasmussen et al. 1994).

In contrast with tasks which are a *user group* characteristic, an important *individual user* characteristic in this application is the level of experience of the user with the system. It influences the ability of the user to locate the needed information (i.e. to find her way in the browsing space), and her search strategy.

2.4 Adapting the Starting Points for Browsing to the Current Task

Every task could be used to index the access to specific information entities needed for the completion of the task. Indexing of information with respect to the individual user's interests, goals or tasks has been investigated in numerous works on adaptive information retrieval (Belew 1986, Kok 1991, Biennier et al. 1990, Crouch et al. 1994, Mathé and Chen 1996, Thomas and Fischer 1996). All these approaches "learn" from user feedback either the goal/task model or the information needs of goals/tasks, or both. In HYNECOSUM the information needs of tasks are not "learned" by the system, but static, "hand-crafted" in advance. The reason is that in this application it is absolutely impossible to expect direct user feedback on the relevance of information to tasks in everyday work. Indirect feedback, for example, the assumption that the more time is spent on an unit, the more interesting it is (Kaplan et al. 1993), can also be unreliable since it is not clear what the user is actually doing in this time. Of course, if she spends too little time, not enough even to read the information, this is an evidence that the user was not interested in it. However, still the question remains whether the reason is that she considers this irrelevant to the goal (indexing has to be changed) or that she has changed her goal in the meantime (a new goal has to be recognized).

In this case the number of user tasks is not large. Also the relevance of information to tasks is stable and does not depend on the individual user. That is why a learning approach in this case is not justified. It is possible to index the information explicitly to the tasks in advance. Still, user feedback is the only possibility when the information space is very large, as in library applications (Crouch et al. 1994, Mathé and Chen 1996) when the set of possible user goals is virtually endless and the relevance of information to goals is varies form individual to individual.

2.5 Adapting the Search Strategy to the
User's Level of Experience

During the testing of HYNECOS and earlier prototypes of HYNECOSUM it became clear that users performing the same tasks may have different information-access strategies. For example, experienced users who had been involved in the design of HYNECOS preferred to be able to access the needed entity with a minimum of clicking and often used the direct queries to the underlying dBase. Users who had some experience, but were not experts with the semantic classification based interface of HYNECOS (shown in figure 2), occasionally complained that it takes too long clicking (through many menus) to reach the needed entity. Novice users had difficulty in *finding* the needed information. For them the optimality of search or the amount of selections was not important; they just wanted to be sure that they would find the needed information. Therefore the individual UM has to support also different ways of accessing information according to the level of experience of the individual user.

2.6 How to Model the User

Stereotypes are the most popular user modeling approaches in practice (Kay 1994) and overlay models are the most practical student modeling approaches for intelligent tutoring systems (Wenger 1987). Such a combination has been considered by many authors (Kobsa and Pohl 1994) as a good basis for user modeling. There is a clear identification of user classes in the hospital domain which is an advantage for user modeling. The different user classes perform different sets of tasks and have different rights of access to information. I decided to represent the user model in HYNECOSUM as a combination of a stereotype (the user class model, representing the typical tasks) and an overlay model (the individual model ensuring the adaptation to the user's level of experience).

2.7 How to Update the User Model

Once a UM has acquired and represented some knowledge about the user, it has to apply it in order to diagnose the current situation (task, goal, etc.) and to suggest relevant information. Other approaches inferring the user's task work under the assumption that the user is able to select correctly the information needed for her task (Croft 1984, Hoppe 1992, Micarrelli and Sciarrone 1996, Oppermann 1994b). However, the goal of the UM in this case is to support exactly the inexperienced users, who are not likely to browse systematically. Such a user would make mistakes, browse occasionally and therefore the system will draw incorrect conclusions about the user's current task from her browsing.

Far more natural is to design the interface in such a way that the users select the task they want to perform directly from a graphical representation on the screen. Because the task-taxonomy and the users' understanding of their tasks in this application are standardized, it is not obscure or unnatural for the users to state what they are doing. With respect to this feature my approach is similar to Kaplan et al. (1993) and Mathé and Chen (1996), where the user interacts with the system by designating her current task. The user in fact sees her model all the time on the screen and manipulates it directly during her interaction with the system. The advantages of this approach are transparency and a clear metaphor ensuring the user's understanding of the UM.

The individual UM must be able to recognize in the user's behavior the transition from novice to expert. The updating of the level of experience of an individual user is based on observing specific patterns in the user's behavior (selection and browsing) which are empirically found. Recently, Micarrelli and Sciarrone (1996) have also proposed a technique based on monitoring user's navigational patterns, but for inferring the user's task rather than her level of experience.

3. Architecture for User Modeling

The architecture for user modeling can be described as a three-layer structure to be added on top of the hypermedia system. The first layer contains the tasks performed by the users. They define "views" over the hypermedia and provide the main context in which a specific UM is situated. The second layer contains information about the user classes. Every user class implies a specific task hierarchy, typical for the representatives of the class. It also provides specific constraints over the rights of access to information and requirements for the form of presentation. The third layer contains the individual user models. Every individual UM contains a reference to the user-class to which the individual user belongs and additional information concerning the user's level of experience and her personal preferences with respect to the type of media.

3.1 Task Hierarchies

The typical tasks performed system users are represented as hierarchies. Every task implies specific information needs (entities). When a user is performing a more specific (closer to the leaf-level) task, she sees a limited view over the hypermedia, which is relevant to the task; moving up in the task-hierarchy, she sees wider views. The information needs of tasks located higher in the hierarchy can be defined as the sum of the information needs of their subtasks ("summary view"). An alternative is that supertasks do not provide direct access to the multimedia, but only to their sub-tasks. Only after selecting a sub-task the user gets the corresponding view to the Hypermedia. This way of defining the information needs of the super-task is called "selective view."

The observations I made with users working with the two aforementioned views showed that in this application the users' level of experience with the system determines their preferred way of viewing. Experienced users prefer a summary view, while inexperienced users prefer selective views. More-

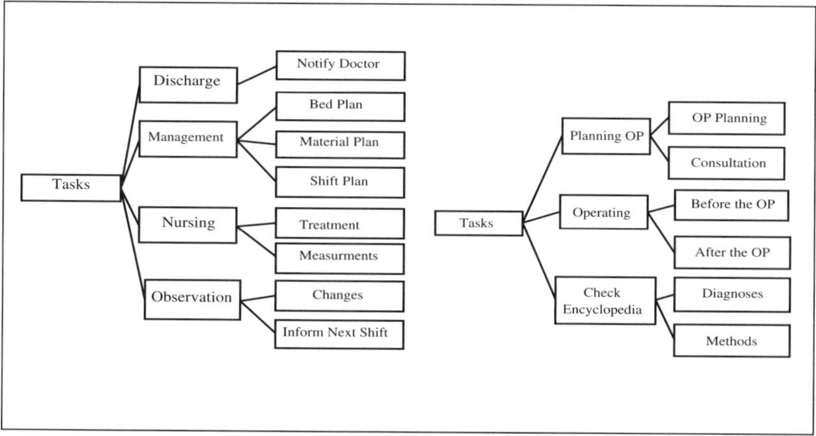

Figure 3. Two examples of task hierarchies:
A nurse and doctor at the ward.

over, it turned out that the level in the task hierarchy from which a provided summary view is comfortable for the users depends on their level of experience. As the users' experience increases, they confidently find the needed information in the summary views provided from more general tasks. That is why the level of the task-hierarchy at which the user is allowed to get a summary view provides a measure of the user's level of experience.

As a knowledge engineering process for creating the task hierarchies I used a structured interview approach. First, I made a scheme describing the main idea of a task-hierarchy and explained it to one enthusiastic user (doctor). He interpreted the scheme according to his understanding and filled it with the tasks which he typically performs and the information he needs for them. With this specific scheme as an example, I interviewed several other users, which I considered as typical representatives of user class. They filled the empty scheme with specific information corresponding to their tasks. In this way I obtained several different task-hierarchies, like the one shown in figure 3.

A task-dependent view over the hypermedia can be defined in two ways:

- "Free browsing with an anchor"—by providing links to the entities that are needed for the task and allowing the user to browse further in the hypermedia following the standard hypermedia links from these entities. In this way the task provides the starting points for browsing.

- "Restricted browsing"—by limiting browsing to the entities linked to one task. In this way the normal hypermedia links outside the view are disabled ("masked").

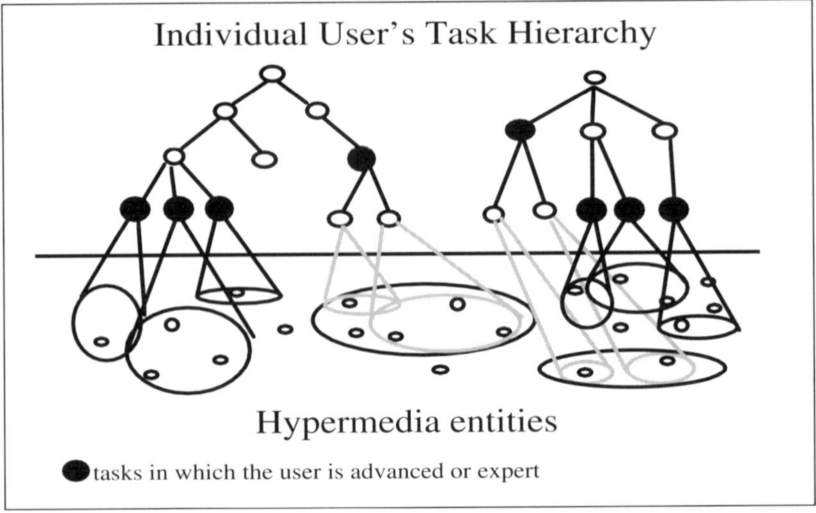

Figure 4. Task-based browsing space definition.

3.2 User Classes

For a hospital information system, the user population can be divided into several partially overlapping user-classes with different information needs, rights of access to information and form of presentation. The factors that define the user class in this case are: profession (doctor, nurse, manager, student, patient), location (outpatient's department, ward), rank (up to 5 stages depending on the profession). A user-class is characterized with a combination of the values of these factors. Every user class can be related to a different task-hierarchy.

The user class can imply also specific presentation (media) preferences. If there are several alternative media representing the same entity, one is chosen that is considered to fit best the needs of the user class. For example, a chief doctor sees a fever curve (in this way she sees the trend in the patient's state), while a nurse gets a list of all measurements (where she can input new data and precisely compare it with previous measurements). This, however, does not restrict the users to one specific presentation, since from the corresponding entity they can easily navigate to the desired multimedia representation of this entity.

3.3 Individual User Models

A user class model can be instantiated in different individual user models. Every individual UM is an overlay over the user class model, representing the user's level of experience and containing parameters which specify individual

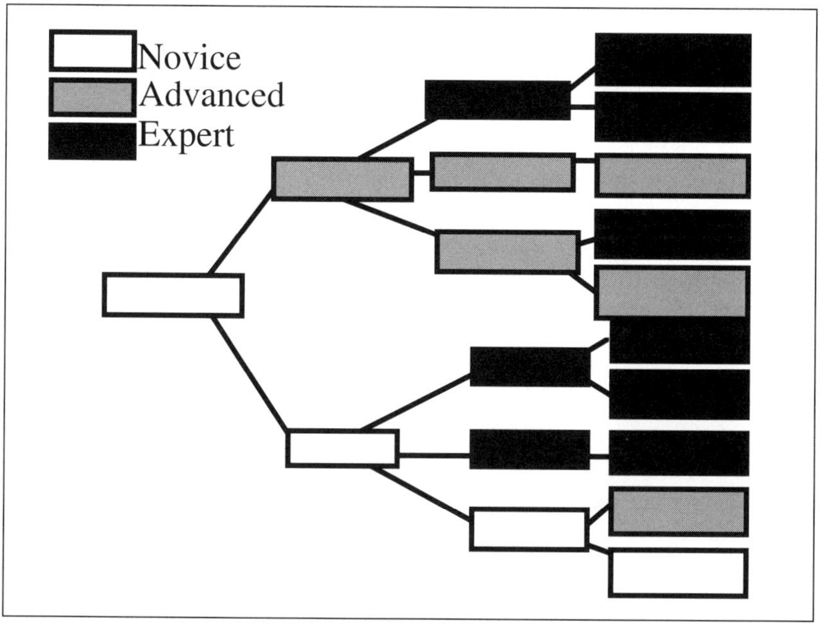

Figure 5. An individual user model: "global" level of experience.

amendments (extensions) of the task hierarchy and the preferred media.

The level of experience is defined locally for each task of the task-hierarchy and can take three values: novice, advanced or expert. The level of experience of the user on a given task defines whether she will get a "selective" or a "summary" view from this task and whether she will get a "restricted browsing" or a "free browsing" type of viewing to the hypermedia. If the user is novice on the task, she gets a "selective" view, i.e. she can only select from the sub-tasks of the current task, but has no access to the hypermedia. The user can not access the hypermedia unless her level of experience on the selected task is at least "advanced" or the task has no subtasks. If the user is advanced or expert on the task, she receives a "summary" view containing all the entities from the subtasks' views and she is free to browse in the hypermedia (i.e. she gets a "free browsing" view to the hypermedia). If the user is "novice" on the task she will get a "restrictive browsing" type of view limited to the entities needed by the current task.

I have described how the local level of experience of the user on every task defines the information context of the task by means of the size of the information space and type of view which enables or disables the possibility of browsing. One can think also of a global level of experience of a user defined across the whole task-hierarchy of the user which grows and propagates upwards through the task hierarchy. The level of experience of a parent task depends on the level of experience of its children-tasks: it is the minimum of the values of its children tasks. The assumption behind this is that the user is not able to cope with the broader view of a general task, if she is not able to cope with the subsets of this view belonging to the single sub-tasks. After some time of work with the system, regions of the user's task hierarchy appear where she is experienced. They are initially closer to the leaf-tasks (see figure 5). With the increasing experience of the user with HYNECOSUM, these regions spread up the task hierarchy towards the most general task (root-task). The global level of experience is the proportion of the tasks with advanced or expert level over the number of all tasks (79% in figure 5).

In summary, the task-based views depending on the user's level of experience provide an appropriate context for information retrieval. This is achieved by managing the size of the task-defined view of the information and the freedom of browsing. By gradually increasing the navigation space together with the user's global experience moving upwards toward the root of the task hierarchy, the user is always interacting with the system in an appropriate context.

4. Designing the Interface

The design of the interface shows the task-hierarchy of the individual user model. The user selects the most general task and then one of its sub-tasks. In this way the user moves deeper in the task hierarchy until a task with "advanced" level of experience or a leaf-task is reached and then she is provided with a menu containing all entities related to this task.

4.1 Task-based Interface Versus Logical-Classification Interface

So far, my main assumption was that the current task performed by the user provides the needed context for browsing and the only difference between experienced and novice users is their ability to cope with wider browsing spaces. However, the differences between the information needs of a novice and an expert concern not only the size of the browsing space, but also the organization of browsing. Users with higher level of experience are more inclined than novice users to browse freely in the hypermedia. Sometimes they switch entirely to a browsing strategy, which is by no means the fastest way to obtain the information. I offer two possible explanations for this:

- The growing confidence of users in their ability to cope with the system pushes them to explore other ways of obtaining the information
- The user is not willing to switch the context of their current task for a small "jump" in the hypermedia

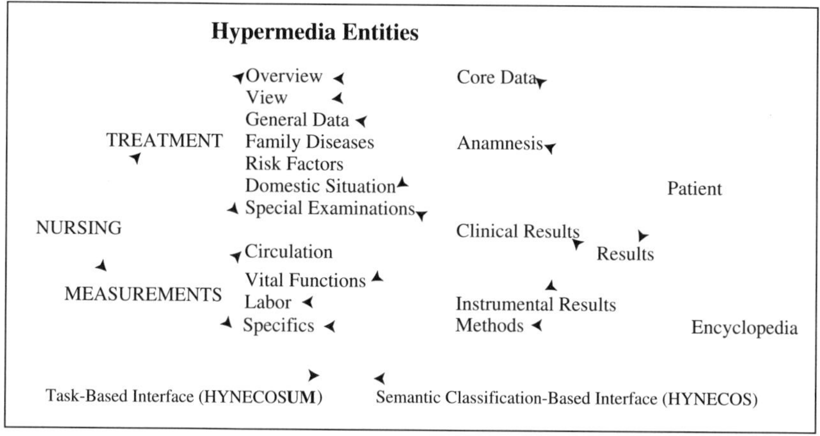

Figure 6. The two types of interfaces to hypermedia entities .

Though the information needs of the users in this application domain are triggered in most of the cases by the standard tasks they are performing, there are cases when users approach the system with a different goal or attitude. For example, while performing the task "Treatment" (see figures 3 and 6), the nurse suddenly wants to know something not directly related with the current task—the amount of a certain type of drug in the storage of the station. Instead of selecting another task—"Management" she tries to find the entity "Materials" by browsing from the current entity (let's say, "Overview"). However, finding the entity "Materials" via browsing in this case is nearly hopeless.

In this case it is more convenient and efficient to use the logical classification interface to find the data, i.e. the original HYNECOS interface. The knowledge of the logical classification of the data is not necessarily related to experience in working with the system. However, the need for alternative search strategies becomes greater with the growing experience (practice and confidence) of the user. Novice users sometimes also approach the system with a goal which differs from their current task. However, in most of the cases they do not dare start a direct browsing search, but try to find in their task hierarchy a task providing them with a view to the needed information. With the growth of their experience they feel encouraged to search for information by browsing directly in the hypermedia, which usually is inefficient. In summary, the task-based interface corresponds to a way of indexing information which is orthogonal to the indexing provided by the semantic classification based interface of HYNECOS (see figure 6). For a user who is searching for a given information out of the context of the specified task, it is easier to use the HYNECOS interface. For a user who approaches with a specific task, it is better to use the task-based interface.

4.2 Experience-based Transition to a Different Search Strategy

In order to help the user to learn how to employ the alternative access strategies, the UM supports a simple teaching facility for novices. In parallel with their increasing level of experience, it provides the users with the opportunity to search with the semantic classification-based interface. It consists of presenting in parallel two alternative interfaces corresponding to the two different access strategies: a graphical representation of the task hierarchy where the user can select the task she wants to perform, and four hierarchically organized menus corresponding to the semantic classification of entities (compare with the original HYNECOS interface in figure 2). For a novice user only the task-based interface is available for selection. However, when an entity is selected from the "Select" (*in German* "Auswahl") window (see figure 8), the HYNECOS menus in the top part of the screen show how this entity is semantically classified by highlighting the corresponding menu items. As users increase in experience level, they are allowed to use the semantic classification-based interface of HYNECOS.

With the growing level of experience of the user, two things happen. First, the HYNECOS menus on the top are progressively enabled for selection. Second, the user gets wider views from higher level tasks, i.e. longer choice of entities in the rightmost menu. This makes the access to the data more direct, but ergonomically more laborious (since the menu-windows have a fixed size, and one has to scroll to select the needed entity). However, the user can reduce dramatically the choice by selecting the logical type of the entity from the standard HYNECOS menus which have now been enabled. At any time the user can select either as before directly from the "Select" menu, or by using the menus corresponding to the logical classification of the entities. If she has difficulty with either of these two options, she can still select a more specific task from the task hierarchy and retrieve a small, more familiar view.

5. Adaptation and Adaptability

Adaptation is a notion referring to the ability of the system to change dynamically according to the changing user's needs (not only with respect to the tasks) in order continually to maintain the appropriate context for interaction (Kuehme 1993). Because one of the most important time-dependent factors is the user's experience (Norcio and Stanley 1989), the system must have means for finding out and reacting to the changes in the user's level of expe-

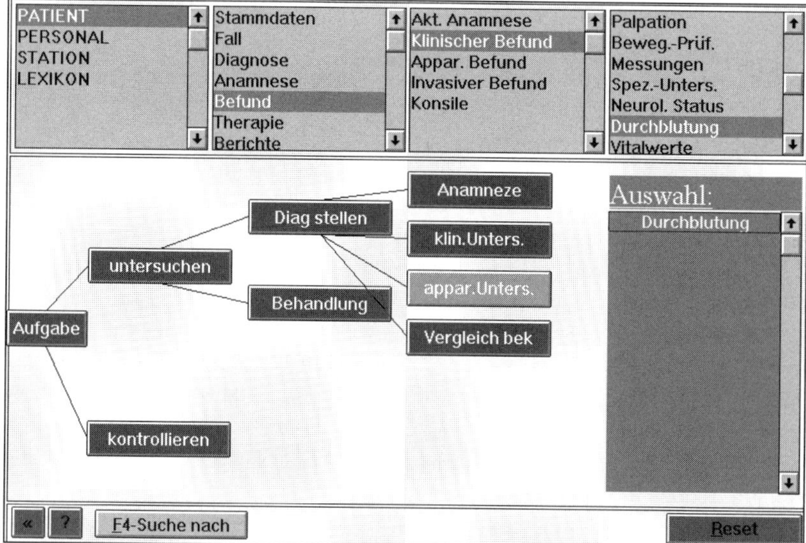

Figure 7. Alternative search strategies in the HYNECOSUM interface.

The user is a doctor at the outpatient's department and novice at the current task "appar.Unters." (Instrumental examinations). The semantic classification menus in the upper part of the screen are not available for selection, but they show how the selected entity from the task-view is classified. Direct search options (button F4 in the lower part of the screen) are currently unavailable (dimmed).

rience. The user's navigation actions are recorded and if patterns are found which imply that the user's proficiency has increased, a flag is set indicating that it seems appropriate to increase the user's recorded level of experience. For example, (see figure 7) if the user navigates down the task hierarchy, selects the task "appar.Unters" (Instrumental Examinations), selects the corresponding entity "Durchblutung" (Circulation), but then immediately (without spending any time to read the contents) clicks on the upper task button "Diag.stellen" (Diagnose), this is a sign that either the user wants to get access to more starting points for browsing (the higher-level task view) or that she is searching for a specific entity without having a specific task in mind. In both cases this means that the user feels more confident in browsing and therefore this leads to increasing the score of the current task.

Increasing the level of experience on the task is suggested by the system after the task score has exceeded a certain threshold. This happens after some period of "good behavior," e.g. selection of a sub-task, then selection of one or more entities from "Select-menu" (not searching too wildly in the hypermedia) and being able to return without using the "Help," "<<" (Back) or "Reset" buttons.

One "symptom" that the user's actual experience on a certain task is lower than the recorded level of experience is that she does not use the provided wider view, but prefers to click on one the sub-tasks and shrink the choice. For example, if the current level of experience of the task "Diag.stellen" (Diagnose) is advanced, the user will get in the "Select-menu" a direct access to all the entities relevant for all four sub-tasks (see figure 7). However, if the user always clicks on the buttons of the subtasks instead of selecting directly from the longer list of entities provided in the task view, this means that it is still too difficult for the user to cope with the choice at this level and therefore she is "punished" by subtracting points from the task-score. Of course, the use of the subtasks to shrink the view might have another explanation: selecting from a too long "Select" menu could be ergonomically inconvenient. The "Select" window has a fixed size and if the task-view involves many entities, one has to scroll to select the needed one. However, in this case the user is supposed to use the semantic classification menus to additionally reduce the choice by selecting the logical type of the entity from the standard HYNECOS menus on the top of the screen which are enabled for her since she is "advanced" at the task. Correct selection from these menus is „rewarded" by adding points to the current task-score. Also the correct/incorrect use of the direct access option ("F4" button) is taken into account. Another significant pattern of behavior is chaotic hypermedia browsing terminating with emergency buttons. "Chaotic" means browsing without coming back to the starting entities (in the "Select-menu") related to the current the task. Use of "Help," "Reset," and "Back" buttons are also "punished" by subtracting points from the current task's score. Once the user is allowed to use the HYNECOS-menus (in the top of the screen), i.e. she is "advanced" at the current task, her way of selecting is taken into account to increase or decrease the task-score. Incorrect selections e.g. selecting dimmed items from the menus, or selecting an already selected item, are punished and may lead to changing the level of experience back to "Novice."

Strongly adaptive systems, however, threaten with a loss of control, and it is difficult for their users to develop coherent models of them (Fischer 1992). A system that is constantly adapting, even if this is supposed to be happening for their own benefit, makes users feel uncomfortable and decreases their confidence. I observed this effect too when the users were working after adaptation has taken place in the user model: the unexpected change in the entities seemed to disturb them more than to help. However, after explaining them the reason and what is actually affected by the change, the users accepted it positively. I believe the policy usually applied in connection with new software releases (which are announced in advance) is accepted by users much better—they need to know what exactly is going to be changed in the system and why. In the medical domain it is sometimes of vital importance to access data quickly; the users therefore want to be able to have absolute confidence in their system. That is why I decided that the system's adaptation to the user's needs has to be carried out not continuously, but at discrete points in time, and only after the user has given specific permission.

When there is evidence that the user's recorded level of experience can be changed, the system does it only after obtaining the user's consent. In this way the system goes along the strategy of adaptively supported adaptability (Oppermann 1994a): supporting the user's adaptation of the system by initial adaptive suggestions showing the rationale for the adaptations and the way of performing them.

Data is collected about the types of media that are retrieved particularly often by the user in order to model the media-preferences of individual users. After a threshold has been exceeded, the user is asked whether she really prefers the type of representation in question. On the basis of her answer, the parameters of her individual preferences are updated.

User-adaptable systems support users in modifying systems according to their own needs (Fischer 1992). My architecture for user modeling enables the users to adapt their individual model in the following ways:

- Defining a task hierarchy through cutting and pasting from a task-library
- Defining new tasks and linking them to existing task aggregates using a specialized task-editor
- Selecting the style of viewing from each task
- Changing the recorded level of experience on each task
- Changing the media preferences in the individual user model

While the availability of tools for adaptation enables creation of highly individualized views, the users have been quite reluctant to use the adaptability tools.

6. Evaluation

My evaluation goal was to see whether the task-based interface of HYNECOSUM provides a better environment for the novice user than the semantic classification-based interface of HYNECOS. The same task was assigned to two groups each including five novice users of the same class: the first group used HYNECOSUM with the task-based interface and the other group used HYNECOS with the semantic classification interface. A task which requires mere input of data was selected, in order to minimize the extraneous influence. The task required access to eleven entities. The participants of each group had to perform the task four times, with data prepared in advance, so that they could perform the task entirely on the computer. Time for accomplishing the task was limited to 15 minutes.

	TB	SCB	TB	SCB	TB	SCB	TB	SCB
Avg. total time task completion	13.3' n=4	>max.	11.2' n=5	15.0' n =1	9.8' n=5	12.2' n=2	8.0' n=5	9.3' n=2
Number of subj. who succeeded	4	0	5	1	5	2	5	2
Avg. time for finding a task-related entity	16'' n=5	12.8' n=5	11'' n=5	10.4' n=5	8'' n=5	7.8' n=5	6'' n=5	7.2' n=5

Table 1. Task-based (TB) versus semantic-classification based (SCB) interfaces. Times are given in min.(') and sec.(''); n = the number of participants for which averages are calculated.

There was no possibility of using external help or manuals.

Overall time and success data (see table 1 and figures 8a and 8b) showed that the task-based interface of HYNECOSUM provided a better environment for novices. All five HYNECOSUM participants managed to complete the task in the assigned time in the second, third and fourth sessions (see figure 8a). Only one participant failed to complete the task in the first session and the reason was that she took too long typing in the data once she had accessed the corresponding entity. In contrast, all five participants working with the semantic classification interface of HYNECOS failed in the first session and only two participants completed the task in the third and fourth session. These two participants achieved an average task completion time similar to the one of the first group. However, they spent *longer time finding* the task-relevant entities than the first group and comparatively *less time in actually working* with the entities, i.e. typing in the data. The third row of the table (presented in figure 8b) shows that the average time (for all attempts made by all participants) to access the task-relevant entities differs dramatically in the two groups while the participants of the task-based interface needed seconds (from 16 down to 6), the participants of the semantic classification-based interface needed minutes (from 13 down to 7)! This can be explained by the more complex cognitive task which the participants of the semantic classification interface have to cope with: they have not only to find their way through the different classes of entities, but also to remem-ber which entities are relevant for completing the task. In summary, this test showed that the task-based interface ensures a higher effectiveness (speed of finding the needed information) than the semantic classification interface.

In order to test whether the different access strategies were really used and whether they satisfied the anticipated needs of users with different levels of experience, I performed a test with a group of participants who could select freely among different strategies. The test involved 7 experienced partici-

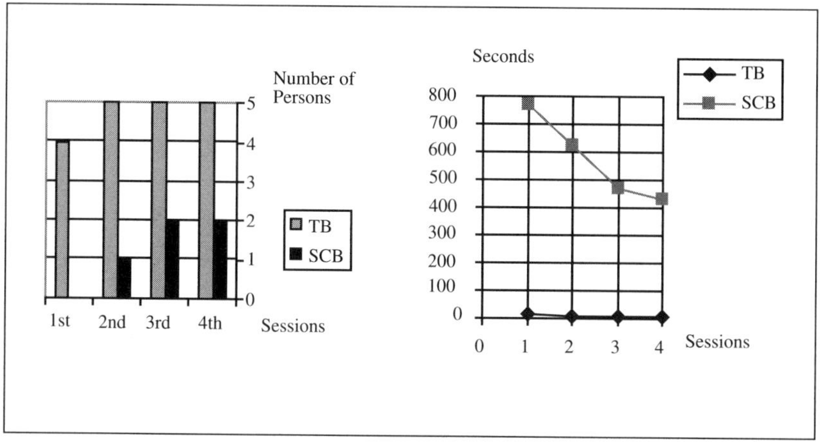

Figure 8 (a—left). Number of persons who succeeded in task-completion / session (b—right). Average time for finding a task-related entity (across all attempts).

pants (with global level of experience more than 70% advanced or expert) from different user classes. Their actions were monitored and recorded. At every information access, the user's current task was automatically recorded (when the participant was working with the task-based interface) and the participant had to say aloud what she was doing. The average (across tasks) usage of different access strategies and their combinations with respect to the user's level of experience on the task are shown in table 2.

The results for tasks in which the user is "advanced" showed that the task-based access strategy was the most popular. This is not surprising: the "advanced" users are bound to use the task-based interface as a basic mode of access since the semantic classification interface and direct query strategies are only available in the context of the current task. A more interesting result is that advanced participants preferred (in 62% versus 25% of the cases) to keep to the restricted-browsing. Advanced users could choose between restricted and free browsing type of view. Their conservatism with respect to the type of viewing could be explained with the suggestion that most of them did not feel a need to browse the hypermedia, since they had all needed entities in the task-views. This suggestion was partially confirmed by the interviews and observations.

The results in the second row of the table (visualized in figure 9) show that most of the users (29%) still prefer to perform task-based access even from tasks where they are experts. However, nearly as often, the participants were combining the task-based access with the semantic classification-based access (23%) and with direct queries (18%). A significant number of participants (all in all 21%) were applying the semantic classification and/or the di-

Interface:	TB	SC	DQ	TB + SC	SC + DQ	TB + DQ	TB+ SC+ DQ
Experience at task:	RB I FB			RB I FB		RB I FB	RB I FB
Advanced	87%	—	—	12%	—	—	1%
	62 I 25%			8% I 4%			— I 1%
Expert	29%	10 %	5 %	23 %	8%	7%	18%
	10 I 19%			1% I 22%		— I 7%	— I 18%

Table 2. Access strategy usage by experience (in % of all entity accesses).
TB=task-based, SC=semantic classification based, DQ=direct query,
RB=restricted browsing, FB=free browsing.

rect query strategies i.e. were using only the options of the original HYNECOS interface. This suggests that expert users do not distinguish between the search strategies but use them freely as alternative routes to information according to the specific situation. This shows that the teaching function of the system has worked well.

7. Conclusions

My approach for media retrieval is quite standard (a-priori, static, content-based indexing) and therefore I do not believe that it contributes to solving the deep problems of content-based image, video and audio retrieval (addressed in sections 1 through 4 of this book). The contribution of the chapter has to be seen in combining various techniques or user modeling and interface design to support the user in *achieving more effective* information retrieval. User Modeling has been applied to solve a problem in an industrial application for information retrieval form large hypermedia documentation system. I have developed an interface based on user modeling and focusing on the tasks performed by the users. It has the following features:

- Provides a task-based context for information retrieval which leads to higher efficiency in document retrieval
- Supports novice users by ensuring a smaller browsing space, while providing to experienced users a larger browsing space and alternative access (search) options
- Provides adaptivity with respect to the individual user's level of experience and only after asking the user and provides tools for adaptability
- Provides a simple teaching function to support the user's learning of alternative search strategies
- The user model is transparent and the user directly manipulates it during interaction with the system

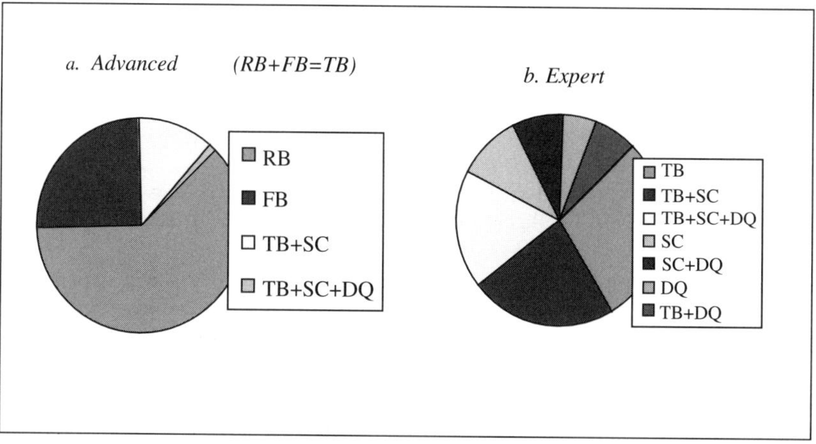

Figure 9. Use of search strategies by expertise in task. (a—left): advanced user (RB+FB=TB). (b—right): expert user.

The evaluation of HYNECOSUM showed that it ensures a higher effectiveness in information access by supporting users with different levels of experience in their browsing and use of different search strategies. This approach is applicable in domains where information retrieval can be related with relatively stable hierarchical task-models, and users are searching for familiar types of information, for example, large, networked office hypermedia-based information systems.

Notes

1. This is a revised and considerably updated version of Vassileva (1994).

2. By "entity" I mean an elementary data type. Following the terminology adopted in Hypertext Design Model (HDM), an entity corresponds to the name of a column in a record in a relational database, i.e. a feature shared by a set of records. For example, the entity "diagnosis" is present in the records of all patients.

References

Beaumont, I. 1994. User Modeling in the Interactive Anatomy Tutoring System ANATOM-TUTOR. *User Modeling and User Adapted Interaction* 4(1): 21-45.

Belew, R. K. 1986. Adaptive Information Retrieval: Machine Learning in Associative Networks. Ph.D. diss., Dept. of Computer and Communication Sciences, University of Michigan, Ann Arbour.

Biennier, F.; Guivarch, M. and Pinon, J.-M. 1990. Browsing in Hyperdocuments with the Assistance of a Neural Network. In *Hypertext: Concepts, Systems and Applications,* eds. Rizk, A. N. Streitz, and J. André, 288–297. Cambridge: Cambridge University Press.

Böcker H. D.; Hohl, H. and Schwab, T. 1990. HYPADAPTER - Individualizing Hypertext. In Proceedings of the Third International Conference of Human Computer Interaction (INTERACT '90), eds. D. Diaper, D. Gilmore, G. Cockton, and Shackel, 931-936. Amsterdam: North-Holland.

Boyle, C. and Encarnacion, A. 1994. MetaDoc: An Adaptive Hypertext Reading System. *User Modeling and User Adapted Interaction* 4(1): 1-19.

Brajnik G.; Guida, G.; Tasso, C. 1990. User Modeling in Expert Man-Machine Interfaces: A Case Study in Intelligent Information Retrieval. *IEEE Transactions on Systems, Man, and Cybernetics* 20(1): 166-185.

Brusilovsky, P.; Pesin, L. and Zyryanov, M. 1993. Towards An Adaptive Hypermedia Component for an Intelligent Learning Environment. In Bass L., J. Gornostaev and C. Unger, eds. *Human Computer Interaction. Lecture Notes in Computer Science No. 753:* 348-358. Berlin: Springer Verlag.

Brusilovsky, P. 1996. Methods and Techniques of Adaptive Hypermedia. *User Modeling and User Adapted Interaction.* 6(2-3): 87-129.

Conklin, J. 1987. Hypertext: An Introduction and Survey. IEEE Computer 20: 17-41.

Croft, B. 1984. The Role of Content and Adaptation in User Interfaces. *International Journal of Man-Machine Studies* 21: 283-292.

Crouch, C.; Crouch, D. and Nareddy, K. 1994. Associative and Adaptive Retrieval in a Connectionist System. *International Journal of Expert Systems* 7 (2): 193-202.

Fischer, G. 1992. Shared Knowledge in Cooperative Problem Solving Systems: Integrating Adaptive and Adaptable Systems. Proceedings UM'92: Third International Conference on User Modeling, 148-161, Dagstuhl, Germany.

Fischer, G. 1995. New Perspectives on Working, Learning and Collaborating and Computational Artifacts in Their Support. In H.-D. Böcker, ed. *Proceedings Software-Ergonomie '95,* 21–41. Stuttgart: Teuber Verlag.

Grazotto, F.; Paolini, P.; and Schwabe, D. 1991. HDM - a Model for the Design of Hypertext Applications. In Proceedings Hypertext '91, 313-328. San Antonio, Texas, ACM Press.

Hoppe, H. 1992. Towards Task Models for Embedded Information Retrieval. in Proceedings CHI'92: 173-180. New York: ACM.

Kaplan, C.; Fenwick, J.; and Chen, J. 1993. Adaptive Hypertext Navigation Based on User Goals and Context. *User Modeling and User-Adapted Interaction* 3 (3): 193-220.

Kay J. 1994. Lies, Damned Lies and Stereotypes: Pragmatic Approximations Of Users. Proceedings of UM'94. 4th International Conference on User Modeling: 175-184. Hyannis. MA.

Kobsa, A. and Pohl, W. 1994. Workshop on Adaptivity and User Modeling in Interactive Software Systems. *User Modeling and User-Adapted Interaction* 3 (4): 359-367.

Kobsa, A.; Nill, A. and Fink, J. 1997. Hypertext and Hypermedia Clients of the User Modeling System BGP-MS. In this volume.

Kok, A. 1991. A Formal Approach to User Modeling in Data-Retrieval. *International Journal of Man-Machine Studies* 35: 675-693.

Kuehme T. 1993. User-Centered Approach To Adaptive Interfaces. *Knowledge-Based Systems* 6(4): 239-248.

Mathé, N. and J. Chen 1996. User-Driven and Context-Based Adaptive Information

Access. *User Modeling and User Adapted Interaction*. 6(2-3): 225-261.

Micarrelli, A. and Sciarrone, F. 1996. A Case-based Toolbox for Guided Hypermedia Navigation. Proceedings UM'96. Fifth International Conference on User Modeling, 129-136. Hawaii.

Norcio, A. and Stanley, J. 1989. Adaptive HCI: A Literature Survey and Perspectives. *IEEE Transactions on Systems, Man and Cybernetic*s 19 (2): 399-408.

Oppermann, R. 1994a. Adaptively Supported Adaptability. *International Journal of Human-Computer Studies*. 40: 455-472.

Oppermann, R. 1994b. *Adaptive User Support*. Hillsdale. NJ: Lawrence Erlbaum Assoc.

Rasmussen, J.; Pejtersen, A. and Goodstein, L. 1994. *Cognitive Systems Engineering*. New York: John Wiley and Sons.

Thomas, C. and Fischer, G. 1996. Using Agents to Improve the Usability and Usefulness of the World-Wide Web. Proceedings UM'96. Fifth International Conference on User Modeling, 5-13. Hawaii.

Thompson, R. H. and Croft, W. B. 1989. Support for Browsing in an Intelligent Text Retrieval System. *International Journal of Man-Machine Studies* 30: 639-668.

Vassileva, J. 1994. A Practical Architecture for User Modeling in a Hypermedia-Based Information System. Proceedings UM'94. Fourth International Conference on User Modeling, 115-120. Hyannis, MA.

Wenger, E. 1987. *Artificial Intelligence and Tutoring Systems*. Los Altos: Morgan Kaufmann.

Chapter 19

Explorations in an Environment for Natural Language Multimodal Information Access

Oliviero Stock, Carlo Strapparava, and Massimo Zancanaro
Istituto per la Ricerca Scientifica e Tecnologica (IRST)

Abstract

This chapter addresses the problem of communication with a multimodal system for information access and exploration, in which communication integrates things other than words, and tries to give a unified and concrete, albeit simplified and limited, working solution for information access dialogues. Communicative acts in multimodal interaction are discussed and the concept of felicity conditions for such a situation is introduced. Felicity conditions make use of the attentional state, considered the most relevant element to model the context of the communicative act. References are made to examples of interaction with ALFRESCO, a working prototype in the art domain.

1. Introduction

This chapter presents a perspective different from the traditional approach to interfaces for information retrieval (IR) systems. It tries to close the gap between user attitudes and needs, on the one hand, and the specific retrieval engines on the other (see also Stein et al., this volume). The emphasis is on flexibility in interaction, information exploration and presentation, all exploiting the multimedia environment.

In multimodal interaction systems (Maybury 1993a) interactivity can mean something that goes beyond what a person is used to in nature: on the one hand the possibility of the computer using different communication media, such as graphics, images, written or synthesized language etc. in a fast and coordinated way extends conceptually the bandwidth of communication toward the person. Quite elaborate theories and prototypes have been proposed for multimodal output (e.g., Wahlster et al. 1992; Wahlster et al. 1993; Maybury, 1993b; Arens et al., 1993; Feiner and McKeown, 1990). On the other hand the possibility of the person directly manipulating entities in combination with language opens new perspectives for human computer interaction (Cohen et al. 1989). We address the problem of communication with a multimodal system, in which communication integrates things other than words, and try to give a unified and concrete, albeit simplified and limited, working solution for information access dialogues.

In a world inhabited by a multitude of available multimedia information travelling on superhighways or stand alone multimedia workstations, content-based indexing is more complex, and certainly of high importance: the chapters by Hauptmann and Witbrock (this volume) and Mani et al. (this volume), for instance, generalize IR methodologies to the multimedia setting, with interesting results. Focusing on users, we believe that exploration of an information space will become more and more the typical interactive attitude. This is the case when language and image-based interaction are integrated with a hypertext capability and when the space of interaction is extended by exploiting the screen functionality for metacommunication. The latter two features are characteristic of the ALFRESCO interactive system and in general of the context of our work (Stock and Team 1993, Zancanaro et al. 1993).

In the next section, we discuss the relation between information retrieval and multimodal dialogues. Then, after a brief review of the ALFRESCO system, we report new developments introduced for communication management. Some notes on evaluation are given before the conclusions.

2. Information Retrieval Interfaces and Multimodal Dialogue

The IR problem has two faces: on one hand it is system-centered, concerned with document (or, more generally, information) indexing while, on the other hand, it is user-centered, concerned with retrieving information relevant for the user. In this chapter, we deal mainly with the user-centered part.

Information needs have been characterized in the IR literature as *verificative needs, conscious topical needs* and *muddled topical needs* (Ingwersen 1992). Passing through a formal interrogation language may be problematic in general, but almost desperate in the last case. Traditionally, query reformulation is used to bring flexibility through iteration. In our approach we take into consideration the dynamic nature of information needs during the interaction.

We face this problem exploiting the metaphor of exploration of a space. Exploring a place means "travelling" to a place you do not yet know, finding out what it is like. Navigating, instead, means working out which direction to go while you are travelling. With the term browsing we mean the process of looking at several things in a casual way, in hope of finding something interesting with no definite target in mind. Following Watherworth and Chignell (1991), there are at least two dimensions for a model of information exploration: structural responsibility and target orientation.

Structural responsibility involves the issue of which agent (i.e. the user or the system) is responsible for carrying out search and for giving structure to information. It gives rise to a dichotomy between navigational and mediated exploration. Navigation is unstructured from the system's point of view; it is the user that gives it structure.

The dimension of target orientation presents a dichotomy between browsing and querying. Browsing is distinguished from querying by the absence of a definite target in the mind of the user. This distinction is determined only by the cognitive state of the user, not by her actions nor by the configuration of the system. In reality there is a continuum of user behaviors varying between querying and browsing. Figure 1 depicts a diagram of this situation, positioning in it traditional question-answering systems and hypertext systems. Some hypertext systems also offer some kind of searching allowing the users to switch to the query state of the target orientation dimension. Also some traditional question-answering systems allow a shift along the target orientation dimension, for instance allowing some kind of "apropos" command.

Our aim is to propose an environment in which interaction moves smoothly along the two dimensions. Dialogue management guarantees communicative action coordination (i.e. proper media usage) and suggests the user shifts along the structural responsibility dimension. The use of natural language allows a more natural way of restricting the search interactively. In section 5.1, we present a model of dialogue structure based on the notion of focus of attention and on different ways of following-up a preceding communicative exchange. In this sense, using natural language is more effective than simply replacing a formal language with a more intuitive tool.

Also, natural language allows moving along the target orientation dimension when the structural responsibility is mediated. For example, instead of querying something like "apropos Siena," the user may ask "tell me something about Siena." In our system, a text describing the town of Siena is generated and linked to an underlying hypertext (see section 3). Now, if the user is in the query state of the target orientation dimension she can smoothly move along the structural responsibility dimension. In the same way, she can exploit the hypertext links to explore the surroundings, and then come back

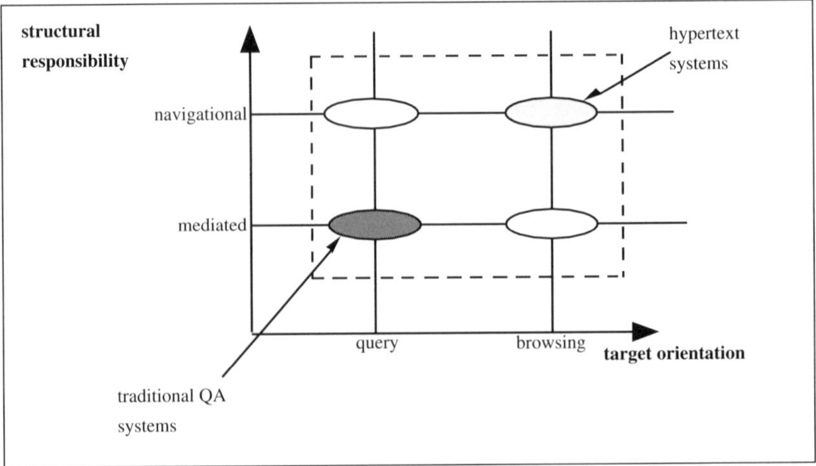

Figure 1. (adapted from Watherworth and Chignell 1991).

to natural language querying as soon as she needs to, thus moving along the target orientation dimension.

3. A Brief Account of ALFRESCO

ALFRESCO (Stock and Team 1993) is an interactive, natural-language centered system for a user interested in frescoes and paintings, with the aim not only of providing information, but also of promoting other masterpieces that may attract the user. It runs on a workstation connected to a videodisc unit and a touch screen. The particular videodisk in use includes images of Fourteenth Century Italian frescoes and monuments. The system knowledge sources (see figure 2) include a knowledge base (defining everything the system can reason about), a database of images and videoclips (on the videodisk), and an hypermedia network. The system, besides understanding and using language, integrates it with hypermedia both in input and output. The user can interact with the system by typing a sentence, navigating in the underlying hypertext, and using the touch screen. In input, our efforts have been focused on combining the interpretation of linguistic deictic references with pointing to images displayed on a touch screen. In output, images and generated text with buttons offer entry points for further hypertext exploration.

The generator is supposed to intervene during a dialogue in which the user is interested in obtaining some detailed information. The output of the generator includes hypertext entry points to an underlying preexisting hypermedia

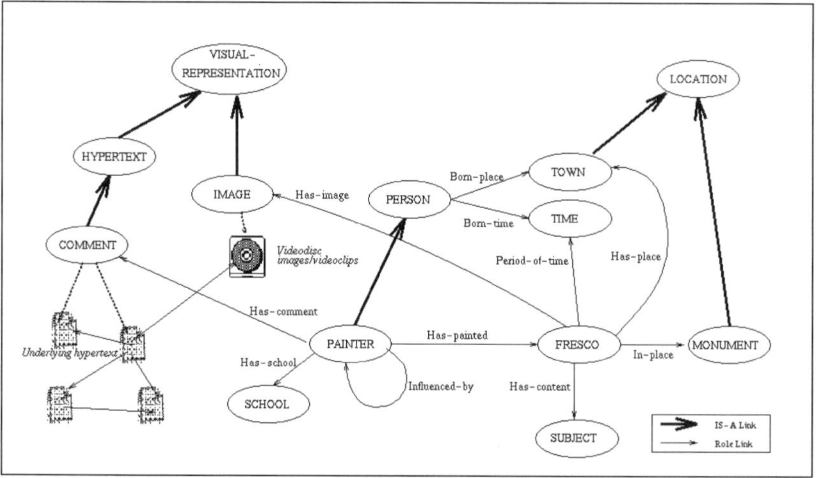

Figure 2. Some elements in ALFRESCO *knowledge sources,*
This is a simplified fragment of the terminolgical box of the ALFRESCO *KB.*
It includes about 250 generic concepts and 200 relations.
Some domain concepts are linked to a media/ representation taxonomy.
The system dynamically selects the most appropriate presentation (see section 4.3).

network. It is concerned with what some art critics say about masterpieces, painters and schools (the static part of the hypertext), and includes links to fresco images and videoclips. The result is a text generated from the knowledge base, tailored for particular user interests, as inferred by the system in the course of the dialogue. Following the links the user can explore the "surroundings" of the focus of her attention. Use of (in our case personalized) text for accessing information presented through diverse media was proven effective in empirical studies (see Sutcliffe et al., this volume).

Fourteenth century frescoes have a content that is almost always centered on a "sacred scene." The scene includes an event that can be reasonably well described (for instance the event "making an announcement" with actor the angel Gabriel and patient Mary, where the content of the message is another event, namely the forthcoming birth of Jesus) and includes a number of well identified recurring characters: humans, animals, saints, angels, etc. The content actually represented is the foreground of the paintings, while nothing is said about the background in which the artist could have expressed any real world scene.

Let us follow an example of an actual interaction with ALFRESCO. The user asks: "Speak to me about Ambrogio Lorenzetti" (see figure 3). ALFRESCO answers producing a generated text with buttons in a hypertext card. A generated text with buttons can be seen as an implicit negotiation. The sys-

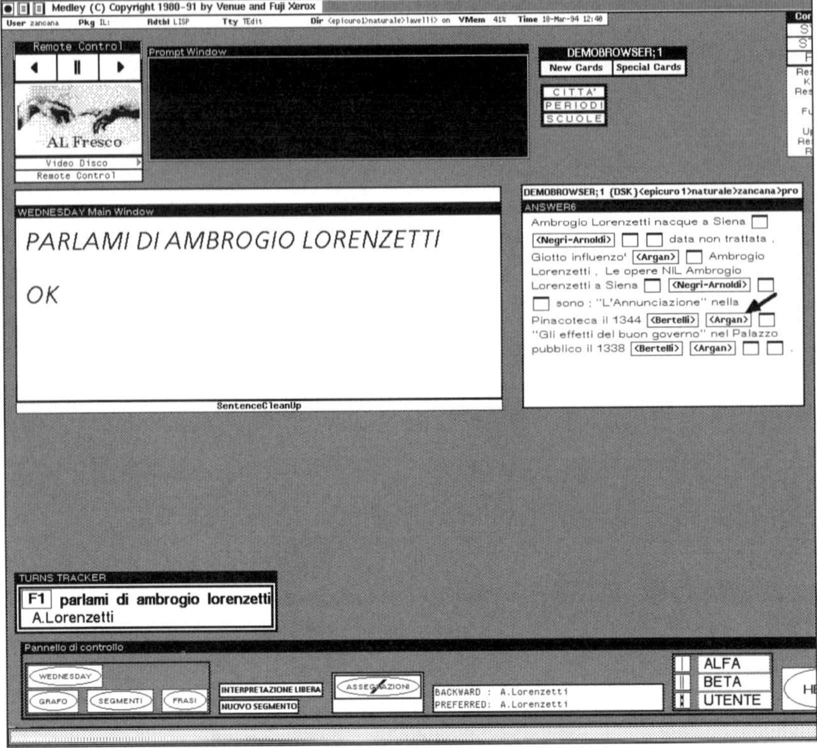

Figure 3. Natural language query (left) and hypertext response (right).

tem proposes the responsibility to the user, but the final decision is left to the user herself: she can choose whether to shift from a mediated to a navigational browsing or not. Let us suppose the user wants to see a comment by Argan (a famous art critic) about the "Annunciation" (a fresco by Lorenzetti) and she clicks on the <Argan> button. The user starts a hypertext navigation.

Once the user has chosen to follow a hypertext link she takes the responsibility of giving structure to information on her own. The system maintains awareness of the changes in the context of the communication: so the user is free to give back the responsibility to the system whenever she wants. In figure 4, the system displays Argan's comment about the "Annunciation." After having read it, the user may want to see the fresco and clicks on the first button of the card. The touchscreen now is displaying the "Annunciation" by Ambrogio Lorenzetti.

A complex nonlinguistic exchange, starting with a clicking act on a hypertext button has taken place which links the subsequent linguistic question to

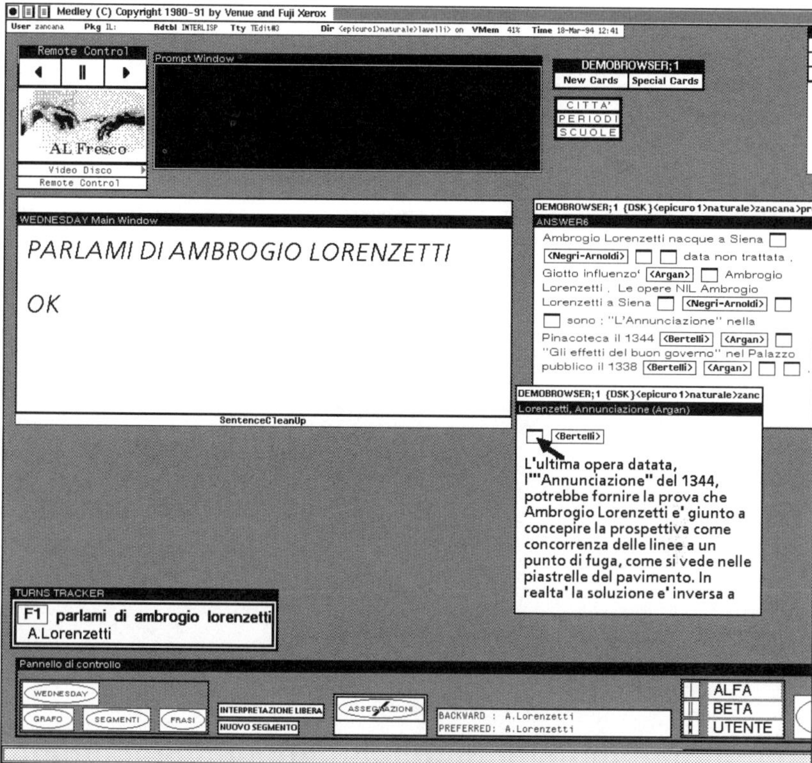

Figure 4. Argan's critique of the "annunciation."

the preceding one. In figure 5 the user switches from hypertext navigation to a NL query and asks: "Who is this ^ person?" touching a character on the fresco (on the touch-screen not represented in the figure). The system answers "Madonna." Querying the system in NL the user is now giving the responsibility back to the system. The system is aware that on the touchscreen the Annunciation is now shown, even if displaying it was not its responsibility. Then the user comes back to the generated hypertext, assuming the responsibility once again, and clicks a button to see "Gli Effetti del Buon Governo" (The Effects of Good Government), another famous fresco painted by Lorenzetti. The touch-screen is now displaying this fresco. "Gli Effetti del Buon Governo" is a large fresco representing scenes from everyday life in a town. Finally (figure 6) the user comes back to a NL query and asks: "What is the town?" "Siena" is the answer from ALFRESCO. Let us note that the new picture on the touchscreen is essential to give sense to the question (the Annunciation does not include a town).

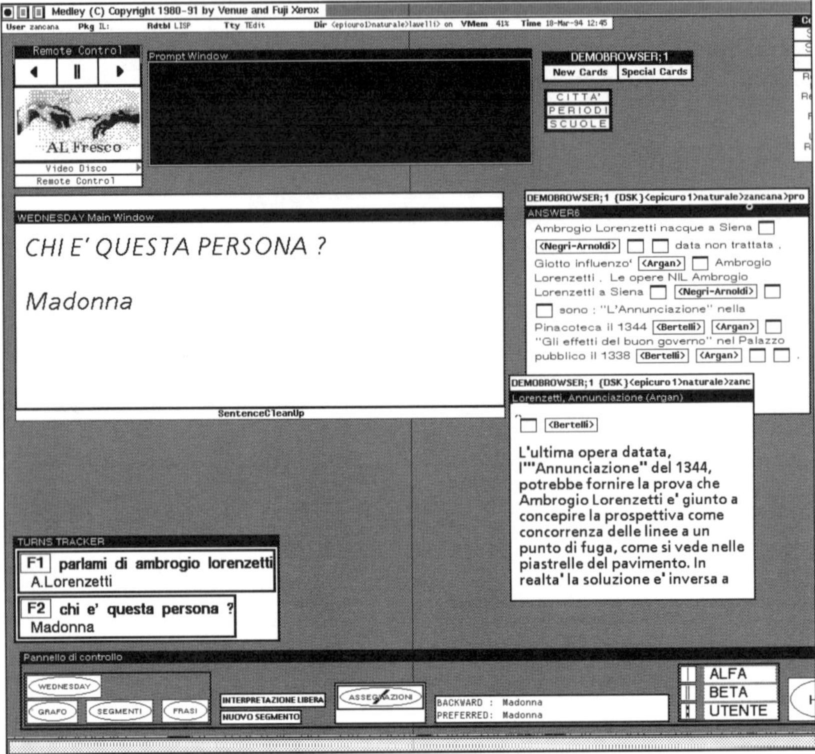

Figure 5. Multimodal (natural language and gesture) query.

Often it is very difficult to have a sophisticated dynamic user model and especially a model of her high level plans. Knowing little of the external context of the user, we may well try to smoothly shift from one plan in our library to another depending on the contents of the user utterances. But it is quite likely that the user is not able to explicitly express the problem at the beginning of the interaction or that she may have no definite target in her mind. Emphasizing plans may be not appropriate.

We propose a level of multimodal acts representation, that we simply call *communicative*, roughly corresponding to what, for strictly linguistic dialogue, is the illocutionary level (Searle 1969). Overall coherence requirements usually produce disambiguation of locutionary acts and also of acts such as mouse clicking. In substance we claim that for these kind of multimodal dialogues a communicative act is interpreted by connecting it appropriately to the multimodal context.

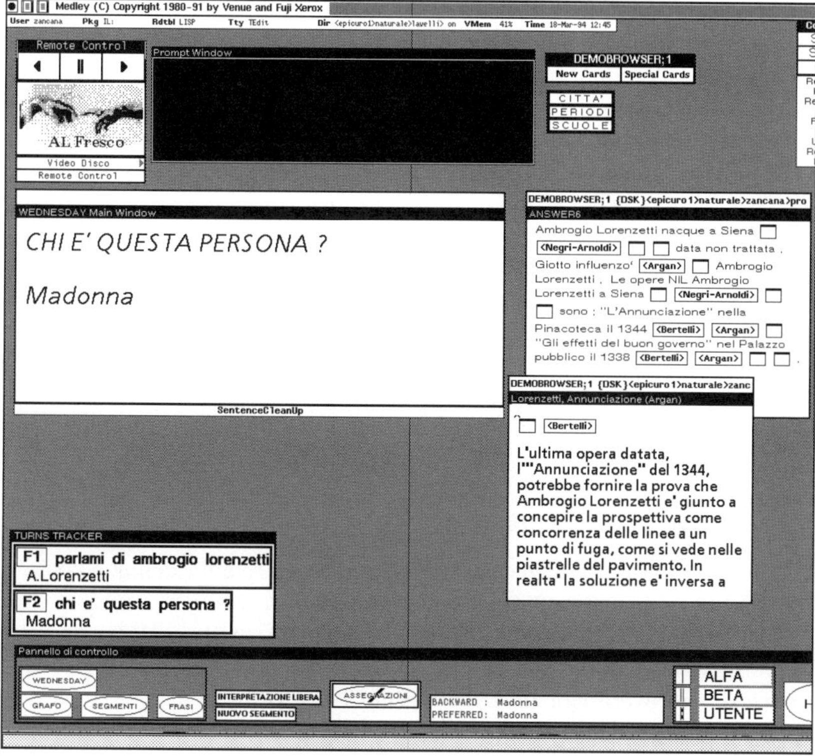

Figure 6. User query: "What is the town?"

4. Multimodal Communicative Acts

Let us briefly introduce some modules in ALFRESCO relevant for our discussion. The domain and some dialogue information are represented in a knowledge representation language based on descriptive logics. Concepts are described in the so called Terminological Box (or Tbox) and instances in the Assertional Box (or Abox).

4.1 User Model

A dynamic user model develops as the dialogue proceeds and contains two kinds of information (represented in two modules called UK and UI): what the user has been exposed to (linguistically or through images) or is assumed to know, and what the user seems to be interested in. The former kind of information is mainly used during the recognition of communicative intentions and the latter is used in the process of output generation.

The user's knowledge model, or UK, is based on an initialization (based on a user profile) and on a model of what the user has become aware of so far. For this purpose, conceptually, a replica of the system's domain Abox is used and takes advantage of the same Tbox and reasoning capability. The system gives an interpretation to every user expression and declares what the user knows in the UK, resulting in a monotonic partial covering of the Domain Abox. In fact the User Abox is split in turn in two parts: what the user knows is true and what the user knows is false. This does not allow us to deal with nested beliefs and some forms of misconceptions (for instance, false presuppositions), but is strong enough for our purposes, as we subsequently discuss.

The user's interest model, or UI, provides a model of the potential interest of the user and consists of an activation/inhibition network the nodes of which are associated with ordered sets of individual concepts.

4.2 Dialogue Cohesion Manager

The dialogue cohesion manager plays an important role for defining context especially for what concerns focus management.

The version used at present is described in Zancanaro et al. (to appear) (see also section 5.1) and is based on an adaptation of the Centering Model (cf. (Joshi and Weinstein 1981; DiEugenio 1990; Grosz et al. 1995)), developed for dialogues in a multimodal environment. Its tasks are (i) to resolve anaphoras (ii) to build a dialogue structure based on cohesion and (iii) to manage focus spaces.

The use of a graphical feedback of the dialogue cohesion status to the user was presented in Zancanaro et al. (1993). This visual representation (a) reassures the user at a glance on the system's interpretation (as such it takes the place of a paraphraser), and (b) allows cooperative recovery from discourse misconceptions by means of a series of "intuitive actions" when this interpretation is not the one the user meant.

Our dialogue model is based on the recognition of some structural relations between pairs of utterances. Although we do not claim that it covers all discourse phenomena, it is very close to the model of thematic developments proposed by Danes (1974). Although the relations are called coherence relations this term is here used in a rather different sense: in this section coherence simply means some kind of structural relation between turns.

4.3 Presentation Actions and Media Coordinator

Communication from the system's part can result in actions such as describing a fresco, showing a picture, indicating on a map how to reach a particular place, and so on. The system must determine how to present the information

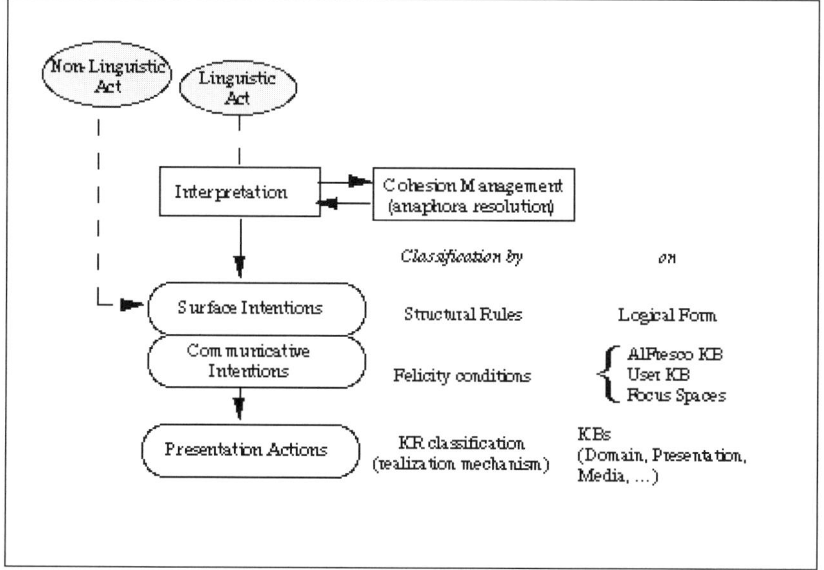

Figure 7. Dialogue management.

to be conveyed. According to Arens et al. (1993), the types of knowledge required for this task are: (a) the nature of the information to be conveyed; (b) the characteristics of the media to be used; (c) the communicative situation (i.e. communicative intention and surface intention).

In our system the presentation action is determined through classification (realization mechanism) in the KB. Taxonomies of presentation actions, media and kinds of objects are defined at the conceptual level and are transportable over domains and situations by adding, if needed, more specific presentations and media. Implicit in the module's output is the offer of a shift between a navigational modality of exploration and a mediated access to information. For instance it may show a hypertext card, giving the user the opportunity of starting a hypertext navigation.

Figure 7 shows the architecture of the pragmatic part of ALFRESCO. An extended explanation of the figure will follow after the definition of the felicity conditions for communicative action.

5. Felicity Conditions

The key point of the theory of Speech Acts (Searle 1969) is that all utterances serve to perform actions. There are many ways in which one could say that in uttering a linguistic expression a speaker was doing something, but there is one privileged level of action that can be called the illocutionary act. Searle claims that communication via language is a form of rule-governed behavior and that illocutionary acts can be specified by a set of necessary and sufficient conditions for their successful performance (*felicity conditions*). He proposes four conditions for a felicitous performance of a speech act: *propositional content conditions*, which specify restrictions on the content of an utterance; *preparatory preconditions*, which are real-world prerequisites to each illocutionary act; *conditions on sincerity*, which state the requisite beliefs, feelings and intentions of the speaker; and, *essential conditions* which state how the speaker intends the utterance to be taken. Searle proposes also a taxonomy of illocutionary forces.

We have developed a taxonomy and a computational treatment of a set of communicative acts in a multimodal setting. The key point for multimodal interaction is provided by the uniform use of felicity conditions, the rules that give meaning to communicative intentions.

We are not talking about goals and beliefs of the actors; we make reference to a highly simplified notion of context, so that the situated occurrence of acts is appropriately interpreted as much as possible without complex inferences. Given an utterance's logical form, LF, we refer to its interpretation in the domain K as $I_K(LF)$. The main domain for interpretation is the system's knowledge model, (henceforth SK). UK is the user's knowledge model (what the system guesses the user knowledge is). Focus of attention is taken into account by means of the *in-focus* predicate.

Propositional content here indicates only the possible surface intention types. *Preparatory* exploits the mechanism of focus spaces, described in Zancanaro et al. (to appear) (see also section 5.1). This mechanism at the same time takes into account the changes in the environment, and the preceding interactions. As far as the first point is concerned, every change in the environment induces an attention shift. We consider this enough for our present purposes. Referring to the preceeding interaction only by means of focus spaces releases us from modality dependent features. *Sincerity* is based on the interpretation values of the expressions in the two domains referred above. For the moment we cannot talk of generic entities (e.g., "what is a fresco?"). We shall not consider *essential* conditions here. In the following we shall just refer to some of the acts in view of explaining the system's behavior in the example reported in section 3. Let us synthetize the essence of felicity conditions of three kinds of requests: describe, find, locate.

request-describe
PROPOSITIONAL CONTENTS: one-of (wh, describe)
PREPARATORY: in-focus($I_{sk}(LF)$)
SINCERITY: $I_{sk}(LF) = I_{uk}(LF)$

Comments: the user asks to have a description about a particular entity; the user already knows which entity satisfies the constraints.

request-find
PROPOSITIONAL CONTENTS: one-of (wh, describe, show, polar with-variable)
PREPARATORY: not in-focus(I_{sk}(LF))
SINCERITY: I_{uk}(LF) = $\emptyset$

Comments: the user asks to find some information about a particular entity; the user doesn't know which entity satisfies the constraints.

request-locate
PROPOSITIONAL CONTENTS: one-of (wh, polar-with-variable)
PREPARATORY: in-focus(I_{sk}(LF))
SINCERITY: I_{uk}(LF) = $\emptyset$

Comments: the user asks to locate an entity among some other entities; in the focus of attention there is an entity which satisfies the constraints and the user knows about it.

The last request in the dialogue shown at the beginning, "Qual è la città ?" (which town is it?), is ambiguous at the surface level in Italian. It is interpreted just as a request-locate, because of the felicity conditions: the image of the town is in focus.

Let us see an example of how a sentence can be interpreted as performing different communicative acts depending on the context in which it is uttered:

U: Is there a painting in Siena?
S: The Effects of Good Government
U: Who is the author?
   (request-find)
S: Ambrogio Lorenzetti.

U: Is there a painting by Ambrogio Lorenzetti?
S: The Effects of Good Government
U: Who is the author?
   (request-describe)
S: <the system generates a text describing Lorenzetti's life and works>

U: Which painters belong to the School of Siena?
S: Simone Martini, Duccio, Ambrogio Lorenzetti.
U: Can you show me a painting?
S: <the system shows "The Annunciation">
U: Who is the author?
   (request-locate)
S: Ambrogio Lorenzetti.

Felicity conditions hold also for non-linguistic communication actions. In that case we can assume *imperative* as the surface intention. For example, with reference to the above dialogue, consider the case that the user, during the hypertext navigation phase, clicks the button for "Gli Effetti del Buon Governo" (the Effects of Good Government). If this fresco has not yet been mentioned in the interaction (as in the considered situation), the system instantiates a *request-find*, shows the fresco on the touch-screen and updates the context. Should the user click again the same button later on, the system instantiates a *request-describe* and generates a linguistic description of the fresco. Let us note that the first click is equivalent to the sentence "Show me this fresco" in that not only the interpretation of the intentions is the same but the context (UK, focus and environment) is updated in the same way.

Let us go back and have a look at the dialogue management architecture depicted in figure 5. Surface intentions, communicative intentions and presentation actions are organized in taxonomies, each involving a classification mechanism. When the user utters a linguistic expression some simple types of presuppositions that affect the user model are computed. Similarly, after action by the system, implicatures may affect the user model. In order to deal with this aspect, we are going to experiment with a Truth Maintenance System.

In the specification of felicity conditions, a key role is played by the *in-focus* predicate. In the next section, a brief account on how focus spaces are managed is given.

5.1. Focus Management

The minimal unit is considered not the utterance but the turn (i.e. the adjacency pairs Question/Answer and Request/Response). Centers are now properties of turns, not of utterances. Every turn T_n is "about" only one entity at a time, the *backward looking center*, $C_b(T_n)$. It is always the confirmation of a previously mentioned entity and it is used to link the turn T_n with a preceding one. A list of *forward looking centers* $C_f(T_n)$ is associated with every turn U_n. This list is made up of all the entities realized in the turn and it is used to link the turn to the following ones. Among the forward-looking centers one is chosen to be the *preferred center* $C_p(T_n)$. It is "the most significative" NP of the turn (i.e. the item realized by it). It is computed by means of structural rules based on the logical form of the user's utterance, usually the wh-focus for wh-questions and the "thing about which we ask" in the other cases.

In an information access dialogue we can imagine that a question is coherent with the preceding dialogue when it is a follow-up of a previous turn. There are at least two ways in which a question may be a follow-up of a turn, either it is about the same subject of the question of that turn, or it is about the same subject of its answer. These *coh-relations* can be defined formally in terms of relations among centers. Given two turns, T_1 and T_2, we define an accessibility relation when there exists a chain of coherent turns from T_1 and T_2. Anaphora resolution is realized in two focus spaces built using the accessibility relation. For more details see Zancanaro et al. (to appear).

As far as deictic demonstratives are concerned a different focus space is adopted. Whenever a deictic context is established, the corresponding turn is marked as a *context creator* (or CC). Only one CC can be active at a given time. For CC turns, all the entities referenceable in the context they establish are added to their centers. This list is called C_d (for deictic centers) and two new relations are defined.

Deictic references and cross-modal anaphoras are resolved using the deictic centers of the current CC. The *in-focus* operator accesses the focus spaces. The order of access depends on contextual rules: for example, after a deictic reference all the elements in the deictic space come before all the elements in the linguistic spaces. As discussed previously, the *in-focus* predicate is an essential part of felicity conditions in our work. Indeed, the attentional state is the most reliable element to model the context of the communicative act as far as (multimodal) information access dialogues are concerned.

6. Notes on Evaluation

For any interactive system the question of evaluation presents itself. In Information Retrieval itself, though, the tradition based on quantitative measurements is more concerned with the retrieval engine (focusing mainly on precision and recall figures) than with user-centered questions.

Certainly, a multimodal system of the kind described here is not easy to evaluate globally in an uncontroversial way. The reason is that before the system is engineered and adopted for a purpose for which some more traditional system exists it is very difficult to make serious overall evaluations with users and comparisons (King 1996). What is next best? Wizard of Oz techniques provide a simulation of the behavior of the final system, so that data on system performance experimented by users that ignore the fact that a hidden human acts as the system, can be recovered. To work for a very complex system you need to have very sophisticated capabilities in the simulation environment, otherwise the wizard cannot operate efficiently enough. In our case we believe it unrealistic to aim directly at global evaluation.

This view is common to other works on multimodality. At this point in time, for this sector of research we believe that the most promising approaches to evaluation are those that isolate some key factor, such as those adopted by Oviatt et al. (1994). For instance, the results of experiments conducted in our team on the preference of deictic references over verbal specifications provide useful indications (DeAngeli et al. 1996).

As an instance of this philosophy, we have devised some experiments that isolate the function of user feedback, concerned with overall interaction cohesion, a key concept in our approach to information exploration. As mentioned before, the "in-focus" feature is of critical importance and used across modalities; it is essential in this respect, so as to guarantee correct interpretation and possible recovery in case of errors. Consistent with the spirit of multimedia integration in communication, we have proposed a multimodal feedback system. Feedback is simple to be perceived and in a form that can be directly manipulated, so that the interpretation can be cooperatively adjusted if the system does not interpret correctly what was meant.

The goal of our experiments is to evaluate the use of the multimodal approach to feedback, with the aim of having a more satisfactory information retrieval dialogue. We want to compare this essentially multimodal and multimedia approach with more traditional approaches (paraphrases, reference binding) by examining its use by different kinds of users. The experimental design has been completed but results of these specific experiments are not available as of this writing.

7. Conclusions

Our aim has been to introduce an approach to multimodal dialogues for information access and exploration, based on a uniform formulation of felicity conditions, simple and computationally feasible. This approach is conceived in particular for an environment suited for exploration of a large information space. In this type of interaction exploitation of the attentional state (Grosz and Sidner 1986) is more realistic than relying in general on the existence of some underlying task for acknowledging coherence. In multimodal information access a key concept is that the user may shift continuously from querying to browsing. The ALFRESCO system is designed specifically to accommodate those changes in target orientation smoothly.

The art domain is among the first ones for which multimedia hypertext has become common, especially in musea. Thus it is among the first to show the inherent limits of that approach taken in isolation. Intelligent interfaces and especially the use of an extended communication paradigm offer some concrete benefits even at this early stage of our understanding of multimodal interaction.

Acknowledgments

We would like to thank all the IRST group that was involved in the various phases of the development of ALFRESCO.

References

Arens, Y.; Hovy, E.; and Vosser, M. 1993. On the Knowledge Underlying Multimedia Presentations. In *Intelligent Multimedia Interfaces*, ed. M. Maybury, 280-306. Menlo Park CA/Cambridge MA: AAAI Press/MIT Press.

Brennan, S. E.; Frieman, M. W.; and Pollard, C. J. 1987. A Centering Approach to Pronouns. In Proceedings of the 25th Annual Meeting of the Association for Computational Linguistics, 155-162. Stanford, CA: ACL.

Cohen, P.; Dalrymple, M.; Moran, D.; Pereira, F.; Sullivan, J.; Gargan, R.; Schlossberg, J.; and Tyler, S. 1989. Synergistic Use of Direct Manipulation and Natural Language. In Proceedings of ACM Human Factors in Computing Systems (CHI'89), 227-233. Austin, TX: Addison-Wesley.

Conklin, J. 1987. Hypertext: an Introduction and Survey. *IEEE Computer* 20:17-41.

Danes, F. 1974. Functional Sentence Perspective and the Organization of the Text. In *Papers on Functional Sentence Perspective*, ed. F. Danes, 106–128. Prague/The Hague: Academia/Mouton.

DeAngeli, A.; Gerbino, W.; and Petrelli, D. 1996. Interface Features Affecting Deixis Production: A Simulation Study. In Proceedings of Workshop on the Integration of Gesture in Language and Speech, 195-204. Wilmington, Delaware. 7-8 October. (http://www.asel.udel.edu/~messing/WIGLS)

Di Eugenio, B. 1990. Centering Theory and the Italian Pronominal System. In Proceedings of COLING '90, 270-275. Helsinki, Finland.

Feiner, S. and McKeown, K. 1990. Coordinating Text and Graphics in Explanation Generation. In Proceedings of Eighth National Conference on Artificial Intelligence (AAAI-90), 442-449. Boston, MA: AAAI.

Grosz, B. J. and Sidner, C. L. 1986. *Attentions, Intentions, and the Structure of Discourse. Computational Linguistics* 12(3):175-204.

Grosz, B. J.; Joshi, A. K.; and Weinstein, S. 1995. Centering: A Framework for Modelling the Local Coherence of Discourse. *Computational Linguistics* 21(2): 203-225.

Hauptmann, A. G. and Witbrock, M. 1997. Informedia: News-on-Demand Multimedia Information Acquisition and Retrieval. In this volume.

Ingwersen, P. 1992. *Information Retrieval Interaction*. London: Taylor Graham.

Joshi, A. and Weinstein, S. 1981. Control of Inference: Role of Some Aspects of Discourse Structure Centering. In Proceedings of the 7th International Joint Conference on Artificial Intelligence, 385-393. Vancouver, Canada: IJCAI.

King, M. 1996. Evaluating Natural Language Processing Systems. *Communications of the ACM* 39(1): 73-79.

Mani, I.; House, D.; Maybury, M.; and Green, M. 1997. Towards Content-Based Browsing of Broadcast News Video. In this volume.

Maybury, M. 1993a. *Intelligent Multimedia Interfaces*. Menlo Park CA/Cambridge MA: AAAI Press/MIT Press.

Maybury, M. 1993b. Planning Multimedia Explanations Using Communicative Acts. In *Intelligent Multimedia Interfaces*, ed. M. Maybury, 59-74. Menlo Park CA/Cambridge MA: AAAI Press/MIT Press.

Oviatt, S. L.; Cohen, P. R.; and Wang, M. 1994. Toward Interface Design for Human Language Technology: Modality and Structure as Determinants of Linguistic Complexity. *Speech Communication* 15(3-4):283-300

Searle, J. 1969. *Speech Acts*. London: Cambridge University Press.

Stein, A.; Gulla, J. A.; Müller, A.; and Thiel, U. 1997. Conversational Interaction for Semantic Access to Multimedia Information. In this volume.

Stock, O. and The AlFresco Project Team. 1993. AlFresco: Enjoying the Combination of NLP and Hypermedia for Information Exploration In *Intelligent Multimedia*

Interfaces, ed. M. Maybury, 195-224. Menlo Park CA/Cambridge MA: AAAI-Press/MIT Press.

Stock, O. 1995. A Third Modality of Natural Language? *Artificial Intelligence Review* 9(2-3): 57-74.

Sutcliffe, A.; Hare, M.; Doubleday, A.; and Ryan, M. 1997. Empirical Studies in Multimedia Information Retrieval. In this volume.

Wahlster, W.; André, E.; Bandyopadyay, S.; Graf, W.; and Rist, T. 1992. WIP: The Coordinated Generation of Multimodal Presentations from a Common Representation. In *Communication from an Artificial Intelligence Perspective: Theoretical and Applied Issues.*, eds. A. Ortony; J. Slack, and O. Stock, 190-231. Berlin: Springer Verlag.

Wahlster, W.; André, E.; Finkler, W.; Profitlich, H. J.; and Rist, T. 1993. Plan-Based Integration of Natural Language and Graphics Generation. *Artificial Intelligence* 63(1-2): 387-427.

Waterworth, J. and Chignell, M. 1991. A Model for Information Exploration. *HYPERMEDIA* 3(1): 35-58.

Zancanaro, M.; Stock, O.; and Strapparava, C. 1993. Dialogue Cohesion Sharing and Adjusting in an Enhanced Multimodal Environment. In Proceedings of 13th International Joint Conference on Artificial Intelligence, 1230-1236. Chambery, France: IJCAI.

Zancanaro, M.; Stock, O.; and Strapparava, C. 1996. Multimodal Interaction for Information Access: Exploiting Cohesion. *Computational Intelligence* 13(4).

Conversational Interaction for Semantic Access to Multimedia Information

Adelheit Stein, Jon Atle Gulla, Adrian Müller, and Ulrich Thiel
GMD-IPSI

Abstract

Effective interaction is essential for effective information retrieval. The entire process of retrieval interaction should be organized in a way that allows the user to concentrate on her primary goals, i.e., clarifying vague information needs, finding appropriate search strategies, and assessing the relevance of retrieved information. Accordingly, an intelligent retrieval system must be capable of interpreting and negotiating ambiguous information needs interactively with the user. The MIRACLE system introduced in this chapter offers semantic access to a large, experimental multimedia information base. Both the retrieval engine and the dialogue manager employ abductive reasoning to generate plausible interpretations of ambiguous user requests/queries and to create coherent interaction options based on a comprehensive dynamic dialogue model. As opposed to most state-of-the-art retrieval systems, MIRACLE supports the user actively on both the pragmatic and the cognitive level.

1. Why Conversational Interaction?

Current multimedia information systems employ a variety of advanced data representation, indexing, and retrieval methods, but mostly apply less elaborate—often simplistic—models of human-computer interaction. Usually, content-based retrieval methods are employed to induce similarity relationships among the available information objects, which can then be inspected by means of browsing operators. However, as the information systems and the human-computer interactions grow increasingly complex, the *entire process* of information search, retrieval, and relevance assessment needs to be actively supported by easy-to-use multimodal user interfaces.

Many users of information retrieval (IR) systems have initially only vague information needs and often encounter problems formulating them precisely. Vague and ambiguous information needs are typical of multimedia retrieval, but occur in text retrieval as well. However, whereas it seems to be acceptable that users discard non-relevant textual items as long as highly relevant documents are shown at the top of the ranking lists, the relevance assessment required in multimedia retrieval imposes an even higher cognitive load on the user. Some data types, e.g., audio and video sequences, may be accessible using standard retrieval methods (based on their speech components, cf. Jones et al., this volume), but they still differ from textual documents, because they cannot easily be skimmed like texts or pictures. In addition, the tacit assumption underlying most text retrieval systems—that relevance can be reduced to topical similarity, which, in turn, is based on the (multiple) occurrences of index terms—has not yet found a convincing counterpart for non-textual media. Instead, there is growing evidence that retrieved data items (including texts) are assessed according to multi-dimensional relevance scales which express the specific needs of users in their current situation. Hence, we claim that clarification of information needs *through* interaction with the system is as important a task as the employment of appropriate indexing and retrieval mechanisms. As this type of interaction includes meta-communication about dialogue goals and strategies, it can be modeled as *conversational interaction* between user and IR system.

From a user-centered point of view, intelligent multimedia retrieval systems should be capable of supporting the user in the following tasks:

- Queries must be disambiguated to assign appropriate retrieval methods
- Different interpretations of the query must be managed, and the relevant information objects must be determined for each of them;
- The information objects must be presented in such a way that the user can relate them to her query and to each other;
- Unexpected problem situations and dialogue strategies should be negotiated and clarified interactively with the user.

The first two issues can be tackled using semantic representations of information objects, linking them to the objects by content-based retrieval operators, and combining them with techniques for query disambiguation (e.g., abduction). Whereas the third issue requires powerful presentation and user guidance facilities, the fourth addresses the pragmatic aspects of information-seeking dialogue. In this chapter we will discuss our approach to combining these levels by *intertwining multimedia IR and dialogue planning*.

The next section gives a brief account of related research in various fields that are relevant for our work. In section 3 we introduce the system architecture of MIRACLE, which integrates a logic-based retrieval engine and dialogue manager as its major components. As both employ abductive reasoning, we discuss the use of this inference technique from the retrieval point of view in section 4, and from the dialogue planning perspective in section 5, analyzing one typical example taken from MIRACLE. A brief summary and outline of future work are given in the conclusions of the chapter.

2. Related Research

As our approach tackles a problem on the borderline between the fields of information retrieval and intelligent interfaces/dialogue systems, we briefly sketch research results from these areas which have been influential for our work.

In IR, we have to regard two lines of research which attempt to overcome the common notion of IR being the task of finding items, usually documents, that match a formal query. A more abstract model put forward by van Rijsbergen (1989) construes the retrieval operation as a *plausible inference,* which requires that relevant items probably imply (parts of) the query. A number of researchers have since then proposed operationalizations of this model using different logics (for an overview see Nie 1992, Thiel et al. 1996). While most of them preferred a deductive framework, in MIRACLE we employ an abductive reasoner, which supports a neat integration of dialogue planning and database access. This is motivated by a second line of research in IR: Over the last two decades the view of *information retrieval as interaction* has been promoted by several researchers in information science and IR (more recently, for example, Belkin and Vickery 1985, Ingwersen 1992). Although most of these studies concentrated on traditional IR systems, and tried to identify ways of enhancing the user-system interaction in this setting, the findings on, for example, retrieval strategies can be employed in the design of intelligent IR systems as well (Belkin et al. 1995).

The interactive development of a proper specification of the information need is supported by a variety of interface designs. Although direct manipulation remains the predominant interaction metaphor (in information systems), the need for more flexible dialogues—including negotiations and explanations—has motivated research into multimodal dialogue (cf. Taylor et al. 1989). Adopting ideas from natural language interfaces, researchers have started to analyze also graphical and linguistic dialogue contributions of user and system as "communicative actions" or "dialogue acts" (Bunt 1989). Thus, an interaction model is achieved that extends the flexibility of the system's reactions beyond the limitations of "adaptive hypertexts" (e.g., Kobsa et al., this volume; Vassileva, this volume): The system cannot only arrange for an appropriate information offer to be explored by the user, but can take a more active part by engaging in a mixed-initiative interaction, for example, by starting clarification sub-dialogues. Based on such an interface design (e.g., Osgood and Bareiss 1993, Stein and Thiel 1993), some information systems prototypes proposed to shift from exploratory IR to *"conversational retrieval"* (Thiel 1995). Other advanced multimodal dialogue systems for information access, such as the AlFresco system (Stock et al., this volume), also pursue a conversational approach and combine graphical with linguistic interaction. AlFresco, however, features mainly explorative information behavior in a natural language environment, whereas the focus in MIRACLE is on the development of more elaborate retrieval mechanisms and the planning of complex information-seeking dialogues.

In a similar vein, intelligent multimedia interfaces aim to "exploit dialogue context" (Maybury 1993, p. 172) in order to make the interaction space transparent to the user and to allow for a collaborative planning of dialogue strategies. To achieve this goal, a theoretically motivated framework for organizing the interaction is needed, i.e., a dynamic model of information-seeking dialogue (Stein and Thiel 1993, Stein and Maier 1995). Many ambitious discourse models have been developed in the field of natural language processing. Apart from those dealing with monologue only, there are some comprehensive models that also apply to collaborative dialogue (e.g., Bunt 1989, Grosz and Sidner 1990, Logan et al. 1994). However, they mainly focus on propositional attitudes and partner/belief modeling, rather than on the organization of the interaction. Other task-independent, dynamic models of dialogue (e.g., Wachtel 1986, Fawcett et al. 1988, Bilange 1991) are closer to our approach, but these models concentrate on natural language interaction within genres other than information retrieval and other application domains (for example, exchanges of factual information within well-defined task settings such as service encounters). For multimedia IR it is paramount that all kinds of interaction are modeled and analyzed from the information seeking/retrieval perspective.

Given this background in intelligent IR and interface research, we would ask: How can this potential be employed to enhance the performance and—what is even more important—the acceptance of multimedia IR systems? A first step towards this goal consists in understanding how users deal with multimedia data. In most cases, textual surrogates are used to index and manage non-textual data (for a survey study see (Lutes et al. 1996). Thus, the multimedia objects are associated with *concepts* that can be expressed in natural language. Our approach to multimedia indexing and retrieval (Müller and Kutschekmanesch 1996) aims at a conceptual retrieval of multimedia documents based on *abductive reasoning*, treating a query as a proposition to be inferred from a rule base by generating *interpretations* of the query in terms of the system's conceptual model. This notion stresses the communicative aspects of the retrieval operation, quite similar to recent approaches in natural language understanding (for example, Hobbs et al. 1993, McRoy and Hirst 1995), which especially solve the task of disambiguating a natural language utterance by abduction.

3. Architecture of MIRACLE

MIRACLE (MultImedia concept Retrieval bAsed on logiCaL query Expansion) is centered around three active components that employ a stratified knowledge base structured according to the tasks supported (see figure 1). The *dialogue manager* acts as a mediator between the user and the abductive retrieval engine; it relies on an explicit representation of the dialogue history employing knowledge about the available dialogue strategies and tactics. The *abductive retrieval engine* accesses a knowledge base comprising a semantic domain model, a model of document structure, and the semantic counterparts to the index terms assigned to the multimedia documents in the database. The *indexer* combines probabilistic text indexing with representation methods for non-textual objects (pictures) (cf. Müller and Kutschekmanesch 1996).

The current version of MIRACLE provides access to a large, experimental *database in the domain of art history*, consisting of SGML texts (biographies, reference articles, etc.), factual knowledge, and descriptions of thousands of works of arts/pictures. MIRACLE is implemented in C, Smalltalk, and Prolog and runs on System V and BSD Unix platforms. The environment is equipped with process-communication facilities, and allows access by users/system developers via a World Wide Web interface.

We distinguish between an intensional (or conceptual) representation of the domain and the extensional level (i.e., instances retrieved from the database). For any ambiguous user query the abductive retrieval engine generates reformulations of the query (query interpretations). Each interpretation is based on a set of additional *hypotheses* which can be seen as the semantic context in which a query will be embedded. If both user and system agree on (some) hypotheses, the corresponding query interpretation(s) can be checked individually by evaluating them with respect to the database's content. Applying this abductive retrieval mechanism, we need to distinguish between at least three global phases of the interaction: query formulation, inspection of the query interpretations, and inspection of instances retrieved from the database. We need, however, a far more complex model of the interaction to deal with unexpected interactions such as embedded clarification dialogues and repair tactics. The dialogue manager dynamically constructs the dialogue history and uses this pragmatic context to plan subsequent steps and flexible interaction options.

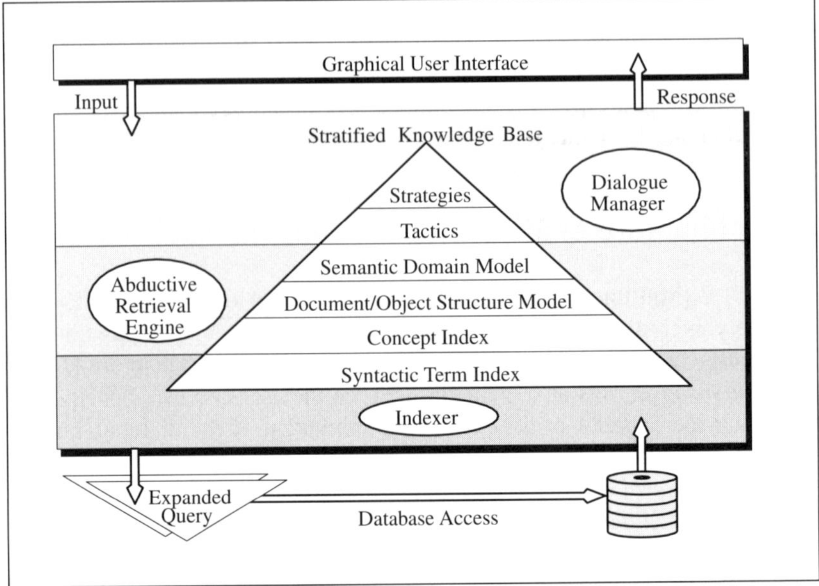

Figure 1. System architecture of MIRACLE.

4. Abductive Multimedia Information Retrieval

Collections of richly structured multimedia information domains demand that a retrieval system act as a mediator between the user's way of expressing information needs and the system's interpretation and computation of the query. Most state-of-the-art document retrieval systems offer as a retrieval result a ranked list of documents, since this is the best feedback available in these approaches (Callan et al. 1993). For instance, in complex domains providing structured documents and multimedia data with fragments of texts, non-textual data and implicit as well as explicit links between them, the user has to cope with a variety of options for handling these information objects. As this can easily distract users from concentrating on retrieval strategies that address their information problem directly, alternative approaches to IR propose retrieval operations on the level of *concepts*, for example, reformulations of queries. Such concepts are semantic entities which may be related to objects of different types. The system must then be capable of identifying these objects, and presenting them to the user. Van Rijsbergen claimed that *"... to design the next generation of IR systems, we will need to have a formal semantics for documents and queries. This semantic representation will interact with other types of knowledge in a controlled way and this way is inference!"* (1989, p. 81)

A widely used technique for reasoning in information retrieval is *deductive inference* (for example, Nie 1992, Hess 1992), mostly within first-order logic or probabilistic logic. Such systems assign a truth value to a given query by computing the deductive closure of a given theory (a set of axioms and rules stored in a knowledge base) and checking whether the query is an element of this closure. A difficult issue for deductive approaches is that they need to provide an accurate model of their domain, and they have to face the fact that changes in any part of the theory might lead to inconsistencies and to parts of the data being unretrievable.

Abductive reasoning has been applied successfully in *unstable* domains like fault analysis of physical systems. The idea of abduction is to process sound and correct proofs (which is of course similar to deductive logics), but to allow in certain cases the grounding of these proofs on specific assumptions, the so-called *abduced* sentences or *hypotheses*. Applying abduction to multimedia IR leads to a natural combination of methods from logic-based IR and object-oriented database theory: Documents are represented as complex structures, containing parts of different data types (texts, pictures, speech, video). They can be represented by systematically rewriting all structured media and hypermedia information in terms of first order logic rules. The rules in MIRACLE's knowledge base thus express properties of the SGML structure, which is the same for all entities of a collection. Elements of this common grammar can be abduced if they are syntactically possible in a certain situation.

The process of abductive information retrieval is characterized as follows: A user query is interpreted as an existential quantified statement which combines elements of the rule base (e.g., SGML elements) to form a new sentence. The abductive retrieval engine attempts to find a proof in terms of an aggregation (D) of multimedia documents, which entails the query Q: D $\Rightarrow$ Q (van Rijsbergen 1989). During the process of proof checking, abduction generates a set of hypothetical explanations (dynamic aggregations of the basic concepts of the rule base) which might imply the consequence (the query). These formulas can be regarded as system-generated interpretations of the user's information need in terms of domain structure and database contents.

The set of additional assumptions (the *hypotheses*) is necessary for deriving evidence that D entails Q within the formal theory describing the structure of the data. These hypotheses model the context in which the human-computer interaction takes place in the following way: A certain query interpretation is only valid within its associated hypothesis (query context). A hypothesis is the collection of assumptions the inference process needs to reformulate a query statement so that it becomes executable for the given database(s).

MIRACLE currently accesses a database consisting of biographies of artists and selected photographs of their works of art. Each biography is concerned with one person, although it might include many references to related persons (teachers, scholars, etc.). A work of art is typically created by one person and is mentioned within this person's biography. Rewriting these assumptions as a set of first-order logic rules allows us to establish a primary domain model. Now consider the following query: *Which artists are concerned with "Impressionism"?* The abductive reasoner infers that one way of executing this query is to retrieve all works of art which are indexed with "Impressionism" and group them by their creators. This inference needed an additional assumption to succeed: The query reformulation is based on the hypothesis that it suffices to process the "group by" command by treating documents as biographies, i.e., to find the creator of a work of art by looking for the subject (the artist) of the corresponding document. This assumption is the context in which this query interpretation is executable. If the user agrees with this assumption, the system is able to process the query in the way described above.

Such a domain model does not suffice for all document types in our prototype (e.g., for survey articles or exhibition catalogues). For example, the inference process for the query on "Impressionism" would fail for documents other than biographies, since here we have no general method for relating impressionistic works of art to individual artists. An additional set of domain rules is needed to capture such cases, which results in different query contexts. As the necessary domain models increase in size and complexity, there will be conflicting rules. A deductive inference process cannot treat inconsistent models properly, since the reasoning process is defined over a sound and complete closure of all rules. The abductive reasoning process, as it is used in the MIRACLE system, provides the means for negotiating the necessary assumptions with the user. The user can select between several query reformulations and assumptions on the domain, which are a prerequisite for computing the corresponding query reformulation. This process resembles the common human search technique of investigating several hypotheses about a given "black box" kind of problem—and thereby ignoring the fact that these hypotheses might be mutually inconsistent.

The retrieval engine and the dialogue manager operate on a set of first-order logic formulas. We will see below examples of such formulas and the way they are presented at the user interface. Each formula expresses one query interpretation, mapping query predicates to applicable retrieval operations. The hypotheses are part of this mapping. They are the additional lemmas—propositions which have been derived during the inference process and which are neither part of the query formulation nor of the database layer of the system—combined conjunctively within that formula. Each formula defines an intensional concept for the given domain, i.e., a way to interpret the query with respect to the database.

The extension of such a formula is computed in a second phase. The inference process is constrained in such a way that only predicates referring to computable functions can form the base of a reformulated query, for example, text retrieval functions as provided by the probabilistic text retrieval system INQUERY (Callan et al. 1992), or picture and audio access methods. Thus, the user's information need is expressed in terms that can be processed efficiently by the underlying data repository. The reformulated query is seen as a formula containing quantified variables which are instantiated during the recursive evaluation of the query. Function calls corresponding to the executable predicates are sent through a process-communication layer to external modules, and, collecting the results bottom-up, the query results are constructed. This design guarantees that each query reformulation is valid, i.e., if there are no results for a given interpretation then this is always due to a lack of data, but not due to a misconception of the underlying data structures.

This retrieval model distinguishes between three global phases of the user-system interaction, which can be illustrated by one typical example dialogue (see below). The example is here paraphrased in natural language, although in MIRACLE the user performs the dialogue acts by filling in query forms and manipulating interface objects (see icons/buttons in figure 2). In the introductory phase of our example, the user selects a domain of interest (here, art and artists), and enters search terms in some slots of the query form offered. Then she suddenly realizes that she has made a mistake, presses the "withdraw" button, and corrects her query[1].

An example dialogue

query formulation phase:

U: Find "parliament" in "Berlin." Start search!
    Sorry, that was wrong. Withdraw!
S: Why? *[displays query form for correction]*
U: Instead, find "Reichstag" after "1945." Start search!
S: I can search for: 1. pictures; 2. biographies; 3. both.
U: Both. *[selects]*

query interpretation phase:

S: Here are some interpretations of your query: $\beta 1$ ... $\beta 6$.
U: *[user inspects the interpretations, asks for explanations, and then selects $\beta 2$]*
    Search database!

inspection and evaluation of retrieved instances:

S: *[shows instances from multimedia database]*
U: Now, I'd like to ...

The revised—but still ambiguous—query can be paraphrased as: *Search for artists who were concerned with the "Reichstag after 1945" (and show their biographies and pictures of their works of art).* The abductive retrieval engine finds six interpretations of this query. Each interpretation consists of a

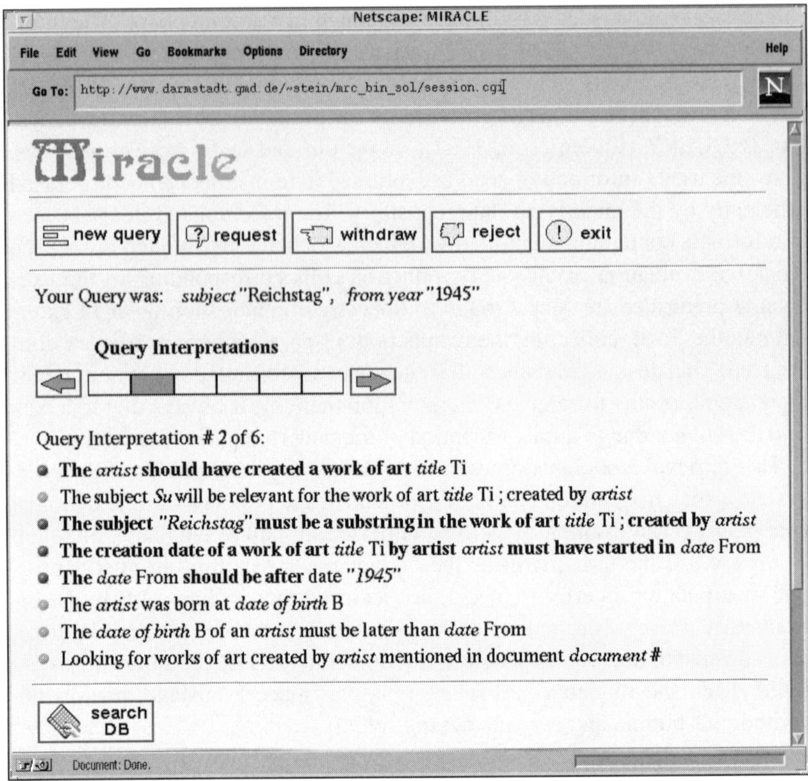

Figure 2. Query interpretation (β2) in MIRACLE.

set of activated formulas and is presented to the user in a textual rule format. The interpretation shown in figure 2 is made up of the rules 1, 3, 4, and 5 (the other rules are inactive), i.e., it interprets "after 1945" as the date of creation of a work of art, and "Reichstag" as part of the textual description of this work. In other interpretations, the date, for instance, is understood as the artist's date of birth. The user can inspect one interpretation after the other, or she can use the buttons on top of the form if for some reason she would like to interrupt the current path.

After selecting β2 as the correct interpretation, the user asks the system to access the database by pressing the "search DB" button. The query interpretation is instantiated in the following manner: First, the system collects all of the biographies that refer to works of art whose titles contain the string "Reichstag." Second, all works of art that were created later than 1945 are returned. Both partial solutions are afterwards combined using a computable relation linking pictures to artists. As a result, all artists are found who creat-

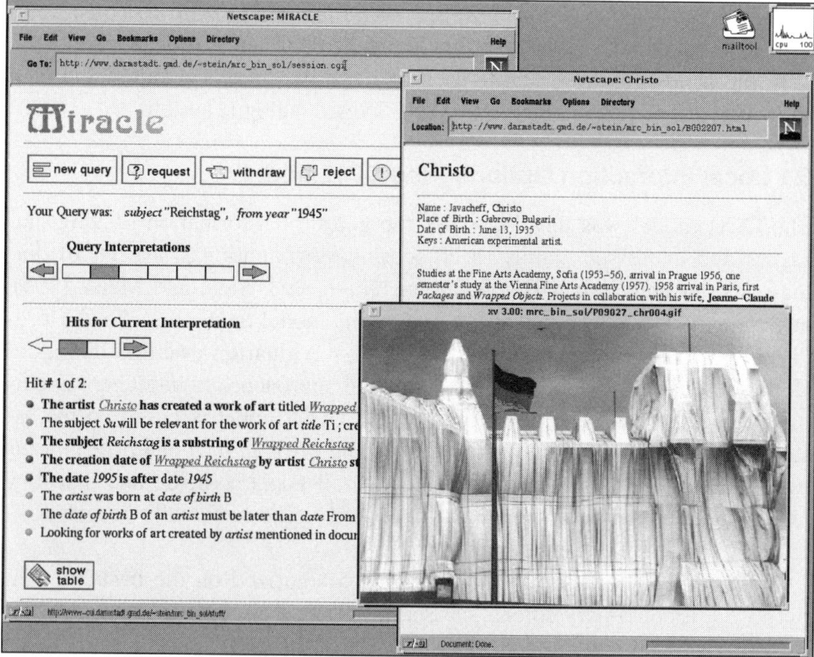

Figure 3. Final set of retrieved instances.

ed works of art that satisfy both conditions, and the system presents the two retrieved hits (left window in figure 2). Clicking on the links "Christo" and "Wrapped Reichstag," the user gets Christo's biography and a picture of the Reichstag taken in June 1995.

5. Dialogue Model and Abductive Dialogue Planning

An intelligent system needs to analyze the dialogue context/history in order to cope with unexpected user actions, to adapt its behavior to changed user strategies, and to allow meta-reasoning about the dialogue and retrieval methods applied. To this end, the dialogue manager must implement an appropriate model of dialogue. Relying on the theoretical framework we have developed—and partly applied—in previous system prototypes (see Stein and Thiel 1993, Stein and Maier 1995), we employ a modified version of this model for MIRACLE:

- Following Belkin et al. (1995), we use a battery of *dialogue scripts* to guide the users through their information retrieval session;

- A *speech-act oriented dialogue model,* COR, is used to construct a structured dialogue history, and to handle deviations from the scripts.

In the following we describe each of these two tiers separately and then show how they are combined into a full-fledged dialogue system.

5.1 Local Interaction Options—the COR Model

The COR model was developed for the genre of information-seeking dialogues and addresses mainly the illocutionary (intentional) aspects of dialogue (Sitter and Stein 1992, Stein and Thiel 1993, Stein and Maier 1995), analogously to the "Conversation for Action" model of Winograd and Flores (1986). In contrast to other genres, such as evaluation-oriented dialogues (Jameson et al. 1995), or non-conversational approaches to intelligent hypermedia access (Vassileva, this volume), the COR model is based on the assumption that the information seeker (A) and provider (B) enter a *cooperative negotiation.* This means that their overall goals coincide and that they take complementary conversational roles to develop a mutually accepted *interpretation* of the current dialogue goal.

COR defines 14 *types of dialogue acts* categorized on the basis of their purpose ("illocutionary force," cf. Searle 1979). This repertoire is small, as the propositional content and specific goals of the participants are not taken into account at the level of COR. It is only by combination with global dialogue scripts that more specific (sub-)types of acts can be distinguished—or, inferred by the dialogue manager. Similar approaches to combine a local exchange model with global discourse structures (strategies) were proposed, for example, by Fawcett et al. (1988) and Bilange (1991), but their repertoire of speech acts is different, as they focus on natural language interaction and other genres.

The basic units of an actual dialogue are individual/atomic dialogue *acts.* They are elements of superordinated complex dialogue contributions, the *moves* which can be assigned the same illocutionary force as the atomic acts. The COR model of the entire *dialogue* is represented as a recursive state transition network (figure 4). For any of the dialogue states the possible follow-up moves and action sequences can thus be described. The initial move is either a "request" for information or an "offer" to search for information and afterwards to present the retrieved items ("inform"). Bold arcs in figure 4 depict *expected moves,* which comply with the role expectations; *unexpected moves* are, for instance, "withdraw" (a previous decision) or "reject" an offer or request—either definitely (quit) or with the intention to continue and begin a new dialogue cycle in state 1.

Moves are also represented as transition networks. The general schema for all moves (except "inform," "promise," and "assert"—which are simpler) is given in figure 5. To represent the instances of this general schema, MOVE

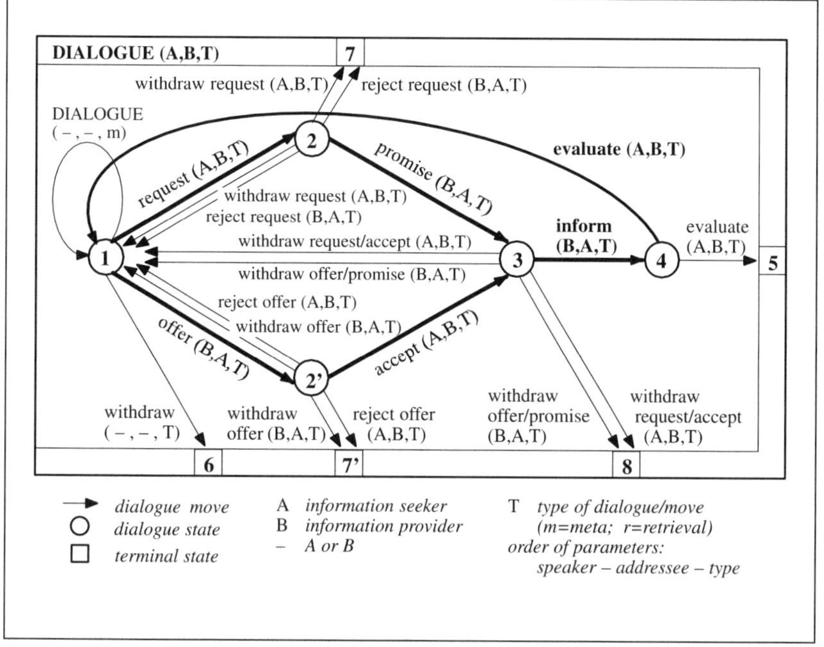

Figure 4. COR network for DIALOGUE.

and ACT are to be replaced by the speech act type to which they correspond, for example, "request." The elements of a move are atomic *acts* (e.g., A: request), other *moves* (assert (A,B,T) to supply context information), and *subdialogues* (dialogue (B,A,T), which is related to the previous act). As "jumps" indicate optional transitions, a move can consist of a single dialogue act, and even the entire move may be omitted in certain situations (for example, a "promise" is unnecessary, if the requested information can be given immediately).

Traversing the COR networks recursively during a dialogue session allows a hierarchical dialogue history to be built up dynamically (see also Hagen and Stein 1996). This history includes all system acts and user acts, puts them in a hierarchical relationship, and records all information (the propositions) exchanged between system and user during the interaction. Both previous queries and their interpretations are stored in the history, where they are referred to as constraints reflecting the user's information needs.

For the example dialogue above, the history tree shown in figure 6 is constructed. The hypothesis C2 underlying the chosen query interpretation is inserted into the tree as constraint information, since the user's choice of an interpretation is understood as a tacit preference of its underlying assumptions

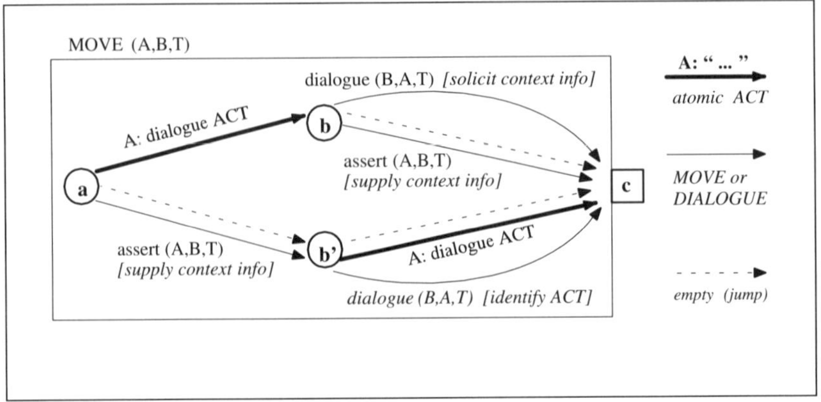

Figure 5. COR network for MOVEs (except inform, promise, and assert).

for the following dialogue. Whereas the COR model itself is realized as a recursive transition network, the dialogue history is a list representation that is accessed as formulas addressing the dialogue acts or the constraints in the history. That is, one can either request formulas specifying all acts that have happened so far in the dialogue, or formulas summing up the constraints found in the tree. The first request performed in the dialogue, for example, is accessed as the formula

$$act(1, request(u,s,r,\alpha)),$$

stating that at step 1 of a retrieval dialogue r, the user u posts a request a .

Modeling communicative acts, our dialogue model is not restricted to interaction in natural language, but also covers other modes (graphical manipulation as in MIRACLE). We assume that the allocation of appropriate modes should be handled by an intelligent presentation component that interacts with the dialogue manager to generate context-dependent multimodal presentations.

5.2 Dialogue Scripts

Scripts are empirically attested prototypical interaction sequences for particular kinds of information-seeking strategies (ISSs). Based on a multi-dimensional classification, Belkin et al. (1995) distinguished between 16 basic ISSs and proposed to define for any of these ISSs at least one prototype dialogue script. Unlike the hierarchical, domain-dependent task models adopted in many other approaches (e.g., Vassileva, this volume), scripts are used as domain-independent *strategic dialogue plans*; they do not define only straightforward (positive) problem-solving paths, but also include some branching points and embedded subdialogues (for example, for negotiating the further

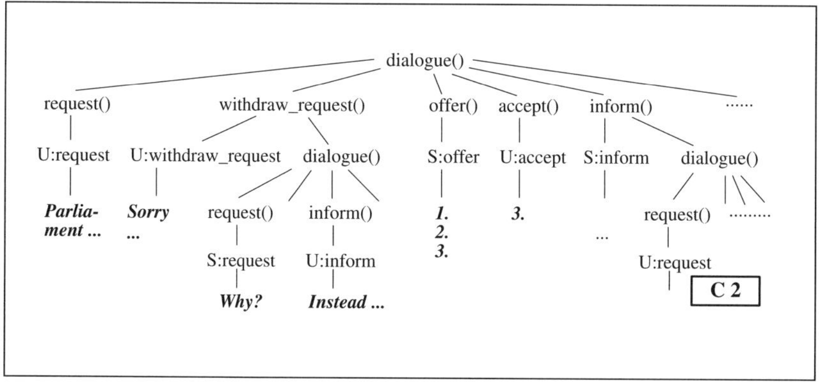

Figure 6. COR dialogue history tree.

strategy or tactic, in case the current strategy fails). The scripts in MIRACLE are realized as recursive transition networks with preconditions and postconditions associated with the transitions.

Our dialogue example above is based on the script paraphrased in figure 7. At each line of the script there is a numbered dialogue step, a list of possible follow-up steps, and the COR act type of this particular act. When alternative follow-up steps of the system are indicated, such as in step 3, preconditions decide which step to go to (forward to 4 or 5 or back to step 1). The COR act type decides how the script act is to be analyzed and recorded in the dialogue history.

5.3 Abductive Dialogue Planning

A major assumption in MIRACLE is that user guidance is not feasible without a corresponding flexibility and robustness towards unexpected user actions. As will be shown below, a speech-act oriented dialogue analysis, like the one used in figure 6 and referred to in the script in figure 7, is all we need to detect and handle acts that are not included in the dialogue scripts. By supplementing the analysis with constraints reflecting the information exchanged during the interaction, the dialogue history also enables a tuning of the system's query interpretation to the context of the dialogue.

When the user wants to perform the task of retrieving some information from the database, she first negotiates her goals with the system (steps 1–4 of the script) to find an appropriate strategy and instantiate a script. A *user guidance module* then executes the script, as user acts and system acts are performed, and produces sets of recommended user acts at each step of the interaction (see figure 8).

In the *dialogue monitoring module*, each act in the dialogue is analyzed, using the COR model, and inserted into the dialogue history. Information ex-

1 S: Here's what we can do ... *[list or menu]*	→ 2	offer
2 U: Let's do this ... *[selects]*	→ 3	accept
3 S: Here's how we'll do it ... *[describes plan]*	→ 4/5/1	inform
4 U: a. OK.	→ 5	evaluate
b. I don't like this.	→ 1	evaluate
5 U: *[fills in query input form]* Start query.	→ 6	request
6 S: a. **One** interpretation: *[shows details]*	→ 7a/7a.2a	inform
b. **Some** interpretations: ... n *[shows list]*	→ 7a/7b	inform
c. **Nothing** found, because ... *[explains]*	→ 5/7c	reject_request
7 U: a. 1. I like this.	→ 9/7a.2a	evaluate
2. Explain this interpretation.	→ 7a.2a/b	request
S: a. *[explains]*	→ 7a.3/4/5	inform
b. I can't explain, because ... *[explains]*	→ 5/7c/11	reject_request
U: 3. Execute this query interpretation.	→ **new script**	request
4. I don't like this.	→ 1/5/7c	evaluate
U: b. 1. Show **this** interpretation. *[selects]*	→ 7a/7b.2	request
...	→ ...	...
S: c. *[list of options to improve results]*	→ 7c.1/2	offer
...	→ ...	...
8 U: a. Execute <u>all</u> query interpretations.	→ **new script**	request
b. ...		
9 S: Shall we save this and continue?	→ 9a–e	request
... ...	→ ...	...
12 S: Goodbye.		

Figure 7. Dialogue script for ISS10.

changed during the interaction, such as query formulas or election of a query interpretation, is inserted into the history together with the corresponding dialogue act. The state of the dialogue is thus given by the state of the COR model and the structure of the dialogue history. During interaction, the dialogue history is actively used to adapt the system's behavior at two different levels.

- The constraints in the dialogue history, such as C2 in figure 6, are used to constrain the interpretation of later queries;

- The dialogue acts in the dialogue history are used to interpret user acts that are not included in the script.

When new queries are entered as follow-ups to earlier ones, we interpret these in light of the knowledge we already have obtained from the user. As the assumptions underlying a previously chosen query interpretation are likely to be valid also for the new ones, the constraints recorded in the dialogue history should be taken into account when new queries are interpreted. Interpreting a query, thus, the abductive retrieval engine first requests all relevant constraints from the dialogue monitoring module. The retrieval engine then

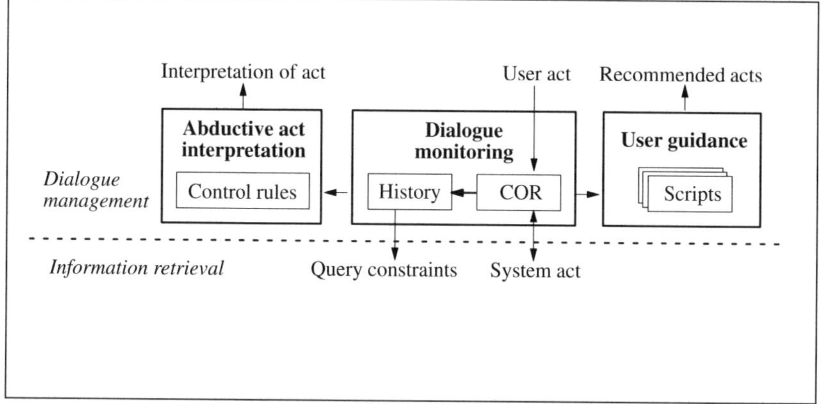

Figure 8. Structure of the dialogue manager.

generates and presents only interpretations of the query that are consistent with these constraints. Consider, for example, the constraints C2 associated with query interpretation β2 (figure 6). C2 is the set of formulas marked as active in the first snapshot of MIRACLE (figure 2); it associates the indicated time period with the creation date of works of art (rather than the date of birth of artists). If the user would later modify the original query, substituting for example "Pont Neuf" for "Reichstag," only β2 is presented as a valid interpretation of the query. The user is thus not asked to make the same choice twice, since we already know from the dialogue history which interpretation she prefers. More details about the use of dialogue-dependent constraints in query interpretation are found in Thiel et al. (1996).

Our example dialogue above showed how the user interrupted the natural flow of the dialogue and did something not determined by the script. This was possible, since the user interface includes both recommended and not recommended acts (see figure 2). Clicking the buttons on top of the window (i.e., "new query," "request," etc.) would invoke functions not recommended in the script, since they do not constitute any necessary steps in the current information-seeking strategy. However, they are important for the flexibility of the user interface and are, therefore, made available to the user (associating them with COR acts). In the example dialogue the user pressed the "withdraw" button to alter the query, but she also could have asked for explanations or rejected a system's offer. After a query interpretation has been shown in MIRACLE, the user may interrupt the retrieval session by posting a new query before even considering the interpretations she has been given. All these acts call for some special treatment, since they are not related to the overall goal of the interaction, are unaware of what has happened earlier in the dialogue, and specify the user's wish only as an illocutionary force.

When the "withdraw" button was used in the dialogue above, the user might just as well have intended to refine the query or perhaps to terminate the session all together.

The *abductive dialogue act interpretation module* (see figure 8) is activated when the dialogue monitoring module receives an act not found in the active script. The interpretation module analyzes the whole history of dialogue acts and employs a set of dialogue control rules to abduce various interpretations of the latest act. When the "withdraw" act is detected in our example dialogue, the interpretation module requests and receives the following formulas H documented in the dialogue history:

act(current,withdraw(request(u,s,r,α))),
act(1,request(u,s,r,α)),
script(current,iss10),

where a refers to the query about artists concerned with parliament in Berlin, and iss10 refers to the activated script shown in figure 7. The term current in the first formula simply marks the withdraw act to be the latest act inserted into the history.

The *dialogue control rules* are the rules used by the system to interpret the deviations from the script. They explain unexpected user acts by referring to concrete system actions and properties of the dialogue history. That is, the concrete actions form hypotheses about what the user really intended by choosing one of the acts not recommended in the script. In the rules below, redo(A), extend(A), and terminate(P) are system actions that all form inter pretations of a simple withdraw act. Since the unexpected act only expresses illocutionary force, there are usually several combinations of system actions that could be the desired one. Formally, we have an abductive reasoning process, where the control rules R and each of the combinations A imply the acts in the dialogue history H:

$R \cup A \Rightarrow H$ where $R \cup A$ is consistent.

Whereas H contains the unexpected, incomplete act from the user, A suggests precise acts that might have been intended by the user. Some of the rules used in this analysis are given below (all variables are universally quantified):

- *change_object(P,A,S)* $\rightarrow$ *act(_,A)* $\wedge$ act(withdraw(current,A))
  If act A in state S of script P is to be changed, both A and withdraw(A) have to be in the dialogue history.

- *redo(A)* $\rightarrow$ *change_object(P,A,S)* $\wedge$ *continue(P)*
  If act A is to be redone, it must be an object of change and be included in a script that is to be continued.

- *extend(A)* $\rightarrow$ *change_object(P,A,S)* $\wedge$ *continue(P)*
  If act A is to be extended with additional information, it must be an ob-

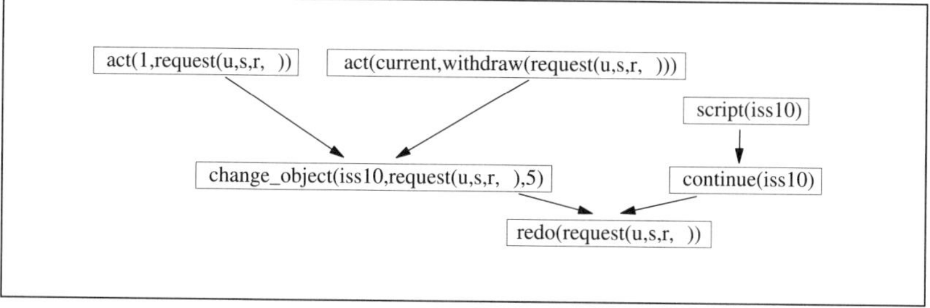

Figure 9. Interpretation of a "withdraw" act.

ject of change and be included in a script that is to be continued.

- *continue(P) → script(P)*
  If script P is to be continued, it must be in the dialogue history.

- *terminate(P,A,S) → script(P) ∧ act(withdraw(current,A))*
  If script P is to be terminated, it must be in the dialogue history and contain an act that is just withdrawn by the user.

After the "withdraw" button has been clicked in our example dialogue, these rules are used to map the act onto a set of system actions. Three different interpretations of this act can be found, one of which is shown in figure 9. The "withdraw" act is mapped here onto a redoing of the query (request). The two other possible interpretations are meant to extend the previous query, or to terminate the active script. Logically, each of the alternatives above implies the unexpected "withdraw" act in this particular context. The system informs the user about the three interpretations computed and displays the query form for the first one (the redo alternative) right away. As this is the interpretation favored by the user, she fills in the new form and asks the system to interpret the modified query.

The principle of the dialogue manager is to offer *guidance* by recommending dialogue moves, and *flexibility* when encountering unexpected moves. All of the expected moves contribute to the achievement of some interaction goal and are consequently included in the scripts elected by the user. Unexpected moves are not goal-directed in the same manner, and they typically express a wish to deviate from the recommendations in the script (see also Alexandersson et al. 1995). We assume that an unexpected move can be interpreted in the light of the dialogue history, and that there may be more than one plausible interpretation of it. Abductive reasoning together with dialogue control rules mapping from system actions to unexpected moves allow us to formalize this dialogue strategy. Since we use abduction, we are able to deal with cases in which the unexpected move or act can be related to many different combinations of previous acts. Most other dialogue systems, as for example (Wachtel 1986), require an exact match between corresponding acts in the dialogue.

This means that the user is always forced to use acts that are unambiguous with respect to the dialogue history, and that buttons in multimodal interfaces have to be associated with specific acts in the dialogue history. As the user may not remember the history and may be uncertain about the consequences of her act, it seems more promising to adopt an approach in which her acts can be negotiated and disambiguated interactively with the system. Another important aspect of MIRACLE's abduction approach is that we get a very clean and simple user interface with a restricted set of user options at the various dialogue states—the user starts out with a rather vague act and gradually refines it into a precise description of what she intends to do.

6. Conclusions

Multimedia information systems face even more complex interface problems than text-based IR systems. Apart from visualization and layout of multimedia documents, the most intriguing issue arises from the fact that non-textual information items may mean different things to different users. Therefore, the risk of retrieving non-relevant items is dramatically increased. As a consequence, one way to ensure the quality of retrieval results is to provide very precise queries, which—on the semantic level—avoid ambiguity, and on the syntactic level take into account the specific way in which non-textual items are indexed. Since this should *not* be left to the user, we claim that the user interface has to act as a mediator between the user's way of expressing information needs and the system's interpretation and evaluation of queries. As a step towards this goal, we have introduced a theoretical framework for *conversational information retrieval*—combining content-based information retrieval with a comprehensive dialogue model—and its application in the multimedia information retrieval prototype MIRACLE. The retrieval engine and the dialogue manager employ abductive reasoning as the main inference technique based on a semantic representation of the information accessed and on the pragmatics of the dialogue.

The abductive retrieval engine of MIRACLE was tested on a large document base comprising several thousand SGML documents and related Web sites with pictures. The rule base used during the abductive query interpretation encompasses a variety of interpretation strategies for ambiguous user queries, which allow the automatic generation of conceptual constraints on the items that are retrieved. The integrated dialogue manager enables MIRACLE to assist users actively during information-seeking dialogue. Based on a two-tiered model of dialogue—the COR model and dialogue scripts—the system monitors and guides the interaction as the dialogue develops. Through examples of the user-system interaction in MIRACLE we demonstrated and discussed how the retrieval engine and the dialogue manager interact with each other to construct a semantically and pragmatically coherent dialogue course.

Future work involves improving the interaction of the system components and the interface design, incorporating a text generation component for natural language explanations, and empirical evaluations of the integrated prototype. In order to directly access non-textual items, the indexer is currently extended by image analysis functionality and an automatic rule-generation component for the derivation of appropriate corpus-dependent interpretation rules. In addition, a more flexible presentation component will be integrated in order to visualize the system's interpretations by automatically generated multimodal presentations.

Note

1. To date, there exists no house of parliament in Berlin, and the user enters the proper name of the historical building ("Reichstag") she is interested in. The building was almost completely destroyed in 1945. It was rebuilt in the sixties and has been a museum since. The "Wrapped Reichstag" project was initiated by Christo and Jeanne–Claude in the seventies and completed in June 1995. Currently, the building is under reconstruction and will, in fact, serve as the future German parliament building.

References

Alexandersson, J.; Maier, E.; and Reithinger, N. 1995. A Robust and Efficient Three-Layered Dialogue Component for a Speech-to-Speech Translation System. In Proceedings of the 7th EACL, 188-193. Dublin, Ireland.

Belkin, N. J.; Cool, C.; Stein, A.; and Thiel, U. 1995. Cases, Scripts, and Information Seeking Strategies: On the Design of Interactive Information Retrieval Systems. *Expert Systems and Applications* 9(3): 379-395.

Belkin, N. J, and Vickery, A. 1985. *Interaction in Information Systems.* London: The British Library.

Bilange, E. 1991. A Task Independent Oral Dialogue Model. In Proceedings of the 5th EACL, 83-88, Berlin, Germany.

Bunt, H. C. 1989. Information Dialogues as Communicative Action in Relation to Partner Modeling and Information Processing. In *The Structure of Multimodal Dialogue,* eds. M. M. Taylor et al., 47-73. Amsterdam: North-Holland.

Callan, J. P.; Croft, W. B.; and Harding, S. M. 1992. The INQUERY Retrieval System. In *Proceedings of the Third International Conference on Database and Expert Systems Application,* 78-83. Berlin: Springer Verlag.

Fawcett, R. P.; van der Mije, A.; and van Wissen, C. 1988. Towards a Systemic Flowchart Model for Discourse. In *New Developments in Systemic Linguistics,* eds. R. P. Fawcett, and D. Young, 116-143. London: Pinter.

Grosz, B. J., and Sidner, C. L. 1990. Plans for Discourse. In *Intentions in Communication. Workshop on Intentions and Plans in Communication and Discourse,* eds. P. R. Cohen et al., 417-444. Cambridge, MA: MIT Press.

Hagen, E., and Stein, A. 1996. Automatic Generation of a Complex Dialogue History.

In Advances in Artificial Intelligence. *Proceedings of the 11th Biennial of the Canadian Society for Computational Studies of Intelligence (AI '96),* Toronto, Canada. ed. G. McCalla, 84-96. Berlin: Springer Verlag..

Hess, M. 1992. An Incrementally Extensible Document Retrieval System Based on Linguistic and Logical Principles. In *Proceedings of the 15th SIGIR,* Pittsburgh, PA, 190-197. New York: ACM Press.

Hobbs, J. R.; Stickel, M.; Appelt, D.; and Martin, P. 1993. Interpretation as Abduction. *Artificial Intelligence* 63(1-2): 69-142.

Ingwersen, P. 1992. *Information Retrieval Interaction.* London: Taylor Graham.

Jameson, A.; Schäfer, R.; Simons, J.; and Weis, T. 1995. Adaptive Provision of Evaluation-Oriented Information: Tasks and Techniques. In *Proceedings of the 14th IJCAI,* 1887-1893. Montreal, Canada. San Mateo, CA: Morgan Kaufman.

Jones, G. J. F.; Foote, J. Sparck Jones, K.; and Young, S. 1997. The Video Mail Retrieval Project: Experiences in Retrieving Spoken Documents. In this volume.

Kobsa, A.; Müller, D.; and Nill, A. 1997. KN-AHS: An Adaptive Hypertext Client of the User Modeling System BGP-MS. In this volume.

Logan, B.; Reece, S.; Cawsey, A.; Galliers, J.; and Sparck Jones, K. 1994. Belief Revision and Dialogue Management in Information Retrieval. Technical Report No. 339, University of Cambridge, Computer Laboratory, June 1994.

Lutes, B.; Kutschekmanesch, S.; Thiel, U.; Berrut, C.; Chiaramella, Y.; Fourel, F.; Haddad, H.; and Mulhem, P. 1995. Study on Non-Textbased Information Retrieval—State of the Art. Available from the European Commission, DG XII, Mr. B. Smith, Batiment Jean Monnet, Kirchberg, 2920 Luxembourg.

Maybury, M. T., ed. 1993. *Intelligent Multimedia Interfaces.* Menlo Park, CA: AAAI Press/The MIT Press.

McRoy, S. W., and Hirst, G. 1995. The Repair of Speech Act Misunderstandings by Abductive Inference. *Computational Linguistics* 21(4): 435-478.

Müller, A., and Kutschekmanesch, S. 1996. Using Abductive Inference and Dynamic Indexing to Retrieve Multimedia SGML Documents. In *MIRO'95. Proceedings of the Final Workshop on Multimedia Information Retrieval* (MIRO'95). Glasgow, Scottland. ed. I. Ruthven. Berlin: Springer Verlag (eWiC, electronic Workshops in Computing series, http://www.springer.co.uk/eWiC/Workshops/MIRO95.html).

Nie, J.-Y. 1992. Towards a Probabilistic Modal Logic for Semantic-based Information Retrieval. In *Proceedings of the 15th SIGIR,* Pittsburgh, PA, 140-151. New York: ACM Press.

Osgood, R., and Bareiss, R. 1993. Automatic Index Generation for Constructing Large-scale Conversational Hypermedia Systems. In: *Proceedings of the 11th AAAI,* 309-314. Menlo Park, CA: AAAI Press/The MIT Press.

van Rijsbergen, C. J. 1989. Towards an Information Logic. In *Proceedings of the 12th SIGIR,* Cambridge, Mass., 77-86. New York: ACM Press.

Searle, J. R. 1979. A Taxonomy of Illocutionary Acts. In *Expression and Meaning. Studies in the Theory of Speech Acts,* ed. J. R. Searle, 1-29. Cambridge, MA: Cambridge University Press.

Sitter, S., and Stein, A. 1992. Modeling the Illocutionary Aspects of Information-Seeking Dialogues. *Information Processing and Management,* 28(2): 165-180.

Stein, A., and Maier, E. 1995. Structuring Collaborative Information-Seeking Dialogues. *Knowledge-Based Systems.* Special Issue on Human-Computer Collaboration 8(2-3): 82-93.

Stein, A., and Thiel, U. 1993. A Conversational Model of Multimodal Interaction in Information Systems. In *Proceedings of the 11th AAAI,* 283-288. Menlo Park, CA: AAAI Press/The MIT Press.

Stock, O.; Strapparava, C.; and Zancanaro, M. Explorations in an Environment for Natural Language MultiModal Information Access. In this volume.

Taylor, M.M.; Néel, F; and Bouwhuis, D. G., eds. 1989. *The Structure of Multimodal Dialogue.* Amsterdam: North-Holland.

Thiel, U. 1995. Interaction in Hypermedia Systems: From Browsing to Conversation. In *Designing User Interfaces for Hypermedia* (Research Reports ESPRIT Project 6532 HIFI, Vol. 1), eds. W. Schuler, J. Hannemann, and N. Streitz, 43-54. Berlin: Springer Verlag.

Thiel, U.; Gulla, J. A.; Müller, A.; and Stein, A. 1996. Dialogue Strategies for Multimedia Retrieval: Intertwining Abductive Reasoning and Dialogue Planning. In *Proceedings of the Final Workshop on Multimedia Information Retrieval (MIRO'95).* Glasgow, Scottland. ed. I. Ruthven. Berlin: Springer Verlag (eWiC, electronic Workshops in Computing series, http://www.springer.co.uk/eWiC/Workshops/MIRO95.html).

Vassileva, J. 1997. Ensuring a Task-based Individualized Interface for Hypermedia Information Retrieval by User Modeling. In this volume.

Wachtel, T. 1986. Pragmatic Sensitivity in NL Interfaces and the Structure of Conversation. In Proceedings of the 11th International Conference on Computational Linguistics (COLING '86), 35-41 Bonn, University of Bonn.

Winograd, T., and Flores, F. 1986. *Understanding Computers and Cognition.* Norwood, NJ: Ablex.

Empirical Evaluations

The chapters in this final section address empirical studies that attempt to tease out principles that could guide the design of intelligent multimedia information retrieval systems. Whereas the first chapter focuses on how users interact with multimedia on-line documentation (and how it could be improved), the second chapter investigates how users seek information from on-line multimedia collections.

In the first chapter, Helmut Horacek (Universität Bielefeld, Germany) reports a study of a multimedia on-line documentation system (the HP-VUE UNIX manual). Horacek focuses on controlled experiments with 20 users with tasks such as window handling (e.g., move, resize, scroll, cut and paste), text editing (e.g., load, insert, spell check, format) and file management (e.g., locate, append, adjust, sort). The experiments were used to confirm or deny hypotheses regarding the most effective use of media for these tasks (e.g., illustrations that give an impression of changes caused by an action will improve user performance, more complex command descriptions will result in reduced user performance). Moreover, user assessments (e.g., of the comprehensibility of graphics, the desire for alternate presentations) and their preferences (e.g., for animations to support particular tasks) were recorded.

Horacek's investigations result in specific multimedia presentation guidelines. For improved descriptions, he argues:

- Use operationally descriptive terms (e.g., referring to "the left mouse button" as opposed to "mouse button 1")
- Use task-oriented statements (e.g., instead of "choose a list item" state "click on the item you wish to choose").

For object identification:

- Ensure explicit connections between textual terms and picture elements (e.g., via arrows)
- Visually distinguish functional elements of pictures (e.g., labels versus

buttons).

In action descriptions:

- Illustrate actions in varying degrees of detail and, if necessary, in several variants
- Articulate non-trivial pre-conditions of an action.

In terms of information organization:

- Link verbal action descriptions which refer to illustration portions
- Partition highly parameterized actions into subparts to enable their composition into user and situation tailored presentations.

Horacek concludes that observations of users performing various tasks requiring access to on-line, mixed media documentation argue for a number of the intelligent methods presented in earlier sections of this book (e.g., user and discourse modeling to enable adaptive hypertext, multimedia presentation planning). These techniques promise user and task tailored documentation, varying in degrees of explicitness and detail, and containing coordinated multimedia illustrations of objects and actions.

Recognizing that not all information will be in extracted form, the final chapter by Alistair Sutcliffe, Matt Hare, Ann Doubleday and Michele Ryan (City University, London) investigates how users search for and extract information from multimedia repositories. Key questions investigated include:

- What is the relationship of users' search behavior to retrieval performance in multimedia databases?
- Does the type of information requested bias which media type users search?
- What kind of performance do users exhibit in complex retrieval situations which require, e.g., negative answers, inference from extracted information, or reference across different media types?
- Do users search all relevant media when seeking information?
- Do users exploit multiple open windows (e.g., to facilitate cross referencing)?

Their studies demonstrate how users may be misled into searching inappropriate media by the way a question is expressed, how explicit cross references between media can help in the extraction of information, as well as showing that well known information retrieval problems such as null result sets are exacerbated by multimedia. Their studies suggest that multimedia information retrieval systems should (1) make the searchable set of media resources visible to the user, (2) widen the scope of searches between media, (3) link related data to queries, and (4) provide history lists of retrieved media. Users may have inappropriate expectations of the type of information that they can extract from different media, which underlines the importance of tools for automatic indexing and querying the content of visual media, reported in earlier chapters. Such tools may counteract the search biases and help provide cross referencing between topics within separate media.

Researches have suggested tentative usability guidelines for how searches may be formulated and for planning presentation of retrieved multimedia data, however, we are still a considerable way from understanding how people browse, search, and extract information from multimedia. Consideration of the users' tasks and information seeking needs should be supported in forming queries, while information delivery might be made more effective by selecting and integrating appropriate media in planned presentations. Unfortunately empirical study to inform design lags technological solutions, such as those presented in earlier sections of the collection. Furthermore, future experiments need to address industrial scale applications with gigabytes of data and thousands of queries. Nevertheless, the studies in this section begin to lay some foundations for more informed, psychologically-based understanding of multimedia information retrieval.

Chapter 21

Empirical Evidence for the Need of Intelligent Methods in Multimedia Information Retrieval

Helmut Horacek
Universitaet des Saarlandes

Abstract

The effectiveness of information retrieval systems depends on the skillful organization of knowledge, the flexibility of text browsers, and the quality of information presentation techniques. Unfortunately, effective information organization and presentation remains challenging—this aspect is rarely covered by design goals, and expert predictions about potential user problems are inherently unreliable. To gain detailed design insight, we have performed a case study that tests a multimedia on-line documentation system in terms of its accuracy and completeness in a few selected domains. By performing these experiments, we have identified potential user problems, the analysis of which has led us to design guidelines which are more concrete than the existing ones. Following these guidelines in an adequate manner requires more than just clever design, and so we argue for and sketch out the use of intelligent methods. Because of the principled nature of the lessons learned, we believe that our study provides useful hints for the design of advanced multimedia on-line information retrieval systems.

1. Introduction

Information retrieval concerns methods for extracting the content of information objects, storing the elaborated structures, accessing these structures, and presenting the results obtained. Classical information retrieval, which aims at accessing documents specified in terms of Boolean expressions built over keywords, subsequently enhanced by probabilistic methods, is being extended by more intelligent retrieval techniques. New developments including full text databases and multimedia call into question the traditional distinction between bibliographic document retrieval and fact retrieval systems. The advantages of hypertext for browsing (Marchionini and Shneiderman 1988) can be synergistically integrated with direct search (Kuhlen 1991), as illustrated in Stock et al. (this volume).

Information retrieval tools as well as on-line documentation need to support users in the task of scanning, understanding, and selecting information. Whereas hypertext support for these tasks has uncovered challenges (e.g., disorientation, inappropriate level of detail), intelligent methods to mitigate these problems need to be carefully applied based on measurable performance improvements because of their potential complexity and expense (e.g., recognizing user plans, building individualized user models).

In order to learn more about the degree of effectiveness of on-line documentation systems regarding these tasks, we have carried out a set of experiments with users to test the accuracy and completeness of a small selection of the facilities provided by the HP-VUE Help Manager. Whereas HP-VUE Help Manager is a graphical interface to HP-UX in English, HP-VUE (HP Visual User Environment) is a set of enhancements of the user interface for the X Window System, a subsystem of UNIX™.

In the experiments, twenty subjects were asked to accomplish a coherently composed sequence of subtasks aided by HP-VUE, with evaluators recording the ratio of success or failure they achieved in accomplishing necessary subtasks. Moreover, we made hypotheses about the expected user performance in some critical subtasks, in order to test the merit and reliability of expert predictions. Pursuing this approach enabled us to identify principled deficits of HP-VUE which improved our knowledge about the design of on-line documentation systems. We have formulated suitable design guidelines abstracting from the particulars of the examples observed. Moreover, the results of our experiments point to areas for the motivated incorporation of intelligent methods.

This chapter is organized as follows. First, we outline the motivations for examining the effectiveness of on-line documentation systems. We briefly assess the capabilities of HP-VUE, and we describe the design of the experiments carried out in connection with this system. Then, we present the results concerning success in accomplishing the given tasks, and we report on assessments and associated demands given by the test subjects. Following this we describe the derived guidelines originating from the deficits identified through our experiments. Finally, we discuss the potential for incorporating intelligent methods.

2. Motivation

It is a well-known fact that good documentation is an invaluable asset (Brockman 1986). Bailey (1983) even estimates that 60% of all human errors with software systems are related in some manner to the quality of the documentation. Earlier on-line documentation systems widely suffered from inflexible information access and from the ignorance of user concerns. Consider, for instance, the *man* function under UNIX™. In response to these deficits, some experimental systems have been developed recently that exhibit a variety of advanced capabilities such as adapting to the user's expertise (Tattersall 1992; Kobsa, Müller and Nill, this volume; Peter and Rösner 1994), applying planned multimedia presentation techniques (Chin et al. 1994, McKeown et al. 1990, Wahlster et al. 1993), and providing active help (Wilensky, Arens, and Chin 1984; Gwei and Foxley 1990; Krause, Mittermaier and Hirschmann 1993).

Multimedia is an important aspect here for two reasons. First, an increasing number of systems combine different types of interaction including command languages, menus, and direct manipulation by using text, icons, graphics, and even video. Second, presentations that exploit multiple human senses have been shown to enhance comprehension (e.g., pictures are considered beneficial for illustrating procedural instructions (Booher 1975)). Nevertheless, little is known yet about how humans make use of multimedia information sources, and what search strategies are beneficial in such an environment. One attempt to gain more insight in this direction is (Sutcliffe et al., this volume).

Despite evaluations that comparatively assess on-line documentation system performance (Krause, Mittermaier and Hirschmann 1993) or design (Duffy, Palmer and Mehlenbacher 1992), there remain serious problems with the organization and presentation of information (e.g., via hypertext nodes and links).[1] Indeed, according to Schriver (1987), most errors in using documentation are a consequence of missing knowledge. In spite of this, perhaps because of this, only a few, vague design goals for on-line help systems address missing knowledge (Duffy, Palmer and Mehlenbacher 1992) and none address the choice and coordination of media. Moreover, tester reliability based on questionnaires (Duffy, Palmer and Mehlenbacher 1992) is low for evaluations of tasks such as *"selecting topics"* (.43), *"obtaining information"* (.47), *and "comprehending information"* (.24).[2] Given tester reliability concerns, we have turned to experiments with the on-line documentation system HP-VUE, in order to identify factors influencing user performance on these key tasks.

3. The System HP-VUE

HP-VUE provides hypertext-based access to on-line information about various system tools including programming languages, icon editors, and mail box tools. Information is presented in textual and graphical form (comprising

Application	T1	T2	T3	T4	T5	T6	T7	T8	Mean
HP-VUE 3.0	.50	.78	.58	.65	.29	.62	.67	.87	.62
PowerPoint 1.0	.25	.55	.82	.75	.47	.78	.34	.82	.60
Microsoft Word 3.0	.25	.28	.38	.68	.47	.67	.42	.19	.58

Table 1. Ratings of help facilities by user task.

colored images of menus and windows), supported by a glossary and a limited key word index.

In order to give the reader an impression of the strengths and weaknesses of HP-VUE, we have evaluated this system according to the questionnaire developed by Duffy, Palmer and Mehlenbacher (1992). In table 1, we present a comparison between HP-VUE and the on-line help facilities of PowerPoint 1.0 and Microsoft Word 3.0 on a Macintosh, which are by far the most similar ones to HP-VUE among the systems tested in (Duffy, Palmer and Mehlenbacher 1992) (the Pearson Product Moment Correlation Coefficients being .44 for PowerPoint 1.0 and .41 for Microsoft Word 3.0). The columns in table 1 represent tasks as distinguished by the rating system in the questionnaire:

- Representing the Problem (T1) (The way topics are named, favoring support for alternate problem representations)
- Accessing the Help System (T2) (Visibility and availability of access to help)
- Selecting a Topic (T3) (Support for alternative search strategies and context sensitivity)
- Searching for Relevant Information (T4) (Overall screen and document design in terms of physical formatting)
- Obtaining the Needed Information (T5) (Completeness and relevance of help content for a topic, such as usage, examples, explanations)
- Comprehending the Information (T6) (Overall quality of writing and graphics)
- Navigating to Other Topics (T7) (Guidance on how to move around, ease of moving around)
- Applying the Help Information (T8) (Ability to use application while in help)

This comparison suggests that HP-VUE is a reasonable system given today's standards, despite the deficits identified in the course of our experiments. It also provides a relative comparison of how well the system supports the tasks addressed by our experiments.

4. Experimental Design

In this section, I discuss the motivations underlying the tasks selected, the tasks to be accomplished by the subjects, and the hypotheses about subject performance that we made.

4.1 Motivations Underlying the Tasks Selected

Since HP-VUE offers information in a variety of heterogeneous areas, we had to pick suitable and representative parts of the documentation for our experiments. We have made our selection on the basis of two orthogonal criteria: we intended to cover a wide range of interaction types, and we favored the inclusion of different kinds of tasks so that a variety of users could be expected to find a task suitable to their degree of experience. On these grounds, we have chosen three areas:

- Operations applied to windows and their contents—the interaction being based on direct manipulation (the "window" experiment)
- Editing and formatting text—the interaction being based on menus (the "editor" experiment)
- Some portions of file management under UNIX™—the interaction being based on a command language (the "UNIX" experiment)

Altogether, we tested 20 subjects, all of them students at the University of Bielefeld and native speakers of German. Students were selected based on their computer expertise (e.g., generally low experience, some experience with command-oriented operating systems). In all cases, the subjects were required to have at most limited experience with those aspects of HP-VUE which have been tested by the experiments. Furthermore, a reasonable command of technical English was required. Because of these restrictive criteria, it was not possible to find a larger number of test subjects.

In each experiment, the subjects were confronted with a coherent sequence of subtasks to accomplish, which took them about half an hour to work on. Each successful completion of a subtask was recorded, as was the failure of doing this within ten minutes. Subjects were assigned to one of the tests based the following:

- Subjects having almost no experience with computers were assigned to the "window" experiment (6 subjects)
- Subjects having some experience with text editors other than the HP-VUE editor were assigned to the "editor" experiment (7 subjects)

- Subjects having reasonable to substantial experience with operating systems, but little or no experience with Unix™ were assigned to the "Unix" experiment (7 subjects)

Due to the significant differences in the degrees of experience required for solving each of these tasks, assigning subjects to individual experiments in a reasonable manner was not difficult. Only the choice between the "window" and the "editor" experiment entailed a few borderline cases. However, in each case we ensured that each subject had no prior experience with the particular environment and was likely to have the intellectual capabilities to solve the given task. All subjects made extensive use of HP-VUE because the on-line documentation apparently enabled them to solve the given problems and, on average, they achieved reasonable success rates. Consequently, an on-line documentation system can be expected to prove its maximal benefit under these circumstances.

4.2 Tasks to be Accomplished by the Subjects

In each experiment the subjects were given a one page description of their task, divided into four subtasks. A checklist associated with each subtask was used to record success or failure.

The "window" group was given two non-optimally positioned windows in a small sized format, one containing an alphabetically ordered set of records with personal data, the other consisting of a single record. The subjects had to appropriately integrate the single record into the sample data. In order to achieve this in a principled manner, they were asked to move the window containing the set of records to a better place, resize this window by enlarging horizontally and vertically, find the appropriate target location in that window where the additional record should be inserted, and cut that record from the other window and paste it into the new location.

In this experiment, the checklist included the following items: identification of objects such as "title bar," "frame," "scroll bar," "mouse key 1," "mouse key 2," performing actions such as scrolling or paging, positioning the mouse, marking the text to cut, and pasting the text into that location.

The "editor" group was initially confronted with an empty editor tablet. The subjects had to compose a letter out of some previously prepared components. In order to achieve this in a principled manner, they were asked to load a file containing the text part of the letter, insert another file including the appropriate header on top of this letter, apply the spell checker to correct typing errors, and format the letter, among others, by indenting the text body by 5 blanks on each side.

In this experiment, the checklist included: positioning the cursor to insert a file, selecting a paragraph to format, and performing indention.

The "Unix" group was given a window with a command line prompt in a specific subdirectory. The subjects had to compose an address file out of some moderately scattered components. In order to achieve this in a principled manner, they were asked to do the following (Note the correspondences and differences between keywords appearing in the task-oriented descriptions given to the subjects and UNIX command names and references to their parameters, as given in the short descriptions provided by HP-VUE):

- *Locate* relevant files with a distinguishing name component (here, headed by "list...") in the given subdirectory (by applying the *find* command)
- *Compose* the two files found (by applying the *cat* command),
- *Align* the left *margins* of all records (by applying the *adjust* command to the margins)
- *Sort* the contents of the composed address file by last name and then by first name (by applying the *sort* command)

In this experiment, the checklist included the following items for each command: identification of the appropriate UNIX command, redirecting the standard output, and specifying the parameters of a command.

When carrying out these tasks, the subjects were given access to a very local portion of HP-VUE by being moved to an initial point most suitable for the task at hand. They were asked to move down the topic hierarchy two levels at most, and external help was provided if they became disoriented because navigation in HP-VUE is challenging for inexperienced users. Moreover, "neutral" single word translations from English to German were provided if a subject explicitly requested them.

4.3 Hypotheses

In order to test to what extent we as experts are able to predict user problems, we made some hypotheses about subject performance in what we considered to be critical subtasks.

Hypothesis 1. A graphical illustration which combines snapshots at two different stages of an action to be performed (e.g., the illustration for resizing a window in HP-VUE) significantly improves the performance of the subjects in comparison to purely static illustrations (e.g., the illustrations of moving and scrolling a window) (the *dynamic graphics* hypothesis).

Hypothesis 2. Given a purely verbal description of the sequence of actions needed to cut and paste text in HP-VUE, subjects will be able to perform approximately half of these subactions correctly. This hypothesis is intended to examine to what extent predicted difficulties can be quantified by external raters (the *cut and paste* hypothesis).

Hypothesis 3. Given the menu-based descriptions in HP-VUE's editor documentation, which look rather similar to one another, performance of the subjects will not vary significantly across individual subtasks. This hypothesis is intended to test whether we as external raters were able to predict reliably where users should have no considerable difficulties (the *editor menu* hypothesis).

Hypothesis 4. Performance in successfully identifying a command keyword in a hierarchically organized set of lists will increase significantly for keywords whose descriptions can easily be matched to task descriptions (e.g., "adjust" and "sort" can be matched almost directly to task descriptions, while "find" and "cut" cannot) (the *concept match* hypothesis).

Hypothesis 5. Given an example that demonstrates the use of redirecting standard output in UNIX using the "cat" command, subjects will make subsequent use of this when applying "adjust" and "sort" commands, even if it does not appear in the help pages describing these commands (the *standard output* hypothesis).

Hypothesis 6. Subjects will perform worse when applying commands with many parameters (e.g., "sort") than those with few (e.g., "find," "cat"). This hypothesis is intended to examine the influence the complexity of a description has on the subjects' performance (the *option variety* hypothesis).

Hence, hypotheses 1 and 2 are tested by the "window" experiment, hypothesis 3 by the "editor" experiment, and hypotheses 4, 5 and 6 by the "UNIX" experiment.

5. Results of the Experiments

In this section, we present detailed experimental results. The discussion includes success rates achieved in accomplishing selected subtasks, and confirmation or denial of hypotheses on the basis of subject performance. All statistics regarding acceptance or rejection of hypotheses were computed according to a t-test (one- or two-tail t-test, depending on the hypothesis made).

5.1 The "Window" Experiment

In the "window" experiment, subjects frequently failed to identify those parts of a window to which they had to apply direct manipulation operations. The graphical display does not contain annotations for establishing a connection between textual descriptions and graphical object referents. Justifying the dynamic graphics hypothesis, the "frame" of a window (see the picture in the left half of figure 1) was identified much more frequently than both, the "title bar" (see the picture in the right half of figure 1) and the "scroll bar" (see the picture in the left half of figure 2). Note, that the graphical display shows relevant parts of the frame pulled out of their original positions to illustrate the required dragging actions. Also the subjects' assessments can be seen as evidence for the interpretation that this dynamic element helped the subjects to identify the frame (see table 4 in section 6). The difference between the sub-

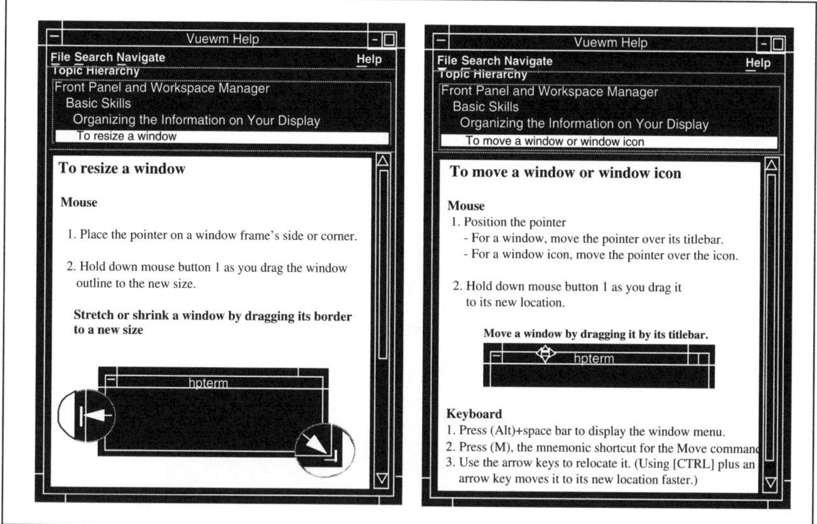

Figure 1. Graphical displays illustrating two window actions.

jects' average performance in identifying the "frame" versus identifying the "scroll bar" and the "title bar" approached significance ($p < 0.06$).

Confronted with the involved and purely textual description of how cutting and pasting text is achieved (see the text in the right half of figure 2), all subjects failed to perform that action in a completely correct way. Almost each subject got only one subaction right; either positioning the mouse, or marking the text to cut, or pasting the text into the target location. No subject was able to correctly position the cursor at the appropriate target location. Since subject performance in cutting and pasting text was below average to a significantly high degree ($p < 0.01$), the cut and paste hypothesis was rejected.

5.2 The "Editor" Experiment

In the "editor" experiment, subjects performed consistently better than in the other experiments. In most subtasks, subjects had only minor difficulties; for instance, a few subjects needed some time to recognize that the text field naming the file selected by its full directory path is related in an appropriate manner to two menus, one exposing directory paths and the other one including the list of files from the current directory (see the left half of figure 3).

Surprisingly, the formatting task led to what was probably the most serious misunderstanding of all experiments. In the task specification, we asked the subjects to *indent* the body of a letter by five blanks on each side. Even though the formatting menu initially defaults "0" and "37" as left and right

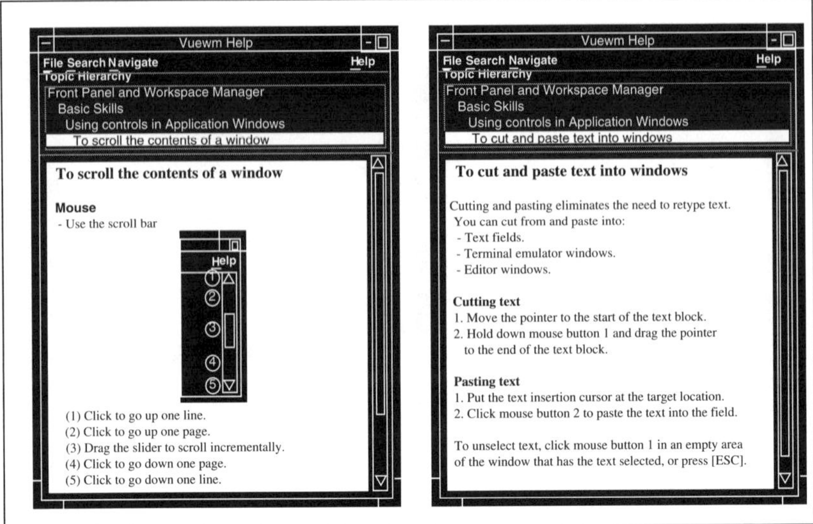

Figure 2. Window manipulations: graphical versus textual display.

margins in the menu (see the menu and the text on the right half of figure 3), the vast majority of the subjects simply entered "5"s in both slots, and they were unable to recover when the whole text consequently disappeared. It is precisely this subtask which endangers the acceptance of the editor menu hypothesis. Comparing the average performance on "Indenting Text" to the subtasks "Opening a File," "Including a File," and "Using the Spell Checker" shows a decrease in performance which approaches significance ($p < 0.08$).

5.3 The "Unix" Experiment

In the "UNIX" experiment, the subjects faced two major issues which many of them failed to accomplish in a satisfactory manner. The first is associated with identifying the "cat" command, and the second with applying the "sort" command to ordering the contents of a file by different fields.

Identifying the "cat" command proved to be difficult, because at least two hypertext links had to be followed in sequence in order to locate the information needed, and each link had to be selected out of a significant number of alternatives (figure 4). Ideally, subjects had to pick up "Editing Files" out of a set of 15 items, each representing a group of actions applicable to files. Usually, subjects accessed information about "cat" by picking the item "Creating Files," either directly or via accessing "Copying Files" first. In the associated text, however, they primarily are told how to type in lines of text to be saved in a file. Only at the end of the second page of this document, two associative

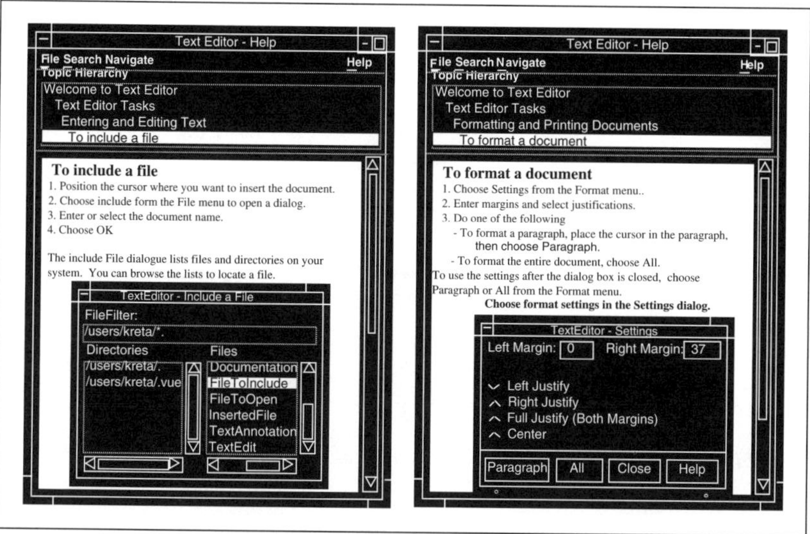

Figure 3. Graphical displays illustrating two editing tasks.

links are offered to "Appending Text to Files" and to "Concatenating Files" (see the arrows on the outer right part of figure 4). Some subjects returned from this node before discovering these links. Among those who succeeded, most pursued this side path, and not the more direct path through "Editing Files." Moreover, some subjects who accessed the document on "Appending Text to Files" failed to recognize the suitability of the example given at the end of the first document page "cat file1 >> file2," probably because the description of this usage of "cat" is tightly integrated in the overall text. In general, most subjects who discovered the information needed about "cat" succeeded by chance rather than by means of a systematic search.

Apart from the "cat" command, the "find" command was also not immediately identifiable in the short command descriptions (see section 4.2 for details), which contrasts with the other two commands, "adjust" and "sort." When comparing the average performance on identifying these pairs of commands (which relate to the concept match hypothesis) the difference proved to be highly significant ($p < 0.01$). Hence, the concept match hypothesis was confirmed.

Most subjects were unable to find the information required for specifying multiple fields for sorting, because this description is embedded deeply in the texts about the "sort" command. In order to access that piece of information, the user has to click on the item "More on Sorting" at the end of the fourth page describing the "sort" command, and then considerably scroll the linked document. Due to the unfortunate organization of the "sort" command de-

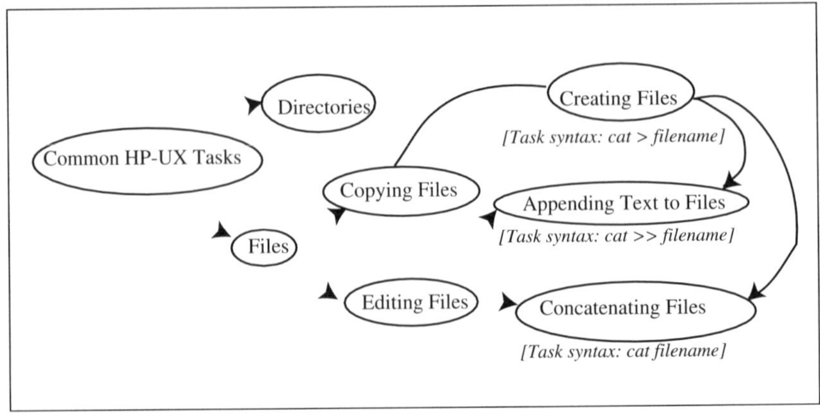

Figure 4. Alternative paths to access information about the "cat" command.

scription, subjects performed worse at applying this command, which is associated with a richer variety of options than the commands "find," "cat" and "adjust." Since the difference in performance proved to be highly significant ($p < 0.01$), the option variety hypothesis was confirmed.

In addition to difficulty using the highly parameterized commands "cat" and "sort," subjects frequently failed to correctly redirect the standard output. This feature is presented differently across command descriptions. Compare, for example, "cat file1 file2 > file3" to "adjust file" and "sort +1 -2 file." The decrease in redirecting the standard output correctly in subsequent command usage (adjust" and "sort") when compared to the first command, where its usage is described explicitly ("cat"), is highly significant ($p < 0.01$). Hence, the standard output hypothesis was rejected.

Table 2 summarizes which of our hypotheses were confirmed or rejected, and by what margin.

6. Assessments Provided by the Test Subjects

After accomplishing each subtask, subjects were asked specific questions about their assessments of selected system features. Most questions concerned the comprehensibility of graphical illustrations and preferences in favor of animations and in favor of more detailed or alternative textual descriptions. Each question was associated with a set of boxes. Answers were recorded using a Likert scale from 1 (strongly agree) to 5 (strongly disagree).

In the course of the "window" and the "editor" experiments, we asked subjects about their expectations concerning the benefit of animations. As ta-

Hypothesis	Assessment	Margin	t-value	Significance
dynamic graphics hypothesis	rejected	very close	t = 1.94	p < 0.06
cut and paste hypothesis	rejected	clear margin	t = 3.10	p < 0.01
editor menu hypothesis	confirmed	very close	t = 2.20	p < 0.08
concept match hypothesis	confirmed	clear margin	t = 3.28	p < 0.01
standard output hypothesis	rejected	clear margin	t = 4.58	p < 0.01
option variety hypothesis	confirmed	clear margin	t = 3.15	p < 0.01

Table 2. Summary of results obtained by hypotheses testing.

bles 3a and 3b illustrate, the answers to this question were rather conclusive. Almost all subjects strongly desired animation in the "window" experiment (the slightly deviant score of the scrolling action is due to one subject who unexpectedly understood that task very quickly). Moreover, subjects were strongly in favor of augmenting the purely textual description of the cut and paste action with a graphical illustration (with a mean of 1.25 and a standard deviation of 0.5). This result can be interpreted as empirical confirmation of the requirement for pictorial information to support action descriptions, as exposed in Booher (1975). In the "editor" experiment, subjects slightly tended to disfavor animations. However, the opinions generally fell into two pronounced clusters, either favoring or disfavoring animations strongly (see the high standard deviation values in the rightmost column in table 3b).

One could argue that the inexperienced subjects participating in our experiments are not very reliable in judging whether animations would be more helpful to them than the information they actually found. We believe that there are several pieces of evidence indicating that the subjects are indeed capable of judging this issue:

- They were given instructions and illustrations by the supervisor as to how to accomplish tasks after they failed to do so, which can be seen as a kind of human animation

- They clearly discriminated between expected benefits and inadequacy of animations

- They assessed animations beneficial also in challenging tasks where they succeeded

Another important concern was the extent to which subjects felt comfortable with the descriptions of the actions to be performed in the "window" experiment. Tables 4a, 4b, 5a, and 5b show the results. Table 4a shows the subjects' preferences for alternative object descriptions, and table 4b the subjects'

Subjects Animation Preferences			Subjects Animation Preferences		
"Window" Experiment	Mean	Standard Deviation	"Editor" Experiment	Mean	Standard Deviation
moving a window	1.16	0.40	*opening a file*	3.60	1.67
resizing a window	1.50	0.89	*including text from a file*	3.58	1.81
scroll a window's contents	2.20	1.79	*using the spell checker*	not asked here	
cutting and pasting text	1.00	0.00	*formatting the text*	2.86	2.03
overall score	1.48	1.03	*overall score*	3.32	1.80

Tables 3a and 3b. User assessments in favor of animations
(scaled from 1 [best score] to 5 [worst score]).

preferences for more detailed action descriptions. Table 5a illustrates the subjects' assessments of the comprehensibility of graphical illustrations, and table 5b correlations of these assessments to the subjects' preferences with respect to variations in object and action descriptions. Again, assessments are scaled from "1" to "5," "1" standing for most comprehensible and strongest preference for alternative descriptions, and "5" standing for the opposite.

However, the degree of the demand for detailed action descriptions does not correlate well with the comprehensibility of the graphics (See value -.34 in the lower right corner of table 5). This circumstance can probably be explained by the complexity of the actions involved: a title bar must merely be moved, a frame is partitioned into regions with different sensitivity to manipulations, and a window can be scrolled by a variety of different actions, that is, by dragging the slider or by clicking in some region of the scroll bar.

On average, users loosely tend to assess graphics as less comprehensible if they have increased difficulty with the task illustrated. Some further details give evidence for the relative importance that graphical illustrations have for task accomplishment. Unlike other subtasks, the success rates achieved in resizing a window correlate strongly with the assessment about the comprehensibility of the graphics illustrating the manipulation operations applicable to the frame of a window (the Pearson Product Moment Correlation Coefficient is .86, in contrast to the corresponding values for the scroll bar (-.45), and for the title bar (-0.02)). Apparently, understanding this graphic was central to accomplishing the task.

Subject Description Preferences
for Alternative Object Descriptions

Object Involved	Mean	Standard Deviation
title bar	2.17	1.83
frame	3.30	1.86
scroll bar	2.00	1.00
total	2.53	1.66

Subject Description Preferences
for More Detailed Action Descriptions

Object Involved	Mean	Standard Deviation
title bar	2.50	1.76
frame	2.00	1.26
scroll bar	1.80	0.84
total	2.12	1.32

Tables 4a and 4b. Subject description preferences
(scaled from 1 [best score] to 5 [worst score]).

Comprehensibility Assessments
for Graphical Illustrations

Object Involved	Mean	Standard Deviation
title bar	3.80	0.98
frame	2.20	1.60
scroll bar	3.40	1.82
total	3.12	1.58

Correlations to Preferences
for Descriptions in a Different Form

Object Involved	Alternatives	More Details
title bar	-.65	-.86
frame	-.49	-.67
scroll bar	-.69	-.73
total	-.60	-.34

Tables 5a and 5b. Subject comprehensibility assessments
(scaled from 1 [best score] to 5 [worst score])
and correlation with subject preferences for different forms.

7. Guidelines Derived

We have grouped the deficits observed and the guidelines derived into four areas: terminology selection, action illustration, object identification, and organization of information distribution. The last three groups prominently involve the coordination or choice of media. We address these groups in turn, and we formulate guidelines that, if followed adequately, should help to avoid these deficits. We also discuss some details about potential improvements. In order to achieve some of these improvements, a certain command of the concepts "context-sensitivity," "adaptability," and "flexible composition of parts" is necessary, which requires the methods applied to exhibit some intelligence.

7.1 Terminology Selection

Like previous researchers, we have observed that the terminology used in presenting information is sometimes inadequate to meet the experience users typically have when they access pieces of information about a particular item described. In our experiments, the editor menu hypothesis and the concept match hypothesis serve as supporting evidence. The most spectacular example in our experiments was the specification of document margins by a pair of numbers, which were interpreted as relative indent counts instead of absolute positions. Some other typical examples are (we also propose better variants):

> The term "terminal emulator window" confused inexperienced users who wanted to know how to cut and paste text. A descriptive phrase like "the window in which you can type in (UNIX) commands" would be more appropriate than the technically exact term. This is consistent with the advice given by Magers (1983) to use jargon-free language.

> Only 2 out of 6 subjects correctly identified "mouse button 1," but they recalled it easily in a later subtask. Nevertheless, half of the subjects failed to generalize that description to identify "mouse button 2" in one of the following subtasks. Hence, the terms "mouse button 1 and 2" should be replaced by "the left button" and "the middle button," respectively.

> Giving the common phrases "choose a list item" and "open a dialog" a contextually meaningful interpretation put too much burden on some of the subjects. For example, "click on the item which you want to choose" is certainly a better phrasing than "choose a list item," thereby following the advice to make task-oriented statements proposed in (Odescalchi 1986a, 1986b). Odescalchi has also demonstrated that the extra effort needed in writing documentation in this style is overcompensated by the productivity gain users can achieve when using task-oriented documentation.

The last set of examples demonstrates that, even though a user might be acquainted with a certain term, they may be unfamiliar with a particular usage or they may be unable to combine some terms in the proper way. Moreover, these abilities may vary significantly across users and groups of users.

From these observations, we can derive the following guidelines:

Guideline 1. Prefer operationally descriptive terms to jargon-like terms and to general terms that have a particular technical meaning in the context considered.

Guideline 2. Provide clarification for the meaning associated with a term by optionally stating consistency requirements, or by explicitly expressing differences to similar terms. Clarification should be made accessible on demand, when the user encounters a problem. Hence, context-sensitivity is an important factor in triggering descriptions from different perspectives.

7.2 Action Illustration

Our experiments demonstrate that some of the illustrations of actions contained in a document are lacking the necessary degree of explicitness to be beneficial to inexperienced users. The cut and paste hypothesis and the standard output hypothesis serve as supporting evidence. Some additional examples are:

- Some subjects were unable to carry out a required mouse action because the associated textual description did not explicitly tell them when to hold down a button and when to release it.

- Another problem is the occurrence of unwanted effects. In HP-VUE, no other manipulations can be carried out once a menu is open. In our experiments, a few subjects opened some menu by chance, so that even correctly applying a dragging action to some manipulation-sensitive window region did not show the expected effect—the menu must be de-activated first.

From these observations, we can derive the following guidelines:

Guideline 3. Provide descriptions of non-trivial action sequences in several variants with increasing degrees of detail and explicitness, all of them being alternatively accessible on demand. A significant amount of adaptability is supported this way.

Guideline 4. Provide access to statements about non-trivial preconditions for applying a described action; this will help users identify obstacles. Context-sensitivity is an important factor here.

7.3 Object Identification

Our experiments also demonstrate that subjects have considerable difficulty in identifying objects using the provided textual descriptions and graphical illustrations. The dynamic graphics hypothesis serves as supporting evidence:

- The prominent window regions "scroll bar" and "title bar" were identified with great difficulty, if at all.

- Graphical annotations may require more explicit description. Particular confusion was caused by the encircled numbers which are intended to point to selected regions of the scroll bar according to their sensitivity to manipulation operations (see the left half of figure 3): several subjects consistently attempted to click on the numbers, apparently expecting some action to happen.

- Frequently, uncertainty about the mouse sensitivity of regions in a graphical display led to misunderstandings. Some subjects attempted to specify a file name directly in the help page that explains the text editor's menu for opening or including a file, instead of accessing the appropriate editor menu.

From these observations, we can derive the following guidelines:

Guideline 5. In order to ensure successful cross media reference, establish a clear connection between occurrences of terms in the text and corresponding parts of the picture (e.g., by using dashes). Alternatively, prominent terms like "scroll bar" and "title bar" could be made mouse-sensitive to provide access to more detailed graphics. In contrast to labeling, which illustrates the portion of a picture by exposing how it is named (clarifying what it is), our guideline aims at getting access to some graphical element from the text referring to it (clarifying where it is and how it looks).

Guideline 6. Design functional elements in a picture in such a way that their meaning is apparent to the user. In particular, labels intended to establish a connection to some portions of text outside of the picture should be distinguished from control buttons in a clear manner.

7.4 Organization of Information Distribution

In several places, the coordination and distribution of information proved to be insufficient for users. The dynamic graphics hypothesis and the option variety hypothesis helped to identify this issue. In some cases, information may be present, but not in the place where it is needed. Consider:

- A rather drastic example is the detailed graphical display including appropriate annotations for the screen regions that apprentices usually find difficult to identify. This picture (see the right part of figure 5) appears at the bottom of an overview page (its upper part is depicted in the left part of figure 5), but the graphical display does not fit on the first page of this document; about half a screen full of text lies between the two document segments displayed in figure 5.

- In the long description including all subtleties of a command, it may be hard to find those features needed for the task at hand (here, this applied to the "sort" command).

- The context between commands presented in different versions and at different places was not always clear to the subjects—for instance, problems with identifying the "cat" command proved to be severe.

From these observations, we can derive the following guidelines:

Guideline 7. Make details of a graphical illustration accessible from those places where action descriptions refer to portions of that illustration. For instance, access should be given to the picture exposed in the right half of figure 5, anchored in the action description found in the screens appearing in figure 1 and in the left part of figure 2. This requires flexible composition of media from smaller parts.

Guideline 8. Partition the presentation of highly parameterized actions into smaller coherent packages enabling flexible composition of parts. In addi-

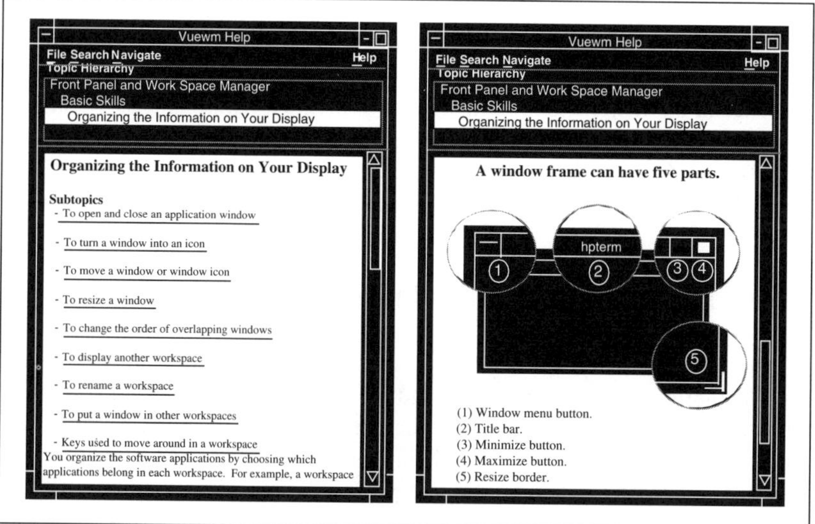

Figure 5. Window manipulation operations: displays from the overview page.

tion, provide overviews to illustrate the connections between usage of individual commands.

These guidelines, which primarily concern the design of graphical illustrations and their coordination with text, can naturally be extended to animations. In contrast to the navigation based organization of information, the temporal order of individual actions and menu-like choice points provide suitable means to coordinate partial information in a dynamic environment. However, applying caution in the choice of media is advisable, since Palmiter, Elkerton and Baggett (1989) have shown that certain kinds of animations do not improve user performance. Nevertheless, in comparison to ordinary graphics, animations provide a richer repertoire for drawing the user's attention to prominent portions of a scene to support the identification of central objects. A basic ingredient in animation design is to stage the action properly, which includes choosing a view that conveys the most information about the events taking place in the animation, and isolating events so that (when possible) only one item at a time occupies the viewer's attention. This rule applies particularly to the demonstration of actions at a high degree of explicitness, which was frequently missing in graphical illustrations and especially in purely verbal descriptions. Finally, animations should provide better means than other media to incorporate and emphasize warnings in a presentation sequence.

Due to limited resources we have only been able to carry out a case study; therefore, the assessments of some of the hypotheses are critical due to the small number of test subjects, and also the number of cases considered is too small to justify the acceptance or the rejection of the hypotheses made in a more general context. Nevertheless, the experiments demonstrate some clear tendencies: the deficits identified are of a principled nature and they enabled us to formulate guidelines for designing hypertext-based on-line help facilities. The rationale underlying our guidelines could certainly be strengthened by performing additional tests with a variety of other similar help systems.

8. Areas for Incorporating Intelligent Methods

In several places where HP-VUE falls short, the guidelines mention the need for adaptability, context-sensitivity, and the flexible composition of parts. We believe that the deficits observed in the course of our experiments with HP-VUE and the design guidelines derived from them give evidence that an on-line documentation system could well profit from the incorporation of intelligent methods. Integrating techniques from adaptive hypertext (Kobsa, Müller and Nill, this volume), multimedia text planning (Wahlster et al. 1993), natural language generation (Bateman and Paris 1989), and user modeling (Chin et al. 1994) would help to generate document versions in varying degrees of explicitness and detail; organize presentations of partial multimedia information and coordinate them appropriately for illustrating objects and actions; and exploit and maintain evidence about the user and his/her actions to select among alternative presentations in a motivated way.

9. Conclusion

In this chapter, we have examined the accuracy and completeness of selected portions of the on-line documentation system HP-VUE, by performing user experiments to discover missing pieces of knowledge in the system and to identify frequently demanded, but missing capabilities. This enterprise was motivated by limited design guidelines for structuring and presenting knowledge in on-line documentation systems and by the attempt to find promising areas for the incorporation of intelligent methods. We have demonstrated that expert assessments with respect to these tasks are unreliable—the hypotheses underlying our experiments also provide evidence for that.

Through our experiments, we have identified several kinds of deficits in the design of HP-VUE. The principled nature of these deficits enabled us to formulate additional and more concrete guidelines for the design of on-line documentation systems. The guidelines derived address the distribution of information over individual documents, their connections by motivated links, and the coordination of text and graphics within a document and across several documents. In some sense, the guidelines presented appear to be rather evident and natural—however, formulating them explicitly seems to meet a particular need since, in practice, the underlying principles are often violated.

Finally, we have argued that there are wide range of areas for beneficially incorporating intelligent methods in on-line documentation systems, including automated text generation, planning multimedia presentations, and user-adaptive documentation. Techniques originating from these areas promise to contribute to the avoidance or, at least, to the reduction of a variety of the deficits observed.

Acknowledgments

We would like to thank Ralf Kowalski for his support in the experiment design and the associated evaluation, and, in particular, for carrying out the vast majority of the time-consuming user experiments Moreover, we have to thank two anonymous referees for their valuable comments, as well as Mark Maybury for his editorial support, especially regarding the graphical illustrations.

Notes

1. This even holds for the next generation of on-line help systems, which attempt to actively participate in the recognition of a user's problem (Krause, Mittermaier and Hirschmann 1993, Wilensky, Arens and Chin 1984). In the scope of this chapter, we concentrate on hypertext-based, passive help systems, because their use is much more common in practice.

2. The measures are calculated in terms of the Pearson Product Moment Correlation Coefficient. That is, the higher the correlation between the judgments given by different testers (1 is the maximum value), the more likely it is that the questionnaire on which these judgments are based is well designed.

References

Bailey, R. 1983. *Human Errors in Computer Systems.* Englewood Cliffs: Prentice-Hall.

Bateman, J. and Paris, C. 1989. Phrasing a Text in Terms the User Can Understand. In Proceedings of the Eleventh International Joint Conference on Artificial Intelligence, 1511-1517. Menlo Park, CA: International Joint Conferences on Artificial Intelligence.

Booher, H. 1975. Relative Comprehensibility of Pictorial Information and Printed Words on Proceduralized Instructions. *Human Factors* 17: 266-277.

Brockman, J. 1986. *Writing Better Computer User Documentation.* New York: John Wiley.

Chin, D.; Inaba, M.; Pareek, H.; Nemoto, K.; Wasson, M.; and Miyamoto, I. 1994. Multi-Dimensional User Models for Multimedia I/O in the Maintenance Consultant. In Proceedings of the Fourth International Conference On User Modeling, 139-144.

ed. A. Kobsa. 15-19 August 1994 Hyannis (Cape Cod), MA.

Duffy, T.; Palmer, J.; and Mehlenbacher, B. 1992. *On-line Help: Design and Evaluation. New York:* Ablex Publishing Corporation.

Gwei, G. and Foxley, E. 1990. Towards a Consultative On-Line Help System. *International Journal of Man-Machine Studies* 32: 363-383.

Kobsa, A.; Müller, D.; and Nill, A. 1997. Hypertext and Hypermedia Clients of the User Modeling System BGP-MS. In this volume.

Krause, J.; Mittermaier, E.; and Hirschmann, A. 1993. The Intelligent System COMFOHELP. *User Modeling and User-Adapted Interaction* 3(3): 249-282.

Kuhlen, R. 1991. Hypertext—Ein nicht-lineares Medium zwischen Buch und Wissensbank. Springer Verlag, Berlin.

Magers, C. 1983. An Experimental Evaluation of On-Line HELP for Non-Programmers. Proceedings of the CHI '83 Conference: Human Factors in Computing Systems, 277-281.

Marchionini, G. and Shneiderman, B. 1988. Finding Facts Versus Browsing Knowledge in Hypertext Systems. *IEEE Computer 21*(1): 70-81.

McKeown, K.; Elhadad, M.; Fukumoto, Y.; Lim, J.; Lombardi, C.; Robin, J.; and Smadja F. 1990. Natural Language Generation in COMET. In *Current Issues in Natural Language Generation,* eds. R. Dale; C. Mellish; M. Zock, 103-139. New York: Academic Press.

Odescalchi E. 1986. Productivity Gain Attained by Task-Oriented Information. Proceedings of the 33rd International Technical Communication Conference, Society for technical Communication, 434-439. Washington DC.

Odescalchi E. 1986. Documentation is the Key to User Success. In *IEEE Transactions on Professional Communication* 29: 16-18.

Palmiter, S.; Elkerton, J.; Baggett, P. 1989. Animated Demonstrations Versus Written Instructions for Learning Procedural Tasks. Technical Report C4E-ONR-2. Center for Ergonomics, University of Michigan, Ann Arbor, MI.

Peter, G.; Rösner, D. 1994. User-Model-Driven Generation of Instructions. *User Modeling and User-Adapted Interaction* 3: 289-319.

Schriver, K. 1987. Teaching Writers to Anticipate the Reader's Needs: Empirically Based Instruction. Doctoral Dissertation in Rhetoric, Carnegie-Mellon University, Pittsburgh, PA.

Stock, O.; Strapparava, C. and Zancanaro, M. 1997. Explorations in an Environment for Natural Language MultiModal Information Access. In this volume

Sutcliffe, A.; Hare, M.; Doubleday, A.; and Ryan M. 1997. Empirical Studies in Multimedia Information Retrieval. In this volume.

Tattersall, C. 1992. Generating Help for Users of Application Software. User Modeling and User-Adapted Interaction 3(2): 211-248.

Wahlster, W.; André, E.; Finkler, W.; Profitlich, H.-J.; Rist, T. 1993. Plan-Based Integration of Natural Language and Graphics Generation. *Artificial Intelligence* (63)1: 387-427.

Wilensky, R.; Arens, Y.; Chin, D. 1984. Talking to UNIX in English: An Overview of UC. Communications of the ACM 27: 574-593.

Chapter 22

Empirical Studies in Multimedia Information Retrieval

Alistair Sutcliffe, Matt Hare, Ann Doubleday and Michele Ryan
School of Informatics, City University

Abstract

Two empirical studies on multimedia information retrieval are reported. The motivation for the experiments was to study how users search different multimedia resources according to an information need, the information seeking strategies they adopt, and preferences for different design options. In the first experiment users were given a set of questions to answer from a set of seven media resources. In the second experiment paper-based scenarios were used to assess performance and preference for different design options in information querying and presentation. Questions appeared to bias users to search inappropriate resources; performance with null answer and linked answer questions was poor. Explicit references between media helped information seeking. Preferences were found for feedback linking questions to retrieved results. Tentative guidelines are proposed from the experimental findings.

1. Introduction

Even though multimedia systems are becoming commonplace we have little understanding about how we interact with composites of text, speech and complex images. Cognitive studies demonstrate that thematic linking of topics in different media via "contact" points (Baggett 1984) is an important facet of the multimedia "reading" process. Different media have biases in terms of human attention, for instance dynamic media (e.g., animation, speech) attract attention much more effectively than static media such as text and still images (Possner 1976, Bieger and Glock 1984).

Sutcliffe and Faraday (1994) have proposed guidelines for information presentation in mixed media. These include how to select appropriate media for specific information types, when to focus attention in visual processing by using markers, highlighting and visual attributes, and methods for linking related information in different media. Similar guidelines have been produced by Feiner and McKeown (1993) and André et al. (1993). Intelligent multimedia planners have been developed for explanations systems (Maybury 1993, André et al. 1993) which employ media selection rules and rhetorically based planning strategies. Intelligence has also been deployed in multimodal interaction, for example, in the Alfresco system described in Stock et al. (this volume), where natural language and diectic input are interpreted in a common semantic framework. In spite of the success of multimedia systems, there have been few empirical studies focused on multimedia interaction so we have little understanding about how users perceive information in different media combinations. A notable exception is the study by Olson et al. (1995) who gave some cognitive principles for building usable multimedia interfaces based on a discourse analysis of user-system interaction with multimedia groupware systems. Further guidelines, based on empirical study of multimedia help systems are reported by Horacek (this volume). Although these studies form useful starting points, we are still a long way from developing principles and guidelines for multimedia interface designs based on sound cognitive science.

Information retrieval from multimedia databases can produce a considerable quantity of information which is difficult to assimilate. Furthermore, multimedia databases exacerbate the problems of query formulation since linguistically expressed query terms often refer to information held in nonlinguistic media. The designer must be consciously aware of each medium, ensuring that it is individually comprehensible, while the organization of media combinations makes a coherent whole (Marks 1995). Williams et al. (1992) demonstrate the difficulty of dealing with a large range and quantity of multimedia data and argue that different media types need to be integrated into a single framework for managing and processing information. For multimedia information retrieval two key questions are "How do people search for information in different types of media?" and "How do they link information fragments across media into a coherent whole?"

Multimedia information retrieval poses users problems in finding appropriate resources and extracting information from within multimedia documents. Text and relational databases can be searched on content and indexing terms. However, to find information in images, video and speech the user is dependent on the extent of the semantic description of the resource assigned by the database indexer. While content directed searching is possible with advanced prototypes, e.g., for spoken language indexing (Weschsler and Schauble 1995; Jones et al., this volume; Hauptmann and Whitbrock, this volume), audio indexing (Blum et al., this volume), video scene boundary browsing (Tonomura et al. 1994; Aigraine et al., this volume), video image indexing (Yoshitaka et al. 1994; Zhang et al., this volume; Pentland, this volume; Flickner et al., this volume), and graphics indexing (Chuah et al., this volume), little is known about how users direct searches according to the semantics of their information needs and query expressions of those needs. User expectations about how to request information are important. For example Holt and Hardwick (1994) argue that searches are often based on what things look like rather than using words to create a description. Foote et al. (1995) report acoustic keyword spotting for audio information retrieval while Tonomura et al. (1994) describe query facilities for visual attributes in video sequences. However, content based retrieval techniques are still in their infancy. Furthermore, we have little understanding about when such techniques may be profitably used in combination with, or instead of, more traditional query languages.

In this chapter we report the results of experimental studies to throw some light on these issues. These studies were conducted within the context of Esprit project INTUITIVE (interactive user interface tools in a visual environment) which produced a reusable library of software for developing front-end user interfaces to multiple, multimedia databases. The experiments were intended to inform both the design of the information retrieval and presentation tools and their configuration for different user needs. The chapter is organized into the following sections. The experimental design is described in section 2. The analysis of the first experiment is described in section 3, followed by the results of the second experiment on user preferences in section 4. In light of the experimental results we identify a number of areas in need of software support at the user interface and discuss the implications for information retrieval tools in section 5.

2. Experimental Design and Methods

The first experiment was undertaken to analyze how users search for and assimilate information stored in a number of different media resources. Two phases of the search process were investigated, first finding the correct media document for the query and second extracting information from one or more media documents. More specifically we wished to shed light on the following questions:

- How do users' search behavior and retrieval performance correlate in multimedia databases?

- Are users biased towards looking for information in a particular media resource according to the information requested in the question?

- How do users perform when queries require negative answers, requiring them to use inference to extract information, and reference to different parts of the answer in separate media resources?

- Do users access all the necessary media resources when seeking information?
- Do users take advantage of having multiple windows open concurrently, to allow cross-referencing and reduce working memory burden?

We were interested in how cues effect users' search behavior and how users extract information from multimedia resources, both when the target information was explicit and when it was not. The experimental system used a 486 PC running Microsoft, Windows™. Multimedia information was presented using Paintbrush™ for still images, Word™ for text and Video for Windows™ for animation. The Paintbrush™ windows had their palette and editing facilities deactivated, while Word™ had its ruler and control bar deactivated, so the users could view, but not change, the media resources. Ten subjects all undergraduates and researchers at City University who were familiar with Microsoft, Windows™, were asked to answer a set of 18 questions using a set of seven multimedia documents. The seven documents contained information relating to a story theme about a retiring racing car driver, and were presented inconised form with a text title (see figure 1).

The multimedia information was related to a storyline about a fictitious, racing car driver (Nigel Dempster) who was retiring after a serious accident, the sponsorship of Dempster by Gateway PLC and his interest in the DOE's project on racing safety. The experimental paradigm was essentially a test of "query by pointing" when the information source is known to the user who has to work out which media resources to query to obtain the answer. The experimental design was composed of the following phases:

- *Exploration.* The subjects were allowed to explore the PC system and the media resources. Exploration was encouraged so all subjects became familiar with the icon and file name cues and the media types in the file name extensions (e.g., DOE.avi indicated a video).
- *Test.* Experimental test in which the subjects started with the initial screen showing the seven iconised multimedia resources (see figure 1) and were then asked to answer 18 questions using the system as they wished. The subjects were audio and video taped and their focus of attention was monitored throughout.
- *Post Test.* Post test questionnaire about their media preferences and debriefing interviews.

The subjects were told that the answers could be found within the information on the screen and that answers should be as detailed as possible. No time limit was given. The questions (see table 1) varied from simple questions designed to elicit a single item of information from a single resource, to complex questions requiring an exhaustive search over several different sources.

The subject performance was scored against a gold standard set of answers, and a log was kept of which media resources they accessed and when.

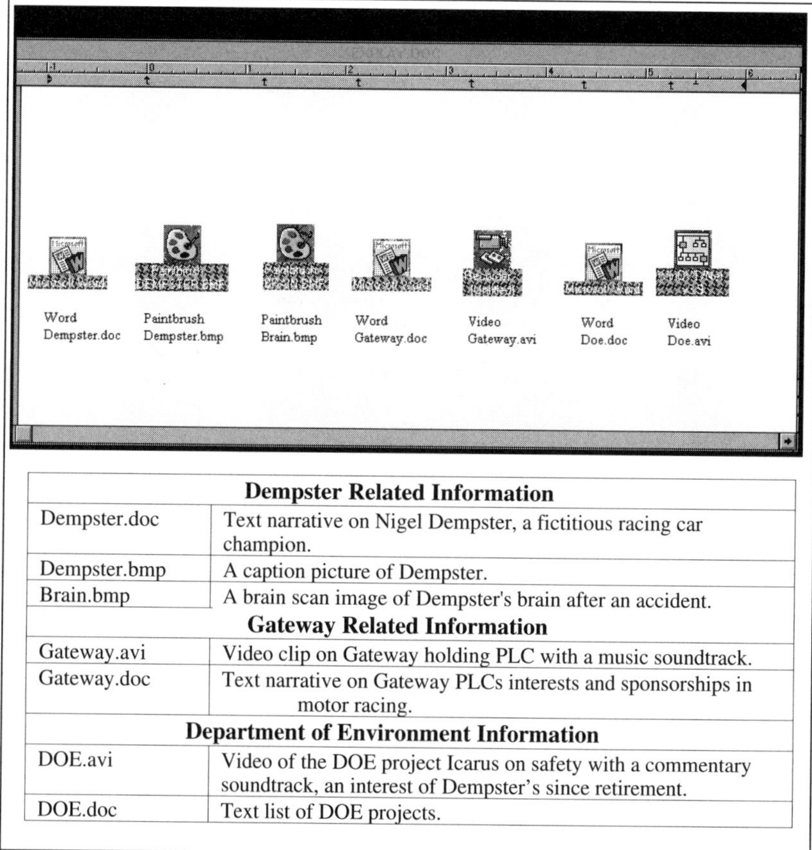

Dempster Related Information	
Dempster.doc	Text narrative on Nigel Dempster, a fictitious racing car champion.
Dempster.bmp	A caption picture of Dempster.
Brain.bmp	A brain scan image of Dempster's brain after an accident.
Gateway Related Information	
Gateway.avi	Video clip on Gateway holding PLC with a music soundtrack.
Gateway.doc	Text narrative on Gateway PLCs interests and sponsorships in motor racing.
Department of Environment Information	
DOE.avi	Video of the DOE project Icarus on safety with a commentary soundtrack, an interest of Dempster's since retirement.
DOE.doc	Text list of DOE projects.

Figure 1. Initial screen layout in experiment 1 (top) and
some of the resources available to answer the questions included (bottom).

A trace of interaction with the system was recorded with the following window operations: Maximize, Normal (display), Iconise, Move, Enlarge, Reduce and Scroll. The trace also logged whether users opened windows concurrently or serially.

In the post test questionnaire subjects were asked to:

- State their preference for the style of window layout for all 7 resources by ranking the following alternatives: (1) All visible in tiled format but reduced in size. (2) All visible in tiled format but clipped with scroll bars. (3) All on screen and full size but overlapped. (4) Presented one at a time, full size, with the others iconised. (5) Any other user-specified strategy.

- Rank the 7 resources in order of perceived difficulty for finding information within the resource.

Question	Search Complexity	Influence	Linked to Question	Number of Resources Required
1	linked facts	explicit cue	-	2
2	simple fact	inference	-	2
3	simple fact	cue bias	from 2	1
4	simple fact	cue bias	from 2,3	1
5	complex facts	inference + bias	-	
6	simple fact	explicit cue	-	1
7	linked facts	explicit cue	from 6	2
8	true/false fact	negative answer	from 6,7	2
9	complex list	completeness	from 6,7,8	2
10	simple fact	display manip	-	1
11	linked facts	inference + bias	weak from 2	2
12	true/false fact	negative answer	-	2
13	linked facts	cue bias	-	1
14	link fact	inference + bias	from 13	1
15	simple fact	inference + bias	from 13, 14	1
16	complex list	cross ref + bias	from 13-15	1
17	complex list	cross ref + bias	from 13-16	1
18	complex list	cue bias	from 13-17	1

Table 1. Classification of search complexity and influence.

- Rank the 7 resources in order of perceived usefulness of the information contained therein for answering the test questions.

3. Results

Overall user performance is shown in tables 2 (totals by question) and 3 (totals by individual subject). The correctness of the subjects' answers varied from 50% (subject 10) to 83% for subjects 2 and 5. Average search times per question varied from 48 to 112 seconds; however, there was no correlation between accuracy of answers and time taken, for instance subject 5 had one of the longer search times. When totals by question are examined it appears that some questions gave more trouble than others. Questions 9 and 13 were answered correctly by only three and four of the subjects respectively. The questions which caused more errors were either those requiring negative answers, compound answers as lists of facts, or those requiring cross reference between information in different media (see table 1 for question types and table 2 for error data).

Overall times to complete the experiment, including reading and other

No.	Question	Average Time to Answer Question	Subjects Answering Correctly
1.	What color T-shirt was Dempster wearing on the day of his retirement announcement?	165.2 secs	10/10
2.	Use the mouse to point out in which part of Dempster's brain the injury is. Say to the experimenter "here" when the mouse is in the correct position.	49.2 secs	5/10
3.	Who was Dempster's doctor?	83.8 secs	8/10
4.	When did Dempster have his brain scan done?	47.0 secs	7/10
5.	Why did Dempster quit Indy Car Racing?	61.3 secs	7/10
6.	Who is Dempster sponsored by?	31.1 secs	9/10
7.	Name the TV family entertainment show host the sponsor has interests in.	152.3 secs	8/10
8.	Is Habitat a company that the sponsor has interests in?	69.8 secs	10/10
9	List as many companies as you can that Dempster's sponsor has shares in.	102.4 secs	3/10
10.	What is the registration number of the white Ford?	74.2 secs	5/10
11.	When and where was Dempster's accident?	62.8 secs	6/10
12.	Did Dempster win the '93 Indianapolis?	48.1 secs	7/10
13.	Name the computer system that Dempster has donated money towards.	90.8 secs	4/10
14.	Describe the end users of this system designed for the fire fighting services.	93.6 secs	6/10
15.	Is the system a single or multi-user environment?	75.1 secs	5/10
16.	What are the incidents that need to be controlled by fire fighters?	101.9 secs	10/10
17.	List the developers of the project.	42.5 secs	7/10
18.	What are Gateway's four defining P-Words for success?	99.6 secs	10/10

Table 2. Questions and average subjects' time and answer accuracy.

Subject Number	Average Time (secs) to Answer Question	Number of Correct Answers	Percent Correct
1	76.4	13/18	72
2	51.1	15/18	83
3	48.5	12/18	66
4	90.9	14/18	77
5	112	15/18	83
6	67.3	12/18	66
7	101	14/18	77
8	51.9	10/18	55
9	97.2	13/18	72
10	95.4	9/18	50

Table 3. Subjects' average time and accuracy in answering questions.

Media Group	Average time (sec)
Document	31.1
Bitmap	64.44
Video	91.31
Document and Bitmap	87.5
Video & Document	87.67

Table 4. Different media information extraction time.

inter-question answering activities, varied from 23–60 minutes, with a mean of 34.7 minutes; however, there was no correlation between speed and accuracy (Spearman correlation coefficient). When question answering times were analyzed according to the media resources required to obtain the answer, text based questions were rapid (31.1 secs), followed by still images (64.4 secs), whereas videos and combined resource questions showed longer response times ranging from 87.5–91 seconds (see table 4).

Frequencies of subjects opening text-based, video-based and still image-based media for searching are shown in table 5. The first column in table 5 expresses the percentage of accesses required for each media type to correctly answer the questions, whereas the second column gives the actual percentage of total access by media type. Subjects accessed text documents more than was necessary; moreover, the percentages hide a tendency for subjects to visit more resources than necessary early in the experiment, and conversely not to visit necessary resources later in the session.

Table 5 shows a significant bias towards searching for information in text-based media (52% against an expected 37.5%). A classic interaction sequence was for subjects to look in a text document, not find the answer, reluctantly go to a video resource to find an answer within it, but then go back to the original text resource in order to double check for answers there. The reverse of this was not true. Once a subject had found what they thought was an answer by reading a text document they did not access any further resources.

More detailed lessons were apparent by investigating how the subjects fared with each question in term of correct replies, media resources they actually accessed, and should have accessed. The subject behavior with individual questions was as follows:

1. What color T-shirt was Dempster wearing on the day of his retirement announcement?

   Answer: Black. This required access to the image (Dempster.bmp) and text

	% Accesses Required to Answer Questions	Actually % Times Opened
Text	37.5	52
Video	37.5	29
Still	25	19

Table 5. Subjects' media access.

(Dempster.doc). All subjects answered this question correctly, and 9/10 accessed the required information optimally, i.e. the document to find out the date of Dempster retirement, followed by the image for the T-shirt color. It is interesting to note that all subjects accessed the text media first, even though color and T-shirt might be strong cues for images resources. Four subjects also accessed all the other media resources, and another one partially so. This may indicate a tendency for users to explore media resources when they first encounter them even though they are not immediately relevant.

2. Point to the Location of Dempster's Brain Injury.

Answer: The location marked as left hand side on the image which was not the left hand side of the image as it appeared to the subject. This required access to an image (Brain.bmp) for location of the injury and possibly the text (Dempster.doc) for the report of the injury. Only half of the subjects answered this question correctly, even though they all accessed the correct resources. Errors were caused by confusion between the orientation from the user's viewpoint as opposed to the image, indicating a lack of attention to image detail as the brain scan contained prominent "L" and "R" cues.

3. Who was Dempster's doctor?

Answer: Dr Guzm. This required access to the image (Brain.bmp) as the doctor's name is on the brain scan. Eight subjects answered this correctly, even though they all accessed the text medium first, showing a strong bias towards text media for information detail.

4. When did Dempster have his brain scan done?

Answer: 3.6.94. This required access to the image (Brain.bmp) as the date appears on the brain scan. Seven subjects gave the correct answer. The previous question gave a strong cue for this question, so the three failures were unexpected. Two subjects accessed the correct image but failed to search for the date, the other subject looked at text documents.

5. Why did Dempster quit Indy Car racing?

Answer: Because of a crash and a row with the Indy car racing association over safety regulations. The answer required access to the text document (Dempster.doc) and caption on the photo image (Dempster.bmp) which described the dispute.

Seven subjects gave the correct answers and another two gave partially correct answers, however, none accessed the Dempster image during this question. This is interesting because it shows a memorization effect, since the subjects had seen the relevant information within the image caption during previous questions (1 and 2).

6. Who is Dempster sponsored by?

Answer: Gateway PLC. From information contained within the text document (Dempster.doc). Nine subjects answered correctly and accessed the text document.

7. Name the TV show host the sponsor has interests in.

Answer: Noel Edmunds. This requires access to text (Gateway.doc) and video (Gateway.avi). The correctness score was 8/10, however the subjects showed some uncertainty about which resource to search. All started with text (three with the inappropriate Dempster.doc), before finding the answer in the video. This indicates that subjects will search video media for specific linguistic based information, providing the cue is sufficiently strong.

8. Does the sponsor have an interest in Habitat?

Answer: No. This negative answer requires search through both the text (Gateway.doc) and video (Gateway.avi) resources. All subjects answered correctly, even though 3/10 did not access both of the required resources. Searches to establish a negative answer may not be complete.

9. List all the companies Dempster's sponsor has shares in.

Answer: The complete list requires access to both text (Gateway.doc) and video (Gateway.avi) resources. Only three subjects gave the complete list, while the rest gave the partial list from the text document. This pattern reflected their access to the video and the text, and demonstrates that once subjects have gained some information they consider the answer adequate. Furthermore, the question may bias them not to look at the video or other resources. This contrasts with question 7 where a strong cue to the video was provided.

10. What is the registration number of the white Ford?

Answer: B54700. The number can be seen on the video (Gateway.avi) but magnifying the image helps. Only half the subjects answered correctly, even though they all accessed the appropriate video. Poor performance was caused by the imperfect image quality, and an apparent usability problem in system operation. The subjects did not use the magnify facility by dragging the window to enlarge it even though they had been shown this in training.

11. When and where was Dempster's accident?

Answer: 6/3/94 at Indianapolis. The location requires access to the text (Dempster.doc), however, the date is shown on the image (Brain.bmp), assuming the scan was taken on the date of the accident. Six subjects answered correctly, and three partially so. Correct answering correlated with information access, as the subjects who gave three partially correct answers did not look at the image. This question may also show a memory priming effect as the subjects remembered the image, since searching for a date in the image is not a strong cue.

12. Did Dempster win the '93 Indianapolis?

Answer: No. Establishing the negative answer required a search through the text, (Dempster.doc) and the image caption (in Brain.bmp). Seven subjects gave the correct answer, but only two of them accessed the image, suggesting people tend to terminate negative type searches early without an exhaustive search.

13. Name the computer system that Dempster has donated money towards.

Answer: Icarus project. This was contained in the video caption and commentary (DOE.avi). Only four subjects found the correct answer, although a partial answer was extracted from the text (Dempster.doc) by five subjects. The question cue biased all subjects to search in text media.

14. Describe the end users of the system.

Answer: New commanders. This was contained in the video commentary (of DOE.avi) although some inference is required to establish the answer. Six subjects found the correct answer, and all but one accessed the correct media resource, probably because of the priming effect from the previous question.

15. Is the system single or multi user?

Answer: Multiuser. But this can only be found implicitly in the video (DOE.avi) which shows the system being used by several people. Half the subjects answered correctly even though all accessed the appropriate video, so they failed to make the correct inference from visual information.

16. What incidents need to be controlled by firefighters?
Answer: Train crash, stadium disaster, house fire. These which required subjects to follow a reference from the video speech commentary "incidents like these" to the visual illustration. All subjects accessed the video (DOE.avi) and answered correctly, so well constructed references between two media work effectively.

17. List the developers on the project.

Answer: W. Midlands Fire Service, Portsmouth Poly, etc. This information had to be extracted from the speech commentary (of DOE.avi). Seven subjects answered correctly, and the three who did not failed to access the video and searched the text document instead.

18. What are Gateway's four defining P-Words?

Answer: Product, packaging, practice, people skills, which were all contained in a graphics caption on the video (Gateway.avi). All subjects answered correctly and accessed the video.

Overall the subjects were remarkably accurate at predicting the correct media resource to search, even when the cues biased them towards the incorrect resource. A possible explanation for this is the role of memory. Four subjects browsed all the resources for question 1 and further random accesses meant that by about question 5 most subjects had viewed all the media. They then used their model of the available resources to direct their search more effectively. The role of memory was also apparent in subject backtracking to fill in answers retrospectively. For instance, question 4 encouraged access to the same information as question 3 and two subjects went back to answer question 3 while attempting number 4. However this was the only instance of backtracking observed in the sessions and was accomplished quickly. There was a persistent bias towards searching text media for questions of identity and descriptive detail, which was only overcome by users forming a model of the media contents.

Information retrieval was only effective for simple questions. When references or cues were explicit, performance was good, but when inference was required performance declined. Questions with negative answers and enumerated lists tended to be incompletely answered, indicating that users quit searching when they have some evidence to confirm their expectations. When enumeration was required in lists, most subjects showed an undisciplined approach and returned partial answers.

3.1 Use of Windows

The optimal pattern for answering several questions should have been to open several windows to cross reference information in parallel. However, subjects rarely opened more than one window at a time, preferring serial search and remembering linked information. They seemed to accept a self imposed burden in working memory when answers required cross references between media resources. After answering a question, on nearly all occasions, the subject returned the screen to its initial iconised state before proceeding to the next question.

The overall pattern of system operation is illustrated in figure 2. This shows a network graph derived from observation of users' actions which were counted and expressed in transition frequencies, e.g., number of times maximize was followed by normal size, etc. The subjects' most frequent behavior pattern was alternating between normal and iconised displays, reflecting serial opening of each resource, with normal to maximize transitions for enlarging images, although not for videos. Other manipulations were infrequent.

3.2 Preference Data

From the post test questionnaire, the subjects' preferred presentation strategies were first for tiled windows with scroll bars, then reduced in size but tiled, with a low rating for window overlapping. Their preference for scroll bars is interesting considering they didn't use this operation or other window commands to manipulate the displays. Video resources were considered to be

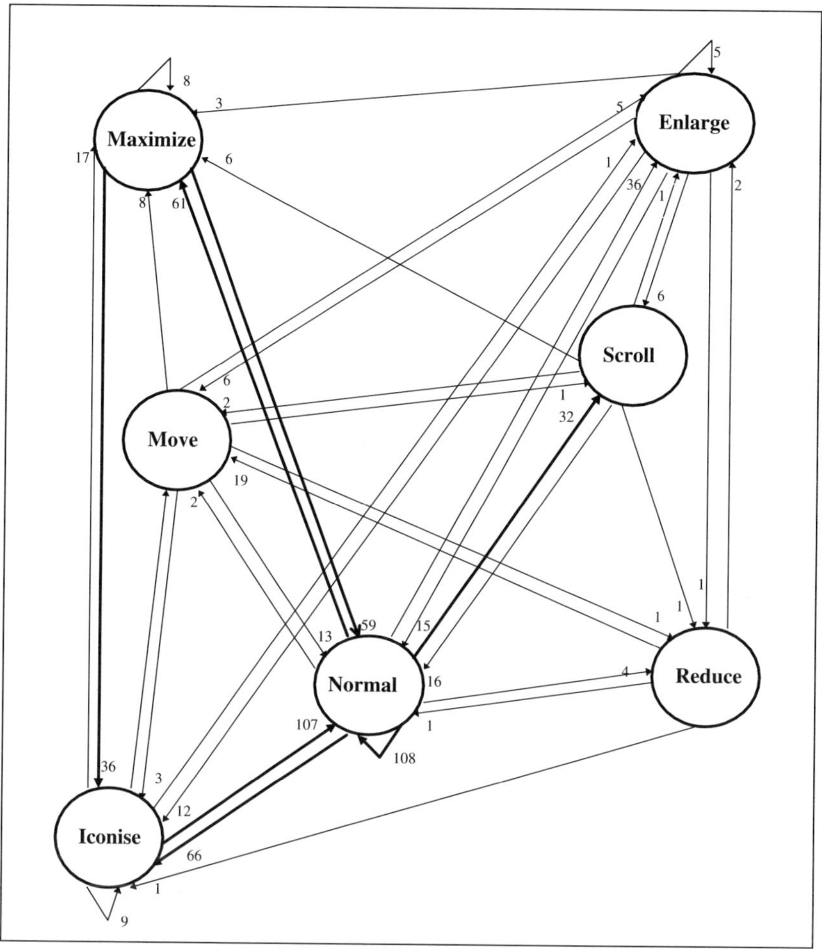

Figure 2. Network diagram for windows manipulations.

more difficult for extracting information, rating 4.8 and 3.7 average score on a 1–7 scale where 7 = most difficult. Text and still image resources showed little difference in difficulty rating (averages in the range 2.6–2.9). Video may have been considered more difficult because it required more control actions, i.e. the subjects had to stop and replay the videos to get the answers to several questions.

When subjects were asked how useful the information contained in each resource was, they rated the videos poorly (averages 2.8, 2.9) and text/still image media better (range 2.7–4.9) apart from the Dempster text resource which received a poor rating of 2.6.

3.3 Discussion of Experiment 1

Even though the subjects were selected for MS®, Windows™ familiarity, they only used a limited number of windowing facilities, concentrating on maximize, minimize and iconise. They rarely viewed windows concurrently and preferred tiled presentations suggesting that users prefer presentations to be optimally laid out to reduce effort. Beard and Walker (1990) have shown that scrolling is much slower than other facilities such as zoom.

Preliminary findings indicate that users' behavior in multimedia information searching tends to be biased towards serial, mono-modal window focused search. They do not readily cross reference information cues in different resources, however, when explicit references are present within a resource searching is more effective, e.g., the speech to video link in question 16. Memory does not seem to be effective in supplying cross referencing cues if these cues are not made explicit in a design. On the other hand, once the subjects have built up a memory of the information contents of the multimedia resources they were able to use that memory effectively, as demonstrated by the decline in cue biased response in later questions.

Interestingly, the subjects did not use window facilities to help build up associations between information in different media. Only one subject opened two or more windows concurrently in order to cross refer between them. The subjects' preference for screen layout, if there was insufficient space to fully display all windows, was to maximize visibility by tiled, reduced windows followed by clipped, scrollable and then overlaid windows. However, the wide variation in individual preferences points to the need for a user configurable system.

Video media may have been perceived as difficult to use for information retrieval because of the extra effort necessary to control dynamic media, i.e. replay and freeze frame to read information in specific video sequences. Salomon (1984) notes that learners invest more mental effort in the media they perceive to be difficult compared to those they perceive as easy. Passive viewing is different from active information retrieval, and it proved harder to extract information from videos than from text.

The bias towards text resources seems to be caused by questions requesting identification and descriptive detail in the answer, information usually associated with linguistic media. However, this bias was not consistent since when subjects learn about the contents of visual media then they correct this bias. Users are cued by the question terms to select a particular media type, e.g., "list all members...," implies text, whereas "show me a selection of cartoons by X" implies image (Cawkell 1993). Cueing need not always be explicit, and users need either to be provided with better information about the diversity of information contained within a set of media resources, or to have tools for rapid exploration of their contents.

4. Experiment 2: Scenarios for Multimedia Presentation

A further experiment using storyboard techniques attempted to measure performance and identify preferences regarding specific design options for intelligent planning in multimedia presentation, in part to investigate the hypothesis that presentation layout could help users more effectively build associations between information.

4.1 Method

Subjects were given screen dumps illustrating mock ups of a multimedia information retrieval system with three design options for information presentation:

- Overlapping vs. Nonoverlapping (i.e. tiled) windows.
- Summarized results in Browsers vs. full sized results in Presenters.
- Spatial linking of windows so queries were placed next to the relevant results vs. nonspatial linking.

The subjects, undergraduate students in Business Computing, were informed that the system would be an "intelligent front end" which could automatically plan to achieve the effects illustrated in the scenarios. The information and media resources were the same as in experiment 1 except that no video could be used in this paper based scenario experiment. Two groups, each with 20 subjects, were used with the following procedure:

- *Group A:* Subjects were given the Overlap, Browser, and Spatial linking scenarios and asked to answer nine questions.
- *Group B:* Subjects were given the Nonoverlap, Presenter and Nonspatial Linked scenarios and asked to answer the same nine questions.

Both groups then received each other's materials so they had a full set of scenarios. The subjects were then requested to rate their preference for each of the design option pairs (e.g., Browser or Presenter) with respect to the question being answered. The scenarios were illustrated by two pages of screen dumps for each set of design options. The subjects were instructed to use the scenarios for each question set although they could refer back to previous images if they wished. Three tools, targeted on specific aspects of information seeking, were shown in separate windows:

- Presenters portrayed text and image results in detail.
- Browsers gave a summary of retrieved results with cues linking them to presenters.
- Selectors for creating queries from pointing to segments of Entity Relationship diagrams and then adding further terms in a form filling dialogue.

The subjects worked at their own pace for 30 minutes to complete the questions and then filled in the preference test questionnaire. A pilot experiment indicated that 30 minutes was an adequate period to complete the nine questions.

4.2 Results

4.2.1 Performance. As indicated in table 6, comparing the design options, overlap and nonoverlap windows showed little difference and Presenters showed no advantage over Browsers. The considerable difference between the Spatial and Nonspatial groups seems to reflect a performance difference with questions that required linking information between Selectors and Presenters. The worst performance in all groups was in answer to the questions requiring a list as answer, which was a factor influencing poor performance in experiment 1. Another factor causing errors was the poor photocopy quality on the scenario screen dumps which hindered searching for information in the image resources.

Analysis of each question showed some differences between the two design options which were masked when totals were compared. The first five questions were answered with the overlap/nonoverlap scenario, questions 6 and 7 used the browser/presenter scenario, while questions 8 and 9 were for the spatial linking scenario. Subject behavior with individual questions was as follows.

1. Where does Dempster live?

Answer type: simple. *Answer:* Palo Alto. Eighteen of the overlap group and sixteen of the nonoverlap group gave the correct answer to this question which was easy to find in the Dempster text document.

2. Write down the side of Dempster's brain injury

Answer type: simple. *Answer:* Left side. Eighteen subjects in both groups answered correctly. Note the prompt in this experiment referred to the location directly rather than asking the subject to point to the left hand side; consequently the orientation error encountered in experiment 1 vanished.

3. Why did Dempster quit Indy car racing?

Answer type: complex, required cross referencing. *Answer:* A serious accident and disagreement over safety regulations. This question received only four correct answers from the overlap group and eight from the nonoverlap group. Many subjects in both groups gave a partially correct answer citing the accident but missed the disagreement which is not stated explicitly as a cause in the text. Tiled presentation showed a better score but the difference was not large.

4. When and where was Dempster's accident?

Answer type: complex, required cross references. *Answer:* 6/3/94 at Indianapolis. Eight subjects in the overlap group and eleven nonoverlap subjects gave the correct answer. The information had to be extracted from the text documents and the date from the brain scan image. As in experiment 1, most subjects

	Overlap	NonOverlap	*Browser*	*Presenter*	Spatial	Nonspatial
Group A Correct Answers	58%	n/a	*72.5%*	*n/a*	62.5%	n/a
Group B Correct Answers	n/a	66%	*n/a*	*67.5%*	n/a	17.5%

Table 6. Percentage of questions answered correctly for the design options

did not expect to find detailed information in visual media, hence they missed the date.

5. What area of research in the DOE did Dempster donate money towards, and which service was the research for?

Answer type: complex, required cross referencing. *Answer:* Technology based training for the fire fighting service. Ten subjects in the overlap group and thirteen nonoverlap subjects found the required information. The poor performance may have been caused by the need to access both the Dempster and DOE texts. Several subjects in both groups gave partially correct answers but missed the connection to the fire fighting service in the DOE text.

6. Name the driver of the number 4 car.

Answer type: simple. *Answer:* Michael Villeneuve. Twelve browser and ten presenter subjects found the answer. Presenter subject errors may have been caused by poor image quality or by the subjects failing to see that the title of the presenter window contained the answer. Browser subjects had to trace the car /driver data from the browser summary to a presenter picture.

7. Name the Indy car team(s), driver(s) and car numbers who are sponsored by Conesco.

Answer type: complex list. *Answer:* Gateway, Nigel Dempster, No 18; Firebird Formula, Scott Pruett, No 27. Seventeen subjects in both conditions answered correctly, even though this answer required several facts in a list.

8. Name the drivers of the AJ Foyt team for the year 1994 and 1995, respectively.

Answer type: complex, required cross referencing. *Answer:* 1994—Andy Lawrence, 1995—Andre Andretti. Fourteen spatial linking subjects answered correctly whereas only one nonspatial linked subject did. This dramatic difference is probably caused by the juxtaposition of the two browsers with the selector windows for the year questions, 1994, 1995. The nonspatial condition did not preserve the link between the query attribute (i.e. the year) and the driver team data in the browser.

9. Which year was the picture of Nigel Dempster taken?

Answer type: complex, required cross referencing between the selector which contained the date and the image in the presenter. *Answer:* 1995. Eleven spatial-linked subjects answered correctly while only six nonlinked subject did so. The

	Overlap	Nonoverlap	No pref-erence	Browser	Presenter	No pref-erence	Spatial	Non-spatial	No pref-erence
Group A Preference	8%	72%	20%	50%	32.5%	17.5%	60%	20%	20%
Group B Preference	23%	61%	16%	47.5%	32.5%	20%	52.5%	7.5%	40%

Table 7. User preferences for nonoverlap, browser and spatial linking.

explanation lies in the proximity between the browser window and picture presenter it was linked to.

4.2.2 Preference. As indicated in table 7, both groups preferred tiled window presentations, although the difference was less marked for browsers over presenters. Spatial linking was strongly preferred by both groups. Although subjects claimed to prefer to browse, selecting from a set of results grouped in a single window, they in fact performed better when results were presented individually. For the other two features, overlapping/nonoverlapping windows and spatial linking, the preferences were in line with performance, a significant positive indication for nonoverlapping and spatially-linked windows. The latter is possibly because subjects were given a time limit to answer each question, so the low number of correct answers in the nonspatial condition could be due to subjects not finding an answer in the allocated time, rather than providing an incorrect answer.

5. Implications for Design of Intelligent Multimedia Retrieval Systems

Implications can be drawn from user preferences and performance in the two experiments at two levels. First, functionality of the user interface to improve usability of retrieved data. Second, task support for users' information seeking and data extraction from retrieved multimedia resources. Although guidelines can be proposed from our empirical studies, as we shall discuss, implementing guidelines in a design for intelligent information retrieval systems can be difficult. We present our findings by first stating the guidelines and then discussing their implication for user interface design.

5.1 User Interface Functionality

- Maximize visibility of information by tiled window presentation to help users assimilate information without having to manipulate windows.

Tiled windows was a strong user preference, even though they tended to view media resources serially. This suggests automatic layout planning may help to encourage more concurrent processing of retrieved media. This may also improve task support by making cross referencing between media easier, an important need as our users rarely cross referenced multiple windows even though the task required this.

- Provide and explain display control functions: users need powerful and flexible means of manipulating retrieved media, so they can extract information more effectively. Explanation of these facilities will be necessary by "intelligent help" to encourage their effective use.

Our users rarely manipulated media presentations to obtain a better view. Providing functions such as "magnify" or "zoom" are necessary for users to manipulate retrieved media effectively, however explanation by the system could be employed to demonstrate, for instance, that dragging a window to enlarge it can make an image more visible. This may overcome the reticence we observed in using such functions.

5.2 Task Support

- Counteract cue bias in multimedia information seeking: users should be encouraged to search media resources other than text for information which is linguistic in nature.

This guideline is easier to state than to solve. In our study the users made many mistakes by choosing inappropriate media for text based information which was contained within other media. They tended to prefer text for most questions which did not overtly cue for spatial/physical data. Furthermore, questions may have provided false cues about the desired target resource. The apparent solution is to exhaustively index all media resources according to their contents, but this incurs a prohibitive cost.

In scaled up databases this problem will be exacerbated by the difficulty in matching indexing terms to the subject matter and the users articulation of their information need, irrespective of media. This is a traditional indexing problem, and even more challenging is visual media and spoken language, as addressed by the many chapters in this collection. Ultimately comprehensive indexing of nontext media (together with support for example based retrieval) is the answer; however, making users aware of nonvisual information in visual media such as captions, text, speech sound tracks, etc., could help overcome some of the problems we observed.

- Validate retrieved datasets for completeness: support extraction of all the information implied by the query from the retrieved media.

Our subjects performed poorly when answers required lists and multipart answers. This problem was a facet of users extracting information, however, they seem to do so more effectively when presented with lists. Hence this problem shares a common origin with others: users do not appear to rigorously extract linguistically based information from nontext media. Again indexing is the ultimate answer, but presenting a summary list of media resources possibly containing appropriate information may help, as may making users aware of captions, embedded text, etc. within visual media. Describing media resources as composite documents is another possible solution.

- Validate negative answers: users need help to ensure that a false negative answer does not happen and that a true negative answer is believed.

Our subjects made several mistakes when questions implied true negative answers, also handling multipart answers posed considerable problems as false negatives. This is a general problem in information retrieval, made worse in multimedia because the information may be present but not found by users. Comprehensive indexing, promoting user awareness of embedded information and encouraging searching retrieved media resources are possible solutions. Searching for negative results encounters a completeness problem which could be dealt with by providing maps of relevant resources, updated to show the resources which have been searched. Such "navigator/browser" tools could also summarize the properties of retrieved items and act as a checklist of media to inspect more closely for detailed information.

- Provide cross references between related information: extraction of related information should be promoted by making associations explicit.

Extracting information gave users problems when inference or following references were required. Assistance in dealing with questions which required references between different types of information could be provided by either searching for related media resources, following relationships on a conceptual schema, or by suggesting strategies for query reformulation to the user, such as narrowing the query if too many results are found. Alternatively, explicit references could be made between media, as implemented in hypermedia, by hot spots in visual media (Cawkell 1993) or stopping of audio on a defined keyword. Unfortunately cross reference links assume the designer knows the users' needs a priori which is often impossible. Intelligent support for linking could be the answer. Horacek (this volume) also argues for closer integration between media to make presentations more coherent. Hypermedia environments which embed preformed queries on links thereby providing an access path to relevant media resources offer one solution to this problem (Li et al. 1992). A more ambitious, but as yet under researched approach, is to attempt dynamic linking of retrieved resources at run time. This would entail analyzing the properties of a set of retrieved media and then establishing links according to user-defined criteria.

- Support exploration of media resources: promoting user memory of searchable resources can help retrieval.

Answers may be found in previously retrieved resources, as observed when our users backtracked to answer previous questions. Furthermore, some questions may have been answered by using knowledge of the contexts of the media resources. Acquisition of a user model of the information resources should be encouraged by providing concept maps of the searchable information space in navigator-browser tools. Guided tours, visit lists as recommended in Hypertext (Nielsen 1995), and dialogue history of previous queries and response sets could facilitate backtracking and query reuse.

6. Conclusions

On reflection, this study provides a mixed message for the role of intelligence in multimedia information retrieval. No doubt relevance feedback would have improved subjects performance as has been demonstrated by Koenemann and Belkin (1996) and others. Feedback should encourage a more rapid formation of a model by the users of the information resources, however we expect the bias in the question content may persist. Further study is required on this point. Many user needs can be satisfied by simple functionality, such as visit lists, designing references and links within media resources, and browsers/navigator maps of media resources. Intelligence could provide considerable assistance in three key areas: presentation planning, query formation and information exploration, and media resource indexing. System support is necessary to help users develop appropriate queries as well as facilitating information extraction from retrieved results. Navigator-browser tools can help exploration of the information space and conceptual model formation to improve retrieval efficiency. Visual media in particular require indexing so users can search them more effectively, however, this is a difficult problem to solve as intelligent auto-indexers require considerable domain knowledge and image recognition capabilities.

Intelligence needs to be applied from the perspective of cooperative assistance. For example in presentation planning, the system shows alternative layouts with different visibility tradeoffs between display all and show detail, clip verses shrink, or trade-off such as the frame rate verses image clarity in video presentation. Intelligent planning needs to be based on sound theory of information seeking strategies as in the MERIT system (Belkin et al. 1995; Stein et al., this volume) and the results we report add to their set of user strategies. Users' needs are hard to anticipate beforehand and often differ between individuals, so intelligence should be delivered either by configurable rule sets or by giving users control of presentation preferences. Adaptive interfaces are necessary with mixed initiative dialogues and user control over system intelligence. Finally, we still understand very little about the cognition of information seeking in multimedia. This study has demonstrated that multimedia pose new problems in retriev-

ing information distributed between media resources such as cue biased searching. Further empirical studies are necessary to advance our insight about how users' needs and behavior can be effectively supported by intelligent systems.

Acknowledgements

The INTUITIVE Project was funded partly by the European Union's ESPRIT program. We acknowledge the help of partners: Cap Gemini Innovation, INRIA (France), Brameur Ltd, Lloyds-Register (UK), Ibermatica (Spain), and SISU (Sweden). We thank Hon Lee, of City University, for contributing to the analysis of the experiments.

References

Aigraine, P.; Joly, P.; and Longueville, V. 1997. Medium Knowledge-Based Macro-Segmentation of Video into Sequences. In this volume.

André, E. and Rist, T. 1993. The Design of Illustrated Documents as a Planning Task. In *Intelligent Multimedia Interfaces*, ed. M. Maybury, 94-116. Cambridge, MA: AAAI/MIT Press.

Baggett, P. 1984. Role of Temporal overlap of Visual and Auditory Material in Forming Dual Media. *Associations Journal of Educational Psychology* 76(3): 408-17.

Beard, D. B. and Walker, J. Q. 1990. Navigational Techniques to Improve the Display of Large 2-Dimensional Spaces. *Behavior and Information Technology* 9(6): 451-466.

Belkin, N. J.; Cool, C.; Stein, A.; and Thiel, U. 1995. Cases, Scripts, and Information-Seeking Strategies: On the Design of Interactive Retrieval Systems. *Expert Systems with Applications* 9(3): 379-395.

Bieger, G. R. and Glock, M. D. 1984. The Information Content of Picture-Text Instructions. *Journal of Experimental Education* 53: 68-76.

Blum, T.; Keislaer, D.; Wheaton, J.; and Wold, E. 1997. Audio Databases with Content-based Retrieval. In this volume.

Cawkell, A. E. 1993. Picture-queries and Picture-databases. *Journal of Information Science*, 19: 409-423.

Chuah, M.; Roth, S.; and Kolojejchick, J. 1997. Sketching, Searching, and Customizing Visualizations: A Content-based Approach to Design Retrieval. In this volume.

Feiner, S. and McKeown, K. R. 1993. Automating the Generation of Co-ordinated Multimedia Explanations. In *Intelligent Multimedia Interfaces*, ed. M. Maybury, 117-38, Cambridge, MA: AAAI/MIT Press.

Flickner, M.; Sawhney, H.; Niblack, W.; Ashley, J.; Huang, Q.; Dom, B.; Gorkani, M.; Hafner, J.; Lee, D.; Petkovic, D.; Steele, D.; and Yanker, P. 1997. Query by Image and Video Content: The QBIC System. In this volume.

Foote J. T.; Brown M. G.; Jones, G. J. F.; Sparck Jones K.; and Young, S. J. 1995. Video Mail Retrieval by Voice: Towards Intelligent Retrieval and Browsing of Multimedia Documents. In Proceedings of the First International Workshop on Intelligence and Multimodality in Multimedia Interfaces: Research and Applications, ed. J. Lee, Session 2, Article 3, 13-14 July, Edinburgh, Scotland.

Hauptmann, A. G. and Witbrock, M. 1997. Informedia: News-on-Demand Multimedia Information Acquisition and Retrieval. In this volume.

Holt B. and Hartwick L. 1994 (October). Retrieving Art Images by Image Content: The UC Davis QBIC Project. *Aslib Proceedings* 46(10): 243-248.

Horacek, H. 1997. Empirical Evidence for the Need of Intelligent Methods in Multi-Media Information Retrieval. In this volume.

Jones, G. J. F.; Foote, J. Sparck Jones, K.; and Young, S. 1997. The Video Mail Retrieval Project: Experiences in Retrieving Spoken Documents. In this volume.

Koenemann, J. and Belkin, N.J. 1996. A Case Study for Interaction. A Study of Interactive Information Retrieval Behavior and Effectiveness. In Proceedings of Human Factors in Computing Systems (CHI-96), eds. B. Nardi and G. van der Veer, 205-212. April 13-18, Vancouver, Canada.

Li, Z.; Davis, H.; and Hall, W. 1992. Hypermedia Links and Information Retrieval. The Department of Electronics and Computer Science, University of Southampton. Presented at British Computer Society 14th Information Retrieval Colloqium, 13-14th April 1992, Lancaster University.

Marks, L. 1995. Structural Issues in Multimedia Design. Tutorial at Interact, 25 - 29 June, Lillehammer, Norway.

Maybury, M.T. 1993. Planning Multimedia Explanations Using Communicative Acts. In *Intelligent Multimedia Interfaces*, ed. M. Maybury, 60-74, Cambridge, MA: AAAI/MIT Press.

Nielsen J. 1995. *Multimedia and Hypertext: The Internet and Beyond.* Chestnut Hill, MA: AP Professional.

Olson, J. S.; Olson, G. M.; and Meader, D. K. 1995. What Mix of Video and Audio is Useful for Small Groups Doing Real Time Design Work. In Proceedings of Human Factors in Computing Systems (CHI-95), 362-370. 7-11th May, Denver, CO. ACM Press.

Pentland, A. 1997. Machine Understanding of Human Behavior. In this volume.

Posner, M. 1976. Visual Dominance: An Information Processing Account of its Origins and Significance. *Psychological Review* 83: 157-171.

Salomon, G. 1984. Television is Easy and Print is Tough: The Differential Investment of Mental Effort in Learning as a Function of Perceptions and Attributions, *Journal of Educational Psychology* 76(4): 647-658.

Stein, A.; Gulla, J. A.; Müller, A.; and Thiel, U. 1997. Conversational Interaction for Semantic Access to Multimedia Information. In this volume.

Stock, O.; Strapparava, C.; and Zancanaro, M. 1997. Explorations in an Environment for Natural Language Multimodal Information Access. In this volume.

Sutcliffe, A. G. and Faraday, P. 1994. Systematic Design for Task related Multimedia Interfaces. *Information and Software Technology* 4(36): 225-234.

Tonomura, Y.; Akutsu, A.; Taniguchi, Y.; and Suzuki, G. 1994. Structured Video Computing. *IEEE Multimedia* 1(3):34-42.

Wechsler, M. and Schauble, P. 1995. Speech Retrieval Based on Automatic Indexing. In Proceedings of the Final Workshop on Multimedia Information Retrieval (MIRO '95), eds. C. J. van Rijsbergen et al. Berlin: Springer Verlag. Glasgow, Scotland, 18-20 September. eWiC, electronic Workshops in Computing Series (http://www.springer.co.uk/eWiC/Workshops/ MIRO95.html)

Williams, N.; Blair; G. S.; and Davies, N. 1992. Distributed Multimedia Computing: An Assessment of the State of the Art. *Information Services and Use*, 11:265-281.

Yoshutaka, A.; Kishida, S.; Hirakawa, M.; and Ichikawa T. 1994. Knowledge Assisted Content-based Retrieval for Multimedia Databases. *IEEE Multimedia* 1(4): 12-21.

Zhang, H. J.; Low, C. Y.; Smoliar, S. 1997. and JianHua, W. Video Parsing, Retrieval and Browsing: An Integrated and Content-based Solution. In this volume.

Index